TENTH ESSENTIALS EDITION

We the People

AN INTRODUCTION TO AMERICAN POLITICS

The 114th Congress, 2015–16*

United States House of Representatives

Democrats: 186   Republicans: 244   Undecided: 5   2014 Election Results: Republicans gained at least 10 seats.*

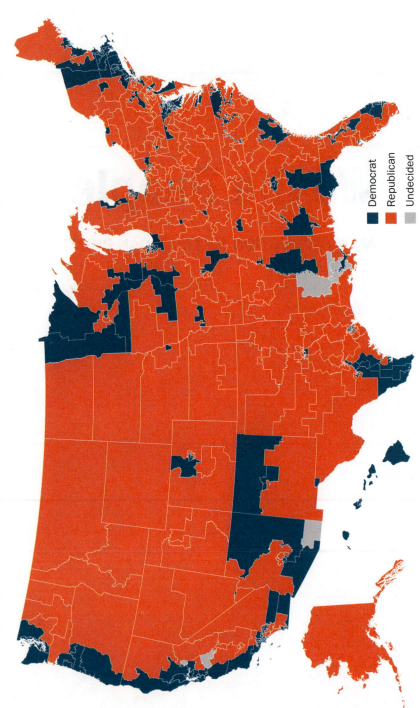

Democrat
Republican
Undecided

United States Senate

Democrats: 44   Republicans: 54   Independents: 2   **2014 Election Results: Republicans gained 9 seats.***

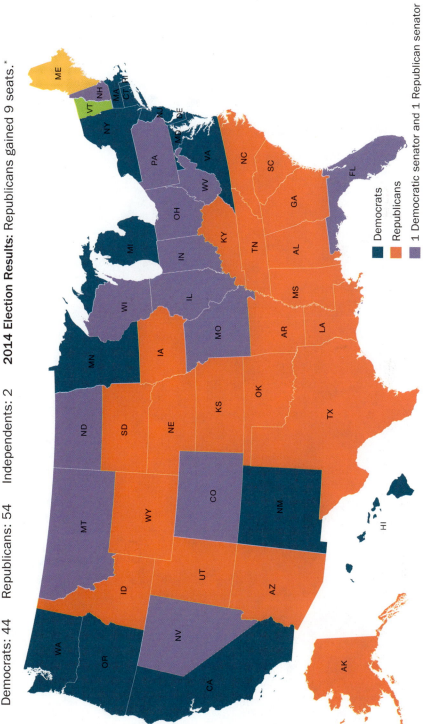

Democrats

Republicans

1 Democratic senator and 1 Republican senator

1 Independent senator and 1 Democratic senator

1 Independent senator and 1 Republican senator

*Data are based on election results as of November 18, 2014. House races in several states remained undecided pending recounts and runoff elections.

TENTH ESSENTIALS EDITION

We the People

AN INTRODUCTION TO AMERICAN POLITICS

Benjamin Ginsberg
JOHNS HOPKINS UNIVERSITY

Theodore J. Lowi
CORNELL UNIVERSITY

Margaret Weir
UNIVERSITY OF CALIFORNIA, BERKELEY

Caroline J. Tolbert
SUNY CORTLAND

Robert J. Spitzer
SUNY CORTLAND

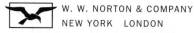
W. W. NORTON & COMPANY
NEW YORK   LONDON

W. W. Norton & Company has been independent since its founding in 1923, when William Warder Norton and Mary D. Herter Norton first published lectures delivered at the People's Institute, the adult education division of New York City's Cooper Union. The firm soon expanded its program beyond the Institute, publishing books by celebrated academics from America and abroad. By mid-century, the two major pillars of Norton's publishing program—trade books and college texts—were firmly established. In the 1950s, the Norton family transferred control of the company to its employees, and today—with a staff of four hundred and a comparable number of trade, college, and professional titles published each year—W. W. Norton & Company stands as the largest and oldest publishing house owned wholly by its employees.

Editor: Lisa Camner McKay
Project Editor: Christine D'Antonio
Editorial Assistants: Sarah Wolf and Samantha Held
Manuscript Editor: Nina Hnatov
Managing Editor, College: Marian Johnson
Managing Editor, College Digital Media: Kim Yi
Senior Production Supervisor, College: Ashley Horna
Media Editor: Toni Magyar
Media Editorial Assistant: Michael Jaoui
Marketing Manager, Political Science: Erin Brown
Art Director: Rubina Yeh
Text Design: Lissi Sigillo
Photo Editor: Evan Luberger
Photo Researcher: Julie Tesser
Permissions Manager: Megan Jackson
Permissions Clearing: Elizabeth Trammell
Information Graphics: Kiss Me I'm Polish LLC, New York
Composition: Graphic World, Inc.
Manufacturing: Courier—Kendallville

Permission to use copyrighted material is included in the credits section of this book, which begins on page A97.

The Library of Congress has cataloged the full edition as follows:

Library of Congress Cataloging-in-Publication Data

Ginsberg, Benjamin.
  We the people: an introduction to American politics/Benjamin Ginsberg, Theodore J. Lowi, Margaret Weir, Caroline Tolbert.—Tenth edition.
    pages cm
  Includes bibliographical references and index.
  ISBN 978-0-393-93703-9 (hardcover)
  1. United States—Politics and government—Textbooks. I. Lowi, Theodore J. II. Weir, Margaret, 1952- III. Tolbert, Caroline J. IV. Title.
  JK276.G55 2015
  320.473—dc23

                                    2014044163

This edition: **ISBN 978-0-393-93705-3**

W. W. Norton & Company, Inc., 500 Fifth Avenue,
New York, N. Y. 10110
www.wwnorton.com

W. W. Norton & Company Ltd., Castle House, 75/76 Wells Street, London W1T 3QT

2 3 4 5 6 7 8 9 0

To Teresa Spitzer

Sandy, Cindy, and Alex Ginsberg

Angele, Anna, and Jason Lowi

Nicholas Ziegler

Dave, Jackie, Eveline, and Eddie Dowling

contents

2 ● The Founding and the Constitution   28

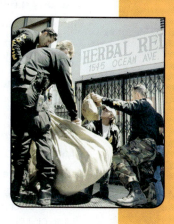

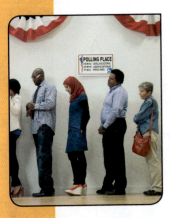

8 ● Interest Groups   242

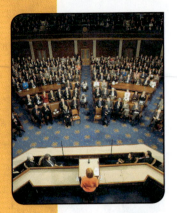

PART III   Institutions

9 ● Congress   270

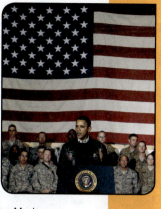

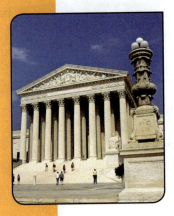

12 ● The Federal Courts   368

PART IV Policy

14 ● Foreign Policy   436

preface

This book has been and continues to be dedicated to developing a satisfactory response to the question more and more Americans are asking: Why should we be engaged with government and politics? Through the first nine editions, we sought to answer this question by making the text directly relevant to the lives of the students who would be reading it. As a result, we tried to make politics interesting by demonstrating that students' interests are at stake and that they therefore need to take a personal, even selfish, interest in the outcomes of government. At the same time, we realized that students needed guidance in how to become politically engaged. Beyond providing students with a core of political knowledge, we needed to show them how they could apply that knowledge as participants in the political process. The "Plug In" sections in each chapter help achieve that goal.

As events from the last several years have reminded us, "what government does" can be a matter of life and death. Recent events have reinforced the centrality of government in citizens' lives. The U.S. government has fought two wars abroad, while claiming sweeping new powers at home that could compromise the liberties of its citizens. America's role in the world is discussed daily both inside and outside the classroom. Moreover, the Internet has opened up new avenues to participation and mobilization. Reflecting all of these trends, this new Tenth Essentials Edition shows more than any other book on the market (1) how students are connected to government; (2) how digital media are changing (or not changing) the way Americans experience politics; and (3) why students should think critically about government and politics. These themes are incorporated in the following ways:

- **New "Politics and Your Future" chapter conclusions give students direct, personal reasons to care about politics.** These sections focus on the political opportunities and challenges that students will face in their lives as a result of emerging social, political, demographic, and technological change. The conclusions reprise the important point made in the chapter introductions that *government matters* and prompt students to consider how political change will impact their futures.

- **New "Plug In" sections show students how to make a difference in politics.** These boxes replace the older "Get Involved" sections with succinct, realistic steps today's students can take—online and off—to *inform* themselves, *express* themselves, *connect* with others, and *act* in politically meaningful ways.

- **New content on how digital media are changing politics is now incorporated throughout the text.** With the Ninth Edition, we added "Digital Citizens" boxes to explore the ways that new information technologies are shaping how we experience politics. In this Tenth Edition, the coverage of digital politics has been integrated into the body of the text, in recognition of the fact that digital media have become an integral part of American politics.

- **New "America Side by Side" boxes use data figures and tables to provide a comparative perspective.** These one-page boxes appear in every chapter and provide a visual presentation of comparative data. By comparing political institutions and behavior across countries, students gain a better understanding of how specific features of the American system shape politics.

- **Chapter introductions focus on "What Government Does and Why It Matters."** In recent decades, cynicism about "big government" has dominated the political zeitgeist. But critics of government often forget that governments do a great deal for citizens. Every year, Americans are the beneficiaries of billions of dollars of goods and services from government programs. Government "does" a lot, and what it does matters a great deal to everyone, including college students. At the start of each chapter, this theme is introduced and applied to the chapter's topic. The goal is to show students that government and politics mean something to their daily lives.

- **Built-in study guides at the end of each chapter offer valuable learning tools.** A practice quiz and glossary definitions help students review the chapter material. Each chapter also includes a list of recommended readings to help the students get started on research projects.

We continue to hope that our book will itself be accepted as a form of enlightened political action. This Tenth Edition is another chance. It is an advancement toward our goal. We promise to keep trying.

acknowledgments

We are especially pleased to acknowledge the many colleagues who had a direct and active role in criticism and preparation of the manuscript. Our thanks go to:

First Edition Reviewers

Sarah Binder, Brookings Institution
Kathleen Gille, Office of Representative David Bonior
Rodney Hero, University of Colorado at Boulder
Robert Katzmann, Brookings Institution
Kathleen Knight, University of Houston
Robin Kolodny, Temple University
Nancy Kral, Tomball College
Robert C. Lieberman, Columbia University
David A. Marcum, University of Wyoming
Laura R. Winsky Mattei, State University of New York at Buffalo
Marilyn S. Mertens, Midwestern State University
Barbara Suhay, Henry Ford Community College
Carolyn Wong, Stanford University
Julian Zelizer, State University of New York at Albany

Second Edition Reviewers

Lydia Andrade, University of North Texas
John Coleman, University of Wisconsin at Madison
Daphne Eastman, Odessa College
Otto Feinstein, Wayne State University
Elizabeth Flores, Delmar College
James Gimpel, University of Maryland at College Park
Jill Glaathar, Southwest Missouri State University
Shaun Herness, University of Florida
William Lyons, University of Tennessee at Knoxville
Andrew Polsky, Hunter College, City University of New York
Grant Reeher, Syracuse University
Richard Rich, Virginia Polytechnic
Bartholomew Sparrow, University of Texas at Austin

Third Edition Reviewers

Bruce R. Drury, Lamar University
Andrew I. E. Ewoh, Prairie View A&M University
Amy Jasperson, University of Texas at San Antonio
Loch Johnson, University of Georgia
Mark Kann, University of Southern California
Robert L. Perry, University of Texas of the Permian Basin
Wayne Pryor, Brazosport College
Elizabeth A. Rexford, Wharton County Junior College
Andrea Simpson, University of Washington
Brian Smentkowski, Southeast Missouri State University
Nelson Wikstrom, Virginia Commonwealth University

Fourth Edition Reviewers

M. E. Banks, Virginia Commonwealth
University
Lynn Brink, North Lake College
Mark Cichock, University of Texas
at Arlington
Del Fields, St. Petersburg College
Nancy Kinney, Washtenaw Community
College
William Klein, St. Petersburg College
Dana Morales, Montgomery College
Christopher Muste, Louisiana State
University
Larry Norris, South Plains College
David Rankin, State University of New
York at Fredonia
Paul Roesler, St. Charles Community
College
J. Philip Rogers, San Antonio College
Greg Shaw, Illinois Wesleyan University
Tracy Skopek, Stephen F. Austin State
University
Don Smith, University of North Texas
Terri Wright, Cal State, Fullerton

Fifth Edition Reviewers

Annie Benifield, Tomball College
Denise Dutton, Southwest Missouri State
University
Rick Kurtz, Central Michigan University
Kelly McDaniel, Three Rivers Community
College
Eric Plutzer, Pennsylvania State University
Daniel Smith, Northwest Missouri State
University
Dara Strolovitch, University of Minnesota
Dennis Toombs, San Jacinto College–
North
Stacy Ulbig, Southwest Missouri State
University

Sixth Edition Reviewers

Janet Adamski, University of Mary
Hardin–Baylor
Greg Andrews, St. Petersburg College
Louis Bolce, Baruch College
Darin Combs, Tulsa Community College
Sean Conroy, University of New Orleans

Paul Cooke, Cy Fair College
Vida Davoudi, Kingwood College
Robert DiClerico, West Virginia University
Corey Ditslear, University of North Texas
Kathy Dolan, University of Wisconsin,
Milwaukee
Randy Glean, Midwestern State University
Nancy Kral, Tomball College
Mark Logas, Valencia Community College
Scott MacDougall, Diablo Valley College
David Mann, College of Charleston
Christopher Muste, University of Montana
Richard Pacelle, Georgia Southern
University
Sarah Poggione, Florida International
University
Richard Rich, Virginia Tech
Thomas Schmeling, Rhode Island College
Scott Spitzer, California State
University–Fullerton
Dennis Toombs, San Jacinto College–
North
John Vento, Antelope Valley College
Robert Wood, University of North Dakota

Seventh Edition Reviewers

Molly Andolina, DePaul University
Nancy Bednar, Antelope Valley College
Paul Blakelock, Kingwood College
Amy Brandon, San Jacinto College
Jim Cauthen, John Jay College
Kevin Davis, North Central Texas College
Louis DeSipio, University of California–
Irvine
Brandon Franke, Blinn College
Steve Garrison, Midwestern State University
Joseph Howard, University of Central
Arkansas
Aaron Knight, Houston Community
College
Paul Labedz, Valencia Community College
Elise Langan, John Jay College
Mark Logas, Valencia Community College
Eric Miller, Blinn College
Anthony O'Regan, Los Angeles Valley
College
David Putz, Kingwood College
Chis Soper, Pepperdine University
Kevin Wagner, Florida Atlantic University
Laura Wood, Tarrant County College

Eighth Edition Reviewers

Andrea Aleman, University of Texas at San Antonio

Stephen Amberg, University of Texas at San Antonio

Steve Anthony, Georgia State University

Brian Arbour, John Jay College, CUNY

Greg Arey, Cape Fear Community College

Ellen Baik, University of Texas–Pan American

David Birch, Lone Star College–Tomball

Bill Carroll, Sam Houston State University

Ed Chervenak, University of New Orleans

Gary Church, Mountain View College

Adrian Stefan Clark, Del Mar College

Casey Klofstad, University of Miami

Annie Cole, Los Angeles City College

Greg Combs, University of Texas at Dallas

Cassandra Cookson, Lee College

Brian Cravens, Blinn College

John Crosby, California State University–Chico

Scott Crosby, Valencia Community College

Courtenay Daum, Colorado State University, Fort Collins

Paul Davis, Truckee Meadows Community College

Peter Doas, University of Texas–Pan American

Vida Davoudi, Lone Star College–Kingwood

John Domino, Sam Houston State University

Doug Dow, University of Texas–Dallas

Jeremy Duff, Midwestern State University

Heather Evans, Sam Houston State University

Hyacinth Ezeamii, Albany State University

Bob Fitrakis, Columbus State Community College

Brian Fletcher, Truckee Meadows Community College

Paul Foote, Eastern Kentucky University

Frank Garrahan, Austin Community College

Jimmy Gleason, Purdue University

Steven Greene, North Carolina State University

Jeannie Grussendorf, Georgia State University

M. Ahad Hayaud-Din, Brookhaven College

Virginia Haysley, Lone Star College–Tomball

Alexander Hogan, Lone Star College–CyFair

Glen Hunt, Austin Community College

Mark Jendrysik, University of North Dakota

Krista Jenkins, Fairleigh Dickinson University

Carlos Juárez, Hawaii Pacific University

Melinda Kovács, Sam Houston State University

Paul Labedz, Valencia Community College

Boyd Lanier, Lamar University

Jeff Lazarus, Georgia State University

Jeffrey Lee, Blinn College

Alan Lehmann, Blinn College

Julie Lester, Macon State College

Steven Lichtman, Shippensburg University

Mark Logas, Valencia Community College

Fred Lokken, Truckee Meadows Community College

Shari MacLachlan, Palm Beach Community College

Guy Martin, Winston-Salem State University

Fred Monardi, College of Southern Nevada

Vincent Moscardelli, University of Connecticut

Jason Mycoff, University of Delaware

Sugumaran Narayanan, Midwestern State University

Adam Newmark, Appalachian State University

Larry Norris, South Plains College

Anthony Nownes, University of Tennessee, Knoxville

Elizabeth Oldmixon, University of North Texas

Anthony O'Regan, Los Angeles Valley College

John Osterman, San Jacinto College–Central

Mark Peplowski, College of Southern Nevada

Maria Victoria Perez-Rios, John Jay College, CUNY

Sara Rinfret, University of Wisconsin, Green Bay

Andre Robinson, Pulaski Technical College

Paul Roesler, St. Charles Community College

Susan Roomberg, University of Texas at San Antonio

Ryan Rynbrandt, Collin County Community College

Mario Salas, Northwest Vista College

Michael Sanchez, San Antonio College

Mary Schander, Pasadena City College

Laura Schneider, Grand Valley State University

Ronnee Schreiber, San Diego State University

Subash Shah, Winston-Salem State University

Mark Shomaker, Blinn College

Roy Slater, St. Petersburg College

Scott Spitzer, California State University–Fullerton

Debra St. John, Collin College

John Vento, Antelope Valley College

Eric Whitaker, Western Washington University

Clay Wiegand, Cisco College

Walter Wilson, University of Texas at San Antonio

Kevan Yenerall, Clarion University

Rogerio Zapata, South Texas College

Ninth Edition Reviewers

Amy Acord, Lone Star College–CyFair

Milan Andrejevich, Ivy Tech Community College

Steve Anthony, Georgia State University

Phillip Ardoin, Appalachian State University

Gregory Arey, Cape Fear Community College

Joan Babcock, Northwest Vista College

Evelyn Ballard, Houston Community College

Robert Ballinger, South Texas College

Mary Barnes-Tilley, Blinn College

Robert Bartels, Evangel University

Nancy Bednar, Antelope Valley College

Annie Benifield, Lone Star College–Tomball

Donna Bennett, Trinity Valley Community College

Amy Brandon, El Paso Community College

Mark Brewer, The University of Maine

Gary Brown, Lone Star College–Montgomery

Joe Campbell, Johnson County Community College

Dewey Clayton, University of Louisville

Jeff Colbert, Elon University

Amanda Cook-Fesperman, Illinois Valley Community College

Kevin Corder, Western Michigan University

Kevin Davis, North Central Texas College

Paul Davis, Truckee Meadows Community College

Terri Davis, Lamar University

Jennifer De Maio, California State University, Northridge

Christopher Durso, Valencia College

Ryan Emenaker, College of the Redwoods

Leslie Feldman, Hofstra University

Glen Findley, Odessa College

Michael Gattis, Gulf Coast State College

Donna Godwin, Trinity Valley Community College

Precious Hall, Truckee Meadows Community College

Sally Hansen, Daytona State College

Tiffany Harper, Collin College

Todd Hartman, Appalachian State University

Virginia Haysley, Lone Star College–Tomball

David Head, John Tyler Community College

Rick Henderson, Texas State University–San Marcos

Richard Herrera, Arizona State University

Thaddaus Hill, Blinn College

Steven Holmes, Bakersfield College

Kevin Holton, South Texas College

Robin Jacobson, University of Puget Sound

Joseph Jozwiak, Texas A & M–Corpus Christi

Casey Klofstad, University of Miami

Samuel Lingrosso, Los Angeles Valley College
Mark Logas, Valencia College
Christopher Marshall, South Texas College
Larry McElvain, South Texas College
Elizabeth McLane, Wharton County Junior College
Eddie Meaders, University of North Texas
Rob Mellen, Mississippi State University
Jalal Nejad, Northwest Vista College
Adam Newmark, Appalachian State University
Stephen Nicholson, University of California, Merced
Cissie Owen, Lamar University
Suzanne Preston, St. Petersburg College
David Putz, Lone Star College–Kingwood
Auksuole Rubavichute, Mountain View College
Ronnee Schreiber, San Diego State University
Ronald Schurin, University of Connecticut
Jason Seitz, Georgia Perimeter College
Jennifer Seitz, Georgia Perimeter College
Shannon Sinegal, The University of New Orleans
John Sides, George Washington University
Thomas Sowers, Lamar University
Jim Startin, University of Texas at San Antonio
Robert Sterken, University of Texas at Tyler
Bobby Summers, Harper College
John Theis, Lone Star College–Kingwood
John Todd, University of North Texas
Delaina Toothman, The University of Maine
David Trussell, Cisco College
Ronald Vardy, University of Houston
Linda Veazey, Midwestern State University
John Vento, Antelope Valley Community College
Clif Wilkinson, Georgia College
John Wood, Rose State College
Michael Young, Trinity Valley Community College
Tyler Young, Collin College

Tenth Edition Reviewers

Stephen P. Amberg, University of Texas at San Antonio
Juan F. Arzola, College of the Sequoias
Thomas J. Baldino, Wilkes University

Christina Bejarano, University of Kansas
Paul T. Bellinger, Jr., University of Missouri
Melanie J. Blumberg, California University of Pennsylvania
Matthew T. Bradley, Indiana University Kokomo
Jeffrey W. Christiansen, Seminole State College
McKinzie Craig, Marietta College
Christopher Cronin, Methodist University
Jenna Duke, Lehigh Carbon Community College
Francisco Durand, University of Texas at San Antonio
Carrie Eaves, Elon University
Paul M. Flor, El Camino College Compton Center
Adam Fuller, Youngstown State University
Christi Gramling, Charleston Southern University
Sally Hansen, Daytona State College
Mary Jane Hatton, Hawai'i Pacific University
David Helpap, University of Wisconsin–Green Bay
Theresa L. Hutchins, Georgia Highlands College
Cryshanna A. Jackson Leftwich, Youngstown State University
Ashlyn Kuersten, Western Michigan University
Kara Lindaman, Winona State University
Timothy Lynch, University of Wisconsin–Milwaukee
Larry McElvain, South Texas College
Corinna R. McKoy, Ventura College
Eddie L. Meaders, University of North Texas
Don D. Mirjanian, College of Southern Nevada
R. Shea Mize, Georgia Highlands College
Nicholas Morgan, Collin College
Matthew Murray, Dutchess Community College
Harold "Trey" Orndorff III, Daytona State College
Randall Parish, University of North Georgia
Michelle Pautz, University of Dayton
Michael Pickering, University of New Orleans
Donald Ranish, Antelope Valley College

Glenn W. Richardson, Jr., Kutztown
    University of Pennsylvania
Jason Robles, Colorado State University
Ionas Aurelian Rus, University of
    Cincinnati–Blue Ash
Robert Sahr, Oregon State University
Kelly B. Shaw, Iowa State University
Captain Michael Slattery, Campbell
    University

Michael Smith, Sam Houston State University
Maryam T. Stevenson, University of
    Indianapolis
Elizabeth Trentanelli, Gulf Coast State
    College
Ronald W. Vardy, University of Houston
Timothy Weaver, University of Louisville
Christina Wolbrecht, University of Notre
    Dame

We are also grateful to Holley Hansen, of Oklahoma State University, who contributed to the "America Side by Side" boxes, and to Gabrielle Ellul for research assistance.

Perhaps above all, we wish to thank those at W. W. Norton. For its first five editions, editor Steve Dunn helped us shape the book in countless ways. Ann Shin carried on the Norton tradition of splendid editorial work on the Sixth through Ninth Editions. Our current editor, Lisa McKay, has brought smart ideas and a keen editorial eye to this Tenth Edition. For our coursepack and other instructor resources for the book, Toni Magyar has been an energetic and visionary editor. Nina Hnatov copyedited the manuscript, and our superb project editor Christine D'Antonio devoted countless hours keeping on top of myriad details. Ashley Horna has been dedicated in managing production. We thank Julie Tesser for finding new photos. Finally, we wish to thank Roby Harrington, the head of Norton's college department.

Benjamin Ginsberg
Theodore J. Lowi
Margaret Weir
Caroline J. Tolbert
Robert J. Spitzer

November 2014

TENTH ESSENTIALS EDITION

We the People

AN INTRODUCTION TO AMERICAN POLITICS

Most Americans share the core political values of liberty, equality, and democracy and want their government and its policies to reflect these values. However, people often disagree on the meaning of these values and what government should do to protect them.

Introduction: The Citizen and Government

WHAT GOVERNMENT DOES AND WHY IT MATTERS Americans some-times appear to believe that the government is an institution that does things to them and from which they need protection. Students may wonder why they have to fill in long, often complicated forms to apply for financial assistance. They may frown when they see the payroll tax deducted from their small pay-check. Like Americans of all ages, they may resent municipal "red-light" cam-eras designed to photograph traffic violators — and send them tickets.

Although most people complain about something that government does *to* them, most everyone wants the government to do a great deal *for* them. Some of the services that people expect from government are big-ticket items, such as providing national security and keeping the nation safe from terrorist at-tacks. We all know that government pays for and directs the military. Students attending a state university know that state and federal public dollars help support their education.

Yet many of the other services that government provides are far less visible, and often it is not even clear that government plays a role at all. For example, students grabbing a quick bite to eat between classes take it for granted that their hamburger will not contain bacteria that might make them sick. With-out federal inspection of meat, however, chances of contracting food-borne illnesses would be much higher and the everyday task of eating would be much riskier. Driving to school would not be possible if not for the tens of billions of dollars spent each year on road construction and maintenance by federal, state, and municipal governments. Like most Americans, young people expect to get reliable information about the weather for the week ahead and warnings about dangerous events such as hurricanes. The National Weather Service and the National Hurricane Center both provide reliable forecasts for such simple calculations as whether to bring an umbrella to more significant calculations made by airlines and air traffic control to get travelers safely where they need to go. These daily decisions don't seem to involve government but in fact they do. Indeed, most Americans would not be here at all if it were not for federal immigration policies, which set the terms for entry into the United States and for obtaining citizenship.

Government is the term generally used to describe the formal institutions through which a land and its people are ruled. As the government seeks to protect its citizens, it faces the challenge of doing so in ways that are true to the key American political values of liberty, equality, and democracy. Liberty means personal freedom and a government whose powers are limited by law. Equality is the idea that all individuals should have the right to participate in political life and society on equivalent terms. Democracy means placing considerable political power in the hands of ordinary people. Most Americans find it easy to affirm all three values in principle. In practice, however, matters are not always so clear. Policies and practices that seem to affirm one of these values may contradict another. Americans, moreover, are sometimes willing to subordinate liberty to security and have frequently tolerated significant departures from the principles of equality and democracy.

chaptergoals

- Explore Americans' attitudes toward government (pp. 5–7)
- Describe the role of the citizen in politics (pp. 7–10)
- Define government and forms of government (pp. 10–13)
- Show how the social composition of the American population has changed over time (pp. 13–18)
- Analyze whether the U.S. system of government upholds American political values (pp. 18–21)

● Government Affects Our Lives Every Day

Explore Americans' attitudes toward government

Since the United States was established as a nation, Americans have been reluctant to grant government too much power, and they have often been suspicious of politicians. But over the course of the nation's history, Americans have also turned to government for assistance in times of need and have strongly supported the government in periods of war. In 1933 the power of the government began to expand to meet the crises created by the stock market crash of 1929, the Great Depression, and the run on banks. Congress passed legislation that brought the government into the businesses of home mortgages, farm mortgages, credit, and relief of personal distress. More recently, when the economy fell into a recession in 2008 and 2009, the federal government stepped in to shore up the financial system, oversee the restructuring of the ailing auto companies, and inject hundreds of billions of dollars into the faltering economy. Today, the national government is an enormous institution with programs and policies reaching into every corner of American life. It oversees the nation's economy; it is the nation's largest employer; it provides citizens with a host of services; it controls the world's most formidable military establishment; and it regulates a wide range of social and commercial activities.

Much of what citizens have come to depend on and take for granted—as, somehow, part of the natural environment—is in fact created by government. Take the example of a typical college student's day, throughout which that student relies on a host of services and activities organized by national, state, and local government agencies. The extent of this dependence on government is illustrated by Table 1.1.

Trust in Government Has Declined

Ironically, even as popular dependence on it has grown, the American public's view of government has turned more sour. Public trust in government has declined, and Americans are now more likely to feel that they can do little to influence the government's actions. Different groups vary somewhat in their levels of trust: African Americans and Latinos express more confidence in the federal government than do whites. But even among the most supportive groups, more than half do not trust the government.[1] These developments are important because politically engaged citizens and public confidence in government are vital for the health of a democracy.

By 2013, only 19 percent of Americans reported trusting the government in Washington "to do what is right" all or most of the time, down from 75 percent in the early 1960s.[2] Several factors contributed to the decline in trust. Revelations about the faulty information that led up to the war in Iraq and ongoing concern about the war had increased Americans' mistrust of government. In March 2007, 54 percent of those surveyed believed that the Bush administration had deliberately misled the American public about whether Iraq had weapons of mass destruction. By 2012, the government's inability to get the economy moving had further undermined trust in government. When political differences over the Affordable Care Act, President Obama's program to reform the American health care system (also called "Obamacare"), led to a two-week partial government

TABLE 1.1

The Presence of Government in the Daily Life of a Student at "State University"

TIME OF DAY	SCHEDULE
7:00 AM	Wake up. Standard time set by the national government.
7:10 AM	Shower. Water courtesy of local government, either a public entity or a regulated private company. Brush your teeth with toothpaste whose cavity-fighting claims have been verified by a federal agency.
7:30 AM	Have a bowl of cereal with milk for breakfast. "Nutrition Facts" on food labels are a federal requirement, pasteurization of milk required by state law, recycling the empty cereal box and milk carton enabled by state or local laws.
8:30 AM	Drive or take public transportation to campus. Air bags and seat belts required by federal and state laws. Roads and bridges paid for by state and local governments, speed and traffic laws set by state and local governments, public transportation subsidized by all levels of government.
8:45 AM	Arrive on campus of large public university. Buildings are 70 percent financed by state taxpayers.
9:00 AM	First class: Chemistry 101. Tuition partially paid by a federal loan (more than half the cost of university instruction is paid for by taxpayers), chemistry lab paid for with grants from the National Science Foundation (a federal agency).
Noon	Eat lunch. College cafeteria financed by state dormitory authority on land grant from federal Department of Agriculture.
2:00 PM	Second class: American Government 101 (your favorite class!). You may be taking this class because it is required by the state legislature or because it fulfills a university requirement.
4:00 PM	Third class: Computer Lab. Free computers, software, and Internet access courtesy of state subsidies plus grants and discounts from IBM and Microsoft, the costs of which are deducted from their corporate income taxes; Internet built in part by federal government.
6:00 PM	Eat hamburger for dinner. Meat inspected by federal agencies.
7:00 PM	Work at part-time job at the campus library. Minimum wage set by federal, state, or local government, books and journals in library paid for by state taxpayers.
8:15 PM	Check the status of your application for a federal student loan (FAFSA) on the Department of Education's website at studentaid.ed.gov.
10:00 PM	Go home. Street lighting paid for by county and city governments, police patrols by city government.
10:15 PM	Watch TV. Networks regulated by federal government, cable public-access channels required by city law. Weather forecast provided to broadcasters by a federal agency.

shutdown in 2013 and the second dramatic showdown over raising the national debt limit in two years (usually a routine matter), public trust once again dipped to historically low levels.[3]

Does it matter if Americans trust their government? For the most part, the answer is yes. As we have seen, most Americans rely on government for a wide range of services and laws that they simply take for granted. But long-term distrust in government can result in public refusal to pay taxes adequate to support such widely approved public activities. Low levels of confidence may also make it difficult for government to attract talented and effective workers to public service.[4] The weakening of government as a result of prolonged levels of distrust may ultimately harm the capacity of the United States to defend its national interest in the world economy and may jeopardize its national security. Likewise, a weak government can do little to assist citizens who need help in weathering periods of sharp economic or technological change.

Political Efficacy Means People Can Make a Difference

Another important trend in American views about government has been a declining sense of **political efficacy**, the belief that ordinary citizens can affect what government does, that they can take action to make government listen to them. In 2014, 78 percent of Americans said that elected officials do not care what people like them think; in 1960, only 25 percent felt so shut out of government.[5] Accompanying this sense that ordinary people cannot be heard is a growing belief that government is not run for the benefit of all the people. In 2012, 57 percent of the public disagreed with the idea that the "government is really run for the benefit of all the people."[6] These views are widely shared across the age spectrum.

This widely felt loss of political efficacy is bad news for American democracy. The feeling that you can't affect government decisions can lead to a self-perpetuating cycle of apathy, declining political participation, and withdrawal from political life. Why bother to participate if you believe it makes no difference? Yet the belief that you can be effective is the first step needed to influence government. Not every effort of ordinary citizens to influence government will succeed, but without any such efforts, government decisions will be made by a smaller and smaller circle of powerful people. Such loss of broad popular influence over government actions undermines the key feature of American democracy: government by the people.

● Citizenship Is Based on Political Knowledge and Participation

Describe the role of the citizen in politics

Beginning with the ancient Greeks, citizenship has meant membership in one's community. In fact, the Greeks did not even conceive of the individual as a complete person. The complete person was the public person, the *citizen*; a noncitizen or a private person was referred to as an *idiōtēs*. Participation in public affairs was virtually the definition of citizenship.

Today, voting is considered the building block of **citizenship**—informed and active membership in a political community—as it is the method by which Americans choose their elected leaders. Citizens can influence their government in many ways, including serving on a jury, lobbying, writing a letter to the editor of a local newspaper, and engaging in a public rally or protest. The point of these activities is to influence the government.

Citizens need political knowledge to figure out how best to act in their own interests. To take a simple example, if the garbage is not collected from in front of people's homes, people need to know that this job is the responsibility of their local government, not the national government. Americans often complain that government does not respond to their needs, but sometimes the failure of government to act may simply result from citizens' lacking the information necessary to present their problems to the correct government office or agency. To put the matter more simply, effective participation requires knowledge. (It should come as no surprise, then, that people who have less knowledge of politics vote at lower rates than those with more knowledge.) Knowledge is the first prerequisite for achieving an increased sense of political efficacy.

When the federal government partially shut down in October 2013, millions of citizens were affected, including visitors who were turned away from the Statue of Liberty. Citizens need political knowledge to understand how such events affect their lives and what policies promote their interests.

Digital Citizenship Is the Newest Way to Participate

As more and more of our social, workplace, and educational activities have migrated online, so too have opportunities for political knowledge and participation, creating a new concept of "digital citizenship." Digital citizenship is the ability to participate in society online, and it is increasingly important in politics. A 2012 Pew survey found that 75 percent of Americans read the news online and more than 6 in 10 look up political information online. People also seek out government information online; 67 percent visit a local, state, or federal government website.[7] Digital citizenship benefits individuals, but it also provides advantages to society as a whole. Digital citizens are more likely to be

Political Knowledge and Trust in Government

In every country, citizens rely on government to provide certain services. But the relationship between a government and its people can vary, as does the level of trust a people have in their government. Trust in government may encourage citizens to pay taxes, engage in civic behavior, or join the government workforce. Lack of trust can make it hard for government officials to achieve public goals by reducing support for spending on public programs. Lack of trust may also cause citizens to be cynical about government and lead them to disengage from public life. In this sense, lack of trust can undermine democracy. At the extreme, lack of trust can lead to social unrest and even revolution.

How much do levels of trust in government vary across countries? Which group is more likely to trust in government, the general population or the informed public? Many of the democracies in the table below, including the United States, have lower levels of trust in government than China, a nondemocratic country. Why would Americans be less trusting of their government than citizens of China, whose government is much less open to public scrutiny?

Country	Percentage Who Trusts Government among General Public	Percentage Who Trusts Government among Informed Public	Difference	Type of Government
China	70	80	−10	Communist state
India	64	71	−7	Parliamentary federal republic
Brazil	51	55	−4	Presidental federal republic
United States	45	59	−14	Presidental federal republic
Germany	44	55	−11	Parliamentary federal republic
Turkey	43	42	1	Republican parliamentary democracy
United Kingdom	43	53	−10	Constitutional monarchy
Poland	34	48	−14	Parliamentary republic
Russia	30	36	−6	Nondemocratic federation

NOTE: The data for the general population are based on 1,000 responses (adults age 18 years and older) per country surveyed. The data for informed publics are based on 500 responses each in China and the United States and 200 responses each in other countries; respondents are adults ages 25–64 who are college educated and in the top 25 percent of household income for their age bracket in their country, and who report significant engagement in business and policy news.

SOURCE: Edelman Trust Barometer Survey, 2013, http://edelmaneditions.com/wp-content/uploads/2013/01/EMBARGOED-2013-Edelman-Trust-Barometer-Global-Deck_FINAL.pdf (accessed 1/14/14).

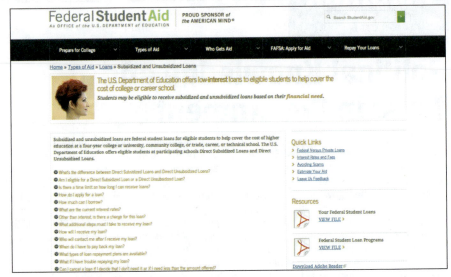

The federal government maintains a large number of websites that provide useful information to citizens on such topics as loans for education, civil service job applications, the inflation rate, and how the weather will affect farming. These sites are just one way in which the government serves its citizens.

interested in politics and to discuss politics with friends, family, and coworkers than individuals who do not use online political information. They are also more likely to vote and participate in other ways in elections. Individuals without Internet access or the skills to participate in politics and the economy online are being left further behind. Exclusion from participation online is referred to as the digital divide. Lower-income and less-educated Americans, racial and ethnic minorities, those living in rural areas, and the elderly are all less likely to have Internet access.

Greater political knowledge increases the ability of people to influence their government. It is to the nature of government that we now turn.

Government Is Made Up of the Institutions and Procedures by Which People Are Ruled

> **Define government and forms of government**

Government refers to the formal institutions and procedures through which a territory and its people are ruled. To govern is to rule. A government may be as simple as a tribal council that meets occasionally to advise the chief, or as complex as the vast establishments—with their forms, rules, and bureaucracies—found in the United States and the countries of Europe. A more complex government is sometimes referred to as "the state." In the history of civilization, governments have not been difficult to establish. There have been thousands of them. The hard part is establishing a government that lasts. Even more difficult is developing a stable government that promotes liberty, equality, and democracy.

Different Forms of Government Are Defined by Power and Freedom

Governments vary in their structure, in their size, and in the way they operate. Two questions are of special importance in determining how governments differ: Who governs? And how much government control is permitted?

In some nations, government power is held by a single individual, such as a king or dictator, or by a small group of powerful individuals, such as military leaders or wealthy landowners. Such a system of government normally pays little attention to popular preferences; it tends to hold power by violence or the threat of violence and is referred to as an **authoritarian** system, meaning that the government recognizes no formal limit but may nevertheless be restrained by the power of other social institutions. A system of government in which the degree of control is even greater is a **totalitarian** system, where the government recognizes no formal limits on its power and seeks to absorb or eliminate other social institutions that might challenge it. Nazi Germany under Adolf Hitler and the Soviet Union under Joseph Stalin are classic examples of totalitarian rule.

In contrast, a **democracy** is a political system that permits citizens to play a significant part in the governmental process, usually through the election of key public officials. Under such a system, **constitutional government** is the norm, in that formal and effective limits are placed on the powers of the government. At times, an authoritarian government might bend to popular wishes, and democratic governments do not automatically follow the wishes of the majority. The point, however, is that these contrasting systems of government are based on very different assumptions and practices.

Americans have the good fortune to live in a nation in which limits are placed on what governments can do and how they can do it. By one measure, just 43 percent of the global population (those living in 90 countries) enjoy sufficient levels of political and personal freedom to be classified as living in a constitutional democracy.[8] And constitutional democracies were unheard of before the modern era. Prior to the eighteenth and nineteenth centuries, governments seldom sought (and rarely received) the support of their ordinary subjects.[9]

Beginning in the seventeenth century, in a handful of Western nations, two important changes began to take place in the character and conduct of government. First, governments began to acknowledge formal limits on their power. Second, a small number of governments began to provide the ordinary citizen with a formal voice in public affairs—through the vote. Obviously, the desirability of limits on government and the expansion of popular influence were at the heart of the American Revolution in 1776. "No taxation without representation" was hotly debated from the beginning of the Revolution through the adoption of the modern Constitution in 1789. But even before the Revolution, a tradition of limiting government and expanding citizen participation in the political process had developed throughout western Europe. Thus, to understand how the relationship between rulers and the ruled was transformed, we must broaden our focus to take into account events in Europe as well as in America. We will divide the transformation into its two separate parts. The first is the effort to put limits on government. The second is the effort to expand the influence of the people through access to government and politics.

Limits on Governments Encouraged Freedom

The key force behind the imposition of limits on government power was a new social class, the bourgeoisie. *Bourgeoisie* is a French word for "freeman of the city," or *bourg*. Being part of the bourgeoisie later became associated with being "middle class" and with involvement in commerce or industry. In order to gain a share of control of government, joining or even displacing the kings, aristocrats, and gentry who had dominated government for centuries, the bourgeoisie sought to change existing institutions—especially parliaments—into instruments of real political participation. Parliaments had existed for centuries but were generally controlled by the aristocrats. The bourgeoisie embraced parliaments as means by which they could exert the weight of their superior numbers and growing economic advantage against their aristocratic rivals. At the same time, the bourgeoisie sought to restrain the capacity of governments to threaten these economic and political interests by placing formal or constitutional limits on governmental power.

Although motivated primarily by the need to protect and defend their own interests, the bourgeoisie advanced many of the principles that became the central underpinnings of individual liberty for all citizens—freedom of speech, freedom of assembly, freedom of conscience, and freedom from arbitrary search and seizure. It is important to note here that the bourgeoisie generally did not favor democracy as we know it. They were advocates of electoral and representative institutions, but they favored property requirements and other restrictions so as to limit political participation to the middle and upper classes. Yet once these institutions of politics and the protection of the right to engage in politics were established, it was difficult to limit them to the bourgeoisie.

Expansion of Participation in America Changed the Political Balance

In America, the expansion of participation to ever-larger segments of society, seen mostly in the expansion of voting rights, occurred because competing segments of the bourgeoisie sought to gain political advantage by reaching out and mobilizing the support of working- and lower-class groups that craved the opportunity to take part in politics—"lining up the unwashed," as one American historian put it.[10] To be sure, excluded groups often agitated for greater participation. But seldom was such agitation, by itself, enough to secure the right to participate. Usually, expansion of voting rights resulted from a combination of pressure from below and help from above.

This pattern of suffrage expansion by groups hoping to derive some political advantage has been typical in American history. After the Civil War, one of the chief reasons that Lincoln's Republican Party moved to enfranchise newly freed slaves was to use the support of the former slaves to maintain Republican control over the defeated southern states. Similarly, in the early twentieth century, upper-middle-class Progressives advocated women's suffrage because they believed that women were likely to support the reforms espoused by the Progressive movement.

The Goal of Politics Is Having a Say in What Happens

Expansion of participation means that more and more people have a legal right to take part in politics. *Politics* is an important term. In its broadest sense, it refers to conflicts over the character, membership, and policies of any organization to which people belong. As Harold Lasswell, a famous political scientist, once put it, politics is the struggle over "who gets what, when, how."[11] Although politics is a phenomenon that can be found in any organization, our concern in this book is narrower. Here, **politics** will be used to refer only to conflicts and struggles over the leadership, structure, and policies of governments. The goal of politics, as we define it, is to have a share or a say in the composition of the government's leadership, how the government is organized, or what its policies are going to be. Having a share is called **power** (influence over a government's leadership, organization, or policies) or influence.

Politics can take many forms, including blogging and posting opinion pieces online, voting, sending emails to government officials, lobbying legislators on behalf of particular programs, and participating in protest marches and even violent demonstrations. A system of government in which the populace selects representatives, who play a significant role in governmental decision making, is usually called a **representative democracy**, or **republic**. A system that permits citizens to vote directly on laws and policies is often called a **direct democracy**. At the national level, America is a representative democracy in which citizens select government officials but do not vote on legislation. Some states and cities, however, have provisions for direct legislation through ballot initiative and popular referendum. In 2014, 158 initiatives appeared on state ballots.

● The Identity of Americans Has Changed over Time

> **Show how the social composition of the American population has changed over time**

While American democracy aims to give the people a voice in government, the meaning of "we the people" has changed over time. Who are Americans? Over the course of American history, politicians, religious leaders, prominent scholars, and ordinary Americans have puzzled over and fought about the answer to this fundamental question. It is not surprising that such a simple question could provoke so much conflict: the American population has increased over eightyfold, from 3.9 million in 1790, the year of the first official census, to 318 million in 2014. As the American population has grown, it has become more diverse in nearly every dimension imaginable.[12]

At the time of the Founding, when the United States consisted of 13 states arrayed along the Eastern Seaboard, 81 percent of Americans counted by the census traced their roots to Europe, mostly England and northern Europe; nearly one in five were of African origin, the vast majority of whom were slaves.[13] There was also an unknown number of Native Americans, not counted by the census because the government did not consider them Americans.[14]

Fast-forward to 1900. The country, now stretched out across the continent, had a sharply altered racial and ethnic composition. Waves of immigrants, mainly from Europe, had boosted the population to 76 million. The black population stood at 12 percent. Residents who traced their origins to Latin America or Asia each accounted for less than 1 percent of the entire population.[15] Although principally of European origin, the American population had become much more ethnically diverse as immigrants, first from Germany, then Ireland, and finally from southern and eastern Europe, made their way to the United States. The foreign-born population of the United States reached its height at 14.7 percent in 1910.[16]

Immigration and Increasing Ethnic Diversity Have Always Caused Intense Debate

As the population grew more diverse, anxiety about Americans' ethnic identity mounted, and much as today, politicians and scholars argued about whether the country could absorb such large numbers of immigrants. The debate encompassed such issues as whether immigrants' political and social values were compatible with American democracy, whether they would learn English, and what diseases they might bring into the United States.

Immigrants' religious affiliations also aroused concern. The first immigrants to the United States were overwhelmingly Protestant, many of them fleeing religious persecution. The arrival of Germans and Irish in the mid-1800s meant increasing numbers of Catholics, and the large-scale immigration of the early twentieth century threatened to reduce the percentage of Protestants significantly: eastern European immigrants pouring into the country were heavily Jewish, while the southern Europeans were mostly Catholic. A more religiously diverse country challenged the implicit Protestantism embedded in many aspects of American public life.

After World War I, Congress responded to the fears swirling around immigration with new laws that sharply limited the number of immigrants who could enter the country each year. Congress also established a new National Origins Quota System based on the nation's population in 1890 before the wave of immigrants from eastern and southern Europe arrived.[17] The new system set up a hierarchy of admissions: northern European countries received generous quotas for new immigrants, whereas eastern and southern European countries were granted very small quotas. These restrictions ratcheted down the numbers of immigrants, so that by 1970, the foreign-born population in the United States reached an all-time low of 5 percent.

Changing Government Criteria for Racial Classification Reflect America's Changing Identity

Official efforts to use racial and ethnic criteria to restrict the American population were not new. The very first census, as we have seen, did not count Native

Americans; in fact, Native Americans were not granted the right to vote until 1924. Most people of African descent were not officially citizens until 1868, when the Fourteenth Amendment to the Constitution conferred citizenship on the freed slaves.

In 1790 the federal government had sought to limit the nonwhite population with a law stipulating that only free whites could become naturalized citizens. Not until 1870 did Congress lift the ban on the naturalization of nonwhites. Restrictions applied to Asians as well. The Chinese Exclusion Act of 1882 outlawed the entry of Chinese laborers to the United States, and additional barriers enacted after World War I meant that virtually no Asians entered the country as immigrants until 1943, when China became our ally in World War II and these provisions were lifted. People of Hispanic origin do not fit simply into the American system of racial classification. In 1930, for example, the census counted people of Mexican origin as nonwhite, but it reversed this decision a decade later. Not until 1970 did the census officially begin counting persons of Hispanic origin, noting that they could be any race.[18]

Today the Country Still Confronts the Question "Who Are Americans?"

Race and Ethnicity By 2000, immigration had profoundly transformed the nation's racial and ethnic profile once again. The primary cause was Congress's decision in 1965 to lift the tight immigration restrictions of the 1920s, a decision that resulted, among other things, in the growth of the Latino population (see Figure 1.1). Census figures for 2012 show that the total Hispanic proportion of the population is now 17 percent, while the black, or African American, population is 13 percent of the total population. Asians make up 5 percent of the population. European Americans account for less than two-thirds of the population—their lowest share ever. Moreover, about 2.5 percent of the population now identifies itself as of "two or more races," a new category added to the census in 2000.[19] Although it is only a small percentage of the population, the multiracial category points toward a future in which the lines separating the traditional labels of racial identification may be blurring.

In 2012, 13 percent of the population was born outside the United States, a figure comparable to the rates of foreign born at the turn of the previous century. Over half of the foreign-born population came from Latin America, with nearly 4 in 10 from Central America (including Mexico). Those born in Asia constituted the next largest group, making up over one-quarter of foreign-born residents. By 2012, less than 12 percent of those born outside the United States came from Europe.[20] These figures represent only legally authorized immigrants, while estimates put the number of undocumented immigrants at almost 12 million, the majority of whom are from Mexico and Central America.[21]

Religion The new patterns of immigration combined with a number of other factors to alter the religious affiliations of Americans. In 1900, 80 percent of the population was Protestant; by 2012, 48 percent of Americans identified themselves

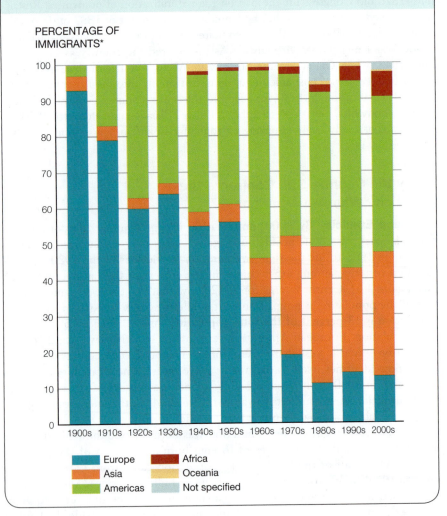

FIGURE 1.1 Immigration by Continent of Origin

Where did most immigrants come from at the start of the twentieth century? How does that compare with immigration in the twenty-first century?

*Less than 1 percent not shown.
SOURCE: Department of Homeland Security, "Yearbook of Immigration Statistics, 2008: Persons Obtaining Legal Permanent Resident Status by State of Residence: Fiscal Years 1999 to 2008," www.dhs.gov (accessed 9/28/09).

PERCENTAGE OF IMMIGRANTS*

Legend: Europe, Asia, Americas, Africa, Oceania, Not specified

as Protestants.[22] Catholics made up 22 percent of the population and Jews accounted for 1.8 percent. A small Muslim population had also grown, to over 0.8 percent of the population. One of the most important changes in religious affiliation during the latter half of the twentieth century was the percentage of people who professed no organized religion. In 2012, 20 percent of the population was not affiliated with an organized church. These changes suggest an important shift in American religious identity: although the United States thinks of itself as a

"Judeo-Christian" nation—and indeed was 95 percent Protestant, Catholic, or Jewish from 1900 to 1968—by 2012 the numbers had fallen to 75 percent of the adult population.[23]

Age As America grew and its population expanded and diversified, the country's age profile shifted with it. In 1900 only 4 percent of the population was over 65. As life expectancy increased, the number of older Americans grew with it: by 2012, nearly 14 percent of the population was over 65. The number of children under the age of 18 also changed; in 1900 this group comprised 43 percent of the American population; by 2012, children 18 and under had fallen to about a quarter of the population.[24] An aging population poses challenges to the United States. As the elderly population grows and the working-age population shrinks, questions arise about how we will fund programs for the elderly such as Social Security.

Geography Over the nation's history, Americans have changed in other ways as well, moving from mostly rural settings and small towns to large urban areas. Before 1920, less than half the population lived in urban areas; today 80.7 percent of Americans do.[25] Critics charge that the American political system, created when America was a largely rural society, underrepresents urban areas. The constitutional provision allocating each state two senators, for example, overrepresents sparsely populated rural states and underrepresents urban states, where the population is far more concentrated. The American population has also shifted regionally. In the past 50 years, especially, many Americans have left the Northeast and Midwest and moved to the South and Southwest. As congressional seats have been reapportioned to reflect the population shift, many problems that particularly plague the Midwest and Northeast, such as the decline of manufacturing jobs, receive less attention in national politics.

Socioeconomic Status Americans have fallen into diverse economic groups throughout American history. For much of American history most people were relatively poor working people, many of them farmers. A small wealthy elite, however, grew larger in the 1890s, in a period called "the gilded age." By 1928, nearly one-quarter of the total annual income went to the top 1 percent of earners; the top 10 percent took home 46 percent of total annual income. After the New Deal in the 1930s, a large middle class took shape and the share going to those at the top dropped sharply. By 1976, the top 1 percent took home only 9 percent of the national annual income. Since then, however, economic inequality has once again widened as a tiny group of super-rich has emerged. By 2012, the top 1 percent earned 20 percent of annual income and the top 10 percent took home more than half of the total national income, the highest ever recorded.[26] At the same time, the incomes of the broad middle class have largely stagnated.[27] And 15 percent of the population remains below the official poverty line. As the middle class has frayed around the edges, the numbers of poor and near poor have swelled to nearly a third of the population.[28]

Population and Representation The shifting contours of the American people have regularly raised challenging questions about our politics and governing arrangements. Population growth has spurred politically charged debates about how the population should be apportioned among congressional districts and has also transformed the close democratic relationship between congressional representatives and their constituents envisioned by the framers. For example, the framers stipulated that the number of representatives in the House "shall not exceed one for every thirty Thousand" constituents; today the average member of Congress represents 721,641 constituents.[29] Immigration and the cultural and religious changes it entails provoked heated debates 100 years ago and still do today. The different languages and customs that immigrants bring to the United States trigger fears that the country is changing in ways that may undermine American values and alter fundamental identities. Yet a changing population has been one of the constants of American history.

America Is Built on the Ideas of Liberty, Equality, and Democracy

Analyze whether the U.S. system of government upholds American political values

A few fundamental values underlie the American system. These values are reflected in such Founding documents as the Declaration of Independence, the Constitution, and the Bill of Rights. The three values on which the American system of government is based are liberty, equality, and democracy.

Liberty Means Freedom

No ideal is more central to American values than liberty. The Declaration of Independence defined three inalienable rights: "Life, Liberty and the pursuit of Happiness." The preamble to the Constitution likewise identified the need to secure "the Blessings of Liberty" as one of the key reasons for which the Constitution was drawn up. For Americans, **liberty** means freedom from government control, and also economic freedom. Both are closely linked to the idea of **limited government**, meaning that powers are defined and limited by a constitution.

The Constitution's first 10 amendments, known collectively as the Bill of Rights, above all preserve individual personal liberties and rights. In fact, liberty has come to mean many of the freedoms guaranteed in the Bill of Rights: freedom of speech and writing, the right to assemble freely, and the right to practice religious beliefs without interference from the government. Over the course of American history, the scope of personal liberties has expanded, as laws have become more tolerant and as individuals have successfully used the courts to challenge restrictions on their individual freedoms. Far fewer restrictions exist today on the press, political speech, and individual moral behavior than in the early years of the nation. Even so, conflicts persist over how personal liberties should be extended and when personal liberties violate community norms. For example, a number of cities have recently passed "sit-lie" ordinances, which limit the freedom of individuals to sit or lie down on sidewalks. Designed to limit the presence of the homeless and make city streets more attractive to pedestrians, the ordinances have also been denounced as infringements on individual liberties.

In addition to personal freedom, the American concept of liberty means economic freedom. Since the Founding, economic freedom has been linked to capitalism, free markets, and the protection of private property. Free competition, the unfettered movement of goods, and the right to enjoy the fruits of one's labor are all essential aspects of economic freedom and American capitalism.[30] In the first century of the republic, support for capitalism often meant support for the doctrine of laissez-faire (literally, "let do" in French), an economic system in which the means of production and distribution are privately owned and operated for profit with minimal or no government interference. **Laissez-faire capitalism** allowed very little room for the national government to regulate trade or restrict the use of private property, even in the public interest. Americans still strongly support capitalism and economic liberty, but they now also endorse some restrictions on economic freedoms to protect the public. Federal and state governments now deploy a wide array of regulations in the name of public protection. These include health and safety laws, environmental rules, and workplace regulations. Not surprisingly, fierce disagreements often erupt over what the proper scope of government regulation should be. What some people regard as protecting the public, others see as an infringement of their own freedom to run their businesses and use their property as they see fit.

Equality Means Treating People Fairly

The Declaration of Independence declares as its first "self-evident" truth that "all men are created equal." As central as it is to the American political creed, however, equality has been a less well-defined ideal than liberty because people interpret "equality" in different ways. Most Americans share the ideal of **equality of opportunity** wherein all people should have the freedom to use whatever talents and wealth they have to reach their fullest potential. Yet it is hard for Americans to reach an agreement on what constitutes equality of opportunity. Must *past* inequalities be remedied in order to ensure equal opportunity in the *present*? Should inequalities in the legal, political, and economic spheres be given the same weight? In contrast to liberty, which requires limits on the role of government, equality implies an *obligation* of the government to the people.[31]

Americans do make clear distinctions between political equality and social or economic equality. **Political equality** refers to the right to participate in politics equally, based on the principle of "one person, one vote." Beginning from a very restricted definition of political community, which originally included only propertied white men, the United States has moved much closer to an ideal of political equality. Broad support for this ideal has helped expand the American political community and extend the right to participate to all. Although considerable conflict remains over whether the political system makes it harder for some people to participate and easier for others and about whether the role of money in politics has drowned out the public voice, Americans agree that all citizens should have an equal opportunity to participate and that government should enforce that right.

In part because Americans believe that individuals are free to work as hard as they choose, they have always been less concerned about social or economic inequality (see Figure 1.2). Many Americans regard economic differences as the consequence of individual choices, virtues, or failures. Because of this, Americans tend to be less supportive than most Europeans of government action to ensure economic equality.

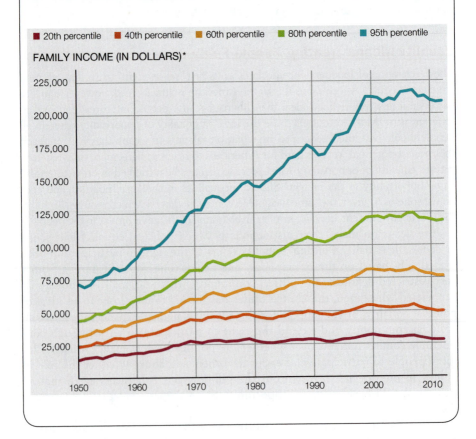

FIGURE 1.2 Income in the United States

The graph shows that while the income of most Americans has risen only slightly since 1950, the income of the richest Americans (the top 5 percent) has increased dramatically. What are some of the ways that this shift might matter for American politics? Does the growing economic gap between the richest groups and most other Americans conflict with the political value of equality?

*Dollar values are given in constant 2012 dollars, which are adjusted for inflation so that we can compare a person's income in 1950 with a person's income today.
SOURCE: U.S. Census Bureau, Current Population Survey, www.census.gov/hhes/www/income/data/historical /inequality/index.html (accessed 1/14/14).

■ 20th percentile   ■ 40th percentile   ■ 60th percentile   ■ 80th percentile   ■ 95th percentile

FAMILY INCOME (IN DOLLARS)*

Democracy Means That What the People Want Matters

The essence of democracy is the participation of the people in choosing their rulers and the people's ability to influence what those rulers do. In a democracy, political power ultimately comes from the people. The principle of democracy in which political authority rests ultimately in the hands of the people is known as **popular sovereignty**. In the United States, popular sovereignty and political equality make politicians accountable to the people. Ideally, democracy envisions an engaged citizenry prepared to exercise its power over rulers. As we noted earlier, the United States is a representative democracy, meaning that the people do not rule directly but instead exercise power through elected representatives. Forms of participation in a democracy vary greatly, but voting is a key element of the representative democracy that the American Founders established.

American democracy rests on the principle of **majority rule** with **minority rights**, the democratic principle that a government follows the preferences of the majority of voters but protects the interests of the minority. Majority rule means that the wishes of the majority determine what government does. The House of Representatives— a large body elected directly by the people—was designed in particular to ensure majority rule. But the Founders feared that popular majorities could turn government into a "tyranny of the majority" in which individual liberties would be violated. Concern for individual rights has thus been a part of American democracy from the beginning. The rights enumerated in the Bill of Rights and enforced through the courts provide an important check on the power of the majority.

American Political Values
and Your Future

Americans express mixed views about government. Almost everyone complains about government, and general trust in government has declined significantly. Despite mounting distrust, when asked about particular government activities or programs, a majority of Americans generally support the activities that government undertakes. These conflicting views reflect the tensions in American political culture: there is no perfect balance between liberty, equality, and democracy. In recent years, finding the right mix of government actions to achieve these different goals has become especially troublesome. Some charge that government initiatives designed to promote equality infringe on individual liberty, while others point to the need for government to take action in the face of growing inequality. Sharp political debate over competing goals alienates many citizens who react by withdrawing from politics. Yet, in contrast to totalitarian and authoritarian forms of government, democracy rests on the principle of popular sovereignty. No true democracy can function properly without knowledgeable and engaged citizens.

The remarkable diversity of the American people represents a great strength for American democracy as well as a formidable challenge. The shifting religious, racial and ethnic, and immigration status of Americans throughout history has

Although most barriers to voting have been removed for Americans ages 18 and up, many people do not vote. In the 2014 election approximately 36 percent of eligible citizens turned out at the polls.

always provoked fears about whether American values could withstand such dramatic shifts. The changing face of America also sparks hopes for an America that embodies its fundamental values more fully.

Demographic changes will continue to raise tough new questions. For example, as the American population grows older, programs for the elderly will take up an increasing share of the federal budget. Yet to be successful, a nation must invest in its young people. And, as any college student knows, the cost of college has risen in recent years. Many students drop out as they discover that the cost of college is too high. Or they graduate and find themselves saddled with loans that will take decades to pay back. Yet, in a world of ever-sharper economic competition, higher education has become increasingly important for individuals seeking economic security. Moreover, an educated population is critical to the future prosperity of the country as a whole. Are there ways to support the elderly and the young at the same time? Is it fair to cut back assistance to the elderly, who have worked a lifetime for their benefits? If we decrease assistance to the elderly, will they stay in the labor market and make the job hunt for young people even more difficult? As these trade-offs suggest, there are no easy answers to these demographic changes.

plug in

Inform

Learn about the demographic diversity of your local area by entering your zip code on the U.S. Census website (http://factfinder2.census.gov/). How does your community compare to the American population as a whole?

Express

Make a list of the most important political values you hold. How do they fit into broader American values?

Connect

See what people across the country are thinking about government and politics at the Pew Research Center's website. Do you think officials in Washington, D.C., pay attention to the public's views?

Act

Rock the Vote helps young people express their political power by organizing concerts, registration drives, and other events. Consider attending or volunteering for one of the events listed for your state at www.rockthevote.com /get-involved/.

studyguide

Practice Quiz

1. Americans' trust in their government *(pp. 5–7)*
   a) has risen steadily since the 1960s.
   b) has declined significantly since the 1960s.
   c) has remained the same over the last 50 years.
   d) has never been studied.
   e) is irrelevant in a democracy.

2. *Political efficacy* is the belief that *(p. 7)*
   a) government operates efficiently.
   b) government has grown too large.
   c) government cannot be trusted.
   d) one can influence what government does.
   e) government is wasteful and corrupt.

3. According to the authors, good citizenship requires *(p. 8)*
   a) political knowledge and political engagement.
   b) political knowledge but not political engagement.
   c) political engagement but not political knowledge.
   d) a good education.
   e) a significant amount of money.

4. What is *digital citizenship*? *(pp. 8–9)*
   a) a new initiative to expand online voter registration
   b) the ability to vote online
   c) the ability to progress through a path to citizenship through an online program
   d) the ability to participate in society online
   e) a new initiative by the government to provide daily updates online

5. What is the difference between a totalitarian government and an authoritarian one? *(p. 11)*
   a) Authoritarian governments allow for popular participation.
   b) Totalitarian governments are generally based on religion.

   c) In an authoritarian government, certain social institutions may restrain the power of the government.
   d) In a totalitarian government, formal and effective limits are placed on the power of the government.
   e) There is no difference between the two.

6. In a constitutional government *(p. 11)*
   a) the government recognizes no formal limits on its power.
   b) presidential elections are always held every four years.
   c) the governmental power is held by a single individual.
   d) formal and effective limits are placed on the powers of government.
   e) the government follows the wishes of the majority.

7. Although not present at the national level, a number of states and cities permit citizens to vote directly on laws and policies. What is this form of rule called? *(p. 13)*
   a) representative democracy
   b) direct democracy
   c) pluralism
   d) laissez-faire capitalism
   e) a republic

8. The percentage of foreign-born individuals living in the United States *(pp. 14–15)*
   a) has increased significantly since reaching its low point in 1970.
   b) has decreased significantly since reaching its high point in 1970.
   c) has remained the same since 1970.
   d) has never been less than the percentage of native-born individuals living in the United States.
   e) has not been studied since 1970.

9. Since 1900, which of the following groups has increased as a percentage of the overall population in the United States? *(pp. 14–15)*
   a) black, Hispanic, and Asian
   b) Hispanic only
   c) Asian only
   d) black only
   e) Hispanic and Asian only

10. As a percentage of the total population in the United States, which age group has increased the most dramatically from 1900 to 2010? *(p. 17)*
    a) children
    b) young adults, ages 20–30
    c) adults, ages 30–44
    d) the elderly
    e) The percentage for each group has remained about the same.

11. What percentage of Americans live in urban areas today? *(p. 17)*
    a) less than 10 percent
    b) about 20 percent
    c) about 40 percent
    d) about 60 percent
    e) about 80 percent

12. Which of the following is *not* related to the American conception of liberty? *(pp. 18–19)*
    a) freedom of speech
    b) economic liberty
    c) freedom of religion
    d) freedom of assembly
    e) All of the above are related to liberty.

13. Which of the following is *not* part of the core value of the American political system? *(pp. 18–21)*
    a) belief in equality of results
    b) belief in equality of opportunity
    c) belief in individual liberty
    d) belief in capitalism
    e) belief in democracy

14. The principle of political equality can be best summed up as *(p. 19)*
    a) "equality of results."
    b) "equality of opportunity."
    c) "one person, one vote."
    d) "equality between the sexes."
    e) "leave everyone alone."

Key Terms

authoritarian government *(p. 11)* a system of rule in which the government recognizes no formal limit but may nevertheless be restrained by the power of other social institutions

citizenship *(p. 8)* informed and active membership in a political community

constitutional government *(p. 11)* a system of rule in which formal and effective limits are placed on the powers of the government

democracy *(p. 11)* a system of rule that permits citizens to play a significant part in the governmental process, usually through the election of key public officials

direct democracy *(p. 13)* a system of rule that permits citizens to vote directly on laws and policies

equality of opportunity *(p. 19)* a widely shared American ideal that all people should have the freedom to use whatever talents and wealth they have to reach their fullest potential

government *(p. 4)* institutions and procedures through which a territory and its people are ruled

laissez-faire capitalism *(p. 19)* an economic system in which the means of production and distribution are privately owned and operated for profit with minimal or no government interference

liberty *(p. 18)* freedom from government control

limited government *(p. 18)* a principle of constitutional government; a government whose powers are defined and limited by a constitution

majority rule/minority rights *(p. 21)* the democratic principle that a government follows the preferences of the majority of voters but protects the interests of the minority

political equality *(p. 19)* the right to participate in politics equally, based on the principle of "one person, one vote"

politics *(p. 13)* conflict over the leadership, structure, and policies of governments

political efficacy *(p. 7)* the ability to influence government and politics

popular sovereignty *(p. 21)* a principle of democracy in which political authority rests ultimately in the hands of the people

power *(p. 13)* influence over a government's leadership, organization, or policies

representative democracy (republic) *(p. 13)* a system of government in which the populace selects representatives, who play a significant role in governmental decision making

totalitarian government *(p. 11)* a system of rule in which the government recognizes no formal limits on its power and seeks to absurb or eliminate other social institutions that might challenge it

For Further Reading

Dahl, Robert. *How Democratic Is the American Constitution?* New Haven, CT: Yale University Press, 2002.

Dalton, Russell. *The Good Citizen: How a Younger Generation Is Reshaping American Politics*. Rev. ed. Washington, DC: CQ Press, 2008.

Delli Carpini, Michael X., and Scott Keeter. *What Americans Know about Politics and Why It Matters*. New Haven, CT: Yale University Press, 1996.

Hochschild, Jennifer L. *Facing Up to the American Dream: Race, Class, and the Soul of the Nation*. Princeton, NJ: Princeton University Press, 1995.

Lasswell, Harold. *Politics: Who Gets What, When, How*. New York: Meridian Books, 1958.

McCarty, Nolan, Keith T. Poole, and Howard Rosenthal, *Polarized America: The Dance of Ideology and Unequal Riches*. Cambridge, MA: MIT Press, 2008.

Mettler, Suzanne. *The Submerged State: How Invisible Government Policies Undermine American Democracy*. Chicago: University of Chicago Press, 2011.

Nye, Joseph S., Jr., Philip D. Zelikow, and David C. King, eds. *Why People Don't Trust Government.* Cambridge, MA: Harvard University Press, 1997.

Page, Benjamin I., and Lawrence R. Jacobs. *Class War? What Americans Really Think about Economic Inequality.* Chicago: University of Chicago Press, 2009.

Tocqueville, Alexis de. *Democracy in America.* Trans. Phillips Bradley. New York: Knopf, Vintage Books, 1945; orig. published 1835.

When the framers of the Constitution met in 1787, they set out to establish a political system that would protect liberty and place limits on government. They also believed a powerful government required a broad, popular base. However, they debated how best to protect liberty and how to balance democracy with other concerns.

The Founding and the Constitution

WHAT GOVERNMENT DOES AND WHY IT MATTERS The framers of the U.S. Constitution knew why government mattered. In the Constitution's preamble, the framers tell us that the purposes of government are to promote justice, to maintain peace at home, to defend the nation from foreign foes, to provide for the welfare of the citizenry, and, above all, to secure the "Blessings of Liberty" for Americans. The remainder of the Constitution spells out a plan for achieving these great objectives. This plan includes provisions for the exercise of legislative, executive, and judicial powers and a recipe for the division of powers among the federal government's branches and between the national and state governments.

Americans often become impatient with the Constitution, as the constitutional separation of powers seems to be a recipe for inaction and "gridlock" when America's major institutions of government are controlled by opposing political forces. This has led to bitter fights that sometimes prevent government from delivering important services. In October 2013, for instance, the federal government partially shut down for 16 days when the House and Senate could not reach agreement on a budget for the federal government. As a result, permit offices across the country no longer took in fees, contractors stopped receiving checks, research projects stalled, and 800,000 federal employees were sent home on unpaid leave—at a cost to the economy of $3.1 billion.

The framers, however, believed that a good constitution not only created a government with the capacity to act forcefully but also promoted compromise and deliberation, sometimes delaying action until tempers cooled and a variety of viewpoints could be heard. The cost of compromise and deliberation encouraged by such constitutional arrangements as the separation of powers might some-times be gridlock, but the benefit may be a government compelled to take many interests and viewpoints into account when it formulates policies.

America's long-standing values of liberty, equality, and democracy were all major themes of the founding period and are all elements of the U.S. Constitu-tion. However, the Constitution was a product of political bargaining and compro-mise, formed in very much the same way political decisions are made today. As this chapter will show, the Constitution reflects high principle as well as political self-interest. It also defines the relationship between American citizens and their government.

chaptergoals

- Describe the events that led to the Declaration of Independence and the Articles of Confederation (pp. 31–36)

- Analyze the reasons for the failure of the Articles of Confederation (pp. 36–41)

- Explain how the Constitution attempted to improve America's governance, and outline the major institutions established by the Constitution (pp. 41–48)

- Present the controversies involved in the struggle for ratification (pp. 48–53)

- Trace how the Constitution has changed over time through the amendment process (pp. 53–56)

● The First Founding: Ideals, Interests, and Conflicts

Describe the events that led to the Declaration of Independence and the Articles of Confederation

The government created by the country's Founders was the product of British legal and political traditions, colonial experience, and new ideas about governance that gained currency in the century before America broke with Britain. While America's leaders were first and foremost practical politicians, they also read political philosophy and were influenced by the important thinkers of their day, including Hobbes, Locke, and Montesquieu.

The seventeenth-century British philosopher Thomas Hobbes (1588–1679) was no advocate of democratic government, but he wrote persuasively in *Leviathan* about the necessity of a government authority as an antidote to human existence in a government-less state of nature, where life was "solitary, poor, nasty, brutish, and short." He also believed that governments should have limits on the powers they exercised and that political systems are based on the idea of "contract theory"—that the people of a country voluntarily give up some freedom in exchange for an ordered society. The monarchs who rule that society derive their legitimacy from this contract, not from a God-given right to rule.

Another British political thinker, John Locke (1632–1704), advanced the principles of republican government by arguing not only that monarchical power was not absolute but that such power was dangerous and should therefore be limited. In a break with Hobbes, Locke argued that the people retain rights despite the social contract they made with the monarch. Preserving safety in society is not enough; people's lives, liberty, and property also require protection. Further, Locke wrote in his *Second Treatise of Civil Government* that the people of a country have a right to overthrow a government they believe to be unjust or tyrannical. This key idea shaped the thinking of the Founders, including Thomas Jefferson, the primary author of the Declaration of Independence, who said that the document was "pure Locke." Locke advanced the important ideas of limited government and consent of the governed.

Baron de la Brède et de Montesquieu (1689–1755) was a French political thinker who advocated the idea that power needed to be balanced by power as a bulwark against tyranny. The way in which this could be achieved was through the separation of governing powers. This idea was already in practice in Britain, where legislative and executive powers were divided between Parliament and the monarch. In *The Spirit of the Laws*, Montesquieu argued for the separation and elevation of judicial power, which in Britain was still held by the monarch. Montesquieu did not argue for a pure separation of powers; rather, basic functions would be separated, but there would also be some overlap of functions. These ideas were central in shaping the three-branch system of government that America's Founders outlined in the Constitution of 1787.

Narrow Interests and Political Conflicts Shaped the First Founding

The American Revolution and the U.S. Constitution were outgrowths of a struggle among competing economic and political forces within the colonies. Five sectors of society had interests that were important in colonial politics: (1) the New England merchants; (2) the southern planters; (3) the "royalists"—holders of royal lands, offices, and patents (licenses to engage in a profession or business activity); (4) shopkeepers, artisans, and laborers; and (5) small farmers. Throughout the eighteenth century, these groups were in conflict over issues of taxation, trade, and commerce. For the most part, however, the southern planters, the New England merchants, and the royal office and patent holders—groups that together made up the colonial elite—were able to maintain a political alliance that held in check the more radical forces representing shopkeepers, laborers, and small farmers. After 1760, however, by seriously threatening the interests of New England merchants and southern planters, British tax and trade policies split the colonial elite, permitting radical forces to expand their political influence, and set in motion a chain of events that culminated in the American Revolution.[1]

British Taxes Hurt Colonial Economic Interests

During the first half of the eighteenth century, Britain ruled its American colonies with a light hand. Evidence of British rule was hardly to be found outside the largest towns and the enterprising colonists had founds ways of evading most of the taxes nominally levied by the distant British government. Beginning in the 1760s, however, the debts and other financial problems faced by the British government forced it to search for new revenue sources. This search rather quickly led to the Crown's North American colonies, which, on the whole, paid remarkably little in taxes to their parent country. Much of Britain's debt arose from the expenses it had incurred in defense of the colonies during the recent French and Indian War (1756–63), as well as from the continuing protection that British forces were giving the colonists from Indian attacks and that the British navy was providing for colonial shipping. Thus, during the 1760s, Great Britain sought to impose new, though relatively modest, taxes on the colonists.

Like most governments of the period, the British regime had limited ways in which to collect revenues. In the mid-eighteenth century, governments relied mainly on tariffs, duties, and other taxes on commerce, and it was to such taxes, including the Stamp Act, that the British turned during the 1760s.

The Stamp Act and other taxes on commerce, such as the Sugar Act of 1764, which taxed sugar, molasses, and other commodities, most heavily affected the two groups in colonial society whose commercial interests and activities were most extensive—the New England merchants and the southern planters. United under the famous slogan "No taxation without representation," the merchants and planters sought to organize opposition to these new taxes. In the course of the struggle against British tax measures, the planters and merchants broke with their royalist allies and turned to their former adversaries—the shopkeepers, laborers, artisans, and small farmers—for help. With the assistance of these groups, the merchants and planters organized demonstrations and a boycott of British goods that ultimately forced the Crown to rescind most of its hated new taxes.

From the perspective of the merchants and planters, this was a victorious conclusion to their struggle with the parent country. They were anxious to end the unrest they had helped to arouse, and they supported the British government's efforts to restore order. Indeed, most respectable Bostonians supported the actions of the British soldiers involved in the Boston Massacre (1770), when those soldiers killed five colonists while attempting to repel an angry mob moving against a government building. In their subsequent trial, the soldiers were defended by John Adams, a pillar of Boston society and a future president of the United States. Adams asserted that the soldiers' actions were entirely justified, provoked as they were by "a motley rabble of saucy boys, negroes and mulattoes, Irish teagues and outlandish Jack tars." All but two of the soldiers were acquitted.[2]

Yet political strife persisted. The more radical forces representing shopkeepers, artisans, laborers, and small farmers, who had been mobilized and energized by the struggle over taxes, continued to agitate for political and social change. These radicals, whose leaders included Samuel Adams, a cousin of John Adams, asserted that British power supported an unjust political and social structure within the colonies and began to advocate an end to British rule.[3]

Political Strife Radicalized the Colonists

The political strife within the colonies was the background for the events of 1773–74. In 1773 the British government granted the politically powerful but ailing East India Company a monopoly on the export of tea from Britain, eliminating a lucrative form of trade for colonial merchants. To add insult to injury, the East India Company sought to sell the tea directly in the colonies instead of working through the colonial merchants. Tea was an extremely important commodity in the 1770s, and these British actions posed a serious threat to the New England merchants. Together with their southern allies, the merchants once again called upon the radicals for support. The most dramatic result was the Boston Tea Party of 1773, when anti-British radicals, led by Samuel Adams (some of them "disguised" as Mohawk Indians), boarded three vessels anchored in Boston Harbor and threw the entire cargo of 342 chests of tea into the harbor.

The British helped radicalize colonists through bad policy decisions in the years before the Revolution. For example, Britain gave the ailing East India Company a monopoly on the tea trade in the American colonies. Colonists feared that the monopoly would hurt colonial merchants' business and protested by throwing East India Company tea into Boston Harbor in 1773.

This event was of decisive importance in American history. The merchants had hoped to force the British government to rescind the Tea Act, but they did not support any demands beyond this one. They certainly did not seek independence from Britain. Samuel Adams and the other radicals, however, hoped to provoke the British government to take actions that would alienate its colonial supporters and pave the way for a rebellion. This was precisely the purpose of the Boston Tea Party, and it succeeded. By dumping the East India Company's tea into Boston Harbor, Adams and his followers goaded the British into enacting a number of harsh reprisals. Within five months of the incident in Boston, the House of Commons passed a series of acts that closed the port of Boston to commerce, changed the provincial government of Massachusetts, provided for the removal of accused persons to Britain for trial, and most important, restricted movement to the West—further alienating the southern planters, who depended upon access to new western lands. These acts of retaliation confirmed the worst criticisms of British rule and helped radicalize Americans. Radicals such as Christopher Gadsden of South Carolina and Samuel Adams had been agitating for more violent measures against the British. But ultimately it was Britain's political repression that fanned support for independence.

Thus, the Boston Tea Party set in motion a cycle of provocation and retaliation that in 1774 resulted in the convening of the First Continental Congress—an assembly of delegates from all parts of the colonies that called for a total boycott of British goods and, under the prodding of the radicals, began to consider the possibility of independence from British rule. The eventual result was the Declaration of Independence.

The Declaration of Independence Explained Why the Colonists Wanted to Break with Great Britain

In 1776, more than a year after open warfare had commenced in Massachusetts, the Second Continental Congress appointed a committee consisting of Thomas Jefferson of Virginia, Benjamin Franklin of Pennsylvania, Roger Sherman of Connecticut, John Adams of Massachusetts, and Robert Livingston of New York to draft a statement of American independence from British rule. The Declaration of Independence, written by Jefferson and adopted by the Second Continental Congress, was an extraordinary philosophical and political document. Philosophically, the Declaration was remarkable for its assertion that certain rights, called "unalienable

The Declaration of Independence's pronouncement that "We hold these truths to be self-evident, that all men are created equal" remains a powerful principle of American democracy. Every year, Americans celebrate the signing of the Declaration on the Fourth of July.

rights"—including life, liberty, and the pursuit of happiness—could not be abridged by governments. In the world of 1776, a world in which some kings still claimed to rule by divine right, this was a dramatic statement. Colonial political thought was heavily influenced by the works of the philosopher John Locke, one of England's foremost liberal theorists of the seventeenth century. In his treatises on government, widely read by educated colonists, Locke asserted that all individuals were equal and possessed a natural right to defend their lives, liberties, and possessions. Individuals created governments to help them protect these rights but, if a government failed in its duties, the citizenry had the right to alter or abolish it. It is easy to see why the colonists found inspiration in Locke's writings as they contemplated altering their relationship to the British Crown.

Politically, the Declaration was remarkable because it identified and focused on grievances, aspirations, and principles that might unify the various colonial groups that were otherwise divided economically, philosophically, and by region. The Declaration was an attempt to identify and articulate a history and set of principles that might help to forge national unity.[4] It also explained to the rest of the world why American colonists were attempting to break away from Great Britain.

The Articles of Confederation Created America's First National Government

Having declared their independence, the colonies needed to establish a governmental structure. In November 1777 the Continental Congress adopted the **Articles of Confederation**, the United States' first written constitution. Although it was not ratified by all the states until 1781, it was the country's operative constitution for almost 12 years, until March 1789.

The Articles of Confederation were concerned primarily with limiting the powers of the central government. The central government, first of all, was based entirely in a Congress. Since it was not intended to be a powerful government, it was given no executive branch. Execution of its laws was to be left to the individual states. Second, the Congress had little power. Its members were not much more than delegates or messengers from the state legislatures. They were chosen by the state legislatures, their salaries were paid out of the state treasuries, and they were subject to immediate recall by state authorities. In addition, each state, regardless of its size, had only a single vote.

The Congress was given the power to declare war and make peace, to make treaties and alliances, to coin or borrow money, and to regulate trade with the Native Americans. It could also appoint the senior officers of the U.S. Army. But it could not levy taxes or regulate commerce among the states. Moreover, the army officers it appointed had no army to serve in because the nation's armed forces were composed of the state militias. And in order to amend the Articles, all 13 states had to agree—a virtual impossibility. Probably the most unfortunate part of the Articles of Confederation was that the central government could not prevent one state from discriminating against other states in the quest for foreign commerce.

The relationship between the Congress and the states under the Articles of Confederation was much like the contemporary relationship between the United Nations and its member states, a relationship in which the states retained virtually all governmental powers. It was properly called a **confederation** (a system of government in which states retain sovereign authority except for the powers expressly delegated to the national government) because, as provided under Article II, "each state retains its sovereignty, freedom and independence, and every Power, Jurisdiction and right, which is not by this confederation expressly delegated to the United States, in Congress assembled." Not only was there no executive, there also was no judicial authority and no other means of enforcing the Congress's will. If there was to be any enforcement at all, the states would do it for the Congress.[5]

● The Failure of the Articles Made the "Second Founding" Necessary

Analyze the reasons for the failure of the Articles of Confederation

The Declaration of Independence and the Articles of Confederation were not sufficient to hold the new nation together as an independent and effective nation-state. From almost the moment of armistice with the British in 1783, moves were afoot to reform and strengthen the Articles of Confederation.

Competition among the states for foreign commerce posed a special problem to the new country, because it allowed the European powers to play the states against one another, which not only made America seem weak and vulnerable abroad but also created confusion on both sides of the Atlantic. At one point during the winter of 1786–87, John Adams of Massachusetts, a leader in the independence struggle, was sent to negotiate a new treaty with the British, one that would cover disputes left over from the war. The British government responded that, because the United States under the Articles of Confederation was unable to enforce existing treaties, it would negotiate with each of the 13 states separately.

At the same time, well-to-do Americans—in particular the New England merchants and southern planters—were troubled by the influence that "radical" forces exercised in the Continental Congress and in the governments of several of the states. The colonists' victory in the Revolutionary War had not only ended British rule but had also significantly changed the balance of political power within the new states. As a result of the Revolution, one key segment of the colonial elite—the royal land, office, and patent holders—was stripped of its economic and political privileges. In fact, many of these individuals, along with tens of thousands of other colonists who considered themselves loyal British subjects, left for Canada after the British surrender. And while the pre-Revolutionary elite was weakened, the pre-Revolutionary radicals were better organized than ever and now controlled such states as Pennsylvania and Rhode Island, where they pursued economic and political policies that struck terror into the hearts of the pre-Revolutionary political establishment. Of course, the central government under the Articles of Confederation was powerless to intervene.

The Annapolis Convention Was Key to Calling a National Convention

The continuation of international weakness and domestic economic turmoil led many Americans to consider whether their newly adopted form of government might not already require revision. In the fall of 1786, many state leaders accepted an invitation from the Virginia legislature for a conference of representatives of all the states, to be held in Annapolis, Maryland. Delegates from only five states actually attended, so nothing substantive could be accomplished. Still, this conference was the first step toward what is now known as the second founding. The one positive thing that came out of the Annapolis Convention was a carefully worded resolution calling on the Congress to send commissioners to Philadelphia at a later time "to devise such further provisions as shall appear to them necessary to render the Constitution of the Federal Government adequate to the exigencies of the Union."[6] But the resolution did not necessarily imply any desire to do more than improve and reform the Articles of Confederation.

The government under the Articles did enact some important measures, including the Land Ordinance of 1785 and the Northwest Ordinance of 1787. The Land Ordinance established the principles of land surveying and land ownership that governed America's westward expansion, and under the Northwest Ordinance the states agreed to surrender their western land claims, which opened the way for the admission of new states to the Union. Still, the young nation's political and economic position deteriorated during the 1780s, and something had to be done.

Shays's Rebellion Showed How Weak the Government Was

It is quite possible that the Constitutional Convention of 1787 in Philadelphia would never have taken place at all except for a single event that occurred during the winter following the Annapolis Convention: Shays's Rebellion.

Daniel Shays, a former army captain, led a mob of farmers in a rebellion against the government of Massachusetts, which had levied heavy taxes against them. The purpose of the rebellion was to prevent foreclosures on farmers' debt-ridden land by keeping the county courts of western Massachusetts from sitting until after the next election. The state militia dispersed the mob, but for several days in February 1787, Shays and his followers terrified the state government by attempting to capture the federal arsenal at Springfield, provoking an appeal to the Congress to help restore order. Within a few days, the state government regained control and captured 14 of the rebels. (All were eventually pardoned.) Later that year, a newly elected Massachusetts legislature granted some of the farmers' demands.

George Washington summed up the effects of this incident: "I am mortified beyond expression that in the moment of our acknowledged

In the winter of 1787, Daniel Shays led a makeshift army against the federal arsenal at Springfield to protest heavy taxes levied by the Massachusetts legislature. The rebellion proved the Articles of Confederation too weak to protect the fledgling nation.

independence we should by our conduct verify the predictions of our transatlantic foe, and render ourselves ridiculous and contemptible in the eyes of all Europe."[7]

The Congress under the Confederation had been unable to act decisively in a time of crisis. This provided critics of the Articles of Confederation with precisely the evidence they needed to push the Annapolis resolution through the Congress. Thus, the states were asked to send representatives to Philadelphia to discuss constitutional revision. Delegates were eventually sent by every state except Rhode Island.

The Constitutional Convention Didn't Start Out to Write a New Constitution

The delegates who convened in Philadelphia in May 1787 had political strife, international embarrassment, national weakness, and local rebellion fixed in their minds. Recognizing that these issues were symptoms of fundamental flaws in the Articles of Confederation, the delegates soon abandoned the plan to revise the Articles and committed themselves to a second founding—a second, and ultimately successful, attempt to create a legitimate and effective national system of government. This effort would occupy the convention for the next five months.

A Marriage of Interest and Principle For years, scholars have disagreed about the motives of the Founders in Philadelphia. Among the most controversial views of the framers' motives is the "economic interpretation" put forward by historian Charles Beard and his disciples.[8] According to Beard's account, America's Founders were a collection of securities speculators and property owners whose only aim was personal enrichment. From this perspective, the Constitution's lofty principles were little more than sophisticated masks behind which the most venal interests sought to enrich themselves.

Contrary to Beard's approach is the view that the framers of the Constitution *were* concerned with philosophical and ethical principles. Indeed, the framers did try to devise a system of government consistent with the dominant philosophical and moral principles of the day. But, in fact, these two views belong together; the Founders' interests were reinforced by their principles. The convention that drafted the American Constitution was chiefly organized by the New England merchants and southern planters. Although the delegates representing these groups did not all hope to profit personally from an increase in the value of their securities, as Beard would have it, they did hope to benefit in the broadest political and economic sense by breaking the power of their radical foes and establishing a system of government more compatible with their long-term economic and political interests. Thus, the framers sought to create a new government capable of promoting commerce and protecting property from radical state legislatures and populist forces hostile to the interests of the commercial and propertied classes.

The Great Compromise The proponents of a new government fired their opening shot on May 29, 1787, when Edmund Randolph of Virginia offered a resolution that proposed corrections and enlargements in the Articles of Confederation. The proposal, reflecting the strong influence of James Madison, was no simple motion; rather, it provided for an entirely new government.

The portion of Randolph's motion that became most controversial was called the **Virginia Plan**. This plan provided for a system of representation in the national legislature based upon the population of each state or the proportion of each state's revenue contribution to the national government, or both. (Randolph also proposed a second chamber of the legislature, to be elected by the members of the first chamber.) Since the states varied enormously in size and wealth, the Virginia Plan was heavily biased in favor of the large states.

While the convention was debating the Virginia Plan, opposition to it began to mount as more delegates arrived in Philadelphia. William Paterson of New Jersey introduced a new resolution known as the **New Jersey Plan**, which called for equal state representation in the national legislature regardless of population. Its main proponents were delegates from the less-populous states, including Delaware, New Jersey, Connecticut, and New York, who asserted that the more populous states, such as Virginia, Pennsylvania, North Carolina, Massachusetts, and Georgia, would dominate the new government if representation were determined by population. The smaller states argued that each state should be equally represented in the new regime regardless of the state's population.

The issue of representation was one that threatened to wreck the entire constitutional enterprise. Delegates conferred, factions maneuvered, and tempers flared. James Wilson of Pennsylvania told the small-state delegates that if they wanted to disrupt the union, they should go ahead. The separation, he said, could "never happen on better grounds." Small-state delegates were equally blunt. Gunning Bedford of Delaware declared that the small states might, if forced, look elsewhere for friends. "The large states," he said, "dare not dissolve the confederation. If they do the small ones will find some foreign ally of more honor and good faith, who will take them by the hand and do them justice." These sentiments were widely shared. The union, as Oliver Ellsworth of Connecticut put it, was "on the verge of dissolution, scarcely held together by the strength of a hair."

The outcome of this debate was the Connecticut Compromise, also known as the **Great Compromise**. Under the terms of this compromise, in the first chamber of Congress, the House of Representatives, the representatives would be apportioned according to the population in each state. This, of course, was what delegates from the large states had sought. But in the second chamber, the Senate, each state would have equal representation regardless of its population; this provision addressed the concerns of the small states. This compromise was not immediately satisfactory to all the delegates. Indeed, two of the most vocal members of the small-state faction, John Lansing and Robert Yates of New York, were so incensed by the concession that their colleagues had made to the large-state forces that they stormed out of the convention. In the end, however, most of the delegates preferred compromise to the breakup of the Union, and the plan was accepted.

The Question of Slavery: The Three-Fifths Compromise Many of the conflicts that emerged during the Constitutional Convention were reflections of the fundamental differences between the slave and the nonslave states—differences that pitted the southern planters against New England merchants. This was the first premonition of the conflict that would later almost destroy the Republic.

Despite the Founders' emphasis on liberty, the new Constitution allowed slavery, counting each slave as three-fifths of a person in apportioning seats in the House of Representatives. In this 1792 painting, Liberty Displaying the Arts and Sciences, *the books, instruments, and classical columns at the left contrast with the kneeling slaves at the right—illustrating the divide between America's rhetoric of liberty and equality and the realities of slavery.*

More than 90 percent of the country's slaves resided in five states—Georgia, Maryland, North Carolina, South Carolina, and Virginia—where they accounted for 30 percent of the total population. In some places, slaves outnumbered non-slaves by as many as 10 to 1. For the Constitution to embody any principle of national supremacy, some basic decisions would have to be made about the place of slavery in the general scheme. James Madison observed,

> It seemed now to be pretty well understood that the real difference of interests lay, not between the large and small but between the northern and southern states. The institution of slavery and its consequences formed the line of discrimination.[9]

Northerners and southerners eventually reached agreement through the **Three-Fifths Compromise**. The seats in the House of Representatives would be apportioned according to a "population" in which five slaves would count as three free persons. The slaves would not be allowed to vote, of course, but the number of representatives would be apportioned accordingly.

The issue of slavery was the most difficult one faced by the framers, and it nearly destroyed the Union. Although some delegates believed slavery to be morally wrong, an evil and oppressive institution that made a mockery of the ideals and values espoused in the Constitution, morality was not the issue that caused the framers to support or oppose the Three-Fifths Compromise. Whatever they thought of the institution of slavery, most delegates from the northern states opposed counting slaves in the distribution of congressional seats. James Wilson of Pennsylvania, for example, argued that if slaves were citizens they should be treated and counted like other citizens. If, on the other hand, they were property, then why should not other forms of property be counted toward the apportionment of representatives? But southern delegates made it clear that if the northerners refused to give in, they would never agree to the new government. William R. Davie of North Carolina heatedly asserted that the people of North Carolina would never enter the Union if slaves were not counted as part of the basis for representation. Without such agreement, he asserted ominously, "the business was at an end." Even southerners such as Edmund Randolph of Virginia, who conceded that slavery was immoral, insisted on including slaves in the allocation of congressional seats. Eventually the North and South compromised on the issue of slavery and representation. Indeed, northerners even agreed to permit a continuation of the odious slave trade until 1808 in order to keep the South in the Union. But eventually, the disparate interests of the North and the South could no longer be reconciled, and a bloody civil war was the result.

● The Constitution Created Both Bold Powers and Sharp Limits on Power

> **Explain how the Constitution attempted to improve America's governance, and outline the major institutions established by the Constitution**

The political significance of the Great Compromise and the Three-Fifths Compromise was to reinforce the unity of the mercantile and planter forces that sought to create a new government. The Great Compromise reassured those who feared that this new governmental framework would reduce the importance of their own local or regional influence. The Three-Fifths Compromise temporarily defused the rivalry between the merchants and planters. Their unity secured, members of the alliance supporting the establishment of a new government moved to fashion a constitutional framework consistent with their economic and political interests.

In particular, the framers sought a new government that, first, would be strong enough to promote commerce and protect property from radical state legislatures such as Rhode Island's. This became the constitutional basis for national control over commerce and finance, and for the establishment of national judicial supremacy and the effort to construct a strong presidency. See Table 2.1 for a comparison of the Articles of Confederation to the Constitution. Second, the framers sought to prevent what they saw as the threat posed by the "excessive democracy" of the state and national governments under the Articles of Confederation. This led to such constitutional principles as **bicameralism** (having a legislative assembly composed of two chambers or houses), **checks and balances** (mechanisms through which each branch of government is able to participate in and influence the activities of the other branches), staggered terms in office with longer terms for senators, and indirect election (selection of

TABLE 2.1

Comparing the Articles of Confederation and the Constitution

MAJOR PROVISIONS	ARTICLES	CONSTITUTION
Executive Branch	None	President of the United States
Judiciary	No federal court system. Judiciary exists only at state level.	Federal judiciary headed by a Supreme Court
Legislature	Unicameral legislature with equal representation for each state. Delegates to the Congress of the Confederation were appointed by the states.	Bicameral legislature consisting of Senate and House of Representatives. Each state is represented by two senators while apportionment in the House is based on state population. Senators are chosen by the state legislatures (changed to popular election in 1913) and House members by popular election.
Fiscal and economic powers	The national government is dependent upon the states to collect taxes. The states are free to coin their own money, print paper money, and sign commercial treaties with foreign governments.	Congress given the power to levy taxes, coin money, and regulate commerce. States prohibited from coining money or entering into treaties with other nations.
Military	The national government is dependent upon state militias and cannot form an army during peacetime.	The national government is authorized to maintain an army and navy.
Legal supremacy	State constitutions and state law are supreme.	National Constitution and national law are supreme.
Constitutional amendment	Must be agreed upon by all states.	Must be agreed upon by three-fourths of the states

the president not by voters directly but by an **electoral college**, whereby presidential electors from each state who meet after the popular election cast ballots for president and vice president; senators also were chosen indirectly, by state legislatures). Third, the framers, lacking the power to force the states or the public at large to accept the new form of government, sought to identify principles that would help to secure support. This became the basis of the constitutional provision for direct popular election of representatives and, subsequently, for the addition of the **Bill of Rights** (the first 10 amendments to the Constitution, ratified in 1791; they ensure certain rights and liberties to the people). Finally, the framers wanted to be certain that the government they created did not pose an even greater threat to its citizens' liberties and property rights than did the radical state legislatures they feared and despised. To prevent the new government from abusing its power, the framers incorporated principles such as the **separation of powers** (the division of governmental power among several institutions that must cooperate in decision making) and **federalism** (a system of government in which power is divided, by a constitution, between a central government and regional governments) into the Constitution. Let us assess the major provisions of the Constitution's seven articles to see how each relates to these objectives.

The Legislative Branch Was Designed to Be the Most Powerful

In Article I, Sections 1–7, the Constitution provided for a Congress consisting of two chambers: a House of Representatives and a Senate. Members of the House of Representatives were given two-year terms in office and were to be elected directly by the people. Members of the Senate were to be appointed by the state legislatures (this was changed in 1913 by the Seventeenth Amendment, which instituted direct election of senators) for six-year terms. These terms were staggered so that the appointments of one-third of the senators would expire every two years. The Constitution assigned somewhat different tasks to the House and Senate. Although the approval of each body was required for the enactment of a law, the Senate alone was given the power to ratify treaties and approve presidential appointments. The House, on the other hand, was given the sole power to originate revenue bills.

The character of the legislative branch was directly related to the framers' major goals. The House of Representatives was designed to be directly responsible to the people in order to encourage popular consent for the new Constitution and to help enhance the power of the new government. At the same time, to guard against "excessive democracy," the Constitution checked the power of the House of Representatives with that of the Senate, whose members were to be appointed by the states for long terms rather than elected directly by the people. The purpose of this provision, according to Alexander Hamilton, was to avoid "an unqualified complaisance to every sudden breeze of passion, or to every transient impulse which the people may receive."[10] Staggered terms of service in the Senate, moreover, were intended to make that body even more resistant to popular pressure. Since only one-third of the senators would be selected at any given time, the composition of the institution would be protected from changes in popular preferences transmitted by the state legislatures. This would prevent what James Madison called "mutability in the public councils arising from a rapid succession of new members."[11] Thus, the structure of the legislative branch was designed to contribute to governmental power, to promote popular consent for the new government, and at the same time to place limits on the popular political currents that many of the framers saw as a radical threat to the economic and social order.

The issues of power and consent were important throughout the Constitution. Section 8 of Article I specifically listed the powers of Congress, which include the authority to collect taxes, borrow money, regulate commerce, declare war, and maintain an army and navy. By granting Congress these powers, the framers indicated very clearly that they intended the new government to be far more powerful than its predecessor. At the same time, by defining the new government's most important powers as belonging to Congress, the framers sought to promote popular acceptance of this critical change by reassuring citizens that their views would be fully represented whenever the government exercised its new powers.

As a further guarantee to the people that the new government would pose no threat to them, the Constitution seemed to say that any powers not listed were not granted at all. Specific powers granted to Congress in the Constitution are **expressed powers**. But the framers intended to create an active and powerful government, and so they also included the necessary and proper clause, sometimes known as the **elastic clause**, which signified that the expressed powers were meant to be a source of strength to the national government, not a limitation on it. In response to the charge that they intended to give the national government too much power, the framers adopted language in the Tenth Amendment stipulating that powers not specifically granted by the Constitution to the federal government were reserved to the states or to the people. As we will see in Chapter 3, the resulting tension between the elastic clause and the Tenth Amendment has been at the heart of constitutional struggles between federal and state powers.

The Executive Branch Created a Brand-New Office

The Articles of Confederation had not provided for an executive branch and the framers viewed this as a source of weakness, so the Constitution provided for the establishment of the presidency in Article II. As Hamilton commented, the presidential article aimed toward "energy in the Executive." It did so in an effort to overcome the natural tendency toward stalemate that was built into the bicameral legislature as well as into the separation of powers among the three branches. The Constitution afforded the president a measure of independence from the people and from the other branches of government—particularly the Congress.

In line with the framers' goal of increased power to the national government, the president was granted the unconditional power to receive ambassadors from other countries, which has amounted to the power to "recognize" other countries. The president was also given the power to negotiate treaties, although their acceptance required the approval of two-thirds of the Senate. The president was given the unconditional right to grant reprieves and pardons, except in cases of impeachment. And the president was provided with the power to appoint major departmental personnel, to convene Congress in special session, and to veto congressional enactments. (The veto power is formidable, but it is not absolute, since Congress can override it by a two-thirds vote.)

The framers hoped to create a presidency that would make the federal government rather than the states the agency capable of timely and decisive action to deal with public issues and problems. At the same time, however, the framers sought to help the presidency withstand excessively democratic pressures by creating a system of indirect rather than direct election through an electoral college.

The Judicial Branch Was a Check on Too Much Democracy

In establishing the judicial branch in Article III, the Constitution reflected the framers' preoccupation with nationalizing governmental power and checking radical democratic impulses while preventing the new national government from interfering with liberty and property.

Under the provisions of Article III, the framers created a court that was to be literally a supreme court of the United States, and not merely the highest court of the national government. The most important expression of this intention was granting the Supreme Court the power to resolve any conflicts that might emerge between federal and state laws. In particular, the Supreme Court was given the right to determine whether a power was exclusive to the national government, concurrent with the states, or exclusive to the states. In addition, the Supreme Court was assigned jurisdiction over controversies between citizens of different states. The long-term significance of this provision was that as the country developed a national economy, it came to rely increasingly on the federal judiciary, rather than on the state courts, for the resolution of disputes.

Judges were given lifetime appointments in order to protect them from popular politics and from interference by the other branches. This, however, did not mean that the judiciary would remain totally impartial to political considerations or to the other branches, for the president was to appoint the judges, and the Senate to approve the appointments. Congress would also have the power to create inferior (lower) courts, change the jurisdiction of the federal courts, add or subtract federal judges, and even change the size of the Supreme Court.

No explicit mention is made in the Constitution of **judicial review**, the power of the courts to review and, if necessary, declare actions of the legislative and executive branches invalid or unconstitutional. The Supreme Court asserted this power in *Marbury v. Madison* (1803). Its assumption of this power, as we shall see in Chapter 12, was based not on the Constitution itself but on the politics of later decades and the membership of the Court.

National Unity and Power Set the New Constitution Apart from the Old Articles

Various provisions in the Constitution addressed the framers' concern with national unity and power, including Article IV's provisions for comity (reciprocity) among states and among citizens of all states. Each state was prohibited from discriminating against the citizens of other states in favor of its own citizens, and the Supreme Court was charged with deciding in each case whether a state had discriminated against goods or people from another state. The Constitution restricted the power of the states in favor of ensuring enough power to the national government to give the country a free-flowing national economy.

The framers' concern with national supremacy was also expressed in Article VI, in the **supremacy clause**, which provided that national laws and treaties "shall be the supreme Law of the Land" and superior to all laws adopted by any state or any subdivision. This meant that states would be expected to respect all laws made under the "Authority of the United States." The supremacy clause also bound the officials of all state and local governments as well as the federal government to take an oath of office to support the national Constitution. This meant that every action taken by the U.S. Congress would have to be applied within each state as though the action were in fact state law.

The Constitution Established the Process for Amendment

The Constitution established procedures for its own revision in Article V. Its provisions are so difficult that the document has been successfully amended only 17 times since 1791, when the first 10 amendments were adopted. Thousands of other amendments have been proposed in Congress, but fewer than 40 of them have even come close to fulfilling the Constitution's requirement of a two-thirds vote in Congress, and only a fraction have gotten anywhere near adoption by three-fourths of the states. Article V also provides that the Constitution can be amended by a constitutional convention. Occasionally, proponents of particular measures, such as a balanced-budget amendment, have called for a constitutional convention to consider their proposals. Whatever the purpose for which it was called, however, such a convention would presumably have the authority to revise America's entire system of government.

The Constitution Set Forth Rules for Its Own Ratification

The rules for the ratification of the Constitution were set forth in Article VII. Nine of the 13 states would have to ratify, or agree to, the terms in order for the Constitution to be formally adopted.

The Constitution Limits the National Government's Power

As we have indicated, although the framers sought to create a powerful national government, they also wanted to guard against possible misuse of that power. To that end, the framers incorporated two key principles into the Constitution: the separation of powers and federalism. A third set of limitations, in the form of the Bill of Rights, was added to the Constitution to help secure its ratification when opponents of the document charged that it paid insufficient attention to citizens' rights.

The Separation of Powers No principle of politics was more widely shared at the time of the 1787 Founding than the principle that power must be used to balance power. As mentioned earlier in the chapter, Montesquieu believed that this balance was an indispensable defense against tyranny. His writings, especially his major work, *The Spirit of the Laws*, "were taken as political gospel" at the Philadelphia convention.[12] Although the principle of the separation of powers was not explicitly stated in the Constitution, the entire structure of the national government was built precisely on Article I (the legislature), Article II (the executive), and Article III (the judiciary; see Figure 2.1).

However, separation of powers is nothing but mere words on parchment without a method to maintain that separation. The method became known by the popular label "checks and balances" (see Figure 2.2). Each branch is given not only its own powers but also some power over the other two branches. Among the most familiar checks and balances are the president's veto as a power over Congress and Congress's power over the president through its control of appointments to high executive posts and to the judiciary. Congress also has power over the president with its control of appropriations (the spending of government money) and the right of approval of treaties (by the Senate). The judiciary was assumed to have the power of judicial review over the other two branches.

Another important feature of the separation of powers is the principle of giving each of the branches a distinctly different constituency. Theorists such as Montesquieu called this a "mixed regime," with the president chosen indirectly by electors, the House by popular vote, the Senate (originally) by state legislature, and the judiciary by presidential appointment. By these means, the occupants of each

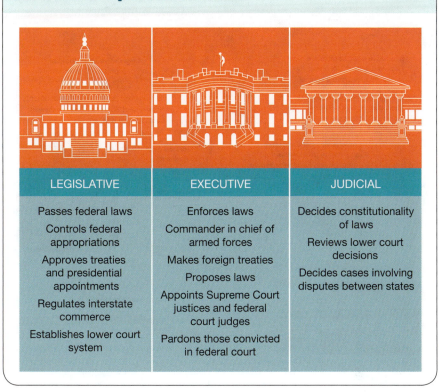

FIGURE 2.1 The Separation of Powers

LEGISLATIVE	EXECUTIVE	JUDICIAL
Passes federal laws	Enforces laws	Decides constitutionality of laws
Controls federal appropriations	Commander in chief of armed forces	Reviews lower court decisions
Approves treaties and presidential appointments	Makes foreign treaties	Decides cases involving disputes between states
Regulates interstate commerce	Proposes laws	
Establishes lower court system	Appoints Supreme Court justices and federal court judges	
	Pardons those convicted in federal court	

branch would tend to develop very different outlooks on how to govern, different definitions of the public interest, and different alliances with private interests.

Federalism Compared to the confederation principle of the Articles of Confederation, federalism was a step toward greater centralization of power. The delegates agreed that they needed to place more power at the national level, without completely undermining the power of the state governments. Thus, they devised a system of two sovereigns—the states and the nation—with the hope that competition between the two would be an effective limitation on the power of both.

The Bill of Rights Late in the Philadelphia convention, a motion was made to include a list of citizens' rights in the Constitution. After a brief debate in which hardly a word was said in its favor and only one speech was made against it, the motion was almost unanimously turned down. Most delegates sincerely believed that since the federal government was already limited to its expressed powers, further protection of citizens was not needed. The delegates argued that the states should adopt bills of rights because their greater powers needed greater limitations. But almost immediately after the Constitution was ratified, there was a movement to adopt a national bill of rights. This is why the Bill of Rights, adopted in 1791, comprises the first 10 amendments to the Constitution rather than being part of the body of it. (We will have a good deal more to say about the Bill of Rights in Chapter 4.)

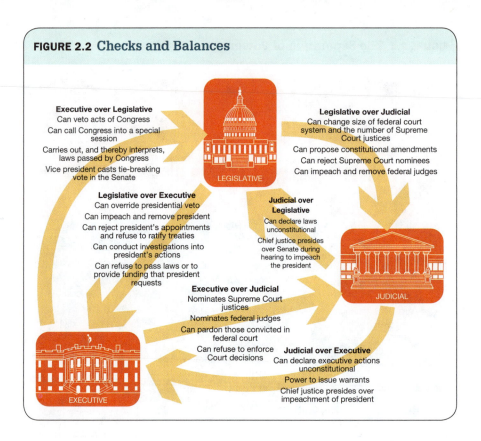

FIGURE 2.2 Checks and Balances

Executive over Legislative
Can veto acts of Congress
Can call Congress into a special session
Carries out, and thereby interprets, laws passed by Congress
Vice president casts tie-breaking vote in the Senate

LEGISLATIVE

Legislative over Judicial
Can change size of federal court system and the number of Supreme Court justices
Can propose constitutional amendments
Can reject Supreme Court nominees
Can impeach and remove federal judges

Legislative over Executive
Can override presidential veto
Can impeach and remove president
Can reject president's appointments and refuse to ratify treaties
Can conduct investigations into president's actions
Can refuse to pass laws or to provide funding that president requests

Judicial over Legislative
Can declare laws unconstitutional
Chief justice presides over Senate during hearing to impeach the president

Executive over Judicial
Nominates Supreme Court justices
Nominates federal judges
Can pardon those convicted in federal court
Can refuse to enforce Court decisions

Judicial over Executive
Can declare executive actions unconstitutional
Power to issue warrants
Chief justice presides over impeachment of president

JUDICIAL

EXECUTIVE

Ratification of the Constitution Was Difficult

Present the controversies involved in the struggle for ratification

The first hurdle faced by the new Constitution was ratification by state conventions of delegates elected by the people of each state. This struggle for ratification was carried out in 13 separate campaigns. Each involved different people, moved at a different pace, and was influenced by local and national considerations. Two sides faced off throughout the states, however; the two sides called themselves Federalists and Antifederalists (see Table 2.2).

The **Federalists** (who more accurately should have called themselves "Nationalists" but who took their name to appear to follow in the Revolutionary tradition) supported the constitution proposed at the American Constitutional Convention of 1787 and preferred a strong national government. The **Antifederalists** favored strong state governments and a weak national government, and opposed the document produced at the Constitutional Convention. They preferred a federal system of government that was decentralized; they took their name by default, in reaction to their better-organized opponents. The Federalists were united in their support of the Constitution, while the Antifederalists were divided over possible alternatives to the Constitution.

TABLE 2.2

Federalists versus Antifederalists

	FEDERALISTS	ANTIFEDERALISTS
Who were they?	Property owners, creditors, merchants	Small farmers, frontiersmen, debtors, shopkeepers, some state government officials
What did they believe?	Believed that elites were most fit to govern; feared "excessive democracy"	Believed that government should be closer to the people; feared concentration of power in hands of the elites
What system of government did they favor?	Favored strong national government; believed in "filtration" so that only elites would obtain governmental power	Favored retention of power by state governments and protection of individual rights
Who were their leaders?	Alexander Hamilton, James Madison, George Washington	Patrick Henry, George Mason, Elbridge Gerry, George Clinton

During the struggle over ratification of the Constitution, Americans argued about great political principles. How much power should the national government be given? What safeguards would most likely prevent the abuse of power? What institutional arrangements could best ensure adequate representation for all Americans? Was tyranny to be feared more from the many or from the few?

Federalists and Antifederalists Fought Bitterly over the Wisdom of the New Document

During the ratification struggle, thousands of essays, speeches, pamphlets, and letters were written in support of and in opposition to the proposed Constitution. The best-known pieces supporting ratification of the Constitution were the 85 essays written, under the name of "Publius," by Alexander Hamilton, James Madison, and John Jay between the fall of 1787 and the spring of 1788—known today as the **Federalist Papers.** They not only defended the principles of the Constitution but also sought to dispel fears of a strong national authority. The Antifederalists published essays of their own, arguing that the new Constitution betrayed the Revolution and was a step toward monarchy. Among the best of the Antifederalist works were the essays, usually attributed to New York Supreme Court justice Robert Yates, that were written under the name of "Brutus" and published in the *New York Journal* at the same time the *Federalist Papers* appeared. The Antifederalist view was also ably presented in the pamphlets and letters written by a former delegate to the Continental Congress and future U.S. senator, Richard Henry Lee of Virginia, using the pen name "The Federal Farmer." These essays highlight the major differences of opinion between Federalists and Antifederalists. Federalists appealed to basic principles of government in support of their nationalist vision. Antifederalists cited equally fundamental precepts to support their vision of a looser confederacy of small republics. Three areas of disagreement were representation, majority tyranny, and governmental power.

Representation The Antifederalists believed that the best and most representative government was that closest to the people, what we would think of as local and state governments. These smaller, more homogeneous governing units would provide "a true picture of the people . . . [possessing] the knowledge of their circumstances and their wants."[13] A strong national government could not represent the interests of the nation as effectively, the Antifederalists argued, because the nation as a whole was simply too large and diverse.

The Federalists, on the other hand, thought that some distance between the people and their representatives might be a good thing, because it would encourage the selection of a few talented and experienced representatives to serve in a national legislature who could balance the wishes of the people with their own considered judgment. In James Madison's view, representatives would not simply mirror society; rather, they must be "[those] who possess [the] most wisdom to discern, and [the] most virtue to pursue, the common good of the society."[14]

Tyranny of the Majority Both Federalists and Antifederalists feared **tyranny**, oppressive and unjust government that employs cruel and arbitrary use of power and authority. But each painted a different picture of what kind of tyranny to fear.

The Antifederalists feared that tyranny would arise from the tendency of all governments to become more "aristocratic," wherein a few individuals in positions of authority would use their positions to gain more and more power over the people. For this reason, Antifederalists were sharply critical of those features of the Constitution that limited direct popular influence over the government, including the election of senators by state legislatures, election of the president by the electoral college, and selection of federal judges by the president and the Senate. Judges, who are appointed for life, were seen as an especially dire threat: "I wonder if the world ever saw . . . a court of justice invested with such immense powers, and yet placed in a situation so little responsible," protested Brutus.[15]

"No taxation without representation" was a rallying cry of the American revolution. The debate over appropriate representation has never been fully resolved, however. Today, residents of Washington, D.C., pay federal income taxes but are not represented in the House or Senate. Presidents Bill Clinton and Barack Obama took a position on the issue by using these D.C. license plates on presidential vehicles.

For the Federalists, tyranny in a republic was less likely to come from aristocrats, and more likely to come from the majority. They feared that a popular majority, "united and actuated by some common impulse of passion, or of interest, adverse to the rights of other citizens," would attempt to "trample on the rules of justice."[16] Those features of the Constitution opposed by the Antifederalists were the very ones that the Federalists defended as the best hope of avoiding tyranny. The sheer size and diversity of the American nation, as represented in the two houses of Congress, would provide a built-in set of balances that would force competing interests to moderate and compromise.

Governmental Power A third difference between Federalists and Antifederalists was over the matter of governmental power. Both sides agreed on the principle of **limited government**, meaning a government whose powers are defined and limited by a constitution, but they differed on how best to limit the government.

Antifederalists wanted the powers of the national government to be carefully specified and limited. Otherwise, the federal government would "swallow up all the power of the state governments." Antifederalists bitterly attacked the supremacy clause and the elastic clause of the Constitution, saying that these provisions gave the national government dangerously unlimited grants of power. They also insisted that a bill of rights be added to the Constitution to place limits on the government's power over citizens.

Federalists favored a national government with broad powers to defend the nation from foreign threats, guard against domestic strife and insurrection, promote commerce, and expand the nation's economy. Federalists agreed that such power could be abused, but believed that the best safeguard against such abuse was through the Constitution's internal checks and controls, not by keeping the national government weak. As Madison put it, "The power surrendered by the people is first divided between two distinct governments [federal and state], and then the portion allotted to each subdivided among distinct and separate departments. Hence, a double security arises to the rights of the people. The different governments will control each other, at the same time that each will be controlled by itself."[17] The Federalists considered a bill of rights to be unnecessary, although this Antifederalist demand was eventually embraced by Federalists, including Madison.

Both Federalists and Antifederalists Contributed to the Success of the New System

In general, the Federalist vision of America triumphed. The Constitution adopted in 1789 created the framework for a powerful national government that for more than 200 years has defended the nation's interests, promoted its commerce, and maintained national unity. In one notable instance, the national government fought and won a bloody war to prevent the nation from breaking apart. And despite this powerful government, the system of internal checks and balances has functioned reasonably well, as the Federalists predicted, to prevent the national government from tyrannizing its citizens.

Although they were defeated in 1789, the Antifederalists present us with an important picture of a road not taken and of an America that might have been. Would Americans in the eighteenth century have been worse off if they had been governed by a confederacy of small republics linked by a national administration with severely limited powers? Were the Antifederalists correct in predicting that a

AMERICA
Side by Side

Comparing Systems of Government

There is tremendous variation among systems of government around the world, even among democracies. All of the countries here share power among three branches—an executive, a legislature, and a judicial. However, the amount of power that each branch has varies. Note that in some systems, no one branch has very much power. In the United States, that is because of the system of checks and balances among the branches. Israel and the United Kingdom, which lack written constitutions, have branches with even less power than in the United States.

Country	Written Constitution?	Year in Effect	Length (in Words)	Federal or Unitary System
Brazil	Yes	1988	51,368	Federal
France	Yes	1958	10,180	Unitary
India	Yes	1950	146,385	Federal
Israel	No	—	—	Unitary
Senegal	Yes	2001	10,866	Unitary
South Africa	Yes	1997	43,062	Unitary
United States	Yes	1789	7,762	Federal
United Kingdom	No	—	—	Unitary

Country	Strength of Executive	Strength of Legislature	Judicial Independence
Brazil	High	Medium	Medium
France	High	Medium	Low
India	Medium	Low	Medium
Israel	Low	Low	Medium
Senegal	High	Medium	Low
South Africa	Medium	Medium	High
United States	Low	Medium	Medium
United Kingdom	Low	Low	Low

SOURCE: Comparative Constitutions Project, "Characteristics of National Constitutions," http://comparativeconstitutionsproject.org/ccp-rankings/ (accessed 2/21/14).

government given great power in the hope that it might do good would, through "insensible progress," inevitably turn to evil purposes?

● Constitutional Amendments Dramatically Changed the Relationship between Citizens and the Government

> **Trace how the Constitution has changed over time through the amendment process**

The Constitution has endured for more than two centuries as the framework of government because it has changed over time. Without change, the Constitution might have become merely a sacred but obsolete relic of a bygone era.

Amendments: Many Are Called; Few Are Chosen

The inevitable need for change was recognized by the framers of the Constitution, and the provisions for **amendment** (a change added to a bill, law, or constitution) were incorporated into Article V. The Constitution has proven to be extremely difficult to amend. In the history of efforts to amend it, the most appropriate characterization is "many are called; few are chosen." Since 1789, more than 11,000 amendments have been formally offered in Congress. Of these, Congress officially proposed only 33, and 27 of these were eventually ratified by the states.

Four methods of amendment are provided for in Article V:

1. Passage in House and Senate by two-thirds vote, then ratification by majority vote of the legislatures of three-fourths (now 38) of the states.

2. Passage in House and Senate by two-thirds vote, then ratification by conventions called for the purpose in three-fourths of the states.

3. Passage in a national convention called by Congress in response to petitions by two-thirds of the states, then ratification by majority vote of the legislatures of three-fourths of the states.

4. Passage in a national convention, as in method (3), then ratification by conventions called for the purpose in three-fourths of the states.

Figure 2.3 illustrates each of these possible methods. Since no amendment has ever been proposed by national convention, routes (3) and (4) have never been employed. And route (2) has only been employed once (the Twenty-First Amendment, which repealed the Eighteenth Amendment, or Prohibition). Thus, route (1) has been used for all the others.

Now it should be clear why it has been so difficult to amend the Constitution. The requirement of a two-thirds vote in the House and the Senate means that any proposal for an amendment in Congress can be killed by only 34 senators or 136 members of the House. What is more, if the necessary two-thirds vote is obtained, the amendment can still be killed by the refusal or inability of only 13 out of 50 state legislatures to ratify it. Since each state has an equal vote regardless of its population, the 13 holdout states may represent a very small fraction of the total American population.

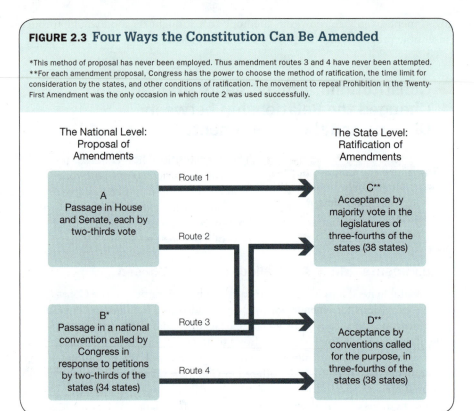

FIGURE 2.3 Four Ways the Constitution Can Be Amended

*This method of proposal has never been employed. Thus amendment routes 3 and 4 have never been attempted.
**For each amendment proposal, Congress has the power to choose the method of ratification, the time limit for consideration by the states, and other conditions of ratification. The movement to repeal Prohibition in the Twenty-First Amendment was the only occasion in which route 2 was used successfully.

The National Level:
Proposal of
Amendments

The State Level:
Ratification of
Amendments

Route 1

Route 2

Route 3

Route 4

A
Passage in House
and Senate, each by
two-thirds vote

B*
Passage in a national
convention called by
Congress in
response to petitions
by two-thirds of the
states (34 states)

C**
Acceptance by
majority vote in the
legislatures of
three-fourths of the
states (38 states)

D**
Acceptance by
conventions called
for the purpose, in
three-fourths of the
states (38 states)

The Amendment Process Reflects "Higher Law"

The very high failure rate of nearly all amendment attempts suggests that only a limited number of changes can actually be made through the Constitution. Most efforts to amend the Constitution have failed because they were simply attempts to use the Constitution as an alternative to legislation for dealing directly with a specific public problem.

Successful amendments, on the other hand, are concerned with the structure or composition of government (see Table 2.3; the first 10 amendments will be discussed in Chapter 4). This is consistent with the dictionary, which defines *constitution* as the makeup or composition of something. And it is consistent with the concept of a constitution as "higher law," because the whole point and purpose of a higher law is to establish a framework within which government and the process of making ordinary law can take place. Even those who would have preferred more changes to the Constitution have to agree that there is great wisdom in this principle. A constitution ought to enable legislation and public policies to be enacted, but it should not determine what that legislation or those public policies ought to be.

For those whose hopes for change center on the Constitution, it must be emphasized that the amendment route to social change is, and always will be, extremely limited. Through a constitution it is possible to establish a working structure of government and basic rights of citizens by placing limitations on the powers of that

TABLE 2.3

Amendments to the Constitution

AMENDMENT	PURPOSE
I	*Limits on Congress:* Congress is not to make any law establishing a religion or abridging speech, press, assembly, or petition freedoms.
II, III, IV	*Limits on Executive:* The executive branch is not to infringe on the right of people to keep arms (II), is not arbitrarily to take houses for a militia (III), and is not to engage in the search or seizure of evidence without a court warrant swearing to belief in the probable existence of a crime (IV).
V, VI, VII, VIII	*Limits on Courts:** The courts are not to hold trials for serious offenses without provision for a grand jury (V), a petit (trial) jury (VII), a speedy trial (VI), presentation of charges (VI), confrontation of hostile witnesses (VI), immunity from testimony against oneself (V), and immunity from more than one trial for the same offense (V). Neither bail nor punishment can be excessive (VIII), and no property can be taken without just compensation (V).
IX, X	*Limits on National Government:* All rights not enumerated are reserved to the states or the people.
XI	Limited jurisdiction of federal courts over suits involving the states.
XII	Provided separate ballot for vice president in the electoral college.
XIII	Eliminated slavery and eliminated the right of states to allow property in persons.**
XIV	(Part 1) Provided a national definition of citizenship.[†]
XIV	(Part 2) Applied due process of Bill of Rights to the states.
XV	Extended voting rights to all races.
XVI	Established national power to tax incomes.
XVII[††]	Provided direct election of senators.
XIX	Extended voting rights to women.
XX	Eliminated "lame duck" session of Congress.
XXII	Limited presidential term.
XXIII	Extended voting rights to residents of the District of Columbia.
XXIV	Extended voting rights to all classes by abolition of poll taxes.
XXV	Provided presidential succession in case of disability.
XXVI	Extended voting rights to citizens aged 18 and over.[†]
XXVII	Limited Congress's power to raise its own salary.

*These amendments also impose limits on the law-enforcement powers of federal (and especially) state and local executive branches.

**The Thirteenth Amendment was proposed January 31, 1865, and adopted less than a year later, on December 18, 1865.

[†]In defining *citizenship*, the Fourteenth Amendment actually provided the constitutional basis for expanding the electorate to include all races, women, and residents of the District of Columbia. Only the "eighteen-year-olds' amendment" should have been necessary, since it changed the definition of citizenship. The fact that additional amendments were required following the Fourteenth suggests that voting is not considered an inherent right of U.S. citizenship. Instead, it is viewed as a privilege.

[††]The Eighteenth Amendment, ratified in 1919, outlawed the sale and transportation of liquor. It was repealed by the Twenty-First Amendment, ratified in 1933.

[†]The Twenty-Sixth Amendment holds the record for speed of adoption. It was proposed on March 23, 1971, and adopted on July 5, 1971.

government. Once these goals have been accomplished, the next problem is how to extend rights to those people who do not already enjoy them. Of course, the Constitution cannot enforce itself. But it can and does have a real influence on everyday life because a right or an obligation set forth in the Constitution can become a cause of action in the hands of an otherwise powerless person.

Private property is an excellent example. Property is one of the most fundamental and well-established rights in the United States, but it is well established not because it is recognized in so many words in the Constitution but because legislatures and courts have made it a crime for anyone, including the government, to trespass or to take away property without compensation.

A constitution is good if it produces the cause of action that leads to good legislation, good court decisions, and appropriate police behavior. A constitution cannot eliminate power. But its principles can be a citizen's dependable defense against the abuse of power.

The Constitution
and Your Future

The Constitution's framers placed individual liberty ahead of all other political values, a concern that led many of the framers to distrust both democracy and equality. They feared that democracy could degenerate into a majority tyranny in which the populace, perhaps led by rabble-rousing demagogues, trampled on liberty. As for equality, the framers were products of their time and place; our contemporary ideas of racial and gender equality would have been foreign to them. By championing liberty, however, the framers virtually guaranteed that democracy and even a measure of equality would sooner or later evolve in the United States. Where they have liberty, more and more people, groups, and interests will almost inevitably engage in politics and gradually overcome whatever restrictions might have been placed on participation.

Unfortunately, liberty can never be taken for granted. It is the duty of each generation to guard its liberty from that which may threaten it. Today, for example, expanding programs of government surveillance may pose a threat to political liberty, as government agencies appear to be recording Americans' emails and phone conversations at an unprecedented level. But our history tells us that citizens' privacy is a prerequisite for effective popular political action, as those who disagree with the groups in power need privacy to plan, organize, and mobilize, lest their plans be anticipated and disrupted. This is a realistic concern given a recent past in which agents of the FBI, seeking to compile damaging information on civil rights leader Dr. Martin Luther King, Jr., secretly taped King's phone calls and meetings.

Thus, as you continue to read this book, ask yourself what you can do to secure the framers' sacrifices and vision. The question of what form of government oversight we ought to tolerate changes over time as technological advances create new opportunities to collaborate with like-minded political actors as well as new opportunities for surveillance. It is the nature of democracy that the party in power today may not be in power tomorrow, thus privacy and liberty in political expression remain a concern for everyone.

plug**in**

Inform

Watch the video "The Constitution, the Articles, and Federalism: Crash Course U.S. History #8" on YouTube, then read the Articles of Confederation and the Constitution (both found in the Appendix to this book) to see the differences for yourself.

Express

Imagine that you are a delegate to the Constitutional Convention. What would you include in (or exclude from) the document, and why?

Connect

Choose a proposed constitutional amendment that you support (find a list at USConstitution.net), and then search online to find the websites of interest groups working to pass the amendment.

Act

Search for "constitutional amendment" on Congress.gov to see what amendments have recently been proposed in Congress, and contact your representatives (via the "Members" tab) to let them know your views on a proposed amendment.

Practice Quiz

1. In their fight against British taxes such as the Stamp Act and the Sugar Act of 1764, New England merchants allied with which of the following groups? *(p. 32)*
   a) artisans, southern planters, and laborers
   b) southern planters only
   c) laborers only
   d) artisans only
   e) southern planters and laborers only

2. How did the British attempt to raise revenue in the North American colonies? *(p. 32)*
   a) income tax
   b) taxes on commerce
   c) expropriation and government sale of land
   d) government asset sales
   e) requests for voluntary donations

3. The first governing document in the United States was *(p. 35)*
   a) the Declaration of Independence.
   b) the Articles of Confederation.
   c) the Constitution.
   d) the Bill of Rights.
   e) the Virginia Plan.

4. Where was the execution of laws conducted under the Articles of Confederation? *(p. 35)*
   a) the presidency
   b) the Congress
   c) the states
   d) the federal judiciary
   e) the federal bureaucracy

5. Which event led directly to the Constitutional Convention by providing evidence that the government created under the Articles of Confederation was unable to act decisively in times of national crisis? *(pp. 37–38)*
   a) the Boston Massacre
   b) the Boston Tea Party
   c) Shays's Rebellion

   d) the Annapolis Convention
   e) the War of 1812

6. Which state's proposal embodied a principle of representing states in the Congress according to their size and wealth? *(p. 39)*
   a) Connecticut
   b) Maryland
   c) New Jersey
   d) Rhode Island
   e) Virginia

7. The agreement reached at the Constitutional Convention that determined that every five slaves would be counted as three free persons for the purposes of taxation and representation in the House of Representatives was called the *(pp. 39–41)*
   a) Virginia Plan.
   b) New Jersey Plan.
   c) Connecticut Compromise.
   d) Three-Fifths Compromise.
   e) Great Compromise.

8. What mechanism was instituted in the Congress to guard against "excessive democracy"? *(pp. 41–42)*
   a) bicameralism
   b) staggered terms in office
   c) appointment of senators for long terms
   d) indirect election of the president
   e) all of the above

9. Which of the following best describes the Supreme Court as understood by the Founders? *(p. 45)*
   a) the body that would choose the president
   b) the highest court of the national government
   c) arbiter of disputes within the Congress
   d) a figurehead commission of elders
   e) a supreme court of the nation and its states

10. Theorists such as Montesquieu referred to the principle of giving each branch of government a distinctly different constituency as *(p. 46)*
   a) mixed regime.
   b) confederation.
   c) laissez-faire.
   d) limited government.
   e) federalism.

11. Which of the following were the Anti-federalists most concerned with? *(pp. 49–51)*
   a) interstate commerce
   b) the protection of property
   c) the distinction between principles and interests
   d) the potential for tyranny in the central government
   e) abolishing slavery

12. Which of the following best describes the process of amending the Constitution? *(p. 53)*
   a) It is difficult and has rarely been used successfully to address specific public problems.
   b) It is difficult and has frequently been used successfully to address specific public problems.
   c) It is easy and has rarely been used successfully to address specific public problems.
   d) It is easy and has frequently been used successfully to address specific public problems.
   e) It is easy, but it has never been used for any purpose.

Key Terms

amendment *(p. 53)* a change added to a bill, law, or constitution

Antifederalists *(p. 48)* those who favored strong state governments and a weak national government and were opponents of the constitution proposed at the American Constitutional Convention of 1787

Articles of Confederation *(p. 35)* America's first written constitution; served as the basis for America's national government until 1789

bicameral *(p. 41)* having a legislative assembly composed of two chambers or houses; distinguished from unicameral

Bill of Rights *(p. 42)* the first 10 amendments to the Constitution, ratified in 1791; they ensure certain rights and liberties to the people

checks and balances *(p. 41)* mechanisms through which each branch of government is able to participate in and influence the activities of the other branches. Major examples include the presidential veto power over congressional legislation, the power of the Senate to approve presidential appointments, and judicial review of congressional enactments

confederation *(p. 35)* a system of government in which states retain sovereign authority except for the powers expressly delegated to the national government

elastic clause *(p. 44)* Article I, Section 8, of the Constitution (also known as the *necessary and proper clause*), which enumerates the powers of Congress and provides Congress with the authority to make all laws "necessary and proper" to carry them out

electoral college *(p. 42)* the electors from each state who meet after the popular election to cast ballots for president and vice president

expressed powers *(p. 44)* specific powers granted by the Constitution to Congress (Article I, Section 8) and to the president (Article II)

federalism *(p. 43)* a system of government in which power is divided, by a constitution, between the central (national) government and regional (state) governments

Federalist Papers *(p. 49)* a series of essays written by James Madison, Alexander Hamilton, and John Jay supporting the ratification of the Constitution

Federalists *(p. 48)* those who favored a strong national government and supported the constitution proposed at the American Constitutional Convention of 1787

Great Compromise *(p. 39)* the agreement reached at the Constitutional Convention of 1787 that gave each state an equal number of senators regardless of its population, but linked representation in the House of Representatives to population

judicial review *(p. 45)* the power of the courts to review and, if necessary, declare actions of the legislative and executive branches invalid or unconstitutional. The Supreme Court asserted this power in *Marbury v. Madison* (1803)

limited government *(p. 51)* a principle of constitutional government; a government whose powers are defined and limited by a constitution

New Jersey Plan *(p. 39)* a framework for the Constitution, introduced by William Paterson, that called for equal state representation in the national legislature regardless of population

separation of powers *(p. 43)* the division of governmental power among several institutions that must cooperate in decision making

supremacy clause *(p. 45)* Article VI of the Constitution, which states that laws passed by the national government and all treaties "shall be the supreme law of the land" and superior to all laws adopted by any state or any subdivision

Three-Fifths Compromise *(p. 40)* the agreement reached at the Constitutional Convention of 1787 that stipulated that for purposes of the apportionment of congressional seats, every slave would be counted as three-fifths of a person

tyranny *(p. 50)* oppressive and unjust government that employs cruel and unjust use of power and authority

Virginia Plan *(p. 39)* a framework for the Constitution, introduced by Edmund Randolph, that called for representation in the national legislature based on the population of each state

For Further Reading

Ackerman, Erin, and Benjamin Ginsberg. *A Guide to the United States Constitution*, 2nd ed. New York: W. W. Norton, 2011.

Beard, Charles. *An Economic Interpretation of the Constitution of the United States*. New York: Macmillan, 1913.

Beeman, Richard. *Plain, Honest Men: The Making of the American Constitution*. New York: Random House, 2009.

Breyer, Stephen. *Active Liberty: Interpreting Our Democratic Constitution*. New York: Knopf, 2005.

Fiske, John. *The American Revolution.* Amazon Digital Services, 2012.

Hamilton, Alexander, James Madison, and John Jay. *The Federalist Papers.* Edited by Isaac Kramnick. New York: Viking, 1987.

Jensen, Merrill. *The Articles of Confederation.* Madison: University of Wisconsin Press, 1963.

Rossiter, Clinton. *1787: Grand Convention.* New York: Macmillan, 1966.

Storing, Herbert, ed. *The Complete Anti-Federalist.* 7 vols. Chicago: University of Chicago Press, 1981.

Wood, Gordon S. *Empire of Liberty: A History of the Early Republic.* New York: Oxford University Press, 2011.

Federalism is at the center of a national debate over marijuana policy: while marijuana remains illegal under federal law, some states permit marijuana for medicinal or recreational use. At the heart of federalism lies the question, which level of government should make policy in a given issue area?

3

Federalism

WHAT GOVERNMENT DOES AND WHY IT MATTERS In 1996, voters in California approved a new law legalizing the cultivation, possession, and use of marijuana for medical purposes. As the idea spread, other states followed suit. By 2014, 23 states and the District of Columbia had approved medical marijuana. In these states, medical clinics selling marijuana have popped up in many cities. With a doctor's prescription, patients can purchase marijuana for personal use. In 2012, two states went even further. Voters in Washington state and Colorado approved measures to legalize the recreational use of marijuana. The laws gave adults over the age of 21 the right to buy limited amounts of marijuana. The following year, Colorado voters agreed to place a hefty tax on marijuana sales. And in the 2014 elections, ballot measures in Alaska, Oregon, and Washington, D.C., also legalized recreational use of marijuana.

States routinely devise their own laws on a wide variety of topics. But the marijuana laws passed over the past two decades are extraordinary because marijuana remains a controlled substance under federal law, making it illegal to grow, sell, or possess marijuana for medical or recreational purposes. States began to legalize marijuana in defiance of clear federal prohibitions.

The federal response to the states has shifted over time. As state laws began to loosen marijuana restrictions, the federal government at first sought to assert its authority. The federal Drug Enforcement Agency staged raids on marijuana clinics and even searched individual homes to enforce the federal law prohibiting marijuana. In 2005, the Supreme Court ruled that these federal actions were constitutional. The Court affirmed the federal government's right to prohibit marijuana even as a growing number of state laws moved in the opposite direction. By 2013, however, the Justice Department, bowing to the states, announced a change of course. The department stated that it would not challenge state laws so long as the states maintained a close watch over their marijuana markets. Instead the federal government would focus its enforcement efforts on specific issues, including trafficking by gangs, sales to minors, and selling across state lines. Washington state's governor, Jay Inslee, issued a joint statement with the state's attorney general noting that the decision "reflects a balanced approach by the federal government that respects the states' interests in implementing these laws and recognizes the federal government's role in fighting illegal drugs and criminal activity."[1]

The debates about marijuana policy engage one of the oldest questions in American government: What is the responsibility of the federal government and what is the responsibility of the states? And when should there be uniformity across the states and when is it better to let the states adopt their own laws based on the preferences of their population, which may result in a diverse set of laws across the nation? The United States is a federal system, in which the national government shares power with lower levels of government. Throughout American history, lawmakers, politicians, and citizens have wrestled with questions about how responsibilities should be allocated across the different levels of government. Some responsibilities, such as foreign policy, clearly lie with the federal government. Others, such as divorce laws, are controlled by state governments. Many government responsibilities are shared in American federalism and require cooperation among local, state, and federal governments. The debate about "who should do what" remains one of the most important discussions in American politics.

chaptergoals

- Describe what the Constitution says about the powers of the national government and of the states (pp. 65–69)

- Trace developments in the federal framework leading to a stronger national government (pp. 69–86)

Federalism Shapes American Politics

Describe what the Constitution says about the powers of the national government and of the states

The Constitution has had its most fundamental influence on American life through **federalism**. Federalism can be defined as the division of powers and functions between the national government and the state governments. Governments can organize power in a variety of ways. One of the most important distinctions is between unitary and federal governments. In a **unitary system**, the central government makes the important decisions, and lower levels of government have little independent power. In such systems, lower levels of government primarily implement decisions made by the central government. In France, for example, the central government was once so involved in the smallest details of local activity that the minister of education boasted that by looking at his watch he could tell what all French schoolchildren were learning at that moment because the central government set the school curriculum. In a **federal system**, by contrast, the central government shares power or functions with lower levels of government, such as regions or states. Nations with diverse ethnic or language groupings, such as Switzerland and Canada, are most likely to have federal arrangements. In federal systems, lower levels of government often have significant independent power to set policy in some areas, such as education and social programs, and to impose taxes. Yet the specific ways in which power is shared vary greatly: no two federal systems are exactly the same.

Federalism Comes from the Constitution

The United States was the first nation to adopt federalism as its governing framework. With federalism, the framers sought to limit the national government by creating a second layer of state governments. American federalism thus recognized two sovereigns in the original Constitution by granting a few **expressed powers** (powers specifically granted to Congress and the president in the Constitution) to the national government and reserving the rest to the states.

The Powers of the National Government As we saw in Chapter 2, the "expressed powers" granted to the national government are found in Article I, Section 8, of the Constitution. These 17 powers include the power to collect taxes, coin money, declare war, and regulate commerce. Article I, Section 8, also contains another important source of power for the national government: the **implied powers** that enable Congress "to make all Laws which shall be necessary and proper for carrying into Execution the foregoing Powers." Such powers are not specifically expressed but are implied through the expansive interpretation of delegated powers. Not until several decades after the Founding did the Supreme Court allow Congress to exercise the power granted in this **necessary and proper clause**, but as we shall see later in this chapter, this doctrine allowed the national government to expand considerably the scope of its authority, although the process was a slow one.

Aside from these powers, the federal government operates with one other advantage over the states: as mentioned in the last chapter, Article VI of the Constitution says that whenever there is a conflict between a national law and a state law, the national law shall prevail. This doctrine of *national supremacy* says that "[t]his Constitution, and the Laws of the United States . . . and all Treaties made . . . shall be the supreme Law of the Land," even extending to state courts and constitutions.

The Powers of State Government One way in which the framers sought to preserve a strong role for the states was through the Tenth Amendment to the Constitution. The Tenth Amendment states that the powers that the Constitution does not delegate to the national government or prohibit to the states are "reserved to the States respectively, or to the people." The Antifederalists, who feared that a strong central government would encroach on individual liberty, repeatedly pressed for such an amendment as a way of limiting national power. Federalists agreed to the amendment because they did not think it would do much harm, given the powers of the Constitution already granted to the national government. The Tenth Amendment is also called the "**reserved powers** amendment" because it aims to reserve powers to the states.

The most fundamental power that the states retain is that of coercion—the power to develop and enforce criminal codes, to administer health and safety rules, and to regulate the family via marriage and divorce laws. The states have the power to regulate individuals' livelihoods; if you're a doctor or a lawyer or a plumber or a hair stylist, you must be licensed by the state. Even more fundamentally, the states have the power to define private property—private property exists because state laws against trespass define who is and is not entitled to use a piece of property. If you own a car, your ownership isn't worth much unless the state is willing to enforce your right to possession by making it a crime for anyone else to drive your car without your permission. These laws are essential to citizens' everyday lives, and the powers of the states regarding such domestic issues are much greater than the powers of the national government, even today.

A state's authority to regulate the health, safety, and morals of its citizens is commonly referred to as the **police power** of the state. Policing is what states do—they coerce you in the name of the community in order to maintain public order. And this was exactly the type of power that the Founders intended the states, rather than the federal government, to exercise.

In some areas, the states share **concurrent powers** (authority possessed by *both* state and national governments) with the national government, whereby they retain and share some power to regulate commerce and to affect the currency—for example, by being able to charter banks, grant or deny corporate charters, grant or deny licenses to engage in a business or practice a trade, and regulate the quality of products or the conditions of labor. Wherever there is a direct conflict of laws between the federal and the state levels, the issue will most likely be resolved in favor of national supremacy.

States' Obligations to One Another The Constitution also creates obligations among the states. These obligations, spelled out in Article IV, were intended to promote national unity. By requiring the states to recognize actions and decisions taken in other states as legal and proper, the framers aimed to make the states less like independent countries and more like parts of a single nation.

Article IV, Section 1, establishes the **full faith and credit clause**, stipulating that each state is normally expected to honor the "public Acts, Records, and judicial Proceedings" that take place in any other state. So, for example, if a person has a restraining order placed on a stalker or batterer in one state, the other states are required to enforce that order as if they had issued it.

The full faith and credit clause has become embroiled in the controversy over same-sex marriage. In 2004, Massachusetts became the first state to legalize gay marriage, as the result of a state court ruling. By 2014, 35 states plus the District of Columbia had legalized gay marriage. Fifteen states have either state constitutional amendments or laws that bar same-sex marriage.[2] The principle of full faith and credit would seem to suggest that states without gay marriage would be obliged to recognize such unions in their states, just as they would recognize heterosexual marriages performed in other states. But to forestall this possibility, in 1996, Congress passed the Defense of Marriage Act (DOMA), which declared that states did *not* have to recognize same-sex marriage even if it is legal in other states. Thus, most states that do not permit same-sex marriage also do not recognize same-sex marriages performed in other states. DOMA also said that the federal government will not recognize gay marriage, even if legal in some states, and that same-sex partners are not eligible for federal benefits such as Medicare and Social Security. In 2013, however, the Supreme Court in *Windsor v. the United States* struck down part of the DOMA, ordering that same-sex married couples receive equal

Public health is a concurrent power. Here, a state health inspector checks that the food in a college cafeteria is at a proper temperature to prevent food-borne illnesses. At the federal level, the Food and Drug Administration regulates some food products, such as baby formula, as well as drugs and other medical devices and procedures.

treatment on issues relating to taxes, inheritance, and other federal laws.[3] It also opened the door for same-sex couples to receive federal social benefits on the same terms as heterosexual married couples. Although the president ordered federal agencies to change their regulations to comply with the ruling, questions remained about whether same-sex couples would receive equal treatment in all social programs that involved both federal and state funding. The court did not rule on whether states have to recognize same-sex marriages in other states.

Article IV, Section 2, known as the "comity clause," also seeks to promote national unity. This clause provides that citizens enjoying the **"privileges and immunities"** of one state should be entitled to similar treatment in other states. What this has come to mean is that a state cannot discriminate against someone from another state or give special privileges to its own residents. For example, in the 1970s, when Alaska passed a law that gave residents preference over nonresidents in obtaining work on the state's oil and gas pipelines, the Supreme Court ruled the law illegal because it discriminated against citizens of other states.[4] The comity clause also regulates criminal justice among the states by requiring states to return fugitives to the states from which they have fled. Thus, in 1952, when an inmate escaped from an Alabama prison and sought to avoid being returned to Alabama on the grounds that he was being subjected to "cruel and unusual punishment" there, the Supreme Court ruled that he must be returned according to Article IV, Section 2.[5] This example highlights the difference between the obligations among states and those among different countries. For example, in 2013, Russia refused to extradite Edward Snowden, a government contractor who leaked important intelligence documents about U.S. government spying. Although the Justice Department stated that it would not seek the death penalty for Snowden, Russia declined to hand Snowden over to American authorities. The Constitution clearly forbids states from doing something similar.

Local Government and the Constitution Local government occupies a peculiar but very important place in the American system. In fact, the status of American local government is probably unique in world experience. First, local governments have no status in the U.S. Constitution. *State* legislatures created local governments, and *state* constitutions and laws permit local governments to take on some of the

Should same-sex marriages performed in one state by legally recognized in another state? The Supreme Court ruled that the federal government must respect same-sex marriages performed in states where the practice is legal, but not all states perform such marriages or recognize those performed in other states.

responsibilities of the state governments. Most states amended their constitutions to give their larger cities **home rule**, powers delegated by the state to a local unit of government to manage its own affairs. But local governments enjoy no such recognition in the federal Constitution. Local governments have always been creatures of the states.[6]

Local governments became administratively important in the early years of the republic because the states relied on local governments (cities and counties) to implement the laws of the state. Local government was an alternative to a state-wide bureaucracy (see Table 3.1).

TABLE 3.1

90,107 Governments in the United States

TYPE	NUMBER
National	1
State	50
County	3,031
Municipal	19,519
Townships	16,360
School districts	12,880
Other special districts	38,266

SOURCE: U.S. Census Bureau, www2.census.gov/govs/cog /g12_org.pdf (accessed 11/02/13).

The Definition of Federalism Has Changed Radically over Time

Trace developments in the federal framework leading to a stronger national government

Many of the fiercest political controversies in American history have revolved around competing views of federalism. The best way to understand these disputes, and how federalism has been redefined throughout American history, is to examine how its conception has changed over time. During the "traditional system" in America, from 1789 to 1937, the political scales clearly favored the states over the federal government. (We call it the "traditional system" because it covered much of American history and because it closely approximated the intentions of the framers of the Constitution.) Then, from the New Deal period of the 1930s to the present, some important limits were placed on state governments, and the federal government exerted far more power than it had under the traditional system, despite efforts to roll back national government powers in recent decades.

Federalism under the "Traditional System" Gave Most Powers to the States

The prevailing view of national government–state government relations under the traditional system was one of **dual federalism**, in which most fundamental governmental powers were shared between the federal and state governments. During this time, the states possessed a vast amount of governing power, and virtually all of the important policies affecting the lives of Americans were made by the state governments. For evidence, look at Table 3.2, which lists the major types of public policies by which Americans were governed for the first century and a half under the Constitution. Under the traditional system, the national government was quite small by comparison both with the state governments and with the governments of other Western nations. Not only was it smaller than most governments of that time, but it was also actually very narrowly specialized in the functions it performed. The national government built or sponsored the construction of roads, canals, and bridges (internal improvements). It provided cash subsidies to shippers and shipbuilders and distributed free or low-priced public land to encourage

TABLE 3.2

The Federal System: Specialization of Governmental Functions in the Traditional System, 1789–1937

NATIONAL GOVERNMENT POLICIES (DOMESTIC)	STATE GOVERNMENT POLICIES	LOCAL GOVERNMENT POLICIES
Internal improvements	Property laws (including slavery)	Adaptation of state laws to local conditions
Subsidies	Estate and inheritance laws	Public works
Tariffs	Commerce laws	Contracts for public works
Public land disposal	Banking and credit laws	
Patents	Corporate laws	Licensing of public accommodation
Currency	Insurance laws	Assessible improvements
	Family laws	Basic public services
	Morality laws	
	Public health laws	
	Education laws	
	General penal laws	
	Eminent domain laws	
	Construction codes	
	Land-use laws	
	Water and mineral laws	
	Criminal procedure laws	
	Electoral and political party laws	
	Local government laws	
	Civil service laws	
	Occupations and professions laws	

western settlement and business ventures. It placed relatively heavy taxes on imported goods (tariffs), not only to raise revenues but also to protect "infant industries" from competition from the more advanced European enterprises. It protected patents and provided for a common currency, which encouraged and facilitated enterprises and helped to expand markets.

What do these functions of the national government reveal? First, virtually all the national government's functions were aimed at assisting commerce. It is quite appropriate to refer to the traditional American system as a "commercial republic." Second, virtually none of the national government's policies directly coerced citizens. The emphasis of governmental programs was on assistance, promotion, and encouragement—the allocation of land or capital to meet the needs of economic development.

Meanwhile, state legislatures were also actively involved in economic regulation during the nineteenth century. In the United States, then and now, private property exists only in state laws and state court decisions regarding property, trespass, and real estate. American capitalism took its form from state property and trespass laws, and from state laws and court decisions regarding contracts, markets, credit, banking, incorporation, and insurance. Laws concerning slavery were a subdivision of property law in states where slavery existed. The practice of important professions, such as law and medicine, was (and is) illegal except as provided for by state law. To educate or not to educate a child has been a decision governed more by state laws than by parents. It is important to note also that most criminal laws, from trespass to murder, have been state laws. Thus, most of the fundamental governing in the United States was done by the states.

Ultimately, the fundamental impact of federalism on the way the United States is governed comes not from any particular provision of the Constitution but from the framework itself, which has determined the flow of government functions and, through that, the political development of the country. By allowing state governments to do most of the fundamental governing, the Constitution saved the national government from many policy decisions that might have proved too divisive for a large and very young country. There is little doubt that if the Constitution had provided for a unitary system rather than a federal system, the war over slavery would have come in 1789 or not long thereafter; and if it had come that early, the South might very well have seceded and established a separate and permanent slaveholding nation.

In helping the national government remain small and apart from the most divisive issues of the day, federalism contributed significantly to the political stability of the young nation, even as the social, economic, and political systems of many of the states and regions of the country were undergoing tremendous, profound, and sometimes violent change.[7] As we shall see, some important aspects of federalism have changed, but the federal framework has survived over two centuries and through a devastating civil war.

The Supreme Court Paved the Way for the End of the "Traditional System"

As the nation grew, disputes arose about the powers of the federal government versus the powers of the states. In the first several decades after the Founding, the

Supreme Court decided several critical cases that expanded federal powers and facilitated trade across the states. These decisions removed barriers to trade in the new nation and laid the groundwork for a national economy. However, by the end of the nineteenth century, as reformers began to enact laws regulating businesses though such measures as child labor restrictions, the Court took a much more restrictive view of federal power. Not until well into the New Deal, in 1937, did the federal government gain the expansive powers it exercises today.

Article I, Section 8, of the Constitution delegates to Congress the power "to regulate Commerce with foreign Nations, and among the several States and with the Indian Tribes." For most of the nineteenth century, the Supreme Court consistently interpreted this **commerce clause** *in favor* of national power over the economy. The first and most important such case was *McCulloch v. Maryland* (1819), which involved the question of whether Congress had the power to charter a national bank, as such an explicit grant of power was nowhere to be found in Article I, Section 8.[8] Chief Justice John Marshall answered that this power could be "implied" from other powers that were expressly delegated to Congress, such as the "powers to lay and collect taxes; to borrow money; to regulate commerce; and to declare and conduct a war."

By allowing Congress to use the necessary and proper clause to interpret its delegated powers expansively, the Supreme Court created the potential for an unprecedented increase in national government power. Marshall also concluded that whenever a state law conflicted with a federal law (as in the case of *McCulloch v. Maryland*), the state law would be deemed invalid, since the Constitution states that "the Laws of the United States . . . shall be the supreme Law of the Land." Both parts of this great case are pro-national, including the verification of the principle of "national supremacy," yet Congress did not immediately seek to expand the policies of the national government.

Another major case, *Gibbons v. Ogden* (1824), reinforced this nationalistic interpretation of the Constitution. The important but relatively narrow issue was whether the state of New York could grant a monopoly to Robert Fulton's steamboat company to operate an exclusive service between New York and New Jersey. Chief Justice Marshall argued that New York state did not have the power to grant this particular monopoly. In reaching this decision, Marshall had to define what Article I, Section 8, meant by "commerce among the several states." He insisted that the definition was "comprehensive," extending to "every species of commercial intercourse." However, this comprehensiveness was limited "to that commerce which concerns more states than one." *Gibbons* is important because it established the supremacy of the national government in all matters affecting what later came to be called "interstate commerce."[9] But the precise meaning of interstate commerce would remain uncertain during several decades of constitutional discourse.

Backed by the implied powers and national supremacy decision in *McCulloch* and by the broad definition of "interstate commerce" in *Gibbons*, Article I, Section 8, was a source of power for the national government as long as Congress sought to facilitate commerce through subsidies, services, and land grants. Later in the nineteenth century, though, the Supreme Court declared any effort of the national government to *regulate* commerce in such areas as fraud, the production of substandard goods, the use of child labor, or the existence of dangerous working conditions or long hours to be unconstitutional as a violation of the concept of interstate commerce. Such legislation meant that the federal government was entering the factory and the workplace—local areas—and was attempting to regulate goods that had not yet passed into interstate commerce. To enter these local workplaces was to exercise police power—a power reserved to the states. No one questioned the power of the national government to regulate businesses that intrinsically involved interstate commerce, such as railroads, gas pipelines, and waterway transportation. But well into the twentieth century, the Supreme Court used the concept of interstate commerce as a barrier against most efforts by Congress to regulate local conditions.

This interpretation of federalism gave the American economy a freedom from federal government control that closely approximated the ideal of free enterprise. The economy was never entirely free, of course; in fact, entrepreneurs themselves did not want complete freedom from government. They needed law and order. They needed a stable currency. They needed courts and police to enforce contracts and prevent trespass. They needed roads, canals, and railroads. But federalism, as interpreted by the Supreme Court for 70 years after the Civil War, made it possible for business to have its cake and eat it, too. Entrepreneurs enjoyed the benefits of national policies facilitating commerce but were shielded by the courts from policies that regulate commerce by protecting the rights of consumers and workers.[10] In addition, the Tenth Amendment was used to bolster arguments about **states' rights**, the principle that the states should oppose the increasing authority of the national government. This principle was most popular in the period before the Civil War.

In the early twentieth century, however, the Tenth Amendment appeared to lose its force as reformers began to press for national regulations to limit the power of large corporations and to protect the health and welfare of citizens, as we shall see next.

FDR's New Deal Remade the Government

The New Deal of the 1930s marked a major change in how the courts interpreted national power. The door to increased federal action opened when states proved unable to cope with the demands brought on by the Great Depression. Before the depression, states and localities took responsibility for addressing the needs of the poor, usually through private charity. But the extent of the need created by the depression quickly exhausted local and state capacities. By 1932, 25 percent of the workforce was unemployed. The jobless lost their homes and settled into camps all over the country, called "Hoovervilles" after President Herbert Hoover. Elected in 1928, the year before the depression hit, Hoover steadfastly maintained that there was little the federal government could do to alleviate these people's misery caused by the depression. It was a matter for state and local governments, he said.

Yet demands mounted for the federal government to take action. When Franklin Delano Roosevelt took office in 1933, he energetically threw the federal government into the business of fighting the depression through a number of proposals

The National School Lunch Program, established by President Harry Truman in 1946, provides nutritious, low-cost lunches to children every day. This program is funded by federal grants to the states.

known collectively as the New Deal. He proposed a variety of temporary measures to provide federal relief and work programs. Most of the programs he proposed were to be financed by the federal government but administered by the states. In addition to these temporary measures, Roosevelt presided over the creation of several important federal programs designed to provide future economic security for Americans. The New Deal signaled the rise of a more active national government.

For the most part, the new national programs that the Roosevelt administration developed did not directly take power away from the states. Instead, Washington typically redirected states by offering them **grants-in-aid**, programs through which Congress provided money to state and local governments on the condition that the funds be employed for purposes defined by the federal government.

Franklin Roosevelt did not invent the idea of grants-in-aid, but his New Deal vastly expanded the range of grants-in-aid to include social programs, providing grants to the states for financial assistance to poor children. Congress added more grants after World War II, creating new programs to help states fund activities such as providing school lunches and building highways. Sometimes the national government required state or local governments to match the national contribution dollar for dollar, but in some programs, such as the development of the interstate highway system, the congressional grants provided 90 percent of the cost of the program.

These types of federal grants-in-aid are called **categorical grants**, because the grants are given to states and localities by the national government on the condition that expenditures be limited to a problem or group specified by law. For the most part, the categorical grants created before the 1960s simply helped the states perform their traditional functions.[11] In the 1960s, however, the national role expanded and federal funding in the form of categorical grants increased dramatically (see Figure 3.1). For example, during the 89th Congress (1965–66) alone, the number of categorical grant-in-aid programs grew from 221 to 379.[12] The *value* of categorical grants also has risen dramatically, from $2.3 billion in 1950 to an estimated $607 billion in 2014. The grants authorized during the 1960s addressed national purposes much more strongly than did earlier grants. One of the most important—and expensive—was the federal Medicaid program, which provides states with grants to pay for medical care for the poor, the disabled, and many nursing home residents.

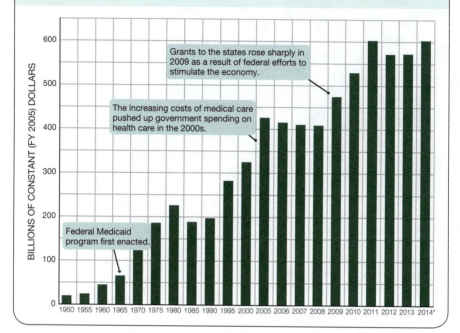

FIGURE 3.1 Historical Trend of Federal Grants-in-Aid,* 1950–2014

Spending on federal grants-in-aid to the states and local governments has grown dramatically since 1990. These increases reflect the growing public expectations about what government should do. What has been the most important cause of the steady increase in these grants?

*Data for 2014 are estimated.

SOURCE: U.S. Budget for Fiscal Year 2015, www.whitehouse.gov/omb/budget/Historicals (accessed 5/15/14).

Changing Court Interpretations of Federalism Helped the New Deal While Preserving States' Rights

In a dramatic change beginning in 1937, the Supreme Court threw out the old distinction between interstate and intrastate commerce on which it had relied in the late 1800s and early 1900s. It converted the commerce clause from a source of limitations to a source of power for the national government. The Court began to refuse to review appeals that challenged acts of Congress protecting the rights of employees to organize and engage in collective bargaining, regulating the amount of farmland in cultivation, extending low-interest credit to small businesses and farmers, and restricting the activities of corporations dealing in the stock market; it upheld many other laws that contributed to the construction of the modern "welfare state."[13]

The Court also reversed its position on the Tenth Amendment, which it had used to strike down national laws as violations of state power. Instead, the Court

approved numerous expansions of national power, to such an extent that the Tenth Amendment appeared irrelevant. In fact, in 1941, Justice Harlan Fiske Stone declared that the Tenth Amendment was simply a "truism" that had no real meaning.[14]

Yet the idea that some powers should be reserved to the states did not go away. Indeed, in the 1950s, southern opponents of the civil rights movement revived the idea of states' rights. In 1956, 96 southern members of Congress issued a "Southern Manifesto" in which they declared that southern states were not constitutionally bound by Supreme Court decisions outlawing racial segregation. They believed that states' rights should override individual rights to liberty and formal equality. With the triumph of the civil rights movement, the slogan of "states' rights" became tarnished by its association with racial inequality.

The 1990s saw a revival of interest in the Tenth Amendment and important Supreme Court decisions limiting federal power. Much of the interest in the Tenth Amendment stemmed from conservatives who believe that a strong federal government encroaches on individual liberties. They believed such freedoms were better protected by returning more power to the states through the process of **devolution**, whereby programs are removed from one level of government by delegating it or passing it down to a lower level of government,

In June 1933, Congress passed the National Industrial Recovery Act, which gave employees the right to engage in collective bargaining with employers over wages and working conditions. Before Roosevelt's New Deal, labor law was largely a state affair, and employees often faced significant barriers to organize and promote their interests.

such as from the national government to the state and local governments. In 1996, Republican presidential candidate Bob Dole carried a copy of the Tenth Amendment in his pocket as he campaigned, pulling it out to read at rallies.[15] The Supreme Court's 1995 ruling in *United States v. Lopez* fueled further interest in the Tenth Amendment. In that case, the Court, stating that Congress had exceeded its authority under the commerce clause, struck down a federal law that barred handguns near schools.[16] This was the first time since the New Deal that the Court had limited congressional powers in this way. In 1997 the Court again relied on the Tenth Amendment to limit federal power in *Printz v. United States.*[17] The decision declared unconstitutional a provision of the Brady Handgun Violence Prevention Act that required state and local law enforcement officials to conduct background checks on handgun purchasers. The Court declared that this provision violated state sovereignty guaranteed in the Tenth Amendment because it required state and local officials to administer a federal regulatory program.

Cooperative Federalism Pushes States to Achieve National Goals

The growth of categorical grants, along with favorable court rulings, created a new kind of federalism. If the traditional system of two sovereigns performing highly different functions could be called dual federalism, historians of federalism suggest that the system since the New Deal could be called **cooperative federalism**, in which grants-in-aid have been used strategically to encourage states and localities to pursue nationally defined goals, with national and state governments sharing powers and resources via intergovernmental cooperation. One political scientist, Morton Grodzins, characterized this as a move from "layer cake federalism" to "marble cake federalism,"[18] in which intergovernmental cooperation and sharing have blurred a once-clear distinguishing line, making it difficult to say where the national government ends and the state and local governments begin (see Figure 3.2).

For a while in the 1960s, it appeared as if the state governments would become increasingly irrelevant to American federalism. Many of the new federal grants bypassed the states and instead sent money directly to local governments and even to local nonprofit organizations. The theme heard repeatedly in Washington was that the states simply could not be trusted to carry out national purposes.[19]

One of the reasons that Washington distrusted the states was because of the way African American citizens were treated in the South. The southern states' forthright defense of segregation, justified on the grounds of states' rights, helped tarnish the image of the states as the civil rights movement gained momentum. The national officials who planned the War on Poverty during the 1960s pointed to the racial exclusion practiced in the southern states as a reason for bypassing state governments. Political scientist James Sundquist described how the "Alabama syndrome" affected the War on Poverty: "In the drafting of the Economic Opportunity Act, an 'Alabama syndrome' developed. Any suggestion within the poverty task force that the states be given a role in the administration of the act was met with

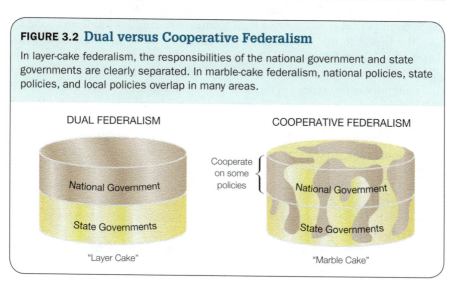

FIGURE 3.2 Dual versus Cooperative Federalism

In layer-cake federalism, the responsibilities of the national government and state governments are clearly separated. In marble-cake federalism, national policies, state policies, and local policies overlap in many areas.

DUAL FEDERALISM

COOPERATIVE FEDERALISM

Cooperate on some policies

National Government

State Governments

National Government

State Governments

"Layer Cake"

"Marble Cake"

the question, 'Do you want to give that kind of power to [then–Alabama governor] George Wallace?'"[20] (Wallace at the time was nationally known for his virulent opposition to the civil rights movement.)

Yet even though many national policies of the 1960s bypassed the states, other new programs, such as Medicaid, relied on state governments for their implementation. In addition, as the national government expanded existing programs run by the states, states had to take on more responsibility. These new responsibilities meant that the states were now playing a very important role in the federal system.

National Standards Have Been Advanced through Federal Programs

Over time, the Supreme Court has pushed for greater uniformity in rules and procedures across the states. In addition to legal decisions, the national government uses two other tools to create similarities across the states: grants-in-aid and regulations.

Grants-in-aid, as we have seen, are incentives: Congress gives money to state and local governments if they agree to spend it for the purposes Congress specifies. But as Congress began to enact legislation in new areas, such as environmental policy, it also imposed additional *regulations* on states and localities. Some political scientists call this a move toward regulated federalism.[21] The effect of these national standards is that state and local policies in the areas of environmental protection, social services, and education are more uniform from coast to coast than are other nationally funded policies.

Some national standards require the federal government to take over areas of regulation formerly overseen by state or local governments. Such **preemption** (the principle that allows the national government to override state or local actions in certain policy areas) occurs when state and local actions are found to be inconsistent with federal requirements. If this occurs, all regulations in the preempted area must henceforth come from the national government. In many cases, the courts determine the scope of the federal authority to preempt. For example, in 1973 the Supreme Court struck down a local ordinance prohibiting jets from taking off from the airport in Burbank, California, between 11:00 PM and 7:00 AM. It ruled that the federal Civil Aeronautics Act granted the Federal Aviation Administration all authority over flight patterns, takeoffs, and landings and that local governments could not impose regulations in this area. As federal regulations increased after the 1970s, Washington increasingly preempted state and local action in many different policy areas. This preemption has escalated since 1994, when Republicans gained control of Congress. Although the Republicans came to power promising to grant more responsibility to the states, they reduced state control in many areas by preemption. For example, in 1998, Congress passed a law that prohibited states and localities from taxing Internet access services. The 1996 Telecommunications Act reduced local control by giving broadcasters and digital companies broad discretion over where they could erect digital television and cellular phone towers even if local citizens objected.[22]

In 2009, after only a few months in office, President Obama reversed the Bush administration's use of federal regulations to limit state laws. Under the new

Government Spending in Federal and Unitary Systems

Both federalism and unitary systems are common among the countries of the world. The key difference between the two systems is in the amount of power that is reserved for state and local governments: federal systems give considerable autonomy to their subnational units, whereas unitary systems tend to be highly centralized.

The graphs here show the percentage of total government revenue that is spent by the central government, state governments, and local governments. The central government of France, a unitary country, spends a larger percentage than Switzerland, Mexico, and the United States, all federal countries. South Korea is a unitary country where local governments operate under a great deal of autonomy, carrying out many of the state's administrative functions. As a result, local government spending in South Korea is comparable to some federal systems. This example shows that while the distinction between federalism and unitary systems is important, it is not the only factor in determining who holds power in a country.

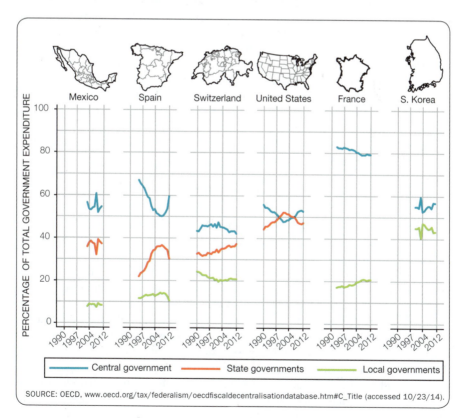

SOURCE: OECD, www.oecd.org/tax/federalism/oecdfiscaldecentralisationdatabase.htm#C_Title (accessed 10/23/14).

policy, federal regulations should preempt state laws only in extraordinary cases. The president directed agency leaders to review the regulations that had been put in place over the past 10 years and consider amending them if they interfered with the "legitimate prerogatives of the states."[23] But as we will see later in this chapter, the Obama administration did use its power of preemption to challenge state immigration laws, charging that states were making laws in a domain reserved for federal authority.

The growth of national standards has created some new problems and has raised questions about how far federal standardization should go. One problem that emerged in the 1980s was the increase in **unfunded mandates**—regulations or new conditions for receiving grants that impose costs on state and local governments for which they are not reimbursed by the national government. The growth of unfunded mandates was the product of a Democratic Congress, which wanted to achieve liberal social objectives, and Republican presidents who opposed increased social spending. Between 1983 and 1991, Congress mandated standards in many policy areas, including social services and environmental regulations, without providing additional funds to meet those standards. Altogether, Congress enacted 27 laws that imposed new regulations or required states to expand existing programs.[24] For example, the 1973 Rehabilitation Act prohibited discrimination against the disabled in programs that were partly funded by the federal government. The new law required state and local governments to make public transit accessible to disabled people with wheelchair lifts in buses, elevators in train stations, and special transportation systems where needed. These requirements were estimated to cost state and local governments $6.8 billion over 30 years.[25] But Congress did not supply additional funding to help states meet these new requirements; the states had to shoulder the increased financial burden themselves. States complained that mandates took up so much of their budgets that they were not able to set their own priorities.[26]

These burdens became part of a rallying cry to reduce the power of the federal government—a cry that took center stage when a Republican Congress was elected in 1994. One of the first measures the new Congress passed was an act to limit the cost of unfunded mandates, the Unfunded Mandates Reform Act (UMRA). Under this law, Congress must estimate the expense for any proposal it believes would exceed the threshold established in UMRA ($73 million in 2012, adjusted for inflation). Congress must then identify funding sources for bills that exceed the threshold established in UMRA.

New national problems inevitably raise the question of who pays. Recently, concern about unfunded mandates has arisen around health care reform. The major health care legislation enacted during Obama's first two years as president, the Affordable Care Act of 2010, called for a major expansion of Medicaid. But because Medicaid is partly funded by the states, any major increase in the number of Medicaid recipients could impose a significant fiscal burden on the states. Although the law provided additional federal aid to support the new requirements, the Medicaid provisions became a target for state challenges to the health care law. One of the central claims in the 26 states' lawsuits charged that the federal government did not have the power to withhold Medicaid funds from states that did not implement the new expansions. The Supreme Court ultimately ruled that states could decline to expand Medicaid coverage without losing their existing Medicaid funds. After the Court's decision, a handful of Republican governors announced that they would not implement the expanded coverage.

New Federalism Means More State Control

Since the 1970s, as states have become more capable of administering large-scale programs, the idea of devolution—transferring responsibility for policy from the federal government to the states and localities—has become popular.

Proponents of more state authority have looked to **block grants** as a way of reducing federal control. Block grants are federal grants-in-aid that allow states considerable discretion in how the funds are spent. President Richard Nixon led the first push for block grants in the early 1970s. Nixon's approach consolidated programs in the areas of job training, community development, and social services into three large block grants. These grants imposed some conditions on states and localities as to how the money should be spent but avoided the narrow regulations contained in the categorical grants discussed earlier. In addition, Congress approved a fourth block grant called **general revenue sharing**, whereby the federal government provided money to local governments and counties with no strings attached; localities could spend the money as they wished. In enacting revenue sharing, Washington acknowledged both the critical role that state and local governments play in implementing national priorities and their need for increased

The debate over national-versus-state control of speed limits arose in 1973, when gas prices skyrocketed and supplies became scarce. Drivers nationwide were forced to wait in long lines at gas stations. The federal government responded to the gas crisis by instituting a national 55-mile-per-hour speed limit.

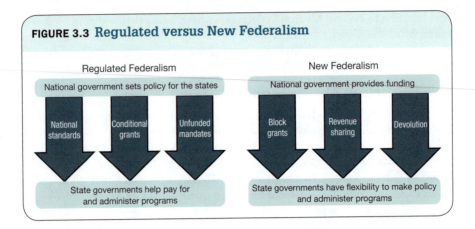

FIGURE 3.3 Regulated versus New Federalism

Regulated Federalism

National government sets policy for the states

National standards | Conditional grants | Unfunded mandates

State governments help pay for and administer programs

New Federalism

National government provides funding

Block grants | Revenue sharing | Devolution

State governments have flexibility to make policy and administer programs

funding and enhanced flexibility in order to carry out that role (see Figure 3.3). Ronald Reagan's version of **New Federalism** (returning power to the states through block grants) similarly aimed to reduce the national government's control. In all, Congress created 12 new block grants between 1981 and 1990.[27]

But this new approach, like those that preceded it, has not provided magic solutions to the problems of federalism. For one thing, there is always a trade-off between accountability—that is, whether the states are using funds for the purposes intended—and flexibility. If the objective is to have accountable and efficient government, it is not clear that state bureaucracies are any more efficient or more capable than national agencies. In Mississippi, for example, the state Department of Human Services spent money from the child care block grant for office furniture and designer salt and pepper shakers that cost $37.50 a pair. As one Mississippi state legislator said, "I've seen too many years of good ol' boy politics to know they shouldn't [transfer money to the states] without stricter controls and requirements."[28] Even after block grants were created, Congress reimposed regulations in order to increase the states' accountability.

At times the federal government has also moved to limit state discretion over spending in cases where it thinks states are too generous. For example, in 2007, President Bush issued regulations that prevented states from providing benefits under the State Child Health Insurance Program (SCHIP) to children in families well above the poverty line. The Bush administration also barred states from providing chemotherapy to illegal immigrants, who are guaranteed emergency medical treatment under Medicaid.[29] These new rules embroiled states and the federal government in sharp conflicts over state discretion in spending decisions, once the hallmark of New Federalism.

There Is No Simple Answer to Finding the Right National-State Balance

As Figure 3.4 indicates, federalism has changed dramatically over the course of American history, even over just the past several decades. Finding the right balance among states and the federal government is an evolving challenge for American

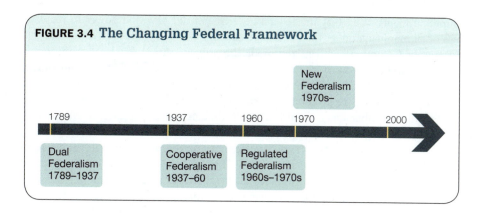

FIGURE 3.4 The Changing Federal Framework

New Federalism 1970s–

1789   1937   1960   1970   2000

Dual Federalism 1789–1937

Cooperative Federalism 1937–60

Regulated Federalism 1960s–1970s

democracy. In recent years, many of the most controversial issues in American politics—including the appropriate size of public social spending, the rights and benefits of immigrants (legal as well as undocumented), what government should do in response to climate change, and questions about whether and how government should regulate business and moral behavior—have been fought out through the federal system. Politicians of all stripes regularly turn to the federal government to override decisions made by states. Likewise, when the federal government proves unable or unwilling to act, activists and politicians try to achieve their goals in states and localities. In many cases, it is up to the courts to decide which level of government should have the final say.

Although conservatives proclaim their preference for a small federal government and their support for more state autonomy, in fact, they often expand the federal government and limit state autonomy. During the presidency of George W. Bush, the growth of government, the activist free-spending Republican Congress, and a series of Supreme Court rulings supporting federal power over the states made it clear that conservatives do not always support small government, nor do they always favor returning power to the states. President Bush, for example, expanded federal control and increased spending in various policy areas. The 2001 No Child Left Behind Act, passed with Democratic support, introduced unprecedented federal intervention in public education, traditionally a state and local responsibility. New detailed federal testing requirements stipulating how states should treat failing schools were major expansions of federal authority in education. When a number of states threatened to defy some of the new federal requirements, Bush's Department of Education relaxed its tough stance and became more flexible in enforcing the act. But the administration did not back down entirely, leading to several legal challenges to different aspects of the law.

In the Supreme Court, too, many decisions supported a stronger federal role over the states. Decisions to uphold the federal Family and Medical Leave Act and the Americans with Disabilities Act asserted federal authority against state claims of immunity from the acts. In one important 2005 case, the Court upheld the right of Congress to ban medical marijuana, even though 11 states had legalized its use. Overturning a lower court ruling that said Congress did not have authority to regulate marijuana when it had been grown for noncommercial purposes in a single state, the

Supreme Court ruled that the federal government did have the power to regulate use of all marijuana under the commerce clause. Even so, by 2014, 23 states and the District of Columbia had legalized medical marijuana. Amid this legal confusion, a medical marijuana industry began to flourish in states that allowed medical use of the drug. In 2012, Colorado and Washington went further by legalizing recreational marijuana even though it is a prohibited substance by federal law. Alaska, Oregon, and the District of Columbia joined them in 2014. Although the federal government has not endorsed these laws, it has made prosecution of marijuana in these states a low priority.

In other policy areas, states and localities have forged their own policies because the federal government has not acted. One of the most controversial of these issues is immigration legislation. In the first half of 2013, for example, state legislatures enacted 377 laws and resolutions related to immigration.[30] Many state and local laws that govern immigration are not controversial, but some raise critical questions about the federal government's role as opposed to the responsibilities of state and local governments. In 2010, Arizona enacted an extremely controversial immigration measure requiring immigrants to carry identity documents and requiring police to ask about immigration status when they stop drivers they suspect of being illegal immigrants. The federal Department of Justice joined several other groups in challenging the law. In the words of then–Attorney General Eric Holder, "It is clearly unconstitutional for a state to set its own immigration policy."[31] In 2012 the Supreme Court ruled that Arizona's law did not preempt federal authority to make immigration law.[32] The court's decision in *Arizona v. United States* did overturn three of four provisions in Arizona's law, but it ruled in favor of the most

The federal government brought Arizona to court over law SB1070, which imposed strict requirements on immigrants. The Supreme Court found that three provisions of the law were preempted by federal law, meaning Arizona did not have the authority to make the regulation. However, the controversial "show me your papers" provision of the law was upheld.

controversial provision, which allows state police to check the immigration status of anyone stopped or arrested.

The Obama administration signaled a much stronger role for the federal government on some dimensions but more flexibility for state action in other matters. The stronger federal role was most evident in the measures to jump-start the failing economy. In 2009, Congress enacted the American Recovery and Reinvestment Act (ARRA), a $787 billion measure that, in addition to tax cuts, offered states substantial one-time funds for a variety of purposes, including education, road building, unemployment insurance, and health care. Many governors, strapped for cash, welcomed the new funds. Others, however, worried that the federal government was using ARRA to dictate state spending priorities. Some of these governors sought to use the funds for purposes not allowed in the legislation or refused parts of the funds that they believed would tie their hands in the future. For example, Governor Mark Sanford of South Carolina, a Republican, asked the federal government for a waiver that would permit his state to use approximately $700 million of its estimated $2.8 billion ARRA allocation to pay down the state's debt. When the waiver was denied, Sanford vowed to reject the federal funds; however, the state legislature overrode his decision.[33] Several states objected to the unemployment funds, which required states to expand eligibility for unemployment insurance to many part-time and temporary workers. A handful of Republican southern governors refused to accept the funds on the grounds that expanded eligibility would place a burden on employers in the future. A majority of states, however, did change their laws in response to the federal requirements.[34]

In other ways, the Obama White House signaled that it would allow the states more leeway for action than they had under the Bush administration. This was particularly true in the domains of social policy and the environment when states sought to enact laws more stringent than those of the federal government. In the memo reversing the Bush policy of preemption, the White House noted, "Throughout our history, State and local governments have frequently protected health, safety, and the environment more aggressively than has the national Government."[35]

The most significant Obama law to affect the states was the 2010 health care overhaul. One controversial part of that legislation required states to expand their Medicaid programs to cover more low-income residents and to offer them additional services. As we saw earlier, the Supreme Court's 2012 ruling in *National Federation of Independent Business v. Sebelius* that the federal government could not impose all-or-nothing conditions on the states—implement the expansion or lose all Medicaid funding—represented a new limit on the national government's power. The ruling mostly upheld the law, but also gave the states more leeway. The other controversial provision of the Affordable Care Act was the "individual mandate," the requirement that individuals without health care insurance be required to purchase such insurance. The 26 states suing the federal government charged that Congress exceeded its power under the commerce clause, arguing that Congress had no power to force individuals to purchase a product and that the act set up a "slippery slope" in which Congress could force individuals to make other purchases. In defending the law, the federal government argued that the complex interactions of the health care market made the individual mandate constitutional under Congress's power to regulate commerce among the states.[36] From the moment a person is born, he or she is part of the health care economy. Even if a person does not have health insurance, federal law requires that hospitals provide treatment in an emergency. Those costs are borne by all of the people who do pay for health insurance.

Taking a more narrow view of the health care market, the Court rejected this argument on the grounds that the federal government cannot regulate economic inactivity, that is, the failure to purchase health insurance. Instead, it found that the Affordable Care Act was constitutional based on Congress's power to tax. The law requires individuals who do not receive insurance from their employers or their parents, and are not eligible for Medicaid, to purchase insurance or pay a penalty. The Court reasoned that the penalty could be considered a tax, and in that sense, it passed constitutional muster. The complex and surprising decision marked a new era in American federalism. The Court placed limits on two of the key powers that have expanded the reach of the federal government since the New Deal—the power to regulate commerce and the power to spend for the general welfare. The decision will surely invite challenges to federal power in new areas.

Federalism
and Your Future

The connections between federalism and our fundamental national values have made federalism a focus of political contention throughout our nation's history. In recent years, sharp differences in Americans' views on many economic and social issues have been reflected in the federal system. Nearly half of the 50 states have legalized medical marijuana, while two have gone further and legalized recreational marijuana. As of 2014, 35 states have legalized same-sex marriage. Some states actively welcome immigrants and seek to opt out of restrictive federal laws; other states go beyond the federal government in enacting restrictive immigration laws.

For young people, these differences across the states provoke important questions about the future. Is the federal government endangering people by allowing states to legalize marijuana? Is it fair to a same-sex couple married in New Jersey that their marriage would not be recognized if they moved to Texas? Each generation confronts a different set of questions about how much variation across the states is appropriate. Are some of the issues on which the states differ fundamental rights that should be uniform across the country? As today's youth help to answer these questions in the coming decades, they will be remaking American federalism.

plugin

Inform

Watch the cartoon "Federal Powers vs. State Powers" on YouTube.

Express

Think about a current issue—such as gun laws, health care, same-sex marriage, or marijuana—that puts state power in contention with national power. Write out your stance on whether the issue should be addressed at the national or state level.

Connect

Find your state-level representatives on your state legislature's website. Most websites also list recent legislation and upcoming votes. Look for bills related to issues that interest you.

Act

Consider emailing your representatives in the state legislature or Congress about the issue you identified and why you think the state or the national government should address it. Contact information is available on the state legislature website or House.gov and Senate.gov.

Practice Quiz

1. Which term describes the sharing of powers between the national government and the state governments? *(p. 65)*
   a) separation of powers
   b) federal system
   c) checks and balances
   d) expressed powers
   e) implied powers

2. Which amendment to the Constitution stated that the powers not delegated to the national government or prohibited to the states were "reserved to the states"? *(p. 66)*
   a) First Amendment
   b) Fifth Amendment
   c) Tenth Amendment
   d) Fourteenth Amendment
   e) Twenty-Sixth Amendment

3. A state government's authority to regulate the health, safety, and morals of its citizens is frequently referred to as *(p. 66)*
   a) the reserved power.
   b) the expressed power.
   c) the police power.
   d) the concurrent power.
   b) the implied power.

4. Which constitutional clause has been central in debates over same-sex marriage because it requires that states normally honor the public acts and judicial decisions of other states? *(p. 67)*
   a) privileges and immunities clause
   b) necessary and proper clause
   c) interstate commerce clause
   d) preemption clause
   e) full faith and credit clause

5. Many states have amended their constitutions to guarantee that large cities will have the authority to manage local affairs without interference from state government. This power is called *(p. 69)*
   a) home rule.
   b) preemption.
   c) devolution.

   d) states' rights.
   e) New Federalism.

6. The system of federalism that allowed states to do most of the fundamental governing from 1789 to 1937 was *(p. 69)*
   a) dual federalism.
   b) regulated federalism.
   c) states' rights.
   d) cooperative federalism.
   e) New Federalism.

7. Beginning in 1937 the Supreme Court laid the groundwork for a stronger federal government by *(pp. 71–73)*
   a) issuing a number of decisions that dramatically narrowed the definition of the commerce clause.
   b) issuing a number of decisions that dramatically expanded the definition of the commerce clause.
   c) issuing a number of decisions that struck down the supremacy clause.
   d) issuing a number of decisions that dramatically expanded the privileges and immunities clause.
   e) issuing a number of decisions that struck down the full faith and credit clause.

8. One of the most powerful tools by which the federal government has attempted to get the states to act in ways that are desired by the federal government is by *(p. 74)*
   a) providing grants-in-aid.
   b) requiring licensing.
   c) granting home rule.
   d) defending states' rights.
   e) general revenue sharing.

9. The process of returning more of the responsibilities of governing from the national level to the state level is known as *(p. 76)*
   a) dual federalism.
   b) devolution.
   c) preemption.
   d) home rule.
   e) incorporation.

10. The form of regulated federalism that allows the federal government to take over areas of regulation formerly overseen by states or local governments is called *(p. 78)*
   a) categorical grants.
   b) devolution.
   c) formula grants.
   d) preemption.
   e) project grants.

11. When state and local governments must conform to costly regulations or conditions in order to receive grants but do not receive reimbursements for their expenditures from the federal government it is called *(p. 80)*
   a) a reciprocal grant.
   b) an unfunded mandate.
   c) general revenue sharing.
   d) a counterfunded mandate.
   e) a concurrent grant.

12. To what does the term *New Federalism* refer? *(p. 82)*
   a) the era of federalism initiated by President Roosevelt during the late 1930s
   b) the national government's regulation of state action through grants-in-aid
   c) the type of federalism relying on categorical grants
   d) efforts to return more policy-making discretion to the states through the use of block grants
   e) the recent emergence of local governments as important political actors

Key Terms

block grants *(p. 81)* federal grants-in-aid that allow states considerable discretion in how the funds are spent

categorical grants *(p. 74)* congressional grants given to states and localities on the condition that expenditures be limited to a problem or group specified by law

commerce clause *(p. 72)* Article I, Section 8, of the Constitution, which delegates to Congress the power "to regulate Commerce with foreign Nations, and among the several States and with the Indian Tribes"; this clause was interpreted by the Supreme Court in favor of national power over the economy

concurrent powers *(p. 66)* authority possessed by both state and national governments, such as the power to levy taxes

cooperative federalism *(p. 77)* a type of federalism existing since the New Deal era in which grants-in-aid have been used strategically to encourage states and localities (without commanding them) to pursue nationally defined goals; also known as "intergovernmental cooperation"

devolution *(p. 76)* a policy to remove a program from one level of government by delegating it or passing it down to a lower level of government, such as from the national government to the state and local governments

dual federalism *(p. 69)* the system of government that prevailed in the United States from 1789 to 1937 in which most fundamental governmental powers were shared between the federal and state governments

expressed powers *(p. 65)* specific powers granted by the Constitution to Congress (Article I, Section 8) and to the president (Article II)

federal system *(p. 65)* a system of government in which the national government shares power with lower levels of government such as states

federalism *(p. 65)* a system of government in which power is divided, by a constitution, between the central (national) government and regional (state) governments

full faith and credit clause *(p. 67)* provision from Article IV, Section 1 of the Constitution requiring that the states normally honor the public acts and judicial decisions that take place in another state

general revenue sharing *(p. 81)* the process by which one unit of government yields a portion of its tax income to another unit of government, according to an established formula; revenue sharing typically involves the national government providing money to state governments

grants-in-aid *(p. 74)* programs through which Congress provides money to state and local governments on the condition that the funds be employed for purposes defined by the federal government

home rule *(p. 69)* power delegated by the state to a local unit of government to manage its own affairs

implied powers *(p. 65)* powers derived from the necessary and proper clause of Article I, Section 8, of the Constitution; such powers are not specifically expressed, but are implied through the expansive interpretation of delegated powers

necessary and proper clause *(p. 65)* provision from Article I, Section 8, of the Constitution providing Congress with the authority to make all laws necessary and proper to carry out its expressed powers

New Federalism *(p. 82)* attempts by presidents Nixon and Reagan to return power to the states through block grants

police power *(p. 66)* power reserved to the state government to regulate the health, safety, and morals of its citizens

preemption *(p. 78)* the principle that allows the national government to override state or local actions in certain policy areas; in foreign policy, the willingness to strike first in order to prevent an enemy attack

privileges and immunities clause *(p. 68)* provision, from Article IV, Section 2, of the Constitution, that a state cannot discriminate against someone from another state or give its own residents special privileges

reserved powers *(p. 66)* powers, derived from the Tenth Amendment to the Constitution, that are not specifically delegated to the national government or denied to the states

states' rights *(p. 73)* the principle that the states should oppose the increasing authority of the national government; this principle was most popular in the period before the Civil War

unfunded mandates *(p. 80)* regulations or conditions for receiving grants that impose costs on state and local governments for which they are not reimbursed by the federal government

unitary system *(p. 65)* a centralized government system in which lower levels of government have little power independent of the national government

For Further Reading

Anton, Thomas. *American Federalism and Public Policy.* Philadelphia: Temple University Press, 1989.

Bensel, Richard. *Sectionalism and American Political Development: 1880–1980.* Madison: University of Wisconsin Press, 1984.

Dye, Thomas R. *American Federalism: Competition among Governments.* Lexington, MA: Lexington Books, 1990.

Elazar, Daniel. *American Federalism: A View from the States.* 3rd ed. New York: Harper & Row, 1984.

Feiock, Richard C., and John T. Scholz. *Self-Organizing Federalism: Collaborative Mechanisms to Mitigate Institutional Collective Action Dilemmas*. New York: Cambridge University Press, 2009.

Gerston, Larry N. *American Federalism: A Concise Introduction*. Armonk, NY: M.E. Sharpe, 2007.

Johnson, Kimberly S. *Governing the American State: Congress and the New Federalism, 1877–1929*. Princeton, NJ: Princeton University Press, 2007.

Kettl, Donald. *The Regulation of American Federalism*. Baltimore: Johns Hopkins University Press, 1987.

Peterson, Paul E. *The Price of Federalism*. Washington, DC: Brookings Institution, 1995.

Pierceson, Jason. *Same-Sex Marriage in the United States: The Road to the Supreme Court*. Lanham, MD: Rowman and Littlefield Publishers, 2013.

Robertson, David Brian. *Federalism and the Making of America*. New York: Routledge, 2011.

Van Horn, Carl E. *The State of the States*. 4th ed. Washington, DC: CQ Press, 2005.

Debates over civil rights date to the country's founding. Today, one of the major contests over civil rights concerns same-sex marriage. As in the past, the Supreme Court has played a key role in determining what civil rights are protected by law.

Civil Liberties and Civil Rights

WHAT GOVERNMENT DOES AND WHY IT MATTERS Today in the United States, we often take for granted the liberties contained in the first 10 amendments to the Constitution, known as the **Bill of Rights**. In fact, few people in recorded history, including American citizens before the 1960s, have enjoyed such protections. And as we shall see in this chapter, guaranteeing the liberties articulated in the Bill of Rights to all Americans required a long struggle. As recently as the early 1960s, many of the freedoms we have today were not guaranteed. At that time, criminal suspects in state cases did not have to be informed of their rights, some states required daily Bible readings and prayers in their public schools, and some communities regularly censored material they deemed to be obscene.

Since the early 1960s the Supreme Court has expanded considerably the scope of **civil liberties**, defined as individual rights and personal freedoms with which governments may not interfere; that is, they are protections for Americans *from* the government. These liberties are constantly subject to judicial interpretation, and their provisions need to be safeguarded vigilantly, especially during times of war or a threat to national security, such as in the aftermath of the terrorist attacks of September 11, 2001.

Civil rights—protections of citizen equality provided *by* the government— have also expanded dramatically since the middle of the twentieth century, when the African American struggle for equal rights took center stage. Many goals of the civil rights movement that once aroused bitter controversy are now widely accepted as part of the American commitment to equal rights. But even today the question of what is meant by "equal rights" is hardly settled. One contemporary example of a contest over civil rights is the issue of same-sex marriage. Some say that all Americans, regardless of gender preference or sexual orientation, should have the right to obtain a state marriage license. Others declare that states should only sanction opposite-sex marriages. As of 2014, 35 states and the District of Columbia allow same-sex marriages, and 15 define marriage as a union between one man and one woman only.[1] At the federal level, in 2013 the Supreme Court struck down portions of the Defense of Marriage Act, which had defined "marriage" and "spouse" to apply only to heterosexual unions. The ruling allowed married same-sex couples to receive federal benefits.[2] This ruling, however, does not force states to make marriage licenses available to same-sex couples. The question of whether same-sex couples do or do not have a constitutional right to marriage is far from settled and sure to generate further debate in the years to come. How can the civil rights of Americans and legal residents be protected as the government enforces immigration laws?

chapter goals

- Explain the origins and evolution of the civil liberties in the Bill of Rights as they apply to the federal government and the states (pp. 95–98)

- Describe how the First Amendment protects freedom of religion (pp. 99–101)

- Describe how the First Amendment protects free speech (pp. 101–8)

- Explore whether the Second Amendment means people have a right to own guns (pp. 108–10)

- Explain the major rights that people have if they are accused of a crime (pp. 110–15)

- Assess whether people have a right to privacy under the Constitution (pp. 115–17)

- Trace the legal developments and social movements that expanded civil rights (pp. 118–25)

- Describe how different groups have fought for and won protection of their civil rights (pp. 125–31)

- Contrast arguments for and against affirmative action (pp. 132–34)

The Origin of the Bill of Rights Lies in Those Who Opposed the Constitution

Explain the origins and evolution of the civil liberties in the Bill of Rights as they apply to the federal government and the states

When the first Congress under the newly ratified Constitution met in April 1789, the most important item of business was the proposal to add a bill of rights to the Constitution. Such a proposal had been turned down with little debate in the waning days of the Philadelphia Constitutional Convention in 1787, not because the delegates were against rights but because—as the Federalists, led by Alexander Hamilton, later argued—such a bill was "not only unnecessary in the proposed Constitution but would even be dangerous."[3] First, according to Hamilton, a bill of rights would be irrelevant to a national government that was given only delegated powers in the first place. To put restraints on "powers which are not granted" could provide a pretext for governments to claim more powers than were in fact granted: "For why declare that things shall not be done which there is no power to do?"[4] Second, the Constitution was to Hamilton and the Federalists a bill of rights in itself, containing provisions that amounted to a bill of rights without requiring additional amendments (see Table 4.1). For example, Article I, Section 9, included the right of **habeas corpus**, a court order demanding that an individual in custody be brought into court and shown the cause for detention. This prohibits the government from depriving a person of liberty without explaining the reason before a judge.

Despite the power of Hamilton's arguments, when the Constitution was submitted to the states for ratification, Antifederalists, most of whom had not been

TABLE 4.1

Rights in the Original Constitution (Not in the Bill of Rights)

CLAUSE	RIGHT ESTABLISHED
Article I, Sec. 9	Guarantee of habeas corpus
Article I, Sec. 9	Prohibition of **bills of attainder**
Article I, Sec. 9	Prohibition of **ex post facto laws**
Article I, Sec. 9	Prohibition against acceptance of titles of nobility, etc., from any foreign state
Article III	Guarantee of trial by jury in state where crime was committed
Article III	Treason defined and limited to the life of the person convicted, not to the person's heirs

delegates in Philadelphia, picked up on the argument of Thomas Jefferson (who also had not been a delegate) that the omission of a bill of rights was a major imperfection of the new Constitution. The Federalists conceded that for the document to gain ratification they would have to make an "unwritten but unequivocal pledge" to add a bill of rights.

The Bill of Rights might well have been titled the "Bill of Liberties," because the provisions that were incorporated in the Bill of Rights were seen as defining a private sphere of personal liberty, free from governmental restrictions.[5] As Jefferson put it, a bill of rights "is what people are entitled to against every government on earth." Note the wording: *against* government. Civil liberties are *protections of citizens from* improper government action. Some of these restraints are substantive liberties, which put limits on *what* the government shall and shall not have power to do—such as establishing a religion, quartering troops in private homes without consent, or seizing private property without just compensation. Other restraints are procedural liberties, which are restraints on *how* the government is supposed to act. These procedural liberties are usually grouped under the general category of **due process of law**, which is the right of every citizen to be protected against arbitrary action by national or state governments. It first appears in the Fifth Amendment provision that "no person shall be . . . deprived of life, liberty, or property, without due process of law." For example, even though the government has the substantive power to declare certain acts to be crimes and to arrest and imprison persons who violate criminal laws, it may not do so without meticulously observing procedures designed to protect the accused person. The best-known procedural rule is that an accused person is presumed innocent until proven guilty. This rule does not question the government's power to punish someone for committing a crime; it questions only the way the government determines who committed the crime. Substantive and procedural restraints together identify the realm of civil liberties.

In contrast, civil rights as a category refers to the obligations imposed on government to *take positive action* to protect citizens from any illegal actions by government agencies and by other private citizens. Civil rights did not become part of the Constitution until 1868, with the adoption of the Fourteenth Amendment, which sought to provide for each citizen "the equal protection of the laws."

The Fourteenth Amendment Created the Doctrine of Incorporation

In the first 70 years of the country's history, the Bill of Rights was understood to apply only to the national government and not to the states. In fact, the Supreme Court said this in a decision in 1833, *Barron v. Baltimore*.[6] But the Civil War cast new light on the large question of state versus national governmental power. After the war, the **Fourteenth Amendment** was added to the Constitution. Part of the amendment reads as though it were meant to tell the states that they must now adhere to the Bill of Rights:

> No *State* shall make or enforce any law which shall abridge the privileges or immunities of citizens of the United States; nor shall any *State* deprive any person of life,

liberty, or property, without due process of law; nor deny to any person within its jurisdiction the equal protection of the laws [emphasis added].

This language sounds like an effort to extend the Bill of Rights to all citizens, wherever they might reside.[7] Yet this was not the Supreme Court's interpretation of the amendment for nearly 100 years. Within five years of ratification of the Fourteenth Amendment, the Court was making decisions as though the amendment had never been adopted.[8]

The first change in civil liberties following the adoption of the Fourteenth Amendment came in 1897, when the Supreme Court held that the due process clause of the Fourteenth Amendment did in fact prohibit states from taking property for a public use without just compensation (a protection found in the Fifth Amendment), overruling the *Barron* case.[9] However, the Supreme Court had selectively "incorporated" under the Fourteenth Amendment only the property protection provision of the Fifth Amendment and no other clause of the Fifth or any other amendment of the Bill of Rights. In other words, although according to the Fifth Amendment "due process" applied to the taking of life and liberty as well as property, only property was incorporated into the Fourteenth Amendment as a limitation on state power.

No further expansion of civil liberties via the Fourteenth Amendment occurred until 1925, when the Supreme Court held that freedom of speech is "among the fundamental personal rights and 'liberties' protected by the due process clause of the Fourteenth Amendment from impairment by the states."[10] In 1931 the Court added freedom of the press to that short list protected by the Bill of Rights from state action; by 1939 it had added freedom of assembly and petitioning the government for redress of grievances.[11] But that was as far as the Court was willing to go.

As Table 4.2 shows, **selective incorporation**—the process by which different protections in the Bill of Rights were incorporated or applied to the states using the Fourteenth Amendment, thus guaranteeing citizens' protection from state as well as national government—continued to occur gradually, up until the last incorporation case in 2010. The final provision of the Bill of Rights to be incorporated by the Supreme Court was the Second Amendment, which protects the right to bear arms.[12] (Incorporation is also sometimes referred to as the "absorption" or the "nationalizing" of the Bill of Rights.)

To make clear that "selective incorporation" should be narrowly interpreted, Justice Benjamin Cardozo, writing for an 8–1 majority in 1937, asserted that although many rights have value and importance, some rights do not represent a "principle of justice so rooted in the traditions and conscience of our people as to be ranked as fundamental." So, until 1961, only the First Amendment and one clause of the Fifth Amendment had been clearly incorporated into the Fourteenth Amendment as binding on the states as well as on the national government.[13]

The best way to examine the Bill of Rights today is the simplest way: to take each of the major provisions one at a time. Some of these provisions are settled areas of law; others are not.

TABLE 4.2

Incorporation of the Bill of Rights into the Fourteenth Amendment

SELECTED PROVISIONS AND AMENDMENTS	INCORPORATED	KEY CASE
Eminent domain (V)	1897	*Chicago, Burlington, and Quincy R.R. v. Chicago*
Freedom of speech (I)	1925	*Gitlow v. New York*
Freedom of press (I)	1931	*Near v. Minnesota*
Free exercise of religion (I)	1934	*Hamilton v. Regents of the University of California*
Freedom of assembly (I) and freedom to petition the government for redress of grievances (I)	1937	*DeJonge v. Oregon*
Freedom of assembly (I)	1939	*Hague v. CIO*
Nonestablishment of state religion (I)	1947	*Everson v. Board of Education*
Freedom from unnecessary search and seizure (IV)	1949	*Wolf v. Colorado*
Freedom from warrantless search and seizure (IV; "exclusionary rule")	1961	*Mapp v. Ohio*
Freedom from cruel and unusual punishment (VIII)	1962	*Robinson v. California*
Right to counsel in any criminal trial (VI)	1963	*Gideon v. Wainwright*
Right against self-incrimination and forced confessions (V)	1964	*Malloy v. Hogan; Escobedo v. Illinois*
Right to counsel and remain silent (V)	1966	*Miranda v. Arizona*
Right against double jeopardy (V)	1969	*Benton v. Maryland*
Right to bear arms (II)	2010	*McDonald v. Chicago*

● The First Amendment Guarantees Freedom of Religion

> **Describe how the First Amendment protects freedom of religion**

Congress shall make no law respecting an establishment of religion, or prohibiting the free exercise thereof; or abridging the freedom of speech, or of the press; or the right of the people peaceably to assemble, and to petition the Government for a redress of grievances.

The Bill of Rights begins by guaranteeing freedom of religion, and the First Amendment provides for that freedom in two distinct clauses: "Congress shall make no law (1) respecting an establishment of religion, or (2) prohibiting the free exercise thereof." The first clause is called the "establishment clause," and the second is called the "free exercise clause."

Separation between Church and State Comes from the First Amendment

The **establishment clause** and the idea of "no law" regarding the establishment of religion can be interpreted in several ways. One interpretation, which probably reflects the views of many of the First Amendment's authors, is that the government is prohibited from establishing an official church. Official state churches, such as the Church of England, were common in the eighteenth century and were viewed by many Americans as inconsistent with a republican form of government. Indeed, many American colonists had fled Europe to escape persecution for having rejected state-sponsored churches. A second interpretation is the view that the government may not take sides among competing religions but may provide assistance to religious institutions or ideas as long as it shows no favoritism. The United States accommodates religious beliefs in a variety of ways, from the reference to God on U.S. currency to the prayer that begins every session of Congress. These forms of establishment have never been struck down by the courts.

The third view regarding religious establishment, which for many years dominated Supreme Court decisions in this realm, is the idea of a "wall of separation" between church and state—Jefferson's formulation—that cannot be breached by the government. For two centuries, Jefferson's words have had a

The First Amendment affects everyday life in a multitude of ways. Because of the amendment's ban on state-sanctioned religion, the Supreme Court ruled in 2000 that student-initiated public prayer in school is illegal. Pregame prayer at public schools violates the establishment clause of the First Amendment.

powerful impact on our understanding of the proper relationship between church and state in America.

Despite the seeming absoluteness of the phrase "wall of separation," there is ample room to disagree on how high or strong this wall is. For example, the Court has been consistently strict in the area of public education in cases of school prayer, striking down such practices as Bible reading,[14] nondenominational prayer,[15] reading prayers over a public address system during a football game,[16] and even a moment of silence for meditation.[17] In each of these cases, the Court reasoned that school-sponsored religious observations, even if nondenominational, are highly suggestive of school sponsorship and therefore violate the prohibition against establishment of religion. On the other hand, the Court has been quite permissive (and some would say inconsistent) about the public display of religious symbols, such as city-sponsored nativity scenes in commercial or municipal areas.[18] And although the Court has consistently disapproved of government financial support for religious schools, even when the purpose has been purely educational and secular, the Court has permitted certain direct aid to students of such schools in the form of busing, for example.

The difficulty in defining what religious establishment means is evident from two cases in 2005 involving government-sponsored displays of religious symbols. In *Van Orden v. Perry*, the Court decided by a 5–4 margin that a display of the Ten Commandments at the Texas State Capitol did not violate the Constitution.[19] However, in *McCreary v. ACLU of Kentucky*, decided at the same time and also by a 5–4 margin, the Court determined that a display of the Ten Commandments inside two Kentucky courthouses was unconstitutional.[20] Justice Stephen Breyer, the swing vote in the two cases, said that the displays in *Van Orden* had a secular purpose, whereas the displays in *McCreary* had a purely religious purpose. The key difference between the two cases is that the Texas display had been exhibited in a large park for 40 years with other monuments related to the development of American law without any objections raised until this case, whereas the Kentucky display was erected much more recently and initially by itself, suggesting to some justices that its posting had a religious purpose. But most observers saw little difference between the two cases, and even Breyer was hard-pressed to explain his shifting votes except to say that *Van Orden* was a "borderline" case.

Free Exercise of Religion Means You Have a Right to Your Beliefs

The **free exercise clause** protects the citizen's right to believe and to practice any religion; it also protects the right to choose not to practice a religion. The precedent-setting case involving free exercise is *West Virginia State Board of Education v. Barnette* (1943), which involved the children of a family of Jehovah's Witnesses who refused to salute and pledge allegiance to the American flag on the grounds that their religious faith did not permit it. Three years earlier, the Court had upheld such a requirement and had permitted schools to expel students for refusing to salute the flag. But the entry of the United States into a war to defend democracy, coupled with the ugly treatment to which the Jehovah's Witnesses children had been subjected, induced the Court to reverse itself and to endorse the free exercise of religion even when it may be offensive to the beliefs of the majority.[21]

Although the Supreme Court has been fairly consistent and strict in protecting the free exercise of religious belief, it has taken pains to distinguish between religious beliefs and *actions* based on those beliefs. In one case, for example, two Native Americans had been fired from their jobs for ingesting peyote, an illegal drug. They claimed that they had been fired from their jobs unlawfully because the use of peyote was a religious sacrament protected by the free exercise clause. The Court disagreed with their claim in an important 1990 decision.[22]

In a different case, Amish parents refused to send their children to school beyond eighth grade because exposing their children to "modern values" would undermine their religious commitment. In this case, the Court decided in favor of the Amish and endorsed a very strong interpretation of the protection of free exercise.[23]

In a 2012 case considered one of the most important religious liberty cases in decades, the Supreme Court ruled unanimously in *Hosanna-Tabor Church v. Equal Employment Opportunity Commission* that employment discrimination laws did not apply to the hiring and firing of church leaders, including those who teach religious subjects at religious educational institutions.[24] This new "ministerial exception" created by the Court left open the question of deciding who was and was not included in this exception.

● The First Amendment and Freedom of Speech and of the Press Ensure the Free Exchange of Ideas

> **Describe how the First Amendment protects free speech**

Congress shall make no law . . . abridging the freedom of speech, or of the press.

Freedom of speech and of the press have a special place in American political thought. To begin with, democracy depends upon the ability of individuals to talk to one another and to disseminate information. A democratic nation could not function without free and open debate. Such debate, moreover, is seen as an essential mechanism for determining the quality or validity of competing ideas. As Justice Oliver Wendell Holmes said, "The best test of truth is the power of the thought to get itself accepted in the competition of the market . . . that at any rate is the theory of our Constitution."[25] What is sometimes called the "marketplace of ideas" receives a good deal of protection from the courts. In 1938 the Supreme Court held that any legislation that attempts to restrict these fundamental freedoms "is to be subjected to a more exacting judicial scrutiny . . . than are most other types of legislation."[26] This higher standard of judicial review came to be called **strict scrutiny**.

The doctrine of strict scrutiny places a heavy burden of proof on the government if it seeks to regulate or restrict speech. Americans are assumed to have the right to speak and to broadcast their ideas unless some compelling reason can be identified to stop them. But strict scrutiny does not mean that speech can never be regulated. According to the courts, although virtually all speech is protected by the Constitution, some forms of speech are entitled to a greater degree of protection than others.

Political Speech Is Consistently Protected

Over the past 200 years, the courts have scrutinized many different forms of speech and constructed different principles and guidelines for each. And of all forms of speech, political speech is the most consistently protected.

Political speech was the activity of greatest concern to the framers of the Constitution, even though some found it the most difficult provision to tolerate. Within seven years of the ratification of the Bill of Rights in 1791, Congress adopted the infamous Alien and Sedition acts, which, among other things, made it a crime to say or publish anything that might tend to defame or bring into disrepute the government of the United States. Quite clearly, the acts' intentions were to criminalize the very conduct given absolute protection by the First Amendment. Fifteen violators, including several newspaper editors, were indicted, and a few were actually convicted before the relevant portions of the acts were allowed to expire.

The first modern free speech case arose immediately after World War I. It involved persons who had been convicted under the federal Espionage Act of 1917 for opposing U.S. involvement in the war. The Supreme Court upheld the Espionage Act and refused to protect the speech rights of the defendants on the grounds that their activities—appeals to draftees to resist the draft—constituted a **"clear and present danger"** to national security.[27] This is the first and most famous "test" for when government intervention or censorship can be permitted.

It was only after the 1920s that real progress toward a genuinely effective First Amendment was made. Since then, the courts have consistently protected political speech even when it has been deemed "insulting" or "outrageous."

A key source of controversy regarding political speech has been the extension of First Amendment protection to the spending of money in political campaigns. In order to limit the corrupting influence of "big money" in political campaigns, Congress has enacted legislation to regulate or limit such spending. (The spending of money in political campaigns has been considered a kind of speech, protected under the First Amendment.) In 2002, Congress passed the Bipartisan Campaign Reform Act (BCRA), which limited "soft money" (money contributed to a political party, not a specific candidate) and regulated "issue advocacy ads" designed to help or hurt candidates but not financed by the candidates. The law survived a constitutional challenge in 2003, but in 2007 the Supreme Court ruled that issue ads could not be restricted. In 2008 it ruled against a part of the law that imposed greater restrictions on giving by wealthy donors.

And in a major decision in 2010, the Supreme Court overturned decades of laws and court cases that had restricted the ability of corporations to spend money from their treasuries on political campaign advertisement. (Corporations have been allowed to spend money on campaigns only through separate political actions committees; see Chapter 8.) In the case of *Citizens United v. Federal Election Commission*, the Supreme Court declared that the First Amendment prohibited BCRA's ban on corporate funding of independent political broadcasts aimed at electing or defeating particular candidates.[28] In its 5–4 decision, the Supreme Court ruled that the Constitution prohibits the government from regulating political speech and that therefore the government could not ban this type of political spending by corporations. In 2014 the Court again expanded its protection of campaign expenditures under the First Amendment by overturning aggregate limits restricting how much money a donor may contribute.[29] The Court's decisions in both cases have been controversial. Republicans hailed the decisions as a victory for free speech, while Democrats denounced the decisions. President Obama called *Citizens United* "a major victory for big oil, Wall Street banks, health insurance companies, and the other powerful interests that marshal their power every day in Washington to drown out the voices of everyday Americans."[30]

Symbolic Speech, Speech Plus, Assembly, and Petition Are Highly Protected

The First Amendment treats the freedoms of religion and political speech as equal to the freedoms of assembly and petition—speech associated with action. Freedom of speech and freedom of assembly are closely related by the "public forum doctrine." In the 1939 case of *Hague v. Committee for Industrial Organization*, the Court declared that the government may not prohibit speech-related activities such as demonstrations or leafleting in public areas traditionally used for that purpose though, of course, the government may impose rules designed to protect the public safety so long as these rules do not discriminate against particular viewpoints.[31]

Generally, the Supreme Court has protected actions that are designed to send a political message. Thus the Court held unconstitutional a California statute making it a felony to display a red Communist flag "as a sign, symbol or emblem of opposition to organized government."[32]

Another example is the burning of the American flag as a symbol of protest. In 1984, at a political rally held during the Republican National Convention in Dallas, Texas, a political protester burned an American flag, thereby violating a Texas law that prohibited desecration of a venerated object. The Supreme Court declared the Texas law unconstitutional on the grounds that flag burning was expressive conduct protected by the First Amendment.[33]

In the 2011 case of *Snyder v. Phelps*, the Court continued to protect symbolic speech. Members of the Westboro Baptist Church had frequently demonstrated at military funerals, claiming that the deaths of soldiers were a sign that God disapproved of acceptance of homosexuality in the United States. They carried signs that included slogans like "Thank God for dead soldiers." The father of a soldier killed in Iraq brought suit against the church and its pastor claiming that the

The Supreme Court has interpreted the freedom of speech as extending to symbolic acts of political protest, such as flag burning. On several occasions—most recently in 2006—a resolution for a constitutional amendment to ban flag burning has passed in the House of Representatives but has never found enough support in the Senate.

demonstrators had caused him and his family severe emotional distress. The Supreme Court ruled, however, that the First Amendment protected this form of speech in a public place against such suits.[34]

Closer to the original intent of the assembly and petition clause is the category of **"speech plus"**—speech accompanied by conduct or physical activity such as sit-ins, picketing, and demonstrating; protection of this form of speech under the First Amendment is conditional, and restrictions imposed by state or local authorities are acceptable if properly balanced by considerations of public order. Courts consistently protect such assemblies under the First Amendment; state and local laws regulating such activities are closely scrutinized and frequently overturned. But the same assembly on private property is quite another matter and can in many circumstances be regulated. For example, the directors of a shopping center can lawfully prohibit an assembly protesting a war or supporting a ban on abortion. Assemblies in public areas can also be restricted in some circumstances, especially when the assembly or demonstration jeopardizes the health, safety, or rights of others. This condition was the basis of the Supreme Court's decision to uphold a lower-court order that restricted the access abortion protesters had to the entrances of abortion clinics.[35]

Speech by Public School Students One group that seems to enjoy only a limited right of free speech is public school students. In 1986 the Supreme Court

The Supreme Court has ruled that high school students' speech can be restricted. In a 2007 case involving a student who displayed the banner pictured, the Court found that the school principal had not violated the student's right to free speech by suspending him.

upheld the punishment of a high school student for making sexually suggestive speech. The Court opinion held that such speech interfered with the school's goal of teaching students the limits of socially acceptable behavior.[36] Two years later, the Supreme Court restricted student speech and press rights even further by defining them as part of the educational process, not to be treated with the same standard as adult speech in a regular public forum.[37] In the 2007 case of *Morse v. Frederick*, the Court held that a principal did not violate a student's free speech rights by suspending him for displaying a banner proclaiming, "BONG HiTS 4 JESUS."[38] The decision affirmed that school officials can censor student speech that advocates or celebrates the use of illegal drugs.

Freedom of the Press Is Broad

For all practical purposes, freedom of speech implies and includes freedom of the press. With the exception of the broadcast media, which are subject to federal regulation, the press is protected under the doctrine against **prior restraint** (efforts by a governmental agency to block the publication of material it deems libelous or harmful in some other way; otherwise known as censorship). Beginning with the landmark 1931 case of *Near v. Minnesota*, the U.S. Supreme Court has held that, except under the most extraordinary circumstances, the First Amendment of the Constitution prohibits government agencies from seeking to prevent newspapers or magazines from publishing whatever they wish.[39] In the case of *New York Times v. United States*, the so-called *Pentagon Papers* case, the Supreme Court ruled that the government could not block publication of secret Defense Department documents given to the *New York Times* by an opponent of the Vietnam War who had obtained the documents illegally.[40]

Another press freedom issue is the question of whether journalists can be compelled to reveal their sources of information. Journalists assert that if they cannot promise to keep the confidentiality of their sources, the flow of information will be reduced and press freedom effectively curtailed. Government agencies, however, assert that the names of news sources may be relevant to criminal or even national security investigations. Nearly all states have "shield laws" that to varying degrees protect journalistic sources. There is, however, no federal shield law, and the Supreme Court has held that the press has no constitutional right to withhold information in court.[41] In 2005, Judith Miller, a *New York Times* reporter, was jailed for contempt of court for refusing to tell a federal grand jury the name of a confidential source in a case involving the leaked identity of the CIA analyst Valerie Plame. Plame's husband, Joseph Wilson, had been critical of the Bush administration's Iraq policies.

Some Speech Has Only Limited Protection

At least four categories of speech fall outside the guarantees of the First Amendment and therefore outside the realm of absolute protection: (1) libel and slander, (2) obscenity and pornography, (3) fighting words, and (4) commercial speech. It should be emphasized once again that these types of speech still enjoy considerable protection by the courts.

Libel and Slander If a written statement is made in "reckless disregard of the truth" and is considered damaging to the victim because it is "malicious, scandalous, and defamatory," it can be punished as **libel**. If an oral statement of such a nature is made, it can be punished as **slander**.

Today, most libel suits involve freedom of the press, and the realm of free press is enormous. Historically, newspapers were subject to the law of libel, which provided that newspapers that printed false and malicious stories could be compelled to pay damages to those they defamed. In recent years, however, American courts have greatly narrowed the meaning of libel and made it extremely difficult, particularly for politicians or other public figures, to win a libel case against a newspaper. In the important 1964 case of *New York Times v. Sullivan*, the Court held that to be deemed libelous, a story about a public official not only had to be untrue but also had to result from "actual malice" or "reckless disregard" for the truth.[42] In other words, the newspaper had to print false and malicious material *deliberately*. In practice, this is a very difficult legal standard to meet.

With the emergence of the Internet as an important communications medium, the courts have had to decide how traditional libel law applies to Internet content. In 1995 the New York courts held that an online bulletin board could be held responsible for the libelous content of material posted by a third party. To protect Internet service providers, Congress subsequently enacted legislation absolving them of responsibility for third-party posts. The federal courts have generally upheld this law and declared that service providers are immune from suits regarding the content of material posted by others.[43]

Obscenity and Pornography If libel and slander cases can be difficult because of the problem of determining the truth of statements and whether those statements are malicious and damaging, cases involving pornography and obscenity can be even trickier. Not until 1957 did the Supreme Court confront these issues, and it did so with a definition of obscenity that may have caused more confusion than it cleared up. Justice William Brennan, in writing the Court's opinion, defined obscenity as speech or writing that appeals to the "prurient interest"—that is, whose purpose is to excite lust as this appears "to the average person, applying contemporary community standards." Even so, Brennan added, the work should be judged obscene only when it is "utterly without redeeming social importance."[44] Brennan's definition, instead of clarifying the Court's view, actually caused more confusion. In 1964, Justice Potter Stewart confessed that, although he found pornography impossible to define, "I know it when I see it."[45]

An effort was made to strengthen the restrictions in 1973, when the Supreme Court expressed its willingness to define pornography as a work that (1) as a whole, is deemed prurient by the "average person" according to "community standards"; (2) depicts sexual conduct "in a patently offensive way"; and (3) lacks "serious literary, artistic, political, or scientific value." This definition meant that pornography would be determined by local rather than national standards. Thus, a local book-seller might be prosecuted for selling a volume that was a best-seller nationally but that was deemed pornographic locally.[46] This new definition of standards did not help much either, and not long after 1973 the Court began again to review all such community antipornography laws, reversing most of them.

In recent years, the battle against obscene speech has targeted "cyberporn," pornography on the Internet. Opponents of this form of expression argue that it should be banned because of the easy access children have to the Internet. The first major effort to regulate the content of the Internet occurred in 1996, when Congress passed the Communications Decency Act (CDA), designed to regulate the online transmission of obscene material. The constitutionality of the CDA was immediately challenged in court by a coalition of interests led by the American Civil Liberties Union (ACLU). In the 1997 Supreme Court case of *Reno v. ACLU*, the Court struck down the CDA, ruling that it suppressed speech that "adults have a constitutional right to receive," saying that "the level of discourse reaching the mailbox simply cannot be limited to that which would be suitable for a sandbox." Supreme Court justice John Paul Stevens described the Internet as the "town crier" of the modern age and said that the Internet was entitled to the greatest degree of First Amendment protection possible.[47] By contrast, radio and television are subject to more control than the Internet. In 2008 the Supreme Court upheld a law that made it a crime to sell child pornography on the Internet.[48]

In 2000 the Supreme Court extended the highest degree of First Amendment protection to cable (not broadcast) television. In *United States v. Playboy Entertainment Group*, the Court struck down a portion of the 1996 Telecommunications Act that required cable TV companies to limit the broadcast of sexually explicit programming to late-night hours. In its decision, the Court noted that the law already provided parents with the means to restrict access to sexually explicit cable channels through various blocking devices. Moreover, such programming could come into the home only if parents decided to purchase such channels in the first place.[49]

Closely related to the issue of obscenity is the matter of violent broadcast content. Here, too, the Court has generally upheld freedom of speech. For example, in the 2011 case of *Brown v. Entertainment Merchants Association* the Court struck down a California law banning the sale of violent video games to children, saying that the law violated the First Amendment.[50]

Fighting Words Speech can also lose its protected position when it moves toward the sphere of action. "Expressive speech," for example, is protected until it moves from the symbolic realm to the realm of actual conduct—to direct incitement of damaging conduct with the use of so-called **fighting words**. In 1942 a man called a police officer a "goddamned racketeer" and "a damn Fascist" and was arrested and convicted of violating a state law forbidding the use of offensive language in public. When his case reached the Supreme Court, the arrest was upheld on the grounds that the First Amendment provides no protection for such offensive language because such words "are no essential part of any exposition of ideas."[51] This decision was reaffirmed in the important 1951 case of *Dennis v. United States*, in which the Supreme Court held that there is no substantial public interest in permitting certain kinds of utterances: the lewd and obscene, the profane, the libelous, and the insulting or "fighting" words—those which by their very utterance inflict injury or tend to incite an immediate breach of the peace.[52] Since that time, however, the Supreme Court has reversed almost every conviction based on arguments that the speaker had used "fighting words."

Commercial Speech Commercial speech, such as newspaper or television advertisements, has only partial First Amendment protection because it cannot be considered political speech. Initially considered to be entirely outside the protection of the First Amendment, commercial speech is subject to regulation, although it is also recognized and protected for the part it plays in the free flow of information. For example, prohibition of false and misleading advertising by the Federal Trade Commission is an old and well-established power of the federal government. The Supreme Court long ago approved the constitutionality of laws prohibiting electronic media from carrying cigarette advertising.[53] It has also upheld city ordinances prohibiting the posting of all signs on public property (as long as the ban is total, so that there is no hint of censorship).[54]

However, the gains outweigh the losses in the effort to expand the protection of commercial speech under the First Amendment. For example, in 1996 the Court struck down Rhode Island laws and regulations banning the advertisement of liquor prices[55] and in 2001 the Court overturned a Massachusetts ban on all cigarette advertising as violations of the First Amendment.[56] These instances of commercial speech indicate the breadth and depth of the freedom today to direct appeals to a large public, to sell goods and services and to mobilize people for political purposes.

● The Second Amendment Now Protects an Individual's Right to Own a Gun

Explore whether the Second Amendment means people have a right to own guns

The Second Amendment was included in the Bill of Rights to provide for "well-regulated" militias to enforce the "security of a free State," which were to be the backing of the government for the maintenance of local public order. "Militia" was understood at the time of the Founding to be a military or police resource for state governments; militias were specifically distinguished from professional armies, which came within the sole constitutional jurisdiction of Congress.

Thus, the right of the people "to keep and bear Arms" is based on and associated with participation in state militias. The reference to citizens keeping arms underscored the fact that in the 1700s, state governments could not be relied on to provide firearms to militia members, so citizens eligible to serve in militias (white males between the ages of 18 and 45) were expected to keep their own firearms at the ready. In the late nineteenth century, some citizens sought to form their own *private* militias, but the Supreme Court cut that short with a ruling that militias are a military or police resource of the government.[57]

After a 1939 Supreme Court case that upheld a federal gun law concluding that the Second Amendment pertained to "the preservation or efficiency of a well regulated militia,"[58] the Court made no Second Amendment decisions for nearly 70 years. Thus, states and localities across the country have very different gun ownership standards. For instance, in Wyoming there is no ban on any type of gun, there is no waiting period to purchase a firearm, and no permit is required for carrying a concealed weapon. In California, by contrast, the possession of assault weapons is banned, there is a 10-day waiting period to purchase a firearm, and a permit is required to carry a concealed weapon (see Figure 4.1).

FIGURE 4.1 Gun Laws and Gun Trafficking

Although state gun laws must conform to the Second Amendment as interpreted by the U.S. Supreme Court, laws concerning gun sales and ownership vary widely from state to state. It is much more difficult to buy a gun in, say, New York or California than in Texas or Kentucky. However, there are few barriers to moving guns from one state to another. The Bureau of Alcohol, Tobacco, and Firearms (ATF) traces guns used in crimes and tracks their movement across states.

SOURCES: Brady Campaign to Prevent Gun Violence, http://bradycampaign.org/?q=programs/million-mom-march/state-gun-laws (accessed 1/14/14); U.S. Bureau of Alcohol, Tobacco, Firearms, and Explosives, www.atf.gov/sites/default/files/assets/statistics/tracedata-2012/source-recovery-by-state.xlsx (accessed 1/14/14).

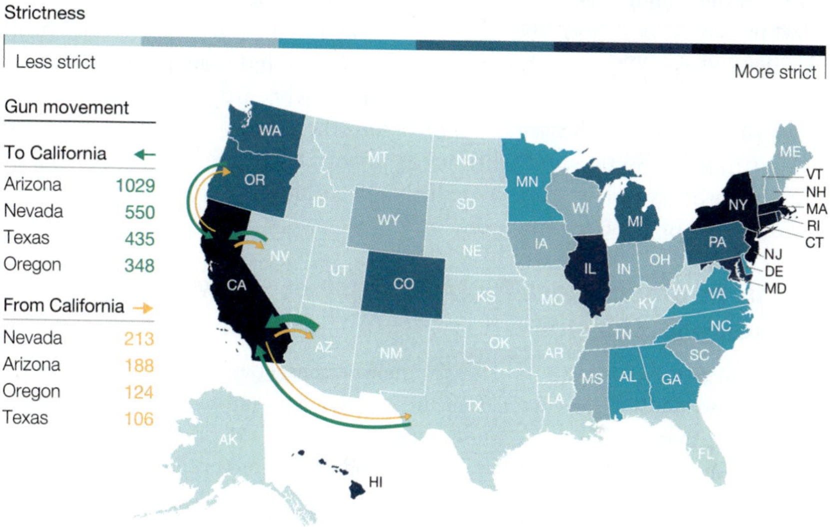

Strictness

Less strict — More strict

Gun movement

To California ←

Arizona	1029
Nevada	550
Texas	435
Oregon	348

From California →

Nevada	213
Arizona	188
Oregon	124
Texas	106

The strictness of state gun laws is based on an analysis of laws aimed at preventing gun violence, such as background checks on all gun sales, permit-to-purchase requirements, and limiting handgun purchases to one a month. The arrows show the inflow and outflow of guns to and from California in 2012. The thickness of the arrow indicates the volume of guns that were used in crimes and tracked by the ATF.

The Court's silence on the application of the Second Amendment ended in 2008, when the Supreme Court made the first of two rulings in favor of expansive rights of gun ownership by individuals. The case of *District of Columbia v. Heller* challenged a strict Washington, D.C., law that banned handguns. In a 5–4 decision, the Court ruled that the Second Amendment provides a constitutional right to keep a loaded handgun at home for self-defense, a view that had long been subject to debate. The Court also said that the decision was not intended to cast doubt on most existing gun laws.[59] Because the District of Columbia is an entity of the federal government, the ruling did not apply to state firearm laws. However, in the 2010 case of *McDonald v. Chicago*, the Court applied the Second Amendment to the states, making this decision the first new incorporation decision by the Court in 40 years (see Table 4.2). The case concerned a Chicago ordinance that made it extremely difficult to own a gun within city limits, and the Court's ruling had the effect of overturning the law.[60]

Despite these rulings, the debate over gun control continues to loom large. A series of tragic shootings in recent years—including the killing of 20 elementary school students in Newtown, Connecticut, and 12 audience members at an Aurora, Colorado, movie theater—has kept the issue of gun laws firmly on the national agenda.

● Rights of the Criminally Accused Are Based on Due Process of Law

Explain the major rights that people have if they are accused of a crime

Except for the First Amendment, most of the battle to apply the Bill of Rights to the states was fought over the various protections granted to individuals who are accused of a crime, who are suspects in the commission of a crime, or who are brought before the court as a witness to a crime. The Fourth, Fifth, Sixth, and Eighth amendments, taken together, are the essence of the due process of law, even though this key phrase does not appear until the very last words of the Fifth Amendment.

The Fourth Amendment Protects against Unlawful Searches and Seizures

The right of the people to be secure in their persons, houses, papers, and effects, against unreasonable searches and seizures, shall not be violated, and no Warrants shall issue, but upon probable cause, supported by Oath or affirmation, and particularly describing the place to be searched, and the persons or things to be seized.

Under what circumstances can the police search an individual's car? The Fourth Amendment protects against "unreasonable searches and seizures," but the Supreme Court has had to interpret what is unreasonable.

The purpose of the Fourth Amendment is to guarantee the security of citizens against unreasonable (that is, improper) searches and seizures. In 1990 the Supreme Court summarized its understanding of the Fourth Amendment brilliantly and succinctly: "A search compromises the individual interest in privacy; a seizure deprives the individual of dominion over his or her person or property."[61] But how are we to define what is reasonable and what is unreasonable?

The 1961 case of *Mapp v. Ohio* illustrates one of the most important principles that has grown out of the Fourth Amendment: the **exclusionary rule**, which is the ability of courts to exclude evidence obtained in violation of the Fourth Amendment, such as barring evidence obtained during an illegal search from being introduced in a trial. Acting on a tip that Dollree Mapp was harboring a suspect in a bombing incident, several police officers forcibly entered Mapp's house claiming they had a warrant to look for the bombing suspect. The police did not find the bombing suspect but did find some materials connected to the local numbers racket (an illegal gambling operation) and a quantity of "obscene materials," in violation of an Ohio law banning possession of such materials. Although no warrant was ever produced, the evidence that had been seized was admitted by a court, and Mapp was charged and convicted for illegal possession of obscene materials.

By the time Mapp's appeal reached the Supreme Court, the question was whether any evidence produced under the circumstances of the search of her home was admissible. The Court's opinion affirmed the exclusionary rule: under the Fourth Amendment (applied to the states through the Fourteenth Amendment), "all evidence obtained by searches and seizures in violation of the Constitution . . . is inadmissible."[62] This means that even people who are clearly guilty of the crime of which they are accused must not be convicted if the only evidence for their conviction was obtained illegally. This idea was expressed by future Supreme Court justice Benjamin Cardozo nearly a century ago when he wrote that "the criminal is to go free because the constable has blundered."[63]

The exclusionary rule is the most dramatic restraint imposed by the courts on police behavior because it rules out precisely the evidence that produces a conviction; it frees those people who are *known* to have committed the crime of which they have been accused because the evidence was obtained improperly. Because it works so dramatically in favor of persons known to have committed a crime, the Court has since softened the application of the rule. In recent years, the federal courts have relied upon a discretionary use of the exclusionary rule, whereby they make a judgment as to the "nature and quality of the intrusion." It is thus difficult to know ahead of time whether a defendant will or will not be protected from an illegal search under the Fourth Amendment.[64] Several recent cases have imposed strict interpretations of a reasonable search. In 2013 the Court held that the use of a drug-sniffing dog on the front porch of a home constituted an improper search in the absence of consent or a warrant. The decision rested on "traditional property notions."[65]

Changes in technology have also had an impact on Fourth Amendment jurisprudence. In the 2012 case of *United States v. Jones*, the Court held that prosecutors violated Jones's rights when they attached a GPS device to his Jeep and monitored his movements for 28 days.[66] On the other hand, in *Maryland v. King*, the Court upheld DNA testing of arrestees without the need for individualized suspicion. Writing for the majority, Justice Anthony Kennedy characterized DNA testing as an administrative tool for identifying the arrestee and thus was legally indistinguishable from photographing and fingerprinting.[67] As new technologies develop, the Court will continue to face the question of what constitutes a reasonable search.

The Fifth Amendment Covers Court-Related Rights

No person shall be held to answer for a capital, or otherwise infamous crime, unless on a presentment or indictment of a Grand Jury, except in cases arising in the land or naval forces, or in the Militia, when in actual service in time of War or public danger; nor shall any person be subject for the same offence to be twice put in jeopardy of life or limb; nor shall be compelled in any criminal case to be a witness against himself, nor be deprived of life, liberty, or property, without due process of law; nor shall private property be taken for public use, without just compensation.

Grand Juries The first clause of the Fifth Amendment sets forth the right to a **grand jury** (a jury that determines whether sufficient evidence is available to justify a trial; grand juries do not rule on the accused's guilt or innocence) to determine whether a trial is warranted. Grand juries play an important role in federal criminal cases. However, the provision for a grand jury is the one important civil liberties provision of the Bill of Rights that was not incorporated by the Fourteenth Amendment to apply to state criminal prosecutions. Thus, some states operate without grand juries. In such states, the prosecuting attorney simply files a "bill of information" affirming that there is sufficient evidence available to justify a trial. If the accused person is to be held in custody, the prosecutor must take the available information before a judge to determine that the evidence shows probable cause.

Double Jeopardy "Nor shall any person be subject for the same offence to be twice put in jeopardy of life or limb" is the constitutional protection from **double jeopardy**, a protection to prevent a person from being tried more than once for the same crime. The protection from double jeopardy was at the heart of the *Palko v. Connecticut* case in 1937. In that case, a Connecticut court had found Frank Palko guilty of second-degree murder and sentenced him to life in prison. Unhappy with the verdict, the state of Connecticut appealed the conviction to its highest state court, won the appeal, got a new trial, and then succeeded in getting Palko convicted of first-degree murder. Palko appealed to the Supreme Court on what seemed an open-and-shut case of double jeopardy. Yet, although the majority of the Court agreed that this could indeed be considered a case of double jeopardy, they decided that double jeopardy was not one of the provisions of the Bill of Rights incorporated in the Fourteenth Amendment as a restriction on the powers of the states.[68] It took more than 30 years for the Court to nationalize the constitutional protection against double jeopardy, when the court overruled *Palko* and declared that double jeopardy now applied to the states (see Table 4.2). Palko was eventually executed for the crime, because he lived in Connecticut rather than in a state whose constitution included a guarantee against double jeopardy.

Self-Incrimination Perhaps the most significant liberty found in the Fifth Amendment, and the one most familiar to many Americans who watch television crime shows, is the guarantee that no citizen "shall be compelled in any criminal case to be a witness against himself." The most famous case concerning self-incrimination involved 23-year-old Ernesto Miranda, who was sentenced to between 20 and 30 years in prison for the kidnapping and rape of an 18-year-old woman. The woman had identified him in a police lineup, and, after two hours of questioning, Miranda confessed, subsequently signing a statement that his confession had been made voluntarily, without threats or promises of immunity. This confession was admitted into evidence, served as the basis for Miranda's conviction, and also served as the basis for the appeal of his conviction all the way to the Supreme Court.[69] Following one of the most intensely and widely criticized decisions ever handed down by the Supreme Court, Miranda's case produced the rules the police must follow before questioning an arrested criminal suspect. The reading of a person's "*Miranda* rights" became a standard scene in every police station and on virtually every dramatization of police action on television and in the movies. *Miranda* advanced the civil liberties of accused persons not only by expanding the scope of the Fifth Amendment clause covering coerced confessions and self-incrimination, but also by confirming the right to counsel (discussed later). The Supreme Court under Warren Burger and William Rehnquist considerably softened the *Miranda* restrictions, but the **Miranda rule** (the requirement, articulated by the Supreme Court in *Miranda v. Arizona*, that persons under arrest must be informed prior to police interrogation of their rights to remain silent and to have the benefit of legal counsel) still stands as a protection against egregious police abuses of arrested persons. However, in the 2010 case of *Berghuis v. Thompkins*, the Supreme Court introduced an important qualification to the Miranda rule, deciding that statements made by suspects who did not expressly waive their rights (usually by signing a form) could be used against them.[70]

Eminent Domain The other fundamental clause of the Fifth Amendment is the "takings clause," which extends to each citizen a protection against the "taking" of private property by the government "without just compensation." Although this part of the Fifth Amendment is not specifically concerned with protecting persons accused of crimes, it is nevertheless a fundamentally important instance where the government and the citizen are adversaries. The power of any government to take private property for public use is called **eminent domain**. The Fifth Amendment puts limits on that inherent power through procedures that require a showing of a public purpose and the provision of fair payment for the taking of someone's property.

The Sixth Amendment's Right to Counsel Is Crucial for a Fair Trial

> In all criminal prosecutions, the accused shall enjoy the right to a speedy and public trial, by an impartial jury of the State and district wherein the crime shall have been committed, which district shall have been ascertained by law, and to be informed of the nature and the cause of the accusation; to be confronted with the witnesses against him; to have compulsory process for obtaining witnesses in his favor, and to have the Assistance of Counsel for his defence.

Like the exclusionary rule of the Fourth Amendment and the self-incrimination clause of the Fifth Amendment, the "right to counsel" provision of the Sixth Amendment is notable for freeing defendants who seem to the public to be guilty as charged. Other provisions of the Sixth Amendment, such as the right to a speedy trial and the right to confront witnesses before an impartial jury, are less controversial.

Gideon v. Wainwright (1963) is the perfect case study because it involved a disreputable person who seemed patently guilty of the crime of which he was convicted. In and out of jails for most of his 51 years, Clarence Earl Gideon received a five-year sentence for breaking and entering a poolroom in Panama City, Florida. While serving time in jail, Gideon became a fairly well-qualified "jailhouse lawyer," made his own appeal on a handwritten petition, and eventually won the landmark ruling on the right to counsel in all felony cases. After the Supreme Court's decision, Gideon was granted a new trial. This time, represented by an attorney, he was found not guilty.[71]

The right to counsel has been expanded during the past few decades, even as the courts have become more conservative. The right to counsel extends beyond serious crimes to any trial, with or without a jury, that holds the possibility of imprisonment.

The Eighth Amendment Bars Cruel and Unusual Punishment

Excessive bail shall not be required, nor excessive fines imposed, nor cruel and unusual punishment inflicted.

Virtually all the debate over Eighth Amendment issues focuses on the last clause of the amendment: the protection from "cruel and unusual punishment." One of the greatest challenges in interpreting this provision consistently arises over the death penalty. In 1972 the Supreme Court overturned several state death-penalty laws, not because they were cruel and unusual but because they were being applied unevenly—that is, blacks were much more likely than whites to be sentenced to death, the poor more likely than the rich, and men more likely than women.[72] Very soon after that decision, a majority of states revised their capital punishment provisions to meet the Court's standards, and the Court reaffirmed that the death penalty could be used if certain standards were met.[73] Since 1976, the Court has consistently upheld state laws providing for capital punishment, although the Court also continues to review death-penalty appeals each year.

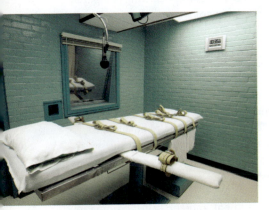

Thirty-two states currently have the death penalty for the most serious crimes. Although a majority of Americans support the death penalty, it has always been controversial and is sometimes seen as a violation of the Eighth Amendment.

Between 1976 and mid-2014, states executed 1,384 people. Most of those executions occurred in southern states, with Texas leading the way at 515. As of 2014, 32 states had statutes providing for capital punishment for specified offenses, a policy supported by a majority of Americans, according to polls. On the other hand, 18 states bar the death penalty, and since the end of the 1990s, both the number of death sentences and the number of executions has declined annually.[74]

Many death-penalty supporters assert its deterrent effects on other would-be criminals. Although studies of capital crimes usually fail to demonstrate any direct deterrent effect, this failure may be due to the lengthy delays (typically years and even decades) between convictions and executions. A system that eliminates undue delays might enhance deterrence. And deterring even one murder or other heinous crime, proponents argue, justifies such laws.

Death-penalty opponents are quick to counter that the death penalty has not been proven to deter crime, either in the United States or abroad. In fact, America is the only Western nation that still executes criminals. If the government is to serve as an example of proper behavior, say foes of capital punishment, it has no business sanctioning killing when incarceration also protects society. Furthermore, execution is time-consuming and expensive—more expensive than life imprisonment—precisely because the government must make every effort to ensure that it is not executing an innocent person. Curtailing legal appeals would make the possibility of a mistake too great. Race also intrudes in death-penalty cases: people of color are disproportionately more likely than whites charged with identical crimes to be given the ultimate punishment.

In recent years, the Court has issued a number of death-penalty opinions, declaring that death was too harsh a penalty for the crime of raping a child[75] and invalidating a death sentence for a black defendant when the prosecutor had improperly excluded African Americans from the jury.[76] The Court also upheld Kentucky's policy of execution by lethal injection despite arguments that this form of execution was likely to cause considerable pain.[77]

● The Right to Privacy Means the Right to Be Left Alone

Assess whether people have a right to privacy under the Constitution

Although the word *privacy* never appears in the Bill of Rights, there is general agreement that a **right to privacy** emanates from the first 10 amendments—even though judges and legal scholars continue to disagree about where the right comes from. The idea behind the right to privacy is simple: people have a right to be left alone from government or other persons' interference in certain personal areas.

The sphere of privacy was drawn by the Supreme Court in 1965, when it ruled that a Connecticut statute forbidding the use of contraceptives violated the right of marital privacy. Estelle Griswold, the executive director of the Planned Parenthood League of Connecticut, was arrested by the state of Connecticut for providing information, instruction, and medical advice about contraception to married couples. She and her associates were found guilty as accessories to the crime and fined $100 each. The Supreme Court reversed the lower-court decisions and declared the Connecticut law unconstitutional because it violated "a right of privacy older than the Bill of Rights—older than our political parties, older than our school system."[78] Justice William O. Douglas, author of the majority decision in the *Griswold v. Connecticut*

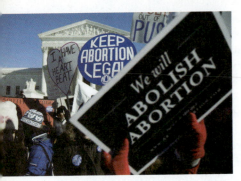

One of the most important cases related to the right to privacy was Roe v. Wade, *which established a woman's right to seek an abortion. However, the decision has remained highly controversial, with opponents arguing that the Constitution does not guarantee this right.*

case, argued that this right of privacy is also grounded in the Constitution, because it fits into a "zone of privacy" created by a combination of the Third, Fourth, and Fifth amendments. A concurring opinion, written by Justice Arthur Goldberg, attempted to strengthen Douglas's argument by adding that "the concept of liberty . . . embraces the right of marital privacy though that right is not mentioned explicitly in the Constitution [and] is supported by numerous decisions of this Court . . . and *by the language and history of the Ninth Amendment* [emphasis added]."[79]

The right to privacy was confirmed and extended in 1973 in an important but controversial privacy decision: *Roe v. Wade.* This decision established a woman's right to seek an abortion and prohibited states from making abortion a criminal act.[80] It is important to emphasize that the preference for privacy rights and for their extension to include the rights of women to control their own bodies was not something invented by the Supreme Court in a vacuum. Most states did not regulate abortions in any fashion until the 1840s, at which time only 6 of the 26 existing states had any regulations governing abortion. In addition, many states had begun to ease their abortion restrictions well before the 1973 *Roe* decision, although in recent years a number of states have reinstated some restrictions on abortion. While the Supreme Court has continued to affirm a woman's right to seek an abortion, the Court has limited the right, approving restrictions as long as they do not pose an "undue burden."

Like any important principle, once privacy was established as an aspect of civil liberties protected by the Bill of Rights through the Fourteenth Amendment, it took on a life of its own. In a number of important decisions, the Supreme Court and the lower federal courts sought to protect rights that could not be found in the text of the Constitution but could be discovered through a study of the philosophic sources of fundamental rights. Increasingly in recent years, right-to-privacy claims have been made by those attempting to preserve the right to obtain legal abortions, by those seeking to obtain greater rights for homosexuals, and by supporters of physician-assisted suicide (also known as the "right to die" movement). In the case of homosexuals, the Supreme Court extended privacy protections to them in 2003 when it ruled that they are "entitled to respect for their private lives" in the case of *Lawrence v. Texas.*[81] The case overturned a Texas law banning certain sexual acts among same-sex partners. The Court concluded, "Petitioners are entitled to respect for their private lives. The State cannot demean their existence or control their destiny by making their private sexual conduct a crime." For the first time, gay men and lesbians could claim right-to-privacy protection.

Civil Liberties around the World

Civil liberties are protected differently around the world. Interestingly, laws protecting freedom of expression and belief tend to be stronger than laws protecting other civil liberties, while the right to an established and equitable system of rule of law tends to be weakest, as the graph here shows. Freedom of association and organization also tends to receive weaker protection, especially in today's climate of fear of terrorism, when governments are concerned with identifying and disrupting terrorist organizations. Why might freedom of belief and expression be more strongly developed than other civil liberties?

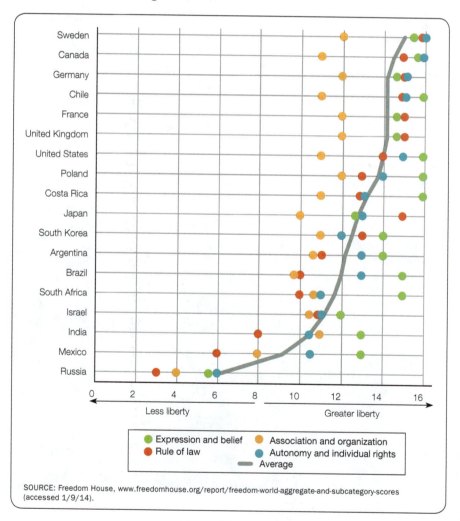

SOURCE: Freedom House, www.freedomhouse.org/report/freedom-world-aggregate-and-subcategory-scores (accessed 1/9/14).

● Civil Rights Are Protections by the Government

Trace the legal developments and social movements that expanded civil rights

With the adoption of the Fourteenth Amendment in 1868, civil rights became part of the Constitution, guaranteed to each citizen through "equal protection of the laws." Together with the **Thirteenth Amendment**, which abolished slavery, and the **Fifteenth Amendment**, which guaranteed voting rights for black men, it seemed to provide a guarantee of civil rights for the newly freed black slaves. But the general language of the Fourteenth Amendment meant that its support for civil rights could be even more far-reaching. The very simplicity of the **equal protection clause** of the Fourteenth Amendment left it open to interpretation:

> No State shall make or enforce any law which shall . . . deny to any person within its jurisdiction the equal protection of the laws.

This provision of the Fourteenth Amendment guarantees citizens "the equal protection of the laws." These words launched a century of political movements and legal efforts to press for racial equality. The African American quest for civil rights in turn inspired many other groups, including members of other racial and ethnic groups, women, the disabled, and gay men, lesbians, and the transgendered, to seek new laws and constitutional guarantees of their civil rights.

Plessy v. Ferguson Established "Separate but Equal"

The Supreme Court was initially no more ready to enforce the civil rights aspects of the Fourteenth Amendment than it was to enforce the civil liberties provisions.

The 1896 Supreme Court case of Plessy v. Ferguson *upheld legal segregation and created the "separate but equal" rule, which fostered national segregation. Overt discrimination in public accommodations was common.*

Resistance to equality for African Americans in the South led Congress to adopt the Civil Rights Act of 1875, which attempted to protect blacks from discrimination by proprietors of hotels, theaters, and other public accommodations. But the Court declared the Civil Rights Act of 1875 unconstitutional on the grounds that the act sought to protect blacks against discrimination by *private* businesses, while the Fourteenth Amendment, according to the Court's interpretation, was intended to protect individuals only from discrimination that arose from actions by *public* officials of state and local governments.

In the infamous case of *Plessy v. Ferguson* (1896), the Court went still further by upholding a Louisiana statute that *required* segregation of the races on trolleys and other public carriers (and, by implication, in all public facilities, including schools). Homer Plessy, a man defined as "one-eighth black," had violated a Louisiana law that provided for "equal but separate accommodations" on trains and a $25 fine for any white passenger who sat in a car reserved for blacks or any black passenger who sat in a car reserved for whites. The Supreme Court held that the Fourteenth Amendment's "equal protection of the laws" was not violated by laws requiring segregation of the races in public accommodations as long as the facilities were equal, thus establishing the **"separate but equal" rule** that prevailed through the mid-twentieth century.[82] People generally pretended that segregated accommodations were equal as long as some accommodation for blacks existed. Thus, racial inequality in the guise of the separate but equal doctrine persisted for decades.

Racial Discrimination Began to Subside after World War II

The Supreme Court had begun to change its position on racial discrimination before World War II by being stricter about the criterion for equal facilities in the "separate but equal" rule. In 1938, for example, the Court rejected Missouri's policy of paying the tuition of qualified blacks to out-of-state law schools rather than admitting them to the University of Missouri Law School.[83] Similar rulings in the 1940s and '50s began to chip away at "separate but equal."

Although none of those pre-1954 cases confronted "separate but equal" and the principle of racial discrimination head on, they were extremely significant to black leaders and gave them encouragement enough to believe that there was at last an opportunity and enough legal precedent to change the constitutional framework itself. Much of this legal work was done by the Legal Defense and Educational Fund of the National Association for the Advancement of Colored People (NAACP). Formed in 1909 to fight discrimination against African Americans, the NAACP was the most important civil rights organization during the first half of the twentieth century.

In the fall of 1952 the Court had on its docket cases from Delaware, the District of Columbia, Kansas, South Carolina, and Virginia challenging the constitutionality of school segregation. Of these, the case filed in Kansas became the chosen one by the NAACP. It seemed to be ahead of the pack in its district court, and it had the special advantage of being located in a state outside the Deep South.[84] Oliver Brown, the father of three girls, lived "across the tracks" in a low-income, racially mixed Topeka neighborhood. Every school day morning, Linda Brown took the school bus to the Monroe School for black children about a mile away. In September 1950, Oliver Brown took Linda to the all-white Sumner School, which was closer to home, to enter her into the third grade in defiance of state law and local segregation rules. When they were refused, Brown took his case to the NAACP, and soon thereafter **Brown v. Board of Education** was born.

In deciding the *Brown* case, the Court, to the surprise of many, basically rejected as inconclusive all the learned arguments about the intent and the history of the Fourteenth Amendment and committed itself instead to considering only the consequences of segregation:

> Does segregation of children in public schools solely on the basis of race, even though the physical facilities and other "tangible" factors may be equal, deprive the children of the minority group of equal educational opportunities? We believe that it does. . . . We conclude that in the field of public education the doctrine of "separate but equal" has no place. Separate educational facilities are inherently unequal.[85]

The *Brown* decision altered the constitutional framework in two fundamental respects. First, after *Brown*, the states no longer had the power to use race as a criterion of discrimination in law. Second, the national government from then on had the power (and eventually the obligation) to intervene with strict regulatory policies against the discriminatory actions of state or local governments, school boards, employers, and many others in the private sector.

The Civil Rights Struggle Escalated after *Brown v. Board of Education*

Brown v. Board of Education withdrew all constitutional authority to use race as a criterion for exclusion, and it signaled more clearly the Court's determination to use the strict scrutiny test in cases related to racial discrimination. This meant that the burden of proof would fall on the government to show that the law in question *was* constitutional—not on the challengers to show the law's *unconstitutionality.*[86] But the historic decision in *Brown v. Board of Education* was merely a small opening move. First, most states refused to cooperate until sued, and many ingenious schemes were employed to delay obedience (such as states paying the tuition for white students to attend newly created "private" academies). Second, while school boards began to cooperate by eliminating legally enforced school segregation (what is referred to as **de jure** segregation, meaning literally "by law" or legally enforced practices), extensive actual segregation remained (what is referred to as **de facto** segregation, meaning literally "by fact," wherein races are still segregated even though the law does not require it). Thus, school segregation in the North as well as in the South remained as a consequence of racially segregated housing patterns that were untouched by the 1954–55 *Brown* principles. Third, discrimination in employment, public accommodations, juries, voting, and other areas of social and economic activity were not directly touched by *Brown*.

Social Protest and Congressional Action Ten years after *Brown*, fewer than 1 percent of black school-age children in the Deep South were attending schools with whites.[87] A decade of frustration made it fairly obvious to all observers that adjudication alone would not succeed. The goal of "equal protection" required positive, or affirmative, action by Congress and by federal agencies. And given massive southern resistance and a generally negative national public opinion toward racial integration, progress would not be made through courts, Congress, or federal agencies without intense, well-organized support. Organized civil rights demonstrations began to mount slowly but surely after *Brown v. Board of Education*. Only a year after Brown, black citizens in Montgomery, Alabama, challenged the city's segregated bus system with a yearlong boycott. The boycott began with the arrest of Rosa Parks, who refused to give up her bus seat for a white man. A seamstress who worked with civil rights groups, Parks eventually became a civil rights icon, as did one of the ministers leading the boycott: Martin Luther King, Jr. After a year of private carpools and walking, Montgomery's bus system desegregated, but only after the Supreme Court ruled the system unconstitutional.

By the 1960s the many organizations that made up the civil rights movement had accumulated experience and built networks capable of launching massive direct-action campaigns against southern segregationists. The Southern Christian Leadership Conference, the Student Nonviolent Coordinating Committee, and many other organizations had built a movement that stretched across the South, using the media to attract nationwide attention and support. The image of protesters being beaten, attacked by police dogs, and set upon with fire hoses did much to win broad sympathy for the cause of black civil rights and to discredit state and local governments in the South. In the massive March on Washington in 1963, the Reverend Martin Luther King, Jr., staked out the movement's moral claims in his famous "I Have a Dream" speech.

The Civil Rights Acts Made Equal Protection a Reality

The right to equal protection of the laws could be established and, to a certain extent, implemented by the courts. But after a decade of very frustrating efforts, the courts and Congress ultimately came to the conclusion that the federal courts alone were not adequate to the task of changing the social rules, and that legislation and administrative action would be needed.

Congress used its legislative powers to help make equal protection of the laws a reality by passing the Civil Rights Act of 1964, prohibiting major forms of discrimination against racial, ethnic, national and religious minorities, and women in voting registration, schools, public accommodations, and the workplace. The act seemed bold at the time, but it was enacted 10 years after the Supreme Court had declared racial discrimination "inherently unequal" under the Fifth and Fourteenth amendments. And it was enacted long after blacks had demonstrated that discrimination was no longer acceptable.

Public Accommodations After the passage of the 1964 Civil Rights Act, public accommodations quickly removed some of the most visible forms of racial discrimination. Signs defining "colored" and "white" restrooms, water fountains, waiting rooms, and seating arrangements were removed and a host of other practices that relegated black people to separate and inferior arrangements were ended. In addition, the federal government filed more than 400 antidiscrimination suits in federal courts against hotels, restaurants, taverns, gas stations, and other "public accommodations."

Many aspects of legalized racial segregation, such as using separate Bibles to swear in black and white witnesses in the courtroom, seem like ancient history today. But the issue of racial discrimination in public settings is by no means over. In 1993, six African American Secret Service agents filed suit after a Denny's restaurant in Annapolis, Maryland, failed to serve them; white Secret Service agents at a nearby table had received prompt service. Similar charges citing discriminatory service at Denny's restaurants surfaced across the country. Faced with evidence of a pattern of systematic discrimination and numerous lawsuits, Denny's paid $45 million in damages to plaintiffs in Maryland and California in what is said to be the largest settlement ever in a public accommodation case.[88] In addition to the settlement, the chain vowed to expand employment and management opportunities for minorities in Denny's restaurants.

School Desegregation The 1964 Civil Rights Act also declared discrimination by private employers and state governments (school boards, etc.) illegal, then went further by providing for administrative agencies to help the courts implement these laws. The act, for example, authorized the executive branch, through the Justice Department, to implement federal court orders to desegregate schools, and to do so without having to wait for individual parents to bring complaints. The act also provided that federal grants-in-aid to state and local governments for education be withheld from any school system practicing racial segregation.

In recent years, a series of court rulings have slowed race-based integration efforts. In 2007 the Supreme Court's ruling in *Parents Involved in Community Schools v. Seattle School District No. 1* limited the measures that can be used to promote school integration.[89] The case involved school assignment plans voluntarily initiated by the city of Seattle and, in another, related case, the city of Louisville, Kentucky. By making race one factor in assigning students to schools, the cities hoped to achieve greater racial balance across the public schools. The court ruled that these plans, even though they were voluntarily adopted by cities, were unconstitutional because they discriminated against white students on the basis of race. Many observers described the decision as the end of the Brown era because it eliminated one of the few public strategies left to promote racial integration. Others argued that Justice Anthony Kennedy's concurring opinion, which recognized the harm of racial isolation, may provide the basis for new efforts to promote integration in the future.[90]

Outlawing Discrimination in Employment The federal courts and the Justice Department also fought employment discrimination through the Civil Rights Act of 1964, which outlawed job discrimination by all private and public employers, including governmental agencies (such as fire and police departments) that employed more than 15 workers. We have already seen (in Chapter 3) that the Supreme Court gave "interstate commerce" such a broad definition that Congress had the constitutional authority to cover discrimination by virtually any local employers.[91] The 1964 act makes it unlawful to discriminate in employment on the basis of color, religion, sex, or national origin, as well as on race.

In order to enforce fair employment practices, the national government could revoke public contracts for goods and services and refuse to engage in contracts with any private company that could not guarantee that its rules for hiring, promotion, and firing were nondiscriminatory.

But one problem was that the complaining party had to show that deliberate discrimination was the cause of the failure to get a job or a training opportunity. Rarely, of course, does an employer explicitly admit discrimination on the basis of race, sex, or any other illegal reason. Recognizing this, the courts have allowed aggrieved parties (the plaintiffs) to make their case if they can show that an employer's hiring practices had the *effect* of exclusion, even if they cannot show the *intention* to discriminate.

Voting Rights Although 1964 was the *most* important year for civil rights legislation, it was not the only important year. In 1965, Congress significantly strengthened legislation protecting voting rights by barring literacy and other tests as a condition for voting in six southern states,[92] by making it a crime to interfere with voting, and by providing for the replacement of local registrars with federally appointed registrars in counties designated by the attorney general as significantly resistant to registering eligible blacks to vote. The right to vote was further strengthened with ratification in 1964 of the Twenty-Fourth Amendment, which abolished the poll tax, and later with legislation permanently outlawing literacy tests in all 50 states and mandating bilingual ballots or oral assistance for speakers of Spanish, Chinese, Japanese, Korean, and Native American and Eskimo languages. This 1965 law finally broke the back of voting discrimination, meaning that it took almost 100 years to carry out the Fifteenth Amendment.

In the long run, the laws extending and protecting voting rights could prove to be the most effective of all the great civil rights legislation, because the progress in black political participation produced by these acts has altered the shape of American politics. In 1965, in the seven states of the Old Confederacy covered by the Voting Rights Act, 29.3 percent of the eligible black residents were registered to vote, compared with 73.4 percent of the white residents (see Table 4.3). In 1967, a mere two years after implementation of the voting rights laws, 52.1 percent of the eligible blacks in the seven states were registered. By 1972 the gap between black and white registration in the seven states was only 11.2 points.

One of the most contentious areas of voting rights today is voter identification laws. Proponents say ID requirements prevent fraud, while opponents argue the rules purposely keep the poor and minorities, who are less likely to have picture ID, from the polls.

TABLE 4.3

Registration by Race and State in Southern States Covered by the Voting Rights Act (VRA)

The VRA had a direct impact on the rate of black voter registration in the southern states, as measured by the gap between white and black voters in each state. Further insights can be gained by examining changes in white registration rates before and after passage of the Voting Rights Act and by comparing the gaps between white and black registration. Why do you think registration rates for whites increased significantly in some states and dropped in others? What impact could the increase in black registration have had on public policy?

	BEFORE THE ACT*			AFTER THE ACT* 1971–72		
	WHITE %	BLACK %	GAP** %	WHITE %	BLACK %	GAP %
Alabama	69.2	19.3	49.9	80.7	57.1	23.6
Georgia	62.6	27.4	35.2	70.6	67.8	2.8
Louisiana	80.5	31.6	48.9	80.0	59.1	20.9
Mississippi	69.9	6.7	63.2	71.6	62.2	9.4
North Carolina	96.8	46.8	50.0	62.2	46.3	15.9
South Carolina	75.7	37.3	38.4	51.2	48.0	3.2
Virginia	61.1	38.3	22.8	61.2	54.0	7.2
TOTAL	73.4	29.3	44.1	67.8	56.6	11.2

*Available registration data as of March 1965 and 1971–72.

**The gap is the percentage-point difference between white and black registration rates.

SOURCE: U.S. Commission on Civil Rights, Political Participation (1968), Appendix VII: Voter Education Project, attachment to press release, October 3, 1972.

A new area of controversy in the realm of voting rights concerns so-called voter ID laws. Some 30 states have enacted legislation requiring voters to show positive identification at the polls. In 2014, seven of these states required photo IDs, like drivers' licenses. Republicans generally support such laws, arguing that they deter voter fraud. Democrats generally oppose such laws, countering that they are particularly burdensome to poor, young, and minority voters, who they say are less likely than others to possess such IDs. Critics also note that virtually no documented cases of voter ID fraud exist, despite intensive efforts to uncover them. Several studies of whether such laws suppress voter turnout have been conducted but have produced inconclusive results.

Housing The Civil Rights Act of 1964 did not address housing, but in 1968, Congress passed another civil rights act specifically to outlaw housing discrimination. Called the Fair Housing Act, the law prohibited discrimination in the sale or rental of most housing, eventually covering nearly all the nation's housing. Housing was among the most controversial of discrimination issues because of deeply entrenched patterns of residential segregation across the United States.

Although it pronounced sweeping goals, the Fair Housing Act had little effect on housing segregation because its enforcement mechanisms were so weak. Individuals believing they had been discriminated against had to file suit themselves. The burden was on the individual to prove that housing discrimination had occurred, even though such discrimination is often subtle and difficult to document. Although local fair-housing groups emerged to assist individuals in their court claims, the procedures for proving discrimination proved a formidable barrier to effective change. These procedures were not altered until 1988, when Congress passed the Fair Housing Amendments Act. This new law put more teeth in the enforcement procedures and allowed the Department of Housing and Urban Development (HUD) to initiate legal action in cases of discrimination.[93]

Even so, another kind of discrimination, related to discriminatory home mortgage–ending practices, remained significant. So-called predatory lending—offering loans with interest rates that are higher than prevailing market rates, including "subprime mortgages"—led to charges that such loans were offered to African Americans and Latinos, while whites with similar incomes were offered loans with lower interest rates. These charges received extensive national attention when the economic downturn of 2008–09 led to widespread mortgage defaults, with many people losing their homes.[94] Lawsuits over these practices have resulted in the largest financial settlements ever issued for lending discrimination.

● The Civil Rights Struggle Was Extended to Other Disadvantaged Groups

> Describe how different groups have fought for and won protection of their civil rights

Even before equal-employment laws began to have a positive effect on the economic situation of blacks, something far more dramatic began to happen: the universalization of civil rights. The right not to be discriminated against was being successfully claimed by the other groups listed in the 1964 Civil Rights Act (those defined by sex, religion, or national origin) and eventually by still other groups (defined by age or sexual orientation). This extension of civil rights became the new frontier of the civil rights struggle, and women emerged with the greatest prominence in this new struggle.

Women Fought Gender Discrimination

In many ways the Civil Rights Act fostered the growth of the women's movement. The first major campaign of the National Organization for Women (NOW) involved picketing the Equal Employment Opportunity Commission (EEOC) for its refusal to ban sex-segregated employment advertisements. NOW also sued the *New York Times* for continuing to publish such ads after the passage

Political equality did not end discrimination against women in the workplace or in society at large. African Americans' struggle for civil rights in the 1950s and '60s spurred a parallel equal rights movement for women in the 1960s and '70s.

of the act. Another organization, the Women's Equity Action League (WEAL), pursued legal action on a wide range of sex discrimination issues, filing lawsuits against law schools and medical schools for discriminatory admission policies, for example.

Building on these victories and the growth of the women's movement, feminist activists sought to add an "Equal Rights Amendment" (ERA) to the Constitution. The proposed amendment was short; it stated that "equality of rights under the law shall not be denied or abridged by the United States or by any State on account of sex." The amendment's supporters believed that such a sweeping guarantee of equal rights was a necessary tool for ending all discrimination against women and for making gender roles more equal. Opponents charged that it would be socially disruptive and would introduce changes (such as unisex restrooms) that most Americans did not want. The amendment easily passed Congress in 1972 and won quick approval in many state legislatures, but it fell 3 states short of the 38 needed to ratify it by the 1982 deadline.[95]

Despite the failure of the ERA, efforts to stop gender discrimination expanded dramatically as an area of civil rights law. In the 1970s the conservative Burger Court (under Chief Justice Warren Burger) helped establish gender discrimination as a major and highly visible civil rights issue. Although the Supreme Court refused to treat gender discrimination as the equivalent of racial discrimination,[96] it did make it easier for plaintiffs to file and win suits on the basis of gender discrimination.

Courts began to find sexual harassment a form of sex discrimination during the late 1970s. Most of the law of sexual harassment has been developed by courts through interpretation of Title VII of the Civil Rights Act of 1964. In 1986 the Supreme Court recognized two forms of sexual harassment: the quid pro quo type, which involves an explicit or strongly implied threat that submission is a condition of continued employment, and the hostile environment type, which involves offensive or intimidating employment conditions amounting to sexual intimidation.[97]

Another major step was taken in 1992, when the Court decided in *Franklin v. Gwinnett County Public Schools* that violations of Title IX of the 1972 Education Act could be remedied with monetary damages.[98] Title IX forbade gender discrimination in education, but it initially sparked little litigation because of its weak enforcement provisions. The Court's 1992 ruling that monetary damages could be awarded for gender discrimination opened the door for more legal action in the area of education. The greatest impact has been in the areas of sexual harassment (the subject of the *Franklin* case) and in equal treatment of women's athletic programs. The potential for monetary damages has made universities and public schools take the problem of sexual harassment more seriously.

In 1996 the Supreme Court made another important decision about gender and education by putting an end to all-male schools supported by public funds. It ruled that the policy of the Virginia Military Institute (VMI) not to admit women was unconstitutional.[99] Along with the Citadel, an all-male military college in South Carolina, VMI had never admitted women in its 157-year history. VMI argued that the unique educational experience it offered—including intense physical training and the harsh treatment of freshmen—would be destroyed if women students were admitted. The Court, however, ruled that the male-only policy denied "substantial equality" to women. Two days after the Court's ruling, the Citadel announced that it would accept women. VMI considered becoming a private institution in order to remain all-male, but in September 1996 the school board finally voted to admit women.

Women have also pressed for civil rights in employment. In particular, women have fought against pay discrimination, which occurs when a male employee is paid more than a female employee of equal qualifications in the same job. In the 1960s, pay discrimination was common. After the Equal Pay Act of 1963 made such discrimination illegal, women's pay slowly moved toward the level of men's pay. In 2007, this movement received a setback when the Supreme Court ruled against a claim of pay discrimination. The case, *Ledbetter v. Goodyear Tire and Rubber Co.*, involved a woman supervisor named Lily Ledbetter, who learned late in her career that she was being paid up to 40 percent less than male supervisors, including those with less seniority. Ledbetter filed a grievance with the EEOC, charging sex discrimination.[100] The Supreme Court denied her claim, ruling that according to the law, workers must file their grievance 180 days after the discrimination occurs. Many observers found the ruling unfair because workers often do not know about pay differentials until well after the initial decision to discriminate has been made. In January 2009, the Lily Ledbetter Fair Pay Act became the first bill that

President Obama signed into law. The new law gave workers expanded rights to sue in cases, such as Ledbetter's, when an employee learns of discriminatory treatment well after it has started.

Latinos and Asian Americans Fight for Rights

Although the Civil Rights Act of 1964 outlawed discrimination on the basis of national origin, limited English proficiency kept many Asian Americans and Latinos from full participation in American life. Two developments in the 1970s, however, established rights for language minorities. In 1974 the Supreme Court ruled in *Lau v. Nichols*, a suit filed on behalf of Chinese students in San Francisco, that school districts have to provide education for students whose English is limited.[101] It did not mandate bilingual education, but it established a duty to provide instruction that the students could understand. And the 1970 amendments to the Voting Rights Act permanently outlawed literacy tests in all 50 states and mandated bilingual ballots or oral assistance for those who speak Spanish, Chinese, Japanese, Korean, or Native American or Eskimo languages.

Asian Americans and Latinos have also been concerned about the impact of immigration laws on their civil rights. Many Asian American and Latino organizations opposed the Immigration Reform and Control Act of 1986 because it imposed sanctions on employers who hire undocumented workers.

Young adults demonstrate their support for the DREAM Act by staging a sit-in protest on the floor of Senator John McCain's headquarters in Tuscon, Arizona. The DREAM Act would provide a path to permanent residency via military service or college attendance for individuals who were brought to the United States illegally as children by their parents.

Such sanctions, they feared, would lead employers to discriminate against Latinos and Asian Americans. These suspicions were confirmed in a 1990 report by the General Accounting Office that found employer sanctions had created a "widespread pattern of discrimination" against Latinos and others who appear foreign.[102]

As we saw in Chapter 3, a number of states, including Arizona, Utah, South Carolina, Georgia, and Alabama have recently passed very strict immigration laws. Civil rights groups have contested the laws in court, and the federal Justice Department has instituted its own legal challenges. Arizona's 2010 law provided the inspiration for these far-reaching state measures. Arizona's law required immigrants to carry identity documents with them at all times, made it a crime for an undocumented immigrant to apply for a job, gave the police greater powers to stop anyone they suspected of being an unauthorized immigrant, and required them to check the immigration status of a person they detain if they suspect that person is an unauthorized immigrant. The Justice Department challenged the law on the grounds that the federal government was responsible for making immigration law, not the states. The Supreme Court's 2012 decision was a partial victory for the federal government. The Court struck down three parts of the Arizona law on the grounds that they preempted federal responsibility. These included the provision that immigrants carry identity papers, that undocumented immigrants cannot apply for jobs, and that police can stop persons they suspect of being undocumented immigrants. The Court let stand the provision that required local police to check the immigration status of an individual detained for other reasons, if they had grounds to suspect that the person was in the country illegally. Opponents of the police checks vowed to challenge that part of the law on the grounds that it led to illegal racial profiling.[103]

Native Americans Have Sovereignty but Still Lack Rights

As a language minority, Native Americans were affected by the 1975 amendments to the Voting Rights Act and the *Lau* decision. The *Lau* decision established the right of Native Americans to be taught in their own languages. This marked quite a change from the period when Native American children attended boarding schools run by the Bureau of Indian Affairs, where they were forbidden from speaking their own languages. In addition to these language-related issues, Native Americans have sought to expand their rights on the basis of their sovereign status. Since the 1920s and '30s, Native American tribes have sued the federal government for illegally seizing land, seeking monetary reparations and land as damages. Both types of damages have been awarded in such suits, but only in small amounts. Native American tribes have been more successful in winning federal recognition of their sovereignty. Sovereign status has, in turn, allowed them to exercise greater self-determination. Most significant economically was a 1987 Supreme Court decision that freed Native American tribes from most state regulations prohibiting gambling. The establishment of casino gambling on Native American lands has brought a substantial flow of new income into some desperately poor reservations.

Disabled Americans Won a Great Victory in 1990

The concept of rights for the disabled began to emerge in the 1970s as the civil rights model spread to other groups. The seed was planted in a little-noticed provision of the 1973 Rehabilitation Act, which outlawed discrimination against individuals on the basis of disabilities. As in many other cases, the law itself helped give rise to the movement demanding rights for the disabled.[104] Modeling it on the NAACP's Legal Defense Fund, the disability movement founded a Disability Rights Education and Defense Fund to press its legal claims. The movement achieved its greatest success with the passage of the Americans with Disabilities Act (ADA) of 1990, which guarantees equal employment rights and access to public businesses for the disabled and bars discrimination in employment, housing, and health care. The EEOC is a body that considers claims of discrimination in violation of this act. The impact of the law has been far-reaching, as businesses and public facilities have installed ramps, elevators, and other devices to meet the act's requirements.[105]

Gay Men and Lesbians Have Gained Significant Legal Ground

In less than 50 years, the lesbian, gay, bisexual, and transgender (LGBT) movement has become one of the largest civil rights movements in contemporary America. For much of the country's history, any sexual orientation other than heterosexuality was considered "deviant" and many states criminalized sexual acts considered to be "unnatural." Homosexuals were often afraid to reveal their sexual orientation for fear of reprisals, including being fired from their jobs, and the police in many cities raided bars and other establishments where it was believed that homosexuals gathered. While no formal restrictions existed on their political participation, homosexuals faced the possibility of ostracism, discrimination, assault, and even prosecution.[106]

The contemporary gay rights movement began in earnest in the 1960s, growing into a well-financed and sophisticated lobby. But until 1996, there was no Supreme Court ruling or national legislation explicitly protecting gays and lesbians from discrimination. The first gay rights case that the Court decided, *Bowers v. Hardwick* (1986), ruled against a right to privacy that would protect consensual homosexual activity.[107] After the *Bowers* decision, the gay and lesbian rights movement sought suitable legal cases to test the constitutionality of discrimination against gay men and lesbians, much as the black civil rights movement did in the late 1940s and '50s. As one advocate put it, "lesbians and gay men are looking for their *Brown v. Board of Education*."[108] In 1996 the Supreme Court, in *Romer v. Evans*, explicitly extended fundamental civil rights protections to gays and lesbians, by declaring unconstitutional a 1992 amendment to the Colorado state constitution that prohibited local governments from passing ordinances to protect gay rights.[109] In its decision, the Court highlighted the connection between gay rights and civil rights as it declared discrimination against gay people unconstitutional.

Homosexuals won another major victory in the 2003 case of *Lawrence v. Texas*, in which the Supreme Court overturned *Bowers* and struck down a Texas law that made certain sexual conduct between consenting partners of the same sex illegal.

Partners for 40 years, Edith Windsor and Thea Spyer were married in 2007. When Thea passed away in 2009, Edith had to pay over $300,000 in taxes because the federal government did not recognize her marriage under the terms of DOMA. In 2013, Edith won her Supreme Court case, which cleared the way for the federal government to recognize same-sex marriages.

Extending the right-to-privacy umbrella to lesbians and gay men, the Court said that "petitioners are entitled to respect for their private lives. The State cannot demean their existence or control their destiny by making their private sexual conduct a crime."[110]

While the ruling in *Lawrence* struck down laws that made homosexual acts a crime, it did not change federal and state laws that deprived homosexuals of full civil rights, including the right to marry. In 2004 the Massachusetts State Supreme Court ordered the state to recognize gay marriage under its state constitution, where it has been legal ever since. As of 2014, 35 states, plus the District of Columbia, have recognized same-sex marriage. In 2013, the Supreme Court struck down a federal law (Defense of Marriage Act, or DOMA) that barred benefits to married same-sex couples, and let stand a California law recognizing gay marriage. Invoking several constitutional protections, the cases significantly strengthened the rights of married gay couples.[111] The federal government subsequently expanded recognition of same-sex marriages for the purpose of federal benefits and legal proceedings, such as survivor benefits, bankruptcies, tax purposes, and immigration. Despite this change at the national level, considerable variation in LGBT civil rights policies continues to exist at the state level.

In 2009 gay rights advocates won a significant victory at the national level: new legislation extended the definition of hate crimes to include crimes against gays and transgender people. Such legislation had been sought since the 1998 murder of Matthew Shepard, a Wyoming college student who was brutally slain because of his sexual orientation. The new law allows for tougher penalties when a crime is designated a hate crime. In another important victory for the gay rights movement, an executive order signed by President Obama in 2011 repealed the U.S. military's "Don't Ask, Don't Tell" policy, a 20-year-old rule that expelled gays and lesbians from the military if they made their sexual orientation known. The new policy allows gays to serve openly in the military.

Affirmative Action Attempts to Right Past Wrongs

Contrast arguments for and against affirmative action

The politics of rights has spread to increasing numbers of groups in American society since the 1960s. The relatively narrow goal of equalizing opportunity by eliminating discriminatory barriers developed toward the far broader goal of **affirmative action**, government policies or programs that seek to redress past injustices against specified groups by making special efforts to provide members of these groups with access to educational and employment opportunities. An affirmative action policy uses two novel approaches: (1) positive or benign discrimination in which race or some other status is actually taken into account as a positive rather than negative factor, and (2) compensatory action to favor members of the disadvantaged group who themselves may never have been the victims of discrimination. President Lyndon Johnson put the case emotionally in 1965: "You do not take a person who, for years, has been hobbled by chains . . . and then say you are free to compete with all the others, and still just believe that you have been completely fair."[112]

Affirmative action also took the form of efforts by the agencies in the Department of Health, Education, and Welfare to shift their focus from "desegregation" to "integration."[113] Federal agencies required school districts to present plans for busing children across district lines, for closing certain schools, and for redistributing faculties as well as students, or face the loss of aid from the federal government. The guidelines constituted preferential treatment to compensate for past discrimination; without this legislatively assisted approach to integration, there would certainly not have been the dramatic increase in the numbers of black children attending integrated classes.

Affirmative action was also initiated in the area of employment opportunity. The EEOC has often required plans whereby employers must attempt to increase the number of minority employees, and the Department of Labor has used the threat of contract revocation for the same purpose.

The Supreme Court Shifts the Burden of Proof in Affirmative Action

Efforts by the executive, legislative, and judicial branches to shape the meaning of affirmative action today tend to center on one key issue: What is the appropriate level of review in affirmative action cases—that is, on whom should the burden of proof be placed, the plaintiff, to show that discrimination has not occurred, or the defendant, to show that discrimination has occurred? Affirmative action was first addressed formally by the Supreme Court in the case of Allan Bakke. Bakke, a white male, brought suit against the University of California at Davis Medical School on the grounds that it denied him admission on the basis of his race. (That year the school had reserved 16 of its 100 available slots for minority applicants.) Bakke argued that his grades and test scores had ranked him well above many students who had been accepted at the school and that the only possible explanation for his rejection was that he was white, whereas those others

Affirmative action remains very controversial in the United States. This cartoon makes the point that admissions offices use a number of preference categories in order to achieve their goal of a diverse class, and minority status is just one of many such categories.

accepted were black or Latino. In 1978, Bakke won his case before the Supreme Court and was admitted to the medical school, but he did not succeed in getting affirmative action declared unconstitutional. The Court accepted the argument that achieving "a diverse student body" was "a compelling public purpose," but it ruled that the method of a rigid quota of student slots assigned on the basis of race was incompatible with the Fourteenth Amendment's equal protection clause. Thus, the Court permitted universities and other hiring authorities to continue to take minority status into consideration, but all but barred the use of quotas.[114]

But in 1995, the Supreme Court's ruling in *Adarand Constructors v. Peña* further weakened affirmative action. This decision stated that race-based policies, such as preferences given by the government to minority contractors, must survive strict scrutiny, placing the burden on the government to show that such affirmative action programs serve a compelling government interest and are narrowly tailored to address identifiable past discrimination.[115]

In 2003 affirmative action again survived court challenge in two cases arising from the University of Michigan. In *Grutter v. Bollinger*, the Court upheld the "holistic" and "individualized" affirmative action program used by Michigan's law school, finding it in keeping with the standard set in the *Bakke* case.[116] Michigan's undergraduate affirmative action program was declared unconstitutional, however, in *Gratz v. Bollinger*, because its ranking system for admissions gave specific points (20 out of 150) to African American, Latino, and Native American applicants.[117] This approach was barred for resembling too closely the specific numerical quota system struck down by *Bakke*. The Court reaffirmed its decision in *Grutter* in 2013 when it decided *Fisher v. University of Texas*, in which a white student challenged the use of race as one factor among many in the admissions decision. In a 7–1 decision, the Court sent the case back to the District Court with instructions to apply "strict scrutiny" to the school's policy, as articulated in *Grutter*.[118]

Civil Liberties, Civil Rights,
and Your Future

Government surveillance of its citizens—encompassing their communications, travel, and personal conduct—is among the major civil liberties questions facing Americans today. Revelations in 2013 of extensive electronic surveillance by the National Security Agency (NSA) of Americans' phone and Internet communications caused an uproar in Congress and in the country.

While many expressed concerns about citizens' privacy, intelligence agencies and police insist that their surveillance activities are of critical importance in the nation's ongoing struggle against terrorism and crime. Testifying before Congress in 2013, NSA officials declared that the agency's eavesdropping program had averted dozens of potential terrorist attacks. But since the matters were highly classified, no actual proof of these assertions was proffered and many members of Congress, including Senate Intelligence Committee Chairman Patrick Leahy (D-Vt.), expressed doubts about the agency's claims. Later, the NSA conceded that its domestic surveillance programs had possibly thwarted only one terrorist plot, rather than the dozens initially claimed. Are worries about privacy overblown, or are the actual threats exaggerated?

For the past several decades, the civil rights revolution has broadened to include not only women and Latinos but sexual orientation and immigration status. As our nation becomes more and more diverse, equal protection of the laws will become more and more important. What civil rights battles now appear on the country's horizon? And how does a country based on the democratic principle of majority rule ensure that the civil rights of minorities are protected?

plug**in**

Inform

Read the Bill of Rights, which is included in the Appendix to this book. Then, learn about how civil liberties apply in the digital age by reading the "Know Your Rights" page on the Electronic Frontier Foundation's website (www.eff.org).

Express

Imagine you are a legislative staffer. Draft a policy memo on the extent of government surveillance of American citizens. Should there be limits on government surveillance in the fight against terrorism?

Connect

Visit the American Civil Liberties Union (ACLU) website, and consider signing up for its mailing list. Which issues interest you?

Act

Click the "Take Action" link on the EFF's website or the "Action" link on the ACLU's site, to sign a petition or learn about other ways to get involved in current civil liberties issues.

studyguide

Practice Quiz

1. Which of the following rights was *not* included in the original Constitution? *(pp. 95–96)*
   a) prohibition of bills of attainder
   b) prohibition of ex post facto laws
   c) guarantee of habeas corpus
   d) guarantee of trial by jury in state where crime was committed
   e) prohibition of warrantless search and seizure

2. Which of the following provided that all of the protections contained in the Bill of Rights applied to the states as well as the national government? *(pp. 96–97)*
   a) the First Amendment
   b) the Fourteenth Amendment
   c) *Palko v. Connecticut*
   d) *Gitlow v. New York*
   e) *Barron v. Baltimore*

3. The process by which some of the liberties in the Bill of Rights were applied to the states (or nationalized) is known as *(p. 97)*
   a) selective incorporation.
   b) judicial activism.
   c) civil liberties.
   d) establishment.
   e) preemption.

4. Which of the following protections are *not* contained in the First Amendment? *(pp. 99–108)*
   a) the establishment clause
   b) the free exercise clause
   c) freedom of the press
   d) the right to peaceably assemble
   e) freedom from unlawful searches and seizures.

5. The judicial doctrine that places a heavy burden of proof on the government when it seeks to regulate or restrict speech is called *(p. 101)*
   a) judicial restraint.
   b) judicial activism.
   c) habeas corpus.
   d) prior restraint.
   e) strict scrutiny.

6. In *McDonald v. Chicago*, the Supreme Court ruled that *(pp. 109–10)*
   a) states can require citizens to own firearms.
   b) federal grants can be used to support the formation of state militias.
   c) felons can be prevented from purchasing assault rifles.
   d) the Second Amendment applies to states as well as the federal government.
   e) the Second Amendment applies only to the federal government and not to states.

7. The Fourth, Fifth, Sixth, and Eighth amendments, taken together, define *(p. 110)*
   a) due process of law.
   b) free speech.
   c) the right to bear arms.
   d) civil rights of minorities.
   e) freedom of religion.

8. In which case did the Supreme Court rule that state governments no longer had the authority to make private sexual behavior a crime? *(p. 116)*
   a) *Webster v. Reproductive Health Services*
   b) *Gonzales v. Oregon*
   c) *Lawrence v. Texas*
   d) *Bowers v. Hardwick*
   e) *Texas v. Johnson*

9. When did civil rights become part of the Constitution? *(p. 118)*
   a) in 1789 at the Founding
   b) with the adoption of the Fourteenth Amendment in 1868
   c) with the adoption of the Nineteenth Amendment in 1920
   d) in the 1954 *Brown v. Board of Education* case
   e) in 2008 when Barack Obama was elected president

10. Which of the following was *not* a way the Twenty-Fourth Amendment of 1964 and the Voting Rights Act of 1965 significantly extended and protected voting rights? *(pp. 123–24)*
    a) barring literacy tests as a condition for voting in six southern states
    b) requiring all voters to register two weeks before any federal election
    c) making it a crime to interfere with voting
    d) abolishing the poll tax
    e) providing for the replacement of local registrars with federally appointed registrars in counties designated as significantly resistant to registering eligible black voters

11. Which of the following is *not* an example of an area in which women have made progress since the 1970s in guaranteeing certain civil rights? *(pp. 125–28)*
    a) sexual harassment
    b) integration into all-male publicly supported universities
    c) more equal funding for college women's varsity athletic programs

d) the passage of the Equal Rights Amendment
    e) None—these are all examples of areas in which women have made progress.

12. The Supreme Court's decision in *Bakke v. Board of Regents* was significant because *(pp. 132–34)*
    a) it stated that race can never be used as a factor in university admissions.
    b) it stated that diversity is a compelling state interest and that university admissions that take racial categories into account are constitutional as long as they are highly individualized.
    c) it permitted quotas and separate university admission standards for members of minority groups.
    d) it evaluated the constitutionality of mechanical point systems that favor minority applicants in university admissions.
    e) it declared that affirmative action policies would no longer be subject to strict scrutiny from the courts.

Key Terms

affirmative action *(p. 132)* government policies or programs that seek to redress past injustices against specified groups by making special efforts to provide members of these groups with access to educational and employment opportunities

Bill of Rights *(p. 93)* the first 10 amendments to the U.S. Constitution, ratified in 1791; they ensure certain rights and liberties to the people

bill of attainder *(p. 95)* a law that declares a person guilty of a crime without a trial

Brown v. Board of Education *(p. 120)* the 1954 Supreme Court decision that struck down the "separate but equal" doctrine as fundamentally unequal; this case eliminated state power to use race as a criterion for discrimination in law and provided the national government with the power to

intervene by exercising strict regulatory policies against discriminatory actions

civil liberties *(p. 93)* areas of personal freedom constitutionally protected from government interference

civil rights *(p. 93)* obligation imposed on government to take positive action to protect citizens from any illegal action of government agencies and of other private citizens

"clear and present danger" test *(p. 102)* test to determine whether speech is protected or unprotected, based on its capacity to present a "clear and present danger" to society

de facto *(p. 120)* literally, "by fact"; practices that occur even when there is no legal enforcement, such as school segregation in much of the United States today

de jure *(p. 120)* literally, "by law"; legally enforced practices, such as school segregation in the South before the 1960s

double jeopardy *(p. 112)* the Fifth Amendment right providing that a person cannot be tried twice for the same crime

due process of law *(p. 96)* the right of every citizen against arbitrary action by national or state governments

eminent domain *(p. 113)* the right of government to take private property for public use

equal protection clause *(p. 118)* provision of the Fourteenth Amendment guaranteeing citizens "the equal protection of the laws"; this clause has served as the basis for the civil rights of African Americans, women, and other groups

establishment clause *(p. 99)* the First Amendment clause that says that "Congress shall make no law respecting an establishment of religion"; this law means that a "wall of separation" exists between church and state

exclusionary rule *(p. 110)* the ability of courts to exclude evidence obtained in violation of the Fourth Amendment

ex post facto laws *(p. 95)* laws that declare an action to be illegal after it has been committed

Fifteenth Amendment *(p. 118)* one of three Civil War amendments; it guaranteed voting rights for African American men

fighting words *(p. 107)* speech that directly incites damaging conduct

Fourteenth Amendment *(p. 96)* one of three Civil War amendments; it guaranteed equal protection and due process

free exercise clause *(p. 100)* the First Amendment clause that protects a citizen's right to believe and practice whatever religion one chooses

grand jury *(p. 112)* jury that determines whether sufficient evidence is available to justify a trial; grand juries do not rule on the accused's guilt or innocence

habeas corpus *(p. 95)* a court order demanding that an individual in custody be brought into court and shown the cause for detention

libel *(p. 106)* a written statement made in "reckless disregard of the truth" that is considered damaging to a victim because it is "malicious, scandalous, and defamatory"

Miranda rule *(p. 113)* the requirement, articulated by the Supreme Court in *Miranda v. Arizona* (1966), that persons under arrest must be informed prior to police interrogation of their rights to remain silent and to have the benefit of legal counsel

prior restraint *(p. 105)* an effort by a governmental agency to block the publication of material it deems libelous or harmful in some other way; censorship; in the United States, the courts forbid prior restraint except under the most extraordinary circumstances

right to privacy *(p. 115)* the right to be left alone, which has been interpreted by the Supreme Court to entail individual access to birth control and abortion

selective incorporation *(p. 97)* the process by which different protections in the Bill of Rights were incorporated into the Fourteenth Amendment, thus guaranteeing citizens protection from state as well as national governments

"separate but equal" rule *(p. 119)* doctrine that public accommodations could be segregated by race but still be considered equal

slander *(p. 106)* an oral statement made in "reckless disregard of the truth" that is considered damaging to the victim because it is "malicious, scandalous, and defamatory"

"speech plus" *(p. 104)* speech accompanied by conduct such as sit-ins, picketing, and demonstrations; protection of this form of speech under the First Amendment is conditional, and restrictions imposed by state or local authorities are acceptable if properly balanced by considerations of public order

strict scrutiny *(p. 101)* a test used by the Supreme Court in racial discrimination cases and other cases involving civil liberties and civil rights that places the burden of proof on the government rather than on the challengers to show that the law in question is constitutional

Thirteenth Amendment *(p. 118)* one of three Civil War amendments; it abolished slavery

For Further Reading

Abraham, Henry J., and Barbara A. Perry. *Freedom and the Court: Civil Rights and Liberties in the United States.* 8th ed. Lawrence: University Press of Kansas, 2004.

Barendt, Eric. *Freedom of Speech.* 2nd ed. New York: Oxford University Press, 2007.

Chen, Anthony S. *The Fifth Freedom: Jobs, Politics, and Civil Rights in the United States, 1941–1972.* Princeton, NJ: Princeton University Press, 2009.

Cook, Byrne. *Reporting the War: Freedom of the Press from the American Revolution to the War on Terror.* New York: Palgrave Macmillan, 2007.

Eisgruber, Christopher. *Religious Freedom and the Constitution.* Cambridge, MA: Harvard University Press, 2010.

Friedman, Barry. *The Will of the People: How Public Opinion Has Influenced the Supreme Court and Shaped the Meaning of the Constitution.* New York: Farrar, Straus and Giroux, 2009.

Friendly, Fred W. *Minnesota Rag: The Dramatic Story of the Landmark Supreme Court Case That Gave New Meaning to Freedom of the Press.* New York: Vintage, 1982.

Greenberg, Jack. *Crusades in the Courts: How a Dedicated Band of Lawyers Fought for the Civil Rights Revolution.* New York: Basic Books, 1994.

Hentoff, Nat. *The First Freedom: The Tumultuous History of Free Speech in America.* New York: Basic Books, 1994.

King, Desmond, and Rogers M. Smith. *Still a House Divided: Race and Politics in Obama's America.* Princeton, NJ: Princeton University Press, 2011.

Lewis, Anthony. *Freedom for the Thought That We Hate: A Biography of the First Amendment.* New York: Basic Books, 2010.

Nichols, Walter. *The Dreamers: How the Undocumented Youth Movement Transformed the Immigrant Rights Debate.* Stanford, CA: Stanford University Press, 2013.

Orth, John. *Due Process of Law: A Brief History.* Lawrence: University Press of Kansas, 2003.

Solove, Daniel. *Nothing to Hide: The False Tradeoff between Privacy and Security.* New Haven, CT: Yale University Press, 2011.

Spitzer, Robert J. *The Right to Bear Arms.* Santa Barbara, CA: ABC-CLIO, 2001.

Spitzer, Robert J. *Saving the Constitution from Lawyers: How Legal Training and Law Reviews Distort Constitutional Meaning.* New York: Cambridge University Press, 2008.

Sundby, Scott. *A Life and Death Decision: A Jury Weighs the Death Penalty.* New York: Palgrave Macmillan, 2007.

How closely should the government follow public opinion? Public opinion on important topics like healthcare and taxes is often sharply divided. In other cases, citizens seem to lack the political knowledge necessary to have informed opinions. These circumstances make it difficult for lawmakers to follow the will of the people.

5

Public Opinion

WHAT GOVERNMENT DOES AND WHY IT MATTERS Economic inequality—a growing gap in income between the very richest Americans and everyone else—is a striking condition of contemporary America. In fact, economic inequality in the United States is the highest it has been since 1928. Political scientist Larry Bartels has shown that the gap between the super rich and everyone else has increased since the 1980s and continues to grow.[1] Between 1993 and 2012, the income of the top 1 percent of Americans grew 86 percent, while the income of the other 99 percent grew less than 7 percent. The median household income of Americans has remained about the same for nearly a decade.[2] The United States has some of the highest economic inequality in the world.[3]

Are Americans aware of this growing economic inequality, and what do they think about it? Public-opinion polls can offer an answer. Polls show that the public's attitude toward growing income inequality has remained mostly unchanged since the 1980s. Less than half of Americans (47 percent) thought the gap between the rich and the poor was a serious problem in 2013.[4] Furthermore, partisanship (see Chapter 7) appears to have a big effect on people's opinions. While 92 percent of Democrats agreed with the statement that "today it's really true that the rich just get richer while the poor get poorer," just 56 percent of Republicans agreed with the statement. The social class of the respondent also shapes public opinion. Of those who describe themselves as lower class, 84 percent agreed that the rich are getting richer, compared with 66 percent of those in the upper class. Those in the upper class also reported being more satisfied and happier.

What does public opinion on inequality mean for American politics? If many Americans are unaware that income inequality is growing, then they may not demand different policies, such as increases in the minimum wage or increased government taxation on the wealthy to support government assistance for the poor. Informed public opinion is crucial in order for citizens to have their preferences heard by elected officials. Low levels of political interest or knowledge may be one reason Americans disagree about the fundamental aspects of social and economic conditions.

In the first four chapters, we have examined the development of the American government. With this chapter, we turn to American politics as it operates in society. We begin with public opinion.

chaptergoals

- Define public opinion, and identify broad types of values and beliefs Americans have about politics (pp. 143–48)

- Explain the major factors that shape specific individual opinions (pp. 148–52)

- Explore when and why public opinion changes and the role that political knowledge plays (pp. 153–55)

- Describe the major forces that shape public opinion (pp. 155–60)

- Describe basic survey methods and other techniques researchers use to measure public opinion (pp. 160–66)

● Public Opinion Represents Attitudes about Politics

Define public opinion, and identify broad types of values and beliefs Americans have about politics

The term **public opinion** refers to the attitudes citizens have about political issues, leaders, institutions, and events. It is useful to distinguish between values and beliefs on the one hand, and attitudes and opinions on the other. **Values (or beliefs)** are the basic principles that shape a person's opinions about political issues and events. They constitute a person's basic orientation to politics. Values underlie deep-rooted goals, aspirations, and ideals that shape an individual's perceptions of political issues and events. Liberty, equality of opportunity, and democracy, for example, are basic political values held by most Americans.

An **attitude (or opinion)** is a specific preference on a particular issue. An individual may have an attitude toward American policy in the Middle East or an opinion about economic inequality in America. The attitude or opinion may have emerged from a broad belief about the purpose of military intervention or about the role of government in the economy, but the opinion itself is very specific. Some attitudes may be short-lived, and can change based on changing circumstances or new information.

Factors such as race, gender, income, age, religion, and region—which not only affect individuals' interests but also shape their experiences and upbringing—influence American's beliefs and opinions. For example, individuals whose incomes differ substantially have correspondingly different views on the desirability of any number of important economic and social programs. In general, the poor—who are the chief beneficiaries of these programs—support them more strongly than do those who are wealthier and pay more of the taxes that fund the programs. Blacks and whites have different views on issues that touch upon civil rights and race relations, such as affirmative action, presumably reflecting differences of interest and historical experience. In recent years, many observers have begun to take note of various differences between the views expressed by men and those expressed by women, especially on foreign policy questions, where women appear to be much more concerned with the dangers of war. Political attitudes are also strongly influenced by partisanship (e.g., Republican versus Democrat) and ideology (e.g., conservative versus liberal).

Opinions about issues and politics have emotional underpinnings as well.[5] Emotional responses to candidates or policies run the gamut from strongly positive to strongly negative, and these emotions are traditionally measured by survey questions asking if a candidate (or individual, event, or issue) makes the respondent feel fearful, anxious, angry, or enthusiastic. Contrary to the idea that public opinion is purely rational, feelings are complicated and often irrational; once individuals become emotionally attached to particular beliefs, they tend to hold on to those beliefs even in the face of contradictory information. Using emotions as a guide, individuals form opinions quickly in response to current events.[6]

As an example, during Barack Obama's first presidential term, about 20 percent of Americans believed that he had been born outside the United States and thus, as a noncitizen, was ineligible for the presidency. Among Republicans, those doubting the president's citizenship numbered more than two in five.[7] This belief persisted even as the verified details of Obama's personal life were widely available and included ample evidence of his American citizenship. To counter the widespread misperception, the White House eventually posted to the Internet a photograph of President Obama's "long-form" birth certificate, showing that he was born in a hospital in Honolulu, Hawaii, on August 4, 1961, at 7:24 P.M.[8] Never in history has a sitting president been forced to prove his citizenship publicly.

Americans Share Common Political Values

Most Americans share a common set of values, including a belief in the principles, if not always the actual practice, of liberty, equality, and democracy. The United States was founded on the principle of individual **liberty**. Americans have always voiced strong support for the idea of liberty and typically support the notion that governmental interference in individuals' lives and property should be kept to a minimum. (Although, in recent years, Americans have grown accustomed to greater levels of governmental intervention than would have been deemed acceptable by the founders of liberal theory.)

Similarly, **equality of opportunity** has always been an important theme in American society. Most Americans believe that all individuals should be allowed to seek personal and material success. Moreover, Americans generally believe that such success should be the result of individual effort and ability, rather than family

Most Americans share certain basic political values, including a belief in equality of opportunity. For example, most people believe that all individuals should be allowed to pursue success based on their own efforts and abilities—and not on their social background.

connections or other forms of special privilege. Quality public education is one of the most important mechanisms for obtaining equality of opportunity in that it allows individuals, regardless of personal or family wealth, a chance to get ahead. Today, the Internet is emerging as an important example of equality of opportunity by providing online access to news, politics, jobs, and other benefits of digital citizenship.[9] Economic opportunity, defined as a good job and a decent standard of living, is a core value in American politics.

Most Americans also believe in **democracy**. They believe that every citizen should have the opportunity to take part in the nation's governmental and policy-making processes and to have some say in determining how he or she is governed, including the right to vote in elections.[10] Figure 5.1 shows there is consensus among Americans on fundamental values.

Obviously, the principles that Americans espouse have not always been put into practice. For 200 years, Americans embraced the principles of individual liberty and equality of opportunity while denying them in practice to generations of African Americans. Yet the strength of the principles ultimately helped overcome practices that deviated from those principles.

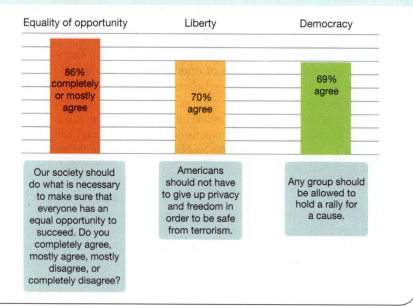

FIGURE 5.1 Americans' Support for Fundamental Values

Americans support equality of opportunity, liberty, and democracy in principle, but do they always support these values in practice? What limits, if any, do you think Americans favor when it comes to equality, liberty, and democracy?

SOURCES: Pew Research Center for the People and the Press Values Survey, www.people-press.org/question-search/?qid=1811658&pid=51&ccid=50#top (accessed 2/5/14). Pew Center/USA Today Poll, January 15–19, 2014, www.pewresearch.org/fact-tank/2014/01/22/most-young-americans-say-snowden-has-served-the-public-interest/(accessed 2/5/2014). First Amendment Center, www.firstamendmentcenter.org (accessed 10/22/12).

Equality of opportunity — Liberty — Democracy

86% completely or mostly agree

70% agree

69% agree

Our society should do what is necessary to make sure that everyone has an equal opportunity to succeed. Do you completely agree, mostly agree, mostly disagree, or completely disagree?

Americans should not have to give up privacy and freedom in order to be safe from terrorism.

Any group should be allowed to hold a rally for a cause.

America's Dominant Political Ideologies Are Liberalism and Conservatism

As we noted in the previous section, Americans share broadly in their fundamental political values. However, the application of these values to specific policies varies quite a bit. The set of underlying orientations, ideas, and beliefs through which we come to understand and interpret politics is called a **political ideology**. In America today, a variety of ideologies compete for attention and support, but two are dominant: liberalism and conservativism.

Liberalism In classical political theory, a *liberal* was someone who favored individual initiative and was suspicious of governments and their ability to manage economic and social affairs—a definition akin to that of today's libertarian. The proponents of a larger and more active government called themselves progressives. In the early twentieth century, many liberals and progressives coalesced around the doctrine of "social liberalism," which represented recognition that government action might be needed to preserve individual liberty. Today's liberals are social liberals rather than classical liberals.

In contemporary politics being **liberal** has come to imply supporting political and social reform; extensive government intervention in the economy; the expansion of federal social services; more vigorous efforts on behalf of the poor, minorities, and women; and greater concern for consumers and the environment. Liberals generally support abortion rights and rights for gays and lesbians, and are concerned with protecting the rights of people accused of crime. Liberals oppose state involvement in religious institutions and state sanction of religious expression. In international affairs, liberals often support arms control, aid to poor nations, and international organizations such as the United Nations and the European Union; liberals generally oppose the development and testing of nuclear weapons, and the use of American troops to influence the affairs of developing nations. Many liberals are opposed to military wars.

Conservatism By contrast, **conservatives** generally support the social and economic status quo and are suspicious of efforts to introduce new political formulae and economic arrangements. They believe strongly that a large and powerful government poses a threat to the freedom of individual citizens. Ironically, today's conservatives espouse the views of classical liberalism. Today, in the domestic arena, conservatives generally oppose the expansion of governmental activity, asserting that solutions to social and economic problems can and should be developed in the private sector. Conservatives particularly oppose efforts to impose government regulation on business, maintaining that regulation frequently leads to economic inefficiency, is costly, and can ultimately lower the entire nation's standard of living. In terms of social policy, many conservatives support school prayer and traditional family arrangements, and are concerned about law and order; conservatives generally oppose abortion, same-sex marriage, and the use of mandatory school busing to achieve the racial integration of schools. In international affairs, conservatism has come to mean support for military intervention and the maintenance of American military power.

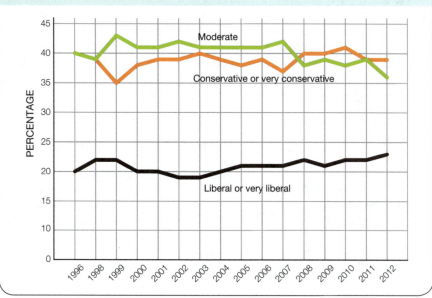

FIGURE 5.2 Americans' Ideology

More Americans identify themselves as "conservatives" than "liberals." During the period shown in this figure, however, Americans have had two Democratic presidents and have several times elected Democratic majorities to a house of Congress. What might account for this apparent discrepancy? What role do moderates play in the electorate? How stable is Americans' ideology over time?

SOURCE: Pew Research Center for the People and the Press, www.pewresearch.org/data-trend/political-attitudes/political-ideology/ (accessed 2/5/14).

Mixing Ideologies Both liberalism and conservatism are far from monolithic ideologies, and until recently most Americans considered themselves moderates, with shades of liberal or conservative values. Many conservatives support at least some government social programs, and many liberals favor strong national defense or oppose government regulations.

Figure 5.2 shows that the percentage of Americans who consider themselves moderates, liberals, or conservatives has remained relatively constant for the past 15 years. Pew surveys indicate that as of 2012, 39 percent of Americans considered themselves conservatives, 37 percent moderates, and 23 percent liberals. These numbers have remained virtually unchanged since the 1990s.

Americans Exhibit Low Trust in Government

One of the most important measures of public opinion in a democracy is trust in government. High levels of political trust create legitimacy for democratic government, whereas very low levels can cause concern. Many scholars and political pundits argue that Americans are becoming more and more disenchanted with traditional political institutions; public approval of Congress reached a low of only 10 percent in 2014.

"Critical citizens" are characterized by high expectations of democracy as an ideal and yet low evaluations of the actual performance of government.[11]

Why does public opinion in the form of trust matter? Declining trust has been linked to declines in political participation and voting. Low confidence in government and elected officials is related to the perception that the government is unable to solve problems, spend money in an effective or efficient way, or represent the interests and policy preferences of average voters.[12]

The Pew Research Center has tracked trust in the federal government from 1958 to 2013 by asking this question on national surveys: "How much of the time do you trust the government in Washington?"[13] The percentage of Americans who indicate they trust the government "just about always or most of the time" has fallen from 73 percent in 1960 to just 19 percent in 2013. These trends span party lines. In 2013, only 10 percent of Republicans indicated they trusted government some or all of the time, compared with 17 percent of Independents and 28 percent of Democrats. (When Republicans hold the White House, slightly more Republicans trust government than Democrats.)

Political Socialization Shapes Public Opinion

Explain the major factors that shape specific individual opinions

People's attitudes about political issues and elected officials tend to be shaped by underlying political beliefs and values. For example, an individual who has negative feelings about government intervention in America's economy and society would probably oppose the development of new social and health care programs. Similarly, someone who distrusts the military would likely be suspicious of any call for the use of U.S. troops. The processes through which these underlying political beliefs and values are formed are collectively called **political socialization**.

Probably no nation, and certainly no democracy, could survive if its citizens did not share some fundamental beliefs. If Americans had few common values or perspectives, it would be very difficult for them to reach agreement on particular issues. In contemporary America, some elements of the socialization process tend to produce differences in outlook, whereas others promote similarities. The **agents of socialization** that shape political beliefs are the family and social networks, social groups and race, political party affiliation, education, and political environment.

The Family and Social Networks Most people acquire their initial orientation to politics from their families. As might be expected, differences in family background tend to produce divergent political perspectives. Although relatively few parents spend much time directly teaching their children about politics, political conversations occur in many households, and children tend to absorb the political views of parents and other caregivers, often without realizing it. Studies find, for example, that political party preferences are initially acquired at home. Children raised in households in which the primary caregivers are Democrats tend to become Democrats, whereas children raised in homes where their caregivers are Republicans tend to favor the Republican Party.[14] Similarly, children reared in politically liberal households are more likely than not to develop a liberal outlook, whereas children raised in politically conservative settings are likely to see the world through conservative

Children are socialized into political environments in ways large and small, from attending political rallies with their parents to hearing off-hand comments at the dinner table. What political opinions did you learn from your parents?

lenses. Family, friends, coworkers, and neighbors are an important source of political orientation for nearly everyone. Online social networks such as Facebook and Twitter likely increase the role of peers in shaping public opinion. One example of the influence of social networks on opinion is the widely shared Facebook meme of an equal sign against a red background, used to symbolize support for same-sex marriage rights. Many individuals changed their profile picture on Facebook to this symbol of marriage equality in June 2013, when the Supreme Court was deciding two cases concerning same-sex marriage. This social media discussion was associated with upticks in public support for gay marriage rights nationally.

Social Groups and Race Another important source of political values is the social groups to which individuals belong. Social groups include those to which individuals belong involuntarily (national, religious, gender, and racial groups, for example) and those they join willingly (such as political parties, labor unions, the military, and environmental, educational, and occupational groups). Group membership gives individuals experiences and perspectives that shape their view of political and social life.

Among the most important of these is race. In American society, for example, the experiences of blacks and whites can differ significantly. Blacks are a minority and have been victims of persecution and discrimination throughout American history. Blacks and whites also have different occupational opportunities, often live in separate communities, and may attend separate schools. Such differences tend to produce distinctive political outlooks. For example, data from CNN, Gallup, and the Pew Center show that blacks and whites differ considerably in their perceptions of the extent of racism in America (see Figure 5.3). Indeed, according to another

FIGURE 5.3 Perception of Fair Treatment across Racial Groups

In the United States, racial groups may not perceive race relations in precisely the same way. How, according to the data in this figure, do blacks and whites differ in their views on race relations? Which group is more likely to think that race relations are good? What factors help to account for these differences in perception?

*12 percent of white and 13 percent of black respondents answered "dont't know."
SOURCES: Pew Research Center, www.pewresearch.org/fact-tank/2013/08/28/the-black-white-and-urban-rural-divides-in-perceptions-of-racial-fairness/ (accessed 2/5/14). Pew Research Center, www.people-press.org/2012/03/30/blacks-view-of-law-enforcement-racial-progress-and-news-coverage-of-race/ (accessed 2/5/14).

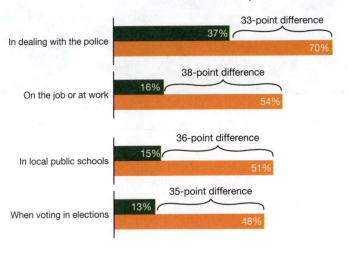

TREATMENT BLACKS RECEIVE

Percentage saying blacks in their community are treated less fairly than whites:

In dealing with the police — White 37%, Black 70% — 33-point difference

On the job or at work — White 16%, Black 54% — 38-point difference

In local public schools — White 15%, Black 51% — 36-point difference

When voting in elections — White 13%, Black 48% — 35-point difference

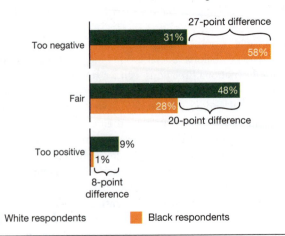

NEWS COVERAGE OF BLACKS

News coverage of blacks is:*

Too negative — White 31%, Black 58% — 27-point difference

Fair — White 48%, Black 28% — 20-point difference

Too positive — White 9%, Black 1% — 8-point difference

■ White respondents   ■ Black respondents

TABLE 5.1

Disagreements among Men and Women on Public Policy Issues

On many policy issues, there is an approximately 10-point gap between the opinion of men and women. What might explain this consistent difference?

POLICY	MEN	WOMEN	GENDER GAP
Agree that same-sex marriage should be legal in all/most cases	40	53	13 points
Agree that religious institutions that object to contraceptive use should be given an exemption from insurance mandate	54	42	12 points
Believe that government does not do enough for poor people	52	62	10 points
Believe the best way to ensure peace is through good diplomacy	53	62	9 points
Believe the country should do whatever it takes to protect the environment	67	75	8 points

SOURCE: Pew Research Center, www.people-press.org/2012/03/29/the-gender-gap-three-decades-old-as-wide-as -ever/ (accessed 2/5/14).

CNN poll, 47 percent of white respondents thought racism fairly or very common, while almost 49 percent thought it was rare in the United States. Among African Americans, on the other hand, fully 86 percent thought racism was common and only 12 percent said it was rare, almost a 40-point difference between blacks and whites.[15] Interestingly, Hispanic Americans, who have also been victims of racism in the United States, are less likely than African Americans to see America as a racist society; in a 2008 survey, 52 percent of Hispanic Americans and 55 percent of white Americans said that race relations in the United States were generally good. Only 29 percent of black Americans agreed.[16]

Men and women have important differences of opinion as well. Reflecting differences in social roles and occupational patterns, women tend to oppose military intervention more than men, are more likely than men to favor policies to protect the environment, and are more likely to support government social and health care programs. Perhaps because of these differences on issues, women are more likely than men to vote for Democratic candidates. This tendency of men's and women's opinions to differ is known as the **gender gap**. Table 5.1 shows that across different policy areas, men's and women's opinions vary fairly consistently by about 10 points.

Party Affiliation Political party membership or loyalty is one of the most important factors affecting political orientation.[17] We can think of partisanship as red-tinted (referring to the Republican Party) or blue-tinted (referring to the Democratic

Party) glasses that color opinion on a vast array of issues. Partisans tend to rely on party leaders and the media for cues on the appropriate positions to take on major political issues.[18] Walter Lippmann, an influential political commentator of the mid-twentieth century, argued that public opinion is but an echo of elite positions on policy issues, and many others studying public opinion agree.

According to recent studies, differences between Democratic and Republican partisans on a variety of political and policy questions are greater today than during any other period for which data are available. On issues of national security, for example, Republicans have become very "hawkish," whereas Democrats have become quite "dovish." In an October 2003 survey, 85 percent of Republicans but only 39 percent of Democrats thought that America's war against Iraq was a good idea.[19] Gaps on social and economic issues are just as broad. Some refer to the ever-widening chasm between the parties as the "politics of extremism." An example is the showdown between congressional Republicans and Democrats over the federal budget and whether to raise the nation's debt ceiling (legal permission for the government to borrow more money to pay its obligations). Republicans insisted on cuts in President Obama's Affordable Care Act; Democrats refused. This clash led to the shutdown of the federal government for two weeks in 2013.

Education Often thought of as a great equalizer, education is also an important source of differences in political perspectives. Governments use public education to try to teach all children a common set of civic values; it is mainly in school that Americans acquire their basic beliefs in liberty, equality, and democracy. In history classes, students are taught that the Founders fought for the principle of liberty. In studying such topics as the Constitution, the Civil War, and the civil rights movement, students are taught the importance of equality. Research finds education to be a strong predictor of tolerance for racial minorities.[20] Through participation in class elections and student government, students are taught the virtues of democracy. These lessons are repeated in every grade, and in many contexts. It is no wonder they constitute such an important element in Americans' beliefs.

At the same time, differences in formal education are strongly associated with differences in political outlook. In particular, those who attend college are often exposed to modes of thought that will distinguish them from their friends and neighbors who do not pursue college diplomas. One of the major differences between college graduates and other Americans is that higher levels of education are associated with greater involvement in politics. College graduates are more likely to vote, join campaigns, take part in protests, and generally make their voices heard.[21]

Political Environment The conditions and events that exist when individuals and groups enter political life shape their political attitudes and values. Although political beliefs are influenced by family background and group membership, the content and character of these views is, to a large extent, determined by political circumstances. For example, the baby-boom generation that came of age in the 1960s was exposed both to the Vietnam War itself and also to widespread antiwar protests, which has made that generation suspicious of foreign wars. The September 11 attacks in 2001 and the war on terrorism helped shape the political lives of those who came of age in the 1990s and 2000s, making them more concerned about security and safety.

Political Knowledge Is Important in Shaping Public Opinion

> **Explore when and why public opinion changes and the role that political knowledge plays**

What best explains whether citizens are generally consistent in their political views or inconsistent and open to the influence of others? In general, knowledgeable citizens are better able to evaluate new information and determine if it is relevant to and consistent with their beliefs and opinions.[22] As a result, better-informed individuals can recognize their political interests and act consistently to further those interests. But political knowledge is generally low in America. In one widely reported survey, 71 percent of Americans could not name their own member of Congress.[23]

This raises the question of how much political knowledge is necessary for one to act as an effective citizen. In an important study of political knowledge in the United States, the political scientists Michael X. Delli Carpini and Scott Keeter found that the average American exhibits little knowledge of political institutions, processes, leaders, and policy debates.[24] Does this ignorance of key political facts matter? Delli Carpini and Keeter also found that political knowledge is not evenly distributed throughout the population. Those with higher education, income, and occupational status and who are members of social or political organizations are more likely to know about and be active in politics. An interest in politics reinforces an individual's sense of political efficacy (the belief that their actions and opinions matter) and provides an incentive to acquire additional knowledge and information about politics. As a result, individuals with higher income and education also have more knowledge and influence and thus are better able to get what they want from government.

Shortcuts and Cues Because being politically informed requires a substantial investment of time and energy, most Americans seek to acquire political information and to make political decisions "on the cheap," making use of shortcuts for political evaluation and decision making rather than engaging in a lengthy process of information gathering. Researchers have found that individuals rely on cues and information from party elites and the media to aid them in attitude formation.[25] Other "inexpensive" ways to become informed include taking cues from trusted friends, relatives, colleagues, or religious leaders.[26] By means of these informational shortcuts, average citizens can form political opinions that are, in most instances, consistent with their underlying preferences. Studies show that even individuals with low levels of political knowledge are able to make relatively informed political choices by relying on these voter cues. Scholars agree that people rely on shortcuts when forming their opinions on politics and public policy.[27]

The public's reliance on elite cues has taken on new significance in today's era of elite polarization. As the political parties and elected officials have become increasingly polarized, has this change affected the way that citizens arrive at their opinions? Political scientists James Druckman, Erik Peterson, and Rune Slothuus have found stark evidence that polarized political environments fundamentally change how citizens make decisions and form opinions. Notably, polarization between the parties means that party endorsements (such as of an issue or candidate) have a larger impact on public opinion formation than they used to. At the same time, polarization decreases the impact of other information on public opinion—that is, party polarization may actually reduce levels of political knowledge. Thus, elite polarization may have negative implications for public opinion formation.[28]

Skim and Scan Another factor affecting political knowledge is the *form* in which people consume information. The transformation of political information in the digital era has had a profound effect on the way the news is reported and how citizens obtain information about politics. A 2012 survey conducted by the Pew Internet and American Life Project found that 36 percent of social networking site users say those sites are important for their political information, and more than three in four Americans read the news online or seek political information online. Recent research also indicates a trend in journalism toward shorter articles and flashier headlines. Americans today are likely to read the news by scanning and skimming multiple headlines online, in bits and bytes, rather than by reading long news articles.

Nicholas Carr's best-selling book, *The Shallows: What the Internet Is Doing to Our Brains*, details the decline in the deep processing that underpins "mindful knowledge acquisition, inductive analysis, critical thinking, imagination, and reflection." He argues that although the Internet may seem to be making us smarter by virtue of giving us access to more data faster than ever, it also threatens the type of intelligence that is measured by depth of thought rather than sheer speed.[29] The habits of browsing, scanning, and reading in a nonlinear fashion have undermined the capacity to immerse oneself in longer works of writing, such as books.

Extending this logic to politics, public opinion may become less rational and more erratic, as individuals will lack a carefully developed understanding on which to base

The public is constantly exposed to competing messages from political elites. Viewers of NBC's popular show Meet the Press *heard different facts and points of view from Democratic senator Kirsten Gillibrand and Republican representative Mike Rogers. Political scientists study the effect of competing messages on public opinion.*

their opinions, despite the overwhelming volume of information about politics online. This trend might explain the significant percentage of Americans who believe political stories that are untrue or based on misinformation, such as the claim that President Obama is not a U.S. citizen. However, as we've seen in this chapter, some research indicates that most individuals use simple cues and shortcuts to process political information. If this is correct, scanning and skimming headlines might provide a reasonable way to be informed about politics without extensive time or effort.

Costs to Democracy? If political scientists are correct in their findings that many citizens base their opinions (and votes) on inadequate knowledge and an overreliance on cues from political elites, this raises a critical question: If political knowledge is necessary for effective citizenship, how does a general lack of such knowledge affect the way we govern ourselves?

Although understandable and, perhaps, inevitable, low levels of political knowledge and engagement weaken American democracy in two ways. First, those who lack political information cannot effectively defend their own political interests and can easily become losers in political struggles. The presence of large numbers of politically inattentive or ignorant individuals means that political power can more easily be manipulated by political elites, the media, and wealthy special interests. If public opinion is easily manipulated, this would not bode well for democracy. But other research has shown that individuals are quite stable and rational in their policy formation. For a closer look at the stability of public opinion on three issues, see Figure 5.4. Notice that even when public opinion has shifted, as in the case of same-sex marriage, the shifts have been relatively steady; we don't see dramatic jumps up and down.

Second, if knowledge is power, then a lack of knowledge can contribute to growing political and economic inequality. When individuals are unaware of their interests or how to pursue them, it is virtually certain that political outcomes will not favor them. As discussed in the introduction, America has one of the largest gaps between the rich and the poor of any nation in the world. But rather than raise taxes, over the past several decades, the United States has substantially reduced the rate of taxation levied on its wealthiest citizens. Political scientist Larry Bartels has shown that, surprisingly, most Americans favored the tax cuts, including millions of middle- and lower-middle-class citizens who did not stand to benefit from the tax policy. The explanation for this odd state of affairs appears to be a lack of political knowledge. Millions of individuals who were unlikely to derive benefit from President Bush's tax policy thought they would.[30]

● The Media and Government Mold Opinion

> **Describe the major forces that shape public opinion**

When individuals attempt to form opinions about particular political issues, events, or personalities, they seldom do so in isolation. Typically, they are confronted with— sometimes bombarded by—the efforts of a host of individuals and groups seeking to persuade them to adopt a particular point of view. During the 2012 presidential election, someone trying to decide what to think about Barack Obama or

FIGURE 5.4

FIGURE 5.4 Stability in Public Opinion

Public opinion on some issues has stayed stable in the last two decades, while opinion on other issues has shifted. What might explain why opinion on same-sex marriage has changed, while opinion on abortion has stayed relatively constant?

SOURCE: Pew Research Center, www.pewresearch.org/data-trend/domestic-issues/abortion/; www.pewresearch .org/data-trend/domestic-issues/gun-control/; www.pewresearch.org/data-trend/national-conditions/personal -finances/; www.pewresearch.org/data-trend/domestic-issues/attitudes-on-gay-marriage/ (accessed 5/1/14).

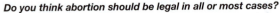

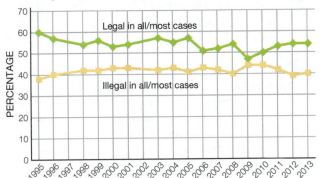

Do you think abortion should be legal in all or most cases?

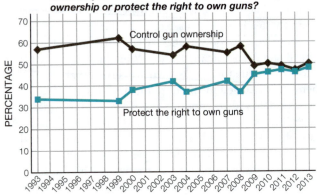

What do you think is more important, to control gun ownership or protect the right to own guns?

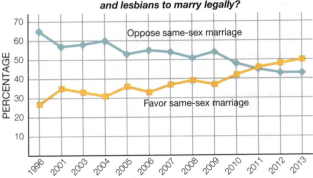

Do you favor or oppose allowing gays and lesbians to marry legally?

Mitt Romney could hardly avoid an avalanche of opinions expressed through the media, in meetings, or in conversations with friends. The **marketplace of ideas** is the interplay of opinions and views that occurs as competing forces attempt to persuade as many people as possible to accept a particular position on a particular issue. Given this constant exposure to the ideas of others, it is virtually impossible for most individuals to resist some modification of their own beliefs. Three forces that play important roles in shaping opinions in the marketplace are the government, private groups, and the news media.[31]

The Government Leads Public Opinion

All governments try to influence, manipulate, or manage their citizens' beliefs. But the extent to which public opinion is actually affected by governmental public relations can be limited. Often, governmental claims are disputed by the media, by interest groups, and at times even by opposing forces within the government itself.

This hasn't stopped modern presidents from focusing a great deal of attention on shaping public opinion to boost support for their policy agendas. Franklin Delano Roosevelt promoted his policy agenda directly to the American people through his famous "fireside chat" radio broadcasts. The George W. Bush administration developed an extensive public-relations program to bolster popular support for its policies, including its war against terrorism. These efforts included presidential speeches, media appearances by administration officials, numerous press conferences, and thousands of press releases presenting the administration's views.[32] Using the runway of an aircraft carrier as his stage, a confident Commander in Chief Bush, dressed in a flight suit, proclaimed the end of the Iraq War in 2003. His statement was premature by eight years, but was effective in maintaining public support for the Iraq War. Like its predecessors, the Obama administration has sought to shape public opinion in the United States and abroad, relying on the power of the president's oratorical skills to build support for his administration's initiatives in domestic and foreign policy. But Obama's White House is unique in using social media to promote the president's policy agenda. Hourly posts on Facebook promote Obama's policies and campaign, and serve to personalize the president.

Private Groups Also Shape Public Opinion

Important political ideas that become prominent in political life are developed and spread not only by government officials but also by important economic and political groups searching for issues that will advance their causes. One especially notable example is the abortion issue, which has inflamed American politics over the past 40 years. The notion of a fetal "right to life," whose proponents seek to outlaw abortion and overturn the Supreme Court's 1973 *Roe v. Wade* decision, was developed by conservative politicians who saw the issue of abortion as a means of uniting Catholic and Protestant conservatives and linking both groups to the Republican Party, along with various right-to-life groups.[33] Catholic and evangelical Protestant religious leaders organized to denounce abortion from their church pulpits and, increasingly, from their television, radio, and Internet pulpits, including the Christian Broadcasting Network (CBN). Religious leaders have also organized demonstrations, pickets, and disruptions at abortion clinics throughout the nation.[34] These efforts have helped win the enactment of stricter abortions laws in many states.

The News Media's Message Impacts Public Opinion

The media are among the most powerful forces operating in the marketplace of ideas. As we shall see in Chapter 6, the mass media are not simply neutral messengers for ideas developed by others. Instead, they are very much opinion makers in their own right and have an enormous impact on popular attitudes. For example, for the past 40 years, since the publication of the Pentagon Papers by the *New York Times* and the exposure of the Watergate scandal led by the *Washington Post*, the national news media have relentlessly investigated personal and official wrongdoing on the part of politicians and public officials. The continual media presentation of corruption in government has undoubtedly contributed to the general attitude of cynicism and distrust that prevails in much of the general public, as discussed above.

At the same time, the ways in which media coverage interprets or "frames" specific events can have a major impact on popular responses and opinions about these events (see Chapter 6). For example, the Bush administration went to great lengths to persuade the media to follow its lead in their coverage of America's response to terrorism in the months following the September 11, 2001, attacks. The media mostly went along, presenting the administration's military campaigns in Afghanistan and Iraq, as well as its domestic antiterrorist efforts, in a positive light. Even supposedly liberal newspapers such as the *New York Times*, which had strongly opposed Bush in the 2000 election, praised his leadership and published articles supportive of the president's bellicose rhetoric against the Iraqi regime prior to March 2003, when President Bush ordered the invasion of Iraq.

Government Policies Also Respond to Public Opinion

Studies generally suggest that elected officials pay attention to the preferences of the public.[35] For example, political scientists Benjamin Page and Robert Shapiro have studied the relationship between changes in opinion toward various political issues and the policy outcomes that most closely correspond to the issues.[36] The results show that shifts in public opinion on particular issues do in fact tend to lead to changes in public policy. One such example is in health care. A July 2009 Pew survey found that 65 percent of Americans favored a law "requiring all Americans to have health insurance, and government aid for those unable to afford it."[37] The federal government adopted the Affordable Health Care Act for America in 2010, which required health insurance for all citizens.

However, there is reason to question whether prevailing public opinion causes politicians to make policies that reflect the general will, or whether government policy in fact causes changes in public opinion. The relationship between government policy and opinion may be dynamic, wherein policy responds to opinion but opinion also shifts based on new government policies.[38] Studies of whether government policy can affect public opinion have found it to have an effect in various policy areas, such as the environment, health care, welfare reform, and smoking bans.

Today, same-sex marriage is one of the most prominent policies engaging opinion on morality and civil rights. Opinion polls show that support for same-sex marriage is

AMERICA
Side by Side

Opinion on the Economy and the Environment

Economic growth and climate change are two important policy issues in countries around the globe. Unlike some issues, which may be on a nation's agenda at one moment but then fade from view, maintaining robust economic growth is almost always a top government priority. But there may be tradeoffs between promoting the economy and other goals such as protecting the environment. The environment often suffers from pollution and other consequences of economic development; at the same time, environmental regulations may slow economic growth if they impose costs on businesses.

A World Values Survey asked individuals around the world which was more important to them: protecting the environment, even if it means sacrificing economic growth, or promoting economic growth, even if it means sacrificing the environment. What might explain the differences in public opinion on this issue across countries?

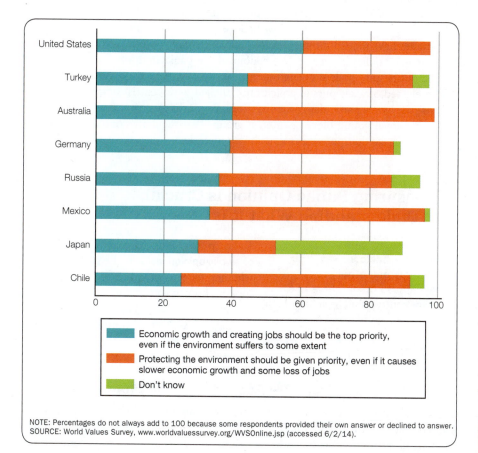

Economic growth and creating jobs should be the top priority, even if the environment suffers to some extent

Protecting the environment should be given priority, even if it causes slower economic growth and some loss of jobs

Don't know

NOTE: Percentages do not always add to 100 because some respondents provided their own answer or declined to answer.
SOURCE: World Values Survey, www.worldvaluessurvey.org/WVSOnline.jsp (accessed 6/2/14).

To what extent do political leaders listen to the opinions of their constituents? To what extent should they listen? Is Calvin's father right that leaders should do what they believe is right, not what the public wants?

increasing. Might it be that state policies send a signal either legitimizing it (in states recognizing same-sex marriage) or stigmatizing it (in states that prohibit same-sex marriage)? Some new research suggests that opinion favoring marriage rights is increasing more quickly in states that have legalized same-sex marriage than in other states. This is an example where state policy may play an important role in changing public opinion.

Of course, sometimes public opinion and policy do not align. At times, officials act on their own preferences if they believe it will benefit government or society, and studies have indeed shown that lawmakers typically do use their own judgment when making policy choices.[39] The bailout of the banks in 2008, for example, was carried out despite polls showing that a majority of Americans opposed this policy. When elected officials pursue policies not aligned with centrist opinion, it is often because they view particular groups of the electorate as more important than others. Inevitably, loyal voting blocs or interest groups that regularly contribute to a candidate may have their interests more closely represented than the general public.[40]

● Measuring Public Opinion Is Crucial to Understanding What It Is

Describe basic survey methods and other techniques researchers use to measure public opinion

Today public officials make extensive use of **public-opinion polls** to help them decide whether to run for office, what policies to support, how to vote on important legislation, and what types of appeals to make in their campaigns. All recent presidents and other major political figures have worked closely with polls and pollsters. In addition, major media outlets and other private organizations make extensive use of polls and polling.

Public-Opinion Surveys Are Accurate If Done Properly

It is not feasible to interview the more than 300 million Americans residing in the United States on their opinions of who should be the next president or what should be done about important policy issues such as how to improve the economy and create jobs. Instead, pollsters take a **sample** of the population and use it to make inferences (e.g., extrapolations and educated guesses) about the preferences of the population as a whole. For a political survey to be an accurate representation of the population, it must meet certain requirements, including an appropriate sampling method, a sufficient sample size, and the avoidance of selection bias.[41]

Representative Samples The most representative sample is what statisticians call a **simple random sample (or probability sample)**, in which every individual in the population has an equal probability of being selected as a respondent. Since we don't have a complete list of all Americans, pollsters use census data, lists of households, and telephone numbers to create lists, drawing samples from regions and then neighborhoods within regions. Just as in a simple random sample, everyone has an equal chance of being selected for the survey. Rolls of registered voters are often used in political surveys designed to predict the outcome of an election.

Another method for drawing samples of the national population is a technique called **random digit dialing** of landline and cell phone numbers, but not business phones or inoperative home telephones. In this method, respondents are selected at random from a list of 10-digit telephone numbers, with every effort made to avoid bias in the construction of the sample. A computer random-number generator is used to produce a list of 10-digit telephone numbers. Given that 98 percent of Americans have telephones (cell phones or landlines), this technique usually results in a random national sample. This allows almost every citizen a chance of being included in the survey. Telephone surveys are fairly accurate, cost-effective, and flexible in the type of questions that can be asked. Websites such as RealClearPolitics.com list the results of every political survey released each day. Every week, the opinions of Americans are measured regarding not just candidates and public policies but also a vast array of products (toothpaste), entertainment (movie-star romances), and even college political science textbooks!

Sample Size A sample must be large enough to provide an accurate representation of the population. Surprisingly, though, the size of the population being measured doesn't matter, only the size of the *sample*. A survey of 1,000 people is just as effective for measuring the opinions of all Texans, a state with 26 million residents, as the opinions of all Americans, with over 314 million residents.

Flipping a coin shows how this works. After tossing a coin 10 times, the number of heads and tails may not be close to 5 and 5. After 100 tosses of the coin, though, the percentage of heads should be close to 50 percent, and after 1,000 tosses, very close to 50 percent. In fact, after 1,000 tosses, there is a 95 percent chance that the number of heads will be somewhere between 46.9 percent and 53.1 percent. This 3.1 percent variation from 50 percent is called the **sampling error (or margin of error)**—a polling error that arises based on the small size of the sample. That is, it is the amount of error we can expect with a typical 1,000-person survey. Normally, samples of 1,000 people are considered sufficient for accurately measuring public opinion through the use of surveys. When the media refer to a "scientific poll" conducted by a highly respected polling firm, they actually mean a poll that has followed the steps just outlined: a poll based on a random (representative) sample of the population that is sufficiently large and avoids selection bias.

Survey Design and Question Wording Even with reliable sampling procedures and a large sample, surveys may fail to reflect the true distribution of opinion within a target population. One frequent source of measurement error is the wording of survey questions. The precise words used in a question can have an enormous impact on the answers that question elicits. The reliability of survey results can also be adversely affected by poor question format, faulty ordering of questions, poor vocabulary, ambiguity of questions, or questions with built-in biases.

Often, seemingly minor differences in the wording of a question can convey vastly different meanings to respondents, and thus produce quite different response patterns (see Box 5.1). For example, for many years the University of Chicago's National Opinion Research Center has asked respondents whether they think the federal government is spending too much, too little, or about the right amount of money on "assistance for the poor." Answering the question posed this way, about two-thirds of all respondents seem to believe that the government is spending too little. However, the same survey also asks whether the government spends too much, too little, or about the right amount for "welfare." When the word *welfare* is substituted for "assistance for the poor," about half of all respondents indicate that too much is being spent.[42] Today, pollsters are increasingly turning to the use of online surveys, often using similar techniques to those of telephone surveys. But while Internet surveys can be more efficient, less costly, and have larger samples, many online surveys do not use probability sampling (random sampling), and thus are not representative of the American population.

Why Are Some Polls Wrong?

The history of polling over the past century contains many instances of getting it wrong and learning valuable lessons in the process. As a result, polling techniques have grown more and more sophisticated, and pollsters have a more and more nuanced understanding of how public opinion is formed and how it is revealed.

Social Desirability Effects Political scientists have found that survey results can be inaccurate when the survey includes questions about sensitive issues for which individuals do not wish to share their true preferences. For example, respondents tend to overreport voting in elections and the frequency of their church attendance. Why? These activities are deemed socially appropriate, so even if the respondents do not vote or attend church regularly, they may feel social pressure to do so, and thus they may respond inaccurately on a survey. Political scientist Adam Berinsky calls this the **social desirability effect**, whereby respondents report what they expect the interviewer wishes to hear or whatever they think is socially acceptable rather than what they actually believe or know to be true.[43] On other topics, respondents may feel self-conscious and so choose not to answer. This happens with questions about people's income.

Questions that ask directly about race or gender are particularly problematic. "Social desirability" makes it difficult to learn voters' true opinions about touchy subjects such as racial attitudes because respondents hide their preferences from

It Depends on How You Ask

THE SITUATION
The public's desire for tax cuts can be hard to measure. In 2000, pollsters asked what should be done with the nation's budget surplus and got different results depending on the specifics of the question.

THE QUESTION
President Clinton has proposed setting aside approximately two-thirds of an expected budget surplus to fix the Social Security system. What do you think the leaders in Washington should do with the remainder of the surplus?

VARIATION 1
Should the money be used for a tax cut, or should it be used to fund new government programs?

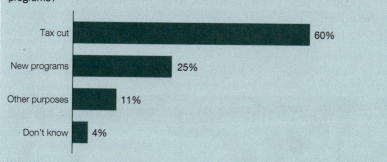

Tax cut	60%
New programs	25%
Other purposes	11%
Don't know	4%

VARIATION 2
Should the money be used for a tax cut, or should it be spent on programs for education, the environment, health care, crime fighting, and military defense?

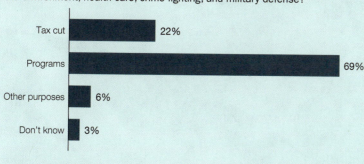

Tax cut	22%
Programs	69%
Other purposes	6%
Don't know	3%

SOURCE: Pew Research Center, reported in the *New York Times*, January 30, 2000, p. WK 3.

the interviewer for fear of social retribution (against what might be deemed "politically incorrect"). However, surveys can be designed to tap respondents' latent or hidden feelings about sensitive issues without directly asking them to express overt opinions. For example, one such survey examined support for a generic black presidential candidate; the study was conducted in mid-2007, well before Barack Obama became president. The survey was designed to tap underlying attitudes toward a black candidate, allowing researchers to compare openly expressed support for such a candidate with unvoiced hidden attitudes toward the same candidate. Results show that 30 percent of Americans exhibited reluctance about voting for a generic black presidential candidate, even though, when asked directly, nearly 85 percent had claimed they would support such a candidate.[44]

Selection Bias The importance of accurate sampling was brought home early in the history of political polling when a 1936 *Literary Digest* poll predicted that the Republican presidential candidate, Alf Landon, would defeat the Democratic incumbent, Franklin Delano Roosevelt, in that year's presidential election. The actual election, of course, ended in a Roosevelt landslide. The main problem with the survey was what is called **selection bias** in drawing the sample. This is a polling error that arises when the sample is not representative of the population being studied, which creates errors in overrepresenting or underrepresenting some opinions. The pollsters had relied on telephone directories and automobile registration rosters to produce the survey sample. During the Great Depression, though, only wealthier Americans owned telephones and automobiles. Thus, the millions

Though public opinion is important, it is not always easy to interpret, and polls often fail to predict accurately how Americans will vote. In 1948 election-night polls showed Thomas Dewey defeating Harry S. Truman for the presidency. The Chicago News Tribune *trusted the polls and incorrectly printed a banner headline proclaiming Dewey the winner, which a triumphant Truman displayed when he won the election by a margin of approximately 4 percent.*

of working-class Americans who constituted Roosevelt's base of support were excluded from the sample.

Selection bias was also at play in preelection polls in the 2012 presidential election, when Gallup significantly overestimated Latino support for Mitt Romney, the Republican candidate, and so predicted a very close race between Romney and the Democratic candidate, President Obama. Blogger Nate Silver, however, predicted Obama would win the election by a comfortable margin. His estimates were based on aggregating information from many different public-opinion polls. Polls designed specifically to measure the opinions of Latinos estimated that 7 in 10 Latinos would vote for Obama over Romney, which was in fact what happened. The Gallup numbers were incorrect because of selection bias (i.e., they had too few Latinos in their sample and therefore their predictions were inaccurate).

In recent years, the issue of selection bias has been complicated by the fact that growing numbers of individuals refuse to answer pollsters' questions, or they use such devices as answering machines and caller ID to screen unwanted callers. Additionally, response rates for surveys (the percentage of calls attempted that are completed) have been falling steeply. Response rates for the Pew Research Center's highly respected surveys, for example, are less than 20 percent. Studies suggest that the views of respondents and nonrespondents can differ, especially along social class lines. Upper-class individuals are often less willing to respond to surveys or less likely to be at home than their working-class counterparts, which can bias telephone surveys. Additionally, women are significantly more likely to answer telephone surveys than men. This can lead to incorrect inferences of public opinion.

Push Polling Push polling introduces a different type of bias into public-opinion polling. Push polls are not scientific polls, as just discussed, and are not intended to yield accurate information about a population. Instead, they involve asking a respondent a loaded question about a political candidate designed to elicit the response sought by the pollster and, simultaneously, to shape the respondent's perception of the candidate in question. One of the most notorious uses of push polling occurred in the 2000 South Carolina Republican presidential primary, in which George W. Bush defeated John McCain and went on to win the presidency. Callers working for Bush supporters asked conservative white voters if they would be more or less likely to vote for McCain if they knew he had fathered an illegitimate black child. Because McCain often campaigned with a daughter whom he and his wife had adopted from Mother Teresa's orphanage in Bangladesh, many voters accepted the premise of the "poll." The purpose of such push polls is not to solicit opinions as much as to plant negative ideas about the opposing candidate to, in this case, "push" McCain voters away from him. More than 100 consulting firms across the nation now specialize in push polling.[45] Push polls may be one reason Americans are becoming increasingly skeptical about the practice of polling and increasingly unwilling to answer pollsters' questions.[46]

The Bandwagon Effect Sometimes polling can even create its own reality. The so-called **bandwagon effect** occurs when polling results influence people to support the candidate marked as the probable victor. This is especially true in the presidential nomination process, where there may be multiple candidates within one party vying to be the party's nominee. A candidate who has "momentum"—that is, one who demonstrates a lead in the polls—usually finds it considerably easier to raise campaign funds than a candidate whose poll standing is low. And with these additional funds, poll leaders can often afford to pay for television time and other campaign activities that will generate positive media attention and thus cement their advantage.

Public Opinion, Democracy,
and Your Future

This chapter has focused on the role of public opinion in American politics. A major purpose of democratic government, with its participatory procedures and representative institutions, is to ensure that political leaders will heed the public will. And, indeed, a good deal of evidence suggests that they do.[47] Some political scientists argue, however, that government policy is much less responsive to public opinion on the issues that really count, and that when the interests of elites are at stake, government officials are much more likely to represent the opinions of the affluent than the poor.[48]

But new technology may be able to help. The migration of politics online has greatly expanded the amount of information available and the ease of becoming informed. Given this new media environment, we might expect public opinion to be more accurate, even about the nuances of public policy. Digital citizenship offers the promise of a more informed electorate, with citizens having multiple venues in which to translate their opinions into political action and demand improved representation from political leaders.

At the same time, the Internet raises concerns about the accuracy and consistency of public opinion. Some research finds that the gap between the haves and the have-nots in terms of political knowledge actually increases with the availability of more information. The implications are significant, given the explosion of political coverage online. The research suggests that with more information, public opinion may actually be less consistent.[49]

Of course, technological change will continue; the media of 2040 will not be the same as the media of 2015. Young adults will face a changing media environment, just as their parents did. Such technological evolution may bring yet further changes to our understanding of the relationship between public opinion, government, and the media. New media may make it easier than ever for citizens to stay informed about the actions of their elected leaders, or new media may make it easier for leaders to learn about their constituents' preferences. What can citizens do to stay informed and make their views known amidst a changing media and political environment?

plugin

Inform

Read about the specific methods used by the pollsters who provide information about public opinion. For example, read the page "How does Gallup polling work?" on gallup.com.

Express

Take the Political Compass test at www.politicalcompass.org or the Pew Research Center's poltical typology quiz at www.people-press .org. These sites rate your political ideology based on your opinions.

Connect

Look up polling results for an issue that you care about to see how your opinion compares with others'. Consider checking poll aggregators like www.pollingreport .com or www.realclearpolitics.com for multiple polls on a range of topics. Pay attention to whether public opinion on your issue has changed over time.

Act

Post a survey question about a political issue on SurveyMonkey or Facebook and send to your class-mates. How do the results of your poll compare to national public opinion on the same issue?

Practice Quiz

1. The term *public opinion* is used to describe *(p. 143)*
   a) the collected speeches and writings made by a president during his or her term in office.
   b) the analysis of events broadcast by news reporters during the evening news.
   c) the beliefs and attitudes that people have about issues.
   d) decisions of the Supreme Court.
   e) any political statement that is made by a citizen outside of his or her private residence or place of employment.

2. Variables such as income, education, race, gender, and ethnicity *(p. 143)*
   a) matter only for people's opinions on moral issues but not for their opinions on economic issues.
   b) have consistently been a challenge to America's core political values.
   c) have little impact on political opinions.
   d) help explain why public-opinion polls are so unreliable.
   e) help explain differences of political opinion in America.

3. Today, the term _____ refers to an ideology that supports social and political reform, greater economic equality, and expansion of government social services. *(p. 146)*
   a) libertarianism
   b) liberalism
   c) conservatism
   d) democracy
   e) moderate

4. The process by which Americans learn political beliefs and values is called *(p. 148)*
   a) brainwashing.
   b) propaganda.
   c) indoctrination.
   d) political socialization.
   e) political development.

5. Which of the following is *not* an agent of socialization? *(p. 148)*
   a) political conditions
   b) political attitudes
   c) social groups
   d) the family
   e) education

6. When men and women respond differently to issues of public policy, this difference is an example of *(p. 151)*
   a) liberalism.
   b) educational differences.
   c) feminism.
   d) party politics.
   e) the gender gap.

7. The fact that the public is inattentive to politics and must frequently rely on informational shortcuts has which of the following effects on American democracy? *(pp. 153–55)*
   a) strengthens it by providing politicians with more freedom to act on a wider variety of issues
   b) strengthens it by increasing the number of people who participate in politics
   c) weakens it by making it easier for various institutions and political actors to manipulate the political process
   d) weakens it by making every citizen equally empowered to produce outcomes that are consistent with their interests on every issue
   e) has no effect on it

8. Which of the following are the most important external influences on how political opinions are formed in the marketplace of ideas? *(pp. 155–60)*
   a) the government, private groups, and the news media
   b) the unemployment rate, the Dow Jones industrial average, and the NASDAQ composite
   c) random digit dialing surveys, push polls, and the bandwagon effect

d) the Constitution, the Declaration of Independence, and the *Federalist Papers*
e) the legislative branch, the executive branch, and the judicial branch

9. Which of the following is the term used in public-opinion polling to denote the small group representing the opinions of the whole population? *(p. 161)*
   a) control group
   b) sample
   c) micropopulation
   d) respondents
   e) median voters

10. A *push poll* is a poll in which *(p. 165)*
    a) the questions are designed to shape the respondent's opinion rather than measure the respondent's opinion.
    b) the questions are designed to measure the respondent's opinion rather than shape the respondent's opinion.

c) the questions are designed to reduce measurement error.
d) the sample is chosen to include only undecided or independent voters.
e) the sample is not representative of the population it is drawn from.

11. A familiar polling problem is the "bandwagon effect," which occurs when *(pp. 165–66)*
    a) the same results are used over and over again.
    b) polling results influence people to support the candidate marked as the probable victor in a campaign.
    c) polling results influence people to support the candidate who is trailing in a campaign.
    d) background noise makes it difficult for a pollster and a respondent to communicate with each other.
    e) a large number of people refuse to answer a pollster's questions.

Key Terms

agents of socialization *(p. 148)* social institutions, including families and schools, that help to shape individuals' basic political beliefs and values

attitude (or opinion) *(p. 143)* a specific preference on a particular issue

bandwagon effect *(p. 165)* a shift in electoral support to the candidate whom public-opinion polls report as the front-runner

conservative *(p. 146)* today this term refers to those who generally support the social and economic status quo and are suspicious of efforts to introduce new political formulae and economic arrangements; conservatives believe that a large and powerful government poses a threat to citizens' freedom

democracy *(p. 145)* a system of rule that permits citizens to play a significant part in

the governmental process, usually through the election of key public officials

equality of opportunity *(p. 144)* a widely shared American ideal that all people should have the freedom to use whatever talents and wealth they have to reach their fullest potential

gender gap *(p. 151)* a distinctive pattern of voting behavior reflecting the differences in views between women and men

liberal *(p. 146)* today this term refers to those who generally support social and political reform; governmental intervention in the economy and more economic equality; the expansion of federal social services; and greater concern for consumers and the environment

liberty *(p. 144)* freedom from governmental control

market place of ideas *(p. 157)* the public forum in which beliefs and ideas are exchanged and compete

political ideology *(p. 146)* a cohesive set of beliefs that forms a general philosophy about the role of government

political socialization *(p. 148)* the induction of individuals into the political culture; learning the underlying beliefs and values on which the political system is based

public opinion *(p. 143)* citizens' attitudes about political issues, leaders, institutions, and events

public-opinion polls *(p. 160)* scientific instruments for measuring public opinion

push polling *(p. 165)* a polling technique in which the questions are designed to shape the respondent's opinion

random digit dialing *(p. 161)* a polling method in which respondents are selected at random from a list of 10-digit telephone numbers, with every effort made to avoid bias in the construction of the sample

sample *(p. 161)* a small group selected by researchers to represent the most important characteristics of an entire population

sampling error (or margin of error) *(p. 161)* polling error that arises based on the small size of the sample

selection bias (surveys) *(p. 164)* polling error that arises when the sample is not representative of the population being studied, which creates errors in overrepresenting or underrepresenting some opinions

simple random sample (or probability sample) *(p. 161)* a method used by pollsters to select a representative sample in which every individual in the population has an equal probability of being selected as a respondent

social desirability effect *(p. 162)* the effect that results when respondents in a survey report what they expect the interviewer wishes to hear rather than what they believe

values (or beliefs) *(p. 143)* basic principles that shape a person's opinions about political issues and events

For Further Reading

Althaus, Scott. *Collective Preferences in Democratic Politics.* New York: Cambridge University Press, 2003.

Asher, Herbert. *Polling and the Public: What Every Citizen Should Know.* 8th ed. Washington, DC: CQ Press, 2011.

Bartels, Larry. *Unequal Democracy.* Princeton, NJ: Princeton University Press, 2008.

Berinsky, Adam. *Silent Voices: Public Opinion and Political Participation in America.* Princeton, NJ: Princeton University Press, 2005.

Bishop, George. *The Illusion of Public Opinion.* New York: Rowman and Littlefield, 2004.

Clawson, Rosalee, and Zoe Oxley. *Public Opinion: Democratic Ideals and Democratic Practice.* Washington, DC: CQ Press, 2008.

Erikson, Robert, and Kent Tedin. *American Public Opinion.* 7th ed. New York: Longman, 2004.

Fiorina, Morris. *Culture War: The Myth of a Polarized America.* New York: Longman, 2005.

Gallup, George. *The Pulse of Democracy.* New York: Simon and Schuster, 1940.

Ginsberg, Benjamin. *The American Lie: Government by the People and Other Political Fables.* Boulder, CO: Paradigm, 2007.

Glynn, Carol, et al., ed. *Public Opinion.* Boulder, CO: Westview, 2004.

Jacobs, Lawrence R., and Robert Y. Shapiro. *Politicians Don't Pander: Political Manipulation and the Loss of Democratic Responsiveness.* Chicago: University of Chicago Press, 2000.

Lee, Taeku. *Mobilizing Public Opinion.* Chicago: University of Chicago Press, 2002.

Lippman, Walter. *Public Opinion.* New York: Harcourt, Brace, 1922.

Norrander, Barbara, and Clyde Wilcox. *Understanding Public Opinion.* Washington, DC: CQ Press, 2009.

Zaller, John. *The Nature and Origins of Mass Opinion.* New York: Cambridge University Press, 1992.

Political candidates who receive positive news coverage gain momentum, which helps them attract campaign contributions and endorsements and eventually win votes. The influence of the media on political campaigns is just one example of its important role in American democracy.

6

The Media

WHAT GOVERNMENT DOES AND WHY IT MATTERS One area in which our government's role is intended to be minimal is the news media. The Constitution's First Amendment guarantees freedom of the press, and most Americans believe that a free press is an essential condition for both liberty and democratic politics. Today the media play a central role in American politics, not only in setting the agenda of topics Americans think about and discuss, but also in swaying opinions on political issues, politicians, and candidates.

Political candidates who receive positive news coverage gain momentum, pick up political endorsements, attract campaign contributions, and win support from voters.[1] In the 2008 campaign for the Democratic Party's presidential nomination, Barack Obama exceeded the media's expectations with his early win in the Iowa caucuses, in which he upset the front-runner, Hillary Clinton, earning him increased press attention and eventually leading the first African American to the White House.[2] But candidates who disappoint media expectations see their political endorsements, campaign contributions, and polling numbers dwindle.

The influence of the media on political candidates is just one example of the media's vitally important role in American democracy. Without the media's investigations, citizens would be forced to rely entirely on the information provided by politicians and the government, and would be deprived of an indispensable opportunity to evaluate issues carefully and to form reasoned opinions.

The rise of the Internet has fundamentally altered the media's role in politics and American democracy. Just 20 years ago the majority of Americans got their political news from a daily newspaper, from radio, or by watching the local evening news and the national evening news from one of the three major networks (ABC, CBS, and NBC). Today, America is becoming a nation of "digital citizens"—daily Internet users who turn to the Internet for politics and news.[3] The Pew Research Center reports that 86 percent of American adults use the Internet, up from 14 percent in 1995. Among Internet users in 2012, 3 in 4 read the news online and 6 in 10 go online for information about politics and campaigns.[4] More Americans now read the news online than read a print newspaper, and those reading online news are more likely to vote and participate in politics in other ways.[5] Today mainstream media must compete with niche media outlets that tailor news to their readers and viewers, and Americans find political content via blogs and social media such as Facebook and Twitter. In 2013 more than 7 in 10 online adults used a social networking site, and as a result, hearing about news from friends and family via social media is a growing trend.[6]

In Chapter 5, we examined the vital question of how public opinion is related to government actions and decisions. We turn now to the most important way in which Americans learn information about their government, which in turn shapes people's opinions. Because most Americans do not have the time, ability, or opportunity to find out directly what their government does on a day-to-day basis, they must rely on the media to inform them.

chaptergoals

- Describe the role of print and broadcast media in providing political information (pp. 175–79)

- Explain how the Internet has transformed the news media (pp. 179–86)

- Analyze how the media, politicians, and public opinion are influenced by one another (pp. 186–92)

● Traditional Media Have Always Mattered in a Democracy

Describe the role of print and broadcast media in providing political information

It is impossible to imagine democratic politics without vigorous media. The public, and therefore public opinion, depends on the news media to publicize and assess the claims of political candidates, to examine government policies and programs, and to reveal wrongdoing by government agencies and public officials. Without the information provided by the media, the public could not possibly know enough to play any role in national politics. Freedom of the press definitely belongs in the First Amendment as one of the first principles of democratic government. As Thomas Jefferson wrote, "The basis of our government being the opinion of the people, the very first object should be to keep that right; and were it left to me to decide whether we should have a government without newspapers or newspapers without a government, I should not hesitate a moment to prefer the latter."[7]

Americans get their news from three main sources: broadcast media (radio and television), print media (newspapers and magazines), and, increasingly, the Internet. Online sources have become a major source of news for Americans, just behind television broadcasts. The Pew Research Center's 2013 biennial media attitudes survey found that half of the public now cites the Internet as a main source for national and international news. Television (69 percent) remains the public's top source for news. Only 28 percent of Americans use newspapers and 23 percent use radio as their main news source. This picture is very different from that of a decade ago, when 44 percent said newspapers were their main source for news and just 24 percent used the Internet as a primary source. The percentage turning to television for news has changed little over the past decade (see Figure 6.1).[8]

Each of these sources has distinctive characteristics. We discuss trends in print and broadcast first, and then we look at online news and how it is changing the media industry and the way Americans get political news.

Print Media

Newspapers, though no longer the primary news source for most Americans, remain important nevertheless because they are influential among the political elite. The broadcast media also rely on leading newspapers such as the *New York Times* and the *Washington Post* to set their news agenda. In fact, the broadcast media engage in relatively little original reporting; they primarily cover stories that have been "broken," or initially reported, by the print media or online media. Print and online media, as written text, also provide more detailed and complete information than radio or television media, offering a better context for analysis. The nation's economic, social, and political elites rely on the detailed coverage provided by the print media to inform and influence their views about important public matters. The print media may have a smaller audience than their cousins in broadcasting, but they have an especially influential audience.

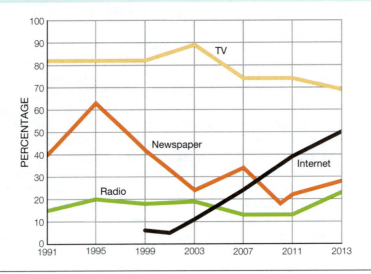

FIGURE 6.1 Americans' Main Sources for News

The media landscape for news has seen remarkable shifts in a short period of time. Twenty years ago, more than 80 percent of Americans watched news on television and more than half read news in a newspaper. Today, fewer Americans watch news on TV and just over a quarter read the newspaper. What media source has gained rather than lost its audience?

SOURCE: Pew Research Center, www.people-press.org/2013/08/08/amid-criticism-support-for-medias-watchdog-role-stands-out (accessed 4/27/14).

For most traditional newspapers, though, recent decades have been ruinous. Competition from broadcast media and, more recently, free content online have combined with declining advertising revenue and circulation levels to undermine the traditional business model of newspapers, bringing financial disaster to traditional print media.[9] Daily newspaper print circulation has declined from 62 million to 49 million nationwide over the past 20 years, while advertising revenue at print newspapers has dropped dramatically since 2006.[10] As a result, newspapers have had to make dramatic cutbacks; estimates indicate the size of newsroom staff is down 30 percent since 2000 industry-wide. Circulation for the *New York Times* dropped more than 10 percent from 2010 to 2011, and in 2011 alone the paper lost 25 percent of its revenue.[11] Major newspapers have sought bankruptcy protection, and others have gone out of business altogether. The *Los Angeles Times* has reduced its news staff by half over the past decade. Newspapers have cut costs by closing their foreign bureaus and their offices in Washington, D.C.

The effects of a decade of newsroom cutbacks are most evident in the political sphere. During the 2012 presidential election, a Pew report revealed that campaign reporters were acting primarily as megaphones, rather than as investigators, of the claims made by the candidates. This meant less reporting by journalists to interpret the claims presented by the candidates. And readers noticed this shift: Pew found that nearly a third of U.S. adults stopped turning to a news outlet because it no longer provided them with the quality of news they were used to receiving.[12]

To counter these trends, traditional media organizations have been forced to adapt, and most now have a significant online presence, blurring the distinction between old media and new. Faced with shrinking revenues from their print versions, a few news organizations, such as the *Washington Post*, the *New York Times*, and the *Wall Street Journal*, charge customers for reading the news online, while others, such as the *Seattle Post-Intelligencer* and the *Christian Science Monitor*, are available online only. Recently, the success of paid digital news that is increasing revenue and improving content, including reviving long-form journalism. The newspaper industry may have finally righted itself in 2012, when 450 of the nation's 1,380 dailies announced plans for paid content subscription, micropayments, or pay wall plans. The metered model allows a certain number of free visits before requiring users to pay. If this approach succeeds, we may see more online subscription newspapers in the future, and a more viable business model for the digital press.

The circulation and newsstand sales of traditional newspapers and newsmagazines has fallen in the last decade. However, because the remaining audience includes political elites and politically engaged citizens, they remain important forums in the marketplace of ideas.

Broadcast Media

Television news reaches more Americans than any other single news source. It is estimated that over 95 percent of Americans have a television, and tens of millions of individuals watch national and local news programs every day. Most television news, however, covers relatively few topics and provides little depth of coverage. Television news is more like a series of newspaper headlines connected to pictures. It serves the extremely important function of alerting viewers to issues and events, but, with exceptions such as the Public Broadcasting System (PBS), it provides little more than a series of "sound bites," brief quotes and short characterizations of the day's events. Because they are aware of the character of television news coverage, politicians and others often seek to manipulate the news by providing the media with sound bites that will dominate news coverage for at least a few days. Twenty-four-hour news stations such as Cable News Network (CNN), MSNBC, and Fox News offer more detail and commentary than the networks' half-hour evening news shows. Even CNN and the others, however, offer more headlines than analysis, especially during their prime-time broadcasts.

Radio news is essentially a headline service, but without pictures. In the short time they devote to news—usually five minutes per hour—radio stations announce the day's major events without providing much detail. In major cities, all-news stations provide more coverage of major stories, but for the most part, these stations fill the day with repetition rather than detail. All-news stations assume that most listeners are in their cars and that, as a result, the people in the audience change throughout the day as listeners reach their destinations. Thus, rather than use their time to flesh out a given set of stories, these stations repeat the same stories each hour to present them to new listeners.

In recent years, radio talk shows have become important sources of commentary and opinion. A number of conservative radio hosts such as Rush Limbaugh and Sean Hannity have huge audiences and have helped mobilize support for conservative political causes and candidates. In the political center or left center, National Public Radio (NPR) is a coveted source for moderate talk radio, providing in-depth political reporting, while the now-defunct Air America hoped to achieve on the left what Limbaugh had achieved on the right.

Comedy talk shows with political content, such as *The Daily Show* and *The Late Show*, have become increasingly important, attracting millions of television viewers. Comedian Stephen Colbert even established a political action committee (PAC) during the 2012 presidential primaries in an effort to draw attention to problems with current campaign finance laws. *The Daily Show* and other late-night talk shows use humor, sarcasm, and social criticism to cover major political events. Yet these talk shows are not just for fun. They have become increasingly important sources of political news, especially for younger viewers. Pew surveys show that many Americans get political news from these shows and that followers of comedic talk shows are well informed about politics.[13]

The broadcast media are also diversifying as they adapt to changes in the American population, especially the growing number of Latinos. In California and Texas, as well as other states, the Latino-oriented television channels Telemundo, Univision, and MSN Latino attract large audiences by focusing on topics or perspectives of particular interest to their audience. Coverage of the Arizona and Alabama illegal immigration laws, for example, in Latino media outlets was significantly different from that of mainstream media. News outlets aimed at other ethnic groups have also become common in many areas. As America has become more multicultural, multiethnic television—a form of niche media—has broadened news media.

More Media Outlets Are Owned by Fewer Companies

The United States boasts nearly 2,000 television stations, approximately 1,400 daily newspapers, and more than 13,000 radio stations (20 percent of which are devoted to news, talk, or public affairs). Despite these substantial numbers overall, the number of traditional news-gathering sources operating nationally is actually quite small—several wire services, four broadcast networks, public radio and television, a few elite newspapers and newsmagazines, and a smattering of other sources such as the national correspondents of a few large local papers and the small independent radio networks. More than three-fourths of the daily newspapers in the United States are owned by large media conglomerates such as the Hearst, McClatchy, or Gannett corporations. Much of the national news published by local newspapers is provided by one wire service, the Associated Press, while additional coverage is provided by services run by several major newspapers, such as the *New York Times* and the *Chicago Tribune*. More than 500 of the nation's television stations are affiliated with one of the four networks and carry that network's evening news programs. Some of the most popular online news outlets are electronic versions of the conventional print or broadcast media.

The trend toward less variety in traditional media has been hastened by changes in media ownership, which became possible in large part as a result of the relaxation of government regulations in the 1980s and '90s. The enactment of the 1996

Telecommunications Act opened the way for further consolidation in the media industry, and a wave of mergers and consolidations has further reduced the field of independent media across the country. For example, the Australian press baron Rupert Murdoch owns the Fox network plus a host of radio, television, and newspaper properties around the world, known collectively as News Corporation, the world's second-largest media conglomerate. In 2007, Murdoch won control of the *Wall Street Journal*, consolidating his position as one of the world's most powerful publishers. News Corporation owns 800 media companies in more than 50 countries and has a net worth of over $5 billion. A small number of giant corporations now control a wide swath of media holdings, including television networks, movie studios, record companies, cable channels and local cable providers, book publishers, magazines, and newspapers. Clear Channel Communications, for example, a Texas-based media conglomerate, owns 850 radio stations—by far the largest number controlled by a single company. These developments have prompted questions about whether enough competition exists among the media to produce a diverse set of views on political and corporate matters, or whether the United States has become the prisoner of media monopolies.[14]

As major newspapers, television stations, and radio networks fall into fewer and fewer hands, the risk increases that politicians and citizens who express less-popular or minority viewpoints will have difficulty finding a public forum. Examples include 2012 Republican presidential candidate Ron Paul, who despite favorable showing in early nominating events, such as the Iowa caucuses and the New Hampshire primary, received little national media coverage because his libertarian ideas were outside the mainstream of his political party. This may also be a reason for the relatively scant mainstream media coverage of the Occupy Wall Street movement, which sought to bring attention to the issue of growing income inequality. The mainstream media are often committed to the status quo, which is why they were less enthusiastic about the Occupy protests or, at the other end of the political spectrum, about the Tea Party. Increasingly, these groups turn to the Internet to express their views. The Internet is an important mechanism for linking communities of adherents, but can it mitigate the traditional media's homogeneous point of view in terms of what is news coverage, or their treatment of opinions that challenge the status quo? Can the diversity of media sources available online, including blogs and social media, help balance the corporate concentration of media ownership?

● The Rise of New Media Has Strongly Influenced How Americans Get Their News

> **Explain how the Internet has transformed the news media**

The twenty-first century has already experienced a profound transformation of the media. The impact of the Internet in mass communication parallels that of the printing press in nineteenth-century America, which saw the rise of the penny press and widespread literacy.[15] Today, even as the newspaper business struggles for its life, readership of online news has soared. The Internet has become the medium of choice for all age groups below 50 years old to consume entertainment, news, and information about politics

The rise of new media has made it easier for Americans with Internet access to get political news, but one in five Americans is still completely offline. For example, there are neighborhoods in large cities like Chicago where over 80 percent of households lack broadband access.

(see Figure 6.2). In 2000, just 35 percent of adult Internet users said they looked for news or information about politics or the upcoming campaigns online. As of 2012 that number had risen to over 60 percent.[16] Among young adults, the number is even higher: 70 percent of 18- to 29-year-olds say that the Internet is their main source of news. Besides online-only newspapers, new forums for news include websites, blogs, social media, YouTube, and Twitter.

The Internet is particularly convenient for obtaining news, and formats for doing so are becoming more diverse and interactive. A Pew 2012 Election Survey found 48 percent of Internet-using registered voters watched news reports online about the presidential election, and 40 percent watched previously recorded videos of a candidate's speech, press conference, or debate. Watching online videos to understand a political issue was equally common. News about politics is often humorous, and 37 percent watched a video parodying a political issue. Watching online campaign ads is common, with this activity reported by one in three Internet users. Live video streaming is a growing substitute for television for some, as 28 percent of this population watched a live online video of a candidate's speech or debate. Presidential addresses are now regularly streamed live, and millions tune in to hear the president in this format.[17]

News watchers have quickly grown accustomed to following world events unfolding in real time. Online media are more diverse and have created a more democratic and participatory press, one in which citizens and nonprofit organizations now play a prominent role. No longer limited to the letters-to-the-editor section in most print publications, readers can now post comments online and participate in a community providing feedback on almost all online news articles. Online media, by representing a wider range of political views than traditional media, have created a more democratic press.

The term *digital citizenship* refers to the ability to participate in society and politics online. In much the same way that education and literacy promoted democracy and economic growth in the nineteenth century, today's Internet has the potential to benefit society as a whole and facilitate political participation by individuals within society. Like education, the Internet helps provide the information and skills needed for democratic engagement and economic opportunity.[18] It facilitates social inclusion through greater access to political information.[19]

However, regular and effective use of the Internet requires high-speed access, technical skills, and literacy to evaluate and use information online.[20] Individuals without access or the skills to use the Internet may be increasingly uninformed

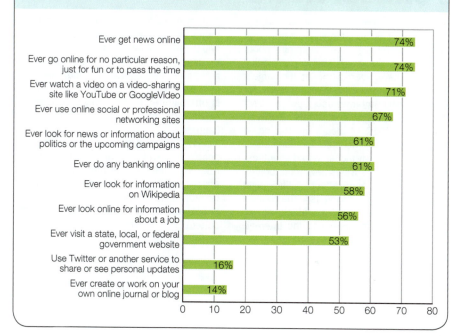

FIGURE 6.2 What Americans Use the Internet For

Obtaining news is one of the major reasons that Americans go online, ahead of job search information and banking. Comparatively few people use the Internet to work on a blog or use Twitter, although these remain important forums for expressing opinion.

NOTE: Data are from surveys in May 2011, February 2012, and December 2012.
SOURCE: Pew Research Project, www.pewinternet.org/data-trend/internet-use/internet-use-over-time/ (accessed 4/27/14).

Category	Percent
Ever get news online	74%
Ever go online for no particular reason, just for fun or to pass the time	74%
Ever watch a video on a video-sharing site like YouTube or GoogleVideo	71%
Ever use online social or professional networking sites	67%
Ever look for news or information about politics or the upcoming campaigns	61%
Ever do any banking online	61%
Ever look for information on Wikipedia	58%
Ever look online for information about a job	56%
Ever visit a state, local, or federal government website	53%
Use Twitter or another service to share or see personal updates	16%
Ever create or work on your own online journal or blog	14%

and excluded from the world of politics online. As of 2013, 7 in 10 Americans were **digital citizens**, individuals with high-speed access at home (beyond mobile access), and more than 8 in 10 Americans used the Internet in some location. As of 2013, 74 percent of whites, 62 percent of blacks, and only 56 percent of Latinos are digital citizens by this definition (home high-speed access). Although only half of the working poor (those earning less than $30,000 a year) had home broadband, 9 out of 10 of those earning more than $75,000 a year did. Fifty-eight percent of high school graduates have home broadband, compared to 90 percent of college graduates.[21] This suggests that there are significant inequalities in access to digital media, what is called the digital divide.

Online News Takes Many Forms

While many traditional news sources, such as newspapers, now publish online, other web news outlets tend to be smaller and more specialized, and have lower personnel and overhead costs than mainstream publishers. The types of online news sources include niche journalism, citizen journalism and blogs, nonprofit journalism, and social media.

Internet Use and Political News

Internet access is increasing around the world, and it is transforming the way that some populations are learning about politics. As the graph shows, developing countries have seen some of the largest increases in Internet use in recent years. For example, while Internet use grew by about 7 percent in the United States between 2008 and 2012, it nearly quintupled in South Africa and doubled in many other developing or newly industrialized countries.

The Internet provides new opportunities for people to learn about politics and become informed participants in the political process. However, within countries, not all groups have equal access to the Internet.

A study of media use in the European Union found that those who are more educated and those employed full time are more likely to use the Internet for news than other groups.[a] In the developing world, this trend is even more extreme, as Internet access is often limited to the highly educated, the wealthy, or the middle class living in urban centers.

Will increasing internet access help people in developing and newly industrialized countries become more informed and effective participants in the political process? Or will it reinforce existing inequalities? Should we be concerned about the same patterns in the United States?

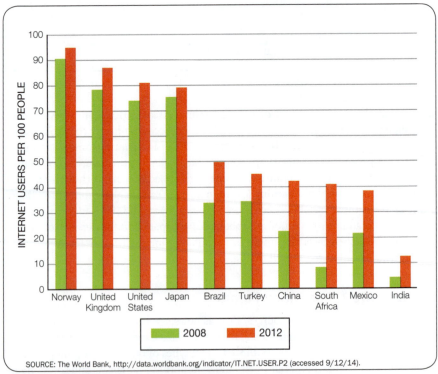

SOURCE: The World Bank, http://data.worldbank.org/indicator/IT.NET.USER.P2 (accessed 9/12/14).

[a]European Commission, "Media Use in the European Union," March 2012, http://ec.europa.eu/public_opinion/archives/eb/eb76/eb76_media_en.pdf (accessed 9/12/14).

Niche Journalism In the gap opened by the decline in traditional print media, the last decade has seen the rise of **niche journalism** (news reporting devoted to a targeted portion of a journalism market sector or for a portion of readers or viewers based on content or ideological presentation) and specialty publications ranging from Slate.com to Politico.com. Bloomberg News, one of the most successful specialty online sources, has hundreds of thousands of readers paying a large annual fee for detailed business-related news. In politics, *Roll Call*, *The Hill*, the *National Journal*, *Congressional Quarterly*, Salon.com, the *Huffington Post*, and *Politico* (the niche leader) have detailed political reporting inside the Beltway (that is, in Washington, D.C., which is encircled by freeways). Niche journalism feeds citizens' interest in politics across the full range of the political spectrum. These niche outlets are supplemented by a rich array of international and foreign online news sources.

Citizen Journalism and Blogs The old media system was dominated by professional journalists, trained in journalism schools, who served as gatekeepers in determining what was front-page news and how political events were to be interpreted. This system had benefits and costs: the quality was high, but the diversity of opinions was relatively low. The media's gatekeeper role continues, but the diversity of online media is changing traditional journalism and the very nature of "news coverage." Even five years ago most establishment journalists took their cues exclusively from a small handful of outlets, but now many of them use a much more extensive and diversified roster of sources, including blogs, Twitter, and independent political commentators. Online news is creating a new generation of whistle-blowers, enhancing the media's traditional role as a watchdog for the people against government corruption, and it is creating new venues for political activism.

A distinguishing feature of the digital media is **citizen journalism**, which is interactive and participatory. Citizen journalism refers simply to news reported and distributed by citizens, rather than professional journalists and for-profit news organizations. It also includes political commentary by ordinary citizens and even crisis coverage from eyewitnesses on the scene. Because it involves a wider range of voices in gathering news and interpreting political events, contemporary news reporting and commentary are more democratic. Magnifying the power of the Internet is the nearly universal availability of digital cameras and camera-equipped cell phones, which give millions of Americans the capacity to photograph or film events and then disseminate them online. When a citizen using a mobile phone captured video of police pepper-spraying peaceful Occupy Wall Street demonstrators at the University of California–Davis in 2011, the video was viewed by millions and became headline news.

Citizen journalism is enhanced by the ease with which anyone can start a blog. There are millions of blogs, covering virtually every topic imaginable, and a large share of these include political news and commentary on local, national, and world events. Many blogs are citizen-run and are more interactive and representative of the diversity of American views than traditional news, which generally reflects the priorities of political elites.

Twitter is also an important tool for citizen journalism. While only 5 to 7 percent of Americans use Twitter for politics, these users tend to be public opinion leaders, and Twitter is the preferred social media platform for political elites and candidates. A study of millions of Twitter messages about Obama during the 2012 presidential election found that the *Washington Post* was the only traditional media corporation cited in the top 10 most frequently cited websites. The other nine

In 2011 an ordinary citizen recorded video of police pepper-spraying peaceful Occupy protesters at the University of California–Davis. The video was widely shared on the Internet, and the story became headline news.

most-cited sites were blogs, YouTube videos, and other alternative online sources. Thus social media and citizen journalism are not replicating traditional media but are giving political activists new voice in shaping the news.

To be sure, the open, freewheeling nature of blogging often means that there is little of the traditional quality control employed by traditional media. Because they do not face the burden of fact-checking required for the mainstream media, even well-meaning bloggers can post false information. This could be one reason misinformation about political issues is higher among blog readers than those reading online news from the mainstream press.[22]

Nonprofit Journalism As traditional news organizations have cut budgets and reduced investigative journalism, political information is increasingly emanating from universities, think tanks, nonprofit organizations, and private foundations. Think tanks such as the Brookings Institution, the Cato Institute, the Hoover Institution, the Heritage Foundation, and the Center for American Progress provide information and analysis on current events in order to influence public debate. Universities have expanded their public outreach, encouraging faculty to explain their findings for a general audience; as a result, university faculty are increasingly cited in the mainstream media, and many are bloggers themselves.

Social Media Social media, such as Twitter and Facebook, are important players in news and political communication. Some 73 percent of online adults used a social networking site of some kind as of 2013 (the percentage increases to

90 percent among 18- to 29-year-olds). Facebook is the dominant social networking platform in sheer number of users, but 42 percent of online adults use multiple social networking sites.[23] Because social media such as Facebook and Twitter are more personalized and interactive than anonymous news organizations, social media are becoming increasingly popular means for Americans to receive political information from the candidates and interest groups they support. In turn, candidates for political office, elected officials, political organizations, and interest groups have been quick to adopt Facebook and Twitter as a means of communicating with their supporters and providing them with a continual feed of new information. In 2007 one of the founders of Facebook helped the Obama presidential campaign establish a Facebook page. The site's fund-raising section allowed visitors to set personal fund-raising goals and to invite other registered friends to help them reach those goals. The Obama site attracted more than a million visitors during the campaign for the 2008 Democratic presidential nomination,[24] and as of 2014, Obama's Facebook page had over 40 million followers.

Both Facebook and Twitter possess important features for political mobilization and information sharing. With these virtual social networks, groups of like-minded individuals, or individuals with shared interests, can quickly and easily share information.

New Media Have Many Benefits

Americans may prefer online news for several reasons. Here we look at four advantages of online news.

Convenience Information online is convenient and always available for those who have regular access to the Internet at home or, increasingly, through mobile devices such as smartphones. Pew surveys show that nearly half of those who use online news and political information cite its convenience.[25] Use of online political information is associated with more interest in politics, greater knowledge of politics, and a greater likelihood of discussing politics with friends and family.[26]

Currency Major news stories regularly break first, and immediately, online and are later reported through print newspapers and television. Social media have accelerated even further the speed with which news travels around the globe. For example, news of Osama bin Laden's death in 2011 spread rapidly through text messaging, smartphones, and social media outlets such as Facebook and Twitter even before it could be verified by traditional media.

Depth Online news provides more information than the 60-second sound bites found in television and radio news. By blending detailed treatment of topics with the visual and emotive appeal of streaming videos, the Internet shares qualities both of print media (promoting knowledge) and of the visual aspects of television (promoting interest and engagement).[27]

Diversity Online sources are much more diverse than those found in the traditional media, and this diversity may increase citizens' political knowledge and interest.[28] While major players online certainly do include mainstream outlets, the Internet remains populated by a wide range of information sources. By making foreign media such as the British

Broadcasting Company (BBC) easily available, the Internet has reduced the importance of physical proximity and created a truly global shared culture. Millions went online to watch live broadcasts of Egyptian citizens protesting for democratic freedoms in 2011.

But New Media Raise Concerns about Investigative Power, News Quality, and Political Tolerance

Despite the benefits of new media, changes to the media arising from the rapid proliferation of the Internet have raised a multitude of concerns.

One such concern is the loss of investigative power. In a democracy, the press is expected to be a watchdog for the people and to inform the citizens of government abuses of power. The greatest challenge for contemporary news organizations is to generate enough revenue to finance traditional investigative journalism.[29] This activity requires more time and resources than other aspects of the news, and yet it may be the most important. By breaking apart mainstream news organizations, online news may actually reduce the media's ability to engage in the kind of sustained, in-depth, and expensive reporting that is critical to the media's watchdog role and thus to the health of American democracy.

Another concern is the variation in the quality of the news. As already noted, the growing diversity of online news has led to wide variation in the quality of available information. The freewheeling nature of the Internet also means that hate speech, rumors, falsehoods, and outdated information can overwhelm thoughtful, original, factual, and civic-oriented voices. Misinformation and unsubstantiated rumors can substitute for objective truth as claims are widely repeated, especially in anonymous and unedited online forums. Perhaps the greatest concern about politics in the digital age goes to the heart of modern democracy: Do online media ultimately help or hinder progress toward a well-informed citizenry that can govern itself effectively? One study has found that while readers of online news from major websites (largely offshoots of the traditional print and broadcast media) are more knowledgeable than average citizens, those who get their political news mainly from blogs are actually worse off.[30] And the very diversity of online news, in fact, may actually *lower* tolerance for social and political diversity. Most new media do not abide by traditional media's principle of objective journalism.

● The Media Affect Power Relations in American Politics

Analyze how the media, politicians, and public opinion are influenced by one another

The content and character of news and public-affairs programming—what the media choose to present and how they present it—can have far-reaching political consequences. The media can shape and modify, if not fully form, the public's perception of events, issues, and institutions. Media coverage can rally support for, or intensify opposition to, national policies on matters as weighty as health care, the economy, and international wars.

The Media Influence Public Opinion through Agenda Setting, Framing, and Priming

Traditional and digital media influence American politics in a number of important ways.[31] The power of all media collectively, both traditional and online, lies in their ability to shape what issues Americans think about (setting the agenda) and what opinions Americans hold about those issues (framing and priming).

Agenda Setting and Selection Bias The first source of media power is **agenda setting**—that is, the power of the media to bring public attention to particular issues and problems. Groups and forces that wish to bring their ideas before the public in order to generate support for policy proposals or political candidacies must secure media coverage. If the media are persuaded that an idea is newsworthy, they may declare it an "issue" that must be confronted or a "problem" to be solved, thus clearing the first hurdle in the policy-making process. If, on the other hand, an idea lacks or loses media appeal, its chance of resulting in new programs or policies is diminished.

For example, in 2008 and 2009 the news agenda was dominated by the global financial crisis and the severe economic recession that ensued. Continuing media attention created enormous pressure for the government to "do something" even as the crisis began to ease, and the new Obama administration's "honeymoon period" was cut short by public frustration over the government's inability to solve the economic problems quickly. In 2010 the media's focus on a massive oil spill in the Gulf of Mexico contributed to widespread anger at the Obama administration's seeming inability to contain the disaster.

Because the media are businesses and because the media seek to attract the largest possible audiences, they naturally tend to cover stories with dramatic or entertainment value, giving less attention to important stories that are less compelling. News coverage thus often focuses on crimes and scandals, especially those involving prominent individuals. This **selection bias**—the tendency to focus news coverage on only one aspect of an event or issue, avoiding coverage of other aspects—means that the media may provide less information about important political issues. The age-old journalistic instinct for sensational stories to tell often trumps the media's responsibility to inform the public about what really matters—and the public's responsibility to demand that from the media.

What the mainstream media decide to report on and what they ignore have important implications. For example, the mainstream media provided little coverage of the Bush tax cuts of 2001 and 2003 (or their extension under President Obama in 2009), although they dramatically increased the federal budget deficit and widened the gap between the super-rich and most other Americans in terms of wealth.[32] It is not surprising that public opinion polls showed 40 percent of Americans had no opinion on whether they favored the massive tax cuts in 2001. The selection bias of traditional media run by professional journalists, however, may be balanced to some degree by the diversity of media sources available online.

Framing **Framing** is the media's ability to influence how the American people interpret events and policies. Politicians take care to choose language that presents their ideas in the most favorable light possible. Public opinion on politics

The way that a story is reported in the news can influence how the audience interprets the event. After Hurricane Sandy hit the Middle Atlantic coast, for instance, the news could write a story focusing on the government's failure to respond in a timely matter or on the government's successful relief efforts. Both stories may be correct—but they leave the reader or viewer with a very different impression.

naturally changes with facts, but few citizens read legislation, so when forming opinions about policy and politics, the public relies on media coverage. This means that arguments made by elected officials and other political actors, or "frames," are critical to the process of forming opinions.

For example, the Obama administration labeled its health care initiative the Patient Protection and Affordable Care Act, thus framing the proposal as a matter of compassionate responsibility and good economic sense. As the bill was debated in Congress, early press coverage framed it as "health care reform." Sensing that Americans generally approve of the idea of "reform," Republican opponents of the legislation chose language that framed it quite differently: the law's provisions for limiting excessive medical testing were labeled as "health care rationing," for example, and committees that were proposed to advise patients about end-of-life care were called "death panels." The language used by Democrats and Republicans framed the debate in different terms: the Democrats framed it as achieving the positive goal of reform, while the Republicans framed it as achieving the negative outcome of rationing.

Priming Another source of media influence on opinion, related to framing, is **priming**. Priming involves "calling attention to some matters while ignoring others."[33] As a result, the public will be *primed* to use certain criteria when evaluating a politician or an issue and to ignore other criteria. For example, the media's intensive focus on terrorism and security in the wake of the September 11, 2001, terrorist attacks primed the public to evaluate President Bush's performance in office based on his ability to defend the nation from terrorism. The public was less likely to assess President Bush based on his ability to manage the economy at the time, as people were not primed to be thinking about the economy. This situation was quite different in 2008, when a serious economic recession received much more extensive media coverage than national security. In the 2008 presidential election, the economy was an important lens through which the public evaluated the candidates, more important than national security.

In the case of political candidates, the media have considerable influence over whether a particular individual will receive public attention and whether a particular individual will be taken seriously as a viable contender. Thus, if the media find a candidate interesting, they may treat him or her as a serious contender despite possible weaknesses and shortcomings. For example, in the 2012 Republican presidential primaries there were positive stories covering New Jersey governor Chris Christie as a possible candidate (though Christie ultimately did not run). After Christie's successful reelection as governor, however, his political coverage switched from positive to negative, as he was the focus of numerous negative stories about an unseemly effort by some in his administration to punish local New Jersey officials by deliberately clogging traffic across the George Washington Bridge (the nation's busiest). These "Bridgegate" stories had a negative priming effect on Christie's formerly positive image, damaging his presidential ambitions.

Leaked Information Can Come from Government Officials or Independent Sources

The media may also report information that is leaked by government officials. A *leak* is the disclosure of confidential information to the news media. Leaks may emanate from a variety of sources, including whistle-blowers, lower-level officials who hope to publicize what they view as their bosses' improper activities. In 1971, for example, a minor Defense Department staffer named Daniel Ellsberg sought to discredit official justifications for U.S. involvement in Vietnam by leaking top-secret documents to the press. The Pentagon Papers—the Defense Department's own secret history of the war, differing widely from the Pentagon's public pronouncements—were published by the *New York Times* and the *Washington Post* after the U.S. Supreme Court ruled that the government could not block their release.[34] Pentagon credibility was severely damaged, hastening the erosion of public support for the war.

Most leaks, though, originate not with low-level whistle-blowers but rather with senior government officials, prominent politicians, and political activists. These individuals cultivate long-term relationships with journalists, to whom they regularly leak confidential information, knowing that it is likely to be published on a priority basis in a form acceptable to them. In turn, of course, journalists are likely to regard high-level sources of confidential information as valuable assets whose favor must be retained. For example, during the George W. Bush administration, Lewis "Scooter" Libby, Vice President Dick Cheney's chief of staff, was apparently such a valuable source of leaks to so many prominent journalists that his name was seldom even mentioned in the newspapers, despite his prominence in Washington and his importance as a decision maker.[35] Through such tacit alliances with journalists, prominent figures can manipulate news coverage and secure the publication of stories that serve their purposes.

New technology and online media have taken the cat-and-mouse game of leaks to a new level. WikiLeaks, an independent nonprofit organization dedicated to publishing classified information, posts leaked documents to its website and uses an anonymous drop-box system so leakers cannot be identified. In recent years, WikiLeaks has released thousands of secret government documents involving instances of government corruption, war crimes in Afghanistan and Iraq, torture at the Guantánamo Bay detention camp, maps of U.S. military drone attacks on civilians around the world, and numerous embarrassing private communiqués sent by U.S. diplomats abroad. WikiLeaks shares its treasure trove of leaked government documents with major international papers, including the *New York Times*. In July 2007 gunners aboard two U.S. Army helicopters killed more than a dozen people, including two Reuters news staffers, in the Iraqi suburb of New Baghdad. Reuters subsequently learned that

Leaks of classified information have sparked significant debate over what the government should classify as "secret" and what deserves to be public knowledge. After Edward Snowden leaked thousands of classified documents, he fled the United States in order to escape arrest and prosecution. His actions have been both defended and denounced.

the U.S. military had video footage of the attack, and the news agency tried to obtain the video through the Freedom of Information Act (FOIA), but without success. The video was leaked to WikiLeaks, however, which released it in April 2010. Shot through an Apache helicopter gunsight, the video clearly shows the slaying of a wounded Reuters employee and his would-be rescuers; it led to a worldwide storm of condemnation of U.S. military action in the Iraq War.

In 2013, Edward Snowden, a former employee of the Central Intelligence Agency (CIA) and contractor for the National Security Agency (NSA), disclosed thousands of classified digital documents to journalists and international media in what has been called the most significant leak in U.S. history. The leaks disclosed widespread global surveillance programs by the U.S. government working with telecommunication companies. The world learned the NSA was searching millions of email and instant messaging contact lists and tracking and mapping the locations of cell phones. For revealing the mass surveillance programs, Snowden has been called a hero, a whistle-blower, a dissident, and a traitor. The leaks garnered intense media attention and sparked heated public debate over government surveillance and privacy of information for individuals.

Critics of WikiLeaks and Snowden argue that posting government documents online is not journalism, that governments must have some secrets, and that the release of some government documents may jeopardize American soldiers and their local allies by revealing their identities. The whistle-blower behind the Pentagon Papers, Daniel Ellsberg, defended WikiLeaks, arguing that it has played a vital role in informing the public of government wrongdoing.

Adversarial Journalism Has Risen in Recent Years

The political power of the news media vis-à-vis the government has greatly increased in recent years through the growing prominence of "adversarial journalism," an aggressive form of investigative journalism that attempts to expose and antagonize the status quo.

The national media's aggressive use of the techniques of investigation, publicity, and exposure allowed them to inform the public about major news stories. Without such aggressive media coverage, would we have known of Bill Clinton's extramarital affair or of Richard Nixon's Committee to Re-elect the President's illegal break-in to the Democratic Party headquarters in the Watergate Building? Would we have known that Iraq did not have weapons of mass destruction (WMDs), despite claims to the contrary by then president George W. Bush? Without aggressive media coverage, would important questions be raised about the conduct of American foreign and domestic policy, including drone attacks, torture, and civil liberty violations? It is easy to criticize the media for their aggressive tactics, but would our democracy function effectively without the critical role of the press? Vigorous and critical media are the "watchdogs" of American politics.

Broadcast Media Are Regulated but Not Print Media

In many countries, such as China, the government controls media content. In other countries, the government owns the broadcast media (e.g., the BBC in Britain) but does not tell the media what to say. In the United States, the government neither owns nor controls the communications networks, but it does regulate the content and ownership of the broadcast media.

In the United States, the print media are essentially free from government interference. The broadcast media, on the other hand, are subject to federal regulation. American radio and television are regulated by the Federal Communications Commission (FCC), an independent regulatory agency established in 1934. Radio and TV stations must have FCC licenses, which must be renewed every five years. Licensing provides a mechanism for allocating radio and TV frequencies to prevent broadcasts from interfering with and garbling one another. License renewals are almost always granted automatically by the FCC. Indeed, renewal requests are now filed by postcard.

Through regulations prohibiting obscenity, indecency, and profanity, the FCC has also sought to prohibit radio and television stations from airing explicit sexual and excretory references between 6 AM and 10 PM, the hours when children are most likely to be in the audience. Generally speaking, FCC regulation applies only to the "over-the-air" broadcast media. It does not apply to cable television, the Internet, or satellite radio. As a result, explicit sexual content and graphic language that would run afoul of the rules on broadcast television are regularly available on cable channels. A number of bills have been introduced in recent Congresses to extend the rules to cable TV and satellite radio, but none has succeeded so far.

For more than 60 years, the FCC also sought to regulate and promote competition in the broadcast industry, but in 1996, Congress passed the Telecommunications Act, a broad effort to do away with most regulations in effect since 1934. The act loosened restrictions on media ownership and allowed telephone companies, cable television providers, and broadcasters to compete with one another for telecommunication services. Following the passage of the act, several mergers between telephone and cable companies and among different segments of the entertainment media produced an even greater concentration of media ownership than had been possible since regulation of the industry began in 1934.

The Telecommunications Act of 1996 also included an attempt to regulate the content of material transmitted over the Internet. This law, known as the Communications Decency Act, made it illegal to make "indecent" sexual material on the Internet accessible to those under 18 years old. The act was immediately denounced by civil libertarians and became the subject of lawsuits. The case reached the Supreme Court in 1997, and the act was ruled an unconstitutional infringement of the First Amendment's right to freedom of speech (see Chapter 4).

Although the government's ability to regulate the content of the electronic media on the Internet has been questioned, the federal government has used its licensing power to impose several regulations that can affect the political content of radio and TV broadcasts. The first of these is the **equal time rule**, under

Federal Communications Commission (FCC) regulations prohibit obscenity, indecency, and profanity in American television and radio broadcasts. The radio personality Howard Stern incurred millions of dollars in FCC fines before moving to satellite radio, which is not regulated by the FCC.

which broadcasters must provide candidates for the same political office equal opportunities to communicate their messages to the public. If, for example, a television station sells commercial time to a state's Republican gubernatorial candidate, it may not refuse to sell time to the Democratic candidate for the same position.

The second regulation affecting the content of broadcasts is the **right of rebuttal**, which requires that individuals be given the opportunity to respond to personal attacks made on a radio or television broadcast. In the 1969 case of *Red Lion Broadcasting Company v. Federal Communications Commission*, for example, the U.S. Supreme Court upheld the FCC's determination that a radio station was required to provide a liberal author with an opportunity to respond to a conservative commentator's attack that the station had aired.[36]

For many years, a third important federal regulation was the **fairness doctrine**. Under this doctrine, broadcasters who aired programs on controversial issues were required to provide time for opposing views. In 1985, however, the FCC stopped enforcing the fairness doctrine on the grounds that there were so many radio and television stations—to say nothing of newspapers and newsmagazines—that in all likelihood many different viewpoints were already being presented without each station's being required to try to present all sides of an argument. Critics of this FCC decision charge that in many media markets the number of competing viewpoints is small. During the past several years, Democratic members of Congress, including Nancy Pelosi, John Kerry, and Richard Durbin, have sought to revive the fairness doctrine in response to what they see as the "unfairness" of conservative talk radio.

The rise of online media challenges our thinking about regulation of the media, as it is more difficult—some say impossible—to regulate political content online. The United Nations recently declared that access to the Internet is a human right.[37] While this came in response to threats by authoritarian governments against Internet access—the Egyptian government, for example, disabled Internet access for the entire nation during protests in 2011—the UN's position demonstrates the significance of information technology in modern life. Many authoritarian countries continue to censor the Internet, sometimes blocking the transmission of stories that contain specific terms or information from specific websites.[38] The government does have the power to regulate the Internet if a website infringes on U.S. copyright law. In January 2012 the U.S. Justice Department shut down a website, Megaupload, that ran services for file storing and viewing. The owners of the Hong Kong–based company, in operation since 2005, were arrested on charges of copyright infringement. The U.S. government claimed it had the right to shut down the website because the company used an Internet server located in Virginia.

The Media, Democracy,
and Your Future

The free media are essential to democratic government. Ordinary citizens depend on the media to investigate wrongdoing, to publicize and explain governmental actions, to evaluate programs and politicians, and to bring to light matters that might otherwise be known to only a handful of governmental insiders. Without free and active media, democratic government would be virtually impossible. Citizens would have few means through which to know or assess the government's actions—other than the claims or pronouncements of the government itself. Moreover, without active (indeed, aggressive) media, citizens would be hard pressed to make informed choices among competing candidates at the polls.

Today's media are not only adversarial but also increasingly partisan. Debates about the liberalism and conservatism of the mass media make it clear that many readers and viewers perceive more and more bias in newspapers, radio, and television. Blogs, niche media, social media, and other Internet outlets, of course, are often highly partisan. To some extent, increasing ideological and partisan stridency is an inevitable result of the expansion and proliferation of news sources. When the news was dominated by three networks and a handful of national papers, each sought to appeal to the entire national audience. This required a moderate and balanced tone so that consumers would not be offended and transfer their attention to a rival network or newspaper. Today, there are so many news sources that few can aim for a national audience. Instead, many target a partisan or ideological niche and aim to develop a strong relationship with consumers in that audience segment by catering to their biases and predispositions. The end result may be to encourage greater division and disharmony among Americans.

Has the rise of citizen journalism, social media, and the Internet fundamentally changed how political information is gathered and distributed? As more and more Americans go online to read the news and learn about politics, even the definition of "journalist" is being challenged. Are Twitter feeds from protesters on the ground in Egypt or in an Occupy Wall Street camp examples of citizen journalism? In an era of online news, regular citizens create content and distribute the news through personal web pages and blogs. Is this real news or just social media gossip on a global scale? Wikipedia, the free online encyclopedia founded by Jimmy Wales, has millions of pages compiled by legions of volunteers that provide content on virtually every political topic imaginable. Social media, Wikipedia, and all Wiki-type sites involve people working collaboratively to write and create information and to transmit knowledge. Is Wikimedia the future of the media?

In the twenty-first century, political campaigns are covered wall to wall by the Internet; on newspapers' sites updated throughout the day; and on blogs, tweets, social media, and cable television. The new digital media are more diverse, more representative of multiple viewpoints, more interactive and participatory, and, to many, more interesting than traditional news media. Time will tell whether the shift to online news strengthens or harms American democracy.

9. *Adversarial journalism* refers to (*pp. 190–91*)
   a) the recent shift in American society away from general purpose sources of information and toward narrowly focused niche sources.
   b) an era in American history when political parties provided all of the financing for newspapers.
   c) an aggressive form of journalism that attempts to expose and antagonize the status quo.
   d) a form of reporting in which the media adopt an accepting and friendly posture toward the government and public officials.
   e) the process of preparing the public to take a particular view of an event or political actor.

10. In general, FCC regulations apply only to (*p. 191*)
    a) cable television.
    b) Internet websites.
    c) over-the-air broadcast media.
    d) satellite radio.
    e) newspapers and magazines.

11. The now-defunct requirement that broadcasters provide time for opposing views when they air programs on controversial issues was called (*p. 192*)
    a) the equal time rule.
    b) the fairness doctrine.
    c) the right of rebuttal.
    d) the response rule.
    e) the free speech doctrine.

12. Which of the following is true of today's media? (*p. 193*)
    a) Print media remain the primary news source for most Americans.
    b) The media are more partisan than in recent years.
    c) Online news readership is in decline.
    d) Virtually all Americans can be considered "digital citizens."
    e) Digital citizenship is equally spread amongst whites, blacks, and Latinos.

Key Terms

agenda setting (*p. 187*) the power of the media to bring public attention to particular issues and problems

citizen journalism (*p. 183*) news reported and distributed by citizens, rather than professional journalists and for-profit news organizations

digital citizen (*p. 181*) a daily Internet user with high-speed home Internet access and the technology and literacy skills to go online for employment, news, politics, entertainment, commerce, and other activities

equal time rule (*p. 191*) the requirement that broadcasters provide candidates for the same political office equal opportunities to communicate their messages to the public

fairness doctrine (*p. 192*) a Federal Communications Commission requirement

for broadcasters who air programs on controversial issues to provide time for opposing views; the FCC ceased enforcing this doctrine in 1985

framing (*p. 187*) the power of the media to influence how events and issues are interpreted

niche journalism (*p. 183*) news reporting devoted to a targeted portion (subset) of a journalism market sector or for a portion of readers or viewers based on content or ideological presentation

priming (*p. 188*) process of preparing the public to take a particular view of an event or political actor

right of rebuttal *(p. 192)* a Federal Communications Commission regulation giving individuals the right to have the opportunity to respond to personal attacks made on a radio or television broadcast

selection bias (news) *(p. 187)* the tendency to focus news coverage on only one aspect of an event or issue, avoiding coverage of other aspects

social media *(p. 184)* web-based and mobile-based technologies that are used to turn communication into interactive dialogue between organizations, communities, and individuals; social media technologies take on many different forms including blogs, Wikis, podcasts, pictures, video, Facebook, and Twitter

For Further Reading

Ansolabehere, Stephen, and Shanto Iyengar. *Going Negative: How Attack Ads Shrink and Polarize the Electorate.* New York: Free Press, 1995.

Campbell, Richard, Christopher Martin, and Bettina Fabos. *Media and Culture.* New York: St. Martin's Press, 2009.

Carr, Nicholas. *The Shallows: What the Internet Is Doing to Our Brains.* New York: W. W. Norton, 2011.

de Zengotita, Thomas. *Mediated: How the Media Shapes Our World and the Way We Live in It.* New York: Bloomsbury, 2006.

Fenton, Tom. *Bad News: The Decline of Reporting, the Business of News, and the Danger to Us All.* New York: HarperCollins, 2005.

Fox, Richard, and Jennifer Ramos. *iPolitics: Citizens, Elections and Governing in the New Media Era.* New York: Cambridge University Press, 2011.

Graber, Doris, and Johanna Dunaway. *Mass Media and American Politics*, 9th ed. Washington, DC: CQ Press, 2014.

Hallin, Daniel C. *The Uncensored War.* Berkeley and Los Angeles: University of California Press, 1986.

Iyengar, Shanto, and Donald Kinder. *News That Matters: Television and American Public Opinion.* Chicago: University of Chicago Press, 2010.

Jenkins, Henry. *Convergence Culture: Where Old and New Media Collide.* New York: New York University Press, 2008.

MacArthur, John. *Second Front: Censorship and Propaganda in the 1991 Gulf War.* Berkeley and Los Angeles: University of California Press, 2004.

Rutherford, Paul. *Weapons of Mass Persuasion.* Toronto: University of Toronto Press, 2004.

Spitzer, Robert J., ed. *Media and Public Policy.* Westport, CT: Praeger, 1993.

West, Darrell M. *Air Wars: Television Advertising in Election Campaigns, 1952–2012.* Washington, DC: CQ Press, 2013.

For much of the country's history, large groups of Americans were denied the right to vote. Most restrictions on voting have been eliminated for Americans age 18 and older, but voter turnout remains relatively low, especially among young voters. Will the rise of online politics increase participation?

POLLING PLACE
投票站 CASILLA ELECTORAL
投票所 LUGAR NG BOTOHAN
투표소 PHÒNG PHIẾU

Political Parties, Participation, and Elections

WHAT GOVERNMENT DOES AND WHY IT MATTERS President Barack Obama was re-elected to a second term as president of the United States in the 2012 election against Republican challenger Mitt Romney. In defeating Romney, Obama won nearly every battleground state, including Colorado, Iowa, Ohio, New Hampshire, Virginia, Wisconsin, and the pivotal state of Florida, the fourth largest state in population. Florida is important not only because of its large number of Electoral College votes but because the numbers of Republicans and Democrats in the state are roughly equal, making it fiercely competitive every four years. What also made Florida unusual in 2012 was the large number of votes cast early, prior to Election Day. Early voting made a difference in 2012 even though new state rules had limited early voting.

Nationwide, 25 percent of all votes were early votes, cast either in person or absentee (by mail ballots). In Florida, 53 percent of votes cast (4.5 million votes of Florida's 8.4 million total votes) were early votes, one of the highest rates in the nation.[1] Early voting is a form of convenience voting: it allows citizens to vote in alternative ways, on their own schedule, rather than requiring that all votes be cast only in person on Election Day. As of 2014, 33 states allow early voting in which any qualified voter may cast a ballot in person during a designated period prior to Election Day.[2] Early voting mattered in

Florida and in the 2012 presidential race in part because Obama's campaign took advantage of early-voting laws, employing a sophisticated voter registration database to get out the vote, and calling, messaging, and emailing supporters until it was confirmed that a ballot had been cast.

But in 2012 the Republican-controlled Florida state legislature significantly reduced the number of days allowed for early voting from 14 days prior to the election to 8. The change eliminated weekend polling hours when many African Americans voted after church, with transportation provided by their congregation to and from the polls. Which voters were negatively affected by this election rule change?

Research by political scientists Michael Herron and Daniel Smith showed that racial minorities, particularly African Americans, as well as individuals registered as Democratic and those registered without party affiliation, had reduced turnout in 2012 compared to 2008.[3] Obama still won Florida, even with reduced turnout of African Americans and Democrats, but the change to early voting rules impacted the race. Elections are determined not just by how people vote, but by *who* votes.

Political parties and elections are all about who controls the government; participation is about who gets involved and why. Social forces work through the parties to gain control over government personnel (meaning those who run the government) and policies. Parties are also a means by which those in government try to influence important groups in society. Political parties, participation, and elections are mechanisms that can help citizens change their government but that may also help leaders consolidate or extend power.

chaptergoals

- Explain the roles that parties play in American elections and government (pp. 201–4)

- Describe the American party system and how it has changed over time (pp. 204–14)

- Identify the most common forms of political participation (pp. 215–220)

- Examine the factors that influence voters' decisions (pp. 221–24)

- Explain the major rules, levels, and types of elections in the United States (pp. 224–26)

- Analyze the strategies, issues, and outcomes of the 2012 and 2014 elections (pp. 226–31)

- Describe how candidates raise the money they need to run (pp. 231–34)

Parties and Elections Have Been Vital to American Politics and Government

Explain the roles that parties play in American elections and government

Political parties, like interest groups, are organized groups that attempt to influence the government by electing their members to government offices. Ordinarily they can be distinguished from interest groups on the basis of their orientation. A party seeks to control the entire government by electing its members to office and thereby controlling the government. Interest groups, by comparison, don't control the operation of government and its personnel, but rather try to influence government policies.

Political Parties Arose from the Electoral Process

Political parties as they are known today developed along with the expansion of suffrage and can be understood only in the context of elections. Political parties and elections are so intertwined that American parties actually take their structure from the electoral process. The shape of party organization in the United States has followed a simple rule: for every district where an election is held, there should be some kind of party unit. Between 1900 and 1952, Republicans failed to maintain party units in most counties of the southern states where the Democratic Party had a near-monopoly; Democrats were similarly unsuccessful in many areas of New England where the Republican Party dominated politics. But for most of the history of the United States, two major parties have had enough of an organized presence to oppose each other in elections in most of the nation's towns, cities, and counties. This makes the American party system one of the oldest political institutions in the history of democracy.

Political parties play a traditionally important role in elections. They recruit candidates to run for office, get their loyal party members out to vote, and work in a variety of ways to promote the causes and issues of the party. In earlier times the parties had near total control over the electoral process. In recent decades, however, they have lost their monopoly to candidates who decide not to work within the party, to **political action committees (PACs)** that raise and distribute millions of dollars for candidates, and to direct appeals through the media.

Parties Recruit Candidates

One of the most important party activities is the recruitment of candidates for thousands of local, state, and national offices. Where they do not have an incumbent running for re-election, party leaders attempt to identify strong candidates and to interest them in entering the campaign.

An ideal candidate will have an unblemished record and the capacity to raise enough money to mount a serious campaign. Party leaders are usually not willing to provide financial backing to candidates who are unable to raise substantial funds on their own. For a U.S. House seat, this can mean several hundred

With no incumbent running for Montana's at-large House district in 2014, the Democrats nominated John Lewis (left), a former congressional aide, and the Republicans nominated Ryan Zinke (right), a state senator.

thousand dollars; for a Senate seat, a serious candidate must be able to raise several million dollars. Often, party leaders have difficulty finding attractive candidates and persuading them to run. Candidate recruitment has become particularly difficult in an era in which **incumbents** (candidates running for re-election to positions that they already hold) are hard to beat, when lengthy political campaigns often involve mudslinging, and when candidates must assume that their personal lives will be intensely scrutinized in the press.[4] Over 20 percent of House races are uncontested (meaning there is only one candidate from one party on the ballot) because challenging incumbents in the House and winning is so difficult. Incumbents in the House on average have more than double the money for their political campaigns than challengers, while Senate incumbents have on average 50 percent more.

Parties Organize Nominations

Article I, Section 4, of the Constitution delegates to the states the power to set the "times, places, and manner" of holding elections, even for U.S. senators and representatives. The Constitution has been amended from time to time to expand the right to participate in elections. Congress has also occasionally passed laws regulating elections, congressional districting, and campaign practices. But the Constitution and the laws are almost completely silent on nominations, setting only citizenship and age requirements for candidates. The president must be at least 35 years of age, a natural-born citizen, and a resident of the United States for 14 years. A senator must be at least 30, a U.S. citizen for at least nine years, and a resident of the state he or she represents. A member of the House must be at least 25, a U.S. citizen for seven years, and a resident of the state he or she represents.

Nomination is the process by which political parties select their candidates for election to public office. The nominating process can precede the election by many months, as it does when the many candidates for the presidency are eliminated from consideration through a grueling series of state primaries until there is only one survivor in each party: the party's nominee.

Parties Help Get Out the Vote

The general election period begins immediately after the nominations. Historically, this has been a time of glory for the political parties, whose popular base of support is fully displayed. All the paraphernalia of party committees (signs, bumper stickers, buttons) is on display, and all the committee members are activated into local party workforces.

The first step involves voter registration. There was a time when party workers were responsible for virtually all this kind of electoral activity, but they have been supplemented by groups such as the League of Women Voters, unions, and chambers of commerce, although the parties frequently mail notices and call voters to ensure that they are registered.

Registered voters then have to decide on Election Day whether to go to the polling place, stand in line, and actually vote for the various candidates and referenda on the ballot. If they are planning to vote by mail in one of the states that allows this, they have to request the ballot, fill it out, and return it. Political parties, candidates, and campaigning can make a big difference in persuading voters to vote. Voter mobilization, once an art, has now become a science. In recent years both parties have developed an extensive database on hundreds of millions of potential voters, allowing the two parties to bring their search for votes, contributions, and campaign help down to named individuals. In the 2008 and 2012 elections the Democrats made their voter files available to state parties, and this technology became one of the keys to their successful mobilization and get-out-the-vote activities those years. Narwhal was the code name for the data platform of the 2012 Obama campaign (Narwhal is the name of a little-known type of whale), allowing campaign workers to track voters and volunteers using Amazon services. Obama's technology team employed elite talent from Twitter, Google, Facebook, Craigslist, and Quora, with most staffers in their 30s. The Republicans too employed technology to enhance their voter mobilization effort, code named Orca (the Orca whale is the only known killer of the Narwhal whale).

Parties Organize Power in Congress

Congress depends more on the party system than is generally recognized. For one thing, power in Congress is organized along party lines. Specifically, the speakership of the House is essentially a party office. All the members of the House take part in the election of the Speaker. But the actual selection is made by the **majority party**, that is, the party that holds the majority of seats in the House or Senate. (The other party is known as the **minority party**, meaning that it holds a minority of legislative seats in either the House or the Senate.) When the majority party presents a nominee to the entire House, its choice is then invariably ratified in a straight vote along party lines.

The committee system of both houses of Congress is also a product of the two-party system. For example, each party is assigned a quota of members for each committee, depending on the percentage of total seats held by the party. The assignment of individual members to these committees is a party decision. Each party has a "committee on committees" to make such decisions. Permission to transfer to another committee is also a party decision, as is advancement up the committee ladder toward the chair. Since the late nineteenth century, most advancements have been automatic—based on the length of continual service on the committee. This seniority system has existed only because of the support of the two parties, however, and either party can deviate from it—that is, pick someone with less seniority to chair a committee—by a simple vote.

Presidents Need Political Parties

Strong presidents with broad popular support can depend on party ties to get their legislation enacted in Congress. Yet there has been a trade-off in using the party machinery to support the president's legislative agenda and building it to support the party in congressional elections. The political scientist Daniel Galvin argues that since the Eisenhower presidency, Republicans have paid much more attention to party building than have Democrats.[5] Given their party's minority status in the electorate for much of the past 50 years, Republican presidents have sought to enhance the party's capabilities to mobilize voters and win elections. George W. Bush's adviser Karl Rove hoped to build a strong party apparatus that would ensure a permanent Republican majority. Democratic presidents have put much less energy into building the party apparatus, focusing instead on their legislative agenda and their own re-election. It was only after their 2004 election defeat that Democrats began to pour their energies into building a stronger party. Under the chairmanship of Howard Dean, a previous presidential candidate and a former Vermont governor, the Democratic National Committee (DNC) invested heavily in new technology and in creating party-mobilizing capabilities in states across the country, not just the traditionally "blue" states that have reliably voted Democratic.

The Obama campaign was able to use this party machinery as a springboard for its own mobilizing organization, Obama for America. With detailed information about Democratic Party activists, Obama for America's database became an important political resource for mobilizing Democrats. After Obama took office, the organization was renamed Organizing for America (OFA) and became an independent project of the DNC. During Obama's first year in office, the president used OFA to mobilize grassroots support for his legislative agenda. OFA took a very active part in lobbying members of Congress to support health care reform. OFA provides training for volunteers to learn how to become organizers, and it has established offices in nearly every state.

● America Is One of the Few Nations with a Two-Party System

> **Describe the American party system and how it has changed over time**

In his 1796 Farewell Address, President George Washington warned his countrymen to shun partisan politics. Nonetheless, a **two-party system**—a political system in which only two parties have a realistic opportunity to compete effectively for control of the government—emerged early in the history of the new Republic. Beginning with the Federalists and the

Jeffersonian Republicans in the 1790s, two major parties have dominated national politics, although which particular two parties they have been has changed with the times and issues. The two-party system today includes Democrats and Republicans.

However, the term *party system* refers to more than just the number of parties competing for power or the set of parties that are important at any given time. It also includes the organization of the parties, the balance of power between and within party coalitions, the parties' social and institutional bases, and the issues and policies around which party competition is organized. Seen from this broader perspective, the character of a nation's party system can change even if the number of parties remains the same and even when the same two parties seem to be competing for power. Today's American party system is very different from the country's party system of 50 years ago, but the Democrats and Republicans continue to be the major competing forces. Over the course of American history, changes in political forces and alignments have produced six distinctive party systems. (see Figure 7.1).

The First Party System: Federalists and Jeffersonian Republicans The first party system emerged in the 1790s and pitted the Federalists against the Jeffersonian Republicans. The Federalists spoke mainly for New England merchants and supported a program of protective tariffs to encourage manufacturing, assumption of the states' Revolutionary War debts, the creation of a national bank, and resumption of commercial ties with Britain. The Jeffersonians, led by southern agricultural interests, opposed these policies and instead favored free trade, the promotion of agricultural over commercial interests, and friendship with France. Over the years, the Federalists gradually weakened and disappeared altogether after the pro-British sympathies of some Federalist leaders during the War of 1812 led to charges of treason against the party.

From the collapse of the Federalists until the 1830s, America had only one political party, the Jeffersonian Republicans, who gradually came to be known as the Democrats. This period of one-party politics had an absence of party competition. Throughout this period, however, there was intense factional conflict within the Democratic Party, particularly between the supporters and opponents of General Andrew Jackson, America's great military hero of the War of 1812. Jackson's opponents united to deny him the presidency in 1824, but Jackson won election in 1828 and again in 1832. Jackson's base of support was in the South and the West, and he generally espoused a program of free trade and policies that would make it easier to borrow money, which appealed to those regions. During the 1830s, groups opposing Jackson united to form a new political force, the Whig Party, thus giving rise to the second American party system.

The Second Party System: Democrats and Whigs Both the Democrats and the Whigs built party organizations throughout the nation, and both sought to enlarge their bases of support by expanding the right to vote. They increased the number of eligible voters through the elimination of property restrictions

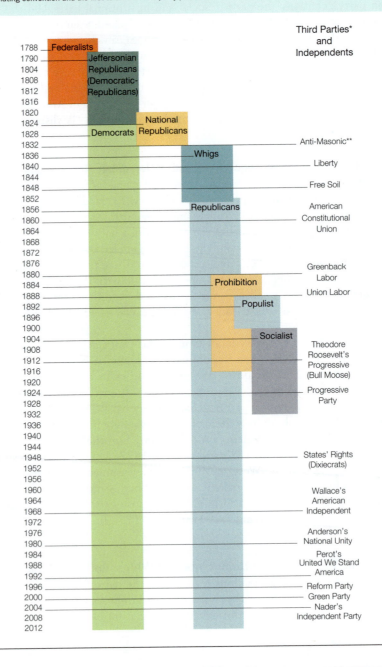

FIGURE 7.1 How the Party System Evolved

During the nineteenth century, the Democrats and the Republicans emerged as the two dominant parties in American politics. As the American party system evolved, many third parties emerged, but few of them remained in existence for very long.

*Or in some cases, fourth parties; most of these parties lasted through only one term.
**The Anti-Masonics had the distinction of being not only the first third party but also the first party to hold a national nominating convention and the first to announce a party platform.

and other barriers to voting—at least voting by white males. Support for the new Whig Party was stronger in the Northeast than in the South and West, and stronger among merchants than among small farmers. Hence, in some measure, the Whigs were the successors of the Federalists. Yet conflict between the two parties revolved more around personalities than policies. The Whigs were a diverse group united more by opposition to the Democrats than by agreement on programs. In 1840 the Whigs won their first presidential election under the leadership of General William Henry Harrison, a military hero known as Old Tippecanoe. The Whig campaign carefully avoided issues—since the party could agree on almost none—and emphasized the personal qualities and heroism of the candidate. The Whigs also invested heavily in campaign rallies and entertainment to win the hearts, if not exactly the minds, of the voters. The 1840 campaign came to be called the "hard cider" campaign because of the practice of using food and especially drink to win votes.

During the late 1840s and early 1850s, conflicts over slavery produced sharp divisions within both the Whig and the Democratic parties, despite the efforts of party leaders to develop compromises. By 1856 the Whig Party had all but disintegrated under the strain, and many Whig politicians and voters, along with antislavery Democrats, joined the new Republican Party, which pledged to ban slavery from the western territories. In 1860 the Republicans nominated Abraham Lincoln for the presidency. Lincoln's victory strengthened southern calls for secession from the Union and, soon thereafter, for all-out civil war.

The Civil War and Post–Civil War Party System: Republicans and Democrats During the course of the war, President Lincoln depended heavily on Republican governors and state legislatures to raise troops, provide funding, and maintain popular support for a long and bloody military conflict. The secession of the South had stripped the Democratic Party of many of its leaders and supporters, but the Democrats remained politically competitive throughout the war and nearly won the 1864 presidential election against Republican Lincoln because of war weariness on the part of the northern public. With the defeat of the Confederacy in 1865, some congressional Republicans sought to convert the South into a Republican bastion through a program of Reconstruction that enfranchised newly freed slaves. This Reconstruction program collapsed in the 1870s as a result of disagreement within the Republican Party in Congress and violent resistance by southern whites. With the end of Reconstruction, the former Confederate states regained full membership in the Union and full control of their internal affairs. Throughout the South, African Americans were deprived of hard-won political rights, including the right to vote, despite post–Civil War constitutional guarantees to the contrary. The post–Civil War South was solidly Democratic in its political affiliation, and with a firm southern base, the national Democratic Party was able to confront the Republicans on a more or less equal basis. From the end of the Civil War to the 1890s, the Republican Party remained the party of the North, with strong business and middle-class support, while the Democrats were the party of the South, with support also from northern working-class and immigrant groups.

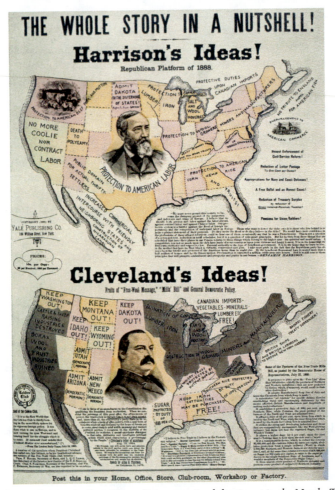

Following the Civil War, the Republican Party remained dominant in the North. This poster supporting Republican Benjamin Harrison in the 1888 election promises protective tariffs and other policies that appealed to the industrial states in the North.

The System of 1896: Republicans and Democrats

During the 1890s profound and rapid social and economic changes led to the emergence of a variety of protest parties, including the Populist Party, which appealed mainly to small farmers but also attracted western mining interests and urban workers. In the 1892 presidential election, the Populist Party carried four states and elected governors in eight. In 1896 the Populist Party effectively merged with the Democrats, who nominated William Jennings Bryan, a Democratic senator with pronounced Populist sympathies, for the presidency. The Republicans nominated the conservative senator William McKinley. In the ensuing campaign, northern and midwestern businesses made an all-out effort to defeat what they saw as a radical threat from the Populist-Democratic alliance. By the time the dust settled, the Republicans had won a resounding victory and confined the Democrats to their smaller bases of support in the South and far West. For the next 36 years, the Republicans were the nation's majority party, carrying seven of nine presidential elections and controlling both houses of Congress in 15 of 18 contests. The Republican Party of this era was very much the party of American business, advocating low taxes, high tariffs on imports, and a minimum of government regulation. The Democrats were far too weak to offer much opposition.

The New Deal Party System: Reversal of Fortune Soon after the Republican presidential candidate Herbert Hoover won the 1928 presidential election, the nation's economy collapsed. The Great Depression, which produced unprecedented economic hardship, stemmed from many causes, but from the perspective of millions of Americans, the Republican Party did not do enough to promote economic recovery. In 1932, Americans elected Franklin Delano Roosevelt (FDR) and a solidly Democratic Congress. FDR developed a program for economic recovery that he dubbed the New Deal. Under the auspices of the New Deal, the size and reach of America's national government increased substantially. The federal government took responsibility for economic management and social welfare to an extent that was unprecedented in American history. Roosevelt designed many of his programs specifically to expand the political base of the Democratic Party. He rebuilt and revitalized the party around a nucleus of unionized workers, upper-middle-class intellectuals and professionals, southern farmers, Jews, Catholics, and African Americans—the so-called New Deal coalition that made the Democrats the nation's majority party for the next 36 years. Groping for a response to the New Deal, Republicans often wound up supporting popular New Deal programs such as Social Security in what was sometimes derided as "me-too" Republicanism. Even the relatively conservative administration of Dwight D. Eisenhower in the 1950s left the principal New Deal programs intact.

The New Deal coalition was severely strained during the 1960s by conflicts over civil rights and the Vietnam War. The struggle over civil rights initially divided northern Democrats who supported the civil rights cause from white southern Democrats who defended the system of racial segregation. The struggle over the Vietnam War further divided the Democrats, with upper-income liberal Democrats strongly opposing the Johnson administration's decision to greatly expand the numbers of U.S. troops fighting in Southeast Asia. These schisms provided an opportunity for the Republicans' "Grand Old Party," or GOP, which returned to power in 1968 under the leadership of Richard Nixon.

The Contemporary American Party System The Republican Party widened its appeal in the second half of the twentieth century (see Figure 7.2). In 1964, for example, the conservative Republican presidential candidate Barry Goldwater argued in favor of substantially reduced levels of taxation and spending, less government regulation of the economy, and the elimination of many federal social programs. Though Goldwater was defeated by Lyndon Johnson, the ideas he espoused continued to be major themes for the Republican Party. It took Richard Nixon's "southern strategy" to give the GOP the votes it needed to end Democratic dominance of national politics. Nixon appealed to disaffected

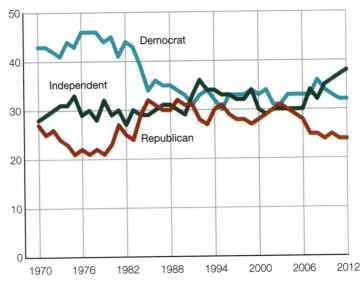

FIGURE 7.2 Americans' Party Identification, 1970–2012

Over time, the Democrats have lost strength as more Americans identified themselves as Republicans and independents. Why do you think the percentage of people identifying themselves as independents grew during the 1970s?

SOURCE: Pew Research Center, www.people-press.org/2012/06/01/trend-in-party-identification-1939-2012/ (accessed 6/24/14).

PERCENTAGE IDENTIFYING THEMSELVES AS . . .

Democrat

Independent

Republican

white southerners, and with the help of the independent candidate and former Alabama governor George Wallace, he sparked the shift of voters that gave the Republican Party a strong position in all the states of the former Confederacy. During the 1980s, under the leadership of President Ronald Reagan, Republicans added two additional important groups to their coalition. The first were religious conservatives, who were offended by Democratic support for abortion and gay rights as well as perceived Democratic disdain for traditional cultural and religious values. The second were working-class whites, who were drawn to Reagan's tough approach to foreign policy and his positions against affirmative action.

While Republicans built a political base around economic and social conservatives and white southerners, the Democratic Party maintained its support among a majority of unionized workers and upper-middle-class intellectuals and professionals. Democrats also appealed strongly to racial minorities. The 1965 Voting Rights Act had greatly increased black voter participation in the South and helped the Democratic Party retain some House and Senate seats in southern states. And whereas the Republicans appealed to social conservatives, the Democrats appealed strongly to Americans concerned with abortion rights, gay rights, women's rights, the environment, and other progressive social causes.

In 2008, Democrats reached beyond their base by appealing to moderate voters in states that had once been Republican strongholds, and they won control of Congress as well as the presidency for the first time since 1995. However, intense party conflict continued to characterize American politics. Republicans won control of the House of Representatives in 2010, and although Obama was re-elected to the presidency in 2012, control of Congress remained divided through 2014, when Republicans won majorities in both houses.

Electoral Realignments Define Party Systems in American History

The points of transition between party systems in American history are sometimes called **electoral realignments**, the points in history when a new party supplants the ruling party, becoming in turn the dominant political force. During these periods, the coalitions that support the parties and the balance of power between the parties are redefined. In historical terms, realignments occur when new issues, combined with economic or political crises, mobilize new voters and persuade large numbers of voters to reexamine their traditional partisan loyalties and permanently shift their support from one party to another.

There is general agreement that five realignments have occurred since the Founding. The first took place around 1790–1800, when the Jeffersonian Republicans defeated the Federalists and became dominant. The second realignment occurred in about 1828, when the Jacksonian Democrats took control of the White House and the Congress. In the third period of realignment, centered on 1860, the newly founded Republican Party, led by Abraham Lincoln, won power and in the process destroyed the Whig Party. Many northern voters who had supported the Whigs or the Democrats on the basis of their economic stands shifted their support to the Republicans as slavery replaced tariffs and economic concerns as the central item on the nation's political agenda. Many southern Whigs shifted their support to the Democrats.

In the 1890s this alignment was at least partially supplanted by an alignment of political forces based on economic and cultural factors, bringing about the fourth electoral realignment. In the election of 1896, the Republican candidate, William McKinley, emphasizing business, industry, and urban interests, defeated the Democrat, William Jennings Bryan, who spoke for sectional interests, farmers, and fundamentalism. Republican dominance lasted until the fifth realignment, during the period 1932–36, when the Democrats, led by FDR, took control of the White House and Congress and, despite sporadic interruptions, maintained control of both through the 1960s. Since that time, American party politics has been characterized primarily by party polarization and by **divided government**, wherein the presidency is controlled by one party while the other party controls one or both houses of Congress.

American Third Parties Have Altered the Shape of the Major Parties

Although the United States has a two-party-dominant system, the country has always had more than two parties. Typically, **third parties** in the United States (parties that organize to compete against the two major American political parties) have represented social and economic interests that, for one reason or another, were not given voice by the two major parties.[6] Such parties often provide new ideas and even party realignment. The Populists, a party centered in the rural areas of the West and Midwest, and the Progressives, spokespeople for the urban middle classes in the late nineteenth and early twentieth centuries, are the most important examples in the past 100 years. More recently, Ross Perot, who ran in 1992 for president as an independent and in 1996 as the Reform Party's nominee, won the votes of almost one in five Americans in 1992. In the extremely close 2000 presidential election, third-party candidate Ralph Nader won just 3 percent of the popular vote, but that was enough to swing the election to Republican George W. Bush. Although most Nader voters preferred Democrat Al Gore, Nader siphoned off enough votes from Gore to throw the election to Bush. Table 7.1 lists the top presidential candidates in 2012, including the top independent and third-party candidates. In addition to the candidates listed in Table 7.1, the Socialist Party, the Prohibition Party, and several other parties nominated candidates for the presidency in 2012.

Although the Republican Party was the only American third party ever to make itself permanent (by replacing the Whigs), other third parties have enjoyed an influence far beyond their electoral size. This was because large parts of their programs were adopted by one or both of the major parties, who sought to appeal to the voters mobilized by the new party to expand their own electoral strength. The Democratic Party, for example, became a great deal more liberal

---

TABLE 7.1

Parties and Candidates in 2012

CANDIDATE	PARTY	VOTE TOTAL	PERCENTAGE OF VOTE
Barack Obama	Democratic	65,907,213	51.06%
Mitt Romney	Republican	60,931,767	47.21
Gary Johnson	Libertarian	1,275,804	0.99
Jill Stein	Green	469,501	0.36
Virgil Goode	Constitution	122,001	0.09

SOURCE: Federal Election Commission, www.fec.gov.

when it adopted most of the Progressive program early in the twentieth century. Many Socialists felt that FDR's New Deal had adopted most of their party's program, including old-age pensions, unemployment compensation, an agricultural marketing program, and laws guaranteeing workers the right to organize into unions.

Although it is not technically a political party, the Tea Party movement had a considerable impact on the Republican Party primaries in 2010, when Tea Party candidates defeated several incumbents and candidates endorsed by Republican Party leaders. Some high-profile Tea Party candidates, including Rand Paul (R-Ky.), then went on to win office in the 2010 midterm elections, but on the whole, the Tea Party succeeded in electing only about 32 percent of its candidates. Though it took the name "Tea Party" and sponsored a national convention, the Tea Party movement is not a formal party. It is an organized challenge to incumbents by the most conservative wing of the Republican Party.[6]

Some proponents of election reform argue that two major parties are not sufficient to represent the varied interests of America's 317 million people, and more political parties would improve representation. Forms of **proportional representation**, multimember districts (more than one candidate elected from each district), or instant runoff voting would increase the probability of third-party representation in America. Yet state ballot-access laws are often a major impediment for third parties, which often fail to meet the criteria to get on the ballot, such as registration fees or petition requirements in which a certain number of voters must sign a petition for a third-party or independent candidate to gain ballot access. States with lower access hurdles, such as Minnesota, have more third-party candidates. Supporters of the current system, on the other hand, contend that America's two-party system creates stability in governing and prevents the need for coalition government, where multiple small parties work together to form a majority to govern.

Group Affiliations Are Based on Voters' Psychological Ties to One of the Parties

One reason parties are so important is that many voters develop **party identification** (an individual voter's psychological ties to one party or another) with one of the political parties. Party identification has been compared to wearing blue- or red-tinted glasses; they color voters' understanding of politics in general and are the most important cue as to how to vote in elections. That is, most Republicans vote for Republican Party candidates, and most Democrats vote for Democratic Party candidates. Although it is an emotional tie, party identification also has a rational component. Voters generally form attachments to parties that reflect their views and interests. Once those attachments are formed, however, they are likely to persist and even to be handed down to children, unless some very strong factors convince individuals that their party is no longer an appropriate object of their affections. Figure 7.3 indicates the relationship between party identification and a number of social criteria.

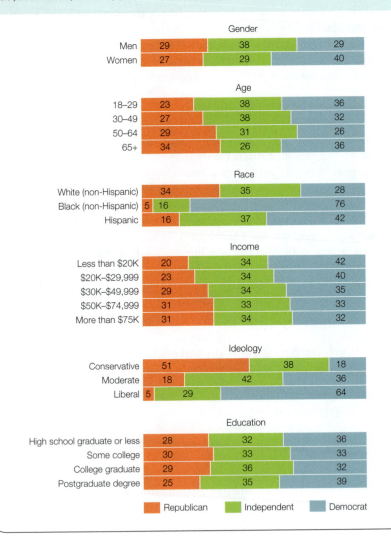

FIGURE 7.3 Who Identifies with Which Party?

Party identification varies by income, race, and gender. For example, as these statistics from 2012 show, Americans with higher incomes are more likely to support the Republican Party. Women are significantly more likely than men to identify with the Democratic Party, whereas more men identify as independents.

NOTE: Percentages do not add to 100 because the category "Other/Don't know" is omitted. In this survey, this category was always between 2 and 5 percent of respondents.
SOURCE: Pew Research Center for the People and the Press, www.people-press.org/2012/08/23/a-closer-look-at-the-parties-in-2012 (accessed 5/9/14).

Gender
	Republican	Independent	Democrat
Men	29	38	29
Women	27	29	40

Age
	Republican	Independent	Democrat
18–29	23	38	36
30–49	27	38	32
50–64	29	31	26
65+	34	26	36

Race
	Republican	Independent	Democrat
White (non-Hispanic)	34	35	28
Black (non-Hispanic)	5	16	76
Hispanic	16	37	42

Income
	Republican	Independent	Democrat
Less than $20K	20	34	42
$20K–$29,999	23	34	40
$30K–$49,999	29	34	35
$50K–$74,999	31	33	33
More than $75K	31	34	32

Ideology
	Republican	Independent	Democrat
Conservative	51	38	18
Moderate	18	42	36
Liberal	5	29	64

Education
	Republican	Independent	Democrat
High school graduate or less	28	32	36
Some college	30	33	33
College graduate	29	36	32
Postgraduate degree	25	35	39

Republican   Independent   Democrat

Political Participation Takes Both Traditional and Online Forms

Identify the most common forms of political participation

Political participation refers to a wide range of activities designed to influence government, politics, and policy. These activities include traditional forms of participation, such as voting and volunteering, as well as newer online forms of participation.

Voting Is the Most Important Form of Traditional Participation

Elections are the hallmark of political participation in a democracy. For most citizens today, voting is the most common form of participation in politics. In addition to voting, citizens can give money to politicians or political organizations, volunteer in campaigns, contact political officials, sign petitions, attend public meetings, join organizations, display campaign signs and pins, write letters to the editor, publish articles, attend rallies, or lobby their representatives in Congress; they can even sue the government or run for elected office. They can also join interest groups, which will be discussed in Chapter 8. These other forms of political action generally require more time, effort, or money than voting. In a 2008 survey of participation, just 22 percent of respondents said they had attended a local community meeting in the previous year; 16 percent said they had contacted a public official. Only 10 percent of those surveyed reported giving money to a candidate's campaign during the election, while 9 percent said they had attended a rally or political meeting. Fewer than 5 percent of those questioned said they had actually spent time volunteering for a political campaign.[7]

Online Political Participation Is Surging

Online political participation is rapidly changing the way Americans experience politics. While traditional forms of participation remain important, the Internet gives citizens greater access to political information about campaigns and candidates and, at least potentially, a greater role in politics than ever before. Many forms of online participation build on traditional forms of participation, but the Internet makes many of these activities easier and gives them greater potential as community-building tools. The Internet has been called a telephone, library, soapbox, storehouse of information, and channel for communication—all in one. As of 2012 nearly 7 in 10 Americans read the news online, and nearly as many used online political information. Smartphones, or Internet-enabled mobile devices, which were used by 40 percent of Americans in 2012, bring the power of the Internet for politics via mobile applications to new heights. Today these online forms of participation have become more common than most of the traditional forms of participation just discussed.[8]

Online participation in elections includes discussing issues or mobilizing supporters through email and Twitter; posting comments on blogs and online news stories; contributing money to candidates; visiting candidate and political party websites; creating and viewing online campaign ads; campaigning on social networking sites; and organizing face-to-face neighborhood meetings on

Like the traditional "I Voted" stickers, political messages shared on social media may remind and encourage others to participate too. In 2012, Facebook users could click an "I Voted" button to announce that they had cast a ballot.

sites such as Meetup.com. The mobile revolution is particularly important for political mobilization and organization. Sixty percent of Americans have Internet-enabled cell phones, or smartphones, that bring the power of digital politics to new heights. Today online forms of participation have become more common than most traditional forms of participation, in that they are performed on a daily or weekly basis. In 2012 every serious presidential candidate had a Facebook page, with millions of fans who received weekly if not daily updates from the campaigns and candidates. These fans, in turn, signaled to their "friends" which candidates they supported for elected office, making politics part of everyday discussion. While only 4 percent of likely voters went online for election information in 1996, 61 percent of Americans reported looking at information online or discussing politics online in 2012, according to Pew's Internet and American Life Project.[9]

Survey data from Pew illustrate how widespread digital politics has become. Sixty-six percent of social media users—or 39 percent of American adults—have engaged in some form of civic or political activity using social media as of 2012. More than one in three social media users have used social media to encourage others to vote, and roughly the same percentage have shared their own thoughts or comments on politics using social media. Roughly the same percentage of Democrats, Republicans, and independents use social media for politics. The young (ages 18 to 29) are significantly more likely than middle-aged and older respondents to use social media for politics.

An important question is whether online political participation influences offline participation, especially voting. Political participation requires that people be motivated and have an interest in the outcome of the election. They must have the knowledge or capacity to understand how to participate, and they must be mobilized.[10] Because digital technology encourages information gathering and interaction between users by combining features of traditional media content with interpersonal communication for discussion and mobilization, the Internet has the potential to promote interest in politics and increase participation.

Voter Turnout in America Is Low

Today voting rights are granted to all American citizens age 18 and older, although some states revoke this right from those who have committed a felony or are mentally incompetent. Despite granting the right to vote, or **suffrage**, to women, racial minorities, and young adults, however, the percentage of eligible individuals who actually vote in America, or **turnout**, is low. Only 6 in 10 eligible Americans vote in presidential elections, and turnout for midterm elections (elections that fall between presidential elections) is typically much lower, around 33 percent of eligible voters; for local elections, turnout is even lower.[11] (See Figure 7.4.) Turnout in state and local races that do not coincide with national contests is typically much lower. In most European countries and other Western democracies, by contrast, national voter turnout is usually between 70 and 90 percent.[12]

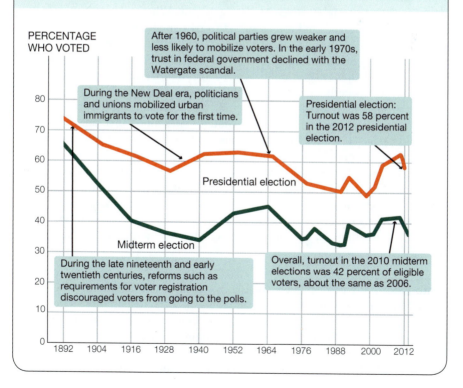

FIGURE 7.4 Voter Turnout in Presidential and Midterm Elections, 1892–2014

Since the 1890s, participation in elections has declined substantially. One pattern is consistent across time: more Americans tend to vote in presidential election years than in years when only congressional and local elections are held. What are some of the reasons that participation rose and fell during the last century?

SOURCE: Erik Austin and Jerome Clubb, *Political Facts of the United States since 1789* (New York: Columbia University Press, 1986); United States Election Project, www.electproject.org (accessed 11/12/14).

PERCENTAGE WHO VOTED

After 1960, political parties grew weaker and less likely to mobilize voters. In the early 1970s, trust in federal government declined with the Watergate scandal.

During the New Deal era, politicians and unions mobilized urban immigrants to vote for the first time.

Presidential election: Turnout was 58 percent in the 2012 presidential election.

Presidential election

Midterm election

During the late nineteenth and early twentieth centuries, reforms such as requirements for voter registration discouraged voters from going to the polls.

Overall, turnout in the 2010 midterm elections was 42 percent of eligible voters, about the same as 2006.

Why Do People Vote?

Three factors organize our understanding of voting in elections: (1) a person's social and demographic background and attitudes about politics, (2) the political environment in which elections take place and whether an election is contested among at least two political candidates, and finally (3) the state electoral laws that shape the political process.

Socioeconomic Status Americans with higher levels of education, more income, and higher-level occupations—collectively, what social scientists call higher **socioeconomic status**—participate much more in politics than do those with less education and less income.[13] Education level is the single most important factor in predicting whether an individual will vote or engage in most other kinds of participation. Income is an important factor (not surprisingly) when it comes to people making campaign contributions. Those with money, time, and capacity to participate effectively in the political system are more likely to do so.[14] Other individual characteristics also affect participation. For example, African Americans and Latinos are less likely to participate than are whites, although when differences in education and income are taken into account, African Americans participate at similar levels to whites.[15] Finally, young people are far less likely to participate in politics than are older people. Individuals with strong partisan ties to one of the major political parties are more likely to vote than nonpartisans or independents.

The Political Environment, Mobilization, and Competition Political environments have increasingly proven to be significant. Whether or not people have resources, feel engaged, and are recruited to participate in politics depends very much on their social setting—what their parents are like, whom they know, what associations they belong to. In the United States, churches are one important social institution for helping foster political participation. A critical aspect of political environments is whether people are mobilized—by parties, candidates, campaigns, interest groups, and social movements. A recent comprehensive study of the decline in political participation in the United States found that half of the drop-off could be accounted for by reduced **mobilization** efforts—the process by which large numbers of people are organized for a political activity.[16]

An additional factor is whether elections are competitive—that is, whether there are at least two candidates actively contesting a position in government.[17] Competitive elections, and the campaign spending and mobilization efforts that go along with them, directly affect turnout rates.[18] Conversely, limited exposure to competitive elections may be one reason for the lower levels of turnout recorded since the 1960s.

State Electoral Laws State electoral laws, which vary widely from state to state, create formal barriers to voting that can reduce participation. In most other democratic nations, where voting rates are higher, citizens are automatically registered to vote, but the United States requires a two-step process: registering to vote and then voting. Registration requirements particularly reduce the voting by the young, those with low education, and those with low incomes because registration requires higher

Several states in the west allow anyone who wishes to vote by mail to do so; in the east, voting by mail is usually only permitted for specific reasons. Voting by mail facilitates voting for those who may find it difficult to make it to the polls—for instance, because they live in a rural area, work long hours, have child care responsibilities, or do not have easy access to transportation.

political involvement, planning, and effort than does the act of voting itself. Those with relatively little education may become interested in politics once the issues of a particular campaign become salient, but by then it may be too late for them to register, especially if they live in states that require registration up to a month before the election. And because young people tend to change residences more often than older people, registration requirements place a greater burden on them. (Look inside the back cover of this book for information on registering to vote in your state.)

In addition to registration, other election regulations have an impact on turnout. For example, whereas most other nations hold elections on weekends, when most people are not working, and Election Day is treated as a holiday, America holds elections during the work week. Many states maintain residency requirements that result in citizens' losing their registration if they move their residences even short distances. Most states purge their voter registration rolls of voters who fail to vote for a given period of time. Americans hold many different elections, often at staggered times throughout the year, such as primary elections and elections for local offices and school budget votes, rather than consolidating elections at a single time. A relatively recent barrier is a requirement that voters provide proof of identity. Thirty-one states now require all voters to show some form of ID before voting. Eight states require a photo ID, while another eight request photo ID but may count the vote with non-photo ID under some circumstances. In the remaining states, non-photo forms of ID are acceptable.[19] Voter identification laws in the states may disproportionately reduce voter turnout of certain groups.[20]

Voter Turnout in Comparison

Over the past 20 years, voter turnout in U.S. national elections has hovered around 45 percent of the voting-age population. While the number is higher in presidential elections than during midterm elections,[a] turnout in the United States still lags behind many democracies.

So why does voter turnout vary so much from country to country? Part of the explanation rests in how we calculate who is eligible to vote. In some countries, it is not enough just to be of voting age. For example, in the United States, noncitizens and ex-felons are denied voting rights. If we exclude those populations from the base when calculating what percentage of people voted, turnout is several percentage points higher.[b]

Another part of the explanation has to do with the rules governing elections and whether they make it easier to vote. In many democracies, citizens are automatically registered to vote when they reach a certain age; in contrast, U.S. citizens have to register to vote and reregister whenever they move. Many countries hold their elections on a Sunday, send their ballots through the mail, or declare their election day a national holiday, so that fewer voters have to choose between going to work or going to the polls. Voting is also compulsory in some countries. Australia, for instance, charges a $20 fee (about $17 in U.S. dollars) unless a citizen can provide a good excuse for why he or she did not vote. These factors and others help explain why turnout is lower in the United States than in many other countries.

Average Turnout in National Elections, 1990–2013

Country	Voting-Age Population Turnout (%)	Compulsory Voting	Weekend or Holiday Voting
Australia	82.3	Yes	Yes
Turkey	79.3	Yes	Yes
Brazil	78.3	Yes	Yes
Germany	71	No	Yes
South Africa	65.6	No	Yes
Japan	64.4	No	Yes
United Kingdom	64.3	No	No
India	61.5	No	Yes
United States	45	No	No
Switzerland	37.9	No	Yes

SOURCE: International Institute for Democracy and Electoral Assistance (IDEA), http://www.idea.int/vt/ (accessed 8/11/14).

[a]International Institute for Democracy and Electoral Assistance (IDEA), "Voter Turnout Data for the United States," www.idea.int/vt/countryview.cfm?id=231 (accessed 9/3/14).
[b]Michael P. McDonald, "National General Election VEP Turnout Rates, 1789–Present," updated 6/11/14, www.electproject.org/national-1789-present (accessed 9/3/14).

● Voters Decide Based on Party, Issues, and Candidate

> **Examine the factors that influence voter's decisions**

Three key factors influence voters' decisions at the polls: party loyalty, issue and policy concerns, and candidate characteristics. The prominence of these three bases for electoral choice varies from contest to contest and voter to voter.

Party Loyalty Is Important

Most voters feel a certain sense of identification or kinship with the Democratic or Republican Party. This sense of identification is often handed down from parents to children and is reinforced by social and cultural ties. Partisan identification predisposes voters in favor of their party's candidates and against those of the opposing party (see Figure 7.5). At the level of the presidential contest, issues and candidate personalities may become very important, although even here many Americans support presidential candidates only because of party loyalty. But partisanship is more likely to be a factor in the less-visible races, where issues and the candidates are not as well known. State legislative races, for

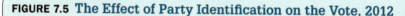

FIGURE 7.5 The Effect of Party Identification on the Vote, 2012

In 2012 more than 90 percent of Democrats and Republicans supported their party's presidential candidate. Should candidates devote their resources to converting voters who identify with the opposition or to winning more support among independents? What factors might make it difficult for candidates to simultaneously pursue both courses of action?

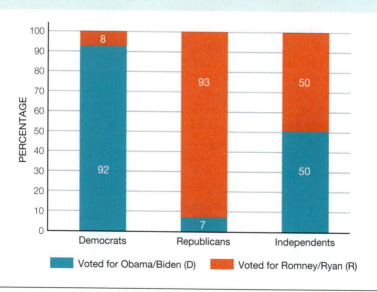

example, are often decided by voters' party ties. Once formed, voters' partisan loyalties seldom change. Voters tend to keep their party affiliations unless some crisis causes them to reexamine the bases for their loyalty and decide to support a different party, such as happened at the beginning of the New Deal era, between 1932 and 1936, when millions of former Republicans transferred their allegiance to FDR and the Democrats.

After the 1960s many analysts expressed concern that American parties had become too weak to play their role in converting popular political participation into effective government. These scholars noted such trends as a decline in partisan attachment within the electorate, a growth in the number of voters identifying as independents, and a rise in so-called split-ticket voting. This overall trend, sometimes termed "dealignment," was seen as a product of growing social diversity and educational attainment, which made voters less reliant on parties to guide their political decision making. The growth of the mass media, particularly television, also seemed to reduce the role of parties in elections, as television tends to focus on the personalities of individual candidates rather than the "institution" of the party. Today, party loyalties in America continue to be in a state of flux. On the one hand, the percentage of voters who declare no party loyalty remains at an all-time high.[21] On the other hand, party identification among a large number of the most active voters has grown stronger.[22]

There is an old saying that politics is the art of compromise, but it is more than that. It is also the challenge of making choices. Parties help to crystallize a world of possible government actions into a set of distinct choices. In so doing, they make it easier for ordinary citizens to understand politics, evaluate candidates, and make their own choices.

Issues Can Shape an Election

Issues and policy preferences are a second factor influencing voters' choices at the polls. Voters may cast their ballots for the candidate whose position on economic issues they believe to be closest to their own, or the candidate who has what they believe to be the best record on foreign policy. Issues are more important in some races than in others. If candidates actually do "take issue" with one another—that is, articulate and publicize very different positions on important public questions— voters are more likely to be able to identify and act on whatever policy preferences they may have.

The ability of voters to make choices on the basis of issue or policy preferences is diminished, however, if competing candidates do not differ substantially or do not focus their campaigns on policy matters. Very often, candidates deliberately take the safe course and emphasize positions that will not offend any voters. Thus, candidates often stress their opposition to corruption, crime, and inflation, since few voters favor these things. Such a strategy, though perfectly reasonable, makes it extremely difficult for voters to make their issue or policy preferences the basis for their choice at the polls.

The most important issue for voters in the 2012 election was the economy. Mitt Romney campaigned on his ability to turn around the deepest economic downturn since the Great Depression, and in exit polls he was seen as the candidate better equipped to handle the economy. The Obama campaign touted

In 2014, Republicans like Joni Ernst appealed to voters who were frustrated with Obama and the Democrats' economic and social policies. Ernst won the Iowa race for the Senate.

the rebound of the auto industry after the president's 2009 bailout package and his health care policy.

Candidate Characteristics Are More Important in the Media Age

Candidates' personal attributes always influence voters' decisions. The important candidate characteristics that affect voters' choices include race, ethnicity, religion, gender, geography, and social background. In general, voters may be proud to see someone of their ethnic, religious, or geographic background in a position of leadership, and they may presume that such candidates are likely to have views and perspectives close to their own. This is why, for many years, politicians sought to "balance the ticket," making certain that their party's ticket included members of as many important groups as possible.

Just as candidates' personal characteristics may attract some voters, they may repel others. Many voters are prejudiced against candidates of certain ethnic, racial, or religious groups. And for many years voters were reluctant to support the candidacies of women, although this appears to be changing. Indeed, the fact that in 2008 the Democratic candidate was a black man and the Republican vice-presidential candidate a woman indicates the increasing diversity of candidates for public office.

Voters also pay attention to candidates' personality characteristics, such as "decisiveness," "honesty," and "vigor." In recent years integrity has become a key election issue. In the 2012 election Obama's opponents painted him as a weak leader, unable to act decisively at home or abroad. Romney's opponents said he only cared about the super-rich, at the expense of the working class. He was also portrayed as antiminority and, in particular, anti-Latino, as his rhetoric was harsh on illegal immigrants when he used the term "self" deportation. However, voters seemed less concerned with these matters than with the ability of the candidates to deal with the nation's economic woes.

The Electoral Process Has Many Levels and Rules

Explain the major rules, levels, and types of elections in the United States

Four types of elections are held in the United States: primary elections, general elections, runoff elections, and initiative and referendum elections; the last are where proposed laws are placed on the ballot for a popular vote.

Primary elections are used to select each party's candidates for the general election. In the case of local and statewide offices, the winners of primary elections face one another as their parties' nominees in the general election. At the presidential level, however, primary elections are indirect because they are used to select state delegates to the national conventions, at which the major party presidential candidates are chosen. The United States is one of the few nations in the world to use primary elections. In most countries, nominations are controlled by party officials, as they once were here. The primary system was introduced at the turn of the twentieth century by Progressive reformers who hoped to weaken the power of party leaders by taking candidate nominations out of their hands.

Under the laws of most states, only registered members of a political party may vote in a primary election to select that party's candidates. This is called a **closed primary**. Other states allow all registered voters to choose on the day of the primary in which party's primary they will participate. This is called an **open primary**.

The primary is followed by the **general election**—the decisive electoral contest. The winner of the general election is elected to office for a specified term. In some states, however, mainly in the Southeast, if no candidate wins an absolute majority in the primary, a runoff election is held before the general election. This situation is most likely to arise if there are more than two candidates, none of whom receives a majority of the votes cast. A runoff election is held between the two candidates who received the largest number of votes.

Beyond presidential and congressional elections, 24 states also provide for the initiative process. **Ballot initiatives** are proposed laws or policy changes placed on the ballot by citizens or interest groups for a popular vote. If a ballot measure receives majority support, it becomes law. Controversial issues frequently appear on the ballots of states that use the initiative process, including proposals to ban same-sex marriage, raise the minimum wage, adopt legislative term limits, and institute election reform, among many others. In recent years voters in several states have voted to cut taxes, to prohibit social services for illegal immigrants, to end affirmative action, to protect open space and the environment, and to prevent offshore drilling. At the turn of the twentieth century, ballot initiatives were used to grant women suffrage (the right to vote), to prevent child labor, to limit the work day to eight hours, and to allow voters to elect U.S. senators directly, rather than having them chosen by state legislatures.

All 50 states have the legislative **referendum**, the practice of referring proposed laws passed by a legislature to the vote of the electorate for approval or rejection. Ballot initiative campaigns often involve high spending by proponents and opponents, and mass media campaigns that can rival those of congressional and presidential candidates within a state. The general referendum and initiative are called direct democracy. They allow voters to govern directly without intervention by government officials or the political parties. The validity of ballot measure results, however, is subject to judicial action. If a court finds that an initiative violates the state or national constitution, it can overturn the result. This happened in the case of a 1995 California initiative curtailing social services to illegal aliens and again in 2012 when the federal courts overturned California's Proposition 8 banning same-sex marriage.[23]

Eighteen states also have legal provisions for **recall** elections, which allow voters to remove governors and other state officials from office prior to the expiration of their terms. Generally, a recall effort begins with a petition campaign. In California, for example, if 12 percent of those who voted in the last general election sign petitions demanding a special recall election, one must be scheduled by the state board of elections. In 2003 many California voters blamed Governor Gray Davis for the state's $38 billion budget deficit, allowing his opponents to secure enough signatures to force a vote. Federal officials, such as the president and members of Congress, are not subject to recall.

The Electoral College Still Organizes Presidential Elections

In the early history of popular voting, nations often made use of indirect elections. In these elections, voters would choose the members of an intermediate body. These members would, in turn, select public officials. The assumption underlying such processes was that ordinary citizens were not really qualified to choose their leaders and could not be trusted to do so directly. The last vestige of this procedure in America is the **electoral college**, the presidential electors from each state who meet after the popular election to cast ballots for president and vice president.

When Americans go to the polls on Election Day, they are technically not voting directly for presidential candidates although they mark ballots for one presidential candidate. Instead, voters within each state are choosing among slates of electors selected by each state's party leadership and who pledge, if elected, to support that party's presidential candidate. These are indirect elections. To win, a U.S. presidential candidate must receive a majority of the votes in the electoral college, which are awarded to states based on the size of their congressional delegation.[24] In each state except Maine and Nebraska, the party candidate who wins the popular vote wins all the electoral college votes for that state, using the winner-take-all rule.[25] Each state has electoral college votes equal to the size of its congressional delegation (House plus Senate), for a total of 538 electoral votes for the 50 states plus the District of Columbia. Occasionally, an elector will break his or her pledge and vote for the other party's candidate. For example, in 1976, when the Republicans carried the State of Washington, one Republican elector from that state refused to vote for Gerald Ford, the Republican presidential nominee. Many states have now enacted statutes formally binding electors to their pledges, but some constitutional authorities doubt whether such statutes are enforceable. The presidential candidate with a majority of the electoral college votes, and not the candidate with the highest number of popular votes, becomes president. No other country uses an electoral college to mediate between a national or direct/popular vote for presidential candidates and the winner.

Throughout history there have been a few cases where the electoral college failed to produce a majority for any candidate. In the election of 1800, Thomas Jefferson was chosen by the House over Aaron Burr after both candidates received an equal number of votes. In 1824, John Quincy Adams was selected over Andrew Jackson, Henry Clay, and William H. Crawford, even though Jackson had won more electoral and popular votes, as none of the four had received an outright majority of electoral votes. On all but three occasions since 1824, the electoral vote has simply ratified the nationwide popular vote. Since electoral votes are won on a state-by-state basis, it is mathematically possible for a candidate who receives a nationwide popular plurality to fail to carry states whose electoral votes would add up to a majority. Thus, in 1876, Rutherford B. Hayes was the winner in the electoral college despite receiving fewer popular votes than his rival, Samuel Tilden. In 1888, Grover Cleveland received more popular votes than Benjamin Harrison, but received fewer electoral votes. And in 2000, Al Gore received 540,000 more popular votes nationwide than his opponent, George W. Bush, but narrowly lost the electoral college by a mere four electoral votes.

● The 2012 and 2014 Elections

Analyze the strategies, issues, and outcomes of the 2012 and 2014 elections

In the fall of 2012, Americans re-elected Barack Obama to the presidency and confirmed the Democratic Party's control of the Senate and the Republican Party's majority in the House of Representatives. Obama won 51 percent of the popular vote, while his Republican challenger, former Massachusetts governor Mitt Romney, received 48 percent. Though the president's margin of victory was about 5 percentage points less than in 2008, it was enough to give him 332 electoral votes to win in the electoral college. However, in 2012 the Republicans maintained their majority in the House of Representative and in the 2014 midterm elections they won majorities in both houses of Congress, taking control of the Senate for the first time in eight years.

The Republican Nomination Process in 2012

The two major political parties have become more ideologically polarized in recent decades, with the Republican Party becoming more consistently conservative and the Democratic Party more consistently liberal than 50 years ago. This is one reason partisan struggles, especially in Congress, have been so intense. However, the growing ideological split between the two parties has not meant that each party is ideologically uniform. The Republican nomination in 2012 was sharply contested by several candidates representing different ideological factions in the party.

From the beginning, Romney's superior organization and financial base made him the front-runner for the Republican nomination. The GOP's social and religious conservatives, though, were unenthusiastic about the former Massachusetts governor. Some saw him as a liberal in Republican clothing while others, particularly evangelical Protestants, were unhappy about the idea of a member of the Mormon faith leading the party. Having won the Republican nomination, Romney moved to reassure the party's social conservatives that he was worthy of their support in the general election. He endorsed a party platform that included a constitutional amendment to ban abortion; elimination of government-funded family planning programs, except for abstinence training;

Candidates for national office hire professional campaign advisers to guide their campaigns and direct volunteers. Here, Mitt Romney collaborates with senior adviser Kevin Madden and chief strategist Stuart Stevens during a strategy meeting en route to a campaign event in 2012.

and a program of detention for "dangerous" aliens. Romney also chose as his vice-presidential running mate congressman Paul Ryan of Wisconsin, who was supported by the GOP's social and fiscal conservatives.

The 2012 General Election

While America, of course, consists of 50 states, presidential elections are usually fought in only 9 or 10 states. This is because some states are solidly Republican (sometimes called the red states) while others are solidly Democratic (known as the blue states). In 2012 opinion polls indicated that only 8 of the 50 states were actually toss-ups, including Colorado, Florida, Iowa, Nevada, New Hampshire, Ohio, Virginia, and Wisconsin. Thus, the 2012 presidential race was waged in 8 to 10 battleground states, where the candidates and their supporters spent hundreds of millions of dollars campaigning.

The Debates Obama and Romney faced each other in three nationally televised presidential debates along with the one vice-presidential debate. In the first presidential debate, both candidates seemed to possess a thorough knowledge of the details of major American domestic policies, but Romney seemed alert and aggressive, while Obama appeared disengaged and listless. In the wake of the first debate, the national polls, which had constantly shown Obama with a slim lead over his Republican opponent, now suggested that the race was neck and neck. The president improved his performance in the next two debates and was generally judged to have been the winner, as was Vice President Biden in his confrontation with Paul Ryan. But Romney had picked up momentum, and Obama had just two weeks after the debates to turn the tables.

Demography and Victory Obama responded by redoubling his efforts in battleground states. Obama shored up support among the working class with speeches and campaign commercials labeling Romney a multimillionaire who was out of touch with ordinary Americans and who sent American jobs overseas. According to exit polls, the president won 63 percent of the votes of those whose family incomes were less than $30,000 per year and 57 percent of those who earned between $30,000 and $49,000 per year.

The Obama campaign also redoubled its efforts among women voters. Democratic ads reminded women that it was the Democratic Party that supported such issues as equal pay. On Election Day, 55 percent of women voters supported Obama, while Romney received the votes of 52 percent of America's men. Finally, Obama campaign workers were determined to ensure high levels of turnout among minority voters, who potentially could be decisive in several battleground states. Not only did Obama capture 93 percent of the African American vote but he also won approximately 70 percent of the Latino vote across the country. Among whites, Romney received 58 percent of the vote. Taken together, working-class voters, women, and minority constituents gave Obama the votes he needed for victory. (See Figure 7.6.)

FIGURE 7.6 Distribution of Electoral Votes in the 2012 Election

Barack Obama defeated Mitt Romney in the 2012 presidential election, winning 332 votes in the electoral college (62 percent of the total). The top map shows who won each state; there, red seems to dominate. However, if we adjust the map to show each state in proportion to its population, blue states—those won by Obama—clearly dominate.

SOURCE: *Washington Post*, www.washingtonpost.com/wp-srv/special/politics/election-map-2012/president/ (accessed 6/8/14).

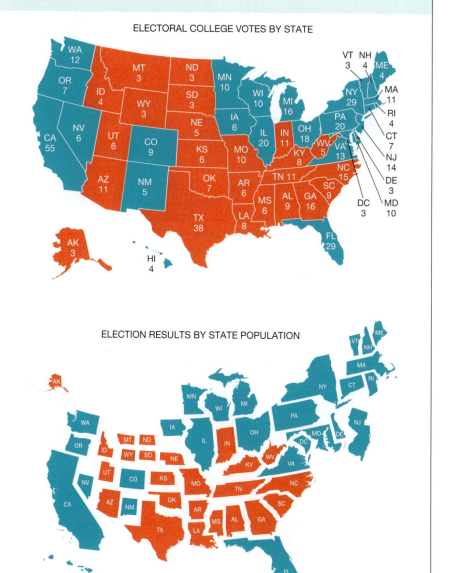

ELECTORAL COLLEGE VOTES BY STATE

ELECTION RESULTS BY STATE POPULATION

For Obama/Biden (D)   For Romney/Ryan (R)

The 2014 Midterm Elections

In 2014 Republicans needed to pick up six additional seats to win a majority in the U.S. Senate, and thus control of both houses of Congress. In fact, the GOP gained nine Senate seats, giving it a solid majority. The Republicans also deepened their advantage in the House of Representatives. Immediately after the election, it was clear that the party had won at least 10 additional seats in the House, pending recounts or run-offs in several districts. After six years of Democrats in the White House and eight in majority control in the Senate, party power in the United States flipped to Republican control of Congress.

What explains Republicans' wins in 2014? First, midterm elections tend to favor the Republican Party because the lower voter turnout for midterm elections means that there is a larger proportion of white, older, and affluent voters (who tend to support the Republican Party) as compared to the electorate in higher-turnout presidential elections, which include more young, minority, and less affluent voters (who are more likely to favor the Democrats). The election of 2014 had the lowest voter turnout in a midterm election since World War II; only about 36 percent of Americans eligible to vote cast a ballot.

Second, President Obama's low approval rating in 2014 contributed to the outcome of the elections, which were widely understood as a referendum on the party of the president. Third, the president's party generally tends to lose seats in midterm elections, giving up some seats that the party gained in the presidential election. This loss is because of the "coattails effect" that occurs in presidential elections: the success of the candidate who wins the presidency helps fellow party members get elected to Congress. Then, in midterm elections, the electorate often reacts against the ideological position and policies of the president's party and supports candidates from the other party. The election results from 2014 fit this pattern.

While the Democrats' losses in Congress may have been expected, the enormous increase in campaign spending was not. A record total of $3.6 billion was spent in the 2014 midterm elections, primarily on 36 Senate races—the most money ever spent on a midterm (non-presidential) election in U.S. history, according to the Center for Responsive Politics.[26] In comparison, the 2012 presidential race between Obama and Romney cost just over $2 billion in total spending by the candidates, parties, and outside groups.

Just a handful of states had highly competitive U.S. Senate races in 2014, and the lion's share of all campaign spending and television advertising was focused on these races. The Senate races in North Carolina was among the most competitive and was also the most expensive Senate race in history with $115 million in total spending. Spending by outside groups not affiliated with the candidates or parties (independent expenditures) accounted for approximately $690 million dollars nationwide, the most ever in a midterm election. The majority of this campaign spending was used for radio and television advertising, much of it negative campaign ads.

In House races, a record total of $119 million was spent by the Republican Party, its outside groups, and candidates, and $110 million by the Democratic Party, its outside groups, and candidates. These off-the-charts numbers represent a post–*Citizens United* political universe, where groups or corporate interests not affiliated with the candidate campaigns can spend unlimited dollars to influence election outcomes. These trends appear to set the stage for exploding spending in the 2016 presidential election, and they raise concerns that the special interests with the most money will determine outcomes in elections.

Many commentators described 2014 as a "Republican wave," as the party also won a majority of the nation's governorships. Although the 2014 election was good for Republicans, it was also good for groups supporting a higher minimum wage. Voters in five states endorsed minimum wage increases on Election Day. Significantly, minimum wage initiatives carried the day even in states where Republicans won statewide offices, including Arkansas, Nebraska, and South Dakota.

● Money Is the Mother's Milk of Politics

> **Describe how candidates raise the money they need to run**

Modern national political campaigns are fueled by enormous amounts of money. The 2012 election shattered previous records for campaign spending: spending by candidates, political parties, and interest groups on the congressional and presidential races was $6 billion combined in 2012, as compared with $5.3 billion in 2008 and $4.2 billion in 2004. Obama, the Democratic National Committee, and its affiliated Super PACs spent approximately $1.1 billion in 2012, while Romney, the Republican National Committee, and its affiliated Super PACs spent around $900 million, swamping previous general election totals. Figure 7.7 shows how the 2012 presidential campaigns spent this money.

Campaign Funds Come from Direct Appeals, the Rich, PACs, and Parties

According to the Center for Responsive Politics, about 10 percent of the $3 billion spent by candidates for federal offices in 2008 came from PACs and the remainder from individual donors. One of the sources of Barack Obama's fund-raising advantage in the 2008 campaign was his ability to generate 3 million small- and medium-sized contributions to his campaign. In 2012 nearly 5 million people contributed money to Obama.[27] Another $500 million in 2008 was raised and spent by individuals and advocacy groups—the so-called 527 and 501(c)(4) groups operating outside the structure of the Democratic and Republican campaigns.

FIGURE 7.7 How Presidential Campaigns Spent Money, 2012

Presidential candidates and the groups that support them spend nearly half of their money on advertising. However, advertising is not the only major expense. The cost of raising money is itself a major line item in the campaign budget.

SOURCE: *Washington Post*, www.washingtonpost.com/wp-srv/special/politics/campaign-finance/ (accessed 6/4/14).

SPENDING BY OBAMA, DEMOCRATIC PARTY, AND DEMOCRATIC SUPER PACS

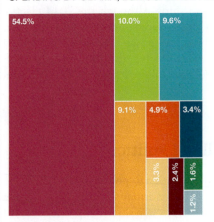

Category	Total spent (millions $)
■ Advertising	580.1
■ Mail	97.3
■ Fund-raising	106.4
■ Payroll	102.3
■ Administration	52.0
■ Travel	35.7
■ Polling	34.9
■ Events	25.3
■ Consultants	13.2
■ Lists	16.8
TOTAL	$1,064.0

SPENDING BY ROMNEY, REPUBLICAN PARTY, AND REPUBLICAN SUPER PACS

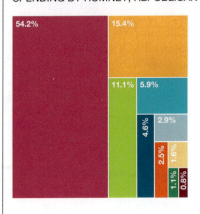

Category	Total spent (millions $)
■ Advertising	470.3
■ Mail	133.4
■ Fund-raising	96.2
■ Payroll	50.8
■ Administration	21.3
■ Travel	39.6
■ Polling	14.2
■ Events	7.0
■ Consultants	24.7
■ Lists	9.6
TOTAL	$867.1

Individual Donors Politicians devote great deal of time to asking people for money. Money is solicited via direct mail, through the Internet, over the phone, and in numerous face-to-face meetings. Under federal law, individuals may donate as much as $2,600 per candidate per election, $5,000 per PAC per calendar year, $32,400 per national party committee per calendar year, and $10,000 to state and local committees per calendar year. There is no limit on the number of candidates or that an individual can give to, however.[28]

Political Action Committees PACs are organizations established by corporations, labor unions, or interest groups to channel the contributions of their members into political campaigns. Under the terms of the 1971 Federal Election Campaign Act, which governs campaign finance in the United States, PACs are permitted to make larger contributions to any given candidate than individuals are allowed to make. Moreover, allied or related PACs often coordinate their campaign contributions, greatly increasing the amount of money a candidate actually receives from the same interest group. More than 4,500 PACs are registered with the Federal Election Commission, which oversees campaign finance practices in the United States. Nearly two-thirds of all PACs represent corporations, trade associations, and other business and professional groups. Alliances of bankers, lawyers, doctors, and merchants all sponsor PACs.

Independent Spending—527, 501(c)(4), and Super PAC Committees Committees known as **527s** and 501(c)(4)s are independent groups that are not covered by the campaign-spending restrictions imposed in 2002 by the Bipartisan Campaign Reform Act (BCRA). These groups, named for the sections of the tax code under which they are organized, can raise and spend unlimited amounts on political advocacy so long as their efforts are not coordinated with those of any candidate's campaign. A 527 is a group established specifically for the purpose of political advocacy, whereas a 501(c)(4) is a nonprofit group such as an environmental or other public interest group that also engages in advocacy. A 501(c)(4) may not spend more than half its revenues for political purposes, but many political activists favor this mode of organization. Unlike a 527, a 501(c)(4) is not required to disclose where it gets its funds or exactly what it does with them. As a result, it has become a common practice for wealthy and corporate donors to route campaign contributions far in excess of the legal limits through 501(c)(4)s. A new form of independent group, the independent expenditure committee, or "Super PAC," came about as a result of a Federal Election Commission ruling that the Supreme Court's 2010 decision in *Citizens United v. Federal Election Commission* permitted individuals and organizations to form committees that could raise unlimited amounts of money to run advertising for and against candidates so long as their efforts were not coordinated with those of the candidates.[29]

In 2014 the Supreme Court removed additional limits on individuals' campaign contributions in its decision in *McCutcheon et al. v. Federal Election Commission*.[30] Outside spending via 527s, 501c(4)s, and Super PACs played an unprecedented role in the 2012 presidential race, as groups ran extensive television ads. The top-spending Super PACs were primarily those advocating against Obama, including American Crossroads ($85 million), the Republican National Committee ($41 million), and Americans for Prosperity ($34 million). Super PACs on both sides relied on very large contributions.

Public Funding The Federal Election Campaign Act also provides for public funding of presidential campaigns. As they seek a major-party presidential nomination, candidates become eligible for public funds by raising at least $5,000 in individual contributions of $250 or less in each of 20 states. Candidates who reach this threshold may apply for federal funds to match, on a dollar-for-dollar basis, all individual contributions of $250 or less that they receive. In 2012 candidates who accepted matching funds could spend no more than $54 million, including matching funds, in their presidential primary campaigns. The funds are drawn from the Presidential Election Campaign Fund. Taxpayers can contribute $3 to this fund, at no additional cost to themselves, by checking a box on the first page of their federal income tax returns. Major-party presidential candidates receive a lump sum (about $91 million in 2012, although neither Obama nor Romney accepted this money in 2012) during the summer prior to the general election. They must meet all their general expenses from this money. Third-party candidates are eligible for public funding only if they received at least 5 percent of the vote in the previous presidential race. This stipulation effectively blocks preelection funding for third-party or independent candidates, although a third party that wins more than 5 percent of the vote can receive public funding after the election.

Under current law, no candidate is required to accept public funding for either the nominating races or the general presidential election. Candidates who do not accept public funding are not bound by any expenditure limits. In 2008, John McCain accepted public funding for the general election campaign, receiving $84 million, but Barack Obama declined, choosing to rely on his own fund-raising prowess. Obama was ultimately able to outspend McCain by a wide margin. The 2008 race was the last time that major-party presidential candidates limited their own fund-raising in favor of public funding. Neither major party candidate accepted public funding in 2012.

The Candidates Themselves On the basis of the Supreme Court's 1976 decision in *Buckley v. Valeo*, the right of individuals to spend their *own* money to campaign for office is a constitutionally protected matter of free speech and is not subject to limitation.[31] Thus, extremely wealthy candidates often contribute millions of dollars to their own campaigns. New York City mayor and billionaire businessman Michael Bloomberg, for example, spent over $75 million in each of his three successful elections, in 2001, 2005, and 2009. The only exception to the *Buckley* rule concerns presidential candidates who accept federal funding for their general election campaigns. Such individuals are limited to $50,000 in personal spending.

In 2014, Shaun McCutcheon successfully challenged the federal limit on the amount of money any one individual can donate to political campaigns and candidates. Many people worry that recent Supreme Court decisions overturning campaign spending reinforce the influence of the very affluent in American politics at the expense of everyone else.

Political Parties, Elections,
and Your Future

While party leaders exercise great control over party platforms, the party message, and often through early money to candidates, who holds elected office and who wins the nomination for president, many aspects of party politics have been turned upside down with the digital revolution in communication. Four resources that political parties use to contest and win elections (time, money, expertise, and organization) have all been altered by the Internet. New media are decentralizing party power, as citizens can volunteer and give money to the party of their choice without ever being contacted by a party official. Online fund-raising allows millions of donors to give small contributions to parties, and new media allow the party to spread its message far and wide online. This is beneficial for parties because more people are involved, but there are more divergent opinions that must be recognized and appeased. At the same time, huge contributions from a handful of very wealthy individuals have increased. Will the ability of the mass public to make their desires known to party leaders mean that party leaders pay more attention to these preferences? Is the two-party system the optimal system for American politics, or should electoral reforms encourage more parties to form and, hence, provide more choice for voters?

The important role played by private funds in American elections affects the balance of power among contending economic groups. Politicians need large amounts of money to campaign successfully for major offices. This fact inevitably ties their interests to the interests of the groups and forces that can provide this money: the affluent. In a nation as large and diverse as the United States, to be sure, campaign contributors represent many different groups and, often, clashing interests. The fact remains, however, that those with more money will be able to give more and speak with a louder voice. Will mass contributions from average people give them a greater voice?

plug**in**

Inform

Find out what's on the ballot in upcoming elections in your state/district, by entering your address at vote411.org (a website from the League of Women Voters).

Express

Write a list of reasons individuals may not vote. In your view, are these obstacles necessary? Consider emailing the editor of your school paper to share your opinion.

Connect

Register to vote. Find the registration forms, deadlines, polling locations, and other information by using the state-by-state URLs listed in the back of this book.

Act

Cast your vote on Election Day. Consider encouraging others to vote too. Research shows that people are most likely to turn out to vote if a friend or family members asks them to.

Practice Quiz

1. A political party is different from an interest group in that a political party *(p. 201)*
   a) seeks to control the entire government by electing its members to office and thereby controlling the government's personnel.
   b) seeks to control only limited, very specific functions of government.
   c) is entirely nonprofit.
   d) has a much larger membership.
   e) has a much smaller membership.

2. Parties today are important in the electoral process in *(pp. 201–2)*
   a) recruiting and nominating candidates for office.
   b) financing all of the campaign's spending.
   c) providing millions of volunteers to mobilize voters.
   d) creating a responsible party government.
   e) changing the electoral laws to make voting easier.

3. Which party was founded as a political expression of the antislavery movement? *(p. 207)*
   a) American Independent
   b) Prohibition
   c) Republican
   d) Democratic
   e) Whig

4. The periodic episodes in American history in which an "old" dominant political party is replaced by a "new" dominant political party are called *(p. 211)*
   a) constitutional revolutions.
   b) party turnovers.
   c) governmental realignments.
   d) presidential elections.
   e) electoral realignments.

5. Third parties have influenced national politics mainly by *(pp. 212–13)*
   a) electing their candidates to the presidency.
   b) electing their candidates to Congress.
   c) supporting the major parties' platforms.
   d) promoting specific issues and ideas.
   e) preventing realignments.

6. Which of the following is *not* a form of traditional political participation? *(p. 215)*
   a) volunteering in a campaign
   b) attending an abortion-rights rally
   c) contributing to the Democratic Party
   d) voting in an election
   e) uploading a political video to YouTube

7. Which of the following factors is *not* currently an obstacle to voting in the United States? *(pp. 218–19)*
   a) registration requirements
   b) that elections occur on Tuesdays
   c) the restriction of voting rights for people who have committed a felony
   d) literacy tests
   e) restrictions in some states on absentee voting

8. Partisan loyalty *(pp. 221–22)*
   a) is often handed down from parents to children.
   b) changes frequently.
   c) is currently much stronger than it was in the 1940s and 1950s.
   d) is mandated in states with closed primaries.
   e) has little impact on voting in congressional and state-level elections.

9. The biggest issue in the 2012 national elections was *(p. 222)*
   a) same-sex marriage.
   b) energy policy.
   c) abortion.
   d) the economy.
   e) Medicare.

10. In the 2012 presidential election, public funding *(p. 234)*
   a) was accepted by both major-party candidates.
   b) was accepted by Barack Obama only.
   c) was accepted by Mitt Romney only.
   d) was declined by both major-party candidates.
   e) was not available.

11. In *Buckley v. Valeo*, the Supreme Court ruled that *(p. 234)*
   a) PAC donations to campaigns are constitutionally protected.
   b) candidates cannot spend any of their own money to run for office.
   c) the right of individuals to spend their own money to campaign is constitutionally protected.
   d) the political system is corrupt.
   e) the entire Federal Elections Campaign Act is unconstitutional.

Key Terms

ballot initiative *(p. 224)* a proposed law or policy change that is placed on the ballot by citizens or interest groups for a popular vote

closed primary *(p. 224)* a primary election in which voters can participate in the nomination of candidates, but only of the party in which they are enrolled for a period of time prior to primary day

divided government *(p. 211)* the condition in American government wherein the presidency is controlled by one party while the opposing party controls one or both houses of Congress

electoral college *(p. 225)* the presidential electors from each state who meet after the popular election to cast ballots for president and vice president

electoral realignment *(p. 211)* the point in history when a new party supplants the ruling party, becoming in turn the dominant political force; in the United States, this has tended to occur roughly every 30 years

527 committees *(p. 233)* nonprofit independent groups that receive and disburse funds to influence the nomination, election, or defeat of candidates; named after Section 527 of the Internal Revenue Code, which defines and provides tax-exempt status for nonprofit advocacy groups

general election *(p. 224)* a regularly scheduled election involving most districts in the nation or state, in which voters select officeholders; in the United States, general elections for national office and most state and local offices are held on the first Tuesday following the first Monday in November in even-numbered years (every four years for presidential elections)

incumbent *(p. 202)* a candidate running for re-election to a position that he or she already holds

majority party *(p. 203)* the party that holds the majority of legislative seats in either the House or the Senate

minority party *(p. 203)* the party that holds a minority of legislative seats in either the House or the Senate

mobilization *(p. 218)* the process by which large numbers of people are organized for a political activity

nomination *(p. 202)* the process by which political parties select their candidates for election to public office

open primary *(p. 224)* a primary election in which the voter can wait until the day of the primary to choose which party to enroll in to select candidates for the general election

party identification *(p. 213)* an individual voter's psychological ties to one party or another

political action committee (PAC) *(p. 201)* a private group that raises and distributes funds for use in election campaigns

political parties *(p. 201)* organized groups that attempt to influence the government by electing their members to important government offices

primary elections *(p. 224)* elections to select a party's candidate for the general election

proportional representation *(p. 213)* a multiple-member district system that allows each political party representation in proportion to its percentage of the total vote

recall *(p. 225)* a procedure to allow voters to remove state officials from office before their terms expire by circulating petitions to call a vote

referendum *(p. 225)* the practice of referring a measure proposed or passed by a legislature to the vote of the electorate for approval or rejection

socioeconomic status *(p. 218)* status in society based on level of education, income, and occupational prestige

suffrage *(p. 217)* the right to vote; also called *franchise*

third parties *(p. 212)* parties that organize to compete against the two major American political parties

turnout *(p. 217)* the percentage of eligible individuals who actually vote

two-party system *(p. 204)* a political system in which only two parties have a realistic opportunity to compete effectively for control of the government

For Further Reading

Aldrich, John W. *Why Parties? The Origin and Transformation of Political Parties in America.* Chicago: University of Chicago Press, 1995.

Crotty, William J., ed. *Winning the Presidency 2012.* Boulder, CO: Paradigm Publishers, 2013.

Ginsberg, Benjamin, and Martin Shefter. *Politics by Other Means: Institutional Conflict and the Declining Significance of Elections in America.* New York: W.W. Norton, 1999.

Heilemann, John, and Mark Halperin. *Game Change: Obama and the Clintons, McCain and Palin, and the Race of a Lifetime.* New York: HarperCollins, 2010.

Maisel, L. Sandy. *Political Parties and Elections: A Very Short Introduction.* New York: Oxford University Press, 2007.

McCarty, Nolan, Keith Poole, and Howard Rosenthal. *Polarized America: The Dance of Ideology and Unequal Riches.* Cambridge, MA: MIT Press, 2006.

Milkis, Sidney. *The President and the Parties: The Transformation of the American Party System since the New Deal.* New York: Oxford University Press, 1993.

Patterson, Thomas E. *The Vanishing Voter: Public Involvement in an Age of Uncertainty.* New York: Vintage Books, 2003.

Shefter, Martin. *Political Parties and the State: The American Historical Experience.* Princeton, NJ: Princeton University Press, 1994.

Wayne, Stephen. *Is This Any Way to Run a Democratic Election?* 5th ed. Washington, DC: CQ Press, 2013.

West, Darrell. *The Next Wave.* Washington, DC: Brookings Institution Press, 2011.

The use of "fracking" to recover gas has brought environmental groups into conflict with the energy industry. Both sides have tried to influence government regulations related to fracking.

Interest Groups

WHAT GOVERNMENT DOES AND WHY IT MATTERS For the past several years, environmental groups and the nation's energy industry have been locked in a struggle over the issue of hydraulic fracturing, or "fracking." This is a method for recovering natural gas trapped in shale formations by pumping millions of gallons of water deep beneath the earth's surface. The energy industry, which stands to make enormous profits from extracting this gas, asserts that fracking is the key to achieving American energy independence. Environmental groups, on the other hand, argue that fracking produces greenhouse gas emissions, undermines air quality, and contaminates drinking water, while discouraging investment in cleaner, renewable forms of energy.

Despite these environmental concerns, large sections of the United States, including tracts in Pennsylvania, Texas, and Ohio, among other states, are being fracked for their natural gas. Environmental groups appear to be losing the battle. Why? The energy industry, organized in groups such as the Natural Gas Alliance, the Independent Petroleum Association of America, and the American Gas Association, has deployed an army of nearly 800 lobbyists, including former members of Congress and other former high-ranking government officials, to promote their cause on Capitol Hill in Washington, D.C., and in the state capitals. The industry has also spent tens of millions of dollars on advertising and campaign contributions—filling the coffers of Democrats and Republicans alike. Even President Obama, a self-proclaimed environmentalist, was moved to declare in his 2011 State of the Union address that natural gas produced in America was an important part of America's energy future.

The case of fracking exemplifies the power of interest groups in action. Tens of thousands of organized groups have formed in the United States, ranging from civic associations to huge nationwide groups such as the National Rifle Association (NRA), whose chief cause is opposition to restrictions on gun ownership, and Common Cause, a public interest group that advocates a variety of liberal political reforms. Despite the array of interest groups in American politics, however, not all interests are represented equally, and the results of competition among various interests are not always consistent with the common good.

The preceding chapter, on political parties, participation, and elections, examined another way in which citizens can influence the government. Yet the interest group process, as we will see, is both more selective and more dynamic: selective because society's "elites" (those with more money, education, and other resources) are better able to exploit the interest group process to their advantage; dynamic because of the explosive growth in the sheer number and diversity of interest groups that have proliferated in the last four decades. In this chapter, we will examine the nature and consequences of interest group politics in the United States.

chaptergoals

- Describe the major types of interest groups and whom they represent (pp. 245–50)
- Describe how groups organize (pp. 250–54)
- Analyze why the number of interest and advocacy groups has grown in recent decades (pp. 254–55)
- Explain how interest groups try to influence government (pp. 255–64)

Interest Groups Form to Advocate for Different Interests

> **Describe the major types of interest groups and whom they represent**

The framers of the U.S. Constitution feared the power that could be wielded by organized interests. Yet they believed that interest groups thrived because of liberty—the freedom that all Americans enjoyed to organize and express their views. If the government were given the power to regulate, restrict, or forbid efforts by organized interests to impose themselves in the political process, it would in effect have the power to suppress liberty. The solution to this dilemma was presented by James Madison in the *Federalist Papers* no. 10:

> Take in a greater variety of parties and interests [and] you make it less probable that a majority of the whole will have a common motive to invade the rights of other citizens. . . . [Hence the advantage] enjoyed by a large over a small republic.[1]

According to the Madisonian theory, a good government encourages multitudes of interests so that no single interest, which Madison called a "faction," can ever tyrannize or dominate the others. The basic assumption is that many competing interests will regulate one another, producing a kind of balance.[2] Today, this Madisonian principle of regulation is called **pluralism**. According to pluralist theory, all interests are and should be free to compete for influence in the United States. While an interest group may lose on one issue, it may win on the next, and overall the vast majority of society will be represented in government. Moreover, according to a pluralist doctrine, the outcome of this competition is compromise and moderation, since no group is likely to be able to achieve any of its goals without accommodating itself to some of the views of its many competitors.[3] Another assumption of pluralism is that all groups have equal access to the political process and that achieving an outcome favorable to a particular group depends only upon that group's strength and resources, not upon biases inherent in the political system. But as we shall see, group politics is a political format that has worked and continues to work more to the advantage of some types of interests than others.

An **interest group** is a group of individuals who organize to influence the government's programs and policies. This definition of interest groups includes membership organizations composed of average citizens, but also businesses, corporations, unions, universities, and other institutions that restrict membership to particular occupational groups or other categories of persons. Individuals form groups in order to increase the chance that their views will be heard and their interests treated favorably by the government.

Interest groups are sometimes referred to as "lobbies." They are also sometimes confused with **political action committees (PACs)**, which are private groups that raise and distribute funds for use in election campaigns. Thus, the purpose of PACs is to influence elections rather than trying to influence the elected. One final distinction is that interest groups are also different from political parties: interest groups tend to concern themselves with the *policies* of government; parties tend to concern themselves with the *personnel* of government.

What Interests Are Represented?

Economic Groups Interest groups come in as many shapes and sizes as the interests they represent. The most obvious are groups with a direct economic interest in government policy. Businesses and corporations make up over 41 percent of those registered to lobby in Washington, with trade associations comprising another 22 percent and labor unions just 2 percent of groups registered to lobby.[4] Trade associations are generally supported by groups of producers or manufacturers in a particular economic sector, such as the National Association of Manufacturers, the American Fuel and Petrochemical Manufacturers Association, and the American Farm Bureau Federation. In addition, specific companies, such as Apple, Microsoft, Exxon, Dow Chemical, and General Motors, lobby on certain issues that are of particular concern to them.

Labor Groups Labor organizations are equally active lobbyists. The AFL-CIO, the United Mine Workers, and the Teamsters are all groups that lobby on behalf

of organized labor. In recent years, groups have organized to further the interests of public employees, such as the American Federation of State, County, and Municipal Employees (AFSCME) and the American Federation of Teachers (AFT). According to one study, however, labor unions represent just 2 percent of the total number of registered lobby groups in Washington.[5] While other economic groups far outweigh unions in sheer number in the nation's capital, average spending on lobbying and campaign contributions tells a somewhat different picture. Unions in fact have the highest average PAC spending, and thus they wield influence through lobbying efforts and targeted contribution to political campaigns.

Although fewer Americans are union members today than 50 years ago, unions continue to influence both local practices as well as state and even national policy in certain sectors. In 2012 Chicago Teachers Union, an affiliate of the American Teachers Federation, went on an eight-day strike over such issues as salary increases, health insurance, and length of the school day and year.

Professional Associations Professional lobbies such as the American Bar Association and the American Medical Association have been particularly successful at furthering their members' interests in Congress and state legislatures. Financial institutions, represented by organizations such as the American Bankers Association and the National Savings and Loan League, although often less visible than other lobbies, also play an important role in shaping legislative policy. These groups comprise 9 percent of all lobby groups in Washington.

Citizen Groups (or Public Interest Groups) Recent years have witnessed the growth of a powerful "public interest" lobby, purporting to represent the general good rather than its own economic interests. **Citizen groups** have been most visible in the consumer protection and environmental policy areas, although public interest groups cover a broad range of issues. The National Resources Defense Council, the Sierra Club, and Common Cause are all examples of citizen groups. Citizen groups comprise 14 percent of registered lobbyists in Washington. Claims to represent only the public interest should be viewed with caution, however: it is not uncommon to find decidedly private interests hiding behind the term *public interest*. For example, the benign-sounding Partnership to Protect Consumer Credit is a coalition of credit card companies fighting for less federal regulation of credit abuses, and Project Protect is a coalition of logging interests promoting increased timber cutting.[6]

Ideological Groups Closely related to and overlapping public interest groups are ideological groups, organized in support of a particular political or philosophical perspective. The National Right to Life Committee and the Christian Coalition focus on conservative social goals, such as opposition to abortion and same-sex marriage. The National Taxpayers Union campaigns to reduce the size of the federal government. Liberal-leaning groups, including EMILY's List and MoveOn.org, support causes such as women's representation and increasing the minimum wage.

Public-Sector Groups The perceived need for representation on Capitol Hill has generated a public-sector lobby in the past several years, including the National League of Cities, the National Conference on State Legislatures, the National Governor's Association, and the "research" lobby. This latter group includes think tanks and universities that have an interest in obtaining government funds for research and support—for example, institutions such as Harvard University, the Brookings Institution, and the American Enterprise Institute. Indeed, universities have expanded their lobbying efforts even as they have reduced faculty positions and course offerings.[7] These groups represent 12 percent of Washington lobby groups.

Some Interests Are Not Represented

It is difficult to categorize unrepresented interests precisely because they are not organized and are not able to present to governments their identity and their demands. The political scientist David Truman referred to these interests as "potential interest groups."[8] And he is undoubtedly correct that at any time, as long as there is freedom, any interest shared by a lot of people can develop through "voluntary association" into a genuine interest group that can demand, usually successfully, to get some representation. But the fact remains that many interests—including some very widely shared interests—do not get organized and recognized. One such group is the homeless and the poor.[9]

Interest Group Membership

In his famous work *Democracy in America,* the French thinker Alexis de Tocqueville stated that "In no country in the world has the principle of association been more successfully used, or more unsparingly applied to a multitude of different objects, than in America."[a] Since then, a multitude of scholars have noted that the United States is a "nation of joiners," with more people active in various groups than almost any other country in the world.

Why is group membership higher in the United States than in many other countries? Part of the explanation has to do with demographics and economics. People who are employed full time, more educated, and wealthier are more likely to join voluntary organizations.[b] This helps explain why membership is lower in developing countries like Turkey or Chile, where much of the population still lacks the time and resources to make joining more feasible. Americans also tend to believe that participation in community affairs is an important part of good citizenship, an idea that some scholars say is related to the institutions of American government and the nature of the Constitution.[c]

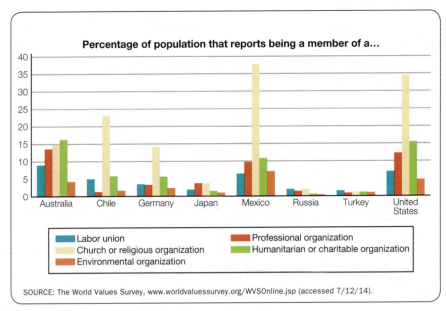

Percentage of population that reports being a member of a...

Legend:
- Labor union
- Church or religious organization
- Environmental organization
- Professional organization
- Humanitarian or charitable organization

SOURCE: The World Values Survey, www.worldvaluessurvey.org/WVSOnline.jsp (accessed 7/12/14).

[a]Alexis de Tocqueville, *Democracy in America* (New York: W. W. Norton, 2007), chap. 12.
[b]James E. Curtis, Edward G. Grabb, and Douglas E. Baer, "Voluntary Association Membership in Fifteen Countries: A Comparative Analysis," American Sociological Review 57, no. 2 (1992): 139–52.
[c]Gabriel Almond and Sidney Verba, *The Civil Culture: Political Attitudes and Democracy in Five Nations* (Newbury Park, CA: Sage Publications, 1989), p. 127.

Not all groups organize to pursue their common interests. Those who are well educated and well-off financially are more likely to have the time, money, and skills needed to organize and mobilize an interest group. One result is that the needs of such groups as the homeless are often not heard in political debate.

Group Membership Has an Upper-Class Bias

Despite the benefits of interest groups in terms of mobilizing and educating the public and the arguments in favor of pluralism, there are concerns about the influence of special interests in the United States. One long-standing critic is E. E. Schattschneider, who argued in a famous quote that "the flaw in the pluralist heaven is that the heavenly chorus sings with a strong upper-class accent."[10] Critics contend pressure politics, or interest group politics, is heavily skewed in favor of corporate, business, and upper-class groups, leaving those with lower socioeconomic status less able to participate in and influence politics.

This is because membership in interest groups is not randomly distributed in the population. People with higher incomes, higher levels of education, and management or professional occupations are much more likely to become members of groups than those who occupy the lower rungs on the socioeconomic ladder.[11] Well-educated, upper-income business- and professional people are more likely to have the time, money, concerns, information, and skills acquired through education that are needed to play a role in a group or association. Moreover, for business- and professional people, group membership may provide personal contacts and access to information that can help advance their careers. At the same time, of course, corporations and businesses usually have ample resources to form or participate in groups that seek to advance their interests.

The result of this elitist tendency is that interest group politics in the United States tends to have a very pronounced class bias. Certainly there are many interest groups and political associations that have a working or lower-class membership (labor organizations or welfare-rights organizations, for example), but the great majority of interest group members are drawn from the middle and upper-middle classes. In general, the "interests" served by interest groups are the interests of society's "haves." Even when interest groups take opposing positions on issues and policies, the conflicting positions they espouse usually reflect divisions among upper-income strata rather than conflicts between the upper and lower classes.

● The Organizational Components of Groups Include Money, Offices, and Members

Describe how groups organize

Although interest groups are many and varied, most share certain key organizational components. These include leadership, money, an agency or office, and members.

First, leadership and decision-making structure is vital for group organization. For some groups, this structure is very simple. For others, it can be quite elaborate and involve hundreds of local chapters that are melded into a national apparatus. Interest group leadership is, in some respects, analogous to business leadership. Political entrepreneurs initially organize and lead groups. Later, these leaders are replaced by a paid professional staff. In the 1960s, for example, Ralph Nader led a loosely organized band of consumer advocates (Nader's Raiders) in a crusade for product safety that resulted in the enactment of a number of pieces of legislation and numerous regulations, such as the requirement that all new cars be equipped with seat belts and other safety devices. Today, Nader's ragtag band of raiders is a well-organized and well-financed phalanx of interlocking groups led by professional staff.

New **netroots** or online advocacy groups often have a streamlined staff structure with little bureaucracy. However, entrepreneurship may be even more important in the world of organizing online. As computer scientist Clay Shirky explains in *Here Comes Everybody*, the Internet has given rise to a proliferation of online organizations without formal organizing structures.[12] Examples include Wikipedia, whose content is provided by volunteers from around the world. But the real impact of the digital media revolution is not politics without groups but is the advent of new forms of organization. Shirky explains that leadership remains a priority because a small group of leader-organizers will contribute the vast majority of effort necessary to make the group a success. Entrepreneurship and leadership are important for all interest groups, but especially so for those with little staff and formal organization, as the leader holds the organization together.

Second, every interest group must build a financial structure capable of sustaining an organization and funding the group's activities, although the costs of maintaining an online organization are lower. Most interest groups rely on membership dues and voluntary contributions from sympathizers. Many also sell services or benefits to members, such as insurance and vacation tours. Third, most groups establish an agency that carries out the group's tasks. This may be a research organization, a public-relations office, or a lobbying office in Washington or a state capital.

Finally, all interest groups must attract and keep members. Somehow, groups must persuade individuals to invest the money, time, energy, or effort required to take part in the group's activities. Members play a larger role in some groups than in others. In **membership associations**, group members play a substantial role, serving on committees and engaging in group projects. In the case of labor unions, members pay dues and may march on picket lines, and in the case of political or ideological groups, members may participate in demonstrations and protests. In another set of groups, **staff organizations**, a professional staff conducts most of the group's activities. Members are called upon only to pay dues and make other contributions. Among well-known public interest groups, some, such as the National Organization for Women (NOW), are membership groups, whereas others, such as Defenders of Wildlife and the Children's Defense Fund, are staff organizations.

The "Free-Rider" Problem Whether they need individuals to volunteer or merely to write checks, interest groups need to recruit and retain members. Yet many groups find this task difficult, even when it comes to recruiting members who agree strongly with the group's goals. Why? As economist Mancur Olson explains, the benefits of a group's success are often broadly available and cannot be denied to nonmembers.[13] Such benefits can be called **collective goods**. Following Olson's own example, suppose a number of private property owners live near a mosquito-infested swamp. Each owner wants this swamp cleared. But if only a few of the owners were to clear the swamp, their actions would benefit all the other owners as well, without any effort on the part of those other owners. Each of the inactive owners would be a **free rider** on the efforts of the ones who cleared the swamp, meaning that they would enjoy the benefits of collective goods but without having participated in acquiring them. Thus, there is a disincentive for any of the owners to undertake the job alone.

Since the number of concerned owners is small in this particular case, they might eventually be able to organize themselves to share the costs as well as enjoy the benefits of clearing the swamp. But suppose the number of interested people increases. Suppose the common concern is not the neighborhood swamp but polluted air or groundwater involving thousands of residents in a region, or millions of residents in a whole nation. National defense is the most obvious collective good whose benefits are shared by all residents, regardless of the taxes they pay or the support they provide. As the number of involved persons increases, or as the size of the group increases, the free-rider problem becomes greater. Individuals do not have much incentive to become active members and supporters of a group if they are already benefiting from the group's activities.

Why Join Groups? To overcome the free-rider problem, interest groups offer numerous incentives to join. Most important, they make various "selective benefits" available only to group members. These benefits can be information related, material, solidary, or purposive. Table 8.1 gives some examples of the range of benefits in each of these categories.

Informational benefits are the most widespread and important category of selective benefits offered to group members. Information is provided through conferences, training programs, online communications, newsletters, and other periodicals sent automatically to those who have paid membership dues.

TABLE 8.1

Selective Benefits of Interest Group Membership

CATEGORY	BENEFITS
Informational benefits	Conferences Professional contacts Training programs Publications Coordination among organizations Research Legal help Professional codes Collective bargaining
Material benefits	Travel packages Insurance Discounts on consumer goods
Solidary benefits	Friendship Networking opportunities
Purposive benefits	Advocacy Representation before government Participation in public affairs

SOURCE: Adapted from Jack Walker, Jr., *Mobilizing Interest Groups in America: Patrons, Professions, and Social Movements* (Ann Arbor: University of Michigan Press, 1991), 86.

Material benefits include anything that can be measured monetarily, such as special goods, services, and even money, provided to members of groups to entice others to join. These benefits often include discount purchasing, shared advertising, and, perhaps most valuable of all, health and retirement insurance.

Another option identified in Table 8.1 is that of **solidary benefits**. These are selective benefits of group membership that include friendship, networking, and consciousness raising, which provides the satisfaction of working toward a common goal with like-minded individuals, a phenomenon often important for netroots groups. One example of the latter can be seen in the claims of many women's organizations that active participation conveys to each female member of the organization an enhanced sense of her own value and a stronger ability to advance individual as well as collective rights. Members of associations based on ethnicity, race, or religion also derive solidary benefits from interacting with individuals they perceive as sharing their own backgrounds, values, and perspectives.

A fourth type of benefit involves the appeal of the purpose of an interest group. These **purposive benefits** emphasize the purpose and accomplishments of the group. For example, people join religious, consumer, environmental, or other civic groups to pursue goals important to them.

Many of the most successful interest groups of the past 20 years have been citizen groups or public interest groups, whose members are brought together largely around shared ideological goals, including government reform, election and campaign reform, civil rights, economic equality, "family values," and even opposition to government itself.

AARP and the Benefits of Membership One group that has been extremely successful in recruiting members and mobilizing them for political action is AARP (formerly called the American Association of Retired Persons). AARP was founded in 1958 as a result of the efforts of a retired California high school principal, Ethel Percy Andrus, to find affordable health insurance for herself and the thousands of members of the National Retired Teachers Association (NRTA).

Today, AARP is a large and powerful organization with 39 million members and an annual budget of over $1 billion. In addition, the organization receives $90 million in federal grants. Its national headquarters in Washington, D.C., staffed by nearly 3,000 full-time employees, is so large that it has its own zip code. Its monthly periodical, *AARP: The Magazine* has a circulation larger than that of America's leading newsmagazines.

How did this large organization overcome the free-rider problem and recruit 39 million older people as members? First, no other organization has ever provided more successfully the selective benefits necessary to overcome the free-rider problem. It helps that AARP began as an organization to provide affordable health insurance for aging members rather than as an organization to influence public policy. But that fact only strengthens the argument that members need short-term individual benefits if they are to invest effort in a longer-term and less concrete set of benefits. As AARP evolved into a political interest group, its leadership added more selective benefits for individual members. They provided guidance against consumer fraud, offered low-interest credit cards, evaluated and endorsed products that were deemed of best value to members, and provided auto insurance and a discounted mail-order pharmacy.

AARP is one of the largest interest groups in the country. One way that AARP attracts members is through selective benefits, such as hotel discounts, affordable health insurance, credit and identity theft protection, and free health tests, like this one in Miami Beach, Florida. These benefits attract members who remain invested in AARP's success because they enjoy tangible benefits from membership.

The Internet Has Changed the Way Interest Groups Foster Participation

Digital media and social media have created a new kind of interest group politics in America that has revolutionized political advocacy. New netroots political associations, such as the liberal-leaning MoveOn.org, have arisen in recent years to play an increasingly important role in citizen participation in politics. Similar conservative groups include Freedomworks and Americans for Prosperity. These grassroots online activist organizations have redefined membership and fund-raising practices via innovative methods for communicating with and measuring the opinions of their members, and moving their members into action.

Traditional interest groups are expensive to organize (which is one reason why group membership has an upper-class bias), and they rely on professional advocates and direct mail. They are also slow to change. By contrast, netroots associations are relatively inexpensive to organize and are quick to adapt to an ever-changing world of politics. Netroots have lower costs than traditional interest groups because they have a streamlined staff structure with fewer staff who often work from virtual offices. This less expensive staff structure engages in different work routines that prioritize communication with members through email, Twitter, and other digital platforms rather than mailing expensive glossy newsletters or engaging in direct lobbying of members of Congress. Netroots associations employ novel grassroots strategies to pressure elected officials, including using online media to organize citizens to attend rallies, fund-raising events, start letter-writing campaigns, organize boycotts, and protests. These tactics have spread across the political advocacy system to more traditional interest groups.

● The Number of Groups Has Increased in Recent Decades

Analyze why the number of interest and advocacy groups has grown in recent decades

Over the past several decades, there has been an enormous increase both in the number of interest groups seeking to play a role in the American political process and in the extent of their influence over that process. This explosion of interest group activity has two basic origins: first, the expansion of the role of government during this period; and second, the coming-of-age of a new dynamic set of political forces in the United States—forces that have relied heavily on public interest groups to advance their causes.

The Expansion of Government Has Spurred the Growth of Groups

Modern governments' extensive economic and social programs have powerful politicizing effects, often sparking the organization of new groups and interests. In other words, interest groups often form as the result of, or in response to, government actions, rather than groups pressing the government to take on new responsibilities. Even when national policies are enacted because of interest group pressure, government involvement in any area can be a powerful stimulus for political organization and action by those whose interests are affected. For example, during the 1970s, expanded federal regulation of the automobile, oil, gas, education, and health care industries impelled each of these interests to increase substantially its efforts to influence the government's behavior. These efforts, in turn, spurred the organization of other groups either to support or to oppose the activities of the first.[14] Similarly, federal social programs have sparked political organization and action by affected groups. For example, federal programs and court decisions in such areas as abortion, school prayer, and same-sex marriage helped spur the rise of fundamentalist religious groups. Thus, the expansion of government in recent decades has also stimulated increased group activity and organization.

Public Interest Groups Grew in the 1960s and '70s

The second factor accounting for the explosion of interest group activity was the emergence of a new set of forces in American politics that can collectively be called the "New Politics" movement.

The **New Politics movement** is made up of upper-middle-class professionals and intellectuals for whom the civil rights and anti–Vietnam War movements of the 1960s were formative experiences. The crusade against racial discrimination and the Vietnam War led these young men and women to see themselves as a political force, focusing their attention on such issues as environmental protection, women's rights, and nuclear disarmament.

Members of the New Politics movement founded or bolstered public interest groups such as Common Cause, the Sierra Club, the Environmental Defense Fund, Physicians for Social Responsibility, NOW, and the various organizations formed by consumer activist Ralph Nader. Through these groups, New Politics forces were able to influence the media, Congress, and the courts, and enjoyed a remarkable degree of success, playing a major role in gaining the passage of environmental, consumer, and occupational health and safety legislation. Technology has also played a role in advancing the New Politics agenda. In the 1970s and '80s, computerized direct-mail campaigns allowed public interest groups to reach hundreds of thousands of potential sympathizers and contributors. Today, the Internet and digital platforms including social media, Twitter, and blogs serve the same function even more efficiently.

● Interest Groups Use Different Strategies to Gain Influence

Explain how interest groups try to influence government

As we have seen, interest groups work to improve the likelihood that their interests will be heard and treated favorably by the government. The quest for political influence or power takes many forms, but among the most frequently used strategies or "tactics of influence" (see Figure 8.1) are lobbying, gaining access to key decision makers, using the courts, mobilizing public opinion, and using electoral politics.

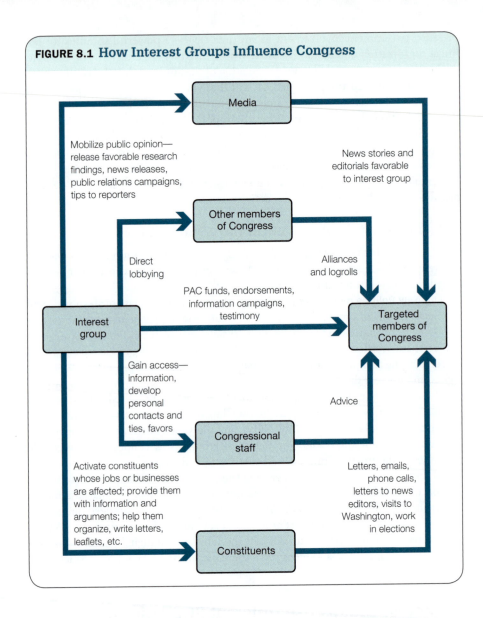

FIGURE 8.1 How Interest Groups Influence Congress

Media

Mobilize public opinion—release favorable research findings, news releases, public relations campaigns, tips to reporters

News stories and editorials favorable to interest group

Other members of Congress

Direct lobbying

Alliances and logrolls

Interest group

PAC funds, endorsements, information campaigns, testimony

Targeted members of Congress

Gain access—information, develop personal contacts and ties, favors

Advice

Congressional staff

Activate constituents whose jobs or businesses are affected; provide them with information and arguments; help them organize, write letters, leaflets, etc.

Letters, emails, phone calls, letters to news editors, visits to Washington, work in elections

Constituents

Many groups employ a mix of strategies. For example, environmental groups such as the Sierra Club lobby members of Congress and key congressional staff members, participate in bureaucratic rule making by offering comments and suggestions to agencies on new environmental rules, and bring lawsuits under various environmental acts such as the Endangered Species Act, which authorizes groups and citizens to come to court if they believe the act is being violated. At the same time, the Sierra Club attempts to influence public opinion through media campaigns and to influence electoral politics by supporting candidates who they believe share their environmental views and by opposing candidates they view as foes of environmentalism.

Direct Lobbying Combines Education, Persuasion, and Pressure

Lobbying is a strategy by which organized interests seek to influence the passage of legislation or other public policy by exerting direct pressure on members of the legislature. Lobbying encompasses a wide range of activities that groups engage in with all sorts of government officials and the public as a whole.

Lobbyists first and foremost provide information to lawmakers about their interests and the legislation at hand.[15] They often testify on behalf of their clients at congressional committee and agency hearings. Lobbyists talk to reporters, place ads in newspapers, and organize letter-writing and email campaigns. They also play an important role in fund-raising, helping to direct clients' contributions to members of Congress and presidential candidates.

Traditionally, the term *lobbyist* referred mainly to individuals who sought to influence the passage of legislation in the Congress. The First Amendment to the Constitution provides for the right to "petition the Government for a redress of grievances." But as early as the 1870s, *lobbying* became the common term for "petitioning." And since petitioning cannot take place on the floor of the House or Senate, petitioners must therefore confront members of Congress in the lobbies of the legislative chamber—hence the term *lobbying*. Although interest groups do not necessarily buy votes, they do buy time, expertise, and influence. Studies have found that those interest groups providing the most money to representatives are more likely to be consulted by that representative and asked to provide information and expertise in discussing a bill pertaining to that group's area of interest. This,

Interest groups may also try to influence the president's decisions. In 2009, President Obama met with business leaders to discuss how a new health care policy would affect their employees' health insurance plans.

in essence, gives interest groups a voice in shaping how legislation is written, and while it cannot ensure votes for laws preferred by the group, it is an effective means for organized interests to influence policy.

The influence of lobbyists, in many instances, is based on personal relationships and the behind-the-scenes services they are able to perform for lawmakers. Many of Washington's top lobbyists have close ties to important members of Congress or are themselves former members of Congress, thus virtually guaranteeing that their clients will have direct access to congressional leaders. Some important lobbyists are married to prominent political figures. For example, Linda Daschle of LHD and Associates is the wife of former Senate majority leader Tom Daschle, and Hadassah Lieberman, wife of former senator Joseph Lieberman, was for many years a lobbyist for the pharmaceutical industry.

Cultivating Access Means Getting the Attention of Decision Makers

In many areas, interest groups, government agencies, and congressional committees routinely work together for mutual benefit. The interest group provides campaign contributions for members of Congress, and it lobbies for larger budgets for the agency. The agency, in turn, provides government contracts for the interest group and constituency services for friendly members of Congress. The congressional committee or subcommittee, meanwhile, supports the agency's budgetary requests and the programs the interest group favors. This so-called **iron triangle** has one angle in an executive branch program, another angle in a Senate or House legislative committee or subcommittee, and a third angle in some highly stable and well-organized interest group. The angles in the triangular relationship are mutually supporting, especially if a committee member has seniority in Congress. Figure 8.2 illustrates one of the most important iron triangles in recent American political history: that of the defense industry. Iron triangles explain how interest groups have influence over both Congress and the government agency directly regulating their interests in many policy areas.

A number of important policy domains, such as the environmental and welfare arenas, are controlled not by highly structured and unified iron triangles but by a jumble of issue networks. These networks consist of like-minded politicians, consultants, public officials, political activists, and interest groups having some concern with the issue in question. Activists and interest groups recognized as being involved in the area (the "stakeholders") are customarily invited to testify before congressional committees or give their views to government agencies considering action in their domain.

Regulating Lobbying Lobbyists' extensive access to members of Congress has led to repeated calls for reform. In 2007, congressional Democrats secured the enactment of a new package of ethics rules designed to fulfill their 2006 campaign promise to bring an end to lobbying abuses. The new rules prohibited lobbyists from paying for most meals, trips, parties, and gifts for members of Congress. Lobbyists were also required to disclose the amounts and sources of small campaign contributions they collected from clients and "bundled" into large contributions. And interest groups were required to disclose the funds they used to rally voters to support or oppose legislative proposals. According to the *Washington Post*, however, within a few weeks lobbyists had learned how to circumvent many of the new rules, and lobbying firms were as busy as ever.[16]

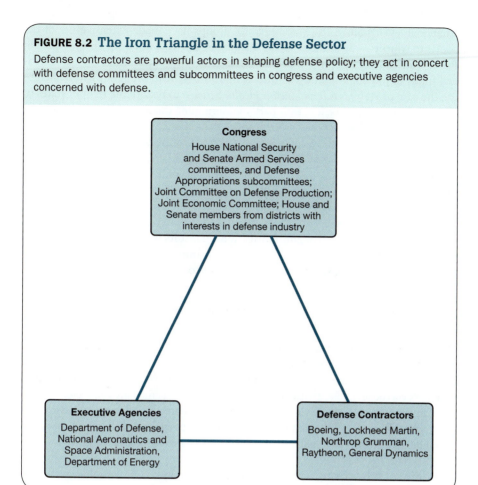

FIGURE 8.2 The Iron Triangle in the Defense Sector
Defense contractors are powerful actors in shaping defense policy; they act in concert with defense committees and subcommittees in congress and executive agencies concerned with defense.

Congress
House National Security and Senate Armed Services committees, and Defense Appropriations subcommittees; Joint Committee on Defense Production; Joint Economic Committee; House and Senate members from districts with interests in defense industry

Executive Agencies
Department of Defense, National Aeronautics and Space Administration, Department of Energy

Defense Contractors
Boeing, Lockheed Martin, Northrop Grumman, Raytheon, General Dynamics

Using the Courts (Litigation) Can Be Highly Effective

Interest groups sometimes turn to litigation when they lack access or when they feel they have insufficient influence to change a law or policy. Interest groups can use the courts to affect public policy in at least three ways: (1) by bringing suit directly on behalf of the group itself, (2) by financing suits brought by individuals, and (3) by filing a companion brief as an *amicus curiae* (literally "friend of the court") to an existing court case.

Among the best-known illustrations of using of the courts as a strategy for political influence is found in the history of the National Association for the Advancement of Colored People (NAACP). The most important of such court cases was, of course, *Brown v. Board of Education of Topeka, Kansas* (1954), in which the U.S. Supreme Court held that legal segregation of the schools was unconstitutional.[17] Later, extensive litigation spearheaded the women's rights movement of the 1960s and the rights of gays and lesbians since the 1990s.

The 1973 Supreme Court case of *Roe v. Wade*, which took away a state's power to ban abortions, sparked a controversy that brought conservatives to the fore on a national level.[18] Since 1973, conservative groups have made extensive use of the courts to whittle away at the scope of the privacy doctrine upon which the ruling in *Roe v. Wade* was based. They won rulings, for example, that prohibit the use of federal funds to pay for voluntary abortions. In 1989, right-to-life groups were able to use the case of *Webster v. Reproductive Health Services* to restore the right of states to place restrictions on abortion, thus partly undermining the *Roe v. Wade* decision (see Chapter 4).[19] The *Webster* case brought more than 300 interest groups on both sides of the abortion issue to the Supreme Court's door. On the other side of the political spectrum, the American Civil Liberties Union (ACLU) regularly uses litigation to challenge state and federal laws that restrict the rights of individuals and groups. This includes recent successful challenges to laws ending affirmative action in the states.

Litigation involving large businesses is voluminous in such areas as taxation, antitrust, interstate transportation, patents, and product quality and standardization. Often a business is brought to litigation against its will by virtue of initiatives taken against it by other businesses or by government agencies. But many individual businesses bring suit themselves in order to influence government policy.

Mobilizing Public Opinion Brings Wider Attention to an Issue

Going public is a strategy that attempts to mobilize the widest and most favorable climate of opinion, and is a favored strategy of citizen groups and netroots or online activist groups. Many groups consider it imperative to maintain political pressure at all times. Citizen groups and online netroot organizations rely heavily on mobilizing their members via social media, Twitter campaigns, and targeted email messages on short notice. On any given day a new viral media story may become headline news, and in most cases an interest group is behind the story. Such groups span the ideological spectrum from liberal to conservative, and can wield significant pressure on elected officials to act.

Institutional Advertising One of the best known ways of going public is the use of **institutional advertising**, which is advertising designed to create a positive image of an organization. A casual scanning of important mass-circulation magazines, newspapers, and television provides numerous examples of expensive and well-designed ads by the major oil companies, automobile and steel companies, other large corporations, and trade associations. The ads show how much these organizations are doing for the country, for the protection of the environment, or for the defense of the American way of life. The ads' purpose is to create and maintain a strongly positive public image in the hope of drawing on these favorable feelings as needed for specific political campaigns later on.

Protests and Demonstrations Many groups resort to going public because they lack the resources, the contacts, or the experience to use other political strategies. The sponsorship of boycotts, sit-ins, mass rallies, and marches by Martin Luther King, Jr.'s Southern Christian Leadership Conference (SCLC) and related organizations in the 1950s and '60s is one of the most significant and successful cases of going public to create a more favorable climate of opinion by calling attention to abuses. The success of these events inspired similar efforts by women's groups. The 2010 GOP takeover of the House of Representatives began with the spontaneous self-organization of the Tea Party movement in 2009 as an angry response to the Obama administration's health care initiatives. In 2011 the Occupy Wall Street movement sparked demonstrations across America and around the world, giving voice to those who were outraged by economic inequality.

Grassroots Mobilization Another form of going public is **grassroots mobilization**. In such a campaign, a lobby group mobilizes its members throughout the country to contact government officials in support of the group's position.

Among the most effective users of the grassroots lobby effort in contemporary American politics is the religious right. Networks of evangelical churches have the capacity to generate hundreds of thousands of letters and phone calls to Congress and the White House. For example, in 2007 a grassroots firm called Grassfire.org led the drive to kill the immigration reform bill supported by President Bush and a number of congressional Democrats that would have legalized the status of many illegal immigrants. Grassfire.org used the Internet and talk radio programs to generate a campaign that yielded 700,000 signatures on petitions opposing the bill. The petitions, along with tens of thousands of phone calls, letters, and emails generated by Grassfire.org and other groups led to the bill's defeat in the U.S. Senate.[20]

One increasingly common way that corporations and interest groups have sought to help themselves politically is by adopting aliases in their advertising efforts. For example, the Save Our Species Alliance is an industry group seeking to weaken the Endangered Species Act, and Citizens for Asbestos Reform seeks to limit the ability of individuals harmed by asbestos from seeking redress in the courts. The Coalition to Protect America's Health Care is a group of for-profit hospitals that runs ads calling for increased federal funding for those entities. Citizens for Better Medicare actually represents the pharmaceutical industry. Voices for Choices was the alias used by a coalition of telecommunications companies that unsuccessfully advertised on behalf of continued regulation of local phone services. Both Americans for Balanced Energy Choices and the Coalition for Clean, Affordable, Reliable Energy sponsor ads promoting the virtues of coal as an energy source. The Partnership to Protect Consumer Credit is an alias used by a coalition of credit card companies seeking higher interest rates, and Americans for Balanced Energy Choices is an alias for a coal industry trade group. As is often the case, the names chosen imply that these organizations are citizen-based, grassroots groups instead of front groups for large corporations. A bill rejected by the Senate in 2006 would have required lobby groups to disclose their actual identities, but it was attacked by the industry as a threat to free speech.

A notorious online grassroots organization is called Anonymous. Anonymous is a loosely associated network of activists and hackers that specializes in online protests. Some consider the group to be outside of the law, as dozens of people have been arrested for involvement in Anonymous cyber attacks in countries around the world. Others consider them freedom fighters or digital Robin Hoods. The group's website describes it as "an internet gathering" with a decentralized organizational structure that operates on ideas rather than directives. The group became known for a series of well-publicized hacks and distributed denial-of-service (DDoS) attacks on government, religious organizations, and corporate websites. Anonymous prioritizes Internet freedom and has mounted protests against antidigital piracy campaigns by motion picture and recording industry trade association and by government. The organization helped promote the global Occupy Wall Street movement and the Arab Spring democratic protests in the Middle East; recently the organization has been active in promoting the rights of gays and lesbians.

Groups Often Use Electoral Politics

In addition to the techniques already discussed, interest groups also seek to use the electoral process to elect sympathetic legislators in the first place and to ensure that those who are elected will owe them a debt of gratitude for their support. While groups invest far more resources in lobbying than in electoral politics, financial support and campaign activism can be important tools for organized interests.

Political Action Committees By far the most common electoral strategy employed by interest groups is that of giving financial support to political parties or to candidates running for office. But such support can easily cross the threshold into outright bribery. Therefore, Congress has occasionally attempted to regulate this strategy. Its most recent effort was the Federal Election Campaign Act of 1971 (amended in 1974). This act limits campaign contributions and requires that each candidate or campaign committee itemize the full name and address, occupation, and principal business of each person who contributes more than $200. These provisions have been effective up to a point, resulting in numerous indictments, resignations, and criminal convictions in the aftermath of the 1972 Watergate scandal.

Reaction to Watergate produced further legislation on campaign finance in 1974 and 1976, but the effect has been to restrict individual rather than interest group campaign activity. Individuals may now contribute no more than $2,600 to any candidate for federal office in any primary or general election. A PAC, however, can contribute $5,000, provided it contributes to at least five different federal candidates each year. Beyond this, the laws permit corporations, unions, and other interest groups to form PACs and to pay the costs of soliciting funds from private citizens for the PACs. In other words, PACs operate in the electoral arena to represent the interests with which they are affiliated.

The flurry of reform legislation of the early and mid-1970s attempted to reduce the influence that special interests had over elections, but the effect has been almost the exact opposite. Electoral spending by interest groups has been increasing steadily. The number of PACs has also increased significantly—from 480 in 1972 to more than 5,500 in 2012. Opportunities for legally influencing campaigns are now widespread.

Given the enormous costs of television commercials, polls, computers, and other elements of the new political technology, most politicians are eager to receive PAC contributions and are at least willing to give a friendly hearing to the needs and interests of contributors. It is probably not the case that most politicians simply sell their votes to the interests that fund their campaigns. But there is considerable evidence to support the contention that interest groups' campaign contributions do influence the overall pattern of political behavior in Congress and in the state legislatures.

Concern about PACs grew through the 1980s and '90s, creating a constant drumbeat for reform of federal election laws. This resulted in the enactment of the McCain-Feingold bill, which became the Bipartisan Campaign Reform Act (BCRA)

The amount of money spent by organized interests on elections has increased dramatically in the last decade. This cartoon raises the concern that political influence is for sale, and only the extremely wealthy can buy it.

of 2002. When it was originally proposed in 1996, the bill was aimed at reducing or eliminating PACs. But in a stunning about-face, when campaign finance reform was adopted in 2002, it did not restrict PACs in any significant way. Rather, it eliminated unrestricted "soft money" donations to the national political parties.

Favorable court rulings in 2010, including the Supreme Court's *Citizens United* case, struck down limits on corporate political spending, which gave rise to so-called Super PACs.[21] These organizations may not contribute money directly to (or coordinate their activities with) campaigns, but may spend unlimited amounts of money on behalf of parties or campaigns they support. These Super PACs are often headed by former party officials. In 2014, Super PACs spent $339 million on House and Senate races.[22] The unlimited money raised and spent by independent political committees makes the formal regulations on PACs and individual contributions almost irrelevant. Spending in U.S. elections is far higher than in any other country in the world.

The Initiative Another political tactic sometimes used by interest groups is sponsorship of ballot initiatives at the state level. The initiative, a device adopted by a number of states around 1900, allows proposed laws to be placed on the general election ballot and submitted directly to the state's voters, bypassing the state legislature and governor. The initiative was originally promoted by late nineteenth-century Populists as a mechanism that would allow the people to govern directly—an antidote to interest group influence in the legislative process.

Ironically studies have suggested that many initiative campaigns today are actually sponsored by interest groups seeking to circumvent legislative opposition to their goals. In recent years, for example, initiative campaigns have been sponsored by the insurance industry, trial lawyers associations, and tobacco companies.[23] Liberal activists have developed their own initiative campaigns to promote issues such as increasing the minimum wage, promoting clean energy, strengthening environmental protection laws, and legalization of marriage rights for same-sex couples.

Groups, Interests,
and Your Future

There is considerable competition among organized groups in the United States. Although the weak and poor do occasionally become organized to assert their rights, interest group politics is generally a form of political competition best suited to the wealthy and powerful. In the realm of group politics, liberty seems inconsistent with equality.

Moreover, although groups sometimes organize to promote broad public concerns, interest groups more often represent relatively narrow, selfish interests. Small, self-interested groups can be organized much more easily than large, more diffuse collectives. For one thing, the members of a relatively small group (say, bankers or hunting enthusiasts) are usually able to recognize their shared interests and the need to pursue them in the political arena. Members of large and more diffuse groups (say, consumers or potential victims of firearms) often find it difficult to recognize their shared interests or the need to engage in collective action to achieve them.[24] This is why causes presented as public interests by their proponents often turn out, upon examination, to be private interests wrapped in a public mantle. Thus the elitist quality of group politics often appears to be inconsistent with democracy.

As this chapter has shown, major changes to political or social institutions can have a significant impact on the number and identity of interest groups. One of the major social trends of our time is demographic change. Notable, the baby boomers, a large generation of Americans born in the period after World War II, are now reaching retirement and old age. Elderly Americans are highly organized and represented by interest groups, such as AARP, that lobby government for benefits, including health care subsidies to keep the cost of their medical care low. Because resources are limited, however, benefits to elderly Americans may come at the expense of social goals that may be more important to other generations. Today's college students are part of the millennial generation, born 1980–2001, who are more numerous than baby boomers. Young people are most affected by the cost of a college education and the job opportunities that exist when they graduate, rather than health care, since the young tend to be relatively healthy but need education and experience. Yet it is difficult to organize college students and the millennial generation on a national or statewide scale to lobby government to spend more on higher education or job opportunities. Why are young people's interests poorly represented and elderly people better represented? Could new organizational routines from netroots help young people organize?

plug**in**

Inform

Find out which groups give the most money to your representatives in Congress by clicking "Congress" at www.opensecrets.org/politicians. You can look up your representatives by zip code.

Express

Imagine you are an aide to a member of Congress. Write a brief policy memo for or against more regulation of lobbying.

Connect

Find an interest group that appeals to you at votesmart.org /interest-groups, then follow that group on Facebook or Twitter.

Act

Join an interest group that works on behalf of a cause you support. Consider forming a campus chapter at your college or university.

studyguide

Practice Quiz

1. The theory that competition among organized interests will produce balance, with all the interests regulating one another is *(p. 245)*
   a) pluralism.
   b) elite power politics.
   c) democracy.
   d) socialism.
   e) libertarianism.

2. Groups that claim to serve the general good, rather than their own particular interests are *(p. 247)*
   a) membership associations.
   b) citizen groups.
   c) professional associations.
   d) ideological groups.
   e) public-sector groups.

3. To overcome the free-rider problem, groups *(p. 251)*
   a) provide general benefits.
   b) litigate.
   c) provide selective benefits.
   d) provide collective goods.
   e) go public.

4. Discount purchasing and health insurance are examples of *(p. 252)*
   a) purposive benefits.
   b) informational benefits.
   c) solidary benefits.
   d) material benefits.
   e) member dues.

5. Friendship and networking are examples of *(p. 252)*
   a) purposive benefits.
   b) informational benefits.
   c) solidary benefits.
   d) material benefits.
   e) member dues.

6. Which of the following is an important reason for the enormous increase in the number of groups seeking to influence the American political system? *(pp. 254–55)*
   a) the decrease in the size and activity of government during the last few decades
   b) the increase in the size and activity of government during the last few decades
   c) the increase in the amount of soft money in election campaigns in recent decades
   d) the increase in legal protection provided to interest groups as a result of the Supreme Court's evolving interpretation of the First Amendment
   e) the increase in the number of people identifying themselves as an independent in recent decades

7. Which of the following is *not* an activity in which interest groups frequently engage? *(pp. 255–64)*
   a) starting their own political party
   b) litigation
   c) sponsoring ballot initiatives at the state level
   d) lobbying
   e) contributing to campaigns

8. Which types of interest groups are most often associated with the New Politics movement? *(p. 255)*
   a) political action committees
   b) professional associations
   c) government groups
   d) labor groups
   e) public interest groups

9. Which of the following best describes the federal government's laws regarding lobbying? *(p. 258)*
   a) Federal law allows lobbying but only on issues related to taxation.
   b) Federal law allows lobbying but only if the lobbyists receive no monetary compensation for their lobbying.
   c) Federal law strictly prohibits any form of lobbying.
   d) Federal law requires all lobbyists to disclose the amounts and sources of small campaign contributions they collect from clients and "bundle" into large contributions, as well as the funds they use to rally voters
   e) There are no laws regulating lobbying because the federal government has never passed any legislation on the legality of the activity.

10. A loose network of elected leaders, public officials, activists, and interest groups drawn together by a public policy issue is referred to as *(p. 258)*
   a) an issue network.
   b) a public interest group.
   c) a political action committee.
   d) pluralism.
   e) an iron triangle.

11. Which of the following is a way that interest groups use the courts to influence public policy? *(pp. 259-60)*
   a) supplying judges with solidary benefits
   b) joining an issue network
   c) creating an iron triangle
   d) forming a political action committee
   e) filing amicus briefs

12. Which of the following are examples of the "going public" strategy? *(pp. 260-62)*
   a) free riding, pluralism, and issue networking
   b) donating money to political parties, endorsing candidates, and sponsoring ballot initiatives
   c) institutional advertising, grassroots advertising, and protests and demonstrations
   d) providing informational benefits, providing solidary benefits, and providing material benefits
   e) filing an amicus brief, bringing a lawsuit, and financing those who are filing a lawsuit

Key Terms

citizen groups *(p. 247)* groups that claim they serve the general good rather than only their own particular interest

collective goods *(p. 251)* benefits, sought by groups, that are broadly available and cannot be denied to nonmembers

free riders *(p. 251)* those who enjoy the benefits of collective goods but did not participate in acquiring them

grassroots mobilization *(p. 261)* a lobbying campaign in which a group mobilizes its membership to contact government officials in support of the group's position

informational benefits *(p. 251)* special newsletters, periodicals, training programs,

conferences, and other information provided to members of groups to entice others to join

institutional advertising *(p. 260)* advertising designed to create a positive image of an organization

interest group *(p. 245)* individuals who organize to influence the government's programs and policies

iron triangle *(p. 258)* the stable, cooperative relationships that often develop among a congressional committee, an administrative agency, and one or more supportive interest groups; not all of these relationships are triangular, but the iron triangle is the most typical

lobbying *(p. 257)* a strategy by which organized interests seek to influence the passage of legislation or other public policy by exerting direct pressure on members of the legislature

material benefits *(p. 252)* special goods, services, or money provided to members of groups to entice others to join

membership association *(p. 251)* an organized group in which members actually play a substantial role, sitting on committees and engaging in group projects

netroots *(p. 250)* grassroots online activist organizations that have redefined membership and fund-raising practices and streamlined staff structure

New Politics movement *(p. 255)* a political movement that began in the 1960s and '70s, made up of professionals and intellectuals for whom the civil rights and antiwar movements were formative experiences; the New Politics movement strengthened public interest groups

pluralism *(p. 245)* the theory that all interests are and should be free to compete for influence in the government; the outcome of this competition is compromise and moderation

political action committee (PAC) *(p. 245)* a private group that raises and distributes funds for use in election campaigns

purposive benefits *(p. 252)* selective benefits of group membership that emphasize the purpose and accomplishments of the group

solidary benefits *(p. 252)* selective benefits of group membership that emphasize friendship, networking, and consciousness raising

staff organization *(p. 251)* type of membership group in which a professional staff conducts most of the group's activities

For Further Reading

Ainsworth, Scott. *Analyzing Interest Groups.* New York: W. W. Norton, 2002.

Baumgartner, Frank, Jeffrey M. Berry, Beth L. Leech, David C. Kimball, and Marie Hojnacki. *Lobbying and Policy Change: Who Wins, Who Loses, and Why.* Chicago: University of Chicago Press, 2009.

Berry, Jeffrey. *Interest Group Society.* 5th ed. New York: Longman, 2008.

Cigler, Allan J., and Burdett A. Loomis, eds. *Interest Group Politics*, 8th ed. Washington, DC: CQ Press, 2011.

Goldstein, Kenneth. *Interest Groups, Lobbying, and Participation in America.* New York: Cambridge University Press, 2008.

Karpf, David. *The MoveOn Effect: The Unexpected Transformation of American Political Advocacy.* New York: Oxford University Press, 2012.

Lessig, Lawrence, *Republic, Lost: How Money Corrupts Politics—and a Plan to Stop It.* New York: Twelve Press, 2011.

Lowi, Theodore J. *The End of Liberalism.* New York: W. W. Norton, 1979.

Olson, Mancur, Jr. *The Logic of Collective Action: Public Goods and the Theory of Groups.* Cambridge, MA: Harvard University Press, 1971.

Scholzman, Kay Lehman, and John T. Tierney. *Organized Interests and American Democracy.* New York: Harper and Row, 1986.

Spitzer, Robert J. *The Politics of Gun Control,* 5th ed. Boulder, CO: Paradigm Publishers, 2012.

Strolovitch, Dara. *Affirmative Advocacy: Race, Class, and Gender in Interest Group Politics.* Chicago: University of Chicago Press, 2007.

In addition to its lawmaking powers, Congress plays a critical role in American democracy as a representative institution. The members of Congress—100 senators and 435 representatives—represent the voices of the people across America. Yet some observers worry that Congress does not represent all voices equally.

Congress

9

WHAT GOVERNMENT DOES AND WHY IT MATTERS As 2013 drew to a close, the price of milk threatened to skyrocket. The cause? Members of Congress could not agree on a farm bill. The bill, which provides subsidies for farmers and funds for the Supplemental Nutrition Assistance Program (SNAP, also called food stamps) for the needy, usually wins support from both Democrats and Republicans. But in 2013, the Republican-controlled House passed a bill that would reduce SNAP benefits by $4 billion a year, while the Democratic-controlled Senate enacted a bill with a cut of only $400 million, a tenth of the size of the Republican cut.[1] As months passed, the two chambers could not reconcile their differences. Yet, the farm bill touched not only SNAP recipients and farmers; failure to pass a farm bill would be widely felt as expiring dairy subsides affected the price of milk for all Americans. Recognizing the widespread consequences of the stalemate, the House ultimately accepted a much smaller cut in food stamps and the sharp increase in diary prices was averted.

On other issues, such as immigration reform, Congress proved unable to reach agreement. Congress last passed comprehensive immigration reform in 1986 and, despite many differences, a growing chorus of voices agreed that it was time for the federal government to take action again. Some groups favor tighter border controls, arguing that illegal immigration puts a burden on basic social services, such as health care, that benefit all Americans. On the other side, "Dreamers"—undocumented young people brought to the United States as children—pushed Congress to create a pathway to citizenship for the more than 11 million undocumented immigrants already in the country. Without such legislation, many young people are unable to seek educational and job opportunities in the country they grew up in. And employers, ranging from farmers to high-tech entrepreneurs, complained that our system for admitting immigrants posed large burdens on business and needed to be updated. In 2013 the Senate responded to these pressures with a comprehensive immigration bill. The bill reflected a compromise on the major elements of reform, including a pathway to citizenship for the undocumented, large sums for improved border security, and an overhaul of the procedures for admitting new legal immigrants, including workers. However, the House could not reach agreement on a bill and the push for comprehensive immigration reform ultimately died.

Congress has vast authority over most aspects of American life. Laws related to federal spending, taxing, and regulation all pass through Congress. While the debates over these laws may seem hard to follow because they are complex and technical or because heated, partisan struggles distract from the substance of the issue, it is important for the American people to learn about what Congress is doing. As the examples of the farm bill and immigration indicate, actions taken—or not taken—in Congress affect the everyday experiences we take for granted. With its power to spend and tax, Congress also affects the choices that people face and the opportunities they can expect in life. In this chapter, we will see how Congress operates, and how forces like interest groups and political parties shape its actions.

chaptergoals

- Describe who serves in Congress and how they represent their constituents (pp. 273–84)
- Explain how party leadership, the committee system, and the staff system help structure congressional business (pp. 284–88)
- Outline the steps in the process of passing a law (pp. 288–93)
- Analyze the factors that influence which laws Congress passes (pp. 293–300)
- Describe Congress's influence over other branches of government (pp. 300–303)

Congress Represents the American People

Describe who serves in Congress and how they represent their constituents

Congress is the most important representative institution in American government. Each member's primary responsibility is to the district, to his **constituency** (the residents in the area from which an official is elected), not to the congressional leadership, a party, or even Congress itself. Yet the task of representation is not a simple one. Views about what constitutes fair and effective representation differ, and constituents can make very different kinds of demands on their representatives. Members of Congress must consider these diverse views and demands as they represent their districts.

The House and Senate Offer Differences in Representation

The framers of the Constitution provided for a **bicameral** legislature—that is, a legislative body consisting of two chambers or houses. The 435 members of the House are elected from districts apportioned according to population; the 100 members of the Senate are elected by their states, with 2 senators from each. Senators have much longer terms in office and usually represent much larger and more diverse constituencies than do their counterparts in the House (see Table 9.1).

Both formal and informal factors contribute to differences between the two chambers of Congress. Differences in the length of terms and requirements for holding office specified by the Constitution in turn generate differences in how members of each body develop their constituencies and exercise their powers of office. The small size and relative homogeneity of their constituencies and the frequency with which they must seek re-election make House members more attuned to the legislative needs of local interest groups. The result is that members of the House most effectively and frequently serve as the agents of well-organized local interests with specific legislative agendas—for instance, used-car dealers seeking relief from regulation, labor unions seeking more favorable legislation,

---

TABLE 9.1

Differences between the House and the Senate

	HOUSE	SENATE
Minimum age of member	25 years	30 years
U.S. citizenship	At least 7 years	At least 9 years
Length of term	2 years	6 years
Number representing each state	1–53 per state (depends on population)	2 per state
Constituency	Local	Local and statewide

or farmers looking for higher subsidies. Because House members seek re-election every two years, they are interested in doing what their constituents want right *now*.

Senators, on the other hand, serve larger and more heterogeneous constituencies. As a result, they are somewhat better able than members of the House to serve as the agents for groups and interests organized on a statewide or national basis. Moreover, with longer terms in office, senators have the luxury of considering "new ideas" or seeking to bring together new coalitions of interests rather than simply serving existing ones.

Representation Can Be Sociological or Agency

We have become so accustomed to the idea of representative government that we tend to forget what a peculiar concept representation really is. A representative claims to act or speak for some other person or group. But how can one person be trusted to speak for another? How do we know that those who call themselves our representatives are actually speaking on our behalf rather than simply pursuing their own interests?

There are two circumstances under which one person reasonably might be trusted to speak for another. The first of these occurs if the two individuals are so similar in background, character, interests, and perspectives that anything said by one would very likely reflect the views of the other as well. This principle is at the heart of what is sometimes called **sociological representation**—a type of representation in which representatives have the same racial, gender, ethnic, religious, or educational backgrounds as their constituents. The assumption is that sociological similarity helps promote good representation; thus, the composition of a properly constituted representative assembly should mirror the composition of society.

The second circumstance under which one person might be trusted to speak for another occurs if the two are formally bound together so that the representative is in some way accountable to those she purports to represent. If representatives can somehow be punished or held to account for failing to represent their constituents properly, then they have an incentive to provide good representation even if their own personal backgrounds, views, and interests differ from those of the people they represent. This principle is called **agency representation**—the sort of representation that takes place when constituents have the power to hire and fire their representatives.

Both sociological and agency representation play a role in the relationship between members of Congress and their constituencies.

The Social Composition of the U.S. Congress The extent to which the U.S. Congress is representative of the American people in a sociological sense can be seen by examining the distribution of important social characteristics in the House and Senate today.

African Americans, women, Latinos, and Asian Americans have increased their congressional representation in the past two decades (see Figure 9.1), but for most of American history, these groups had no representatives in Congress. Even now,

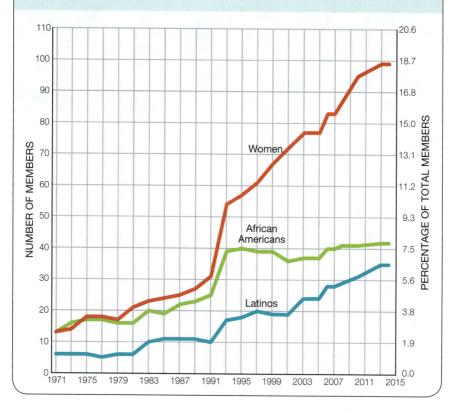

FIGURE 9.1 Women, African Americans, and Latinos in the U.S. Congress, 1971–2014

Congress has become more socially diverse since the 1970s. After a gradual increase from 1971 to 1990, the number of women and African American members grew quickly during the first half of the 1990s. How closely does the number of female, African American, and Latino representatives reflect their proportion of the total U.S. population?

SOURCES: Harold W. Stanley and Richard G. Niemi, eds., *Vital Statistics on American Politics, 2003–2004* (Washington, DC: CQ Press, 2003), 207, Table 5–2; and Jennifer E. Manning, Membership of the 113th Congress: A Profile, Congressional Research Service 7-5700, January 13, 2014, www.tas.org/sgp/crs/misc/R42964.pdf (accessed 2/24/14).

their representation in Congress is still not comparable to the proportions in the general population. After the Democrats won control of the House in the 2006 election, California Democrat Nancy Pelosi became the first woman Speaker of the House of Representatives. She held that position through 2010. Following the 2012 elections, the 113th Congress (2013–14) included 79 women in the House of Representatives and 20 women in the Senate, an all-time high. Since many important contemporary national issues do cut along racial and gender lines, a considerable clamor for reform in the representative process is likely to continue until these groups are fully represented.

To more effectively promote a legislative agenda that addresses issues that disproportionately affect racial and ethnic minority groups, members of Congress from those groups have formed caucuses. Here, members of the Congressional Black Caucus discuss economic opportunity at a town meeting in Miami Gardens, Florida.

The occupational backgrounds of members of Congress have always been a matter of interest because so many issues cut along economic lines that are relevant to occupations and industries. The legal profession is the dominant career of most members of Congress prior to their election. Public service or politics is also a significant background. In addition, many members of Congress also have important ties to business and industry.[2] One composite portrait of a typical member of Congress has been that of "a middle-aged male lawyer whose father was of the professional or managerial class; a native-born 'white,' or—if he cannot avoid being an immigrant—a product of northwestern or central Europe or Canada, rather than of eastern or southern Europe, Latin America, Africa, or Asia."[3] This is not a portrait of the U.S. population at large.

Is Congress still able to legislate fairly or take account of a diversity of views and interests if it is not a sociologically representative assembly? The task is certainly much more difficult. Yet there is reason to believe it can. Representatives can serve as the agents of their constituents, even if they do not precisely mirror their sociological attributes.

Representatives as Agents A good deal of evidence indicates that whether or not members of Congress share their constituents' sociological characteristics, they do work very hard to speak for their constituents' views and serve their constituents' interests in the governmental process. The idea of representative as agent is similar to the relationship of lawyer and client. True, the relationship between the member of Congress and an average of 710,767 "clients" in the district, or the senator and millions of "clients" in the state, is very different from that of the lawyer and client. But the criteria of performance are comparable. One expects at the very least that each representative will constantly be seeking to discover the interests of the constituency and will take those interests into account as she governs.[4] Whether members of Congress always represent the interests of their constituents is another matter, as we will see later in this chapter.

There is constant communication between constituents and congressional offices, and the volume of email from constituents and advocacy groups has grown so large so quickly that congressional offices have struggled to find effective ways to respond in a timely manner.[5] At the same time, members of Congress have found new ways to communicate with constituents. They have created websites describing their achievements, established a presence on social networking sites, and issued e-newsletters that alert constituents to current issues. Many have also set up blogs and use Twitter accounts to establish a more informal style of communication with constituents.

The seriousness with which members of the House attempt to behave as representatives can be seen in the amount of time spent on behalf of their constituents. Well over a quarter of their time and nearly two-thirds of the time of their staff members is devoted to constituency service (called "casework"). This service is not merely a matter of writing and mailing letters. It includes talking to constituents, providing them with minor services, presenting special bills for them, attempting to influence decisions by regulatory commissions on their behalf, helping them apply for federal benefits, such as Social Security and Small Business Administration loans, and assisting them with immigration cases.[6]

In many districts there are two or three issues on which constituents have such pronounced opinions that representatives feel they have little freedom of choice. For example, representatives from districts that grow wheat, cotton, or tobacco probably will not want to exercise a great deal of independence on relevant agricultural legislation. In oil-rich states such as Oklahoma, Texas, and California, senators and members of the House are likely to be leading advocates of oil interests. For one thing, representatives are probably fearful of voting against their district interests; for another, the districts are unlikely to have elected representatives who would *want* to vote against them. On the other hand, on many issues, constituents do not have very strong views, so representatives are free to act as they think best. Foreign policy issues often fall into this category.

The influence of constituencies is so pervasive that both parties have strongly embraced the informal rule that nothing should be done, with regard to constituencies, that would endanger the re-election chances of any member. Party leaders obey this rule fairly consistently by not asking any member to vote in a way that might conflict with a district interest.

The Electoral Connection Hinges on Incumbency

The sociological composition of Congress and the activities of representatives once they are in office are very much influenced by electoral considerations. Two factors related to the U.S. electoral system affect who gets elected and what they do once in office. The first factor is that of incumbency advantage. The second is the way congressional district lines are drawn, which can greatly affect the outcome of an election. Let us examine more closely the impact that these considerations have on representation.

Incumbency—holding a political office for which one is running—plays a very important role in the American electoral system and in the kind of representation citizens get in Washington. Once in office, members of Congress gain access to an array of tools that they can use to stack the deck in favor of their re-election. The most important of these is constituency service—taking care of the problems and requests of individual voters. Congressional offices will intervene on behalf of constituents when they have problems with federal programs or agencies, in such areas as Social Security benefits, veterans' benefits, passports, and the like. When congressional offices contact federal agencies dealing with such matters, the offices usually respond with extra speed, knowing that members of Congress can embarrass or penalize an agency that doesn't do its job properly. Through such services and through regular e-newsletters, the incumbent seeks to establish a "personal" relationship with his constituents. The success of this strategy is evident in the high rates of re-election for congressional incumbents, which are as high as 98 percent for House members and 96 percent for members of the Senate in recent years (see Figure 9.2). It is also evident in what is called "sophomore surge"—the tendency

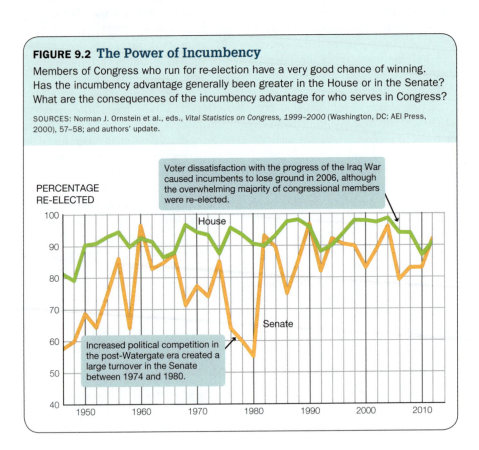

FIGURE 9.2 The Power of Incumbency

Members of Congress who run for re-election have a very good chance of winning. Has the incumbency advantage generally been greater in the House or in the Senate? What are the consequences of the incumbency advantage for who serves in Congress?

SOURCES: Norman J. Ornstein et al., eds., *Vital Statistics on Congress, 1999–2000* (Washington, DC: AEI Press, 2000), 57–58; and authors' update.

Voter dissatisfaction with the progress of the Iraq War caused incumbents to lose ground in 2006, although the overwhelming majority of congressional members were re-elected.

PERCENTAGE RE-ELECTED

House

Senate

Increased political competition in the post-Watergate era created a large turnover in the Senate between 1974 and 1980.

for incumbent candidates to win a higher percentage of the vote when seeking future terms in office.

Incumbency re-election dipped some in the 2006 elections, when 94 percent of House incumbents and 79 percent of Senate incumbents were re-elected. This relative drop was caused by voter dissatisfaction with Republican rule, the unpopularity of President Bush, and widespread dissatisfaction with the Iraq War. As a result, the Democrats won control of both houses for the first time since 1994. Every incumbent defeated in 2006 was a Republican. In 2010, Democrats were particularly vulnerable since their party controlled the presidency and both houses of Congress in a year when economic woes contributed to strong anti-incumbent sentiment. As a result, 54 incumbent Democratic members of the House and 2 incumbent Democratic senators lost their seats in 2010, and the Republicans regained control of the House. In the 2012 elections, approximately 90 percent of incumbents in the House and 91 percent in the Senate were re-elected. Furthermore, incumbents often won by large margins: only 64 of the 435 House races were decided by a margin of less than 10 percent. The average margin of victory across all congressional contests was 31.85 percent.[7]

Incumbency can also help a candidate by scaring off potential challengers. In many races, potential candidates may decide not to run because they fear that the incumbent simply has too much money or is too well liked or too well known. Potentially strong challengers may also decide that a district's partisan leanings are too unfavorable. The efforts of incumbents to raise funds to ward off potential challengers start early. Connecticut Democratic House member Joe Courtney won his seat in 2006 by a very small margin, with only 91 more votes than his opponent. He began fund-raising for the 2008 election even before he was sworn in for his first term. In addition, the Democratic Congressional Campaign Committee placed him on its "Frontline" team, a group of the 29 most vulnerable Democrats—these representatives were given high-profile speaking assignments and important committee appointments to elevate their profiles. In 2008, Courtney was re-elected by a 2-to-1 margin over his opponent and was easily re-elected in 2010 and 2012.

The advantage of incumbency thus tends to preserve the status quo in Congress. This fact has implications for the social composition of Congress. For example, incumbency advantage makes it harder for women to increase their numbers in Congress, because most incumbents are men. Women who run for open seats (that is, seats for which there are no incumbents) are just as likely to win as male candidates.[8] Supporters of **term limits** (legally prescribed limits on the number of terms an elected official can serve) argue that such limits are the only way to get new faces into Congress.

Apportionment and Redistricting Another major factor that affects who wins a seat in Congress is the way congressional districts are drawn. Every 10 years, state legislatures must redraw election districts and redistribute legislative representatives to reflect population changes or in response to legal challenges to existing districts. Because the number of congressional seats has been fixed at 435 since 1929, redistricting is a zero-sum process; for one state to gain a seat, another must lose one. The

Redrawing legislative districts is a difficult task because it has political implications for who will be elected. Here, the attorney for Arizona's Independent Redistricting Commission discusses a possible layout with a city council member from Casa Grande. Arizona gained one congressional seat following the 2010 census.

process of allocating congressional seats among the 50 states is called **apportionment**. Over the past several decades, the shift of the American population to the South and the West has greatly increased the size of the congressional delegations from those regions. This trend continued after the 2010 census (see Figure 9.3). Texas emerged as the biggest winner, with a gain of four additional seats, while Florida added two seats and Arizona, Georgia, Nevada, South Carolina, Utah, and Washington all added one seat.[9] Latino voters are nearly three times as prevalent in states that gained seats than in states that lost seats, suggesting that the growth of the Latino population is a major factor in the American political landscape.[10]

States that gain or lose seats must then redraw their Congressional district borders. This is a highly political process: districts are shaped to create an advantage for the party with a majority in the state legislature, which controls the **redistricting** process. In this complex process, those charged with drawing districts use sophisticated computer technologies to come up with the most favorable district boundaries. Redistricting can create open seats and pit incumbents of the same party against one another, ensuring that one of them will lose. Redistricting can also give an advantage to one party by clustering voters with certain ideological or sociological characteristics in a single district, or by diluting the influence of voter blocs by separating those voters into two or more districts. The manipulation of electoral districts to serve the interests of a particular group is known as **gerrymandering**.

Since the passage of the 1982 amendments to the 1964 Civil Rights Act, race has become a major (and controversial) consideration in drawing voting districts. These amendments, which encouraged the creation of districts in which members of racial

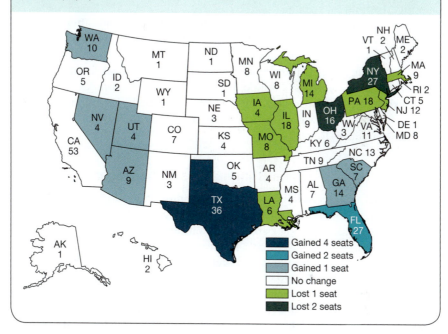

FIGURE 9.3 Results of Congressional Reapportionment, 2010

States in the West and parts of the South were the big winners in the reapportionment of House seats following the 2010 census. The old manufacturing states in the Midwest and Mid-Atlantic regions were the biggest losers. Which states have the greatest number of House seats?

SOURCE: U.S. Census Bureau, 2010 Census and Census 2000, www.census.gov/population/apportionment/data (accessed 6/26/14).

minorities have decisive majorities, have greatly increased the number of minority representatives in Congress. After the 1991–92 redistricting, the number of predominantly minority districts doubled, rising from 26 to 52. Among the most fervent supporters of the new minority districts were white Republicans, who used the opportunity to create more districts dominated by white Republican voters. These developments raise thorny questions about representation. Some analysts argue that the system may grant minorities greater sociological representation, but it has made it more difficult for them to win substantive policy goals. This was a common argument after the sweeping Republican victories in the 1994 congressional elections. Others dispute this argument, noting that the strong surge of Republican voters was a more significant factor in those elections than any Democratic losses due to racial redistricting.[11]

In the case of *Miller v. Johnson* (1995), the Supreme Court limited racial redistricting by ruling that race could not be the predominant factor in creating electoral districts.[12] The distinction between race being a "predominant" factor and its being one factor among many is very hazy. As a result, concerns about redistricting and representation persist.[13] Questions about minority representation emerged in 2011 in Texas, which gained four new seats as a result of reapportionment. The Republican legislature drew a map that advantaged Republicans in three of those districts. But the plan drew a legal challenge on the grounds that it underrepresented Hispanic voters, who accounted for most of the state's population growth. Although federal judges drew a map more favorable to minorities (and Democrats), the Supreme Court ruled that the state did not have to use the map drawn by judges. The state ultimately agreed to a map that added two Latino-dominated districts. However, federal courts ruled that this map also weakened Latino and African American political power by creating too few minority districts.

The future of race in redistricting became more uncertain after the 2013 Supreme Court decision in *Shelby County v. Holder*. That decision invalidated a section of the Voting Rights Act requiring that the Justice Department approve the redistricting plans of jurisdictions with a history of racial discrimination.[14] Many Democrats expressed disappointment with the decision, fearing that the previously covered states, several of which are controlled by Republican majorities, might try to redraw district lines to partisan ends and further bias districts toward Republicans.[15]

Direct Patronage Means Bringing Home the Bacon

Members of Congress have numerous opportunities to provide direct benefits, or **patronage**, for their constituents. Patronage resources are available to higher officials, and include making partisan appointments to offices and conferring grants, licenses, or special favors to supporters. The most important such opportunity for direct patronage is in so-called **pork barrel legislation (or pork)**—appropriations made by legislative bodies for local projects that are often not needed but that are created to help local representatives win re-election in their home districts. This type of legislation specifies a project to be funded, and the location of the project within a particular district. Many observers of Congress argue that pork-barrel bills are the only ones that some members are serious about moving toward actual passage, because they are seen as so important to members' re-election bids.

A common form of pork barreling is the "earmark," the practice through which members of Congress insert into bills language that provides special benefits for their own constituents. Highway bills are a favorite vehicle for congressional pork-barrel spending. The 2005 highway bill was full of such items, containing more than 6,000 projects earmarked for specific congressional districts. These measures often have little to do with transportation needs, instead serving as evidence for constituents that congressional members can bring federal dollars back home. Perhaps the most extravagant item in the 2005 bill—and the one least needed for transportation—was a bridge in Alaska designed to connect a barely populated island to the town of Ketchikan, whose population is just short of 8,000. At a cost that could have soared to $2 billion, the bridge would have replaced an existing five-minute ferry ride. After Hurricane Katrina, "the bridge to nowhere" became a symbol of wasteful congressional spending. Sensitive to this criticism, Congress removed the earmarks for the bridge from the final legislation. Even so, it allowed Alaska to keep the funds for other, unspecified transportation projects. In 2007 the state quietly dropped the project.

When Democrats took over Congress in 2007, they vowed to limit the use of earmarks, which had grown from 1,439 per year in 1995 to 15,268 in 2006. More troubling, earmarks were connected to congressional scandals. For example, Republican House member Randy "Duke" Cunningham (R-Calif.) was sent to jail in 2005 for accepting bribes by companies hoping to receive earmarks in return.[16] The House passed a new rule requiring that those representatives supporting each earmark identify themselves and guarantee that they have no personal financial stake in the requested project. A new ethics law applies similar provisions to the Senate. The new requirements appear to have had some impact: the 2007 military bill, for example, cut in half the earmark spending contained in the military bill passed in 2006. But in the midst of the sharp economic downturn in 2009, Congress passed a bill designed to stimulate the economy that contained more than 8,000 earmarks. In many cases, Republicans and some Democrats who voted against the bill were later happy to take credit from their constituents for the earmarks they had placed in it. In his 2010 State of the Union address, President Obama called for Congress to publish a list of all earmark requests on a single website. Congress not only failed to enact such legislation, in 2010 it set a new record by passing 11,320 earmarks, worth $32 billion. But in 2011 the House and the Senate agreed to a two-year moratorium on earmarks in spending bills, and renewed the ban in 2012 for the 113th Congress.[17] Despite the moratorium, some members of Congress charged that special provisions were creeping back into legislation, and few members of Congress supported making the moratorium permanent.[18]

There are a few other types of direct patronage (see Figure 9.4). One important form of constituency service is intervention with federal administrative agencies on behalf of constituents. Members of the House and Senate and their staffs spend a great deal of time on the telephone and in administrative offices seeking to secure favorable treatment for constituents and supporters. For example, members of Congress can assist senior citizens who are having Social Security or Medicare benefit eligibility problems. They may also help constituents find federal grants for which they may be eligible to apply. As Representative Pete Stark (D-Calif.) puts it on his website, "We cannot make the decision for a federal agency on such matters, but we can make sure that you get a fair shake."[19] A small but related form of patronage is securing an appointment to one of the military academies for the child of a constituent. Traditionally, these appointments are allocated one to a district.

A different form of patronage is the **private bill**—a proposal in Congress to provide a specific person with some kind of relief, such as a special exemption from immigration quotas. It is distinguished from a public bill, which is supposed to deal with general rules and categories of behavior, people, and institutions. As many as 75 percent of all private bills introduced (and one-third of those that pass) are concerned with obtaining citizenship for foreign nationals who cannot get permanent visas to the United States because the immigration quota for their country is filled or because of something unusual about their particular situation.[20] For example, in 2012, a private bill granted a Nigerian immigrant—who was living in Michigan on an expired visa after coming to the United States as a teenager to undergo treatment for life-threatening facial tumors—a green card that would allow him to attend an Ohio medical school.[21]

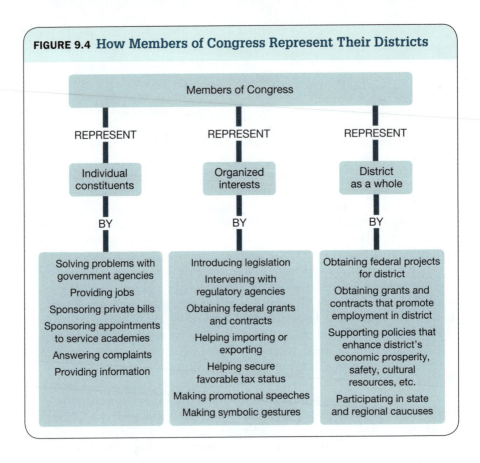

FIGURE 9.4 How Members of Congress Represent Their Districts

Members of Congress

REPRESENT — Individual constituents — BY
- Solving problems with government agencies
- Providing jobs
- Sponsoring private bills
- Sponsoring appointments to service academies
- Answering complaints
- Providing information

REPRESENT — Organized interests — BY
- Introducing legislation
- Intervening with regulatory agencies
- Obtaining federal grants and contracts
- Helping importing or exporting
- Helping secure favorable tax status
- Making promotional speeches
- Making symbolic gestures

REPRESENT — District as a whole — BY
- Obtaining federal projects for district
- Obtaining grants and contracts that promote employment in district
- Supporting policies that enhance district's economic prosperity, safety, cultural resources, etc.
- Participating in state and regional caucuses

● The Organization of Congress Is Shaped by Party

Explain how party leadership, the committee system, and the staff system help structure congressional business

The U.S. Congress is not only a representative assembly, it is also a legislative body. For Americans, representation and legislation go hand in hand; however, many parliamentary bodies in other countries are representative without the power to make laws. It is no small achievement that the U.S. Congress both represents *and* governs.

To exercise its power to make laws, Congress must first bring about something close to an organizational miracle. The building blocks of congressional organization include the political parties, the committee system, congressional staff, the caucuses, and the parliamentary rules of the House and Senate. Each of these factors plays a key role in the organization of Congress and in the process through which Congress formulates and enacts laws.

Party Leadership in the House and the Senate Organizes Power

Every two years, at the beginning of a new Congress, the members of each party in the House of Representatives gather to elect their leaders. House Republicans call their gathering the **conference**. House Democrats call theirs the caucus. The elected leader of the majority party is later proposed to the whole House and is automatically elected to the position of **Speaker of the House**, with voting along straight party lines. The Speaker is the most important party and House leader and can influence the legislative agenda, the fate of individual pieces of legislation, and members' positions within the House. The House majority conference or caucus then also elects a **majority leader**, the elected leader of the majority party in the House of Representatives or in the Senate. (In the House, the majority leader is subordinate in the party hierarchy to the Speaker of the House.) The minority party goes through the same process and selects the **minority leader**, who is the elected leader of the minority party in the House or Senate. Both parties also elect assistants to their party leaders, called **whips**, who are responsible for coordinating the party's legislative strategy, building support for key issues, and counting votes.

Next in line of importance for each party after the Speaker and majority or minority leader is what Democrats call the Steering and Policy Committee—Republicans have a separate steering committee and a separate policy committee—whose tasks are to assign new legislators to committees and to deal with the requests of incumbent members for transfers from one committee to another.

Generally, members of Congress seek assignments that will allow them to influence decisions of special importance to their districts. Representatives from farm districts, for example, may request seats on the Agriculture Committee.[22] Seats on powerful committees such as Ways and Means, which is responsible for tax legislation, and Appropriations are especially popular.

Within the Senate, the majority party usually designates a member with the greatest seniority to serve as president pro tempore, a position of primarily ceremonial leadership. Real power is in the hands of the majority leader and minority leader, each elected by party conference. Together they control the Senate's calendar, or agenda for legislation. Each party also elects a Policy Committee, which advises the leadership on legislative priorities.

As Speaker of the House, John Boehner attempted to keep his party unified, despite disagreements between the Tea Party members and other Republicans. These disagreements were pronounced in debates over the federal government's 2014 budget.

The Committee System Is the Core of Congress

The committee system is central to the operation of Congress. At each stage of the legislative process, Congress relies on committees and subcommittees to do the hard work of sorting through alternatives and writing legislation. There are several different kinds of congressional committees; these include standing committees, select committees, joint committees, and conference committees.

Standing committees are the most important arenas of congressional policy making. These permanent committees remain in existence from one session of Congress to the next; they have the power to propose and write legislation. The jurisdiction of each standing committee covers a particular subject matter, such as finance or agriculture, which in most cases parallels the major departments or agencies in the executive branch. Among the most important standing committees are those in charge of finances. The House Ways and Means Committee and the Senate Finance Committee are powerful because of their jurisdiction over taxes, trade, and expensive entitlement programs such as Social Security and Medicare. The Senate and House Appropriations committees also play important ongoing roles because they decide how much funding various programs will actually receive; they also determine exactly how the money will be spent. A seat on the Appropriations Committee allows a member the opportunity to direct funds to a favored program—perhaps one in her home district.

Except for the House Rules Committee, all standing committees receive proposals for legislation and process them into official bills. The House Rules Committee decides the order in which bills come up for a vote on the House floor and determines the specific rules that govern the length of debate and opportunity for amendments. The Senate, which has less formal organization and fewer rules, does not have a rules committee.

Select committees are usually temporary and normally do not have the power to present legislation to the full Congress, but rather are set up to highlight or investigate a particular issue or address an issue not within the jurisdiction of existing committees. (The House and Senate Select Intelligence committees are permanent, however, and do have the power to report legislation, which means they can send legislation to the full House or Senate for consideration.) These committees may hold hearings and serve as focal points for the issues they are charged with considering. Congressional leaders form select committees when they want to take up issues that fall between the jurisdictions of existing committees, to highlight an issue, or to investigate a particular problem. Examples of select committees investigating political scandals include the Senate Watergate Committee of 1973, the committees set up in 1987 to investigate the Iran-Contra affair, and the Whitewater Committee of 1995–96. Select committees set up to highlight ongoing issues have included the House Select Committee on Hunger, established in 1984, and the House Select Committee on Energy Independence and Global Warming, created in 2007 but abolished in 2011, when Republicans assumed control of the House. In 2003, Congress created the House Select Committee on Homeland Security to oversee the new cabinet department, Homeland Security. This committee also has the power to report legislation and is now permanent.

Joint committees are formed of members of both the Senate and the House. There are four such committees: economic, taxation, library, and printing. These joint committees are permanent, but they do not have the power to report legislation. The Joint Economic Committee and the Joint Taxation Committee have often played important roles in collecting information and holding hearings on economic and financial issues. In 2011, Congress created the Joint Select Committee on Deficit

Reduction and, in an unusual move, gave the committee the power to write and report legislation. Informally known as "the supercommittee," the committee was charged with coming up with $1.2 trillion in debt reduction. Formed after a contentious debate about raising the debt limit (usually a routine matter) the supercommittee proved unable to come to an agreement and disbanded less than four months after it was created.

Finally, **conference committees** are temporary joint committees whose members are appointed by the Speaker of the House and the presiding officer of the Senate. These committees are charged with working out a compromise on legislation that has been passed by the House and the Senate, but in different versions. Conference committees play an extremely important role in determining what laws are actually passed, because they must reconcile any differences in the legislation passed by the House and Senate.

When control of Congress is divided between two parties, each is guaranteed significant representation in conference committees. When a single party controls both houses, the majority party is not obligated to offer such representation to the minority party. In 2003, Democrats complained that Republicans took this power to the extreme by excluding them and adding new provisions to legislation at the conference committee stage. Democrats even prevented several conference committees from convening to protest their near exclusion from conference committees on major energy, health care, and transportation laws. After the Democrats returned to power in 2007, they largely bypassed the conference committees; when their early efforts to reach compromises in the conference were derailed by partisan differences, the Democrats began making closed-door agreements between top leaders in the House and the Senate. Although the process facilitated compromises across the two chambers, it meant that important changes to bills were made in private, without the transparency that would have been part of the conference committee process. After 2010, Congress continued to avoid conference committees. Instead, the Republican House and Democratic Senate exchanged amendments as they sought to reach agreement on the final version of a bill, a practice known informally as "ping pong."[23]

Within each committee, hierarchy is based on seniority. **Seniority** is the ranking given to an individual on the basis of length of continuous service on a committee in Congress. In general, each committee is chaired by the most senior member of the majority party. But the principle of seniority is not absolute. Both Democrats and Republicans have violated it on occasion. In 1995, when the Republicans won control of the House, then-Speaker Newt Gingrich instituted a new practice of frequent seniority violations, often selecting committee chairs based on loyalty or fund-raising abilities, a practice that subsequent Republican leaders have maintained. In 2007 the Democrats returned to the seniority principle to select committee chairs but altered traditional practices in other ways by offering freshman Democrats choice committee assignments to increase their chances of re-election.[24]

The Staff System Is the Power behind the Power

The congressional institution second in importance only to the committee system is the staff system. Every member of Congress employs a large number of staff members, whose tasks include handling constituent requests and, to a large and growing extent, dealing with legislative details and the activities of administrative agencies. Increasingly,

Members of Congress rely heavily on their personal staffs and on committee staffs, who often play an important role in the legislative process.

staffers bear the primary responsibility for formulating and drafting proposals, organizing hearings, dealing with administrative agencies, and negotiating with lobbyists. Indeed, legislators typically deal with one another through staff rather than through direct, personal contact. Today, staffers develop policy ideas, draft legislation, and have a good deal of influence over the legislative process.

Representatives and senators together employ about 11,500 staffers in their Washington and home offices. In addition, Congress employs more than 2,000 committee staffers. These individuals make up the permanent staff, who stay attached to every House and Senate committee regardless of turnover in Congress and who are responsible for organizing and administering the committee's work, including researching, scheduling, organizing hearings, and drafting legislation. Committee staffers also play key roles in the legislative process.

● Rules of Lawmaking Explain How a Bill Becomes a Law

> **Outline the steps in the process of passing a law**

The institutional structure of Congress is one key factor that helps shape the legislative process. A second and equally important set of factors is the rules of congressional procedure. These rules govern everything from the introduction of a **bill** (a proposed law that has been sponsored by a member of Congress and submitted to the clerk of the House or Senate) through its submission to the president for signing (see Figure 9.5).

FIGURE 9.5 How a Bill Becomes a Law

*Points at which a bill can be amended.
**If the president neither signs nor vetoes a bill within 10 days, it automatically becomes law.
†Points at which a bill can die.

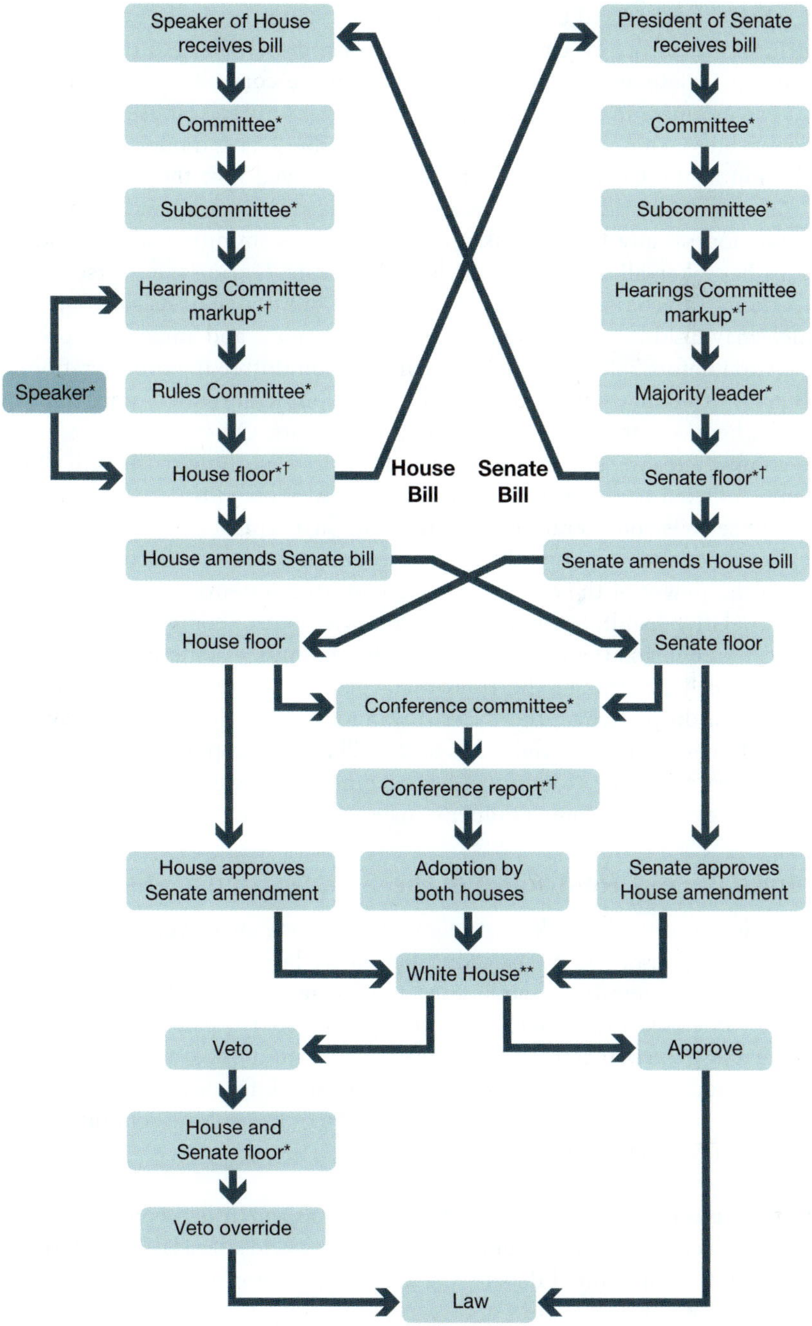

Speaker of House receives bill → Committee* → Subcommittee* → Hearings Committee markup*† → Rules Committee* → House floor*†

Speaker*

President of Senate receives bill → Committee* → Subcommittee* → Hearings Committee markup*† → Majority leader* → Senate floor*†

House Bill   Senate Bill

House amends Senate bill   Senate amends House bill

House floor   Senate floor

Conference committee*

Conference report*†

House approves Senate amendment   Adoption by both houses   Senate approves House amendment

White House**

Veto   Approve

House and Senate floor*

Veto override

Law

Not only do these regulations influence the fate of each and every bill but they also help determine the distribution of power in the Congress.

The First Step Is Committee Deliberation

Even if a member of Congress, the White House, or a federal agency has spent months developing and drafting a piece of legislation, it does not become a bill until it is submitted officially by a senator or representative to the clerk of the House or Senate and referred to the appropriate committee for deliberation. Bills can originate in the House or the Senate but only the House can introduce "money bills": those that spend or raise revenues. The framers' inserted this provision in the Constitution because they believed that the chamber closest to the people should exercise greater authority over taxing and spending. No floor action on any bill can take place until the committee with jurisdiction over it has taken all the time it needs to deliberate. During the course of its deliberations, the committee typically refers the bill to one of its subcommittees, which may hold hearings, listen to expert testimony, and amend the proposed legislation before referring the bill to the full committee for consideration. The full committee may accept the recommendation of the subcommittee or hold its own hearings and prepare its own amendments. Or, even more frequently, the committee and subcommittee may do little or nothing with a bill that has been submitted to them. Many bills are simply allowed to "die in committee" without serious consideration given to them. In a typical congressional session, 95 percent of the roughly 8,000 bills introduced die in committee—an indication of the power of the congressional committee system.

The relative handful of bills that are reported out of committee must, in the House, pass one additional hurdle within the committee system: the Rules Committee, which determines the rules that will govern action on the bill on the House floor. In particular, the Rules Committee allots the time for debate and decides to what extent amendments to the bill can be proposed from the floor. In recent years, the Rules Committee has become less powerful because the House leadership exercises so much influence over its decisions.

Debate Is Less Restricted in the Senate Than in the House

In the House, virtually all the time allotted for debate on a given bill is controlled by the bill's sponsor and by its leading opponent. In almost every case, these two people are the committee chair and the ranking minority member of the committee that processed the bill—or those they designate. These two participants are, by rule and tradition, granted the power to allocate most of the debate time in small amounts to members who are seeking to speak for or against the measure. Preference in the allocation of time goes to the members of the committee whose jurisdiction covers the bill.

The Filibuster In the Senate, the leadership has much less control over floor debate. Indeed, the Senate is unique among the world's legislative bodies for its commitment to unlimited debate. Once given the floor, a senator may speak as long as he wishes. On a number of memorable occasions, senators have used the right to talk without interruption for as long as they want to prevent action on legislation they opposed. Through this tactic, called the **filibuster**, members of the Senate can prevent action on legislation they oppose by continuously holding the floor and speaking until the majority backs down (or the filibustering senator gives up). Once given the floor, senators have unlimited time to speak. A vote of three-fifths of the Senate is required to end a filibuster. During the 1950s and '60s, opponents of civil rights legislation often sought to block its passage by staging filibusters. Democrats used the threat of a filibuster to block some of President George W. Bush's judicial nominees, much as Republicans used the same tactic to derail Clinton nominees. In 2003, Senate Republicans staged a 30-hour filibuster marathon, bringing cots and sleeping bags into the Senate to protest Democratic use of the tactic. Senate Democrats staged a similar marathon session, cots and all, when they held the Senate majority in 2007. The votes of three-fifths of the Senate, or 60 votes, are needed to end a filibuster. This procedure to end a filibuster is called **cloture.**

For much of American history, senators used the filibuster only rarely. In the last 20 years, however, the filibuster has become so common that observers routinely note that it takes 60 votes (instead of a simple majority of 51) to pass anything in the Senate. The 110th Congress (2007–08) set a new record, with 112 cloture votes (the vote to end a filibuster). The 113th Congress (2013–14) broke the record, with 178 cloture votes as of November 2014. In contrast, the 109th Congress (2005–06) held only 54 cloture votes.[25]

In 2013 the Democratic Senate leader Harry Reid (Nev.) mobilized his party to alter the filibuster rules for the first time in many decades. Frustrated by the repeated failure of the Senate to vote on many of President Obama's nominees to fill positions in the executive branch, as well as judgeships to important federal courts, Reid invoked what senators had come to call "the nuclear option," a change to the filibuster rules in the middle of the session by simple majority vote. Under the new rules, nominees for executive branch appointments and federal court nominees—except the Supreme Court—cannot be filibustered, meaning that they can be approved by a simple majority vote. Not surprisingly, the two parties had different views on the decision. Reid defended it as necessary, and Republicans denounced the new rule.

Voting Once debate is concluded on the floor of the House and the Senate, the leaders schedule it for a vote on the floor of each chamber. By this time, congressional leaders know what the vote will be; leaders do not bring legislation to the floor unless they are fairly certain it is going to pass. As a consequence, it is unusual for the leadership to lose a bill on the floor. On rare occasions, the last moments of the floor vote can be very dramatic, as each party's leadership puts its whip organization into action to make sure that wavering members vote with the party. In September 2008 the House of Representatives surprisingly rejected a $700 billion bank rescue plan, which led the Dow Jones Industrial Index to decline nearly 7 percent in a single day—one of the biggest drops in recent history. As the *New York Times* reported, lawmakers were "almost speechless" on hearing that the bill had not passed; not only did the White House and the congressional leadership of both parties expect the bill to prevail, albeit narrowly, but so did even the most ardent opponents of the bill. As the end of the voting period for members drew close, it was clear that the bill was going down to defeat, with 205 votes for it and 228 against. Since members of the House can change their votes until the voting period ends, the Speaker decided to extend the time to 40 minutes in order to corral votes from members. Despite the efforts of both Democratic and Republican leaders, they could not persuade enough members to switch their votes. A few days later, the House passed a revised version of the bill by 263 to 171 votes.[26]

Conference Committees Reconcile House and Senate Versions of Legislation

Getting a bill out of committee and through both houses of Congress is no guarantee that it will be enacted into law. Before a bill can be sent to the president, both houses must pass it in the identical form. Frequently, bills that began with similar provisions in both chambers emerge with little resemblance to each other. Alternatively, a bill may be passed by one chamber but undergo substantial revision in the other chamber. In such a case, a conference committee composed of the senior members of the committees or subcommittees that initiated the bill may be convened to iron out differences between the two pieces of legislation.

When a bill comes out of conference, it faces one more hurdle. Before it can be sent to the president for signing, the House-Senate conference committee's version of the bill must be approved on the floor of each chamber. Usually such approval is given quickly. Occasionally, however, a bill's opponents use this round of approval as one last opportunity to defeat a piece of legislation. In recent years, as we have seen, polarization in Congress has led to much less reliance on conference committees. Instead, leaders exchange amendments in hopes of reaching agreement.

The President's Veto Controls the Flow of Legislation

Once adopted by the House and Senate, a bill goes to the president, who may choose to sign it into law or **veto** it. If the president neither signs nor vetoes it within 10 days, and Congress is in session, the bill automatically becomes law. The veto is the president's constitutional power to reject a piece of legislation. To veto a bill, the president returns it unsigned within 10 days to the house of Congress in which it originated. If Congress adjourns during the 10-day period, such that congressional adjournment prevents the president from returning the bill to Congress, the bill is also considered to be vetoed. This latter method is known as the **pocket veto**. Unlike a regular or return veto, a pocket-vetoed bill cannot be overridden; the bill simply dies. The possibility of a presidential veto affects how willing members of Congress are to push for different pieces of legislation at different times. If they think a proposal is likely to be vetoed, they might shelve it for a later time, or alter it to suit the president's preferences.

A presidential veto may be overridden by a two-thirds vote in both the House and the Senate. Successful overrides are rare, but are a blow to the president.

● Several Factors Influence How Congress Decides

Analyze the factors that influence which laws Congress passes

What determines the kinds of legislation that Congress ultimately produces? According to the simplest theories of representation, members of Congress respond to the views of their constituents. In fact, creating a legislative agenda, drawing up a list of possible measures, and deciding among them is a complex process in which a variety of influences from inside and outside government play important roles. External influences include a legislator's constituency and various interest groups. Influences from inside government include party leadership, congressional colleagues, and the president. Let us examine each of these influences individually and then consider how they interact to produce congressional policy decisions.

Constituents Matter

Because members of Congress, for the most part, want to be re-elected, we would expect the views of their constituents to be a primary influence on the decisions those legislators make. Yet most constituents pay little attention to politics and often do not even know what policies their representatives support. Nonetheless, members of Congress spend a lot of time worrying about what their constituents think, because these representatives realize that the choices they make may be scrutinized in a future election and used as ammunition by an opposing candidate. Because of this possibility, members of Congress do try to anticipate their constituents' policy views.[27]

Interest Groups Influence Constituents and Congress

Interest groups are another important external influence on congressional policies. Members of Congress pay close attention to interest groups for a number of reasons: interest groups can mobilize constituents, serve as watchdogs on congressional action,

Representatives often spend a lot of time meeting with constituents in their districts in order to explain how they have helped their district and to learn what issues their constituents care about. Such meetings are often informal affairs at local restaurants or fairs.

and supply candidates with money. When members of Congress are making voting decisions, those interest groups that have some connection to constituents or that can mobilize followers in particular members' districts are most likely to be influential.

Interest groups also have substantial influence in setting the legislative agenda and helping craft specific language in legislation. Today, sophisticated lobbyists win influence by providing information about policies to busy members of Congress. In the 2009–10 health care reform effort, the biotechnology firm Genentech ghostwrote statements that more than a dozen members of Congress placed into the *Congressional Record*. Genentech's role came to light when it became evident that some members had used the exact same language in their *Congressional Record* entries.[28] In recent years, interest groups have also begun to build broader coalitions and comprehensive campaigns around particular policy issues. These coalitions do not rise from the grass roots but instead are put together by Washington lobbyists who launch comprehensive lobbying campaigns that combine simulated grassroots activity with information and campaign funding for members of Congress.

Concerns that special interests exert too much influence led Congress to enact new ethics legislation in 2007. The new law set new restrictions on the gifts lobbyists can bestow on lawmakers and limited privately funded travel. The law also prohibited members of Congress from lobbying for two years after they retired (it had been one year) and required lawmakers to identify the earmarks they inserted in legislation. Further, it aimed to shine light on the practice of "bundling," in which lobbyists assemble money from a number of clients to make a single political donation. Now lobbyists will be required to disclose the names of the individual contributors to these political donations. Although the new law provides additional transparency, revealing more about the relationship between lobbyists and members of Congress, it does not fundamentally alter the fact that wealthy interest groups continue to exercise tremendous influence in Congress.

Moreover, the large sums of cash raised by Super PACs—discussed in Chapter 7—have introduced a whole new set of questions about the role of special interests in politics, especially because donors to Super PACs can remain anonymous. Although they cannot openly coordinate with candidates, Super PACs can endorse candidates by name and are often run by people close to the candidates they support. In 2012, Super PACs poured unprecedented sums of money into the race for president, but they also targeted key congressional contests, in an effort to affect the balance of power between the parties in Congress.[29] This pattern continued in 2014, when Super PACs poured $33 million into congressional races.

Party Leaders Rely on Party Discipline

In both the House and the Senate, party leaders have a good deal of influence over the behavior of their party members. This influence, sometimes called "party discipline," was once so powerful that it dominated the lawmaking process. In the 1800s party leaders could often command the allegiance of more than 90 percent of their members. A vote in which half or more of the members of one party take one position while at least half of the members of the other party take the opposing position is called a **party unity vote**. At the beginning of the twentieth century, nearly half of all **roll-call votes** (votes in which each legislator's yes or no vote is recorded as the clerk calls the names of the members alphabetically) in the House of Representatives were party votes. While party voting is rarer today than a century ago, in the last decade it has been fairly common to find at least a majority of the Democrats opposing a majority of the Republicans on any given issue.

Typically, party unity is greater in the House than in the Senate. House rules give more power to the majority party leaders, which gives them more influence over House members. In the Senate, however, the leadership has few controls over its members. Former Senate majority leader Tom Daschle once observed that a Senate leader seeking to influence other senators has as incentives "a bushel full of carrots and a few twigs."[30]

Party unity has been on the rise in recent years because the divisions between the parties have deepened on many high-profile issues such as abortion, affirmative action, the minimum wage, and school vouchers (see Figure 9.6), and because

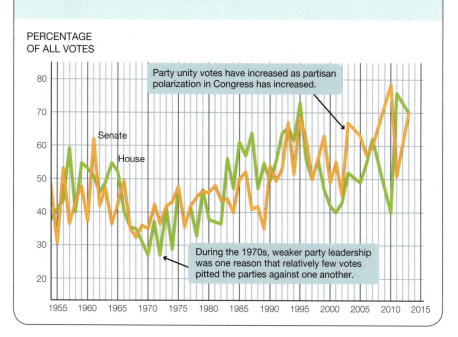

FIGURE 9.6 Party Unity Votes by Chamber

Party unity votes are roll-call votes in which a majority of one party lines up against a majority of the other party. Party unity votes increase when the parties are polarized and when the party leadership can enforce discipline. Why did the percentage of party unity votes decline in the 1970s? Why has it risen in recent years?

SOURCE: Congressional Quarterly, http://media.cq.com/votestudies (accessed 6/9/14).

PERCENTAGE OF ALL VOTES

Party unity votes have increased as partisan polarization in Congress has increased.

Senate

House

During the 1970s, weaker party leadership was one reason that relatively few votes pitted the parties against one another.

the majority-minority party difference has been small in recent years. In 2013, House Democrats voted with the majority 88 percent of the time, close to their all-time high of 92 percent in 2008. In 2013, Senate Democrats set a record for party unity by voting with their caucus 94 percent of the time. Republicans were also very united. In 2013, House Republicans voted with their party 92 percent of the time, their all-time high; Senate Republicans voted with their party 86 percent of the time.[31]

Although party organization has weakened since the turn of the twentieth century, today's party leaders still have resources to reward loyal members who vote with the party: (1) leadership PACs, (2) committee assignments, (3) access to the floor, (4) the whip system, (5) logrolling, and (6) the presidency.

Leadership PACs Leaders have increased their influence over members in recent years with aggressive use of leadership political action committees. Leadership PACs are organizations that members of Congress use to raise funds that they then distribute to other members of their party running for election. Republican congressional leaders pioneered the aggressive use of leadership PACs to win their congressional majority in 1995, and the practice has spread widely since that time. Money from leadership PACs can be directed to the most vulnerable candidates or to candidates who are having trouble raising money. They can also be used to influence primary elections. In 2010 and 2012 conservatives in the House and Senate used leadership PACS to support conservative candidates in Republican primaries. Although leadership PACs have traditionally enhanced the power of the party and created a bond between the leaders and the members who receive their help, the aggressive use of PACs by Republican conservatives highlights their use for wings of the party who want to increase their power.[32]

Committee Assignments Party leaders can create debts among members by helping them get favorable committee assignments. These assignments are made early in the congressional careers of most members and cannot be taken from them if they later go against party discipline. Nevertheless, if the leadership goes out of its way to get the right assignment for a member, this effort is likely to create a bond of obligation that can be called upon without any other payments or favors. This is one reason the Republican leadership gave freshmen favorable assignments when the Republicans took over Congress in 1995. When the Democrats won control of Congress in 2007, House Speaker Nancy Pelosi gave desirable and prestigious committee assignments to Democratic House members who faced competitive re-election races, to assist them in their home districts and increase their loyalty.

Access to the Floor The most important everyday resource available to the parties is control over access to the floor. With thousands of bills awaiting passage and most members clamoring for access in order to influence a bill or to publicize themselves, floor time is precious. In the Senate, the leadership allows ranking committee members to influence the allocation of floor time—who will speak for how long; in the House, the Speaker, as head of the majority party (in consultation with the minority leader), allocates large blocks of floor time. Thus, floor time is allocated in both houses of Congress by the majority and minority leaders. More important, the Speaker of the House and the majority leader in the Senate possess the power of recognition—that is, they decide who may and may not speak on the floor. This seemingly insubstantial authority is, in fact, quite formidable and can be used to stymie a piece of legislation completely or to frustrate a member's attempts to speak on a particular issue. Because the power is significant, members of Congress usually attempt to stay on good terms with the Speaker and the majority leader in order to ensure that they will continue to be recognized.

The Whip System Some influence accrues to party leaders through the whip system, which is primarily a communications network in each house of Congress for conveying the leaders' wishes and plans to the members. Between 12 and 20 assistant and regional whips are selected to operate at the direction of the majority or minority leader and the whip. They take polls of all the members to learn their intentions on specific bills, enabling the leaders to know whether they have enough support to allow a vote as well as whether the vote is so close that they need to put pressure on undecided members. In those instances, the Speaker or a lieutenant will go to a few party members who have indicated they will switch if their vote is essential—an expedient that the leaders try to limit to a few times per session.

The whip system helps maintain party unity in both houses of Congress, but it is particularly critical in the House of Representatives because of the large number of legislators whose positions and votes must be accounted for. The majority and minority whips and their assistants must be adept at inducing compromise among legislators who hold widely differing viewpoints.

Since Republicans retook control of the House in 2010, the whip operation has been faced with significant challenges from the unusually large number of freshmen members of Congress elected in 2010. Of the 87 newly elected freshmen, 40 percent had never held elected office before, calling themselves "citizen politicians." More important, many of these new members had identified themselves as members of the conservative Tea Party movement. Given the divisions between more experienced and moderate members in leadership and the new influx of conservative freshmen, Speaker John Boehner adopted an unusually loose approach to party discipline, as typified by his statement "Let the House work its will."[33] This approach created problems for the leadership, forcing the Speaker to end his "grand bargain" negotiations with President Obama surrounding deficit reduction and a raise in the debt ceiling in the summer of 2011. These problems only became worse for Boehner in 2012 and 2013, when conservative members repeatedly voted down bills that the Speaker supported.

Logrolling A legislative practice wherein agreements are made between legislators in voting for or against a bill is called **logrolling**. Unlike with bargaining, legislators who are logrolling have nothing in common but their desire to exchange support. The agreement states, in effect, "You support me on bill X, and I'll support you on bill Y." Since party leaders are the center of the communications networks in the two chambers, they can help members create large logrolling coalitions. Hundreds of logrolling deals are made each year, and although there are no official record-keeping books, it would be a poor party leader whose whips did not know who owed what to whom.

The Presidency Of all the influences that maintain the clarity of party lines in Congress, the influence of the presidency is probably the most important. Indeed, the office is a touchstone of party discipline in Congress. Since the late 1940s, under President Harry Truman, presidents each year have identified a number of bills to be considered part of their administration's program. By the mid-1950s, both parties in Congress began to look to the president for these proposals, which became the most significant part of Congress's agenda. The president's support is an important criterion for party loyalty, and party leaders are able to use it to rally some members. Since 2011, with the presidency in Democratic hands and the House of Representatives controlled by Republicans, party polarization has limited the president's agenda-setting powers. Instead, his proposals have become targets for congressional opponents.

Partisanship Has Thwarted the Ability of Congress to Decide

In November 2013, Congress received the lowest levels of approval ever recorded in public opinion polls. Just 9 percent approved of the job Congress was doing, while 86 percent expressed disapproval.[34] Two concerns lay behind the public's dissatisfaction with Congress. The first was the inability of the Republican House and the Democratic Senate to make decisions on numerous issues. The second was the pervasive belief that members of Congress listen more to special interests than to the American public.

By the end of 2013, the 113th Congress was on track to be the least productive Congress in modern history. The 112th Congress had held the record but in 2013, Congress enacted fewer than 60 new laws, making it the least productive single year on record. The previous record low was in 1995, when just 88 laws were enacted.[35] Indeed, many high-profile bills ended in failure throughout 2012 and 2013. In 2012 when Republican leader John Boehner attempted to strike a "grand bargain" with President Obama over taxes and spending—one very favorable to Republicans—conservative Republicans in the House rejected it as not going far enough. The political standoff that resulted included regular threats of a government shutdown, which led to the decision by rating agency Moody's to downgrade the U.S. credit rating for the first time in history. The impasse continued into 2013 when House Republicans refused to pass a bill funding government operations or extending the debt ceiling unless the spending bill included language delaying implementation of the Affordable Care Act (ACA).[36] As a consequence, the federal government shut down for the first time in almost two decades. Despite House

Passing legislation is difficult. Efforts to pass immigration reform in 2013 ultimately failed, even though the Senate passed a bill that was supported by House Minority Leader Nancy Pelosi (D-Calif.) and the Congressional Hispanic Caucus. The opposition of House Republicans meant the bill was not brought for a vote in the House, however.

Speaker John Boehner's warnings to the Republican conference that the GOP would be blamed for the shutdown and his attempts to negotiate with Senate Democrats and the White House to reopen the government, House Republicans stood firm on their insistence to tie any deal to delaying the ACA.[37] As public ire rose over the continued shutdown, the House voted to pass a Senate bill—which contained virtually no concessions to the GOP—to reopen the government and extend the debt limit, just hours before the United States was set to cross the debt-ceiling deadline.[38] Democrats and Republicans succeeded in averting a second showdown over the debt ceiling when both sides agreed on a budget deal in late 2013.

The public's disapproval of Congress was intensified by the belief that members of Congress pay attention to special interests. Much of the dissatisfaction with Congress appeared to be directed at members of Congress, not at the institution itself. In fact, a 2011 poll found that nearly half of those responding believed that most members of Congress are corrupt.[39] Both Occupy Wall Street on the left and the Tea Party movement on the right charge that Congress has been captured by special interests. This sense has been intensified by the rise of Super PACs after 2010, when several court decisions, including *Citizens United v. Federal Election Commission*, allowed outside groups and individuals to spend unlimited amounts of money on elections.[40]

Congressional Polarization Congress's inability to decide reflects the deep ideological differences that separate the two parties. Efforts to measure the ideological distance between the two parties show that since the mid-1970s, Republicans and Democrats have been diverging sharply and are now more polarized than at any time in the last century. Democrats have become more liberal and Republicans have become more conservative on issues related to the economy and the role of government.[41] The Republican Party has experienced the greatest ideological shift, becoming sharply more conservative. Moreover, because congressional districts are increasingly homogeneous in their ideology—in part due to gerrymandering but mainly because of natural clustering of the population—most members of Congress are in safe seats. Their constituents will not punish them for failing to compromise. Moreover, active mobilization by organizations on the right, such as the Club for Growth, means that Republican members of Congress who support compromises might be punished. These outside organizations have financed alternative candidates to challenge members who vote against the organizations' positions.

● Much Congressional Energy Goes to Tasks Other Than Lawmaking

Describe Congress's influence over other branches of government

In addition to the power to make the law, Congress has at its disposal an array of other instruments through which to influence the process of government. The Constitution gives the Senate the power to approve treaties and appointments. And Congress has a number of other powers through which it can share with the other branches the capacity to administer the laws.

Congress Oversees How Legislation Is Implemented

Oversight refers to the effort by Congress, through hearings, investigations, and other techniques, to exercise control over the activities of executive agencies. Oversight is carried out by committees or subcommittees of the Senate or the House, which conduct hearings and investigations to analyze and evaluate bureaucratic agencies and the effectiveness of their programs. Their purpose may be to locate inefficiencies or abuses of power, to explore the relationship between what an agency does and what a law intends, or to change or abolish a program. Most programs and agencies are subject to some oversight every year during the course of hearings on **appropriations**—that is, the amounts of money approved by Congress in statutes (bills) that each unit or agency of government can spend.

Committees or subcommittees have the power to subpoena witnesses, administer oaths, cross-examine, compel testimony, and bring criminal charges for contempt (refusing to cooperate) and perjury (lying). Hearings and investigations resemble each other in many ways, but they differ on one fundamental point.

Public Opinion of the Legislature

The U.S. Congress suffers from very low approval ratings: very few Americans approve of the way Congress is handling its job. Are all legislatures equally unpopular? The World Values Survey has asked respondents around the world for their level of confidence in their legislative branch of government. In the United States, Japan, Australia, Chile, and Mexico, citizens report a low degree of confidence in their legislatures. Only in Turkey does a majority of the public report "a great deal" or "quite a lot" of confidence in the legislature. Mexico is notable in that 38 percent of the public reports no confidence in the legislature.

In democracies, the legislatures are usually expected to be the branch of government that is closest to the people. So why do people around the world consistently report low levels of confidence in the legislature? One explanation might be cultural change: younger generations may be less deferential to authority and more skeptical of governmental power than older generations. Others have pointed to corruption scandals affecting members of legislatures as a possible cause.[a] Perhaps the most convincing argument is reflected in the adage, "familiarity breeds contempt." As legislatures become more and more transparent in their operations, the media are able to report easily on the conflict and controversy that legislatures engage in when attempting to pass legislation. As a result of all this (perhaps overly negative) media attention, the public has developed a negative attitude about legislative institutions.[b]

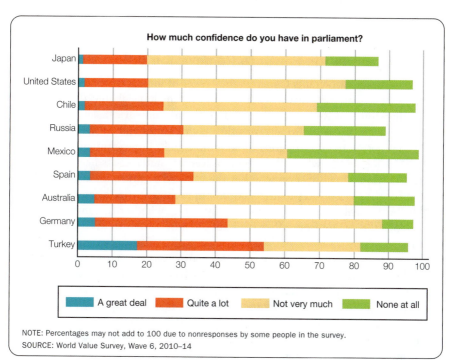

NOTE: Percentages may not add to 100 due to nonresponses by some people in the survey.

SOURCE: World Value Survey, Wave 6, 2010–14

[a]Pippa Norris, ed. *Critical Citizens: Global Support for Democratic Governance?* (New York: Oxford University Press, 1999).
[b]See Richard E. Neustadt, "The Politics of Mistrust" in *Why People Don't Trust Government,* ed. Joseph S. Nye, Jr., Philip D. Zelikow, and David C. King (Cambridge, MA: Harvard University Press, 1997), and Russell J. Dalton, *Democratic Challenges, Democratic Choices:* The Erosion of Political Support in Advanced Industrial Democracies (New York: Oxford University Press, 2004).

A hearing is usually held on a specific bill, and the questions asked there are usually intended to build a record with regard to that bill. In an investigation, the committee or subcommittee does not begin with a particular bill, but examines a broad area or problem and then concludes its investigation with one or more proposed bills.

Oversight hearings can serve as political tools. In 2012, with the presidential race looming, Republican House Speaker John Boehner urged Republicans to use their oversight powers aggressively, telling them, "Our obligation is to use our majority to shine a spotlight on the places where the president's failed policies are getting in the way of American job creation. And that means stepped-up oversight of the Obama administration's policies."[42]

Special Senate Powers Include Advice and Consent

The Constitution has given the Senate a special power, one that is not based on lawmaking. The president has the power to make treaties and to appoint top executive officers, ambassadors, and federal judges—but only "with the Advice and Consent of the Senate" (Article II, Section 2). For treaties, two-thirds of senators present must concur; for appointments, a simple majority is required.

The power to approve or reject presidential requests includes the power to set conditions. The Senate only occasionally exercises its power to reject treaties and appointments, and usually that is when opposite parties control the Senate and the White House. For example, only nine judicial nominees have been rejected by the Senate during the past century, whereas thousands have been approved.

Impeachment Is the Power to Remove Top Officials

The Constitution also grants Congress the power of **impeachment** over the president, vice president, top executive branch officials, and judicial officials. To impeach means the House of Representatives charges a government official (president or otherwise) with "Treason, Bribery, or other high Crimes and Misdemeanors" and brings that person before Congress to determine guilt. Impeachment is thus like a criminal indictment in which the House of Representatives acts like a grand jury, voting (by simple majority) on whether the accused ought to be impeached. If a majority of the House votes to impeach, an impeachment trial is conducted in and by the Senate, which acts like a trial jury by voting whether to convict and forcibly remove the person from office (this vote requires a two-thirds majority of the Senate).

Controversy over Congress's impeachment power has arisen over the grounds for impeachment, especially the meaning of "high Crimes and Misdemeanors." A strict reading of the Constitution suggests that the only impeachable offense is an actual crime. But a more common working definition is that "an impeachable offense is whatever the majority of the House of Representatives considers it to be at a given moment in history."[43] In other words, impeachment, especially impeachment of a president, is a political decision.

The political nature of impeachment was very clear in the two instances of presidential impeachment that have occurred in American history. In 1867,

President Andrew Johnson, a southern Democrat who had battled a congressional Republican majority over Reconstruction, was impeached by the House but saved from conviction by one vote in the Senate. On December 19, 1998, the House of Representatives approved two articles of impeachment against President Bill Clinton, accusing him of lying under oath and obstructing justice during the investigation of his affair with White House intern Monica Lewinsky. The vote was highly partisan, with only five Democrats voting for impeachment on each charge. In the Senate, where a two-thirds majority was needed to convict the president, only 45 senators voted to convict on the first count of lying and 50 voted to convict on the second charge of obstructing justice. As in the House, the vote for impeachment was highly partisan, with all Democrats and only five Republicans supporting the president's ultimate acquittal.

Congress
and Your Future

When Congress is ineffective, American democracy suffers. As we have seen in this chapter, prolonged stalemates in Congress have led to a reduction in America's credit rating and a costly government shutdown. Moreover, Americans have lost confidence in Congress as it has lurched from crisis to crisis. Is it time for some major changes to make Congress work better? Disillusionment with congressional gridlock has led some to say that the United States should become a parliamentary system, where the winning party can enact the legislation it promised in its party platform. Such a system is more accountable to voters and less prone to stalemate. But Americans would have to jettison the presidency and become a unicameral body to operate as a true parliamentary system, like that of Britain.

Short of such major institutional transformations, are there changes that would make Congress work better? One measure that might lead to more bipartisan agreement—the appointment of citizen commissions to reapportion congressional district lines—has been adopted in some states. If this practice became more widespread, it is possible that it would lead to election of more moderate candidates, making it easier to compromise in Congress. Changes in the way Congress conducts its business could also promote more bipartisan decision making. For example, House Speaker John Boehner decided that he would only bring legislation to the floor if a majority of Republicans supported it. The "Hastert Rule," as this practice is called, after former speaker Dennis Hastert, is not a formal rule of Congress, but a norm that Boehner decided to implement. It is a practice that could easily be abandoned, allowing bipartisan majorities to enact legislation. Another significant change—eliminating the filibuster in the Senate—would heighten partisan differences but ease gridlock. As we have seen, the Senate voted to eliminate the filibuster for executive branch appointments and judicial candidates (except for the Supreme Court) in 2013. Abandoning the filibuster altogether would allow legislation to move more smoothly through the Senate. Will any of these changes—or other measures—be adopted? Each carries risks to political parties and to politicians. Yet, gridlock carries political risks as well, as the public grows frustrated with congressional inaction on important policy areas. How politicians weigh these different choices will shape how—and whether—Congress fills its central position in American democracy.

plug in

Inform

Find out who represents your state in the Senate (by entering your state at senate.gov) and in the House of Representatives (by entering your zip code at house.gov).

Express

Look up your representative's recent voting record in the *Washington Post*'s U.S. Congress Votes Database (http://projects .washingtonpost.com/congress /113/). Make a list of five issues he or she voted on, and state whether you would have voted the same way on behalf of your district.

Connect

Follow your members of Congress on social media. Pay attention to which issues they address in their posts, and consider posting a comment if you have an opinion.

Act

Let your member of Congress know about issues that are important to you by sending them an email and encouraging friends and family to do so as well. Members' email addresses are given on their web pages.

studyguide

Practice Quiz

1. Because they have larger and more heterogeneous constituencies, senators *(p. 274)*
   a) have less freedom to consider "new ideas" or to bring together new coalitions of interests.
   b) are more attuned to the needs of localized interest groups.
   c) care more about re-election than House members.
   d) can better represent the national interest.
   e) face less competition in elections than House members.

2. Which type of representation is described when constituents have the power to hire and fire their representative? *(p. 274)*
   a) agency representation
   b) sociological representation
   c) democratic representation
   d) trustee representation
   e) economic representation

3. Which of these is an advantage in getting re-elected afforded by incumbency? *(p. 278)*
   a) Incumbents are allowed to spend more money campaigning than their challengers.
   b) Incumbents can provide constituency services during their tenure.
   c) Term limits for incumbents mean they know when an election will be their last.
   d) The courts allow legislators to gerrymander districts.
   e) Incumbents have no advantage over challengers in winning office.

4. Some have argued that the creation of minority congressional districts has *(p. 281)*
   a) lessened the sociological representation of minorities in Congress.
   b) made it more difficult for minorities to win substantive policy goals.
   c) been a result of the media's impact on state legislative politics.

   d) lessened the problem of "pork-barrel" politics.
   e) had no impact on representation.

5. One way members of Congress can work as agents of their constituents is by *(p. 282)*
   a) providing direct patronage.
   b) taking part in a party vote.
   c) joining a caucus.
   d) supporting term limits.
   e) engaging in gerrymandering.

6. Which of the following types of committees includes members of both the House and the Senate on the same committee? *(p. 287)*
   a) standing committee
   b) conference committee
   c) select committee
   d) All committees include both House members and senators.
   e) No committees include both House members and senators.

7. Which of the following is a technique that can be used to block action on legislation in the Senate? *(p. 291)*
   a) filibuster
   b) conference
   c) roll-call voting
   d) cloture
   e) logrolling

8. Which of the following is *not* an important influence on how members of Congress vote on legislation? *(pp. 293–94)*
   a) the media
   b) constituency
   c) the president
   d) interest groups
   e) party leaders

9. Which of the following is *not* a resource that party leaders in Congress use to create party discipline? *(pp. 294–98)*
   a) leadership PACs
   b) committee assignments
   c) access to the floor
   d) the whip system
   e) roll-call votes

10. An agreement between members of Congress to trade support for each other's bills is known as *(p. 297)*
    a) oversight.
    b) filibuster.
    c) logrolling.
    d) patronage.
    e) cloture.

11. When Congress conducts an investigation to explore the relationship between what a law intended and what an executive agency has done, it is engaged in *(p. 300)*
    a) oversight.
    b) advice and consent.
    c) appropriations.
    d) executive agreement.
    e) direct patronage.

12. Which of the following statements about impeachment is *not* true? *(pp. 302–3)*
    a) The president is the only official who can be impeached by Congress.
    b) Impeachment means to charge a government official with "Treason, Bribery, or other high Crimes and Misdemeanors."
    c) The House of Representatives decides by simple majority vote whether the accused ought to be impeached.
    d) The Senate decides whether to convict and remove the person from office.
    e) There have only been two instances of impeachment in American history.

Key Terms

agency representation *(p. 274)* a type of representation in which a representative is held accountable to a constituency if he or she fails to represent that constituency properly; this is incentive for good representation when the personal backgrounds, views, and interests of the representative differ from those of his or her constituency

apportionment *(p. 280)* the process, occurring after every decennial census, that allocates congressional seats among the 50 states

appropriations *(p. 300)* the amounts of money approved by Congress in statutes (bills) that each unit or agency of government can spend

bicameral *(p. 273)* having a legislative assembly composed of two chambers or houses; distinguished from *unicameral*

bill *(p. 288)* a proposed law that has been sponsored by a member of Congress and submitted to the clerk of the House or Senate

cloture *(p. 291)* a rule or process in a legislative body aimed at ending debate on a given bill; in the U.S. Senate, 60 senators (three-fifths) must agree in order to impose a time limit and end debate

conference committees *(p. 287)* joint committees created to work out a compromise on House and Senate versions of a piece of legislation

conference *(p. 285)* a gathering of House Republicans every two years to elect their House leaders; Democrats call their gathering the caucus

constituency *(p. 273)* the residents in the area from which an official is elected

filibuster *(p. 291)* a tactic used by members of the Senate to prevent action on legislation they oppose by continuously holding the floor and speaking until the majority backs down; once given the floor, senators have unlimited time to speak, and it requires a vote of three-fifths of the Senate to end a filibuster

gerrymandering *(p. 280)* the apportionment of voters in districts in such a way as to give unfair advantage to one racial or ethnic group or political party

impeachment *(p. 302)* the formal charge by the House of Representatives that a government official has committed "Treason, Bribery, or other high Crimes and Misdemeanors"

incumbency *(p. 278)* holding the political office for which one is running

joint committees *(p. 286)* legislative committees formed of members of both the House and Senate

logrolling *(p. 297)* a legislative practice whereby agreements are made between legislators in voting for or against a bill; vote trading

majority leader *(p. 285)* the elected leader of the majority party in the House of Representatives or in the Senate; in the House, the majority leader is subordinate in the party hierarchy to the Speaker of the House

minority leader *(p. 285)* the elected leader of the minority party in the House or Senate

oversight *(p. 300)* the effort by Congress, through hearings, investigations, and other techniques, to exercise control over the activities of executive agencies

party unity vote *(p. 295)* a roll-call vote in the House or Senate in which at least 50 percent of the members of one party take a particular position and are opposed by at least 50 percent of the members of the other party

patronage *(p. 282)* the resources available to higher officials, usually opportunities to make partisan appointments to offices and to confer grants, licenses, or special favors to supporters

pocket veto *(p. 292)* a presidential veto that is automatically triggered if the president does not act on a given piece of legislation passed during the final 10 days of a legislative session

pork barrel legislation (or pork) *(p. 282)* appropriations made by legislative bodies for local projects that are often not needed but that are created so that local representatives can win re-election in their home districts

private bill *(p. 283)* a proposal in Congress to provide a specific person with some kind of relief, such as a special exemption from immigration quotas

redistricting *(p. 280)* the process of redrawing election districts and redistributing legislative representatives; this happens every 10 years to reflect shifts in population or in response to legal challenges to existing districts

roll-call vote *(p. 295)* a vote in which each legislator's yes or no vote is recorded as the clerk calls the names of the members alphabetically

select committees *(p. 286)* (usually) temporary legislative committees set up to highlight or investigate a particular issue or address an issue not within the jurisdiction of existing committees

seniority *(p. 287)* the ranking given to an individual on the basis of length of continuous service on a committee in Congress

sociological representation *(p. 274)* a type of representation in which representatives have the same racial, gender, ethnic, religious, or educational backgrounds as their constituents. It is based on the principle that if two individuals are similar in background, character, interests, and perspectives, then one can correctly represent the other's views

Speaker of the House *(p. 285)* the chief presiding officer of the House of Representatives; the Speaker is the most important party and House leader, and can influence the legislative agenda, the fate of individual pieces of legislation, and members' positions within the House

standing committee *(p. 286)* a permanent committee with the power to propose and write legislation that covers a particular subject, such as finance or agriculture

term limits *(p. 279)* legally prescribed limits on the number of terms an elected official can serve

veto *(p. 292)* the president's constitutional power to prevent a bill from becoming a law; a presidential veto may be overridden by a two-thirds vote of each house of Congress

whip *(p. 285)* a party member in the House or Senate responsible for coordinating the party's legislative strategy, building support for key issues, and counting votes

For Further Reading

Berg, John C. *Class, Gender, Race, and Power in the U.S. Congress.* Boulder, CO: Westview, 1994.

Burrell, Barbara C. *A Woman's Place Is in the House: Campaigning for Congress in the Feminist Era.* Ann Arbor: University of Michigan Press, 1994.

Dodd, Lawrence, and Bruce I. Oppenheimer, eds. *Congress Reconsidered*, 10th ed. Washington, DC: CQ Press, 2012.

Dodson, Debra L. *The Impact of Women in Congress.* New York: Oxford University Press, 2006.

Fenno, Richard F. *Homestyle: House Members in Their Districts.* Boston: Little, Brown, 1978.

Fiorina, Morris. *Congress: Keystone of the Washington Establishment*, 2nd ed. New Haven, CT: Yale University Press, 1989.

Fowler, Linda, and Robert McClure. *Political Ambition: Who Decides to Run for Congress?* New Haven, CT: Yale University Press, 1989.

Koger, Gregory. *Filibustering: A Political History of Obstruction in the House and Senate.* Chicago: University of Chicago Press, 2010.

Mann, Thomas E., and Norman J. Ornstein. *It's Even Worse Than It Looks: How the American Constitutional System Collided with the New Politics of Extremism.* New York: Basic Books, 2012.

Mayhew, David R. *Congress: The Electoral Connection.* New Haven, CT: Yale University Press, 1974.

Palmer, Barbara, and Denise Simon. *Breaking the Political Glass Ceiling: Women and Congressional Elections*, 2nd ed. New York: Routledge, 2008.

Sinclair, Barbara. *Unorthodox Lawmaking*, 4th ed. Washington, DC: CQ Press, 2011.

Smith, Steven S., and Christopher Deering. *Committees in Congress*, 3rd ed. Washington, DC: CQ Press, 1997.

Spitzer, Robert J. *President and Congress.* New York: McGraw-Hill, 1993.

One of the president's important roles is to serve as commander in chief of the armed forces. Times of war and national emergency have often served to strengthen the office of the presidency.

10

The Presidency

WHAT GOVERNMENT DOES AND WHY IT MATTERS By 2016, President Barack Obama will be able to look back over his two terms as president and point to a solid record of policy triumphs, often enacted over determined Republican opposition. Under the president's leadership, the nation's health care system was significantly redesigned so that beginning in 2014, health insurance was offered to 32 million previously uninsured Americans. With the president's signature in 2010, the Dodd-Frank Wall Street Reform and Consumer Protection Act imposed a major set of new regulations on the financial services sector, whose practices had been blamed for the "Great Recession" of 2008. The president ended the war in Iraq and brought most American troops home from Afghanistan. Terrorist mastermind Osama bin Laden was killed by U.S. special operations troops. And, in pitched battles with congressional Republicans, the president forced Congress to end the 2013 government shutdown, to accept an increase in the national debt limit, and to accept several of his most controversial judicial and executive branch nominees. This last victory came when Senate Democrats were able to partially eliminate the Senate's historic filibuster rule, which had allowed Republicans to prevent debate on the president's nominations (see Chapter 9).

These policy triumphs reflect the considerable power of contemporary presidents. But President Obama also suffered a number of significant failures. Despite throwing his full political weight behind popular new gun control legislation just after his re-election, Congress failed to act. His efforts to bring about immigration reform and increase the federal minimum wage were blunted. Some of the president's actions, such as his agreement to reduce economic sanctions against Iran in exchange for an Iranian promise to slow the development of nuclear weapons, remained highly controversial. Even the president's health care triumph was dampened by the errors, mismanagement, and confusion surrounding the rollout of the program in 2014. Thus despite Obama's efforts and notable policy successes, the president and the nation continued to confront major problems, including budget deficits, unemployment, failing schools, and challenges abroad.

President Obama's record of successes and failures is a reflection of the strengths and limits of the institution. Obama inherited a presidency considerably more powerful than the institution imagined by the framers of the U.S. Constitution. In this chapter, we will examine the foundations, powers, and limits of the presidency. Ironically, national emergencies present some of the biggest challenges to presidents, but have also strengthened the office.

chaptergoals

- Outline the powers the Constitution gives the president (pp. 313–23)
- Identify the institutional resources presidents have to help them exercise their powers (pp. 323–27)
- Explain how modern presidents have become even more powerful (pp. 327–35)

● Presidential Power Is Rooted in the Constitution

Outline the powers the Constitution gives the president

The presidency was established by Article II of the Constitution, which begins by asserting "The executive power shall be vested in a President of the United States of America." The article goes on to describe the manner in which the president is to be chosen and defines the basic powers of the presidency. By vesting the executive power in a single president, the framers were emphatically rejecting proposals for various forms of collective leadership.

The presidential selection process defined by Article II resulted from a struggle between those delegates who wanted the president to be selected by, and thus responsible to, Congress and those who preferred that the president be elected directly by the people. Direct popular election would create a more independent and more powerful presidency. With the adoption of a scheme of indirect election through an electoral college, in which the electors would be selected by the state legislatures (and close elections would be resolved in the House of Representatives), the framers hoped to achieve a "republican" solution: a strong president responsible to state and national legislators rather than directly to the electorate. This indirect method of electing the president probably did dampen the power of most presidents in the nineteenth century. This conclusion is supported by the fact that, as we shall see later in this chapter, presidential power increased as the president developed a closer and more direct relationship with a mass electorate.

The framers' idea that electors would be chosen by the state legislatures gave way during the nineteenth century to various systems of popular selection of the electors. This made the presidency a more democratic institution and made the president more directly responsible to the American people than to the states. Today, in 48 of the 50 states, the candidate who wins a state's popular vote wins all of that state's electoral college votes. The presidential candidate with a majority of votes in the electoral college—not necessarily the candidate with the most votes

The election of the American president does not formally conclude on Election Day in November. In December, electors from each state cast their votes for president. The state electoral votes are then counted in January in the House of Representatives, which announces the victor.

from the people—becomes president. The number of electors per state is equal to its number of delegates in the House and Senate, thus small states are overrepresented in the electoral college. As a result, the electoral college system can sometimes distort the outcomes of presidential races, although it does not undermine the principle of popular selection of the nation's leaders.

While Section 1 of Article II explains how the president is to be chosen, Sections 2 and 3 outline the powers and duties of the president. These two sections identify two sources of presidential power. Some presidential powers are specifically established by the language of the Constitution. For example, the Constitution authorizes the president to make treaties, grant pardons, and nominate judges and other public officials. These specifically defined powers granted to the president in the Constitution are called the **expressed powers** of the office and cannot be revoked by the Congress or any other agency without an amendment to the Constitution. Other expressed powers include the power to receive ambassadors and command of the military forces of the United States.

In addition to the president's expressed powers, Article II declares that the president "shall take Care that the Laws be faithfully executed." Since the laws are enacted by Congress, this language implies that Congress is to delegate to the president the power to implement or execute its will. Powers given to the president by Congress are called **delegated powers** (constitutional powers that are assigned to one governmental agency but that are exercised by another agency with the express permission of the first). In principle, Congress delegates to the president only the power the president needs to carry out congressional decisions. So, for example, if Congress determines that air quality should be improved, it might delegate to the executive branch the power to identify the best means of bringing about such an improvement and the power to implement the actual cleanup process. In practice, of course, decisions about how to clean the air are likely to have an enormous impact on businesses, organizations, and individuals throughout the nation. By delegating power to the executive branch, Congress substantially enhances the importance of the presidency. In most cases, Congress delegates power to executive agencies rather than to the president, but as we shall see, contemporary presidents have found ways to capture a good deal of this delegated power for themselves.

Expressed Powers Come Directly from the Words of the Constitution

The president's expressed powers, as defined by Sections 2 and 3 of Article II, fall into several categories:

1. *Military.* Article II, Section 2, provides for the power as "Commander in Chief of the Army and Navy of the United States, and of the Militia of the several States, when called into the actual Service of the United States."

2. *Judicial.* Article II, Section 2, also provides the power to "grant Reprieves and Pardons for Offenses against the United States, except in Cases of Impeachment."

3. *Diplomatic.* Article II, Section 2, also provides the power "by and with the Advice and Consent of the Senate, to make Treaties." Article II, Section 3, provides the power to "receive Ambassadors and other public Ministers."

4. *Executive.* Article II, Section 3, authorizes the president to see to it that all the laws are faithfully executed; Section 2 gives the chief executive the power to appoint, remove, and supervise all executive officers and to appoint all federal judges.

5. *Legislative.* Article I, Section 7, and Article II, Section 3, give the president the power to participate authoritatively in the legislative process.

Military The president's military powers are among the most important exercised by the chief executive. The position of **commander in chief** (the role of the president as commander of the national military and the state National Guard units when called into service) makes the president the highest military authority in the United States. Within the executive branch, the president directs the secretary of defense, who heads the vast Defense Department, encompassing all the military branches of service. The president also directs the nation's intelligence network, which includes not only the Central Intelligence Agency (CIA) but also the National Security Council (NSC), the National Security Agency (NSA), the Federal Bureau of Investigation (FBI), and a host of less well-known but very powerful international and domestic security agencies.

Military Sources of Domestic Power The president's military powers extend into the domestic sphere. Article IV, Section 4, provides that the "United States shall [protect] every State . . . against Invasion . . . and . . . domestic Violence," and

One of the president's responsibilities is the maintenance of public order. After Hurricane Katrina devastated the Gulf Coast in 2005, President Bush declared a federal state of emergency in Louisiana and sent troops to the region to rescue residents, provide food and medicine, and keep order.

Congress has made this an explicit presidential power through statutes directing the president as commander in chief to discharge these obligations.[1] The Constitution restrains the president's use of domestic force by providing that a state legislature (or governor, when the legislature is not in session) must request federal troops before the president can send them into the state to provide public order. Yet this proviso is not absolute. First, presidents are not obligated to deploy national troops merely because the state legislature or governor makes such a request. More important, the president may deploy troops in a state or city without a specific request from the state legislature or governor if the president considers it necessary to maintain an essential national service during an emergency, enforce a federal judicial order, or protect federally guaranteed civil rights.

One historic example of the unilateral use of presidential emergency power, even when the state didn't request it, was the decision by President Dwight Eisenhower in 1957 to send troops into Little Rock, Arkansas, against the wishes of the state of Arkansas, to enforce court orders to integrate Little Rock's Central High School. The governor of Arkansas, Orval Faubus, had actually posted the Arkansas National Guard at the entrance of Central High School to prevent the court-ordered admission of nine black students. After an effort to negotiate with Governor Faubus failed, President Eisenhower reluctantly sent 1,000 paratroopers to Little Rock, who stood watch while the black students took their places in the all-white classrooms.

Military emergencies have typically also led to expansion of the domestic powers of the executive branch. This was true during the First and Second World Wars and in the wake of the war on terrorism as well. Within a month of the September 11 attacks, the White House had drafted and Congress had enacted the USA PATRIOT Act, expanding the power of government agencies to engage in domestic surveillance activities, including electronic surveillance, and restricting judicial review of such efforts. The act also gave the attorney general greater authority to detain and deport aliens suspected of having terrorist affiliations. The following year, Congress created the Department of Homeland Security, combining offices from 22 federal agencies into one huge new cabinet department responsible for protecting the nation from attack and responding to other emergencies. The new agency includes the U.S. Coast Guard, Transportation Security Administration, Federal Emergency Management Agency, Customs and Border Protection, Immigration and Customs Enforcement, U.S. Citizenship and Immigration Services, and offices from the departments of Agriculture, Energy, Transportation, Justice, Health and Human Services, Commerce, and the General Services Administration. The White House drafted the actual reorganization plan, but Congress weighed in to make certain that the new agency's workers had civil service and union protections.

Judicial The presidential power to grant reprieves, pardons, and amnesty involves the power of life and death over all individuals who may be a threat to the security of the United States. Presidents may use this power on behalf of a particular individual, as did Gerald Ford when he pardoned Richard Nixon in 1974 "for all offenses against the United States which he . . . has committed or may have committed." Or they may use it on a large scale, as did President Andrew Johnson in 1868, when he gave full amnesty to all southerners who had participated in the

"Late Rebellion," and President Carter in 1977, when he declared an amnesty for all the draft evaders of the Vietnam War. President Clinton created great controversy with a large number of last-minute pardons issued in the final days of his presidency in 2000. President George W. Bush, on the other hand, issued fewer pardons than any president in modern times.[2]

Diplomatic The president is America's "head of state"—its chief representative in dealings with other nations. As head of state, the president has the power to make treaties for the United States (with the advice and consent of the Senate). When President Washington received Edmond Genêt ("Citizen Genêt") as the formal emissary of the revolutionary government of France in 1793 and had his cabinet officers and Congress back his decision, he established a greatly expanded interpretation of the power to "receive Ambassadors and other public Ministers," extending it to the power to "recognize" other countries. That power gives the president the almost unconditional authority to review the claims of any new ruling groups in order to determine if they indeed control the territory and population of their country, so that they can commit it to treaties and other agreements.

In recent years, presidents have expanded the practice of using executive agreements instead of treaties to establish relations with other countries.[3] An **executive agreement** is exactly like a treaty because it is a contract between two countries that has the force of a treaty, but it does not require the Senate's "advice and consent." (Senate treaty approval requires a two-thirds vote.) Ordinarily, executive agreements are used to carry out commitments already made in treaties or laws, or to arrange for matters well below the level of policy. But when presidents have found it expedient to use an executive agreement in place of a treaty, Congress has typically acquiesced.

Executive Power The most important basis of the president's power as chief executive is to be found in Article II, Section 3, which stipulates that the president must see that all the laws are faithfully executed, and Section 2, which provides that the president will appoint, remove, and supervise all executive officers, and appoint all federal judges (with Senate approval). The power to appoint the principal executive officers and to require each of them to report to the president on subjects relating to the duties of their departments makes the president the true chief executive officer (CEO) of the nation. In this manner, the Constitution focuses executive power and legal responsibility on the president. The famous sign on President Truman's desk, "The Buck Stops Here," was not merely an assertion of Truman's personal sense of responsibility but was in fact recognition by him of the legal and constitutional responsibility of the president. The president is subject to some limitations, because the appointment of all such officers, including ambassadors, ministers, and federal judges, is subject to a majority approval by the Senate. But these appointments are at the discretion of the president, and these appointees are generally loyal to the president.

Legislative Power The president plays a role not only in the administration of government but also in the legislative process. Two constitutional provisions are the primary sources of the president's power in the legislative arena. The first of these is the provision in Article II, Section 3, providing that the president "shall from time to time give to the Congress Information of the State of the Union, and recommend to their Consideration such Measures as he shall judge necessary and expedient."

Delivering a State of the Union address may at first appear to be little more than the president's obligation to make recommendations for Congress's consideration. But as political and social conditions began to favor an increasingly prominent presidential role, each president, especially since Franklin Delano Roosevelt, began to rely on this provision in order to become the primary initiator of proposals for congressional action and the principal source for public awareness of national issues. Few today doubt that the president and the executive branch together are the primary source for many important congressional actions.[4]

The second of the president's legislative powers is the veto power assigned by Article I, Section 7.[5] The **veto** power is the president's constitutional power to prevent a bill from becoming a law (see Figure 10.1). It makes the president the single most important legislative leader.[6] No bill vetoed by the president can become law unless both the House and the Senate override the veto by a two-thirds vote. In the case of a **pocket veto**, Congress does not have the option of overriding the veto but must reintroduce the bill in the next session. A pocket veto is a presidential veto that is automatically triggered if the president does not act on a given piece of legislation passed during the final 10 days of a legislative session. Usually, if a president does not sign a bill within 10 days, it automatically becomes law. But this is true only while Congress is in session. If a president chooses not to sign a bill presented within the last 10 days of a legislative session, and Congress is out of session when the 10-day limit expires, instead of becoming law, the bill is vetoed and dies.

Use of the veto varies according to the political situation each president confronts. President Bush vetoed only 12 bills in his eight-year presidency, the lowest per-year average of any president since the nineteenth century. Eleven of those vetoes came during his last two years in office, when the Democratic Party controlled both houses of Congress. President Obama, who had a Democratic majority in the Senate in his first six years, has used his veto power only twice. The veto power is effective: more than 90 percent of all vetoes in history have been upheld.

Although not explicitly stated, the Constitution implies that the president has the power of **legislative initiative**—the president's implied power to bring a legislative agenda before Congress. To "initiate" means to originate, and in government that can mean power. "Initiative" obviously suggests the ability to formulate proposals for important policies, and the president, as an individual with a great deal of staff assistance, is able to initiate decisive action more frequently than Congress, with its large assemblies that have to deliberate and debate before taking action. With some important exceptions, Congress depends on the president to set the agenda of public policy. For example, during the weeks following September 11, 2001, George W. Bush took many presidential initiatives to Congress, and each was given nearly unanimous support—from commitments to pursue Al Qaeda, remove the Taliban, and reconstitute the Afghan regime, to almost unlimited approval for the mobilization of military force and the power to regulate American civil liberties.

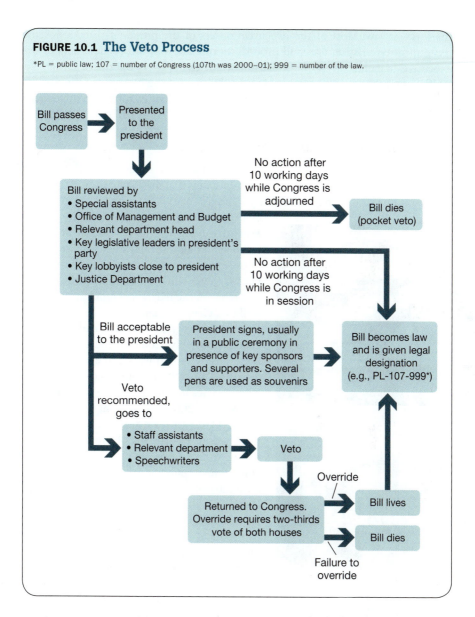

FIGURE 10.1 The Veto Process

*PL = public law; 107 = number of Congress (107th was 2000–01); 999 = number of the law.

Bill passes Congress → Presented to the president

Bill reviewed by
- Special assistants
- Office of Management and Budget
- Relevant department head
- Key legislative leaders in president's party
- Key lobbyists close to president
- Justice Department

No action after 10 working days while Congress is adjourned → Bill dies (pocket veto)

No action after 10 working days while Congress is in session

Bill acceptable to the president

President signs, usually in a public ceremony in presence of key sponsors and supporters. Several pens are used as souvenirs

Bill becomes law and is given legal designation (e.g., PL-107-999*)

Veto recommended, goes to
- Staff assistants
- Relevant department
- Speechwriters
→ Veto

Returned to Congress. Override requires two-thirds vote of both houses

Override → Bill lives

Failure to override → Bill dies

The president's initiative does not end with congressional policy making and the making of laws in the ordinary sense of the term. The president has still another legislative role (in all but name) within the executive branch. This is designated as the power to issue **executive orders**. The executive order is a rule or regulation issued by the president that has the effect and formal status of legislation, except that it is limited to the executive branch. It is first and foremost a normal tool of management, a power possessed by virtually any CEO to make "company policy": rules setting procedures, etiquette, chains of command, functional responsibilities, and so on. But evolving out of this normal management practice is a recognized presidential power to promulgate rules governing the executive branch that have the force of law. Most of the executive orders of the president provide for the reorganization of structures and procedures or otherwise direct the affairs of the executive branch. One of the most important examples is Executive Order No. 8248, September 8, 1939, establishing the divisions of the Executive Office of the President. Another one of similar importance is President Nixon's executive order establishing the Environmental Protection Agency (EPA) in 1970–71.

Delegated Powers Come from Congress

Many of the powers exercised by the president and the executive branch are not found in the Constitution but are the products of congressional statutes (laws) and resolutions. Over the past century, Congress has voluntarily delegated a great deal of its own legislative authority to the executive branch. This delegation of power has been an almost inescapable consequence of the expansion of government activity in the United States since the New Deal. Given the vast range of the federal government's responsibilities, Congress cannot execute and administer all the programs it creates and the laws it enacts. Inevitably, Congress must turn to the hundreds of departments and agencies in the executive branch or, when necessary, create new agencies to implement its goals. Thus, for example, in 2002, when Congress sought to protect America from terrorist attacks, it established a Department of Homeland Security with broad powers in the realms of law enforcement, public health, and immigration. Similarly, in 1972, when Congress enacted legislation designed to protect consumers from unreasonable or substantial risks posed by products, it assigned the task of developing safety standards and ordering product recalls to the Consumer Product Safety Commission.

The president and the executive branch are responsible for the implementation of many laws that Congress passes. These delegated powers extend to health care, as the executive branch orchestrated the health insurance enrollment process for millions of Americans under the Affordable Care Act. It also extends to consumer safety when the Consumer Product Safety Commission issues recalls for hazardous products like this surge protector, which could overheat, smoke, and melt.

Modern Presidents Have Claimed Inherent Powers

Presidents have claimed a third source of power beyond expressed and delegated powers. These are powers not specified in the Constitution or the law but are "powers over and beyond those expressly granted in the Constitution or reasonably to be implied from express grants."[7] These powers claimed by a president that are not expressed or implied in the Constitution, but are seen to "inhere" in the office, are referred to as the **inherent powers** of the presidency and have been asserted by recent presidents in times of war or national emergency. Yet not all powerful presidents claimed inherent powers.

For example, after the outbreak of the Civil War in 1861, President Abraham Lincoln issued a series of executive orders for which he had no clear legal basis. Without Congress in session, Lincoln combined the state militias into a 90-day national volunteer force, called for 40,000 new volunteers, enlarged the regular army and navy, diverted $2 million in unspent appropriations to military needs, instituted censorship of the U.S. mail, ordered a blockade of southern ports, suspended the writ of habeas corpus in the border states, and ordered the arrest by military police of individuals whom he deemed to be guilty of engaging in or even just contemplating treasonous actions.[8] Lincoln asserted that these extraordinary measures were necessary to confront this crisis. When Congress convened in July, he reported his actions to it, saying that they could only be legal if Congress passed a law making them so, which it did. Even though Lincoln never claimed inherent powers, his example was used by later presidents as justification.[9]

When North Korean forces invaded South Korea in June 1950, Congress was actually prepared to declare war, but President Harry S. Truman decided not to ask for congressional action. Instead, Truman asserted the principle that the president and not Congress could decide when and where to deploy America's military might. Truman dispatched American forces to Korea without a congressional declaration, and in the face of the emergency, Congress felt it had to acquiesce, and approved money to finance the conflict. The wars in Vietnam, Bosnia, Afghanistan, Iraq, and a host of lesser conflicts were all fought without formal declarations of war, usually with Congress enacting legislation giving authorization. When Truman ordered federal troops to take over a striking steel mill in 1952, citing the need for steel to support the Korean War effort, his administration claimed the "inherent" power to do so. (The Supreme Court ruled against Truman's seizure attempt.)

In 1973, Congress responded to presidential unilateralism by passing the **War Powers Resolution** over President Richard Nixon's veto. This law states that the president can send troops into action abroad only by authorization of Congress, or if American troops are already under attack or serious threat. It reasserted the principle of congressional war power, required the president to inform Congress of any planned military campaign, and stipulated that forces must be withdrawn within 60 days unless Congress acts to extend military action. Presidents, however, have often ignored the War Powers Resolution, claiming inherent executive power to defend the nation.

President George W. Bush responded to the 2001 attacks by Islamic terrorists by organizing a major military campaign to overthrow the Taliban regime in Afghanistan, which had sheltered the terrorists. In 2003, Bush ordered the invasion of Iraq, which he accused of posing a threat to the United States. U.S. forces overthrew the government of the Iraqi dictator, Saddam Hussein, and occupied the country. In both instances, Congress passed resolutions approving the president's actions beforehand, but the president was careful to assert that he did not need congressional authorization.

In 2011, President Obama ordered U.S. air strikes and drone attacks in Libya against the military forces of Libyan dictator Mu'ammar Qaddafi as they moved

Presidential Powers

Many countries around the world have a president at the head of government. But the powers of the president are not constant from country to country. This chapter has described the constitutional powers of the American president in detail. The table here compares these powers to the powers of the presidents of France, Germany, and South Africa. Both Germany and South Africa have parliamentary systems of government, meaning that the most powerful executive position is the prime minister (who is the leader of and is elected by the legislature and thus part of the legislative branch). In Germany the most powerful position is held by the chancellor while the president plays a mostly ceremonial role, similar to the United Kingdom's queen. South Africa's president is actually more analogous to a prime minister, as he leads the legislature (and is elected by it) and runs the government, but the position also involves a ceremonial role. Finally, France's system is called "semi-presidential," which is an executive system that divides power between a president and a prime minister, who have different but (theoretically) equal powers.

	United States	France	Germany	South Africa
Type of executive system	Presidential	Semi-presidential	Parliamentary	Parliamentary
Elected by	Electoral college (indirectly by the voters)	The voters	The parliament[a]	The parliament
Legislative power	Can sign or veto legislation	Appoints prime minister, but cannot dismiss him/her	Can sign law but only on behalf of the chancellor	Can sign bills or send them back to the parliament for reconsideration
	Responsible for enacting legislation	Can sign bills or send them back to the parliament for reconsideration	Position is largely ceremonial	Considerable legislative powers
		Can initiate referendum		
Power to appoint justices	Yes	Yes	No	Yes
Power to declare war	No	No	No[b]	Yes
Power to call new parliamentary elections	No	Yes	Yes	Yes
Term limits	Two four-year terms	Two consecutive five-year terms	Two five-year terms	Two five-year terms

[a] Germany's president is elected by a special federal convention, which includes all the members of Germany's Bundestag (lower house of parliament), as well as an equal number of representatives sent by the regional legislatures.

[b] One of the most famous clauses of the German constitution is their neutrality requirement; the country may only maintain weapons for defensive purposes

SOURCES: Basic Law for the Federal Republic of Germany, 1949: www.gesetz-eim-internet.de/englisch_gg /englisch_gg.html; Constitution of the Republic of South Africa, 1996: www.gov.za/documents/constitution/1996 /a108-96.pdf; Constitution of the Fifth Republic, 1958: www.assemblee-nationale.fr/english/ (all accessed 10/16/14).

against Libyan rebels who sought to overthrow the brutal Qaddafi regime. While no American forces landed in Libya, the air attacks were still a military attack on another nation—what the War Powers Resolution calls "hostilities." The strikes continued more than 60 days without any congressional approval, and in violation of the law. Yet Congress failed to take action against Obama, and the president was mostly praised for helping Libyans overthrow Qaddafi at the cost of no American lives.

Institutional Resources of Presidential Power Are Numerous

> **Identify the institutional resources presidents have to help them exercise their powers**

Constitutional sources of power are not the only resources available to the president. Presidents have at their disposal a variety of other formal and informal resources that have important implications for their ability to govern (see Figure 10.2). Indeed, without these other resources, presidents would lack the ability—the tools of management and public mobilization—to make much use of the power and responsibility given to them by Congress. Let us first consider the president's formal institutional resources and then, in the section following, turn to the more informal political resources that affect a president's capacity to govern, in particular the president's base of popular support.

The Cabinet Is Often Distant from the President

In the American system of government, the **Cabinet** is the traditional but informal designation for the heads (secretaries, or chief administrators) of all the major federal government departments. Cabinet secretaries are appointed by the president with the consent of the Senate. The Cabinet has no constitutional status. Unlike in Great Britain and many other parliamentary countries, where the Cabinet *is* the government, the American Cabinet meets but it makes no decisions as a group. The Senate must approve each appointment, but Cabinet members are responsible to the president, not to the Senate or to Congress at large. Since Cabinet appointees generally have not shared political careers with the president or one another, and since they may meet literally for the first time only after their selection, the formation of an effective governing group out of this diverse collection of appointments is highly unlikely.

The White House Staff Constitutes the President's Eyes and Ears

The **White House staff** is composed mainly of analysts and advisers who are closest to, and most responsive to, the president's needs and preferences.[10] Although many of the top White House staff members are given the title "special assistant" for a particular task or sector, the types of judgments they are expected to make and the kinds

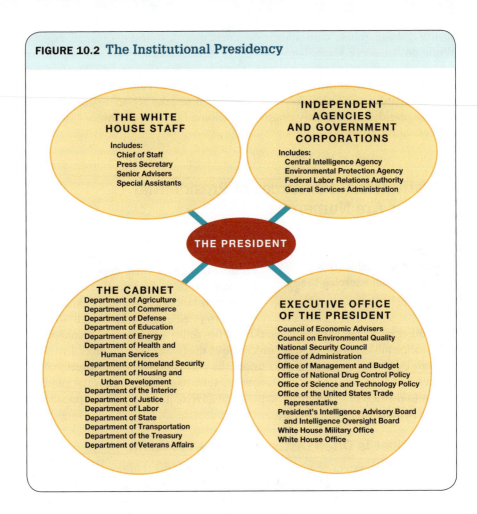

FIGURE 10.2 The Institutional Presidency

THE WHITE HOUSE STAFF

Includes:
Chief of Staff
Press Secretary
Senior Advisers
Special Assistants

INDEPENDENT AGENCIES AND GOVERNMENT CORPORATIONS

Includes:
Central Intelligence Agency
Environmental Protection Agency
Federal Labor Relations Authority
General Services Administration

THE PRESIDENT

THE CABINET

Department of Agriculture
Department of Commerce
Department of Defense
Department of Education
Department of Energy
Department of Health and
    Human Services
Department of Homeland Security
Department of Housing and
    Urban Development
Department of the Interior
Department of Justice
Department of Labor
Department of State
Department of Transportation
Department of the Treasury
Department of Veterans Affairs

EXECUTIVE OFFICE OF THE PRESIDENT

Council of Economic Advisers
Council on Environmental Quality
National Security Council
Office of Administration
Office of Management and Budget
Office of National Drug Control Policy
Office of Science and Technology Policy
Office of the United States Trade
    Representative
President's Intelligence Advisory Board
    and Intelligence Oversight Board
White House Military Office
White House Office

of advice they are supposed to provide are a good deal broader and more generally political than those coming from the Executive Office of the President or from the cabinet departments. The members of the White House staff also tend to be more closely associated with the president than are other presidentially appointed officials.

From an informal group of fewer than a dozen people (popularly called the **Kitchen Cabinet**—advisers to whom the president turns for counsel and guidance; members of the official Cabinet may or may not also be members of the Kitchen Cabinet) and no more than four dozen at its height during the Roosevelt presidency in 1937, the White House staff has grown substantially.[11] Nixon employed 550 people in 1972. President Carter, who found so many of the trappings of presidential power distasteful, and who publicly vowed to keep his staff small and decentralized, built an even larger and more centralized staff. President Clinton reduced the White House staff by 20 percent, but a large White House staff is still essential. In Obama's second term, the White House staff numbered approximately 450. In the spirit of transparency, the White House lists their names, position, and salary on the White House website.

The Executive Office of the President Is a Visible Sign of the Modern Strong Presidency

The **Executive Office of the President (EOP)** is a major part of what is often called the "institutional presidency"—the permanent agencies that perform defined management tasks for the president. Created in 1939, the EOP is composed of between 1,500 and 2,000 highly specialized people who work for EOP agencies. The most important and largest EOP agency is the Office of Management and Budget (OMB). Its roles in preparing the national budget, designing the president's program, reporting on agency activities, and overseeing regulatory proposals make OMB personnel part of virtually every conceivable presidential responsibility. The status and power of the OMB have grown in importance with each successive president. The process of budgeting at one time was a "bottom-up" procedure, with expenditure and program requests passing from the lowest bureaus through the departments to "clearance" in the OMB and hence to Congress, where each agency could be called in to reveal what its "original request" was before the OMB revised it. Now the budgeting process is "top-down": the OMB sets priorities for agencies as well as for Congress.

The staff of the Council of Economic Advisers (CEA) constantly analyzes the economy and economic trends and attempts to give the president the ability to anticipate events rather than waiting and reacting to them. The Council on Environmental Quality was designed to do for environmental issues what the CEA does for economic issues. The National Security Council (NSC) is composed of designated cabinet officials and others spanning military, diplomatic, and intelligence areas who meet regularly with the president to give advice on national security matters. Other EOP agencies perform more specialized tasks.

The Vice Presidency Has Become More Important since the 1970s

The vice presidency is a constitutional anomaly even though the Constitution created the office along with the presidency. The vice president exists for two purposes only: to succeed the president in case of death, resignation, or incapacity; and to preside over the Senate, casting a tie-breaking vote when necessary.[12]

The main value of the vice president as a political resource for the president is electoral. Traditionally, presidential candidates choose running mates who can win the support of at least one state (preferably a large one) not otherwise likely to support the ticket. It is very doubtful that John Kennedy would have won in 1960 without his vice-presidential candidate, Texan Lyndon Johnson, and the contribution Johnson made to winning his home state. Another rule holds that the vice-presidential nominee should provide some regional balance and, wherever possible, some balance among various ideological or ethnic subsections of the party. In 2008, Barack Obama chose Senator Joseph Biden of Delaware to be his running mate for a number of reasons. To begin with, Biden is Catholic and has blue-collar origins. Obama believed correctly that Biden would appeal to these important groups in such must-win states as Pennsylvania and Ohio. Perhaps even more important, Biden possessed enormous foreign policy experience and chaired the Senate Foreign Relations Committee. The Republicans had often pointed to Obama's lack of experience in the international realm as indicating that he was not ready to be president. Democrats hoped that Biden's presence on the ticket would put the "experience" issue to rest.

As the institutional presidency has grown in size and complexity, most presidents of the past 25 years have sought to use their vice presidents as a management resource after the election. President Clinton, for example, relied greatly on his vice president, Al Gore, to oversee the National Performance Review (NPR), an ambitious program to "reinvent" the way the federal government conducts its affairs. President George W. Bush granted unprecedented power and responsibility to his vice president, Dick Cheney, who helped shape the "war on terror." In the Obama White House, Vice President Joe Biden is said to be regarded as the "skeptic-in-chief."[13] Biden's role is to question and criticize policy recommendations made to the president until, of course, the president makes a decision, at which point the vice president falls loyally in step.

The First Spouse Has Become Important to Policy

The president serves as both chief executive and chief of state—the equivalent of Great Britain's prime minister and monarch rolled into one, simultaneously leading the government and representing the nation at official ceremonies and functions.

Because they are generally associated with the head-of-state aspect of America's presidency, presidential spouses are usually not subject to the same degree of media scrutiny or partisan attack as the president. Traditionally, most first ladies have limited their activities to the ceremonial portion of the presidency. First ladies greet foreign dignitaries, visit other countries, and attend important national ceremonies.

First Lady Michelle Obama has focused her attention on children's health with her "Let's Move!" campaign. This campaign emphasizes physical activity and healthy eating to combat childhood obesity. In Iowa, more than 10,000 school-aged children joined Michelle for an exercise class.

Some first spouses, however, have had considerable influence over policy. Franklin Roosevelt's wife, Eleanor, was widely popular, but also widely criticized for her active role in many elements of her husband's presidency. During the 1992 campaign, Bill Clinton often implied that his wife would be active in the administration; he joked that voters would get "two for the price of one." And indeed, after the election, Hillary Clinton took a leading role in many policy areas, most notably heading the administration's health care reform effort. She also became the first first lady to win public office on her own, winning a seat in the U.S. Senate from New York in 2000. She also ran for the presidency in 2008, and was appointed secretary of state by Obama in 2009. Barack Obama's wife, Michelle, is an attorney and served for a number of years as a senior administrator at the University of Chicago's Pritzker School of Medicine. Michelle Obama has emerged as a visible and active administration figure, as when she launched an anti-childhood-obesity campaign in 2010.

Party, Popular Mobilization, and Administration Make Presidents Stronger

During the nineteenth century, Congress was America's dominant institution of government, and members of Congress sometimes treated the president with disdain. Today, however, no one would assert that the presidency is unimportant. Presidents seek to dominate the policy-making process and claim the inherent power to lead the nation in time of war. The expansion of presidential power over the course of the past century has come about not by accident but as the result of an ongoing effort by successive presidents to enlarge the powers of the office. Some of these efforts have succeeded and others have failed. As the framers of the Constitution predicted, presidential *ambition* has been a powerful and unrelenting force in American politics.

Generally, presidents can expand their power in two ways: through popular mobilization and through the administration. First, presidents may use popular appeals to create a mass base of support that will allow them to dominate their political foes, a tactic called "going public."[14] Second, presidents may seek to bolster their control of established executive agencies or to create new administrative institutions and procedures that will reduce their dependence on Congress and give them a more independent governing and policy-making capability. Perhaps the most obvious example of this is the use of executive orders to achieve policy goals in lieu of seeking to persuade Congress to enact legislation.

Presidents have a third tool: their political party. Each president has relied on his own party to implement his legislative agenda. President Obama, for instance, relied on Democrats in the Senate to help his approvals to the federal judiciary win appointment. However, the president does not control his party; party members have considerable autonomy. Moreover, in America's system of separated powers, the president's party may be in the minority in Congress and unable to do much for the chief executive's programs. Consequently, although their party is valuable to chief executives, it has not been a fully reliable presidential tool. As a result, contemporary presidents are more likely to use the two other methods, popular mobilization and executive administration, to achieve their political goals.

Going Public Means Trying to Whip Up the People

During the nineteenth century, it was considered inappropriate for presidents to engage in personal campaigning on their own behalf or in support of programs and policies. When Andrew Johnson broke this unwritten rule and made a series of speeches vehemently seeking public support for his Reconstruction program, even some of Johnson's most ardent supporters were shocked at what they saw as his lack of

President Franklin Delano Roosevelt's direct appeals to the American people allowed him to "reach over the heads" of congressional opponents and force them to follow his lead because their constituents demanded it.

decorum and dignity. The president's opponents cited his "inflammatory" speeches in one of the articles of impeachment drafted by the Congress pursuant to the first impeachment trial of a president in history.[15]

In the twentieth century, though, popular mobilization became a favored weapon in the political arsenals of most presidents. Among modern presidents, the one who used public appeals most effectively was Franklin Delano Roosevelt. The political scientist Sidney Milkis observes that FDR was "firmly persuaded of the need to form a direct link between the executive office and the public."[16] Roosevelt developed a number of tactics aimed at forging such a link. He made important use of the new electronic medium, the radio, to reach millions of Americans. In his famous "fireside chats," the president, or at least his voice, came into every living room in the country to discuss programs and policies and generally to assure Americans that he was aware of their difficulties and working diligently toward solutions.

Roosevelt was also an innovator in the realm of what is now called press relations. When he entered the White House, FDR faced a mainly hostile press typically controlled by conservative members of the business establishment. As the president wrote, "All the fat-cat newspapers—85 percent of the whole—have been utterly opposed to everything the Administration is seeking."[17] Roosevelt hoped to use the press to mold public opinion, but to do so he needed to circumvent the editors and publishers who were generally unsympathetic to his goals. To this end, he worked to cultivate the reporters who covered the White House. Roosevelt made himself available for biweekly press conferences, where he offered candid answers to reporters' questions and made certain to make important policy announcements that would provide the reporters with significant stories for their papers.[18]

Every president since FDR sought to craft a public-relations strategy that would emphasize the incumbent's strengths and maximize his popular appeal. For John F. Kennedy, handsome and quick-witted, the televised press conference was an excellent public-relations vehicle. Johnson and Nixon lacked Kennedy's charisma, but both were effective television speakers, usually reading from a prepared text. Bill Clinton made extensive use of televised town meetings—carefully staged events that gave the president an opportunity to appear to consult with rank-and-file citizens about his goals and policies without having to face the sorts of pointed questions preferred by reporters. President Obama is a talented and effective speaker who often relies on his own speaking abilities rather than material crafted by the Communications Office.

Going Public Online President Barack Obama has also been the first to make full use of a new communication medium—in this case, the Internet. Drawing on the interactive tools of the Web, Obama's 2008 and 2012 campaigns changed the way politicians organize supporters, advertise to voters, defend against attacks, and communicate with their constituents.[19] The Internet has not only changed the way modern presidents campaign but also how they govern. The Whitehouse.gov website keeps the president's constituents abreast of his policy agenda with a weekly streaming video address by the president, press briefings, speeches and remarks, a daily blog, photos of the president, the White House schedule, and other information. Virtually everything the president does is recorded online. YouTube airs Obama's press conferences and public appearances on a daily basis. Every presidential address is now streamed live online.

Circumventing television and other traditional media, the Internet allows the president to reach citizens directly. In March 2014, Obama broke new media ground again, appearing on the comic website's *Funny or Die* program "Between Two Ferns," where he was interviewed by comic actor Zach Galifianakis. Obama's purpose was to reach out to uninsured young people to prod them to sign up for medical insurance. Obama's Facebook page personalizes the president's connection with his constituents and the causes they care about. As of 2014, Barack Obama's Facebook page had more than 39 million "likes." In 2014, Obama had 42 million Twitter followers. Websites, podcasts, Facebook, and other new media forums facilitate direct communication between the president and the people, creating a virtual network of constituents. Like FDR in the 1930s and '40s, and Kennedy in the 1960s, Obama may have changed how presidents govern for some time to come.

The Limits of Going Public Some presidents have been able to make effective use of popular appeals to overcome congressional opposition. Popular support, though, has not been a firm foundation for presidential power. The public is notoriously fickle. After America's triumph in the 1990 Persian Gulf War, President George H. W. Bush scored a remarkable 90 percent approval rating in the polls. Two years later, however, after the 1991 budget crisis, Bush's support plummeted and the president was defeated in his bid for re-election. President George W. Bush maintained an approval rating of over 70 percent for more than a year following the September 11, 2001, terrorist attacks. By the end of 2005, however, President Bush's approval rating had dropped to 39 percent as a result of the growing unpopularity of the Iraq War, the administration's inept handling of hurricane relief, and several White House scandals, including the conviction of Vice President Cheney's chief of staff on charges of lying to a federal grand jury. Between the time President Obama took office in 2009 and 2014, his public approval ranged from a high of 65 percent to a low of 40 percent.[20] Such declines in popular approval during a president's term in office are nearly inevitable and follow a predictable pattern.[21] Presidents generate popular support by promising to undertake important programs that will contribute directly to the well-being of large numbers of Americans. Almost without exception, presidential performance falls short of promises and popular expectations, leading to a decline in public support and the ensuing weakening of presidential influence.[22] It is a rare American president, such as Bill Clinton, who exits the White House more popular than when he went in.

The Administrative Strategy Increases Presidential Control

Contemporary presidents have increased the administrative capabilities of their office in four ways. First, they have enhanced the reach and power of the EOP. Second, they have sought to increase White House control over the federal bureaucracy. Third, they have expanded the role of executive orders. Fourth, they have made frequent use of signing statements and other instruments of direct presidential governance. Taken together, these four components of what might be called the White House "administrative strategy" have given presidents a capacity to achieve their programmatic and policy goals even when they are unable to secure congressional approval. Indeed, some recent presidents have been able to accomplish a great deal with remarkably little congressional, partisan, or even public support.

The Executive Office of the President The EOP has grown from six administrative assistants in 1939 to today's several hundred employees working directly for the president in the White House office along with some 2,500 individuals staffing the divisions of the Executive Office.[23] The creation and growth of the White House staff gives the president an enormously enhanced capacity to gather information, plan programs and strategies, communicate with constituencies, and exercise supervision over the executive branch. The staff multiplies the president's eyes, ears, and arms, becoming a critical instrument of presidential power.[24]

In particular, the OMB serves as a potential instrument of presidential control over federal spending and hence a mechanism through which the White House has greatly expanded its power. In addition to its power over the federal budget process (discussed earlier), the OMB has the capacity to analyze and approve all legislative proposals, not only budgetary requests, emanating from all federal agencies before they are submitted to Congress. This procedure, now a matter of routine, greatly enhances the president's control over the entire executive branch. All legislation originating in the White House and all executive orders also go through the OMB.[25] Thus, through one White House agency, the president has the means to exert major influence over the flow of money and the shape and content of national legislation.

Regulatory Review A second tactic that presidents have used to increase their power and reach is the process of regulatory review, through which they have sought to seize control of rule making by the agencies of the executive branch (see also Chapter 11). Whenever Congress enacts a statute, the statute's actual implementation requires the promulgation of hundreds of rules by the agency charged with administering the law and giving effect to the will of Congress. Some congressional statutes are quite detailed and leave agencies with relatively little discretion. Typically, however, Congress enacts a relatively broad statement of legislative intent and delegates to the appropriate administrative agency the power to fill in many important details.[26] In other words, Congress typically says to an administrative agency, "Here is the problem: deal with it."[27]

The discretion Congress delegates to administrative agencies has provided recent presidents with an important avenue for expanding their own power. For example, President Clinton believed the president had full authority to order agencies of the executive branch to adopt such rules as the president thought appropriate. During the course of his presidency, Clinton issued 107 directives to administrators ordering them to propose specific rules and regulations. In some instances, the language of the rule to be proposed was drafted by the White House staff; in other cases, the president asserted a priority but left it to the agency to draft the precise language of the proposal. President George W. Bush continued the Clinton-era practice of issuing presidential directives to agencies to spur them to issue new rules and regulations. Obama's first regulatory director, Cass Sunstein, not only issued a number of major regulatory directives to federal agencies but also launched a "look back" program. Under this program, the administration sought to eliminate several hundred existing rules it deemed obsolete.[28]

Governing by Decree: Executive Orders

Another mechanism through which contemporary presidents have sought to enhance their power to govern unilaterally is the use of executive orders and other forms of presidential decrees, including executive agreements, national security findings and directives, proclamations, reorganization plans, signing statements, and a host of other tools.[29] Executive orders have a long history in the United States and have been the vehicles for a number of important government policies, including the purchase of Louisiana, the annexation of Texas, the emancipation of the slaves, the internment of people of Japanese descent, the desegregation of the military, the initiation of affirmative action, and the creation of important federal agencies, among them the EPA, the FDA, and the Peace Corps.[30]

Presidents may not use executive orders to issue whatever commands they please. The use of such decrees is bound by law. If a president issues an executive order, proclamation, directive, or the like, in principle he does so pursuant to the powers granted to him by the Constitution or delegated to him by Congress, usually through a statute. When presidents issue such orders, they generally state the constitutional

In 2013, Obama issued an executive order to prepare the United States for the impacts of climate change. Here, scientists use time-lapse cameras to document and analyze the rate at which this Alaskan glacier is shrinking.

or statutory basis for their actions. For example, when President Truman ordered the desegregation of the armed services, he did so pursuant to his constitutional powers as commander in chief. In a similar vein, when President Johnson issued Executive Order No. 11246, he asserted that the order was designed to implement the 1964 Civil Rights Act, which prohibited employment discrimination. Where an executive order has no statutory or constitutional basis, the courts have held it to be void.[31]

President George W. Bush did not hesitate to use executive orders, issuing nearly 300 during his two terms. During his first months in office, Bush issued orders prohibiting the use of federal funds to support international family planning groups that provided abortion counseling services and limiting the use of embryonic stem cells in federally funded research projects. Throughout his administration, Bush made very aggressive use of executive orders in response to the threat of terrorism. In November 2001, for example, he issued a directive authorizing the creation of military tribunals to try noncitizens accused of involvement in acts of terrorism against the United States. President Obama issued 164 executive orders between 2009 and 2013, using some of them to reverse executive orders of his predecessor (just as Bush reversed some of those of the Clinton years). Obama's executive orders authorized stem cell research, restored funding for international family planning organizations, opened access to presidential papers, and barred improper interrogation methods of detainees captured by the United States.[32] In 2012, Obama issued an order designed to halt the deportation of undocumented immigrants who had come to the United States as children. These individuals would become eligible for work permits. Immigrant rights groups hailed the order while Republicans criticized the president for circumventing Congress. In 2013, Obama issued over 20 orders to enhance federal gun regulations.

Signing Statements To negate congressional actions to which they object, recent presidents have made frequent and calculated use of presidential **signing statements**.[33] The signing statement is an announcement made by the president at the time of signing a congressional enactment into law, often presenting the president's interpretation of the law in addition to the usually innocuous remarks about the many benefits the law will bring the nation. Occasionally presidents have used signing statements to point to sections of the law they deem improper or even unconstitutional and to instruct executive branch agencies how to execute the law.[34] President Harry Truman, for example, accompanied his approval of the 1946 Hobbs Anti-Racketeering Act with a message offering his interpretation of ambiguous sections of the statute and indicating how the federal government would implement the law.[35]

Presidents have made signing statements throughout American history, though many were not recorded and did not become part of the official legislative record. Ronald Reagan's attorney general, Edwin Meese, is generally credited with transforming the signing statement into a significant tool of presidential direct action.[36]

With the way paved, Reagan and his successors proceeded to use detailed and artfully designed signing statements (prepared by the Department of Justice) to attempt actually to reinterpret congressional enactments. For example, when signing the Safe Drinking Water Act Amendments of 1986, President Reagan issued a statement that interpreted sections of the act to allow discretionary enforcement when the Congress seemed to call for mandatory enforcement.[37] Reagan hoped the courts would accept his version of the statute when examining subsequent enforcement decisions. In other cases, Reagan used his signing statements to attempt to nullify portions of statutes. George W. Bush issued 161 signing statements. Within these 161 statements, however, Bush inserted nearly 1,200 specific signing statement provisions—more than twice as many provisions as all past presidents combined—using them to rewrite the law on numerous occasions. As a candidate, Obama criticized Bush's prolific use of signing statements but did not entirely abandon the practice as president. In his first five years in office, Obama issued 25 signing statements containing 74 specific provisions.[38]

Presidential Power Has Limits

Though the "administrative strategy" has provided presidents with a host of new powers, presidents are not dictators or kings. Their power continues to be limited by Congress and, especially, by the congressional power of the purse. In 2011 and again in 2013, Congress demonstrated that its control over federal spending and borrowing papers could force the president to pay attention to the legislative branch. In the budget battle of 2013, Republicans used their control of the House of Representatives to shut down most government agencies for more than two weeks until a budgetary compromise was reached.

Another area in which the president has limited influence is the overall state of the national economy. The public frequently blames or rewards the president for economic performance; the Consumer Confidence Index, a measure of how optimistic consumers are about the future of the economy, is a very good indicator of a sitting president's chances for re-election. But the president's actual impact on the economy is limited. Unemployment and inflation, two important indicators of economic health, are subject to macroeconomic conditions largely outside the president's control, such as consumer demand or the productivity of workers. What influence the federal government does have is exercised mainly by the chair of the Federal Reserve, an independent agency.

The president is also limited in the implementation of his legislative agenda by the party in control of the House and Senate. As Figure 10.3 shows, presidential success on congressional votes is much higher when his party is in the majority in

National Park Service
U.S. Department of the Interior

Because of the
Federal Government SHUTDOWN,
**All National Parks
Are CLOSED**.

While presidents are more powerful today than they were 200 years ago, they are still subject to constitutional checks and balances. This process can lead to frustration, such as the 2013 government shutdown.

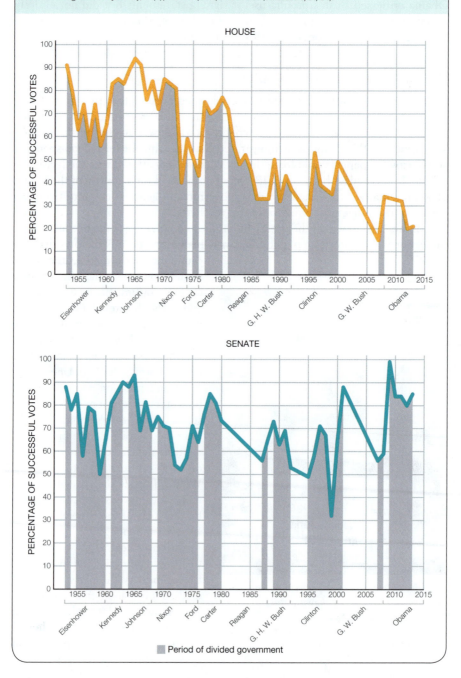

FIGURE 10.3 Presidential Success on Congressional Votes, 1953–2013*

Presidents have more success in Congress when their party is in the majority. Can you identify the periods when presidents had majority support in Congress and when they did not?

*Percentages based on votes on which presidents took a position.
SOURCE: Congressional Quarterly, http://media.cq.com/votestudies (accessed 3/17/14).

HOUSE

SENATE

■ Period of divided government

Congress. In periods of divided government, when one or both houses of Congress are controlled by the opposition party, the president has much more difficulty implementing his agenda.

The Presidency
and Your Future

The framers of the Constitution created a system of government in which the Congress and the executive branch were to share power. At least since the New Deal of the 1930s, however, the powers of Congress have waned whereas those of the presidency have expanded. Louis Fisher, a leading authority on the separation of powers, recently observed that in what are arguably the two most important policy arenas, national defense and the federal budget, the powers of Congress have been in decline for at least the past 50 years. The last time Congress exercised its constitutional power to declare war was 1942, and yet, since that time, American forces have been committed to numerous conflicts around the world by order of the president.

What might the growth of presidential power mean for students reading this book today? It might mean that policies they favor can more easily become the law of the land. Congress works slowly while the president can work quickly—making law by the stroke of a pen. Some advocates, for example, have asserted that President Obama can issue executive orders legalizing the status of America's estimated 11 million undocumented immigrants even though Congress has failed to enact legislation on immigration reform. Presidential strength works both ways, however: for those who oppose a particular policy or have qualms about some aspect of it, the stroke of the presidential pen might seem hasty and autocratic. Proponents of quick and unilateral presidential action should be careful what they wish for. They may not always welcome the action.

plugin

Inform

Watch a few recent presidential speeches, including this year's State of the Union address, on YouTube. What problems does the president consider most pressing? What solutions does he propose?

Express

Make a list of powers claimed by modern presidents that are not in the Constitution. Explain why you think the president should or should not have each of these powers.

Connect

Follow the president and/or vice president on social media. What issues are highlighted in posts from the past week? What solutions are proposed?

Act

Create a petition at whitehouse .gov (currently found under the "Participation" tab) regarding an issue you care about, and try to get as many signatures as possible. Can you get past the threshold necessary for an official White House response?

Practice Quiz

1. Which article of the Constitution establishes the presidency? *(p. 313)*
   a) Article I
   b) Article II
   c) Article III
   d) Article IV
   e) Article V

2. The Founders chose to select the president through an indirect election in order to *(p. 313)*
   a) increase the strength and influence of political parties.
   b) build an imperial presidency that would overwhelm the power of Congress.
   c) force the president to be responsive to the will of the people.
   d) make the president responsible to the state and national legislatures.
   e) create a more independent chief executive.

3. Which of the following military and war powers does the Constitution *not* assign to the president? *(pp. 315–16)*
   a) command of the army and navy of the United States
   b) the power to declare war
   c) command of the state militias
   d) the power to make treaties
   e) The Constitution assigns all of the powers above to the president.

4. Executive agreements are exactly like treaties except that *(p. 317)*
   a) executive agreements involve only domestic, not international, affairs.
   b) the Constitution explicitly mentions the president's ability to make executive agreements.
   c) executive agreements do not require the Senate's "advice and consent."
   d) executive agreements are ordinarily used to carry out commitments not already made in treaties or laws.
   e) executive agreements require a two-thirds approval vote in the Senate.

5. What are the requirements for overriding a presidential veto? *(p. 318)*
   a) 50 percent plus one vote in both houses of Congress
   b) two-thirds vote in both houses of Congress
   c) two-thirds vote in the Senate only
   d) three-fourths vote in both houses of Congress
   e) A presidential veto cannot be overridden by Congress.

6. When the president issues a rule or regulation that reorganizes or otherwise directs the affairs of the executive branch, it is called *(pp. 319–20)*
   a) an executive agreement.
   b) an executive order.
   c) an executive mandate.
   d) administrative oversight.
   e) legislative initiative.

7. The War Powers Resolution of 1973 was an act passed by Congress that *(p. 321)*
   a) required the CIA to collect intelligence on all Americans born in a foreign country.
   b) outlawed presidential use of executive agreements.
   c) created the National Security Council.
   d) granted the president the authority to declare war.
   e) stipulated military forces must be withdrawn within 60 days in the absence of a specific congressional authorization for their continued deployment.

8. Approximately how many people work for agencies within the Executive Office of the President? *(p. 325)*
   a) 25 to 50
   b) 500 to 750
   c) 1,500 to 2,000
   d) 4,500 to 5,000
   e) over 10,000

9. The Office of Management and Budget is part of *(p. 325)*
   a) the Executive Office of the President.
   b) the White House staff.
   c) the Cabinet.
   d) the Council of Economic Advisers.
   e) the Kitchen Cabinet

10. Which of the following statements about vice presidents is not true? *(pp. 326–27)*
   a) The vice president succeeds the president in case of death, resignation, or incapacitation.
   b) The vice president casts the tie-breaking vote in the Senate when necessary.
   c) The vice president also serves as an honorary member of the Supreme Court.
   d) Modern presidents often use their vice presidents as a management resource.
   e) Presidential candidates typically select a vice presidential candidate who is likely to bring the support of a state that would not otherwise support the ticket.

11. What are two ways that presidents can expand their power? *(p. 327)*
   a) avoiding popular appeals and loosening their control of executive agencies
   b) using popular appeals and bolstering their control of executive agencies
   c) using popular appeals and loosening their control of executive agencies
   d) avoiding popular appeals and bolstering their control of executive agencies
   e) weakening national partisan institutions and bolstering their control of executive agencies

12. When the president makes an announcement about his interpretation of a congressional enactment that he is signing into law, it is called *(p. 332)*
   a) a signing statement.
   b) a line item veto.
   c) an executive order.
   d) legislative initiative.
   e) executive privilege.

Key Terms

Cabinet *(p. 323)* the secretaries, or chief administrators, of the major departments of the federal government; cabinet secretaries are appointed by the president with the consent of the Senate

commander in chief *(p. 315)* the role of the president as commander of the national military and the state National Guard units (when called into service)

delegated powers *(p. 314)* constitutional powers that are assigned to one governmental agency but that are exercised by another agency with the express permission of the first

executive agreement *(p. 317)* an agreement, made between the president and another country, that has the force of a treaty but does not require the Senate's "advice and consent"

Executive Office of the President (EOP) *(p. 325)* the permanent agencies that perform defined management tasks for the president. Created in 1939, the EOP includes the OMB, the CEA, the NSC, and other agencies

executive order *(p. 319)* a rule or regulation issued by the president that has the effect and formal status of legislation

expressed powers *(p. 314)* specific powers granted by the Constitution to Congress (Article I, Section 8) and to the president (Article II)

inherent powers *(p. 319)* powers claimed by a president that are not expressed in the Constitution but are inferred from it

Kitchen Cabinet *(p. 324)* an informal group of advisers to whom the president turns for counsel and guidance; members of the official Cabinet may or may not also be members of the Kitchen Cabinet

legislative initiative *(p. 318)* the president's implied power to bring a legislative agenda before Congress

pocket veto *(p. 318)* a presidential veto that is automatically triggered if the president does not act on a given piece of legislation passed during the final 10 days of a legislative session

signing statements *(p. 332)* announcements made by the president when signing bills into law, often presenting the president's interpretation of the law

veto *(p. 318)* the president's constitutional power to prevent a bill from becoming a law; a presidential veto may be overridden by a two-thirds vote of each house of Congress

War Powers Resolution *(p. 319)* a resolution of Congress that the president can send troops into action abroad only by authorization of Congress, or if American troops are already under attack or serious threat

White House staff *(p. 323)* analysts and advisers to the president, each of whom is often given the title "special assistant"

For Further Reading

Crenson, Matthew, and Benjamin Ginsberg. *Presidential Power: Unchecked and Unbalanced.* New York: W. W. Norton, 2007.

Crouch, Jeffrey P. *The Presidential Pardon Power.* Lawrence: University Press of Kansas, 2009.

Dodds, Graham. *Take Up Your Pen: Unilateral Presidential Directives in American Politics.* Philadelphia: University of Pennsylvania Press, 2013.

Edwards, George. *Why the Electoral College Is Bad for America.* New Haven, CT: Yale University Press, 2004.

Fisher, Louis. *The Law of the Executive Branch.* New York: Oxford University Press, 2014.

Genovese, Michael, and Robert J. Spitzer. *The Presidency and the Constitution.* New York: Palgrave/Macmillan, 2005.

Han, Lori Cox, and Diane Heith. *Presidents and the American Presidency.* New York: Oxford University Press, 2013.

Kernell, Samuel. *Going Public: New Strategies of Presidential Leadership.* Washington, DC: CQ Press, 2006.

Neustadt, Richard E. *Presidential Power: The Politics of Leadership from Roosevelt to Reagan.* Rev. ed. New York: Free Press, 1990.

Spitzer, Robert J. *The Presidential Veto: Touchstone of the American Presidency.* Albany: State University of New York Press, 1988.

Government bureaucracies affect ordinary Americans in countless ways. For example, the Environmental Protection Agency (EPA) proposes and enforces regulations that protect Americans' health and the environment. Here, an EPA worker vacuums a gasoline-like substance that contains the cancer-causing chemical benzene from the South Platte River, north of Denver, Colorado.

Bureaucracy

11

WHAT GOVERNMENT DOES AND WHY IT MATTERS Americans depend on government bureaucracies to accomplish the most spectacular achievements as well as the most mundane. Yet they often do not realize that public bureaucracies are essential for providing the services they use every day and rely on in emergencies. On a typical day, a college student might check the weather forecast, drive on an interstate highway, mail the rent check, drink from a public water fountain, check the calories on the side of a yogurt container, attend a class, log on to the Internet, and meet a relative at the airport. Each of these activities is possible because of the work of a government bureaucracy: the U.S. Weather Service, the U.S. Department of Transportation, the U.S. Postal Service, the Environmental Protection Agency, the Food and Drug Administration (FDA), the student loan programs of the U.S. Department of Education, the Advanced Research Projects Agency (which developed the Internet in the 1960s), and the Federal Aviation Administration. Without the ongoing work of these agencies, many of these common activities would be impossible, unreliable, or more expensive. Even though bureaucracies provide essential services that all Americans rely on, they are often disparaged by politicians and the general public alike.

In emergencies, the national perspective on bureaucracy and, indeed, on "big government" shifts. After the September 11, 2011, terrorist attacks, all eyes turned to Washington. The federal government responded by strengthening and reorganizing the bureaucracy to undertake a whole new set of responsibilities designed to keep America safe. In the biggest government reorganization in over half a century, Congress created the Department of Homeland Security in 2002. The massive new department merged 22 existing agencies into a single department employing nearly 170,000 workers. Although the Bush administration presided over the creation of the Department of Homeland Security, Bush, like his Republican predecessors Ronald Reagan and George H. W. Bush, sought to roll back the regulatory role of the government.

In Chapters 9 and 10, we examined the two branches of government that exercise ultimate responsibility over the bureaucracy: Congress and the presidency. The numerous departments, agencies, offices, and bureaus that make up the bureaucracy exist because Congress created them by legal enactment. Congress oversees the activities of agencies, controls their funding, and can even rearrange or dismantle them. The president, as chief executive, can appoint top agency officials (with Senate approval), issue rules to govern agency behavior, control agency funding requests, and apply various other political pressures to compel agencies to respond to presidential priorities. Yet despite these many controls, members of Congress and presidents often express frustration at what they claim are the severe limits on the powers they can exercise to control the bureaucracy. These tensions suggest a separation of powers approach to studying the relationships among these three parts of the government.

chaptergoals

- Define bureaucracy, and describe the basic features of the executive branch (pp. 343–50)
- Describe the major goals we expect federal agencies to promote (pp. 350–58)
- Explain why it is often difficult to control the bureaucracy (pp. 358–63)

Bureaucracy Exists to Improve Efficiency

> **Define bureaucracy, and describe the basic features of the executive branch**

Bureaucracy is simply a form of organization. *Bureau*, a French word, can mean either "office" or "desk." *Cracy* is the Greek word for "rule" or "form of rule." Putting *bureau* and *cracy* together produces a very interesting definition: rule by offices and desks. In fact, **bureaucracy** is the complex structure of offices, tasks, rules, and principles of organization that are employed by all large-scale institutions to coordinate effectively the work of their personnel. Each member of an organization has an office, meaning a place as well as a set of responsibilities. That is, each "office" is made up of a set of tasks that are specialized to the needs of the organization, and the person holding that office (or position) performs those specialized tasks. Specialization and repetition are essential to the efficiency of any organization. Therefore, when an organization is inefficient, it is almost certainly because it is not bureaucratized enough!

Bureaucracies not only perform specialized tasks that require routine action but also undertake politically controversial tasks that require them to exercise a great deal of discretion and professional judgment. In many areas of policy, Congress writes laws that are very broad, and it is up to the bureaucracy to define what the laws will mean in practice. The decisions that bureaucrats make, often based on professional judgments, can themselves become politically contentious.

Both routine and exceptional tasks require the organization, specialization, and expertise found in bureaucracies. To provide these services, government

The Department of Homeland Security is tasked with the broad goal of keeping America safe. Its 240,000 employees work in jobs as diverse as aviation security, emergency response, and chemical facility inspection. DHS also provided security at MetLife Stadium for the 2014 Super Bowl, an event attended by approximately 82,000 people.

bureaucracies employ specialists such as meteorologists, doctors, and scientists. To do their job effectively, these specialists require resources and tools (ranging from paper to complex computer software); they have to coordinate their work with others (e.g., traffic engineers must communicate with construction engineers); and there must be effective outreach to the public (e.g., doctors must be made aware of health warnings). Bureaucracy is a means of coordinating the many different parts that must work together to provide useful services.

Bureaucrats Fulfill Important Roles

Congress is responsible for making the laws, but in most cases legislation only sets the broad parameters for government action. Bureaucracies are responsible for filling in the blanks by determining how the laws should be implemented. This requires bureaucracies to draw up much more detailed rules that guide the process of **implementation** (the efforts of departments and agencies to translate laws into specific bureaucratic rules and actions) and also to play a key role in enforcing the laws. Congress needs the bureaucracy to engage in rule making and implementation for several reasons. One is that bureaucracies employ people who have much more specialized expertise in specific policy areas than do members of Congress. Decisions about how to achieve many policy goals—from managing the national parks to regulating air quality to ensuring a sound economy—rest on the judgment of specialized experts. A second reason that Congress needs bureaucracy is that because updating legislation can take many years, bureaucratic flexibility can ensure that laws are administered in ways that take new conditions into account. Finally, members of Congress often prefer to delegate politically difficult decision making to bureaucrats.

Bureaucrats Make Rules One of the most important things that government agencies do is issue rules that provide more detailed and specific indications of what a given congressional policy will actually mean. For example, the Clean Air Act empowers the Environmental Protection Agency (EPA) to assess whether current or projected levels of air pollutants pose a threat to public health, to identify whether motor vehicle emissions are contributing to such pollution, and to create rules designed to regulate these emissions. Under the George W. Bush administration, the EPA claimed it did not have the authority to regulate a specific group of pollutants commonly referred to as "greenhouse gases" (for example, carbon dioxide). In 2007 the Supreme Court ruled that the EPA did have that authority and had to provide a justification for not regulating such emissions.[1] In the first year of the Obama administration, the agency ruled that greenhouse gases did pose a threat to public health and that the emissions from motor vehicles contributed to greenhouse gas pollution.[2] The agency then proposed new emission standards for automobiles, which would raise the average per-vehicle fuel economy for new vehicles to 35.5 miles per gallon starting in 2016, a standard later boosted to 54.4 miles per gallon by 2025.[3] Not only will this finding by the EPA have a significant effect on the automobile industry, but it could lead to far-reaching regulations governing all industries that generate greenhouse gases. Not surprisingly, the agency's findings soon faced legal challenges by industries affected by the ruling.[4]

Once a new law is passed, the agency studies the legislation and proposes a set of rules to guide implementation. These proposed rules are then open to comment by anyone who wishes to weigh in. Representatives for the regulated industries and advocates of all sorts commonly submit comments. But anyone who wants to can go to www.regulations.gov to read proposed rules, enter his own comments, and view the comments of others. Once rules are approved, they are published in the *Federal Register* and have the force of law.

Bureaucrats Enforce Laws In addition to rule making, bureaucracies play an essential role in enforcing the laws. In doing so, bureaucracies exercise considerable power over private actors. For example, in 2013 the auto manufacturers Hyundai and Kia reached a settlement with the EPA after the agency, which monitors fuel economy tests for all vehicles sold in the United States, found that the companies overstated the mileage claims for their cars. Hyundai and Kia agreed to reimburse nearly 1 million customers for the shortfall in the fuel economy, totaling approximately $400 million.[5]

The Merit System: How to Become a Bureaucrat Public bureaucrats are rewarded with greater job security than employees of most private organizations. More than a century ago, the federal government attempted to imitate business by passing the Civil Service Act of 1883, which was followed by almost universal adoption of equivalent laws in state and local governments. These laws required that appointees to public office be qualified, as measured by competitive examinations, for the job to which they were appointed. This policy came to be called the **merit system**; its purpose was to put an end to political appointments under the "spoils system," when government jobs were given out based on political connections rather than merit. Under the old spoils system, presidents filled up to 200,000 federal jobs with political friends and supporters. In 1881, President James A. Garfield wrote, "My day is frittered away with the personal seeking of people when it ought to be given to the great problems which concern the whole country."[6] Ironically, the final push to enact civil service reform occurred when a frustrated office seeker shot and killed President Garfield in 1881. At the higher levels of government agencies, including such posts as cabinet secretaries and assistant secretaries, many jobs are filled with political appointees and are not part of the merit system.

As a further safeguard against political interference (and to compensate for the lower-than-average pay given to public employees), merit system employees—genuine civil servants—were given legal protection against being fired without a show of cause. Reasonable people may disagree about the value of such security and how far it should extend in the civil service, but the justifiable objective of this job protection (cleansing bureaucracy of political interference while upgrading performance) cannot be disputed.

The Size of the Federal Service Has Actually Declined

For decades, politicians from both parties have asserted that the federal government is too big. Ronald Reagan led the way with his 1981 statement that government was the problem, not the solution. Fifteen years later, President Bill Clinton abandoned the traditional Democratic defense of government, declaring that "the era of big government is over." President George W. Bush voiced similar sentiments when he accepted his party's nomination for president in 2000, proclaiming, "Big government is not the answer!" President Obama struck a different tone. Addressing Congress on the topic of health care reform, he noted that while Americans had a "healthy skepticism about government," they also believed that "hard work and responsibility should be rewarded by some measure of security and fair play," and he recognized "that sometimes government has to step in to help deliver that promise."[7] Despite fears of bureaucratic growth getting out of hand, however, the federal service has hardly grown at all during the past 35 years; it reached its peak postwar level in 1968 with 3.0 million civilian employees plus 3.6 million military personnel (a figure swollen by the war in Vietnam). The number of civilian federal employees has since fallen to less than 2.8 million in 2012; the number of military personnel totals 1.4 million.[8]

The growth of the federal service over the past 50 years is even less imposing when placed in the context of the total workforce and when compared with the size of state and local public employment. Figure 11.1 indicates that since 1950, the ratio of federal employment to the total workforce has in fact *declined* slightly in the past 60 years. Meanwhile, state and local employment has grown: in 1950 there were 4.3 million state and local civil service employees (about 6.5 percent

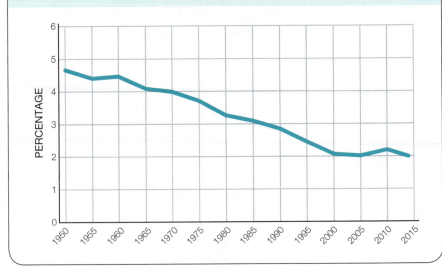

FIGURE 11.1 Employees in the Federal Service as a Percentage of the National Workforce, 1950–2014

Since 1950, the ratio of federal employment to the total workforce has gradually declined. Today federal employees make up less than 2 percent of the total workforce in the United States. Even at its height, federal employees made up less than 6 percent. What do these numbers suggest about the size of the federal government today?

NOTE: Employment numbers are for December of each year.
SOURCE: Bureau of Labor Statistics, http://bls.gov/webapps/legacy/cesbtab1.htm (accessed 3/20/14).

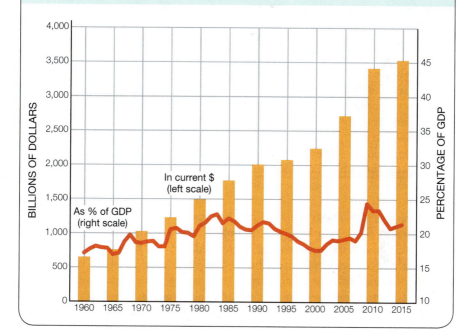

FIGURE 11.2 Annual Federal Outlays, 1960–2015*

As the bars in the figure indicate, when measured in dollars, federal government spending has gone up over time, from $423 billion in 1950 to over $3 trillion in 2013. (The amounts here are measured in constant 2009 dollars, which means the numbers have been adjusted for inflation.) But as the red line shows, federal spending as a percent of gross domestic product has moved up and down just slightly over time. Thus while government spending has grown, it has basically kept pace with the growing size of the U.S. economy.

*Data for 2014 and 2015 are estimated.
SOURCE: Office of Management and Budget, www.whitehouse.gov/omb/budget/historicals (accessed 3/20/14).

of the country's workforce). In 2011 there were close to 20 million state and local employees (nearly 14 percent of the nation's employed workforce).[9] Federal employment, in contrast, exceeded 6 percent of the workforce only during World War II, and almost all of that temporary growth was military.

Another useful comparison is illustrated in Figure 11.2. Although the dollar increase in federal spending shown by the bars looks impressive, the trend line indicating the relation of federal spending to the gross domestic product (GDP) remained close to what it had been in 1960. This changed in 2009, when the recession pushed spending up dramatically, as the federal government sought to stimulate the economy, and spending rose on other recession-related programs, such as unemployment insurance. After 2009 the budget also reflected the costs of the wars in Iraq and Afghanistan, which had not been included in the Bush administration's budgets.

In sum, the national government is indeed "very large," but it has not been growing any faster than the economy or society. The same is roughly true of the growth pattern of state and local public personnel. Bureaucracy keeps pace with society, despite people's seeming dislike of it, because the control towers, the prisons, the Social Security system, and other essential elements of modern-day society cannot be operated without bureaucracy.

The Executive Branch Is Organized Hierarchically

Cabinet departments, agencies, and bureaus are the operating parts of the bureaucratic whole. A **department** is the largest subunit of the executive branch. At the top is the head of the department, who in the United States is called the "secretary" of the department.[10] Below the secretary and the deputy secretary are the "undersecretaries" who have management responsibilities for one or more operating agencies. Those operating agencies are the most directly responsible for shaping the department's actual programs and are collectively and generally called the "bureau level." Each bureau-level agency usually operates under the statute adopted by Congress that set up the agency and gave it its authority and jurisdiction. The names of these bureau-level agencies are often quite well known to the public—the Forest Service and the Agricultural Research Service, for example. These are the so-called line agencies, or agencies that deal directly with the public. Each bureau or agency is, of course, subdivided into still other units, known as divisions, offices, or units—all are parts of the bureaucratic hierarchy.

Not all government agencies are part of cabinet departments. Some **independent agencies** are set up by Congress outside the departmental structure altogether, even though the president appoints and directs the heads of these agencies. Independent agencies usually have broad powers to provide public services that are either too expensive or too important to be left to private initiatives. Some examples of independent agencies are the National Aeronautics and Space Administration (NASA), the Central Intelligence Agency (CIA), and the EPA. **Government corporations** are a third type of government agency but are more like private businesses in performing and charging for a market service, such as transporting railroad passengers (Amtrak).

Yet a fourth type of agency is the independent regulatory commission, given broad discretion to make rules. The first regulatory agencies established by Congress, beginning with the Interstate Commerce Commission in 1887, were set up as independent regulatory commissions because Congress recognized that regulatory agencies are "mini-legislatures," whose rules are exactly the same as legislation but require the kind of expertise and full-time attention that is beyond the capacity of Congress. Until the 1960s most of the regulatory agencies that were set up by Congress, such as the Federal Trade Commission (1914) and the Federal Communications Commission (FCC; 1934), were independent regulatory commissions. But beginning in the late 1960s and the early 1970s, all new regulatory programs, with two or three exceptions (such as the Federal Election Commission), were placed within existing departments and made directly responsible to the president. The first new major regulatory agency established

Bureaucracy in Comparison

As one of the world's largest and most populous countries, the United States has a vast bureaucracy to run government programs and services. However, as a percentage of the labor force, the number of government employees in the United States is not especially high. As the first graph below shows, the size of government bureaucracies, relative to each country's work force, varies widely. For example, the Norwegian government employs roughly 30 percent of the labor force, whereas only around 6 percent of Japanese workers work for the government. We can also see differences in whether most government employees work at the national level or the subnational level in each country. In the United States, most government employees work at the state or local level, rather than the national level. In other countries like Italy or Turkey, most bureaucrats work for the national government. What do you think accounts for these differences? How does federalism influence American bureaucracy, and what differences do we see in countries like France that do not have federalist systems?

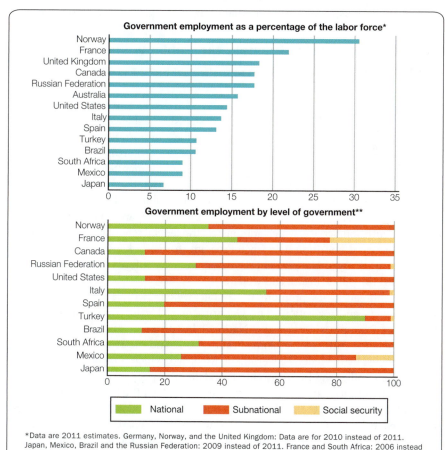

Government employment as a percentage of the labor force*

Norway, France, United Kingdom, Canada, Russian Federation, Australia, United States, Italy, Spain, Turkey, Brazil, South Africa, Mexico, Japan

Government employment by level of government**

Norway, France, Canada, Russian Federation, United States, Italy, Spain, Turkey, Brazil, South Africa, Mexico, Japan

National | Subnational | Social security

*Data are 2011 estimates. Germany, Norway, and the United Kingdom: Data are for 2010 instead of 2011. Japan, Mexico, Brazil and the Russian Federation: 2009 instead of 2011. France and South Africa: 2006 instead of 2011.

**Data are for 2011. Data on the United Kingdom and Australia are not available.

SOURCE: OECD, www.oecd-ilibrary.org/governance/government-at-a-glance-2013_gov_glance-2013-en (accessed 6/30/14).

in decades was approved by Congress in 2010 as part of the Dodd-Frank Wall Street Reform and Consumer Protection Act. The Consumer Financial Protection Bureau was created to protect consumers by carrying out federal consumer financial protection laws. It functions as an independent unit within the U.S. Federal Reserve.

● Federal Bureaucracies Promote Welfare and Security

Describe the major goals we expect federal agencies to promote

The different agencies of the executive branch can be classified into three main groups based on the services they provide to the American public. The first category of agencies provides services and products that seek to promote the public welfare. The second group provides services that help maintain a strong economy. The third group of agencies works to promote national security. Let us look more closely at what each set of agencies offers to the public.

Federal Bureaucracies Promote the Public Welfare

One of the most important activities of the federal bureaucracy is to promote the public welfare. Americans often think of government welfare as a single program that goes only to the very poor, but a number of federal agencies provide services, build infrastructure, and enact regulations designed to enhance the well-being of the vast majority of citizens. Departments that have important responsibilities for promoting the public welfare in this sense include the Department of Housing and Urban Development, the Department of Health and Human Services, the Department of Veterans' Affairs, the Department of the Interior, the Department of Education, and the Department of Labor. Ensuring the public welfare is also the main activity of agencies in other departments, such as the Department of Agriculture's Food and Nutrition Service, which administers the federal school lunch program and the Supplemental Nutrition Assistance Program (formerly known as food stamps). In addition, a variety of independent regulatory agencies enforce regulations that aim to safeguard the public health and welfare.

Federal bureaucracies promote the public welfare with a diverse set of services, products, and regulations. The Department of Health and Human Services (HHS), for example, oversees the National Institutes of Health (NIH), which is responsible for cutting-edge biomedical research, and the two major health programs provided by the federal government: Medicaid, which provides health care for low-income families and for many elderly and disabled people; and Medicare, which is the health insurance available to most elderly people in the United States.

A different notion of the public welfare, but one highly valued by most Americans, is provided by the National Park Service, under the Department of the Interior. Created in 1916, the National Park Service is responsible for the care and upkeep of national parks. Since the nineteenth century, Americans have seen protection of the natural environment as an important public goal and have looked to federal agencies to implement laws and administer programs that preserve natural areas and keep them open to the public.

The federal bureaucracy also promotes public welfare through the watchdog activities of many **regulatory agencies**—departments, bureaus, or independent agencies whose primary mission is to impose limits, restrictions, or other obligations on the conduct of individuals or companies in the private sector. These include the FDA within the Department of Health and Human Services, the Occupational Safety and Health Administration (OSHA) in the Department of Labor, and independent regulatory commissions, such as the FCC and the EPA. An agency or commission is regulatory if Congress delegates to it relatively broad powers over a sector of the economy or a type of commercial activity and authorizes it to make rules within that jurisdiction. Rules made by regulatory agencies have the force of law. (Figure 11.3 shows spending by selected regulatory agencies.)

Often working behind the scenes, these agencies seek to promote the welfare of all Americans. The EPA, for example, works to protect public health by ensuring the provision of clean and safe drinking water. Just as the agency sets standards to limit emissions from automobiles to protect the public from

The National Institutes of Health is an example of a federal bureaucracy that promotes the public welfare by conducting cutting-edge biomedical research. NIH research has helped doctors to treat diabetes and cardiovascular disease, among many other illnesses. This scientist is studying pancreatic beta cells, which play a role in diabetes.

air pollutants, as we saw earlier, the EPA also sets national water quality standards to protect against contaminants that may pose health risks. The safety standards apply to the more than 170,000 public water systems around the country that support our access to safe drinking water and are implemented by states, local governments, and water suppliers—all of which are overseen by the EPA to ensure compliance.[11] Unsafe drinking water may seem like a concern of less-developed countries, but in 2014 a chemical spill in West Virginia made the tap water undrinkable for some 300,000 people for weeks.

As we saw in Chapters 8 and 9, government agencies often develop close ties to the groups in society that they are supposed to regulate. This close political connection is known as an **iron triangle**: the stable, cooperative relationships that often develop among a congressional committee, an administrative agency, and one or more interest groups (see Figure 11.4). These relationships may push policies in a direction favorable to particular interests but inimical to the public interest.

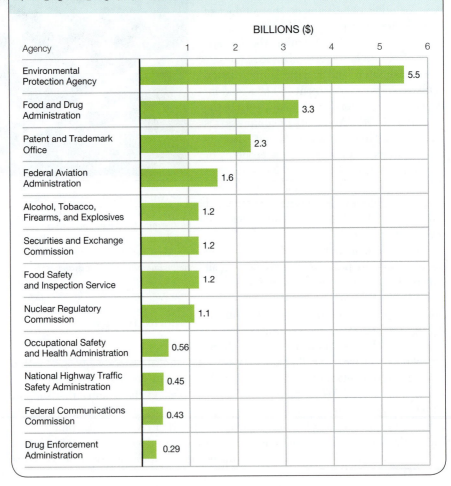

FIGURE 11.3 Spending on Regulation by Selected Agencies

One way bureaucratic agencies promote the public welfare is by regulating the activities of individuals or companies. There are costs and benets associated with regulation. Calculating the benets (in such terms as food-borne illnesses avoided or trafc accidents prevented) is difcult, but regulatory agencies' expenditures offer one way to look at costs. This gure shows the expenditures of selected agencies that regulate activities in a variety of areas. Do any of the data here surprise you, either because of how much or how little is spent by a certain agency?

SOURCE: Susan Dudley and Melinda Warren, http://regulatorystudies.columbian.gwu.edu/files/downloads/2014_Regulators_Budget.pdf (accessed 8/26/14).

BILLIONS ($)

Agency	Spending
Environmental Protection Agency	5.5
Food and Drug Administration	3.3
Patent and Trademark Office	2.3
Federal Aviation Administration	1.6
Alcohol, Tobacco, Firearms, and Explosives	1.2
Securities and Exchange Commission	1.2
Food Safety and Inspection Service	1.2
Nuclear Regulatory Commission	1.1
Occupational Safety and Health Administration	0.56
National Highway Traffic Safety Administration	0.45
Federal Communications Commission	0.43
Drug Enforcement Administration	0.29

Federal Agencies Provide for National Security

One of the remarkable features of American federalism is that the most vital agencies for providing security for the American people (namely, the police) are located in state and local governments. But some agencies vital to maintaining national security are located in the national government, and they can be grouped into two categories: (1) agencies to confront threats to internal national security and (2) agencies to

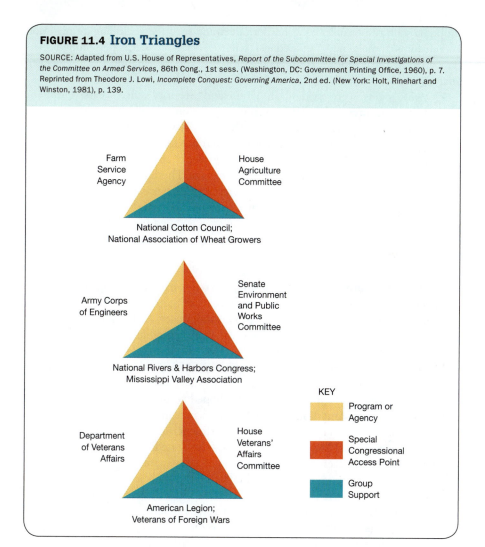

FIGURE 11.4 Iron Triangles

SOURCE: Adapted from U.S. House of Representatives, *Report of the Subcommittee for Special Investigations of the Committee on Armed Services*, 86th Cong., 1st sess. (Washington, DC: Government Printing Office, 1960), p. 7. Reprinted from Theodore J. Lowi, *Incomplete Conquest: Governing America*, 2nd ed. (New York: Holt, Rinehart and Winston, 1981), p. 139.

Farm Service Agency

House Agriculture Committee

National Cotton Council; National Association of Wheat Growers

Army Corps of Engineers

Senate Environment and Public Works Committee

National Rivers & Harbors Congress; Mississippi Valley Association

KEY

Program or Agency

Special Congressional Access Point

Group Support

Department of Veterans Affairs

House Veterans' Affairs Committee

American Legion; Veterans of Foreign Wars

defend American security from external threats. The departments of greatest influence in these two areas are Homeland Security, Justice, Defense, and State.

Agencies for Internal Security The task of maintaining domestic security changed dramatically after the terrorist attacks of September 11, 2001. The creation of the Department of Homeland Security (DHS) in late 2002 signaled the high priority that domestic security would now have. The orientation of domestic agencies shifted as well, as agencies geared up to prevent terrorism, a task that differed greatly from their former charge of investigating crime. With this shift in responsibility came broad new powers, many of them controversial—including the power to detain terrorist suspects and to engage in extensive domestic intelligence-gathering about possible terrorists. Since its creation, the Department of Homeland Security has also assumed a large role in domestic security, bringing under its umbrella such responsibilities as border safety and security (including immigration and customs); emergency preparedness; science-related concerns pertaining in particular to chemical, biological, and nuclear threats; and information and intelligence analysis and assessment.

Growing pains were evident in Homeland Security's first years. Different bureaucratic cultures, now part of a single operation, quickly became embroiled in turf battles with one another and with the FBI (which remained in the Justice Department) as the two departments attempted to sort out their respective responsibilities. These early problems signaled deeper challenges that the Department of Homeland Security has continued to face. The DHS has been unable to establish itself as a strong institutionally coherent presence capable of coordinating government action. Part of the problem is that the DHS portfolio of responsibilities is both large and vague. In addition, the agency failed to establish strong links with state and local agencies whose activities remain critical to its on-the-ground capabilities.

Agencies for External National Security Two departments occupy center stage in maintaining national security: the departments of State and Defense.

The State Department's primary mission is diplomacy. As the most visible public representative of American diplomacy, the secretary of state works to promote American perspectives and interests in the world. For example, in 2013, Secretary of State John Kerry made a closely watched stop in Egypt, the first visit by a high-ranking American official since a coup by the Egyptian military deposed the country's first democratically elected president. Kerry hoped to defuse anti-American sentiment and underscore American support for democracy in that country. Although diplomacy is the primary task of the State Department, diplomatic missions are only one of its organizational dimensions. As of 2014 the State Department also included 35 bureau-level units, each under the direction of an assistant secretary.

These bureaus support the responsibilities of the elite foreign service officers (FSOs), who staff U.S. embassies around the world and who hold almost all the most powerful positions in the department below the rank of ambassador.[12] The ambassadorial positions, especially the plum positions in the major capitals of the world, are filled by presidential appointees, many of whom get their positions by having been important donors to victorious political campaigns.

Despite the importance of the State Department in foreign affairs, fewer than 20 percent of all U.S. government employees working abroad are directly under its authority. By far the largest number of career government professionals working abroad are under the authority of the Defense Department. In 2002 the Defense Department created the U.S. Northern Command, a regional command charged with ensuring homeland defense, directing military operations inside the nation's borders, and providing emergency backup to state and local governments, which are the first responders to any security disaster. The creation of a regional command within the United States was an unprecedented move, breaching a long-standing line between domestic law enforcement and foreign military operations.

As the creation of a military capacity within the United States suggests, addressing the threat of terrorism calls for greater coordination of internal and external security. In 2004 the National Commission on Terrorist Attacks upon the United States (the

9/11 Commission) issued a widely read report that called for a major reorganization of bureaucratic responsibilities for internal and external security. The report revealed that different departments of the American government had information that, if handled properly, might have prevented the attacks of September 11, 2001.

The 9/11 Commission's work prompted a major reorganization of the fragmented intelligence community. In 2005 a new office, the Director of National Intelligence (DNI), took over responsibility for coordinating the efforts of the 16 different agencies that gather intelligence. The DNI reports directly to the president each morning.

National Security and Democracy Of all the agencies in the federal bureaucracy, those charged with providing national security most often come into conflict with the norms and expectations of American democracy. Two issues in particular arise as these agencies work to ensure national security: (1) the trade-offs between respecting the personal rights of individuals versus protecting the general public, and (2) the need for secrecy in matters of national security versus the public's right to know what the government is doing.

Protecting national security often requires the government to conduct its activities in secret. Yet, as Americans have come to expect a more open government in the past three decades, many believe that federal agencies charged with national security keep too many secrets from the American public. As one critic put it, "the United States government must rest, in the words of the Declaration of Independence, on 'the consent of the governed.' And there can be no meaningful consent where those who are governed do not know to what they are consenting."[13] The effort to make information related to national security more available to the public began in 1966 with the passage of the Freedom of Information Act (FOIA). The information obtained through FOIA often reveals unflattering or unsuccessful aspects of national security activities. One private organization, the National Security Archive, makes extensive use of FOIA to obtain information about the activities of national security agencies. For example, the organization's website contains "The Torture Archive," a searchable database of documents related to the detention of individuals in the war on terrorism and the authorized use of torture by the American government.

The tension between secrecy and democracy has sharpened dramatically with the threat of terrorism. FOIA has been curtailed, and the range of information deemed sensitive has greatly expanded. President George W. Bush defended the new secrecy, declaring, "We're an open society, but we're at war. Foreign terrorists and agents must never again be allowed to use our freedoms against us." Although most Americans agreed that enhanced secrecy was needed to ensure domestic security, concerns about excessive secrecy mounted. Some analysts worried that secrecy would prevent Congress from carrying out its basic oversight responsibilities. They also claimed that much of the secrecy had nothing to do with national security. The day after President Obama's election, he implemented an Open Government Directive. He also instructed federal agencies that they should administer FOIA liberally: when in doubt, err on the side of openness. And in the most substantive change, Obama issued an executive order designed to promote more rapid declassification of secret documents.

The U.S. media have used Freedom of Information Act requests to obtain important information, such as federal drug safety reports and conditions at local jails. Americans are likely to always debate just how much secrecy their government is entitled to.

However, the Obama administration also continued some of the secrecy practices initiated in the Bush years. Most notably, it invoked the state secrets privilege to prevent lawsuits related to warrantless wiretapping and torture from going to trial.[14] Massive leaks of sensitive national security documents by national security contractor Edward Snowden in 2013 exposed the extent, and potential illegality, of the National Security Agency's (NSA) global surveillance operations. They showed that the NSA was collecting private data on millions of Americans and foreign nationals, including the tracking of phone calls, email messages, web browser history, and personal contacts. The revelations prompted outrage at home and abroad.[15]

Federal Bureaucracies Help to Maintain a Strong National Economy

In our capitalist economic system, the government does not directly run the economy. Yet many federal government activities are critical to maintaining a strong economy. Foremost among these are the agencies that are responsible for fiscal and monetary policy. Other agencies, such as the Internal Revenue Service (IRS), collect private resources into federal funds for public purposes. Tax policy may also strengthen the economy through decisions about whom to tax, how much, and when. Finally, the federal government, through such agencies as the Department of Transportation, the Commerce Department, and the Energy Department, may directly provide services or goods that bolster the economy.

Fiscal and Monetary Agencies Fiscal policy—the government's use of taxing, monetary, and spending powers to manipulate the economy—can refer to any government policy having to do with public finance. However, Americans often reserve the word *fiscal* for taxing and spending policies and use the term *monetary* for policies having to do with banks, credit, and currency.

While the responsibility for making fiscal policy lies with Congress, the administration of fiscal policy occurs primarily in the Treasury Department. In addition to collecting income, corporate, and other taxes, the Treasury manages the national debt—over $17 trillion in 2014.[16] The Treasury Department is also responsible for printing the U.S. currency, but currency represents only a tiny proportion of the entire money economy. Most of the trillions of dollars used in the transactions of the private and public sectors of the U.S. economy exist in computerized accounts rather than actual currency.

A key monetary agency is the **Federal Reserve System**, a system of 12 Federal Reserve banks, headed by the Federal Reserve Board, that facilitates exchanges of cash, checks, and credit; regulates member banks; and uses monetary policies to fight inflation and deflation. The Federal Reserve System (called simply the Fed) has authority over the interest rates and lending activities of the nation's most important banks. Congress established the Fed in 1913 as a clearinghouse responsible for adjusting the supply of money and credit to the needs of commerce and industry in different regions of the country. The Fed is also responsible for ensuring that banks do not overextend themselves, a policy that guards against bank failures during a sudden economic scare, such as occurred in 1929 and again in 2008. The Treasury and the Federal Reserve took center stage in 2008 when a string of bank failures threatened economic catastrophe. These agencies designed a $700 billion bailout package and persuaded Congress that a rapid response was needed to avert a worldwide depression. Although the Treasury and the Federal Reserve sprang into action when economic calamity loomed, critics charged that the crisis could have been prevented if these agencies had exercised more regulatory oversight over the financial sector during the previous decade. In 2010, Congress and the president created the Financial Stability Oversight Council to indentify system-wide risks to the financial sector. The financial industry has kept a close eye on these developments, aiming to limit the regulatory reach of the new council.[17]

Revenue Agencies Revenue agencies are responsible for collecting taxes. Examples include the Bureau of Alcohol, Tobacco, Firearms and Explosives, for collection of taxes on the sales of those particular products, and federal customs agents (part of the DHS), who oversee the collection of taxes on imports at every U.S. seaport and international airport. But far and away the most important of the revenue agencies is the Internal Revenue Service (IRS), which collects income taxes.

The IRS is the government agency that Americans love to hate. As one expert put it, "Probably no organization in the country, public or private, creates as much clientele *dis*favor as the Internal Revenue Service. The very nature of its work brings it into an adversarial relationship with vast numbers of Americans every year [emphasis added]."[18] Taxpayers complain about the IRS's needless complexity, its lack of sensitivity and responsiveness to individual taxpayers, and its overall lack of efficiency. Such complaints led Congress to pass the IRS Restructuring and Reform Act of 1998, which instituted a number of new protections for taxpayers.

● Several Forces Control Bureaucracy

Explain why it is often difficult to control the bureaucracy

By their very nature, bureaucracies pose challenges to democratic governance. Although they provide the expertise needed to implement the public will, they can also become entrenched organizations that serve their own interests. The task is neither to retreat from bureaucracy nor to attack it, but to take advantage of its strengths while making it more accountable to the demands of democratic politics and representative government.

We must return to James Madison's observation: "You must first enable the government to control the governed; and in the next place oblige it to control itself."[19] Today the problem is the same, only now the process has a name: administrative accountability. Accountability implies that some higher authority will guide and judge the actions of the bureaucracy. The highest authority in a democracy is *demos* ("the people"), and the guidance for bureaucratic action is the popular will. But that ideal of accountability must be translated into practical terms by the president and the Congress.

The President as Chief Executive Can Direct Agencies

In 1937, President Franklin Roosevelt's Committee on Administrative Management officially addressed a plea that had been growing increasingly urgent: "The president needs help." The national government had grown rapidly during the preceding 25 years, but the structures and procedures necessary to manage the burgeoning executive branch had not yet been established. The response to the call for "help" for the president initially took the form of three management policies: (1) all communications and decisions that related to executive policy decisions must pass through the White House; (2) in order to cope with such a flow, the White House must have adequate staffs of specialists in research, analysis, legislative and legal writing, and public affairs; and (3) the White House must have additional staff to ensure that presidential decisions are made, communicated to Congress, and carried out by the appropriate agency.

Making the Managerial Presidency The story of the modern presidency can be told largely as a series of responses to the plea for managerial help. Indeed, each expansion of the national government into new policies and programs in the twentieth and twenty-first centuries has been accompanied by a parallel expansion of the president's management authority.[20]

President Jimmy Carter, in particular, was probably more preoccupied with administrative reform and reorganization than any other twentieth-century president. His reorganization of the civil service will long be recognized as one of the most significant contributions of his presidency. The Civil Service Reform Act of 1978 was the first major revamping of the federal civil service since its creation in 1883. The 1978 act created the Merit Systems Protection Board (MSPB) to defend competitive merit recruitment and promotion from political encroachment. A separate Federal Labor Relations Authority (FLRA) was set up to administer collective bargaining and individual personnel grievances. The third new agency, the Office of Personnel Management (OPM), was created to manage recruiting, testing, training, and the retirement system. The Senior Executive Service—a top management rank for civil servants—was also created at this time to recognize and foster "public management" as a profession and to facilitate the movement of top, "supergrade" career officials across agencies and departments.[21]

Carter also tried to impose a stringent budgetary process on all executive agencies. Called "zero-base budgeting," it was a method of budgeting from the bottom up, wherein each agency was required to rejustify its entire mission rather than merely its increase for the next year. Zero-base budgeting did not succeed, but the effort was not lost on President Reagan. From Carter's "bottom-up" approach, Reagan went to a "top-down" approach, whereby the initial budgetary decisions would be made in the White House and the agencies would be required to abide by those decisions. This process converted the Office of Management and Budget (OMB) into an agency of policy determination and presidential management.[22] President George H. W. Bush took Reagan's centralization strategy even further in using the White House staff instead of cabinet secretaries for managing the executive branch.[23]

President Clinton engaged in the most systematic effort to "change the way the government does business," a phrase he used often to describe the goal of his National Performance Review (NPR), one of the most important administrative reform efforts of the twentieth century. President Clinton launched the NPR to make the federal bureaucracy more efficient, accountable, and effective. The NPR sought to prod federal agencies into adopting flexible, goal-driven practices. Clinton promised that the result would be a government that would "work better and cost less." Virtually all observers agreed that the NPR made substantial progress. Its original goal was to save more than $100 billion over five years, in large part by cutting the federal workforce by 12 percent (more than 270,000 jobs) by the end of 1999. By the end of 2000, $136 billion in savings was achieved, and the federal workforce had been cut by 426,200.[24]

Like his predecessors, George W. Bush pursued a strategy different from those of previous presidents, dismantling Clinton's NPR and favoring **privatization**—the transfer of all or part of a program from the public sector to the private sector. Bush was the first president with a degree in business, and his management strategy followed a standard business school dictum: select skilled subordinates and delegate responsibility to them. Bush followed this model closely in his appointment of highly experienced officials to cabinet positions and in his selection of Dick Cheney for vice president. But critics contended that the Bush administration's distrust of the bureaucracy led it to exercise inappropriate political control.

Since Obama took office, his administration has sought to reinvigorate federal agencies, which reflects the Democrats' greater support for strong government institutions. Obama's approach to the managerial presidency features a deep belief

In recent decades there have been several attempts to "reinvent" government. In 1993, President Bill Clinton and Vice President Al Gore established the National Performance Review to reinvent government. Gore promoted this on David Letterman's show, where he railed against the government's procurement requirements, which even specified the number of pieces into which a government ashtray may shatter.

in the importance of scientific expertise in government service. The president's appointees to head key regulatory agencies, including the EPA, OSHA, and the FDA, reflect this conviction. Some of the new agency leaders are well-known academic experts.

Congress Promotes Responsible Bureaucracy

Congress is constitutionally essential to responsible bureaucracy because the key to bureaucratic responsibility is legislation. When a law is passed and its intent is clear, the accountability for implementation of that law is also clear. Then the president knows what to "faithfully execute," and the responsible agency understands what is expected of it. But when Congress enacts vague legislation, agencies must resort to their own interpretations. The president and the federal courts often step in to tell agencies what the legislation intended. And so do interest groups. Yet when everybody, from president to courts to interest groups, gets involved in the actual interpretation of legislative intent, to whom and to what is the agency accountable?

Congress's answer is **oversight**—the effort by Congress, through hearings, investigations, and other techniques, to exercise control over the activities of executive agencies. The more power Congress has delegated to the executive, the more it has sought to reinvolve itself in directing the interpretation of laws through committee and subcommittee oversight of each agency. The standing committee system in Congress is well suited for oversight, inasmuch as most of the congressional committees and subcommittees have jurisdictions roughly parallel to one or more departments and agencies, and members of Congress who sit on these committees can develop expertise equal to that of the bureaucrats.

The most visible indication of Congress's oversight efforts is the use of public hearings, before which bureaucrats and other witnesses are summoned to discuss and defend agency budgets and past decisions. In 2013 and 2014, for example, Congress held high-profile hearings on topics as diverse as the attack on the American mission in Benghazi, Libya; reform of the Postal Service; and security concerns about the Department of Health and Human Services' new Healthcare.gov website.

The data drawn from studies of congressional committee and subcommittee hearings and meetings show quite dramatically that Congress has tried through oversight to keep pace with the expansion of the executive branch. The annual number of oversight hearings has grown over time as the bureaucracy has expanded. Oversight hearings in both the Senate and the House increased dramatically in the 1970s, in the aftermath of the Watergate scandal. In recent years, oversight has become a topic of substantial political concern. After the Republicans took over Congress in 1995, they concentrated their oversight power on investigating scandal. When George W. Bush became president in 2001, congressional oversight virtually disappeared. In the words of the congressional scholars Thomas Mann and Norman Ornstein, Republican members of Congress saw "themselves as field lieutenants in the president's army far more than they [did] as members of a separate and independent branch of government."[25] In Mann and Ornstein's view, Congress's failure to exercise its oversight role led to poor government performance and bureaucracies that were not accountable to the American people. After winning back Congress in 2006, the Democrats revived the oversight role, holding hearings on such issues as the use of government contractors in the Iraq and Afghanistan wars and the Troubled Asset Relief Program (TARP), which was instituted to help bail out the banks in 2008. When Republicans took control of the House in 2010, oversight hearings focused on the Democratic administration's programs, such as the Consumer Financial Protection Bureau, and in 2013 hearings focused on the troubled rollout of the Affordable Care Act.

In addition, Congress has created for itself three large agencies whose obligations are to engage in constant research on problems taking place in or confronted by

After a shooting at the Washington Navy Yard in 2013, the Senate Homeland Security and Governmental Affairs Committee interviewed administrators from several agencies on procedures for government clearances and background checks.

the executive branch. These are the Government Accountability Office (GAO), the Congressional Research Service (CRS), and the Congressional Budget Office (CBO). Each of these agencies is designed to give Congress information independent of the information it can get directly from the executive branch through hearings and other communications.[26] Another source of information for oversight comes directly from citizens through FOIA, which, as we have seen, gives ordinary citizens the right of access to agency files and agency data.

Can the Bureaucracy Be Reformed?

When citizens complain that government is too bureaucratic, what they often mean is that government bureaucracies seem inefficient and waste money. Do these frustrations mean that bureaucracy needs to be reformed? In a sense, bureaucracy is always in need of reform. Yet, reforms may be more difficult to implement in the public sector because the government is held to much higher standards of accountability than are private companies. The government has sought to find various ways to make the federal bureaucracy more efficient. The key strategies used to promote reform include termination, devolution, and privatization. In general, Democratic administrations have aimed to make the existing bureaucracy work more effectively, whereas Republican administrations have sought to sideline the bureaucracy, especially by contracting out government work to private companies.

The only *certain* way to reduce the size of the bureaucracy is to eliminate programs. But termination is extraordinarily difficult. Even in the 12 years of the Reagan and George H. W. Bush administrations, both of which proclaimed a strong commitment to the reduction of the national government, not a single national government agency or program was terminated. In the 1990s, Republicans did succeed in eliminating two small agencies.

The next most effective approach to genuinely reducing the size of the federal bureaucracy is **devolution**, downsizing the federal bureaucracy by delegating the implementation of programs to state and local governments. Often the central aim of devolution is to provide more efficient and flexible government services. Yet by its very nature, devolution entails variation across the states. Up to a point, variation can be considered one of the virtues of federalism. But in a democracy, it is inherently dangerous to have large variations in the provision of services and benefits.

Privatization simply means that a formerly public activity is picked up under contract by a private company or companies. But such programs are still very much government programs—paid for by government and supervised by government. Privatization downsizes the government only in that the workers providing the service are no longer counted as part of the government bureaucracy. When private contractors can perform a task as well as government can but for less money, taxpayers win. But private firms are not necessarily more efficient or less costly than government, especially when there is little competition among private firms and when public bureaucracies are not granted a fair chance to bid in the contracting competition. In addition, concerns about adequate government oversight and accountability of private contractors have escalated as the scale of contracting has dramatically increased. Congress and presidents have reacted to these concerns in several ways, but conducting adequate oversight of contractors remains a challenge.

Bureaucracy, Democracy,
and Your Future

Reconciling bureaucracy and democracy requires clear rules and laws, maximum openness in agency decisions, clear rationales for those decisions, and accessible means for questioning and appealing those decisions. One important way for Congress to ensure accountability of the bureaucracy is for Congress to spend more time clarifying its legislative intent. Bureaucrats are more responsive to clear legislative guidance than to anything else, and when Congress and the president are at odds about the interpretation of laws, bureaucrats can evade responsibility by playing off one branch against another. Moreover, clearer laws from Congress and clearer rules and decisions made by administrative agencies would reduce the need for courts to review those laws and decisions, which is expensive and time consuming. Adequate congressional oversight is also important because a bureaucracy that is shielded from the public eye may wind up pursuing its own interests or those of narrowly focused private interests rather than those of the public.

The emergence of "big data" is likely to change the way bureaucracies operate in the future. Big data refers to huge data sets that compile information on a wide range of topics including climate, traffic, and health and the NSA's massive database of phone calls and use of social media. Big data has the potential to improve government performance by linking sources of information that were previously unconnected. It also allows the government to analyze information that was stored as text or went uncollected. Advances in government's ability to implement programs in public health, food safety, and transportation are only the beginning of what big data promises. At the same time, however, big data poses a threat to individual privacy, as the revelations about the NSA's data suggest. As bureaucracies tap into the promise of big data to create more effective programs, a close public eye on the implications for the right to privacy will be needed. How might big data improve the government's delivery of services in the future? What additional safeguards might be needed to protect individuals' privacy?

plug**in**

Inform

Learn about the role of the American bureaucracy at www.ushistory.org/gov/8.asp.

Express

Identify three federal or state bureaucratic institutions that have directly affected your life—such as the DMV, the IRS, the FAA, the FDA, or any of the other agencies mentioned in this chapter. Write a couple of sentences about your interaction with each agency and whether it performed its role well in your experience.

Connect

Find at least one federal agency's Facebook page, and see what types of information members of the bureaucracy are posting. Consider posting a response if the rules and regulations being discussed affect you.

Act

Share information from a federal agency's website, such as the Department of Education's Federal Student Aid page or the Department of Justice's FOIA page, with friends or classmates, along with your thoughts on why it is important.

studyguide

Practice Quiz

1. What task must bureaucrats perform if Congress charges them with enforcing a law through detailed directions? *(p. 344)*
   a) constitutional revisions
   b) implementation
   c) interpretation
   d) lawmaking
   e) quasi-judicial decision making

2. Which of the following best describes the growth of the federal service in the past 35 years? *(p. 346)*
   a) rampant, exponential growth
   b) little growth to slight decline
   c) There are nearly half as many federal employees as 35 years ago.
   d) vast, compared to the growth of the economy and the society
   e) The federal service has been eliminated in favor of more state government employees.

3. The Civil Service Act of 1883 mandated that appointees to public office *(p. 345)*
   a) pledge an oath of loyalty to the United States.
   b) be qualified for the job to which they are appointed.
   c) not belong to any political party.
   d) cannot be fired for any reason.
   e) cannot serve more than 4 years.

4. Which of the following is an example of a government corporation? *(p. 348)*
   a) National Aeronautics and Space Administration
   b) National Science Foundation
   c) Social Security Administration
   d) Amtrak
   e) Federal Express

5. A stable relationship between a bureaucratic agency, a clientele group, and a legislative committee is called *(p. 351)*
   a) a standing committee.
   b) a conference committee.

   c) a cabinet.
   d) an issue network.
   e) an iron triangle.

6. The State Department's primary mission is *(p. 354)*
   a) gathering intelligence.
   b) unifying the nation's military departments.
   c) engaging in diplomacy.
   d) investigating terrorism.
   e) overseeing domestic security efforts.

7. Which of the following is true regarding the Freedom of Information Act (FOIA)? *(pp. 355–56)*
   a) It was passed following the September 11, 2001 terrorist attacks.
   b) It grew out of the Open Government Directive.
   c) The range of information deemed sensitive has been heavily reduced since the year 2000.
   d) The range of information deemed sensitive has been greatly expanded since the year 2000.
   e) It enabled lawsuits related to warrantless wiretapping and torture to go to trial.

8. Americans refer to government policy about banks, credit, and currency as *(p. 357)*
   a) monetary policy.
   b) deficit policy.
   c) fiscal policy.
   d) interstate commerce policy.
   e) regulatory policy.

9. Which of the following is an example of a revenue agency? *(p. 357)*
   a) the OMB
   b) the Financial Stability Oversight Council
   c) the Fed
   d) the IRS
   e) the Commerce Department

10. Which president instituted the bureaucratic reform of the National Performance Review? *(p. 359)*
    a) Richard Nixon
    b) Lyndon Johnson
    c) Jimmy Carter
    d) Bill Clinton
    e) George W. Bush

11. The concept of *oversight* refers to the effort made by *(pp. 360–61)*
    a) Congress to make executive agencies accountable for their actions.
    b) the president to make executive agencies accountable for their actions.
    c) the president to make Congress accountable for its actions.
    d) the courts to make executive agencies responsible for their actions.
    e) the states to make the executive branch accountable for its actions.

12. *Devolution* refers to *(p. 362)*
    a) the gradual decline in efficiency that always comes when government begins to implement a new program.
    b) moving all or part of a program from the public sector to the private sector.
    c) a policy of reducing or eliminating regulatory restraints on the conduct of individuals or private institutions.
    d) a policy to remove a program from one level of government by passing it down to a lower level of government.
    e) reducing the overall number of regulatory agencies in the federal bureaucracy.

Key Terms

bureaucracy *(p. 343)* the complex structure of offices, tasks, rules, and principles of organization that are employed by all large-scale institutions to coordinate effectively the work of their personnel

department *(p. 348)* the largest subunit of the executive branch. The secretaries of the 15 departments form the Cabinet

devolution *(p. 362)* a policy to remove a program from one level of government by delegating it or passing it down to a lower level of government, such as from the national government to the state and local governments

Federal Reserve System *(p. 357)* a system of 12 Federal Reserve banks that facilitates exchanges of cash, checks, and credit; regulates member banks; and uses monetary policies to fight inflation and deflation

fiscal policy *(p. 357)* the government's use of taxing, monetary, and spending powers to manipulate the economy

government corporation *(p. 348)* government agency that performs a service normally provided by the private sector

implementation *(p. 344)* the efforts of departments and agencies to translate laws into specific bureaucratic rules and actions

independent agency *(p. 348)* agency that is not part of a cabinet department

iron triangle *(p. 351)* the stable, cooperative relationships that often develop among a congressional committee, an administrative agency, and one or more supportive interest groups; not all of these relationships are triangular, but the iron triangle is the most typical

merit system *(p. 345)* a product of civil service reform, in which appointees to positions in public bureaucracies must objectively be deemed qualified for those positions

oversight *(p. 360)* the effort by Congress, through hearings, investigations, and other techniques, to exercise control over the activities of executive agencies

privatization *(p. 359)* the transfer of all or part of a program from the public sector to the private sector

regulatory agency *(p. 351)* a department, bureau, or independent agency whose primary mission is to impose limits, restrictions, or other obligations on the conduct of individuals or companies in the private sector

revenue agency *(p. 357)* an agency responsible for collecting taxes; examples include the Internal Revenue Service for income taxes, the U.S. Customs Service for tariffs and other taxes on imported goods, and the Bureau of Alcohol, Tobacco, Firearms and Explosives for collection of taxes on the sales of those particular products

For Further Reading

Arnold, Peri E. *Making the Managerial Presidency: Comprehensive Organization Planning.* Princeton, NJ: Princeton University Press, 1986.

Gormley, William, and Stephen Balla. *Bureaucracy and Democracy: Accountability and Performance.* 3rd ed. Washington, DC: CQ Press, 2012.

Kettl, Donald F. *The Politics of the Administrative Process.* 5th ed. Washington, DC: CQ Press, 2011.

Kettl, Donald F. *System Under Stress: The Challenge to 21st Century Governance.* 3rd ed. Los Angeles: Sage/CQ Press, 2014.

Light, Paul C. *A Government Ill Executed: The Decline of the Federal Service and How to Reverse It.* Cambridge, MA: Harvard University Press, 2008.

Lowi, Theodore J. *The End of Liberalism.* New York: W. W. Norton, 1979.

Skowronek, Stephen. *Building a New American State: The Expansion of National Administrative Capacities, 1877–1920.* New York: Cambridge University Press, 1982.

Verkuil, Paul. *Outsourcing Sovereignty: Why Privatization of Government Functions Threatens Democracy and What We Can Do about It.* New York: Cambridge University Press, 2007.

Weiner, Tom. *Legacy of Ashes: The History of the CIA.* New York: Doubleday, 2007.

Wildavsky, Aaron, and Naomi Caiden. *The New Politics of the Budgetary Process.* New York: Longman, 2003.

Wood, B. Dan. *Bureaucratic Dynamics: The Role of Bureaucracy in a Democracy.* Boulder, CO: Westview, 1994.

The Supreme Court is America's highest court. Although the Court is often viewed as the least political of the three branches, its rulings touch on major political issues and affect ordinary Americans in many ways, from health care to immigration to free speech.

The Federal Courts

WHAT GOVERNMENT DOES AND WHY IT MATTERS The Supreme Court sits at the top of the judicial branch of the U.S. federal government. Many Americans view the Supreme Court as aloof and apolitical, because unlike the president and members of Congress, the judges who sit on the Supreme Court are appointed, not elected. Thus they do not need to raise money or campaign the way that politicians do. But the issues that the Supreme Court decides are often as political as those voted on in the House and Senate, and the Supreme Court is often asked to hear questions that touch the lives of ordinary Americans, including students, in a very direct and meaningful way. One recent example is the 2007 case of *Morse v. Frederick*.[1] This case dealt with the policies of Juneau-Douglas High School in Juneau, Alaska. In 2002 the Olympic torch relay passed through Juneau on its way to Salt Lake City for the opening of the Winter Olympics. As the torch passed Juneau-Douglas High, a senior, Joseph Frederick, unfurled a banner that read, "Bong Hits 4 Jesus." The school's principal promptly suspended Frederick, who then brought suit for reinstatement, alleging that his free speech rights had been violated (see Chapter 4).[2]

Like most of America's public schools, Juneau-Douglas High prohibits on school grounds any assemblies or expressions that advocate illegal drug use. Civil libertarians see such policies as restricting students' right to free speech—a right that has been recognized by the Supreme Court since a 1969 case in which it ruled that an Iowa public school could not prohibit students from wearing antiwar armbands. Unfortunately for Joseph Frederick, today's Supreme Court is more conservative than its 1969 counterpart. Speaking for the Court's majority, Chief Justice John Roberts said that the First Amendment did not require schools to permit students to advocate illegal drug use. This decision affected not only Joseph Frederick but millions of other students whose views might be seen as inappropriate by school administrators. Far from being a remote institution, the Supreme Court turns out to have reached into every public school in America.

Unlike the two branches of government examined in Chapters 10 and 11, the courts are fundamentally undemocratic: their members are not elected (Supreme Court members serve for "lifetime during good behavior") and they are therefore insulated from public pressures. That does not mean that politics has no effect on court decisions—far from it. In addition, both Congress and the president have a hand in making law; judges can affect the meaning of law only through interpretation. That power, however, is an important one, as examples in this chapter will demonstrate. The courts not only interpret the laws passed by Congress and the decisions of presidents when challenges arise but also interpret and apply fundamental rights.

chaptergoals

- Identify the general types of cases and types of courts in our legal system (pp. 371–75)

- Describe the different levels of federal courts and their functions (pp. 375–80)

- Explain how the Supreme Court exercises the power of judicial review (pp. 380–84)

- Describe the process the Supreme Court follows in the exercise of its power of judicial review (pp. 384–90)

- Consider the personal and political influences on judges and the courts (pp. 391–94)

● The Legal System Settles Disputes

Originally, a "court" was the place where a sovereign ruled—where the king or queen governed. Settling disputes between citizens was part of governing. In modern democracies, courts and judges have taken over from monarchs the power to resolve disputes by hearing the facts on both sides and deciding which side possesses greater merit. But since judges are not monarchs, they must have a basis for their authority. That basis in the United States is the Constitution and the law. Courts decide cases by hearing the facts on both sides of a quarrel and applying the relevant law or principle to the facts.

Court Cases Proceed under Criminal and Civil Law

Court cases in the United States proceed under two broad categories of law: criminal law and civil law.

Cases of **criminal law** deal with disputes or actions involving criminal penalties. Criminal law regulates the conduct of individuals, defines crimes, and specifies punishment for criminal acts. The government charges an individual with violating a statute (a law) that has been enacted to protect the public health, safety, morals, or welfare. In criminal cases, the government is always the **plaintiff** (the individual or organization that brings a complaint in court) and alleges that a criminal violation has been committed by a named **defendant** (the one against whom a complaint is brought in a criminal or civil case). Most criminal cases arise in state and

In criminal cases, the government charges an individual with violating a statute protecting health, safety, morals, or welfare. Most such cases arise in state and municipal courts. Here, an Illinois county court hears testimony in a murder case.

municipal courts and involve matters ranging from traffic offenses to robbery and murder. While the great bulk of criminal law is still a state matter, a large and growing body of federal criminal law deals with infringements from tax evasion and mail fraud to acts of terrorism and the sale of narcotics. Defendants found guilty of criminal violations may be fined or sent to prison.

Cases of **civil law** involve disputes among individuals or between individuals and the government that do not involve criminal penalties. Unlike criminal cases, the losers in civil cases cannot be fined or sent to prison, although they may be required to pay monetary damages for their actions. In a civil case, the one who brings a complaint is the plaintiff and the one against whom the complaint is brought is the defendant. The two most common types of civil cases involve contracts and torts. In a typical contract case, an individual or a corporation charges that it has suffered because of another's violation of a specific agreement between the two. For example, the Smith Manufacturing Corporation may charge that Jones Distributors failed to honor an agreement to deliver raw materials at a specified time, causing Smith to lose business. Smith asks the court to order Jones to compensate it for the damage it allegedly suffered. In a typical tort case, one individual charges that he or she has been injured by another's negligence or malfeasance. Medical malpractice suits are one example of tort cases. Another important area of civil law is administrative law, which involves disputes over the jurisdiction, procedures, or authority of administrative agencies. A plaintiff may assert, for example, that an agency did not follow proper procedures when issuing new rules and regulations. A court will then examine the agency's conduct in light of the Administrative Procedure Act, the legislation that governs agency rule making.

In deciding cases, courts apply statutes (laws) and legal **precedents** (prior cases whose principles are used by judges as the basis for their decisions in present cases). State and federal statutes, for example, often govern the conditions under which contracts are and are not legally binding. Jones Distributors might argue that it was not obliged to fulfill its contract with the Smith Manufacturing Corporation because actions by Smith, such as the failure to make promised payments, constituted fraud under state law. Attorneys for a physician being sued for malpractice, meanwhile, may search for prior instances in which courts ruled that actions similar to those of their client did not constitute negligence. Such precedents are applied under the doctrine of **stare decisis**, a Latin phrase meaning "let the decision stand." It is the doctrine that a previous decision by a court applies as a precedent in similar cases until that decision is overruled.

Types of Courts Include Trial, Appellate, and Supreme

In the United States, systems of courts have been established both by the federal government and by the governments of the individual states. Both systems have several levels, as shown in Figure 12.1. More than 99 percent of all court cases in the United States are heard in state courts. The overwhelming majority of criminal cases, for example, involve violations of state laws prohibiting such actions as murder, robbery, fraud, theft, and assault. If such a case is brought to trial, it will be heard in a state **trial court** (the first court to hear a criminal or civil case), in front of a judge and sometimes a jury, who will determine whether the defendant violated state law. If the

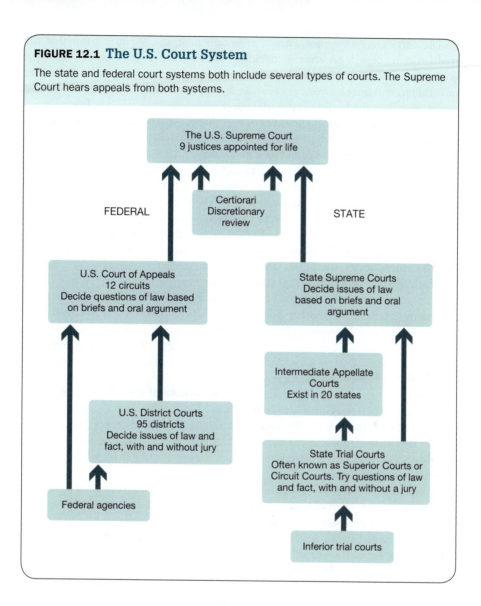

FIGURE 12.1 The U.S. Court System

The state and federal court systems both include several types of courts. The Supreme Court hears appeals from both systems.

The U.S. Supreme Court
9 justices appointed for life

FEDERAL

Certiorari
Discretionary
review

STATE

U.S. Court of Appeals
12 circuits
Decide questions of law based
on briefs and oral argument

State Supreme Courts
Decide issues of law
based on briefs and oral
argument

Intermediate Appellate
Courts
Exist in 20 states

U.S. District Courts
95 districts
Decide issues of law and
fact, with and without jury

State Trial Courts
Often known as Superior Courts or
Circuit Courts. Try questions of law
and fact, with and without a jury

Federal agencies

Inferior trial courts

defendant is convicted, he or she may appeal the conviction to a higher court, such as a state **court of appeals** (a court that hears the appeals of trial court decisions), and from there to a state's **supreme court** (the highest court in a particular state or in the United States, which primarily serves an appellate function). The government is not entitled to appeal if the defendant is found not guilty in a criminal case.

Similarly, in civil cases, most litigation is brought in the courts established by the state in which the activity in question took place. For example, a patient bringing suit against a physician for malpractice would file the suit in the appropriate court in the state where the alleged malpractice occurred. The judge hearing the case would apply state law and state precedent to the matter at hand. In a civil case, such as malpractice, either side may appeal the verdict if it loses.

The party filing an appeal, known as an appellant, usually must show that the trial court made a legal error in deciding the case. Appeals courts do not hear witnesses or examine additional evidence and will only consider new facts under unusual circumstances. Thus, for example, a physician who loses a malpractice case might appeal on the basis that the trial court misapplied the relevant law or incorrectly instructed the jury. It should be noted that most criminal and civil cases are settled before trial through negotiated agreements between the parties. In criminal cases, these agreements are called **plea bargains**.

Cases are heard in the federal courts if they involve federal laws, treaties with other nations, or the U.S. Constitution; these areas are the official **jurisdiction** (the sphere of a court's power and authority) of the federal courts. In addition, any case in which the U.S. government is a party is heard in the federal courts. If, for example, an individual is accused of violating a federal criminal statute, such as evading the payment of income taxes, a federal prosecutor would bring charges before a federal judge. Civil cases involving the citizens of more than one state and in which more than $75,000 is at stake may be heard in either the federal or the state courts, usually depending on the preference of the plaintiff.

Federal courts serve another purpose in addition to trying cases within their jurisdiction: that of hearing appeals from state-level courts. In both civil and criminal cases, a decision of the highest state court can be appealed to the U.S. Supreme Court by raising a federal issue. A defendant who appeals a lower-court decision in federal court might assert, for example, that he or she was denied the right to counsel or was otherwise deprived of the **due process of law** (the right of every citizen against arbitrary action by national or state governments) guaranteed by the federal Constitution, or the defendant might assert that important issues of federal law were at stake in the case. The U.S. Supreme Court is not obligated to accept such appeals and will do so only if it believes that the matter has considerable national significance.

In addition, in criminal cases, defendants who have been convicted in a state court may request a **writ of habeas corpus** from a federal district court. Sometimes known as the "Great Writ," habeas corpus is a court order that the individual in custody be brought into court and shown the cause for his or her detention. It instructs the authorities to release a prisoner deemed to be held in violation of his or her legal rights. Habeas corpus is guaranteed by the Constitution and can be suspended only in cases of rebellion or invasion. In 1867, Congress's distrust of southern courts led it to authorize federal district judges to issue such writs to prisoners who they believed had been deprived of constitutional rights in state court. Generally speaking, state defendants seeking a federal writ of habeas corpus must show that they have exhausted all available state remedies and must raise issues not previously raised in their state appeals. Federal courts of appeal and, ultimately, the U.S. Supreme Court have appellate jurisdiction for federal district court habeas decisions.

Although the federal courts hear only a small fraction of all the civil and criminal cases decided each year in the United States, their decisions are extremely important. It is in the federal courts that the Constitution and federal laws that govern all Americans are interpreted and their meaning and significance established. Moreover, it is in the federal courts that the powers and limitations of the increasingly powerful national government are tested. Finally, through their power to review the decisions of the state courts, it is ultimately the federal courts that dominate the American judicial system.

The Federal Courts Hear a Small Percentage of All Cases

Describe the different levels of federal courts and their functions

In 2013 federal district courts (the lowest federal level) received 375,870 cases. Though large, this number is approximately 1 percent of the number of cases heard by state courts. The federal courts of appeal listened to 56,475 cases in 2013, and about 16 percent of the verdicts were appealed to the U.S. Supreme Court. Most of the cases filed with the Supreme Court are dismissed without a ruling on their merits. The Court has broad latitude to decide what cases it will hear and generally listens to only those cases it deems to raise the most important issues. Only 77 cases were given full-dress Supreme Court review in the Court's 2012–13 term.[3]

The Lower Federal Courts Handle Most Cases

Most of the cases of original federal jurisdiction are handled by the federal district courts. **Original jurisdiction** is the authority to initially consider a case. It is distinguished from appellate jurisdiction, which is the authority to hear appeals from a lower court's decision. Courts of original jurisdiction are the courts that are responsible for discovering the facts in a controversy and creating the record on which a judgment is based. In courts that have appellate jurisdiction, judges receive cases after the factual record is established by the trial court. Ordinarily, new facts cannot be presented before appellate courts. Article III of the Constitution gives the Supreme Court original jurisdiction in a limited number of cases including (1) cases between the United States and one of the 50 states, (2) cases between two or more states, (3) cases involving foreign ambassadors or other ministers, and (4) cases brought by one state against citizens of another state or against a foreign country. Article III assigns original jurisdiction in all other federal cases to the lower courts that Congress was authorized to establish. Importantly, the Constitution gives the Supreme Court appellate jurisdiction in *all* federal cases.

The 94 federal district courts are staffed by 679 federal district judges. District judges are assigned to district courts according to the workload; the busiest of these courts may have as many as 28 judges. Only one judge is assigned to each case, except where statutes provide for three-judge courts to deal with special issues. The routines and procedures of the federal district courts are essentially the same as those of the lower state courts, except that federal procedural requirements tend to be stricter. States, for example, do not have to provide a grand jury, a 12-member trial jury, or a unanimous jury verdict. Federal courts must follow all these procedures.

The Appellate Courts Hear 20 Percent of Lower Court Cases

Roughly 20 percent of all lower court and federal agency cases are accepted for review by the federal appeals courts and by the Supreme Court in its capacity as an appellate court. There are 13 U.S. Court of Appeals judicial districts, or circuits (with a total of 179 judges). Those districts consist of 11 that divide up the nation geographically plus one for the District of Columbia and one federal circuit that deals with patents, trademarks, international trade, and claims against the federal government (see Figure 12.2).

Except for cases selected for review by the Supreme Court, decisions made by the appeals courts are final. Because of this finality, certain safeguards have been built into the system. The most important is the provision of more than one judge for every appeals case. Each court of appeals has from 6 to 28 permanent judgeships, depending on the workload of the circuit. Although normally three judges hear appealed cases, in some instances a larger number of judges sit together en banc.

Another safeguard is provided by the assignment of a Supreme Court justice as the circuit justice for each of the circuits. Since the creation of the appeals court

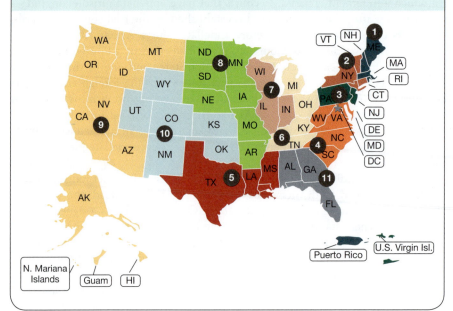

FIGURE 12.2 Federal Appellate Court Circuits

The 94 federal district courts are organized into 12 regional circuits: the 11 shown here plus the District of Columbia, which has its own circuit. Each circuit court hears appeals from lower federal courts within the circuit. A 13th federal circuit court, the U.S. Court of Appeals for the Federal Circuit, hears appeals from a number of specialized courts such as the U.S. Court of Federal Claims.

SOURCE: www.uscourts.gov/court_locator.aspx (accessed 7/27/10).

in 1891, the circuit justice's primary duty has been to review appeals arising in the circuit in order to expedite Supreme Court action. The most frequent and best-known action of circuit justices is that of reviewing requests for stays of execution when the full Court is unable to do so—primarily during the summer, when the Court is in recess.

The Supreme Court Is the Court of Final Appeal

The Supreme Court is America's highest court. Article III of the Constitution vests "the judicial power of the United States" in the Supreme Court, and this court is supreme in fact as well as form. The Supreme Court is the only federal court established by the Constitution. The lower federal courts were created by Congress and can be restructured or, presumably, even abolished by the legislative branch. The Supreme Court is made up of a chief justice and eight associate justices (see Table 12.1). The **chief justice** presides over the Court's public sessions and conferences. In the Court's actual deliberations and decisions, however, the chief justice has no more authority than his or her colleagues. Each justice casts one vote. The chief justice, though, is the first to speak and vote. Voting then proceeds from most to least senior. To some extent, the influence of the chief justice is a function of his or her own leadership ability. Some chief justices, such as the late Earl Warren, have been able to lead the Court in a new direction. In other instances, forceful associate justices, such as the late Felix Frankfurter, are the dominant figures on the Court.

The Constitution does not specify the number of justices who should sit on the Supreme Court; Congress has the authority to change the Court's size. In the early nineteenth century, there were six Supreme Court justices; later there were seven.

TABLE 12.1

Supreme Court Justices, 2012 (in Order of Seniority)

NAME	YEAR OF BIRTH	PRIOR EXPERIENCE	APPOINTED BY	YEAR OF APPOINTMENT
Antonin Scalia	1936	Law professor, federal judge	Reagan	1986
Anthony Kennedy	1936	Federal judge	Reagan	1988
Clarence Thomas	1948	Federal judge	G. H. W. Bush	1991
Ruth Bader Ginsburg	1933	Federal judge	Clinton	1993
Stephen Breyer	1938	Federal judge	Clinton	1994
John Roberts Jr. (Chief Justice)	1955	Federal judge	G. W. Bush	2005
Samuel Alito	1950	Federal judge	G. W. Bush	2006
Sonia Sotomayor	1954	Federal judge	Obama	2009
Elena Kagan	1960	Solicitor General	Obama	2010

Congress set the number of justices at nine in 1869, and the Court has remained that size ever since. In 1937, President Franklin Roosevelt, infuriated by several Supreme Court decisions that struck down New Deal programs, asked Congress to enlarge the Court so that he could add a few sympathetic justices to the bench. Although Congress balked at Roosevelt's "court packing" plan, the Court gave in to FDR's pressure and began to take a more favorable view of his policy initiatives. The president, in turn, dropped his efforts to enlarge the Court. The Court's surrender to FDR came to be known as "the switch in time that saved nine."

Judges Are Appointed by the President and Approved by the Senate

Federal judges are appointed by the president and are generally selected from among the more prominent or politically active members of the legal profession. Many federal judges previously served as state court judges or state or local prosecutors. Before the president makes a formal nomination, however, the senators from the candidate's own state must indicate that they support the nominee. This is an informal but seldom violated practice called **senatorial courtesy.** If one or both senators from a prospective nominee's home state belong to the president's political party, the president will almost invariably consult them and secure their blessing for the nomination. Because the president's party in the Senate will rarely approve a nominee opposed by a home-state senator from its ranks, the president will usually not bother to present such a nomination to the Senate. Through this arrangement, senators are able to exercise veto power over appointments to the federal bench from their own states. If the state has no senator from the president's party, the governor or members of the state's House delegation may make suggestions. The practice of "courtesy" generally does not apply to Supreme Court appointments, only to district and circuit court nominations.

Federal appeals court nominations follow much the same pattern. Since appeals court judges preside over jurisdictions that include several states, however, senators do not have as strong a role in proposing potential candidates. Instead, potential appeals court candidates are generally suggested to the president by the Justice Department or by important members of the administration. The senators from the nominee's own state are still consulted, however, before the president formally acts.

There are no formal qualifications for service as a federal judge. In general, presidents endeavor to appoint judges who possess legal experience and good character and whose partisan and ideological views are similar to their own. Once the president has formally nominated an individual, the nominee must be considered by the Senate Judiciary Committee and confirmed by a majority vote in the full Senate. In recent years the judicial appointments process has been affected by increasing partisan conflict. Senate Democrats have sought to prevent Republican presidents from appointing conservative judges, while Senate Republicans have worked to prevent Democratic presidents from appointing liberal judges. During the early months of the Obama administration, Republicans were able to slow the judicial appointment process through filibusters and other procedural maneuvers so that only 3 of the president's 23 nominations for federal judgeships were confirmed by the Senate.[4] Obama's allies urged the president to take a more aggressive stance or risk allowing Republicans to block what had been considered a key Democratic priority. In 2013 the Senate voted 52 to 48 to end the use of the filibuster against all executive branch and judicial nominees except those to the Supreme Court. By the beginning of his sixth year in office, Obama had won the appointment of 184 new district court judges and 44 new appeals court judges.[5]

If political factors play an important role in the selection of district and appellate court judges, they are decisive when it comes to Supreme Court appointments. Because the high court has so much influence over American law and politics, virtually all presidents have made an effort to select justices who share their political philosophies.

As of 2014, five of the nine current justices were appointed by Republican presidents. This conservative majority, consisting of Chief Justice John Roberts and Justices Samuel Alito, Anthony Kennedy, Antonin Scalia, and Clarence Thomas, has propelled the Court in a more conservative direction in a variety of areas. In 2009 and 2010, for example, in a series of 5–4 decisions, the Court overturned limits on corporate campaign spending, ruled that the Federal Communications Commission (FCC) was justified in penalizing the use of expletives on the airwaves, and blocked a suit against former attorney general John Ashcroft by a terrorist suspect alleging that he had been mistreated in prison. In 2011 and 2012, however, Chief Justice Roberts responded to charges that the Court's decisions were political rather than judicial by joining the liberal bloc in two important cases. The first was the Court's decision to invalidate portions of an Arizona law designed to identify and apprehend illegal aliens.[6] The second was the Court's 5–4 decision to uphold the Affordable Care Act, President Obama's major legislative achievement. Critics had charged that the act's requirement that all Americans purchase health insurance was unconstitutional. Roberts wrote that this requirement was just another federal tax.[7]

The number of justices varied during the first 80 years of American history, but has held at nine since 1869. The justices hear and decide all cases as a group. Despite ideological differences, in recent years approximately half of all cases were decided by a unanimous vote of 9 to 0.

Supreme Court nominations have come to involve intense partisan struggle in recent decades. Typically, after the president has named a nominee, interest groups opposed to the nomination have mobilized opposition in the media, among the public, and in the Senate. When President George H. W. Bush proposed conservative judge Clarence Thomas for the Court, for example, liberal groups launched a campaign to discredit Thomas. After extensive research into his background, opponents of the nomination were able to produce evidence suggesting that Thomas had sexually harassed a former subordinate, Anita Hill. Thomas denied the charge. After contentious Senate Judiciary Committee hearings, highlighted by testimony from both Thomas and Hill, Thomas narrowly won confirmation.

In 2009, when President Obama nominated federal judge Sonia Sotomayor to replace retiring justice David Souter, conservatives denounced Sotomayor as a "reverse racist" for her support of affirmative action. Many Republican senators, however, were reluctant to oppose a Hispanic nominee. For several years, the GOP has made efforts to attract America's rapidly growing Hispanic population. Republicans feared that opposing Sotomayor would undermine these efforts.[8] In the end, Sotomayor was easily confirmed, as was Obama's second nominee to the Court, Elena Kagan.

● The Power of the Supreme Court Is Judicial Review

Explain how the Supreme Court exercises the power of judicial review

The term **judicial review** refers to the power of the judiciary to review and, if necessary, declare actions of the legislative and executive branches invalid or unconstitutional. It is sometimes also used to describe the scrutiny that appellate courts give to the actions of trial courts, but strictly speaking, this is improper usage. A higher court's examination of a lower court's decisions might be called "appellate review," but it is not judicial review.

Judicial Review Covers Acts of Congress

Because the Constitution does not give the Supreme Court the power of judicial review over congressional enactments, the Court's exercise of it is something of a usurpation. It is not known whether the framers of the Constitution opposed judicial review, but "if they intended to provide for it in the Constitution, they did so in a most obscure fashion."[9] Disputes over the intentions of the framers were settled in 1803 in the case of *Marbury v. Madison*.[10] The Court said,

> It is emphatically the province and duty of the Judicial Department [the judicial branch] to say what the law is. Those who apply the rule to particular cases must, of necessity, expound and interpret that rule. If two laws conflict with each other, the Courts must decide on the operation of each. . . . So, if a law [e.g., a statute or treaty] be in opposition to the Constitution, if both the law and the Constitution apply to a particular case, so that the Court must either decide that case conformably to the law, disregarding the Constitution, or conformably to the Constitution, disregarding

Judicial Review across the Globe

In 1946 only about a quarter of democracies had a court that possessed judicial review; by 2006 almost 90 percent did.[a] The type of judicial review varies by county. The United States has concrete judicial review, which means that a specific case must be brought to the Supreme Court before it can declare a law unconstitutional. Other countries, such as France, have abstract judicial review, which means the constitutional court does not have to wait for a specific court case in order to declare a law unconstitutional. Instead, the court usually responds to a request by an elected official, such as a member of parliament or local government, in ruling whether a law is unconstitutional. Some countries, such as Germany and South Africa, possess both types of judicial review.

Not all democracies have judicial review. For example, the judiciary in the United Kingdom officially lacks this power. The United Kingdom is one of the few remaining democracies with parliamentary sovereignty, meaning that, while local laws can be declared unconstitutional, no court can overturn a law passed by the national parliament. British courts can rule a law passed by parliament as "incompatible" with European Union law or other treaty obligations, but this does not automatically strike the law down. Instead, the law stays "on the books" and the parliament is asked to reconsider the law and amend it so it does not contradict other laws.[b]

Country/ Court	Concrete Review	Abstract Review	What Can Be Reviewed
United States *Supreme Court*	Yes	No	• National legislation • Actions of other national government institutions (e.g., executive orders) • State and local laws • Lower court decisions and appeals
Germany *Federal Constitutional Court*	Yes	Yes	• National legislation • Actions of other national government institutions • State and local laws • Constitutional amendments • Election law violations
France *Constitutional Council*	Limited*	Yes	• National legislation *prior to being signed into law* • Legislation pertaining to cases before the other high courts
United Kingdom *Supreme Court***	No	No	• Actions of other government institutions ("secondary legislation") • Local laws

*A 2009 reform allows some concrete review. For more information, see Ordinance No. 58-1067 at www.conseil-constitutionnel.fr/conseil-constitutionnel/root/bank_mm/ anglais/en_ordinance_58_1067.pdf (accessed 9/12/14).
**Prior to 2009, the role of the "high court" was performed by the United Kingdom's House of Lords (the 12 "Law Lords").

[a]David S. Law and Mila Versteeg, "The Evolution and Ideology of Global Constitutionalism," *California Law Review*, 99, no. 5 (2010): 1163–257.
[b]United Kingdom Judicial Office, "About the Judiciary: Judges and Parliament," www.judiciary.gov.uk/about-the-judiciary/the-judiciary-the-government-and-the-constitution/ jud-acc-ind/judges-and-parliament/ (accessed 9/12/14).

the law, the Court must determine which of these conflicting rules governs the case. This is of the very essence of judicial duty.

The Court's legal power to review acts of Congress has not been seriously questioned since 1803 in part because the Supreme Court makes a self-conscious effort to give acts of Congress an interpretation that will make them constitutional. For example, in its 2012 decision upholding the constitutionality of the Affordable Care Act, the Court agreed with the many legal scholars who had argued that Congress had no power under the Constitution's commerce clause to order Americans to purchase health insurance. But rather than invalidate the act, the Court declared that the law's requirement that all Americans purchase insurance was actually a tax and, thus, represented a constitutionally acceptable use of Congress's power to levy taxes.[11]

In more than two centuries, the Court has concluded that only 175 acts of Congress directly violate the Constitution.[12] These cases are often highly controversial. For example, in 2007, 2010, and 2014, the high court struck down key portions of the bipartisan Campaign Reform Act, through which Congress had sought to regulate spending in political campaigns.[13] The Court found that provisions of the act limiting political advertising violated the First Amendment. These cases are unusual in that Supreme Court rarely overturns acts of Congress.

Judicial Review Applies to Presidential Actions

The federal courts also review presidential actions from time to time. In recent decades, the courts have, more often than not, upheld presidential power in such areas as foreign policy, war and emergency powers, legislative power, and administrative authority. But the Supreme Court ruled on three cases involving President George W. Bush's antiterrorism initiatives and claims of executive power, and in two of the three cases placed some limits on presidential authority.

One important case was *Hamdi v. Rumsfeld*.[14] Yaser Esam Hamdi, apparently a Taliban soldier, was captured by American forces in Afghanistan and brought to the United States, where he was incarcerated at the Norfolk Naval Station. Hamdi was classified as an enemy combatant and denied civil rights, including the right to counsel, despite the fact that he had been born in the U.S. and was a U.S. citizen. In 2004 the Supreme Court ruled that Hamdi was entitled to a lawyer and "a fair opportunity to rebut the government's factual assertions." Thus, the Court imposed restrictions on the president's power, although it also affirmed the president's most important claim: the unilateral power to declare individuals, including U.S. citizens, "enemy combatants" who could be detained by the United States.

In the 2006 case of *Hamdan v. Rumsfeld*,[15] Salim Hamdan, a Taliban fighter, was captured in Afghanistan and held at the Guantánamo Bay naval base. The Bush administration planned to try Hamdan before a military commission created by a 2002 presidential order. The Supreme Court ruled that this presidentially created commission violated federal law and U.S. treaty obligations. In response, Bush pressed Congress to rewrite the law, which it did, enacting the Military Commissions Act. This law gave the president legal authority for his actions. Section 7 of the law said that Guantánamo prisoners could not bring habeas corpus petitions

In 2011 the Supreme Court struck down a California law that regulated the sale of violent video games to children, saying the law violated the First Amendment. California state senator Leland Yee, who proposed the ban, held up some of the games the law would have regulated.

to federal courts to seek their release. In the 2008 case of *Boumediene v. Bush*,[16] however, the Supreme Court struck down Section 7, saying that habeas corpus was a fundamental right.

Judicial Review Also Applies to State Actions

The logic of the **supremacy clause** of Article VI of the Constitution, which states that laws passed by the national government and all treaties "shall be the supreme Law of the Land" and superior to all laws adopted by any state or any subdivision, implies that the Court may review the constitutionality of state laws. Furthermore, in the Judiciary Act of 1789, Congress conferred on the Supreme Court the power to reverse state constitutions and laws whenever they are clearly in conflict with the U.S. Constitution, federal laws, or treaties.[17] This power gives the Supreme Court appellate jurisdiction over all of the millions of cases handled by U.S. courts each year.

The supremacy clause of the Constitution also provides that "the Judges in every State shall be bound thereby, any Thing in the Constitution or Laws of any State to the Contrary notwithstanding." Under this authority, the Supreme Court has frequently overturned state constitutional provisions or statutes and state court decisions it deems contrary to the federal Constitution or federal statutes.

The civil rights arena abounds with examples of state laws that were overturned because the statutes violated guarantees of due process and equal protection contained in the Fourteenth Amendment to the Constitution. For example, in the

1954 case of *Brown v. Board of Education*, the Court overturned statutes from Kansas, South Carolina, Virginia, and Delaware that either required or permitted segregated public schools, on the basis that such statutes denied black schoolchildren equal protection of the law.[18] In 2003 the Court ruled that Texas's law criminalizing sodomy violated the right to liberty protected by the due process clause.[19]

Sometimes Court decisions are so broad and sweeping that they have the effect of changing the law, and legal practices, across the country. In the 1973 Supreme Court case of *Roe v. Wade*, for example, the Court ruled that a safe, legal abortion was a constitutionally protected right for women under most circumstances. This decision had the effect of striking down restrictive abortion laws in more than 40 states.

Almost all of the dramatic changes in the treatment of criminals and those accused of crimes have been made by the appellate courts, especially the Supreme Court. For example, in *Miranda v. Arizona* (1966), the Supreme Court set forth what is known as the *Miranda* rule: arrested people must be informed prior to police interrogation that they have the right to remain silent, the right to be informed that anything they say can be held against them, and the right to counsel before and during police interrogation (see Chapter 4).[20] Over the years the Supreme Court has developed a number of principles regulating police conduct to ensure that the police do not violate constitutional liberties. These principles, however, must often be updated to keep pace with changes in technology. In the 2012 case of *United States v. Jones*, the Supreme Court found that police use of a GPS tracker—a device invented more than two centuries after the adoption of the Bill of Rights—constituted a "search" as defined by the Fourth Amendment. The Court ruled that the police were prohibited from attaching a global-positioning device to a car belonging to a suspected drug dealer without first obtaining a valid warrant.[21] Many of the Supreme Court's recent decisions overturning state law have come in cases concerning criminal punishments. For example, in 2012 the Court struck down Alabama and Arkansas statutes that mandated a sentence of life in prison without possibility of parole for minors who were found guilty of homicide. The Court held this statute violated the Eighth Amendment's prohibition of cruel and unusual punishment.[22]

● Most Cases Reach the Supreme Court by Appeal

> **Describe the process the Supreme Court follows in the exercise of its power of judicial review**

Article III of the Constitution and Supreme Court decisions define judicial power as extending only to "cases and controversies." This means that the case before a court must be an actual controversy, not a hypothetical one, with two truly adversarial parties. The courts have interpreted this language to mean that they do not have the power to render advisory opinions to legislatures or agencies about the constitutionality of proposed laws or regulations. Furthermore, even after a law is enacted, the courts will generally refuse to consider its constitutionality until it is actually applied. Even with this provision, given that millions of disputes arise every year, the job of the Supreme Court would be impossible if it were not able to control the flow of cases and its own caseload. As noted earlier, cases that come first to the Supreme Court are very few in number.

Most cases reach the Supreme Court through the **writ of certiorari**, which is granted whenever four of the nine justices agree to review a decision of a lower court. (*Certiorari* comes from the Latin for "to make more certain.") The term *certiorari* is sometimes shortened to *cert*, and cases deemed to merit certiorari are referred to as "certworthy." An individual who loses in a lower federal court or state court and wants the Supreme Court to review the decision has 90 days to file a petition for a writ of certiorari with the clerk of the U.S. Supreme Court. Petitions for thousands of cases are filed with the Court every year.

Since 1972 most of the justices have participated in a "certiorari pool" in which their law clerks work together to evaluate the petitions. Each petition is reviewed by one clerk, who writes a memo for all the justices participating in the pool summarizing the facts and issues and making a recommendation. Clerks for the other justices add their comments to the memo. After the justices have reviewed the memos, any one of them may place any case on the discuss list, which is circulated by the chief justice. If a case is not placed on the discuss list, it is automatically denied certiorari. Cases placed on the discuss list are considered and voted on during the justices' closed-door conference.

For certiorari to be granted, four justices must be convinced that the case satisfies Rule 10 of the Rules of the U.S. Supreme Court. Rule 10 states that certiorari is not a matter of right but is to be granted only when there are special and compelling reasons. These include conflicting decisions by two or more circuit courts, conflicts between circuit courts and state courts of last resort, conflicting decisions by two or more state courts of last resort, decisions by circuit courts on matters of federal law that should be settled by the Supreme Court, a circuit court decision on an important question that conflicts with Supreme Court decisions, cases that present important questions of civil rights or civil liberties, and cases in which the federal government is an appellant. It should be clear from this list that the Court will usually take action under only the most compelling circumstances—when there are conflicts among the lower courts about what the law should be, when an important legal question has been raised in the lower courts but not definitively answered, or when a lower court deviates from the principles and precedents established by the high court. Ultimately, however, the question of which cases to accept can come down to the preferences and priorities of the justices.

As Figure 12.3 shows, the Court is inundated by appeals, and the number of appeals has skyrocketed over the years, even though the Court actually rules on less than 1 percent of these appeals.

The Solicitor General, Law Clerks, and Interest Groups Also Influence the Flow of Cases

In addition to the judges themselves, three other entities play an important role in shaping the flow of cases through the federal courts: the solicitor general, federal law clerks, and interest groups.

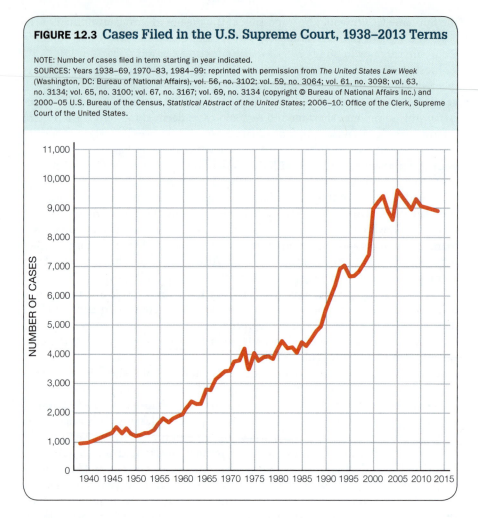

FIGURE 12.3 Cases Filed in the U.S. Supreme Court, 1938–2013 Terms

NOTE: Number of cases filed in term starting in year indicated.
SOURCES: Years 1938–69, 1970–83, 1984–99: reprinted with permission from *The United States Law Week* (Washington, DC: Bureau of National Affairs), vol. 56, no. 3102; vol. 59, no. 3064; vol. 61, no. 3098; vol. 63, no. 3134; vol. 65, no. 3100; vol. 67, no. 3167; vol. 69, no. 3134 (copyright © Bureau of National Affairs Inc.) and 2000–05 U.S. Bureau of the Census, *Statistical Abstract of the United States*; 2006–10: Office of the Clerk, Supreme Court of the United States.

The Solicitor General If any single person has greater influence than individual judges over the federal courts, it is the **solicitor general** of the United States. The solicitor general is the third-ranking official in the Justice Department (below the attorney general and the deputy attorney general) but the top government lawyer in virtually all cases before the Supreme Court in which the government is a party. The solicitor general controls the flow of cases by screening them before any agency of the federal government can appeal them to the Supreme Court; indeed, the justices rely on the solicitor general to "screen out undeserving litigation and furnish them with an agenda to government cases that deserve serious consideration."[23] More than half of the Supreme Court's total workload consists of cases under the direct charge of the solicitor general. Typically, more requests for appeals are rejected than are accepted by the solicitor general. Without the solicitor general's support, requests directly from government agencies are seldom reviewed by the Court.

The solicitor general can enter a case even when the federal government is not a direct litigant, by writing an **amicus curiae** ("friend of the court") brief. A "friend of the court" is not a direct party to a case but seeks to assist the Supreme Court in reaching a decision by presenting additional briefs. Other interested parties may file amicus briefs as well.

In addition to exercising substantial control over the flow of cases, the solicitor general can shape the arguments used before the federal courts. Indeed, the Supreme Court tends to give special attention to the way the solicitor general characterizes the issues.

Law Clerks Every federal judge employs law clerks to research legal issues and assist with the preparation of opinions. Each Supreme Court justice is assigned four clerks. The clerks are almost always honors graduates from the nation's most prestigious law schools. A clerkship with a Supreme Court justice is a great honor and generally indicates that the fortunate individual is likely to reach the very top of the legal profession. The work of the Supreme Court clerks is a closely guarded secret, but some justices rely heavily on their clerks for advice in writing opinions and in deciding whether specific cases ought to be heard by the Court. In a recent book, a former law clerk to the late justice Harry Blackmun charged that Supreme Court justices yielded "excessive power to immature, ideologically driven clerks, who in turn use that power to manipulate their bosses."[24]

Lobbying for Access: Interests and the Court At the same time that the Court exercises discretion over which cases it will review, groups and forces in society often seek to persuade the justices to listen to their problems. Lawyers representing interest groups try to choose the proper client and the proper case, so that the issues in question are most dramatically and appropriately portrayed. When possible, they also pick a district with a sympathetic judge in which to bring the case. Sometimes they wait for an appropriate political climate.

Group litigants have to plan carefully when to use and when to avoid publicity. They must also attempt to develop a proper record at the trial court level, one that includes some constitutional arguments and even, when possible, errors on the part of the trial court. One of the most effective strategies that litigants use in getting cases accepted for review by the appellate courts is to bring the same type of suit in more than one circuit (that is, to develop a "pattern of cases"), in the hope that inconsistent treatment by two different courts will improve the chance of a Supreme Court review.

The two most notable users of the "pattern of cases" strategy in recent years have been the National Association for the Advancement of Colored People (NAACP) and the American Civil Liberties Union (ACLU). For many years, the NAACP (and its Defense Fund—now a separate group) has worked through local chapters and with many individuals to encourage litigation on issues of racial discrimination and segregation. Sometimes it distributes petitions to be signed by parents and filed with local school boards and courts, deliberately sowing the seeds of future litigation. The NAACP and the ACLU often encourage private parties to bring suit and then join the suit as amici curiae.

The Supreme Court's Procedures Mean Cases May Take Months or Years

The Preparation The Supreme Court's decision to accept a case is the beginning of what can be a lengthy and complex process (see Figure 12.4). First, the attorneys on both sides must prepare **briefs**—written documents that may be several hundred pages long in which the attorneys explain, using case precedents, why the Court should rule in favor of their client. Briefs are filled with referrals to precedents specifically chosen to show that other courts have frequently ruled in the same way that the Supreme Court is being asked to rule. The attorneys for both sides muster the most compelling precedents they can in support of their arguments.

As the attorneys prepare their briefs, they often ask sympathetic interest groups for help. Groups are asked to file amicus curiae (friend of the court) briefs that support the claims of one or the other litigant. In a case involving separation of church and state, for example, liberal groups such as the ACLU and Citizens for the American Way are likely to be asked to file amicus briefs in support of strict separation, whereas conservative religious groups are likely to file amicus briefs advocating increased public support for religious ideas. Often dozens of briefs will be filed on each side of a major case. Amicus filings are a primary method used by interest groups to lobby the Court.

Oral Argument The next stage of a case is **oral argument**, in which attorneys for both sides appear before the Court to present their positions and answer questions posed by justices. Each attorney has only a half hour to present his or her case, and this time includes interruptions for questions. Certain members of the Court, such as Justice Scalia, are known to interrupt attorneys dozens of times. Others, such as Justice Thomas, seldom ask questions. For an attorney, the opportunity to argue a case before the Supreme Court is a singular honor and a mark of professional distinction. It can also be a harrowing experience, as justices interrupt a carefully prepared presentation to ask pointed questions. Oral argument can be very important to the outcome of a case. It allows justices to better understand the heart of the case and to raise questions that might not have been addressed in the opposing side's briefs. It is not uncommon for justices to go beyond the strictly legal issues and ask opposing counsel to discuss the implications of the case for the Court and the nation at large.

The Conference Following oral argument, the Court discusses the case in its Wednesday or Friday conference, a strictly private meeting that no outsiders are permitted to attend. The chief justice presides over the conference and speaks first; the other justices follow in order of seniority. The justices discuss the case and eventually reach a decision on the basis of a majority vote. If the Court is divided, a number of votes may be taken before a final decision is reached. As the case is

FIGURE 12.4 Time Line of a Supreme Court Case

This calendar of events in the case of *Chamber of Commerce v. Environmental Protection Agency* illustrates the steps of the process a case goes through as it moves through the Supreme Court.

SOURCE: www.scotusblog.com/case-files/cases/chamber-of-commerce-of-the-united-states-v-environmental-protection-agency/ (accessed 6/9/14).

April 19, 2013

The Chamber of Commerce filed a petition for a writ of certiorari in the case *Chamber of Commerce of the United States of America, et. al. v. Environmental Protection Agency, et al.*

May 2013

Filing of briefs and amicus curiae briefs in support of the petitioner, including the Institute for Trade, Standards, and Sustainable Development and Nobel Prize–winning economist Thomas C. Shelling

July 2013

Brief of the solicitor general on behalf of the Environmental Protection Agency (the respondent)

August 7, 2013

The case is distributed for conference.

October 15, 2013

The petition (certiorari) is granted.

November 25, 2013

Date for oral argument is set for February 24, 2014.

December 2013

Briefs and amicus curiae briefs are filed on behalf of petitioner.

January 2014

Briefs and amicus curiae briefs are filed on behalf of respondent.

February 24, 2014

Oral argument of one hour

June 2014

Decision

discussed, justices may try to influence or change one another's opinions. At times, this may result in compromise decisions.

Opinion Writing After a decision has been reached, one of the members of the majority is assigned to write the **opinion**—the written explanation of the Supreme Court's decision in a particular case. This assignment is made by the chief justice, or by the most senior justice in the majority if the chief justice is on the losing side. The assignment of the opinion can make a significant difference to the interpretation of a decision. Lawyers and judges in the lower courts will examine the opinion carefully to ascertain the Supreme Court's intent. Differences in wording and emphasis can have important implications for future litigation. Once the majority opinion is drafted, it is circulated to the other justices. Some members of the majority may decide that they do not agree with all the language of the opinion and therefore write "concurring" opinions that support the decision but offer a different rationale or emphasis. In assigning an opinion, serious thought must be given to the impression the case will make on lawyers and the public, and to the probability that one justice's opinion will be more widely accepted than another's.

One of the more dramatic instances of this tactical consideration occurred in 1944, when Chief Justice Harlan F. Stone chose Justice Felix Frankfurter to write the opinion in the "white primary" case *Smith v. Allwright*. The chief justice believed that this sensitive case, which overturned the southern practice of prohibiting black participation in nominating primaries, required the efforts of the most brilliant and scholarly jurist on the Court. But the day after Stone made the assignment, Justice Robert H. Jackson wrote a letter to Stone urging a change of assignment. In his letter, Jackson argued that Frankfurter, a foreign-born Jew from New England, would not win the South with his opinion, regardless of its brilliance. Stone accepted the advice and substituted Justice Stanley Reed, an American-born Protestant from Kentucky and a southern Democrat in good standing.[25]

Dissent Justices who disagree with the majority decision of the Court may choose to publicize their disagreement in the form of a **dissenting opinion** (a decision written by a justice in the minority in a particular case in which the justice wishes to express his or her reasoning in the case). Dissents can be used to express opposition to an outcome or to signal to defeated political forces in the nation that their position is supported by at least some members of the Court. Because there is no need to please a majority, dissenting opinions can be more eloquent and less guarded than majority opinions. The current Supreme Court often produces 5–4 decisions, with dissenters writing long and detailed opinions that, they hope, will help them to persuade a swing justice to join their side on the next round of cases dealing with a similar topic. During the Court's 2006–07 term, Justice Ruth Bader Ginsburg was so unhappy about the majority's decisions in a number of cases that she twice violated her own long-standing practice and read forceful dissents from the bench, thus underscoring her disagreement with current legal trends and pointing the way toward other possibilities.

Supreme Court Decisions Are Influenced by Activism and Ideology

Consider the personal and political influences on judges and the courts

The Supreme Court explains its decisions in terms of law and precedent. But although law and precedent do have an effect on the Court's deliberations and eventual decisions, throughout its history, the Court has shaped and reshaped the law. In the late nineteenth and early twentieth centuries, for example, the Supreme Court held that the Constitution, law, and precedent permitted racial segregation in the United States. Beginning in the late 1950s, however, the Court found that the Constitution prohibited segregation on the basis of race and ruled that racial categories in legislation were always suspect. By the 1970s and '80s the Court once again held that the Constitution permitted the use of racial categories—when such categories were needed to help members of minority groups achieve full participation in American society. In the 1990s the Court began to retreat from this position, too, indicating that governmental efforts to provide extra help to racial minorities could represent an unconstitutional infringement on the rights of the majority.

Institutional Interests The Supreme Court's justices are acutely aware of the Court's place in history, and they care about protecting the Court's power and reputation. This desire to protect the institutional integrity of the Court can sometimes influence judicial thinking. Chief Justice John Roberts seemed to have institutional concerns in mind when he surprised fellow conservatives by casting the deciding vote in favor of the constitutionality of the Affordable Care Act in 2012. Roberts had been widely expected to oppose the president's health care reform effort. However, the Court's conservative majority had come under increasing political fire for its positions on such matters as campaign finance and affirmative action. Roberts, according to one commentator, saw himself as "uniquely entrusted with the custodianship of the court's legitimacy, reputation, and stature" and was determined to show that the Court stood above mere political ideology.[26]

Activism and Restraint The judicial philosophy of judges plays an important role in their decision making. One element of judicial philosophy is the issue of activism versus restraint. Over the years, some justices have believed that courts should narrowly interpret the Constitution according to the stated intentions of its framers and defer to the views of Congress when interpreting federal statutes. Justice Frankfurter, for example, advocated judicial deference to legislative bodies and avoidance of the "political thicket" in which the Court would entangle itself by deciding questions that were essentially political rather than legal in character. Advocates of **judicial restraint** are sometimes called "strict constructionists," because they refuse to go beyond the clear words of the Constitution in interpreting the document's meaning.

The alternative to restraint is **judicial activism**. Activist judges, such as the former chief justice Earl Warren, believe that the Court should go beyond the words of the Constitution or a statute to consider the broader societal implications of its decisions. Activist judges sometimes strike out in new directions, promulgating new interpretations or inventing new legal and constitutional concepts when they believe these to be socially desirable. For example, Justice Harry Blackmun's opinion in *Roe v. Wade* was based on a constitutional right to privacy that is not found in the words of the Constitution but was, rather, from the Court's prior decision in *Griswold v. Connecticut*.[27] Blackmun and the other members of the majority in the *Roe* case argued that the right to privacy was implied by other constitutional provisions. In this instance of judicial activism, the Court knew the result it wanted to achieve and was not afraid to make the law conform to the desired outcome.

Activism and restraint are sometimes confused with liberalism and conservatism. For example, conservative politicians often castigate "liberal activist" judges and call for the appointment of conservative jurists who will refrain from reinterpreting the law. To be sure, some liberal jurists are activists and some conservatives have been advocates of restraint, but the reverse is also true—liberals can be restrained, and conservatives activist. Indeed, the Rehnquist Court, dominated by conservatives, was among the most activist courts in American history, striking out in new directions in such areas as federalism and election law. The Roberts Court is continuing along the same route. As the examples of these conservative courts illustrate, a judge may be philosophically conservative and believe in strict construction of the Constitution but also be jurisprudentially activist and believe that the courts must play an active and energetic role in policy making, if necessary striking down acts of Congress to ensure that the intent of the framers is fulfilled.

Political Ideology and Partisanship The philosophy of activism versus restraint is sometimes a smokescreen for political ideology, and indeed, the liberal or conservative attitudes of justices play an important role in their decisions. A study by three political scientists

In 2012 the Supreme Court heard the case of Evan Miller (right), who was sentenced to life imprisonment without parole for a crime he allegedly committed when he was 14 years old. The Court ruled that a life-without-parole sentence for a 14-year-old violates the Eighth Amendment's prohibition against cruel and unusual punishment.

found that in First Amendment free speech cases that came before the Supreme Court between 1953 and 2011, liberal justices were more likely to vote to support the free speech rights of liberals, and conservative justices were more likely to support the free speech rights of conservative speakers. This trend, however, was even stronger for conservative justices than liberal justices. For example, conservative justice Antonin Scalia voted in favor of conservative speakers 65 percent of the time, but in favor of liberal speakers 21 percent. The study, commented one legal analyst, "shows how much justices' ideology influences the speech they are willing to protect."[28]

Historically, liberal judges have been activists, willing to use the law to achieve social and political change, whereas conservatives have been associated with judicial restraint. In recent years, however, some conservative justices who have long called for restraint have actually become activists in seeking to undo some of the work of liberal jurists over the past several decades.

From the 1950s to the '80s the Supreme Court took an activist role in such areas as civil rights, civil liberties, abortion, voting rights, and police procedures. For example, the Supreme Court was more responsible than any other governmental institution for breaking down America's system of racial segregation. The Supreme Court virtually prohibited states from interfering with the right of a woman to seek an abortion and sharply curtailed state restrictions on voting rights. And it was the Supreme Court that placed restrictions on the behavior

Today, the Supreme Court is frequently at the center of major political issues. In 2014 it decided the case Burwell v. Hobby Lobby, *in which arguments for religious freedom under the First Amendment came into play. The Court decided that employers with religious objections were not required to provide employees with no-cost access to contraception.*

of local police and prosecutors in criminal cases. In a series of decisions between 1989 and 2008, however, the conservative justices appointed by Ronald Reagan, George H. W. Bush, and George W. Bush were able to swing the Court to a more conservative position on civil rights, affirmative action, abortion rights, property rights, criminal procedure, voting rights, desegregation, and the power of the national government.

The Federal Judiciary
and Your Future

In the original conception of the framers, the judiciary was to be the institution that would protect individual liberty from the government. As we saw in Chapter 2, the framers believed that in a democracy, the great danger was what they termed "tyranny of the majority"—the possibility that a popular majority, "united or actuated by some common impulse or passion," would "trample on the rules of justice."[29] The framers hoped that the courts would protect liberty from the potential excesses of democracy. And for most of American history, this was precisely the role played by the federal courts. The courts' most important decisions were those that protected the freedoms—to speak, worship, publish, vote, and attend school—of groups and individuals whose political views, religious beliefs, or racial or ethnic backgrounds made them unpopular.

Today, Americans of all political persuasions seem to view the courts as useful instruments through which to pursue their goals rather than as protectors of individual rights. Conservatives want to ban abortion and help business maintain its profitability, whereas liberals want to promote school integration and help enhance the power of workers in the workplace. These may all be noble goals, but they present a basic dilemma for students of American government. If the courts are simply one more set of policy-making institutions, then who is left to protect the liberty of individuals?

Students should realize that the decisions made by the Supreme Court today will have important consequences for their lives and futures. The Court's campaign finance decisions will have consequences for who will govern the nation you inherit. The Court's decisions in the realm of equal protection will have an impact upon your life and career chances. The Court's decisions in the realm of immigration will affect who will and will not be able to call themselves Americans. The Court's decisions in the realm of presidential war powers may or may not send some of you to distant battlefields. The Supreme Court is not an abstract entity in far-off Washington. It reaches directly into your life.

plug**in**

Inform

Watch the Standard Deviants' five-minute "Judicial Branch Intro" on YouTube for a review of which features of the court system were established in the Constitution versus the Judiciary Act.

Express

Identify one Supreme Court case that affects your life and explain how. For ideas, search www.uscourts.gov for their "Landmark Supreme Court Cases about Students" page.

Connect

Visit www.uscourts.gov /Court_Locator.aspx, and find your nearest federal court. What does this court do? Find a link to your state's judicial/court system home page by searching online or through www.ncsc.org/Information -and-Resources/Browse-by-State /State-Court-Websites.aspx. What do state and local courts in your area do?

Act

Do you have a legal question? You can ask a question about court procedures and the law on the FindLaw website, browse answers to many common questions, and even find legal counsel.

studyguide

Practice Quiz

1. What is the name for the body of law that involves disputes among individuals? *(p. 372)*
   a) civil law
   b) privacy law
   c) plea bargains
   d) household law
   e) common law

2. By what term is the practice of the courts to uphold precedent known? *(p. 372)*
   a) habeas corpus
   b) certiorari
   c) stare decisis
   d) rule of four
   e) senatorial courtesy

3. The term *writ of habeas corpus* refers to *(p. 374)*
   a) a criterion used by courts to screen cases that no longer require resolution.
   b) a decision of at least four of the nine Supreme Court justices to review a decision of a lower court.
   c) a short, unsigned decision by an appellate court, usually rejecting a petition to review the decision of a lower court.
   d) a brief filed by the solicitor general when the federal government is not a direct litigant in a Supreme Court case.
   e) a court order that an individual in custody be brought into court and shown the cause for his or her detention.

4. Where do most trials in America take place? *(p. 375)*
   a) state courts
   b) appellate courts
   c) federal courts
   d) federal circuit courts
   e) the Supreme Court

5. Under what authority is the number of Supreme Court justices decided? *(pp. 377–78)*
   a) the president
   b) the chief justice
   c) the Department of Justice
   d) Congress
   e) the Constitution

6. The Supreme Court's decision in *Marbury v. Madison* was important because *(pp. 380–82)*
   a) it invalidated state laws prohibiting interracial marriage.
   b) it ruled that the recitation of prayers in public schools are unconstitutional under the establishment clause of the First Amendment.
   c) it established that arrested people have the right to remain silent, the right to be informed that anything they say can be held against them, and the right to counsel before and during police interrogation.
   d) if provided an expansive definition of *commerce* under the interstate commerce clause.
   e) it established the power of judicial review.

7. The Supreme Court rules on what percentage of the appeals it receives in an average year? *(p. 385)*
   a) less than 1 percent
   b) less than 20 percent
   c) about 50 percent
   d) about 75 percent
   e) 100 percent

8. Which of the following influences the flow of cases heard by the Supreme Court? *(pp. 385–88)*
   a) the attorney general and the Secretary of State
   b) the solicitor general and law clerks
   c) the president and Congress
   d) state legislatures
   e) the federal district and circuit courts

9. Which government official is responsible for arguing the federal government's position in cases before the Supreme Court? *(p. 386)*
   a) the vice president
   b) the solicitor general
   c) the attorney general
   d) the chief justice
   e) the U.S. district attorney

10. Which of the following is a brief submitted to the Supreme Court by someone other than one of the parties in the case? *(p. 387)*
    a) amicus curiae
    b) habeas corpus
    c) writ of certiorari
    d) ex post brief
    e) de jure brief

11. A dissenting opinion is written by *(p. 390)*
    a) the chief justice of the Supreme Court.

b) a Supreme Court justice who agrees with the majority's ultimate decision but wishes to emphasize a different rationale or emphasis.
c) a Supreme Court justice who disagrees with the majority decision.
d) the solicitor general.
e) a Supreme Court justice assigned by the chief justice.

12. Justices who favor going beyond the words of the Constitution to consider the broader societal implications of the Supreme Court's decisions are considered advocates of which judicial philosophy? *(p. 392)*
    a) original intent
    b) judicial restraint
    c) judicial activism
    d) judicial constitutionalism
    e) stare decisis

Key Terms

amicus curiae *(p. 387)* literally, "friend of the court"; individuals or groups who are not parties to a lawsuit but who seek to assist the Supreme Court in reaching a decision by presenting additional briefs

briefs *(p. 388)* written documents in which attorneys explain, using case precedents, why the court should find in favor of their client

chief justice *(p. 377)* justice on the Supreme Court who presides over the Court's public sessions and whose official title is chief justice of the United States

civil law *(p. 372)* the branch of law that deals with disputes that do not involve criminal penalties

court of appeals *(p. 373)* a court that hears the appeals of trial court decisions

criminal law *(p. 371)* the branch of law that regulates the conduct of individuals, defines crimes, and specifies punishment for criminal acts

defendant *(p. 371)* the one against whom a complaint is brought in a criminal or civil case

dissenting opinion *(p. 390)* a decision written by a justice in the minority in a particular case in which the justice wishes to express his or her reasoning in the case

due process of law *(p. 374)* the right of every citizen against arbitrary action by national or state governments

judicial activism *(p. 392)* judicial philosophy that posits that the Court should go beyond the words of the Constitution or a statute to consider the broader societal implications of its decisions

judicial restraint *(p. 391)* judicial philosophy whose adherents refuse to go beyond the clear words of the Constitution in interpreting the document's meaning

judicial review *(p. 380)* the power of the courts to review and, if necessary, declare actions of the legislative and executive branches invalid or unconstitutional; the Supreme Court asserted this power in *Marbury v. Madison*

jurisdiction *(p. 374)* the sphere of a court's power and authority

opinion *(p. 390)* the written explanation of the Supreme Court's decision in a particular case

oral argument *(p. 388)* the stage in Supreme Court procedure in which attorneys for both sides appear before the Court to present their positions and answer questions posed by justices

original jurisdiction *(p. 375)* the authority to initially consider a case; distinguished from appellate jurisdiction, which is the authority to hear appeals from a lower court's decision

plaintiff *(p. 371)* the individual or organization that brings a complaint in court

plea bargain *(p. 374)* a negotiated agreement in a criminal case in a which a defendant agrees to plead guilty in return for the state's agreement to reduce the severity of the criminal charge the defendant is facing

precedent *(p. 372)* prior case whose principles are used by judges as the basis for their decisions in present cases

senatorial courtesy *(p. 378)* the practice whereby the president, before formally nominating a person for a federal judgeship, seeks the indication that senators from the candidate's own state support the nomination

solicitor general *(p. 386)* the top government lawyer in all cases before the Supreme Court in which the government is a party

stare decisis *(p. 372)* literally, "let the decision stand"; the doctrine that a previous decision by a court applies as a precedent in similar cases until that decision is overruled

supremacy clause *(p. 383)* Article VI of the Constitution, which states that laws passed by the national government and all treaties "shall be the supreme Law of the Land" and superior to all laws adopted by any state or any subdivision

supreme court *(p. 373)* the highest court in a particular state or in the United States; this court primarily serves an appellate function

trial court *(p. 372)* the first court to hear a criminal or civil case

writ of certiorari *(p. 385)* a decision of at least four of the nine Supreme Court justices to review a decision of a lower court; *certiorari* is Latin, meaning "to make more certain"

writ of habeas corpus *(p. 374)* a court order that the individual in custody be brought into court and shown the cause for detention; habeas corpus is guaranteed by the Constitution and can be suspended only in cases of rebellion or invasion

For Further Reading

Abraham, Henry. *The Judicial Process*, 7th ed. New York: Oxford University Press, 1998.

Baum, Lawrence. *The Supreme Court*, 10th ed. Washington, DC: CQ Press, 2009.

Epstein, Lee. *Constitutional Law for a Changing America*. Washington, DC: CQ Press, 2007.

Fisher, Louis. *Constitutional Dialogues*. Princeton, NJ: Princeton University Press, 1988.

Greenberg, Jan Crawford. *Supreme Conflict: The Inside Story of the United States Supreme Court*. New York: Penguin, 2008.

Hall, Kermit L., James Ely, and Joel Grossman. *The Oxford Companion to the Supreme Court*. New York: Oxford University Press, 2005.

Irons, Peter. *A People's History of the Supreme Court*. New York: Penguin, 2006.

Johnson, Timothy R. *Oral Arguments and Decision Making on the U.S. Supreme Court*. Albany, NY: SUNY Press, 2004.

O'Brien, David M. *Storm Center: The Supreme Court in American Politics*, 8th ed. New York: W. W. Norton, 2008.

Spitzer, Robert J., ed. *Politics and Constitutionalism*. Albany, NY: SUNY Press, 2000.

Spitzer, Robert J. *Saving the Constitution from Lawyers*. New York: Cambridge University Press, 2008.

Stevens, John Paul. *Six Amendments: How and Why We Should Change the Constitution*. Boston: Little, Brown, 2014.

Sunstein, Cass. *Are Judges Political?* Washington, DC: Brookings Institution, 2006.

Toobin, Jeffrey. *The Oath: The Obama White House and the Supreme Court*. New York: Anchor, 2013.

Ward, Artemus. *Deciding to Leave: The Politics of Retirement from the U.S. Supreme Court*. Albany, NY: SUNY Press, 2003.

Health care is an area of social policy that has been controversial. Although most Americans support universal access to health care, they disagree about the best way to ensure high-quality health care. As Congress considered various proposals in 2009 and 2010, the debate heated up.

13

Domestic Policy

WHAT GOVERNMENT DOES AND WHY IT MATTERS Public policy refers to the decisions, rules, and regulations produced by the government. This chapter gives much of its attention to one broad subcategory of public policy: social policy. Social policies are important because they promote a range of public goals found in most public policies. The first is to protect against the risks and insecurities that most people face over the course of their lives. These include illness, disability, temporary unemployment, and the reduced earning capability that comes with old age. Most spending on social welfare in the United States goes to programs that serve these purposes, such as Social Security and medical insurance for the elderly. These are widely regarded as successful and popular (though expensive) programs.

Comprehensive health care reform is more controversial. Most Americans support universal access to health care, but when it comes to specific proposals, they often express doubts. Democrats experienced the public's ambivalence about health care reform after they enacted major changes to the system in 2010. The Patient Protection and Affordable Care Act is complex legislation that many people find hard to understand. Some parts of it are clearly popular, such as the provisions that allow young people to remain on their parents' insurance until they reach the age of 26 and that provide full coverage of many preventive health services for adults and children. Other features, such as the requirement that everyone purchase insurance—with federal assistance—remain unpopular. Even after the law was fully implemented in 2014, the public was split, with 46 percent of Americans holding an unfavorable view of the law and 38 percent holding a favorable view (the remaining 16 percent didn't have an opinion or didn't answer). Two years after its enactment, Americans could not agree about the role government should play in ensuring health care for all.[1]

In the last several chapters, we examined the parts of the government that make policy: Congress, the presidency, the bureaucracy, and the courts. This chapter and Chapter 14 examine that which is produced by the government—namely, public policy. Many, many books have been written about public policy, and it is not possible to cover the whole range of policies in a single chapter. So this chapter and Chapter 14 will divide the subject in half and focus on a few selected examples. This chapter will focus on domestic policy, meaning policies that shape what happens within our nation's borders. Chapter 14 will examine foreign policy, meaning policies that shape America's relations with the other nations of the world.

In this chapter, we will examine the different approaches to achieving policy goals. We will then examine one broad area of domestic public policy, called social policy. We focus on social policy because much of the government's annual budget goes to social programs, because such spending is often controversial, and because this process illustrates how the government tries to accomplish its goals.

chaptergoals

- Explain how different kinds of public policies achieve their goals using different means (pp. 403–11)

- Trace the history of government programs designed to help the poor (pp. 411–17)

- Describe how education, health, and housing policies try to promote equality of opportunity (pp. 417–24)

- Explain how contributory and noncontributory programs benefit different groups of Americans (pp. 424–29)

The Tools for Making Policy Are Techniques of Control

> **Explain how different kinds of public policies achieve their goals using different means**

Most of this book has focused on how government gets things done. This chapter, and Chapter 14, will focus on what the government produces, called **public policy**. Public policy can be defined simply as a law, a rule, a statute, or an edict that expresses the government's goals and provides for rewards and punishments to promote those goals' attainment. Public policy can include a law passed by Congress, a presidential directive, a Supreme Court ruling, or a rule issued by a bureaucratic agency.

In trying to achieve some purpose, public policy is inherently coercive, even when motivated by the best and most benign intentions. Note that the word *policy* shares a root with the word *police*. Both terms come from the Greek words *polis* and *politeia*, which refer to the political community and the sources of public authority. So it is important to remember that although the idea of coercion seems inherently negative, it is in fact a vital and necessary part of governing. (If overused or misused, however, coercion can obviously be harmful.)

Techniques of control are to policy makers what tools are to a carpenter. There are a limited number of techniques that the government can use, each with its own logic and limitations. An accumulation of experience helps us to understand when a certain technique is likely to work. Still, just as carpenters will have different ideas about the best tool for a job, so policy makers will disagree about which techniques work best and when. What we offer here is a workable elementary handbook of techniques that will be useful for analyzing policy.

Table 13.1 lists some important techniques of control available to policy makers. These techniques can be grouped into three categories: promotional, regulatory, and redistributive policies.

Promotional Policies Get People to Do Things by Giving Them Rewards

Promotional policies are the carrots of public policy. Their purpose is to encourage people to do something they might not otherwise do or to get people to do more of what they are already doing. Sometimes the purpose is merely to compensate people for something done in the past. Promotional techniques can be classified into at least two separate types: subsidies and contracting.

Subsidies **Subsidies** are simply government grants of cash or other valuable commodities, such as land, to individuals or an organization that are used to promote activities desired by the government, to reward political support, or to buy off political opposition. Subsidies were the dominant form of public policy of the national government and the state and local governments throughout the nineteenth century. They continue to be an important category of public policy at all levels of government.

During the nineteenth century, subsidies in the form of land grants were given to farmers and to railroad companies to encourage western settlement. Substantial cash

TABLE 13.1

Techniques of Public Control

TYPE OF POLICY	TECHNIQUES	DEFINITIONS AND EXAMPLES
Promotional	Subsidies and grants of cash, land, etc.	"Patronage"—the promotion of private activity through what recipients consider "benefits" (example: in the nineteenth century the government encouraged westward settlement by granting land to those who went west)
	Contracts	Agreements with individuals or firms in the "private sector" to purchase goods or services
	Licenses	Unconditional permission to do something that is otherwise illegal (franchise, permit)
Regulatory	Criminal penalties	Heavy fines or imprisonment, loss of citizenship
	Civil penalties	Less onerous fines, probation, public exposure, restitution
	Administrative regulations	The setting of interest rates, maintenance of health and safety standards, and investigation and publicizing of wrongdoing
	Subsidies and contracts	Can be considered regulatory when certain conditions are attached (example: the government refuses to award a contract to firms that show no evidence of affirmative action in hiring)
	Regulatory taxes	Taxes that keep down consumption or production (liquor, gas, cigarette taxes)
	Expropriation	"Eminent domain"—the power to take private property for public use
Redistributive	Taxes	Alteration of the redistribution of money by changing taxes or tax rules
	Budgeting and spending through subsidies and contracts	Deficit spending to pump money into the economy when it needs a boost; creation of a budget surplus by cutting spending or increasing taxes to discourage consumption in inflationary times
	Fiscal use of credit and interest (monetary techniques)	Change in interest rates to affect both demand for money and consumption (example: the Federal Reserve Board raises interest rates to slow economic growth and ward off inflation)

subsidies have traditionally been given to shipbuilders to help build the commercial fleet and to guarantee the use of their ships as military personnel carriers in time of war. Policies using the subsidy technique have continued to be plentiful in the twentieth century and into the twenty-first, even after the 1990s, when there was widespread public and official hostility toward subsidies. For example, in 2007 the annual value of corporate subsidies, not including agriculture, was estimated at $92 billion.[2]

Subsidies have always been a technique favored by politicians because they can be treated as benefits that can be spread widely in response to many demands that might otherwise produce profound political conflict. Subsidies can, in other words, be used to buy off the opposition. And once subsidies exist, the threat of their removal becomes a very significant technique of control.

Contracting Like any corporation, a government agency must purchase goods and services by contract. The law requires open bidding for a substantial proportion of these contracts because government contracts are extremely valuable to businesses in the private sector and because the opportunities and incentives for abuse are very great. Yet contracting is more than a method of buying goods and services. It is also an important technique of policy because government agencies are often authorized to use their **contracting power** (the power of government to set conditions on companies seeking to sell goods or services to government agencies) as a means of encouraging corporations to improve themselves, as a means of helping to build up whole sectors of the economy, and as a means of encouraging certain desirable goals or behavior, such as equal employment opportunity. For example, the infant airline industry of the 1930s was nurtured by the national government's lucrative contracts to carry airmail.

Military contracting has long been a major element in government spending. So tight was the connection between defense contractors and the federal government during the Cold War that as he was leaving office, President Eisenhower warned the nation to beware of the powerful "military-industrial complex." After the Cold War, as military spending and production declined, major defense contractors began to look for alternative business activities to supplement the reduced demand for weapons. For example, Lockheed Martin, the nation's largest defense contractor, began to bid on contracts related to welfare reform. Since the terrorist attacks of 2001, however, the military budget has been awash in new funds, and military contractors are flooded with business. President Bush increased the Pentagon budget by more than 7 percent a year, requesting so many weapons systems that one observer called the budget a "weapons smorgasbord."[3] Military contractors geared up to produce not only weapons for foreign warfare but also surveillance systems to enhance domestic security.

Regulatory Policies Are Rules Backed by Penalties

If promotional policies are the carrots of public policy, regulatory policies can be considered the sticks. Regulation is a technique of control in which the government adopts rules imposing restrictions on the conduct of private citizens. They come in several forms, but every regulatory technique shares a common trait: direct government control of conduct. The conduct may be regulated because people feel it is harmful to others, or threatens to be, such as drunk driving or false advertising. Or the conduct may be regulated because people think it's immoral, whether it harms others or not, such as prostitution, gambling, or drinking. Because there are many forms of regulation, we have subdivided them here: (1) police regulation, through civil and criminal penalties; (2) administrative regulation; (3) regulatory taxation; and (4) expropriation.

Police Regulation "Police regulation" comes closest to the traditional exercise of police power—a power traditionally reserved to the states to regulate the health, safety, and morals of its citizens. After a person's arrest and conviction, these techniques are administered by courts and, where necessary, penal institutions. They are regulatory techniques.

Civil penalties usually refer to fines or some other form of material restitution (such as public service) as a sanction for violating civil laws or common law principles, or committing negligence. Civil penalties can range from a five-dollar fine for a parking violation to a more onerous penalty for late payment of income taxes to the much more onerous penalties for violating antitrust laws against unfair competition or environmental protection laws against pollution. Criminal penalties usually refer to imprisonment but can also involve heavy fines and the loss of certain civil rights and liberties, such as the right to vote.

Administrative Regulation Police regulation addresses conduct considered immoral. In order to eliminate such conduct, strict laws have been passed and severe sanctions enacted. But what about conduct that is not considered morally wrong but that may have harmful consequences? For example, there is nothing morally wrong with radio or television broadcasting. But government regulates broadcasting on a particular frequency or channel because there would be virtual chaos if everybody could broadcast on any frequency at any time.

This kind of conduct is thought of less as *policed* conduct and more as *regulated* conduct. When conduct is said to be regulated, the purpose is rarely to eliminate the conduct but rather to influence it toward more appropriate channels, toward more appropriate locations, or toward certain qualified types of persons, all for the purpose of minimizing injuries or inconveniences. This type of regulation is sometimes called administrative regulation because the controls are given over to civilian agencies rather than to the police, and the rules are made by regulatory agencies and commissions. Each regulatory agency has extensive powers to keep a sector of the economy under surveillance and also has powers to make rules dealing with the behavior of individual companies and people. But these administrative agencies have fewer powers of punishment than the police and the courts have, and the administrative agencies generally rely on the courts to issue orders enforcing the rules and decisions made by the agencies.

Table 13.1 lists subsidies and contracts as examples of both promotional and regulatory policies; although these techniques might normally be thought of as strictly promotional policies, they can also be used as techniques of administrative regulation. It all depends on whether the law sets serious conditions on eligibility for the subsidy or contract. To put it another way, the government can use the threat of losing a valuable subsidy or contract to improve compliance with the goals of regulation. For example, the threat of removal of the subsidies called "federal aid to education" has had a very significant influence on the willingness of schools to cooperate in the desegregation of their student bodies and faculties. For another example, social welfare subsidies (benefits) can be lowered to encourage or force people to take low-paying jobs, or they can be increased to calm political unrest when people are engaging in political protest.[4]

Regulatory Taxation In many instances, the primary purpose of a tax is not to raise revenue but to influence conduct, often to discourage or eliminate an activity altogether by making it too expensive for most people. Such taxes are called regulatory taxes. For example, since the end of Prohibition, although there has been no penalty for the production or sale of alcoholic beverages, the alcohol industry has not been free from regulation. First, all alcoholic beverages have to be licensed, allowing only those companies that are "bonded" to put their product on the market. Beyond that, federal and state taxes on alcohol are made disproportionately high, on the theory that, in addition to the revenue gained, less alcohol will be consumed. The same is true of cigarette taxes.

Expropriation Confiscation of property with or without compensation for a public use, or expropriation, is a widely used technique of control in the United States, especially in land-use regulation. Almost all public works, from highways to parks to government office buildings, involve the forceful taking of some private property in order to assemble sufficient land and the correct distribution of land for the necessary construction.

We generally call the power to expropriate eminent domain (the right of government to take private property for public use), a power that is recognized as inherent in any government. The Fifth Amendment of the U.S. Constitution provides an important safeguard against abuse, saying that private property cannot be taken for public use "without just compensation." Thus, the government is not permitted to use that power except through a strict due process, and it must offer "fair market value" for the land sought.[5]

Forcing individuals to work for a public purpose is another form of expropriation. The draft of young men for the armed forces, court orders to strikers to return to work, and sentences for convicted felons to do community service are examples of the regular use of expropriation in the United States.

Redistributive Policies Affect Broad Classes of People

Redistributive policies (also called macroeconomic policies) are usually of two types, monetary and fiscal, but they have a common purpose: to control people by manipulating the entire economy rather than by regulating *people* directly. (Macroeconomic refers to the economy as a whole.) Whereas regulatory policies focus on individual conduct, redistributive policies seek to control conduct more indirectly by altering the conditions of conduct or manipulating the environment of conduct.

Monetary Policies **Monetary policies** allow government to regulate the economy through the manipulation of the supply of money and credit. America's most powerful institution in this area of monetary policy is the Federal Reserve Board (the Fed), the governing board of the **Federal Reserve System**, consisting of a chair and six other members, all appointed by the president with the consent of the Senate. The Fed can affect the total amount of credit available through the interest (called the federal funds rate) that member banks charge one another for loans. If the Fed significantly decreases the federal funds rate, it can give a boost to a sagging economy. During 2001 the Fed cut interest rates eleven times to combat the combined effects of recession and the terrorist attacks. In the steep recession that began in 2008, the Fed acted aggressively. By December 2008 it had cut rates nine times, from a high in September 2007 of 4.75 percent to a historically low zero percentage rate. Moreover, the Federal Reserve kept interest rates at or near that level well into 2014, in an attempt to encourage new lending and thus economic growth.[6] If the Fed raises the federal funds rate, it can put a brake on the economy, because the higher discount rate also increases the general interest rates charged by leading private banks to their customers. Although the Federal Reserve is responsible for ensuring high employment as well as price stability, it has been particularly important in fighting inflation. During the late 1970s and early '80s, with inflation at record-high levels, Federal Reserve chairman Paul Volcker aggressively raised interest rates in order to dampen inflation. Although his actions provoked a sharp recession, they raised the stature of the Fed, demonstrating its ability to manage the economy.

The chair of the Federal Reserve is one of the most important people in Washington, as the Fed plays an important role in maintaining a strong national economy. At her confirmation hearing in 2013, Janet Yellen discussed the role of the Fed in reducing unemployment and in keeping inflation at approximately 2 percent a year.

Fiscal Policies **Fiscal policies** are the government's use of taxing, monetary, and spending powers to manipulate the economy. Personal and corporate income taxes, which raise most of the U.S. government's revenues, are the most prominent examples. While the direct purpose of an income tax is to raise revenue, each tax has a different impact on the economy, and government can plan for that impact. Although the primary purpose of the graduated income tax is, of course, to raise revenue, an important second objective is to collect revenue in such a way as to reduce the disparities of wealth between the lowest and the highest income brackets. We call this a policy of redistribution. Another policy objective of the income tax is the encouragement of the capitalist economy by rewarding investment. The tax laws allow individuals or companies to deduct from their taxable income any money they can justify as an investment or a "business expense"; this gives an incentive to individuals and companies to spend money to expand their production, their advertising, or their staff, and reduces the income taxes that businesses have to pay.

Americans have long debated the appropriate levels of taxation on individual and corporate income. After passing major income tax cuts in 2001, President Bush proposed and Congress passed a sweeping new round of cuts in 2003. Bush's plan was intended to promote investment by reducing taxes on most stock dividends, to spur business activity by offering tax breaks to small businesses, and to stimulate the economy by reducing the tax rates for all taxpayers. In 2006, Congress extended the rate reductions on dividends and capital gains, a move that estimates showed would cost the treasury $70 billion over five years.

President Obama and the Democratic leadership proposed extending the tax cuts for everyone with annual incomes under $250,000; those making more would have their income taxes revert back to the rates in the 1990s. Republicans and some Democrats preferred to extend the tax cuts for everyone. At the end of 2010, Obama and Congress reached a deal to extend the Bush tax cuts for two years. In 2013 they were extended again and made permanent.

Spending Power as Fiscal Policy Perhaps the most important redistributive technique of all is the most familiar one: the "spending power," which is a combination of subsidies and contracts. Government can use these techniques to achieve policy goals far beyond buying goods and services and regulating individual conduct. This is why subsidies and contracts show up yet again in Table 13.1 as redistributive techniques.

Agricultural subsidies are one example of the national government's use of its purchasing power as a fiscal or redistributive technique. Since the 1930s the federal government has attempted to raise and to stabilize the prices of several important agricultural products, such as corn and wheat, by authorizing the Department of Agriculture to buy enormous amounts of these commodities if prices on the market fall below a fixed level.

Should the Government Intervene in the Economy?

All politicians want a healthy economy, but they often differ in their views about how to attain it. Addressing economic challenges and maintaining a strong economy

Tax Rates around the World

How do tax rates in the United States compare to those in other countries? Focusing just on personal income taxes, different countries have different tax rates depending on income, and individuals may receive tax relief if they are married or have children. As the first figure here shows, U.S. income tax rates (federal plus average state income taxes) are slightly below average when compared to other countries in the Organization for Economic Cooperation and Development (OECD).

However, when we look at the total tax burden as a share of the country's economy (GDP), the tax burden in the United States is significantly less than in other wealthy countries. The second figure shows how the United States compares to selected OECD countries and the average for all OECD countries. When we compare total tax revenue as a percentage of GDP,[a] Chile and Mexico are the only OECD members that have a lower tax burden than the United States.[b]

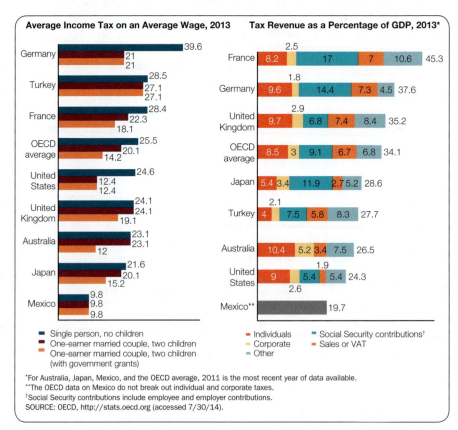

Average Income Tax on an Average Wage, 2013

Country	Single person, no children	One-earner married couple, two children	One-earner married couple, two children (with government grants)
Germany	39.6	21	21
Turkey	28.5	27.1	27.1
France	28.4	22.3	18.1
OECD average	25.5	20.1	14.2
United States	24.6	12.4	12.4
United Kingdom	24.1	24.1	19.1
Australia	23.1	23.1	12
Japan	21.6	20.1	15.2
Mexico	9.8	9.8	9.8

Tax Revenue as a Percentage of GDP, 2013*

Country	Individuals	Corporate	Social Security contributions[†]	Sales or VAT	Other	Total
France	8.2	2.5	17	7	10.6	45.3
Germany	9.6	1.8	14.4	7.3	4.5	37.6
United Kingdom	9.7	2.9	6.8	7.4	8.4	35.2
OECD average	8.5	3	9.1	6.7	6.8	34.1
Japan	5.4	3.4	11.9	2.7	5.2	28.6
Turkey	4	2.1	7.5	5.8	8.3	27.7
Australia	10.4		5.2	3.4	7.5	26.5
United States	9	1.9	5.4	5.4	2.6	24.3
Mexico**					19.7	19.7

*For Australia, Japan, Mexico, and the OECD average, 2011 is the most recent year of data available.

**The OECD data on Mexico do not break out individual and corporate taxes.

[†]Social Security contributions include employee and employer contributions.

SOURCE: OECD, http://stats.oecd.org (accessed 7/30/14).

[a]Since larger, wealthier economies generate more tax revenue than smaller and poorer countries, controlling for GDP gives us a more comparable measure of tax burdens across different types of economies.

[b]OECD.StatExtract, "All-In Average Personal Income Tax Rates at Average Wage by Family Type," Table I.6, http://stats.oecd.org/index.aspx?DataSetCode=TABLE_I6 (accessed 7/31/14).

are extremely important to political leaders. Until 1929 most Americans believed that government had little to do with actively managing the economy. The world was guided by the theory that the economy, if left to its own devices, would produce full employment and maximum production. This traditional view of the relationship between government and the economy crumbled in 1929 before the stark reality of the Great Depression of 1929–33. When President Franklin Delano Roosevelt took office in 1933, he energetically threw the federal government into the business of fighting the Depression. One of the main ways that the federal government sought to keep the economy healthy was through decisions about taxing and spending in accordance with the ideas of the British economist John Maynard Keynes. Keynesians argue that by pumping money into the economy, particularly by running deficits during periods of recession, government can stimulate demand and create a cycle of increased production and jobs that will pull the economy out of recession.

In the 1980s growing numbers of Republicans began to reject the idea that government could help ensure economic prosperity. Instead, they argued that freeing markets from government intervention would produce the best economic results. As Ronald Reagan put it in his first inaugural address, "Government is not the solution to our problem, government is the problem."[7] Many Democrats, on the other hand, continued to believe that government has an important role to play in promoting a strong economy. This fundamental disagreement between the parties over the appropriate role of government underlies the fierce contemporary political debates over the government's role in the economy.

Today some of the most intense conflicts between Democrats and Republicans concern taxes. As Republicans embraced the idea that reducing the role of government in the economy would promote investment and spur economic growth, they made tax cuts their highest priority. Because no one really likes to pay taxes, Republican support for tax cuts creates a political dilemma for Democrats. How can they defend taxes? Polls show that most of the time—although not always—a majority of Americans think that their taxes are too high.[8] Aware of the political damage that might come from opposing tax cuts, many Democratic members of Congress have supported tax cuts. But because most Democrats favor higher levels of public spending than do Republicans, they ultimately need taxes to fund government programs. To resolve this political problem, Democrats have sought to increase taxes on the wealthy. One reliable finding in public opinion polls is that the majority of Americans agree that upper-income people are not paying their fair share of taxes.[9] Raising taxes on the wealthy involves boosting taxes on investment income, which accounts for a much greater share of the income for the wealthy.

● Social Policy and the Welfare System Buttress Equality

Trace the history of government programs designed to help the poor

For much of American history, local governments and private charities—not the federal government—were in charge of caring for the poor. During the 1930s, when this largely private system of charity collapsed in the face of widespread economic destitution, the federal government created the beginnings of an American welfare state. The idea of the welfare system was new; it meant that the national government would oversee programs designed to promote economic security for all Americans—not just for the poor. The American system of social welfare includes many different policies enacted over the years since the Great Depression. Because each program is governed by distinct rules, the kind and level of assistance available vary widely.

The History of the Government Welfare System Dates Only to the 1930s

There has always been a welfare system in America, but until 1935 it was almost entirely private, composed of an extensive system of voluntary philanthropy through churches and other religious groups, ethnic and fraternal societies, communities and neighborhoods, and philanthropically inclined rich individuals. Most often it was called charity, and although it was private and voluntary, it was thought of as a public obligation.

The traditional approach of charity crumbled in the face of the stark reality of the Great Depression. During the Depression, misfortune became so widespread and private wealth shrank so drastically that private charity was out of the question and the distinction between deserving and undeserving became impossible to

In the early days of the Depression, much of the assistance for the destitute was provided by private groups, through projects such as New York City soup kitchens. Just a few years later, the government became responsible for providing food to needy families.

draw. Following the crash of 1929 around 20 percent of the workforce immediately became unemployed; this figure grew as the Depression stretched into years. Moreover, few of the unemployed had any monetary resources or any family farm on which to fall back. Banks failed, wiping out the savings of millions who had been prudent enough or fortunate enough to have any savings at all. Thousands of businesses failed as well, throwing middle-class Americans onto the bread lines along with unemployed laborers, dispossessed farmers, and those who had never worked in any capacity whatsoever. The Great Depression proved to Americans that poverty could be a result of imperfections in the economic system as well as of individual irresponsibility. It also forced Americans to drastically alter their standards regarding who was deserving and who was not.

Once poverty and dependency were accepted as problems inherent in the economic system, a large-scale public policy approach was not far away. By the time President Franklin Delano Roosevelt took office in 1933, the question was not whether there was to be a public welfare system but how generous or restrictive that system would be.

The Social Security Act of 1935 Was the Foundation of the Welfare System

The modern welfare state in the U.S. began with the enactment of the Social Security Act of 1935. This act created two separate categories of welfare: contributory and noncontributory.

Contributory Programs The category of welfare programs that are financed by taxation or other mandatory contributions by their present or future recipients can justifiably be called "forced savings" because these programs force working Americans to contribute a portion of their earnings to provide income and benefits during their retirement years. These **contributory programs** are what most people have in mind when they refer to **Social Security** or social insurance, a contributory welfare program into which working Americans contribute a percentage of their wages and from which they receive cash benefits after retirement. Under the original contributory program, old-age insurance, the employer and the employee were each required to pay equal amounts, which in 1937 were set at 1 percent of the first $3,000 of wages, to be deducted from the paycheck of each employee and matched by the same amount from the employer. This percentage has increased over the years; the contribution in 2014 was 7.65 percent subdivided as follows: 6.2 percent on the first $117,100 of income for Social Security benefits, plus 1.45 percent on all earnings for Medicare.[10] Starting in 2014 households earning over $250,000 a year paid an extra 0.9 percent in Medicare taxes as a result of a provision in the Affordable Care Act. In the short term, Social Security redistributes money from younger workers to older retirees: the taxes of current workers are paying for the benefits received by retirees.

Congress increased Social Security benefits every two or three years during the 1950s and '60s. The biggest single expansion in contributory programs since 1935 was the establishment in 1965 of **Medicare**, a form of national health insurance for the elderly and the disabled that provides substantial medical services to elderly persons who are already eligible to receive old-age, survivors', and disability insurance under the original Social Security system. In 2003, Congress added a prescription drug benefit to the package of health benefits for the elderly. Social Security benefits and costs are adjusted through **indexing** (a periodic process of adjusting of social benefits or wages to account for increases in the cost of living), whereby benefits paid out under contributory programs are modified annually by **cost-of-living adjustments (COLAs)**—changes made to the level of benefits of a government program based on the rate of inflation. Of course, Social Security taxes (contributions) also increased after almost every benefit increase.

Noncontributory Programs Social programs that provide assistance to people based on demonstrated need rather than any contribution they have made—**noncontributory programs**—are also known as "public assistance programs," or more commonly as "welfare." Until 1996 the most important noncontributory program was Aid to Families with Dependent Children (AFDC, originally called Aid to Dependent Children), which provided federal funds, administered by the states, for children living with parents or relatives who fell below state standards of need. It was founded in 1935 by the original Social Security Act. In 1996, Congress abolished AFDC and replaced it with the Temporary Assistance to Needy Families (TANF) block grant. Eligibility for public assistance is determined by **means testing**, a procedure that requires applicants to show a financial need for assistance. Between 1935 and 1965 the government created programs to provide housing assistance, school lunches, and food stamps to other needy Americans.

As with contributory programs, the noncontributory public assistance programs made their most significant advances in the 1960s and '70s. The largest single category of expansion was the establishment in 1965 of **Medicaid**, a federally and state-funded, state-operated program that provides extended medical services to low-income Americans. Noncontributory programs underwent another major transformation in the 1970s in the level of benefits they provide. Besides being means tested, noncontributory programs are state based; grants-in-aid are provided by the federal government to the states as incentives to establish the programs, but states retain considerable leeway to establish eligibility criteria (see Chapter 3). Thus from the beginning there were considerable disparities in benefits from state to state. The national government sought to rectify the disparities in levels of old-age benefits in 1974 by creating the Supplemental Security Income (SSI) program to augment benefits for the aged, the blind, and the disabled. SSI provides uniform minimum benefits across the entire nation and includes mandatory COLAs. States are allowed to be more generous if they wish, but no state is permitted to provide benefits below the minimum level set by the national government. As a result, 25 states increased their own SSI benefits to the mandated level.

The TANF program is also administered by the states and, as with the old-age benefits just discussed, benefit levels vary widely from state to state (see Figure 13.1). In 2013 the states' monthly TANF benefits varied from $170 in Mississippi to $923 in Alaska.[11] Even the most generous TANF payments are well below the federal poverty line. In 2014 the poverty level for a family of three included those earning $19,790 a year, or $1,649 a month.[12]

The number of people receiving AFDC benefits expanded in the 1970s, in part because new welfare programs had been established in the mid-1960s: Medicaid

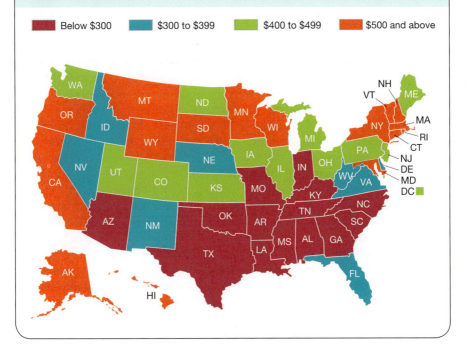

(discussed earlier) and the **Supplemental Nutrition Assistance Program (SNAP)**, which is still sometimes called by its old name, food stamps. SNAP is the largest anti-poverty program, which provides recipients with a debit card for food at most grocery stores. Collectively, these programs provide what are called **in-kind benefits**—noncash goods and services provided by the government that the beneficiary would otherwise have to pay for in cash. Because AFDC recipients automatically received Medicaid and food stamps, these new program created an incentive for poor Americans to establish their eligibility for AFDC.

Welfare Reform Has Dominated the Welfare Agenda in Recent Years

From the 1960s to the 1990s, opinion polls consistently showed that the public viewed welfare beneficiaries as "undeserving."[13] Underlying that judgment was the belief that welfare recipients did not want to work. These negative assessments were amplified by racial stereotypes. By 1973, 46 percent of welfare recipients were African American. Although the majority of recipients were white, media portrayals helped to create the widespread perception that the vast majority of welfare recipients were black. A careful study by Martin Gilens has shown how racial stereotypes of blacks as uncommitted to the work ethic reinforced public opposition to welfare.[14]

Despite this public opposition, it proved difficult to reform welfare, and welfare rolls reached an all-time high in 1994. Sensing continuing public frustration with welfare, when Bill Clinton was a presidential candidate he vowed "to end welfare as we know it," an unusual promise for a Democrat. Once in office, Clinton found it difficult to design a plan that would provide an adequate safety net for recipients who were unable to find work. Clinton's major achievement in the welfare field was to increase the Earned Income Tax Credit (EITC). This credit now allows working parents whose annual income falls below $49,078 (for a family of three or more) to file through their income tax return for an income supplement of up to $5,751, depending on their income and family size. It was a first step toward realizing Clinton's campaign promise to ensure that "if you work, you shouldn't be poor."

Congressional Republicans proposed a much more dramatic reform of welfare, which Clinton, facing a campaign for re-election in 1996, signed. The Personal Responsibility and Work Opportunity Reconciliation Act (PRWORA) repealed AFDC and replaced it with the Temporary Assistance to Needy Families (TANF) program. In place of the individual entitlement to assistance, the new law created block grants to the states and allowed states much more discretion in designing their cash-assistance programs to needy families. The new law also established time limits, restricting recipients to two years of assistance and creating a lifetime limit of five years. It imposed new work requirements on those receiving welfare, and it restricted most legal immigrants from receiving benefits. The aim of the new law was to reduce welfare caseloads, promote work, and reduce out-of-wedlock births. Notably, reducing poverty was not one of its stated objectives.

After this law was enacted, the number of families receiving assistance dropped by 60 percent nationwide, from 5.1 million families in 1994 to 1.9 million families in 2005.[15] The sharp decline in the number of recipients was widely hailed as a sign that welfare reform was working. Indeed, former welfare recipients have been more successful at finding and keeping jobs than many critics of the law predicted. One important indicator of how welfare has changed is the proportion of funds it provides in cash assistance. Before the 1996 reform, assistance was provided largely in the form of a cash grant. By 2008, 70 percent of welfare funds were

In recent decades, welfare reform has emphasized work requirements and training for unemployed recipients. Here, an instructor provides training in using power tools as part of a Detroit-area welfare-to-work program funded by the federal government.

allocated for noncash assistance and 30 percent for cash assistance. This means that an increasing proportion of welfare funds is spent on such costs as assistance with transportation to work, temporary shelter, or onetime payments for emergencies so that people do not end up on the welfare rolls. The orientation of assistance has shifted away from subsidizing people who are not in the labor force and toward addressing temporary problems that low-income people face and providing assistance that facilitates work.[16] But critics point out that most former welfare recipients are not paid enough to pull their families out of poverty. While the 1996 law has helped reduce welfare caseloads, it has done little to reduce the underlying problem of poverty.[17]

As the economy soured in 2008 and 2009, the number of people on welfare rolls began to move upward, but at a very slow rate. The American Recovery and Reinvestment Act of 2009 included a TANF Emergency Fund that provided money for states to create subsidized jobs for low-income parents and young adults. Despite these measures, many advocates for the poor worried that the state TANF programs were not assisting enough poor families. After the Emergency Fund expired in 2011, advocates for the poor charged that, with states making deep cuts to their budgets, TANF was not keeping pace with the growth of poverty caused by the recession. They contrasted spending on TANF to the growth of the supplemental nutrition program (SNAP, or food stamps), whose growth closely tracked the rise in unemployment and poverty during the recession. In 2007, before the recession took hold, approximately 26.3 million individuals a month received SNAP benefits. By 2014 that number had risen to more than 46.9 million people a month, close to 15 percent of all Americans.[18]

● The Cycle of Poverty Can Be Broken by Education, Health, and Housing Policies

Describe how education, health, and housing policies try to promote equality of opportunity

The welfare state not only supplies a measure of economic security but also provides opportunity. The American belief in equality of opportunity makes such programs particularly important. Programs that provide opportunity keep people from falling into poverty, and they offer a hand up to those who are poor. At their best, opportunity policies allow all individuals to rise as high as their talents will take them. Three types of policies are most significant in opening opportunity: education policies, health policies, and housing policies.

Education Policies Provide Life Tools

Education is highly valued in America, a belief reflected in the fact that the vast majority of the education provided to Americans comes from public educational institutions financed through state, local, and (to a lesser extent) national government education policy. Less well appreciated is the fact that education is an extremely important factor in shaping the distribution and redistribution of wealth and opportunity in America.

Compared to state and local efforts, the role of national government education policy has been limited for most of American history. Moreover, the most important national education policies have come only since World War II: the GI Bill of Rights of 1944, the National Defense Education Act (NDEA) of 1958, the Elementary and Secondary Education Act (ESEA) of 1965, and various youth and adult vocational training acts since 1958. Note, however, that because the GI Bill was aimed almost entirely at postsecondary schooling, the national government did not really enter the field of elementary education until after 1957.[19]

What finally brought the national government into elementary education was embarrassment over the fact that the Soviet Union had beaten the United States into space with the launching of the world's first satellite, Sputnik. As a result, the federal government adopted the policy under NDEA of improving education in science and mathematics. At the same time, the federal government recognized the role of education in promoting equal opportunity. In 1965 the ESEA offered federal aid for education by allocating funds to school districts with substantial numbers of children from families who were unemployed or earning less than $2,000 a year. Today the federal government spends $74.9 billion, 12 percent of all spending on K–12 education; states and localities each account for 44 percent of spending. Over time, however, federal education funds have become less targeted on low-income districts as Congress has failed to update the formula for allocating funds.[20]

The federal role was substantially increased in 2001 by President George W. Bush's signature education act, No Child Left Behind (NCLB). Supported by Democrats and Republicans, the law sought to combine the goals of higher standards and equality of opportunity. It aimed to improve standards through stronger federal requirements for student testing and school accountability. Every child in grades 3 through 8 had to be tested yearly for proficiency in math and reading. The law aimed to promote equality of opportunity with two provisions: first, for a school to be judged a success, it had to show positive test results for all subcategories of children—minority race and ethnicity, English learners, and disability—not just overall averages. Second, parents with children in schools whose scores are poor had the right to transfer their children to a better school or to get funds for tutoring and summer programs.

NCLB initially attracted broad bipartisan support, but it quickly generated considerable controversy. Many states branded it an "unfunded mandate," noting that the law placed expensive new obligations on schools to improve their performance but provided woefully inadequate resources. Teachers objected that "teaching to the test" undermined critical-thinking skills. In some states, up to half of the schools failed to meet the new standards, which resulted in a costly remedial challenge. Under the federal law, they were required to improve student performance by providing such new services as supplemental tutoring, longer school days, and additional summer school. Critics also charged that NCLB actually undermined equal opportunity because it ended up punishing underperforming schools—mostly those schools that bear the greatest burden for teaching the neediest students.[21]

Faced with these conflicts, the Obama administration sought a major overhaul of NCLB. The president announced that states could apply for waivers that would exempt them from some of the requirements of NCLB. Waivers would be granted if states could show that they had their own plans for

Education policy is the most important means of providing equal opportunity for all Americans. President Obama sought to overhaul some problematic aspects of the No Child Left Behind Act, but Congress struggled to agree on the new provisions.

improving student achievement. By 2014, 45 states had been granted waivers from NCLB.[22]

But waivers did not signal a movement away from a standards-based approach to equality of opportunity. In fact, Obama's education initiatives have drawn many of the same criticisms that surrounded NCLB, especially the emphasis on high-stakes testing. As a condition of receiving waivers, states were required to show that they had adopted a strong set of educational standards and that they linked teacher evaluations to test results. Most states endorsed a set of standards known as the Common Core State Standards. Drawn up by representatives of the National Governors Association and the Council of Chief State School Officers in 2010, the standards set out clear markers for student knowledge. While many educators believed that the standards could serve as a tool for promoting equality of opportunity by improving education in all schools, the testing regime associated with the common core drew sharp criticisms from conservatives and liberals, and some education experts, as a return to the failed policies of NCLB. Some states and school districts withdrew from the program.[23]

The Obama administration had also put its own imprint on schools with its strong support for charter schools—publicly funded schools that are free from the bureaucratic rules and regulations of the school district in which they are located and free to design specialized curricula and to use resources in ways they think most effective. The Obama administration put its weight behind charter schools in one of its first pieces of legislation, the American Recovery and Reinvestment Act, sometimes called the stimulus bill. The act included a new $4.3 billion program called Race to the Top, which offered competitive grants to state education systems. The administration awarded sizable grants to 11 states and to Washington, D.C., praising the states for proposing bold new programs for assessing teachers and overhauling failing schools.[24] Several years after the program began, it was clear that states had promised more than they could do in the limited time that the funds were provided.[25]

Health Policies Mean Fewer Sick Days

Until recent decades, no government in the United States—national, state, or local—concerned itself directly with individual health. But public responsibility was always accepted for *public* health. After New York City's newly created Board of Health was credited with holding down a cholera epidemic in 1867, most states created statewide public health agencies. Within a decade, the results were obvious. Between 1884 and 1894, for example, Massachusetts's rate of infant mortality dropped from 161.3 per 1,000 to 141.4 per 1,000.[26]

The U.S. Public Health Service (USPHS) has been in existence since 1798 but was only a small part of public health policy until after World War II. Established in 1937, but little noticed for 20 years, was the National Institutes of Health (NIH), an agency within the USPHS created to do biomedical research. Between 1950 and 2012, NIH expenditures by the national government increased from $160.0 million to $30.9 billion. NIH research on the link between smoking and disease led to one of the most visible public-health campaigns in American history. Today, NIH's focus has turned to cancer and human immunodeficiency virus/acquired immune deficiency syndrome (HIV/AIDS). As with smoking, this work on HIV/AIDS has resulted in massive public-health education as well as new products and regulations. In 2013 federal spending on HIV/AIDS-related programs was $28 billion.[27]

Other recent commitments to the improvement of public health are the numerous laws aimed at cleaning up and defending the environment (including the creation in 1970 of the Environmental Protection Agency) and laws attempting to improve the health and safety of consumer products (regulated by the Consumer Product Safety Commission, created in 1972). Health policies aimed directly at the poor include Medicaid and nutritional programs, particularly food stamps and the school lunch program. As Figure 13.2 shows, the government has committed large resources to health care programs. While they yield great benefits by providing health care to millions, these programs have seen their costs rise dramatically in recent years—far more than the rate of inflation—prompting growing calls for major changes in spending and funding.

After the 2008 election the Obama administration and the Democratic Congress pressed forward with comprehensive health care reform. Seeking to avoid the conflicts that broke out in Congress over the Clintons' failed health care reform proposal, Obama offered Congress broad principles for reform, not a detailed proposal. The administration aimed to cover most Americans who lacked health insurance with a reform strategy that built on the existing system. The plan that ultimately passed, the Affordable Care Act (ACA), had three key features: the first was the creation of new state-based insurance exchanges where individuals could buy health insurance, along with insurance regulation that would prohibit

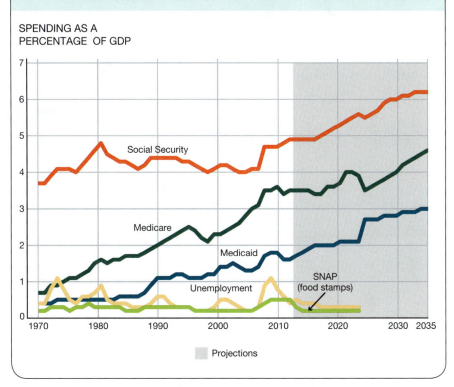

FIGURE 13.2 **The Size of the Welfare State**

Spending on Medicare, Medicaid, and Social Security are all projected to rise as a percent of GDP. Social Security, a contributory program that provides income to the elderly, is by far the largest welfare program in the United States. Which program is the smallest?

SOURCE: Congressional Budget Office, www.cbo.gov/publication/44521 (accessed 4/29/14); Congressional Budget Office, www.cbo.gov/publication/45229 (accessed 4/29/14); Office of Management and Budget, www.whitehouse.gov/omb/budget/historicals (accessed 4/29/14).

SPENDING AS A
PERCENTAGE OF GDP

Social Security

Medicare

Medicaid

Unemployment

SNAP
(food stamps)

Projections

insurers from denying benefits for a variety of reasons such as preexisting conditions. With a few exceptions, the legislation also makes insurers cover preventive medicine in full. The second provision of the ACA, known as "the individual mandate," required uninsured individuals to purchase health insurance; those who do not have insurance are subject to a fine (scheduled to rise over time) of 1 percent of yearly household income or $95, whichever was larger. The third major provision of the ACA was a set of subsidies to help the uninsured and small businesses purchase insurance as well as an expansion of the public programs Medicaid and the State Children's Health Insurance Program (SCHIP). The Medicaid expansion made more people eligible for the program by opening it to people with incomes at or below 138 percent of the poverty level. This meant that individuals making up to $16,000 a year would be eligible to receive Medicaid. The reform also allowed working-aged adults without dependent children to qualify for the program for the first time. This provision was intended to provide health insurance for many of the country's uninsured. Figure 13.3 shows the projected number of insured Americans with and without the ACA in 2024.

Even after its enactment, the law remained highly controversial. All the new Republican House members elected in 2010 favored repeal of the measure, and 2012 Republican presidential candidate Mitt Romney likewise pledged to roll back the measure. The rollout of the state insurance exchanges in fall 2013 damaged already skeptical public perceptions of the ACA. Massive computer problems with the main website, heathcare.gov, meant that some applicants working through the online system were cut off after hours of effort; others could not even get started on their applications. These problems affected applicants from the 27 states that did not set up their own insurance exchanges but relied on the federal website. Some of the state exchanges, such as Covered California, worked largely as intended but others, such as Oregon's, failed altogether. Only after a major reworking of the online system did the federal insurance exchanges begin to work as intended. The administration extended the sign-up deadline, and by April 2014 it announced that more than 8 million people had signed up through the exchanges, a number

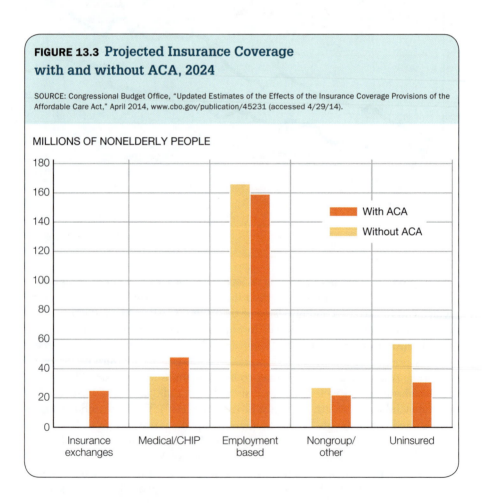

FIGURE 13.3 Projected Insurance Coverage with and without ACA, 2024

SOURCE: Congressional Budget Office, "Updated Estimates of the Effects of the Insurance Coverage Provisions of the Affordable Care Act," April 2014, www.cbo.gov/publication/45231 (accessed 4/29/14).

MILLIONS OF NONELDERLY PEOPLE

that exceeded initial expectations.[28] Even so, the disastrous launch of the insurance exchanges represented a missed opportunity for the administration to change public perceptions of the ACA, and more Americans reported an unfavorable view of the ACA than a favorable view into 2014.[29]

The new health care reform law faced challenges not only in public opinion but from state governments soon after it was enacted. Twenty-one state attorneys general filed lawsuits against the legislation on the grounds that the provision requiring individuals to purchase health insurance expanded the commerce clause beyond its constitutional limits. The states also objected to provisions that required them to expand their Medicaid programs to cover more poor people.

The Supreme Court decided these suits in 2012, ruling that most of the act was constitutional.[30] Chief Justice John Roberts, regarded as a conservative, surprised many observers by writing the decision that declared the individual mandate constitutional. However, the decision found that the mandate could not be justified as constitutional under the commerce clause, which the administration relied on in its arguments before the Court. Because the mandate regulated economic *inactivity* (i.e., failure to purchase health insurance), Roberts argued that it could not be justified under the commerce clause, which regulates economic *activity*. Instead the Court ruled that the requirement to purchase insurance was legal under Congress's taxing powers (since, under the law, failure to purchase insurance results in a penalty). The decision on Medicaid, the second contested feature of the act, also came as a surprise. The Court ruled that Congress did not have the power to take existing Medicaid funds away from states if they did not comply with the expansion requirements. In response, 21 states decided not to expand their Medicaid programs. These state decisions left 5.7 million people who would have qualified for Medicaid without access to health care.[31]

Housing Policies Provide Residential Stability

The United States has one of the highest rates of homeownership in the world, and the central thrust of federal housing policy has been to promote homeownership. The federal government has traditionally done much less to provide housing for low-income Americans who cannot afford to buy homes. Federal housing programs were first created in the 1930s depression period, when many Americans found themselves unable to afford housing. Through public housing for low-income families, which originated in 1937 with the Wagner-Steagall National Housing Act, and subsidized private housing after 1950, the percentage of American families living in overcrowded conditions was reduced from 20 percent in 1940 to 9 percent in 1970. Federal policies made an even greater contribution to reducing "substandard" housing, defined by the U.S. Census Bureau as dilapidated houses without hot running water and without some other plumbing. In 1940 almost 50 percent of American households lived in substandard housing. By 1950 this had been reduced to 35 percent; by 1975 the figure was reduced further, to 8 percent.[32] Despite these improvements in housing standards, federal housing policy until the 1970s was largely seen as a failure. Restricted to the poorest of the poor and marked by racial segregation and inadequate spending, public housing contributed to the problems of the poor by isolating them from shopping, jobs, and urban amenities. Dilapidated high-rise housing projects stood as a symbol of the failed American policy of "warehousing the poor." By the 1980s the orientation of housing policy had changed: most federal housing policy for low-income Americans came in the form of housing choice vouchers (formerly called Section 8 vouchers), which provided recipients with support to rent in the private market. While this program did not promote the same isolation of the poor, it was often useless in expensive housing markets, where the vouchers provided too little money to cover rental costs.

Beginning in 2007 and 2008 a home loan crisis presented the government with a different kind of housing problem. During the housing boom of the early 2000s, many homeowners received loans that they later could not afford to repay. This was caused in part by the deregulation of the mortgage industry in 1999, which allowed many new mortgage companies to form, offering loans that cost little at first but required large payments from homeowners later. This "predatory lending" targeted unsophisticated buyers and made it very hard for borrowers to understand the terms of the loans. Lending standards were relaxed to the point that rising numbers of borrowers were offered "no-doc" loans, which required no documentation of the borrowers' income. As more and more Americans took out such loans, demand for housing rose, and housing prices skyrocketed. This was the housing bubble—a bubble that was bound to burst, because so many borrowers would not be able to pay back their loans. As growing numbers of homeowners began to default on their loans in 2007, banks foreclosed on their houses and the value of housing began to drop. This downward spiral set off the major recession that began in 2007. As borrowers defaulted, banks holding that debt—including the biggest banks in America—teetered on the edge of failure and threatened to destabilize the entire economy. Many of the new mortgage companies went bankrupt. As unemployment rose, more families, unable to pay their mortgages, lost their homes. Many homeowners found that their homes were "underwater," meaning that the homeowners owed more on their mortgages than the homes were now worth. By 2014 nearly 5 million homes had been lost to foreclosure.[33]

● Social Policy Spending Benefits the Middle Class More Than the Poor

Explain how contributory and noncontributory programs benefit different groups of Americans

The two categories of social policy, contributory and noncontributory, generally serve different groups of people. We can understand much about the development of social policy by examining which constituencies benefit from different policies.

The strongest and most generous programs are those in which the beneficiaries are widely perceived as deserving of assistance and also are politically powerful. Because Americans prize work, constituencies who have "earned" their benefits in some way or those who cannot work because of a disability are usually seen as most deserving of government assistance. Politically powerful constituencies are those who vote as a group, lobby effectively, and mobilize to protect the programs from which they benefit.

When we study social policies from a group perspective, we can see that senior citizens and the middle class receive the most benefits from the government's social policies, and that children and the working poor receive the fewest. In addition, America's social policies do little to change the fact that minorities and women are more likely to be poor than white Americans and men.

Senior Citizens Receive over a Third of All Federal Dollars

The elderly are the beneficiaries of the two strongest and most generous social policies: old-age pensions (what we call Social Security) and Medicare (medical care for the elderly). As these programs have grown, they have provided most elderly Americans with economic security and have dramatically reduced the poverty rate among the elderly. In 1959, before very many people over the age of 65 received social insurance, the poverty rate for the elderly was 35 percent; by 2012 it had dropped to 9 percent.[34] Because of this progress, many people call Social Security the most effective anti-poverty program in the United States. This does not mean that the elderly are rich, however; in 2012 the median income of elderly households was $33,848, well below the national median income. The aim of these programs is to provide security and prevent poverty.[35]

One reason that Social Security and Medicare are politically strong is that senior citizens are widely seen as a deserving population. Because of their age, they are not expected to work. Moreover, both programs are contributory, and a work history is a requirement for receiving a Social Security pension. But these programs

AARP has been highly effective in representing the interests of the elderly in social policy. Here, AARP members demonstrate in favor of the right to buy cheaper prescription drugs from Canada under Medicare.

are also strong because they serve a constituency that has become quite powerful. The elderly are a very large group: in 2013 there were 41.5 million Americans over the age of 65. Because Social Security and Medicare are not means tested, they are available to all former workers and their spouses over the age of 65, whether they are poor or not. The size of this group is of such political importance also because the elderly turn out to vote in higher numbers than the rest of the population.

In addition, the elderly have developed strong and sophisticated lobbying organizations that can influence policy making and mobilize elderly Americans to defend these programs against proposals to cut them. One important and influential organization is AARP (formerly the American Association of Retired Persons; it changed its name to its initials because 44 percent of its members work full or part time). AARP had more than 40 million members in 2014, amounting to one-fifth of all voters. It also has a sophisticated lobbying organization in Washington that employs 63 lobbyists and a staff of 165 policy analysts.[36]

Lobbying groups for seniors are among the most powerful in America. They mobilize their supporters and work with legislators to block changes they believe will hurt the elderly. In the case of Medicare reform, for example, AARP had long opposed any reform that allowed private health care firms to provide Medicaid benefits. But in 2003, AARP switched its position and endorsed the Bush administration's bill to provide prescription drug benefits through the involvement of private firms. AARP's endorsement of the plan was decisive to the bill's passage. In 2005, AARP's opposition to President Bush's plan to partially privatize Social Security was decisive in killing that plan. In 2009 and 2010, AARP came out in support of health care reform, although it avoided endorsing any specific bill. Thousands of members left the organization in protest, but AARP is so large that their actions had little impact.

The Middle and Upper Classes Benefit from Social Policies

Americans don't usually think of the middle or upper classes as benefiting from social policies, but government action promotes the social welfare of these groups in a variety of ways. First, medical care and pensions for the elderly help the middle class by relieving them of the burden of caring for elderly relatives. Before these programs existed, old people were more likely to live with and depend financially on their adult children. Many middle-class families whose parents and grandparents are in nursing homes rely on Medicaid to pay nursing home bills.

In addition, the middle and upper classes benefit from what some analysts call the "shadow welfare state."[37] These are the social benefits that private employers offer to their workers—medical insurance and pensions, for example. The federal government subsidizes such benefits by not taxing the payments that employers and employees make for health insurance and pensions. These **tax expenditures**, as they are called, are an important way in which the federal government helps ensure the social welfare of the middle and upper classes. Such programs are called "tax expenditures" because the federal government helps finance them through the tax system rather than by direct spending, by providing tax deductions for private employers for amounts spent on health insurance and other benefits. Another key tax expenditure that helps those more well off is the tax exemption on mortgage interest payments: taxpayers can deduct the amount they have paid in interest on a mortgage from the income they report on their tax return. By allowing these payments to be counted as deductions, the government makes homeownership less expensive.

People often don't think of these tax expenditures as part of social policy because they are not as visible as the programs that provide direct payments or services to beneficiaries. But tax expenditures represent a significant federal investment: they cost the national treasury some $1.26 trillion a year and make it easier and less expensive for working Americans to obtain health care, save for retirement, and buy homes. These programs are very popular with the middle and upper classes, so Congress rarely considers reducing them. On the few occasions when public officials have tried to limit these programs—with proposals to limit the amount of mortgage interest that can be deducted, for example—they have quickly retreated. These programs are simply too popular among Americans whose power comes from their numbers at the polling booth.

The Working Poor Receive Fewer Benefits

People who are working but are poor or are just above the poverty line receive only limited assistance from government social programs. This is somewhat surprising, given that Americans value work so highly. But the working poor are typically employed in jobs that do not provide pensions or health care; often they are renters because they cannot afford to buy homes. This means they cannot benefit from the shadow welfare state that subsidizes the social benefits enjoyed by most middle-class Americans. At the same time, however, they cannot get assistance through programs such as Medicaid and TANF, which are largely restricted to the nonworking poor.

Three government programs do assist the working poor: the Affordable Care Act (discussed earlier), the Earned Income Tax Credit (EITC), and SNAP (formerly known as food stamps). The EITC was implemented in 1976 to provide poor workers some relief from increases in the taxes that pay for Social Security. As it has expanded, the EITC has provided a modest wage supplement for the working poor, allowing them to catch up on utility bills or pay for children's clothing. Poor workers can also receive benefits from the SNAP program. To be eligible, households must earn below 130 percent of the poverty line (about $25,400 a year for a three-person family in 2014). The average monthly benefit for a family of three is $395 a month.[38] Food advocates such as Feeding America have encouraged people to take "the SNAP Challenge," in which people who do not need food stamps spend $1.50 a meal (the average for SNAP recipients) for a week. In the words of one high-profile participant, "I was hungry last week—laser-focused on how much food was left in the fridge and how many dollars were left in my wallet. I was scared about eating portions that were too big, and wasn't sure what to do if my food ran out."[39] Even though the working poor may be seen as deserving, they lack political power because they are not organized. There is no equivalent to AARP for the poor. Nonetheless, because work is highly valued in American society, politicians find it difficult to cut the few social programs that help the working poor. In 1995 efforts to cut the EITC were defeated by coalitions of Democrats and moderate Republicans, although Congress did place new restrictions on food stamps and reduced the level of spending on this type of aid.

Spending for the Nonworking Poor Is Declining

The only nonworking, able-bodied poor people who receive federal cash assistance are parents who are caring for children. The primary source of cash assistance for these families was AFDC and now is the state-run TANF program, but they also rely on the SNAP program and Medicaid. Able-bodied adults who are not caring for children are not eligible for federal assistance other than food stamps. Many states provide small amounts of cash assistance to such individuals through programs called "general assistance," but in the past decade, many states have abolished or greatly reduced their general assistance programs in an effort to encourage these adults to work. Americans don't like to subsidize adults who are not working, but they do not want to harm children.

AFDC was the most unpopular social spending program, and as a result, spending on it declined after 1980. Under TANF, states receive a fixed amount of federal funds, whether the welfare rolls rise or fall. Because the number of people on welfare has declined so dramatically since 1994—by over 50 percent—states have had generous levels of federal resources for the remaining welfare recipients. Many states, however, have used the windfall of federal dollars to cut taxes and indirectly support programs that benefit the middle class, not the poor.[40] Welfare recipients have little political power to resist cuts in their benefits. In 2014 more than 46.9 million people (15 percent of the population) received SNAP benefits.[41]

Minorities, Women, and Children Are Most Likely to Face Poverty

Minorities, women, and children are disproportionately poor. Much of this poverty is the result of disadvantages rooted in the position of these groups in the labor market. In 2012 the poverty rate for African Americans was 27.2 percent, and for Latinos it was 25.6 percent. For non-Hispanic whites, it was 9.7 percent.[42] Much of this economic inequality stems from the fact that minority workers tend to have low-wage jobs. Minorities are also more likely to become unemployed and to remain unemployed for longer periods of time than are white Americans. African Americans, for example, typically have experienced twice as much unemployment as have other Americans. The combination of low-wage jobs and unemployment often means that minorities are less likely to have jobs that give them access to the shadow welfare state. They are more likely to fall into the precarious categories of the working poor or the nonworking poor.

In the past several decades, policy analysts have begun to talk about the "feminization of poverty," or the fact that women are more likely than men to be poor. This problem is particularly acute for single mothers, who are more than twice as likely as the average American to fall below the poverty line (see Figure 13.4). When the Social Security Act was passed in 1935, the main programs for poor women were ADC and survivors' insurance for widows. The framers of the act believed that ADC would gradually disappear as more women became eligible for survivors' insurance. The social model behind the Social Security Act was that of a male breadwinner with a wife and children. Women were not expected to work, and if a woman's husband died, ADC or survivors' insurance would help her stay at home and raise her children. The framers of Social Security did not envision today's large number of single women

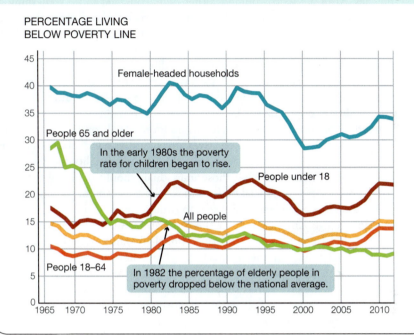

FIGURE 13.4 Poverty Levels in the United States, 1966–2012

Poverty rates in the U.S. population vary considerably. The rate of poverty among female-headed households declined significantly in the 1990s but has been increasing again since 2000. Which group has seen the greatest reduction in its poverty level since 1966?

SOURCES: U.S. Census Bureau, www.census.gov/hhes/www/poverty/data/historical/people.html (accessed 4/29/14).

PERCENTAGE LIVING
BELOW POVERTY LINE

Female-headed households

People 65 and older

In the early 1980s the poverty rate for children began to rise.

People under 18

All people

People 18–64

In 1982 the percentage of elderly people in poverty dropped below the national average.

heading families. At the same time, they did not envision that so many women with children would also be working. This combination of changes helped make AFDC (the successor program to ADC) more controversial. Many people asked why welfare recipients shouldn't work, if the majority of women who were not on welfare worked. Such questions led to the welfare reform of 1996, which created TANF.

One of the most troubling issues related to American social policy is the number of American children who live in poverty. The rate of child poverty in 2012 was 21.8 percent—6.8 percent higher than that of the population as a whole. These high rates of poverty stem in part from the design of American social policies. Because these policies do not generously assist able-bodied adults who aren't working and because these policies offer little help to the working poor, the children of these adults are likely to be poor as well.

As child poverty has grown, several lobbying groups have emerged to represent children's interests; the best known of these is the Children's Defense Fund. But even with a sophisticated lobbying operation and although their numbers are large, poor children do not vote and therefore wield little political power.

Social Policy
and Your Future

Public policy encompasses many different ways for the government to achieve its objectives. All public policies are tools of government control, but the means chosen to achieve their goals can have a major effect on how the public feels about those policies. After all, who wouldn't rather be encouraged to do something by being paid to do it instead of being told that failure to do the very same thing may result in jail time? This might lead you to think that the government should do everything by relying on payments or subsidies, but for many areas of public life, this is simply not possible—not to mention incredibly expensive.

Social policies, established in the 1930s, have stirred up much controversy. Liberals often argue that more generous social policies are needed if America is truly to ensure equality of opportunity, saying that the government needs to go beyond simply providing opportunity and should ensure more equal conditions, especially where children are concerned. Conservatives, on the other hand, often argue that social policies that offer income support take the ideal of equality too far and, in the process, do for individuals what those individuals should be doing for themselves. From this perspective, social policies make the government too big, and big government is seen as a fundamental threat to Americans' liberties.

Where do average Americans fit in these debates? Americans are often said to be philosophical conservatives and operational liberals.[43] When asked about government social policy in the abstract, they say they disapprove of activist government—a conservative view. But when they must evaluate particular programs, Americans generally express support—a liberal perspective. Some programs are more popular than others. Policies in which the recipients are regarded as deserving, such as programs for the elderly, receive more support than those that assist working-age people. Programs that have a reputation for effectiveness and those that require people to help themselves through work are also viewed favorably.[44]

Yet reform is often difficult to achieve. The most pressing social policy issue in the coming decades—the rising cost of health care—has been notoriously difficult to address. The United States spends more on health care than any other advanced nation, but many Americans remain without access to care, even after the expansions in the Affordable Care Act. The share of our economy devoted to health care rose from 7.2 percent in 1970 to 17.9 percent in 2010, and it appears to be growing again after a brief slowdown.[45] The causes of increasing health care costs are many, including new technology, administrative complexity, greater coverage for more people, and an aging population. Can we reap the advantages of our highly advanced health care system and reduce costs at the same time? While most Americans might prefer this outcome, it is very difficult to reach agreement on the reforms needed to attain this goal. What strategies might be used to initiate a national discussion of health care? What are the consequences of inaction for today's young adults?

plugin

Inform

Check the newspaper or a news website to see what economic and social policies are in the news. Look for stories on taxes, employment, economic growth, poverty, health, education, and housing.

Express

Write a list of how you expect economic and social policies to affect your life in the next five years.

Connect

Join an organization that promotes fiscal responsibility in government, such as the Concord Coalition, or one that promotes economic justice, such as the Sargent Shriver National Center on Poverty Law (www.povertylaw.org).

Act

Share information about higher education policies that affect you and your fellow students. For example, the Student Aid Alliance website provides information about the federal government's role in student aid—and offers several ways to take action if you are concerned.

Practice Quiz

1. Which of the following is *not* a type of regulatory policy? *(pp. 405–7)*
   a) criminal penalties
   b) civil penalties
   c) administrative regulations
   d) expropriation
   e) redistribution

2. Monetary policy seeks to influence the economy through *(p. 407)*
   a) taxing and spending.
   b) privatizing and nationalizing selected industries.
   c) the availability of credit and money.
   d) foreign exchange of currency.
   e) administrative regulation.

3. Monetary policy is handled largely by *(pp. 407–8)*
   a) Congress.
   b) the Department of the Treasury.
   c) the federal judiciary.
   d) the Federal Reserve System.
   e) the president.

4. A situation in which the government attempts to affect the economy through taxing and spending is an example of *(p. 409)*
   a) a reserve requirement.
   b) an expropriation policy.
   c) a monetary policy.
   d) a fiscal policy.
   e) eminent domain.

5. America's welfare state was constructed initially in response to *(pp. 411–12)*
   a) the Civil War.
   b) World War II.
   c) political reforms of the Progressive era.
   d) the Great Depression.
   e) the growth of the military-industrial complex.

6. Which of the following is an example of a contributory program? *(pp. 413–14)*
   a) Medicaid
   b) Social Security
   c) Temporary Assistance for Needy Families
   d) Supplemental Nutrition Assistance Program
   e) School Lunch Program

7. Means testing requires that applicants for welfare benefits show *(p. 414)*
   a) that they are capable of getting to and from their workplace.
   b) that they have the ability to store and prepare food.
   c) some definite need for assistance plus an inability to provide for it.
   d) that they have the time and resources to take full advantage of federal educational opportunities.
   e) that they are natural-born citizens who have never been convicted of a felony.

8. Which of the following are examples of in-kind benefits? *(p. 415)*
   a) Medicaid and SNAP
   b) Social Security payments and cost-of-living adjustments
   c) Medicare and unemployment compensation
   d) the GI Bill of Rights and the Equal Rights Amendment
   e) the Earned Income Tax Credit and No Child Left Behind

9. In 1996, as part of welfare reform, Aid to Families with Dependent Children was abolished and replaced by *(p. 416)*
   a) the Earned Income Tax Credit.
   b) Aid to Dependent Children.
   c) the Affordable Care Act.
   d) Supplemental Security Income.
   e) Temporary Assistance for Needy Families.

10. Which of the following was not part of the No Child Left Behind Act of 2001? *(p. 418)*
    a) a provision allowing parents whose child is attending a failing school to transfer the child to a better school
    b) a requirement that all students be proficient in reading and math by 2014
    c) a requirement that schools show positive results for all subcategories of students and not just positive overall averages
    d) a requirement that a national test be used to evaluate every student around the country
    e) a requirement that every child in grades 3 through 8 be tested yearly for proficiency in math and reading

11. In terms of receiving benefits of social policies, what distinguishes the elderly from the working poor? *(p. 427)*
    a) The elderly are perceived as deserving, whereas the working poor are not.
    b) The elderly receive fewer benefits from the government's social policies.
    c) The elderly are more organized and more politically powerful than are the working poor.
    d) The elderly are less organized and less politically powerful than are the working poor.
    e) There is no significant difference between these two groups.

12. Which of the following statements about the poverty in the United States is most accurate? *(p. 428)*
    a) African Americans have a lower poverty rate than whites.
    b) Hispanics have a lower poverty rate than whites.
    c) Hispanics have a higher poverty rate than whites.
    d) The rate of child poverty is less than the rate of adult poverty.
    e) Women are less likely than men to fall below the poverty line.

Key Terms

contracting power *(p. 405)* the power of government to set conditions on companies seeking to sell goods or services to government agencies

contributory programs *(p. 413)* social programs financed in whole or in part by taxation or other mandatory contributions by their present or future recipients

cost-of-living adjustments (COLAs) *(p. 414)* changes made to the level of benefits of a government program based on the rate of inflation

Federal Reserve System *(p. 408)* a system of 12 Federal Reserve banks that facilitates exchanges of cash, checks, and credit; regulates member banks; and uses monetary policies to fight inflation and deflation

fiscal policy *(p. 409)* the government's use of taxing, monetary, and spending powers to manipulate the economy

indexing *(p. 414)* periodic process of adjusting of social benefits or wages to account for increases in the cost of living

in-kind benefits *(p. 415)* noncash goods and services provided to needy individuals and families by the federal government

means testing *(p. 414)* a procedure by which potential beneficiaries of a public assistance program establish their eligibility by demonstrating a genuine need for the assistance

Medicaid *(p. 414)* a federally and state-financed, state-operated program providing medical services to low-income people

Medicare *(p. 413)* a form of national health insurance for the elderly and the disabled

monetary policies *(p. 407)* efforts to regulate the economy through the manipulation of the supply of money and credit; America's most powerful institution in this area of monetary policy is the Federal Reserve Board

noncontributory programs *(p. 414)* social programs that provide assistance to people based on demonstrated need rather than any contribution they have made

public policy *(p. 403)* a law, a rule, a statute, or an edict that expresses the government's goals and provides for rewards and punishments to promote those goals' attainment

Social Security *(p. 413)* a contributory welfare program into which working Americans contribute a percentage of their wages and from which they receive cash benefits after retirement or if they become disabled

subsidies *(p. 403)* government grants of cash or other valuable commodities, such as land, to individuals or an organization; used to promote activities desired by the government, to reward political support, or to buy off political opposition

Supplemental Nutrition Assistance Program (SNAP) *(p. 415)* the largest anti-poverty program, which provides recipients with a debit card for food at most grocery stores; formerly known as *food stamps*

tax expenditures *(p. 426)* government subsidies provided to employers and employees through tax deductions for amounts spent on health insurance and other benefits

For Further Reading

Baldwin, Robert, Martin Cave, and Martin Lodge. *Understanding Regulation*. New York: Oxford University Press, 2012.

Campbell, Andrea Louise. *How Policies Make Citizens: Senior Political Activism and the American Welfare State*. Princeton, NJ: Princeton University Press, 2005.

Cohen, David K., and Susan L. Moffitt. *The Ordeal of Equality: Did Federal Regulation Fix the Schools?* Cambridge, MA: Harvard University Press, 2009.

Hacker, Jacob S. *The Great Risk Shift: Why American Jobs, Families, Health Care, and Retirement Aren't Secure—and How We Can Fight Back*. New York: Oxford University Press, 2006.

Howard, Christopher. *The Welfare State Nobody Knows: Debunking Myths about U.S. Social Policy*. Princeton, NJ: Princeton University Press, 2007.

Katz, Michael. *In the Shadow of the Poorhouse: A Social History of Welfare in America*. New York: Basic Books, 1986.

Krugman, Paul. *Peddling Prosperity: Economic Sense and Nonsense in the Age of Diminished Expectations*. New York: W. W. Norton, 1994.

Light, Paul. *Artful Work: The Politics of Social Security Reform*. New York: Random House, 1985.

Marmor, Theodore R., Jerry L. Mashaw, and Phillip L. Harvey. *America's Misunderstood Welfare State*. New York: Basic Books, 1990.

Mettler, Suzanne. *Degrees of Inequality: How the Politics of Higher Education Sabotaged the American Dream*. New York: Basic Books, 2014.

Patterson, James T. *America's Struggle against Poverty, 1900–1994*. Cambridge, MA: Harvard University Press, 1994.

Ravitch, Diane. *Reign of Error: The Hoax of the Privatization Movement and the Danger to America's Public Schools.* New York: Knopf, 2013.

Schwarz, John E. *America's Hidden Success: A Reassessment of Twenty Years of Public Policy.* New York: W. W. Norton, 1988.

Soss, Joe, Richard C. Fording, and Sanford F. Schramm. *Disciplining the Poor: Neoliberal Paternalism and the Persistent Power of Race.* Chicago: University of Chicago Press, 2011.

Spitzer, Robert J. *Guns across America.* New York: Oxford University Press, 2015.

Weir, Margaret, Ann Orloff, and Theda Skocpol, eds. *The Politics of Social Policy in the United States.* Princeton, NJ: Princeton University Press, 1988.

The United States spends hundreds of billions of dollars—far more than any other country—on its military and weapons. However, Americans often disagree on when and how their government should act in international affairs, especially when it comes to deploying the U.S. military.

14

Foreign Policy

WHAT GOVERNMENT DOES AND WHY IT MATTERS Ever since George Washington, in his Farewell Address, warned the American people "to have . . . as little political connection as possible" with foreign nations and to "steer clear of permanent alliances," Americans have been distrustful of foreign policy. Despite their distrust, the United States has been forced to pursue its national interests in the world through a variety of means, including diplomacy, economic policy, military action, and the sorts of entangling alliances with other nations and international organizations that would have troubled Washington.

To some college students, foreign policy may seem like a distant or abstract matter, but not too long ago tens of thousands of students were drafted and sent to serve in Korea and Vietnam. Even today, in the era of the all-volunteer military, thousands of recent college graduates (and numerous current college students) have served in America's military forces in Iraq and Afghanistan, and many others know someone who has been wounded or killed on distant battlefields.

War is only one aspect of American foreign policy, but America has fought many wars. Though Americans like to regard themselves as a peaceful people, since our own Civil War, American forces have been deployed abroad on hundreds of occasions for major conflicts and minor skirmishes. Writing in 1989, historian Geoffrey Perret commented that no other nation "has had as much experience of war as the United States."[1] America has not become less warlike in the years since Perret published his observation. America currently spends approximately $640 billion per year on its military and weapons programs—a figure that represents over one-third of the world's total military expenditure and over three times the amount spent by the People's Republic of China, the nation that currently ranks second to the United States in overall military outlays.[2]

Foreign policy, especially military policy, is often a major political issue in the United States. An old American adage asserts that "politics stops at the water's edge." The point of this saying is that America suffers as a nation if it fails to set aside its political and partisan differences when dealing with the rest of the world. In today's world, however, the water's edge does not neatly demarcate the difference of interests between "us" and "them." As the global economic crisis that deepened in 2008 revealed, "our" economic interests and "their" economic interests are intertwined. Environmental concerns are global, not national. And even in the realm of security interests, some risks and threats are shared and require international rather than national responses. Our national government must find ways to act internationally and strike the right balance between competition and cooperation in the international arena.

In this chapter, we will first examine the main goals and purposes of American foreign policy. We will then discuss the actors and institutions that shape foreign policy. Next, we will analyze the instruments that policy makers have at their disposal to implement foreign policy.

chaptergoals

- Explain how foreign policy is designed to promote security, prosperity, and humanitarian goals (pp. 439–46)
- Identify the major players in foreign-policy making, and describe their roles (pp. 446–51)
- Describe the means the United States uses to carry out foreign policy (pp. 451–57)

Foreign Policy Goals Are Related

Explain how foreign policy is designed to promote security, prosperity, and humanitarian goals

The term *foreign policy* refers to the programs and policies that determine America's relations with other nations and foreign entities. Foreign policy includes diplomacy, military and security policy, international human rights policies, and various forms of economic policy such as trade policy and international energy policy. Of course, foreign policy and domestic policy are not completely separate categories but are, instead, closely intertwined. Take security policy, for example. Defending the nation requires the design and manufacture of tens of billions of dollars in military hardware. The manufacture of this military equipment provides jobs in American communities where the equipment is built, while paying for it involves raising taxes or choosing not to fund other programs.

Although U.S. foreign policy has a number of purposes, three main, interrelated goals stand out. These are security, prosperity, and the creation of a better world.

Security Is Based on Military Strength

To many Americans, the chief purpose of the nation's foreign policy is protection of America's security in an often hostile world. Traditionally, the United States has been concerned about threats that might emanate from other countries, such as Nazi Germany during the 1940s and then Soviet Russia until the Soviet Union's collapse in 1991. Today American security policy is concerned not only with the actions of other nations but also with the activities of terrorist groups and other hostile **non-state actors**.[3] To protect the nation's security from foreign threats, the United States has built an enormous military apparatus and a complex array of intelligence-gathering institutions, such as the Central Intelligence Agency (CIA), charged with evaluating and anticipating challenges from abroad.[4]

During the eighteenth and nineteenth centuries, American security was based mainly on the geographic isolation of the United States. We were separated by two oceans from European and Asian powers, and many Americans thought that our security would be best preserved by remaining aloof from international power struggles. This policy of avoiding involvement in the affairs of other nations was known as **isolationism**. In his 1796 Farewell Address, President George Washington warned Americans to avoid permanent alliances with foreign powers, and in 1823, President James Monroe warned foreign powers not to meddle in the Western Hemisphere. Washington's warning and what came to be called the Monroe Doctrine were the cornerstones of the U.S. foreign policy of isolationism until the end of the nineteenth century. The United States saw itself as the dominant power in the Western Hemisphere and, indeed, believed that its "manifest destiny" was to expand from sea to sea. The rest of the world, however, should remain at arm's length.

In the twentieth century, technology made oceans less a barrier to foreign threats, and the world's growing economic interdependence meant that the

United States could no longer ignore events abroad. At the beginning of the twentieth century, despite its isolationist sentiments, the United States entered World War I on the side of Great Britain and France when the Wilson administration concluded that America's economic and security interests would be adversely affected by a German victory. In 1941, America was drawn into World War II when Japan attacked the U.S. Pacific fleet anchored at Pearl Harbor, Hawaii. Even before the Japanese attack forced America to fight, the Roosevelt administration had already concluded that the United States needed to act to prevent a victory by the German-Japanese-Italian Axis alliance.

In the aftermath of World War II, the United States developed a new security policy known as **containment** to check or "contain" the growing power of the Soviet Union. By the end of the 1940s the Soviets had built a huge empire and enormous military forces. Most threatening of all, it had built nuclear weapons and intercontinental bombers capable of attacking the United States. The United States was committed to maintaining its own military might as a means of **deterrence**, to discourage the Soviets from attacking the United States or its allies. Some Americans wanted a more aggressive policy, arguing that we should attack the Soviets before it was too late. Others said that we should show our peaceful intentions and attempt to placate the Soviets. This policy is called **appeasement**.

The policies that the United States adopted, deterrence and containment, could be seen as midway between aggression and appeasement. A nation pursuing a policy of deterrence, on the one hand, signals its peaceful intentions, but on the other hand it indicates its willingness and ability to fight if attacked. Thus, during the era of confrontation with the Soviet Union between the late 1940s and 1990, known as the **Cold War**, the United States frequently asserted that it had no intention of attacking the Soviet Union. At the same time, however, the United States built a huge military force, including a vast arsenal of nuclear weapons and intercontinental missiles, and frequently asserted that in the event of a Soviet attack, it would respond with overwhelming force. The Soviet Union announced that its nuclear weapons were also intended for deterrent purposes. Eventually the two sides possessed such enormous arsenals of nuclear missiles that each potentially had the ability to destroy the other in the event of war. This heavily armed standoff came to be called a posture of mutually assured destruction. During the 1962 "Cuban missile crisis," the United States and the USSR came to the brink of war when President Kennedy declared that the Soviet Union must remove its nuclear missiles from Cuba and threatened to use force if the Soviets refused. After an extremely intense several weeks, the crisis was defused by a negotiated compromise in which the Soviets agreed to remove their missiles in exchange for a guarantee from the United States that it would not invade Cuba. The two superpowers had come so close to nuclear war that afterward the leaders of both nations sought ways to reduceing tensions. This effort led to a period of détente, in which a number of arms control agreements were signed and the threat of war was reduced.

In 1991 the Soviet Union collapsed, partly because its huge military expenditures undermined its creaky and inefficient centrally planned economy. The new Russia, though still a formidable and sometimes unfriendly power, posed less of a threat to the United States. Americans celebrated the end of the Cold War and believed that the enormous expense of America's own military forces might be reduced. Within several years of the Soviet collapse, however, a new set of security threats emerged, requiring new policy responses. The September 11, 2001, terrorist attacks demonstrated a threat against which some security scholars had long warned: that non-state actors and so-called rogue states might acquire significant military capabilities, including nuclear weapons, and would not be affected by America's deterrent capabilities.

Unlike **nation-states** (political entities consisting of a people with some common cultural experience who also share a common political authority, recognized by other sovereignties), which have governments and fixed borders, terrorist groups are non-state actors having no fixed geographic location that can be attacked. Terrorists may believe that they can attack and melt away, leaving the United States with no one against whom to retaliate. Hence, the threat of massive retaliation does not deter them. Rogue states are nations with unstable and erratic leaders who seem to pursue policies driven by ideological or religious fervor rather than careful consideration of economic or human costs. The United States considers North Korea and Iran to be rogue states.

To counter these new security threats, the George W. Bush administration shifted from a policy of deterrence to one of **preventive war**—the willingness to strike first in order to prevent an enemy attack. The United States declared that it would not wait to be attacked but would, if necessary, take action to disable terrorist groups and rogue states before they could develop the ability to do it harm. The Bush administration's "Global War on Terror" is an expression of this notion of prevention, as was the U.S. invasion of Iraq. The United States has also refused to rule

The U.S. invasion of Iraq in 2003 was an example of preventive war. The Bush administration argued that it had to strike Iraq first, before Iraq used weapons of mass destruction to attack American interests.

out the possibility that it would attack North Korea or Iran if it deemed those nations' nuclear programs to be an imminent threat to American security interests. Accompanying this shift in military doctrine was a significant increase in overall U.S. military spending (see Figure 14.1).

In a 2014 speech President Obama signaled a shift in American military policy. The president declared that U.S. policy had led to too many "military adventures." In the future, said the president, American policy would be based on collective action and restraint. While a military option would remain available if Americans were directly threatened, the president said that nonmilitary options, including diplomacy and economic sanctions, should always be tried first. This emphasis on diplomacy, sanctions, and collective action summarized the president's responses to major foreign policy problems, including the civil war in Syria, Russia's annexation of the Crimean area of Ukraine, the Iranian

FIGURE 14.1 U.S. Spending on National Defense since 2000

The United States has long spent large sums of money on national defense. During the 1990s the budget for national defense declined as the country enjoyed a "peace dividend" following the conclusion of the Cold War. After the attacks of September 11 and the commencement of the war on terrorism, however, national defense spending rose steadily; in a decade, spending increased by 70 percent.

*Data for 2014 are estimated.
SOURCE: Office of Management and Budget, Table 6.1, www.whitehouse.gov/omb/budget/historicals (accessed 6/12/14).

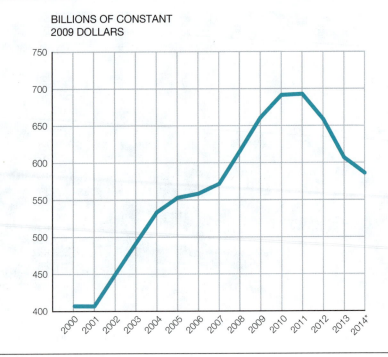

nuclear program, and the North Korean effort to build missiles capable of carrying nuclear warheads.

Between 2012 and 2014, Americans debated what to do for Syria, which was locked in a brutal civil war. The United States vacillated over its response. Ultimately the U.S. limited its efforts to humanitarian assistance and a successful effort to force Syrian leader Bashar al-Assad to surrender his chemical weapons, which he had used against the rebels. In fall 2014, Obama ordered airstrikes against Islamic militants, known as ISIS (Islamic State in Iraq and Syria). ISIS had overrun large areas of Iraq and Syria was deemed by the president to be a threat to U.S. interests.

Economic Prosperity Helps All Nations

A second major goal of U.S. foreign policy is promoting American prosperity. America's international economic policies are intended to expand employment opportunities in the United States, to maintain access to foreign energy supplies at a reasonable cost, to promote foreign investment in the United States, and to lower the prices Americans pay for goods and services.

The most important international organization for promoting free trade is the **World Trade Organization (WTO)**, which officially came into being in 1995. The WTO grew out of the **General Agreement on Tariffs and Trade (GATT)**, established in 1947, which set many of the rules governing international trade. Since World War II, GATT had brought together a wide range of nations for regular negotiations designed to reduce barriers to trade. Such barriers, many believed, had contributed to the breakdown of the world economy in the 1930s and had helped cause World War II. The WTO has 159 members worldwide, including the United States. Similar policy goals are pursued in regional arrangements, such as the **North American Free Trade Agreement (NAFTA)**, a trade treaty among the United States, Canada, and Mexico to lower and eliminate tariffs among the three countries.

Working toward freer trade has been an important goal of each presidential administration since World War II. Yet as globalization has advanced, concerns about free trade, and about the operation of the WTO in particular, have grown. Trade policy is complicated because most Americans benefit from a policy of free trade, which tends to reduce the cost of goods and services. One reason that consumer electronics are so inexpensive is that televisions, smartphones, and other gadgets are imported from all over the world, driving down their prices. However, many American industries and their employees are hurt by free trade if it results in factories and jobs moving abroad. Hence trade policy always produces huge political battles between those who stand to benefit and those who stand to lose from particular policies. Trade is an area where the line between domestic and foreign policy is blurred. Furthermore, critics believe that the WTO does not pay sufficient attention to the concerns of developing nations or to such issues as environmental degradation, human rights, and labor practices, including the use of child labor in many countries. The major problem in WTO negotiations has been conflicts between poor, developing nations and rich, developed countries.

America Seeks a More Humane World

A third goal of American policy is to make the world a better place for all its inhabitants. The main forms of policy that address this goal are international environmental policy, international human rights policy, and international peacekeeping. The United States also contributes to international organizations that work for global health and against hunger, such as the World Health Organization. These policies are often seen as secondary to the other goals of American foreign policy and are forced to give way if they interfere with security or foreign economic policy. Moreover, while the United States spends billions annually on security policy and hundreds of millions on trade policy, it spends relatively little on environmental, human rights, and peacekeeping efforts. Some critics charge that America has the wrong priorities, spending far more to make war than to protect human rights and the global environment. Nevertheless, a number of important American foreign policy efforts are, at least in part, designed to make the world a better place (see Figure 14.2).

In the realm of international environmental policy, the United States supports a number of international efforts to protect the environment. These include the United Nations Framework Convention on Climate Change, an international agreement to study and ameliorate harmful changes in the global environment, and the Montreal Protocol, an agreement signed by more than 150 countries to limit the production of substances potentially harmful to the world's ozone layer. Other nations have severely criticized the United States for withdrawing from the 1997 Kyoto Protocol, an agreement setting limits on emissions of greenhouse gases from industrial countries. The United States has asserted that the Kyoto Protocol would be harmful to American economic interests. Although the United States is concerned with the global environment, national economic interests took precedence in this case. In preparation for the 2012 expiration of the Kyoto agreement, world leaders gathered in Copenhagen, Denmark, in 2009 to begin the process of negotiating a new climate treaty. The Copenhagen Climate Summit, however, failed to produce a binding international agreement and ended with the United States, Europe, and China blaming one another for the lack of concrete results.

The same national priorities seem apparent in the area of human rights policy. The United States has a long-standing commitment to human rights and is a party to most major international human rights agreements. These include the International Covenant on Civil and Political Rights, the UN Convention against Torture, the International Convention on the Elimination of All Forms of Racial Discrimination, and various agreements to protect children. The State Department's Bureau of Democracy, Human Rights, and Labor works cooperatively with international organizations to investigate and focus attention on human rights abuses. In 1998 the United States enacted the International Religious Freedom Act, which calls on all governments to respect religious freedom.

Another form of U.S. policy designed to improve the condition of the world is support for international peacekeeping efforts. At any point in time, a number of border wars, civil wars, and guerrilla conflicts are flaring somewhere in the world, usually in its poorer regions. These wars often generate humanitarian crises in the form of casualties, disease, and refugees. In cooperation with international agencies and other nations, the United States funds a number of efforts to keep the peace in

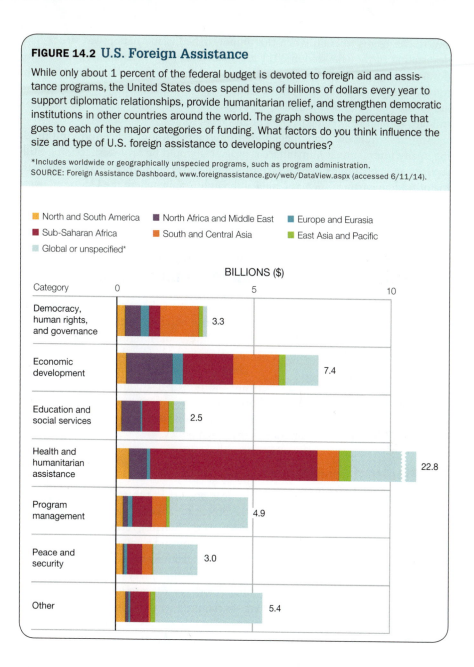

FIGURE 14.2 U.S. Foreign Assistance

While only about 1 percent of the federal budget is devoted to foreign aid and assistance programs, the United States does spend tens of billions of dollars every year to support diplomatic relationships, provide humanitarian relief, and strengthen democratic institutions in other countries around the world. The graph shows the percentage that goes to each of the major categories of funding. What factors do you think influence the size and type of U.S. foreign assistance to developing countries?

*Includes worldwide or geographically unspecied programs, such as program administration.
SOURCE: Foreign Assistance Dashboard, www.foreignassistance.gov/web/DataView.aspx (accessed 6/11/14).

■ North and South America   ■ North Africa and Middle East   ■ Europe and Eurasia
■ Sub-Saharan Africa   ■ South and Central Asia   ■ East Asia and Pacific
■ Global or unspecified*

BILLIONS ($)

Category		
Democracy, human rights, and governance	3.3
Economic development	7.4
Education and social services	2.5
Health and humanitarian assistance	22.8
Program management	4.9
Peace and security	3.0
Other	5.4

volatile regions and to deal with the health care and refugee problems associated with conflict. In 2013 the United States provided more than $2 billion in funding for United Nations peacekeeping operations in the Democratic Republic of Congo, Kosovo, Lebanon, Mali, and elsewhere. As the world's wealthiest nation, the United States also recognizes an obligation to render assistance to nations facing crises and emergencies. In 2010, for example, the United States sent medical aid, food relief, and rescue teams to Haiti when that impoverished island nation was struck by a devastating earthquake, and in 2011 it provided support to Japan when a tsunami devastated a portion of the Japanese coast and damaged the Fukushima Daiichi nuclear reactor. In 2014 the United States pledged $300 million in humanitarian aid to the people of South Sudan, a population at grave risk of famine caused by military conflict between government and rebel forces.

America's humanitarian policies are important. Without U.S. efforts and funding, many international humanitarian programs would be far less successful. Still, security and economic interests take precedence over humanitarian concerns with major trading partners such as China and Saudi Arabia, where the U.S. often overlooks human rights violations.

American Foreign Policy Is Shaped by Government and Nongovernment Actors

> **Identify the major players in foreign-policy making, and describe their roles**

As we have seen, domestic policies are made by governmental institutions and influenced by a variety of interest groups, political movements, and even the mass media. The same is true in the realm of foreign policy. The president and his chief advisers are the principal architects of U.S. foreign policy. However, the Congress, the bureaucracy, the courts, political parties, interest groups, and trade associations also play important roles in this realm. Often, the president and Congress are at odds over foreign policy.

The President Leads Foreign Policy

The Constitution assigns the president clear powers in the realm of foreign and security policy. The president is given the power to make treaties and appoint ambassadors (both with the advice and consent of the Senate), receive foreign ambassadors, and serve as commander in chief of the army and navy of the United States. Presidents have expanded upon these powers, claiming that their obligation to defend the nation serves as the basis for presidential primacy in all matters affecting America's international interests. Since World War II, presidents have declined to ask Congress for a declaration of war as required by the Constitution and have, instead, relied on congressionally enacted "authorizations of the use of military force." In some instances, presidents have committed American forces to foreign conflicts under their own authority.

Most American presidents have been domestic politicians who set out to make their place in history through achievements in domestic policy. A standard joke during Bill Clinton's 1992 campaign was that he had learned his foreign policy at the International House of Pancakes. Thus, it was not unusual that his successor, President George W. Bush, had virtually no foreign policy preparation prior to taking office. He had traveled very little outside the United States and had had almost no foreign experience as governor of Texas.

Nonetheless, Bush was decisive in the initiatives he took to define America's national interest for his administration. Examples include revival of the controversial nuclear missile shield ("Star Wars"); abandonment of the Anti-Ballistic Missile (ABM) treaty, which alienated Russia; changes in policy priorities away from humanitarian and environmental goals and toward a far stronger emphasis on national security; and turning America's concerns (by degree or emphasis) away from Europe and toward an "Asia-first" policy.

September 11 and its aftermath immensely accentuated the president's role and his place in foreign policy.[5] By 2002 foreign policy was the centerpiece of the Bush administration's agenda. In a June 1 speech at West Point, the **Bush Doctrine** of preemptive war was announced. Bush argued that "our security will require all Americans . . . to be ready for preemptive action when necessary to defend our liberty and to defend our lives." Bush's statement was clearly intended to justify his administration's plans to invade Iraq, but it had much wider implications for international relations and for the central role of the American president in guiding foreign policy.

By 2010, President Barack Obama had put his own stamp on American foreign policy, altering the conduct of America's war in Afghanistan and seeking to compel the Israelis and Palestinians to accept a Middle East peace deal. Obama also sought to engage more fully America's allies, who had been miffed by the previous administration's tendency to engage in unilateral action. Thus, the United States worked closely with its NATO allies in 2011 in a successful multilateral effort to end the Libyan dictatorship of Mu'ammar Qaddafi.

By the end of 2011, Obama ended direct U.S. military involvement in Iraq and had begun to withdraw American forces from Afghanistan. One of his triumphs was the 2011 military raid that resulted in the killing of Osama bin Laden, who had long been sought by the United States as the mastermind of the September 11 terrorist attacks. Yet President Obama faced a number of challenges as he neared the end of his presidency. Russian prime minister Vladimir Putin upset the international order in Europe by seizing the Crimean Peninsula of Ukraine. North Korea continued to test missiles, Iran had not definitively halted its nuclear weapons program, Israel and the Palestinians fought a war in Gaza, and ISIS militants sought to win control of Iraq, Syria, and Lebanon. These and new problems would challenge Obama's successors. Presidents have come to dominate American foreign policy, but America's foreign policies are never able to cure the ills of the world.

The Bureaucracy Implements and Informs Policy Decisions

The major foreign policy actors in the bureaucracy are the secretaries of the departments of State, Defense, and the Treasury; the Joint Chiefs of Staff (JCS), especially the chair of the JCS; and the director of the CIA. Since 1947 a separate unit in the White House has overseen the vast foreign policy establishment for the purpose of synthesizing all the messages arising out of the bureaucracy and helping the president make his own foreign policy. This is the National Security Council (NSC). It is a "subcabinet" made up of the major players just listed plus others whom each president appoints. Since the profound shake-up of September 11, two additional key players have been added. The first is the secretary of the new Department of Homeland Security (DHS). The second was imposed at the top as the war in Iraq was becoming a quagmire: a director of national intelligence, to collate and coordinate intelligence coming in from multiple sources and to report a synthesis of all this to the president on a daily basis.

Since the creation of the CIA and the Department of Defense in 1947, the secretary of defense and the director of the CIA have often been rivals engaged in power struggles for control of the intelligence community.[6] For the most part, secretaries of defense have prevailed in these battles, and the Defense Department today controls more than 80 percent of the nation's intelligence capabilities and funds. The creation of the position of director of national intelligence in 2005 to coordinate all intelligence activities set off new Washington power struggles as the "intelligence czar" faced opposition from both the CIA and the Department of Defense.

In the wake of September 11, military and law enforcement agencies increased their role in America's foreign-policy making.[7] In recent years American ambassadors have complained that they have been relegated to secondary status as the White House has looked to military commanders for information, advice, and policy implementation. For every region of the world, the U.S. military has assigned a "combatant commander," usually a senior general or admiral, to take charge of operations in that area. In many instances these combatant commanders, who control troops, equipment, and intelligence capabilities, have become the real eyes, ears, and voices for American foreign policy in their designated regions.

Congress's Legal Authority Can Be Decisive

Although the Constitution gives Congress the power to declare war (see Table 14.1), Congress has exercised this power on only five occasions: the War of 1812, the Mexican War (1846), the Spanish-American War (1898), World War I (1917), and World War II (1941). For the first 150 years of American history, Congress's role in foreign policy was limited because the United States' role in world affairs was limited. The treaty power was and is an important entrée of the Senate into foreign-policy making. But since World War II and the continual involvement of the United States in international security and foreign aid, Congress as a whole has become a major foreign-policy maker because most modern foreign policies require financing, which requires action by both the House of Representatives and the Senate. For example, Congress's first act after the September 11, 2001, attacks was to authorize the president to use "all necessary and appropriate force," coupled with a $40 billion emergency appropriations bill for homeland defense. Although President Bush believed he possessed the constitutional authority to invade Iraq, he still sought congressional approval, which he received in October 2002.

Not only does the president need Congress to provide funding for foreign and military policy initiatives, but also, under the Constitution, many presidential agreements with foreign nations have to be approved by Congress. Article II, Section 2, of the Constitution declares that proposed treaties with other nations must be submitted by the president to the Senate and approved by a two-thirds vote. Because this "supermajority" is usually difficult to achieve, presidents generally prefer a different type of agreement with other nations, called an **executive agreement**. An executive agreement is similar to a treaty and has the force of law but is almost always based on authority from a prior law passed by Congress or Senate-approved treaty.

TABLE 14.1

Principal Foreign Policy Provisions of the Constitution

	POWERS GRANTED	
	PRESIDENT	CONGRESS
War power	Commander in chief of armed forces	Provide for the common defense; declare war
Treaties	Negotiate treaties	Ratification of treaties by two-thirds majority (Senate)
Appointments	Nominate high-level government officials	Confirm president's appointments (Senate)
Foreign commerce	No explicit powers, but treaty negotiation and appointment powers pertain	Explicit power "to regulate foreign commerce"
General powers	Executive power; veto	Legislative power; power of the purse; oversight and investigation

Another aspect of Congress's role in foreign policy is the Senate's power to confirm the president's nominations of cabinet members, ambassadors, and other high-ranking officials (such as the director of the CIA, but not the director of the NSC). A final constitutional power of Congress is the regulation of "commerce with foreign nations."

Other congressional players are the foreign policy, military policy, and intelligence committees: in the Senate, these are the Foreign Relations Committee, the Armed Services Committee, the Intelligence Committee and the Homeland Security and Governmental Affairs Committee; in the House, these are the Foreign Affairs Committee, the Intelligence Committee the Homeland Security Committee, and the Armed Services Committee. Usually a few members of these committees who have spent years specializing in foreign affairs become trusted members of the foreign policy establishment and are influential makers of foreign policy. In fact, several members of Congress have left the legislature to become key foreign affairs cabinet members.

Interest Groups Pressure Foreign Policy Decision Makers

Although the president, the executive branch "bureaucracy," and Congress are the true makers of foreign policy, the "foreign policy establishment" is a much larger arena, including what can properly be called the shapers of foreign policy: a host of unofficial, informal players who possess varying degrees of influence depending on their prestige, reputation, and socioeconomic standing and, most important, the party and ideology that are dominant at a given moment.

By far the most important category of nonofficial player is the interest group—that is, the interest group to which one or more foreign policy issues are of long-standing and vital relevance. Most of these groups are "single-issue" economic groups, such as the tobacco industry and the computer hardware and software industries, which become most active when their particular issue is on the agenda.

Another type of interest group with a well-founded reputation for influence in foreign policy is made up of people with strong attachments to and identification with their country of national origin. The interest group with the reputation for the greatest influence is Jewish Americans, whose family and emotional ties to Israel make them one of the most alert and active interest groups in all of foreign policy. In 2010 a dispute between Israel and the Obama administration over Israel's construction of new Jewish housing in Jerusalem led to an intense effort by American Jews to generate congressional support for Israel's position. Similarly, Americans of Irish heritage, despite having lived in the United States for two, three, or four generations, still maintain vigilance about American policies toward Ireland and Northern Ireland. A third type of interest group is devoted to human rights. Such groups are made up of people who, instead of having self-serving economic or ethnic interests in foreign policy, are genuinely concerned about the welfare and treatment of people throughout the world—particularly those who suffer under harsh political regimes. A relatively small but often quite influential example is Amnesty International, whose exposés of human rights abuses have altered the practices of many regimes around the world. In recent years the Christian right has been a vocal advocate for the human rights of Christians who are persecuted in other parts of the world for their religious beliefs, most notably in China. For example, in the 1990s the Christian Coalition joined groups such as Amnesty International in lobbying Congress to restrict trade with countries that permit attacks against religious believers.

A final actor in the realm of foreign policy is public opinion. For the most part, the public is not engaged in foreign policy issues, as most Americans are concerned mainly with domestic issues. However, public opinion does begin to count when the nation is at war. Americans are often impatient with military actions that seem long and drawn out, producing costs and casualties for reasons that no longer seem clear. Fear of public opinion is one reason that presidents have favored professional military forces and technologies like drones that would reduce the immediacy of war to America's general public.

Members of Amnesty International asked the U.S. government to take action to support a global arms trade treaty. Interest groups such as Amnesty International may influence foreign policy by lobbying the government directly and by raising public awareness of certain issues.

Putting It Together

Let's make a few tentative generalizations to frame the remainder of this chapter. First, when an important foreign policy decision has to be made under conditions of crisis—where time is of the essence—the influence of the presidency is at its strongest. Second, within these time constraints, access to the decision is limited almost exclusively to the narrowest definition of the foreign policy establishment. The arena for participation is tiny; any discussion at all is limited to the officially and constitutionally designated players.[8] As time becomes less restricted, even when the decision to be made is of great importance, the arena of participation expands to include more government players and more nonofficial, informal players—the most concerned interest groups and the most important journalists. In other words, the arena becomes more pluralistic and, therefore, less distinguishable from the politics of domestic-policy making. Third, because there are so many other countries with power and interests on any given issue, there are severe limits on the choices the United States can make. As one author concludes, in foreign affairs, "policy takes precedence over politics."[9] Thus, even though foreign-policy making in noncrisis situations may closely resemble the pluralistic politics of domestic-policy making, foreign-policy making is still a narrower, more elitist arena with fewer participants.

● Tools of American Foreign Policy Include Diplomacy, Force, and Money

> **Describe the means the United States uses to carry out foreign policy**

We will deal here with those instruments of American foreign policy most important in the modern epoch: diplomacy, the United Nations, the international monetary structure, economic aid and sanctions, collective security, military deterrence, and arbitration. Each of these instruments will be evaluated in this section for its utility in the conduct of American foreign policy, and each will be assessed in light of the history and development of American values.

Diplomacy Is the Master Policy Tool

We begin this treatment of instruments with diplomacy. **Diplomacy** is the representation of a government to other foreign governments. Its purpose is to promote national values or interests by peaceful means. According to Hans Morgenthau, "a diplomacy that ends in war has failed in its primary objective."[10]

Diplomacy, by its very nature, is overshadowed by spectacular international events, dramatic initiatives, and meetings among heads of state or their direct personal representatives. The traditional American distrust of diplomacy continues today, albeit in weaker form. Impatience with or downright distrust of diplomacy has been built not only into all the other instruments of foreign policy but also into the modern presidential system itself.[11] So much personal responsibility has been heaped on the presidency that it is difficult for presidents to entrust any of their authority or responsibility in foreign policy to professional diplomats in the State Department and other bureaucracies.

In 2008 both parties' presidential candidates criticized the Bush administration for having failed to use diplomacy to secure greater international support for the Iraq war. Both promised to revitalize American diplomacy. President Obama appointed Hillary Clinton secretary of state, in part to underline the importance he attached to diplomacy by choosing such a prominent figure as America's chief diplomat.

The significance of diplomacy and its vulnerability to politics may be better appreciated as we proceed to the other instruments. Diplomacy was an instrument more or less imposed on Americans as the prevailing method of dealing among nation-states in the nineteenth century. The other instruments to be identified and assessed below are instruments that Americans self-consciously crafted for themselves to take care of their own chosen place in the world affairs of the second half of the twentieth century and beyond. They therefore better reflect American culture and values than diplomacy does.

The United Nations Is the World's Congress

The utility of the **United Nations (UN)** to the United States as an instrument of foreign policy can be too easily underestimated, because the UN is a very large and unwieldy institution with few powers and no armed forces to implement its rules and resolutions. It is an organization of nations founded in 1945 to be a channel for negotiation and a means of settling international disputes peaceably. The UN can serve as a useful forum for international discussions and an instrument for multilateral action. Most peacekeeping efforts to which the United States contributes, for example, are undertaken under UN auspices.

The UN's supreme body is the UN General Assembly, comprising one representative of each of the 193 member states; each member representative has one vote, regardless of the size of the country. Important issues require a two-thirds-majority vote, and the annual session of the General Assembly runs only from September

The United Nations is not always but can be an important instrument of American foreign policy. In trying to build international support for the U.S. case against Iraq, President Bush went before the General Assembly and urged the United Nations to compel Iraq to disarm. Two months later, the UN Security Council gave its qualified support to Bush's position.

to December (although it can call extra sessions). The General Assembly has little organization that can make it an effective decision-making body, with only six standing committees, few tight rules of procedure, and no political parties to provide priorities and discipline. Its defenders are quick to add that although it lacks armed forces, it relies on the power of world opinion—and this is not to be taken lightly. The powers of the UN devolve mainly to the organization's "executive committee," the UN Security Council, which alone has the real power to make decisions and rulings that member states are obligated by the UN Charter to implement. The Security Council may be called into session at any time, and each member (or a designated alternate) must be present at UN headquarters in New York at all times. The council is composed of 15 members: 5 are permanent (the victors of World War II), and 10 are elected by the General Assembly for unrepeatable two-year terms. The 5 permanent members are China, France, Russia, the United Kingdom, and the United States. Each of the 15 members has only one vote, and a nine-vote majority of the 15 is required on all substantive matters. But each of the 5 permanent members also has a negative vote, a "veto," and one veto is sufficient to reject any substantive proposal.

The International Monetary Structure Helps Provide Economic Stability

Fear of a repeat of the economic devastation that followed World War I brought the United States together with its allies (except the USSR) to Bretton Woods, New Hampshire, in 1944 to create a new international economic structure for the postwar world. The result was two institutions: the International Bank for Reconstruction and Development (commonly called the World Bank) and the International Monetary Fund.

The World Bank was set up to finance long-term capital. Leading nations took on the obligation of contributing funds to enable the World Bank to make loans to capital-hungry countries. (The U.S. quota has been about one-third of the total.) The **International Monetary Fund (IMF)** was set up to provide for the short-term flow of money. It provides loans and facilitates international monetary exchanges. After the war, the dollar, instead of gold, was the chief means by which the currencies of one country would be "changed into" currencies of another country for purposes of making international transactions. To permit debtor countries with no international balances to make purchases and investments, the IMF was set up to lend dollars or other appropriate currencies to such needy member countries to help them overcome temporary trade deficits.

During the 1990s the importance of the IMF increased through its efforts to reform some of the largest debtor nations and formerly Communist countries, to bring them more fully into the global capitalist economy. The future of the IMF, the World Bank, and all other private sources of international investment will depend in part on extension of more credit to the developing world, because credit means investment and productivity. But the future may depend even more on reducing the debt that is already there from previous extensions of credit.

Economic Aid Has Two Sides

Every year, the United States provides nearly $30 billion in economic assistance to other nations. Some aid has a humanitarian purpose, such as helping to provide health care, shelter for refugees, or famine relief. Much American aid, however, is

The United States is the most influential member of the World Bank, which provides loans and other assistance to developing countries. Here, workers in Afghanistan work to improve roads. The World Bank has provided hundreds of millions of dollars to help rebuild Afghanistan over the past decade.

designed to promote American security interests or economic concerns. For example, the United States provides military assistance to a number of its allies in the form of advanced weapons or loans to help them purchase such weapons. These loans generally stipulate that the recipient must purchase the designated weapons from American firms. In this way the United States hopes to bolster its security and economic interests with one grant. The two largest recipients of American military assistance are Israel and Egypt, American allies that fought two wars against each other. The United States believes that its military assistance allows both countries to feel sufficiently secure to remain at peace with each other.

Aid is an economic carrot. Sanctions are an economic stick. Economic sanctions that the United States employs against other nations include trade embargoes, bans on investment, and efforts to prevent the World Bank or other international institutions from extending credit to a nation against which the United States has a grievance. Sanctions are most often employed when the United States seeks to weaken what it considers a hostile regime or when it is attempting to compel some particular action by another regime. In recent years the United States has maintained economic sanctions against Iran and North Korea in an effort to prevent those nations from pursuing nuclear weapons programs. The United States also uses economic sanctions to advance its international humanitarian policy goals. The United States currently has sanctions in place against Sudan, Zimbabwe, Belarus, and Myanmar, four countries with records of serious violations of civil and political rights.[12]

Collective Security Is Designed to Deter War

In 1947 most Americans hoped that the United States could meet its world obligations through the UN and economic structures alone. But most foreign-policy makers anticipated the need for military entanglements at the time of drafting the original UN Charter by insisting on language that recognized the right of all nations to provide for their mutual defense independent of the UN. Almost immediately after enactment of the Marshall Plan, designed to promote European economic recovery, the White House and other top officials urgently requested the Senate to ratify and both houses of Congress to finance mutual defense alliances.

The Senate, at first reluctant to approve treaties providing for national security alliances, ultimately agreed with the executive branch. The first collective security agreement was the Rio Treaty (ratified by the Senate in 1947), which created the Organization of American States (OAS). This was the model treaty, anticipating all succeeding collective security treaties by providing that an armed attack against any of its members "shall be considered as an attack against all the American States," including the United States. A more significant break with U.S. tradition of avoiding peacetime entanglements came with the North Atlantic Treaty (signed in 1949), which created the **North Atlantic Treaty Organization (NATO)**. Comprising the United States, Canada, and most of Western Europe, NATO was formed to counter the perceived threat from the Soviet Union. Other collective security treaties followed.

In addition to these multilateral treaties, the United States entered into a number of **bilateral treaties** (treaties made between two nations), such as the treaty with Vietnam that resulted in ultimately unsuccessful American military action to protect that nation's government. As one author has observed, the United States has been a *producer* of security, whereas most of its allies have been *consumers* of security.[13]

This pattern has continued in the post–Cold War era, and its best illustration is in the 1991 Persian Gulf War, where the United States provided the initiative, the leadership, and most of the armed forces, even though its allies reimbursed over 90 percent of the cost.

It is difficult to evaluate collective security and its treaties because the purpose of collective security as an instrument of foreign policy is prevention, and success of this kind has to be measured in terms of what has *not* happened. Critics have argued that U.S. collective security treaties posed a threat of encirclement to the Soviet Union, forcing it to produce its own collective security, particularly the Warsaw Pact.[14] Nevertheless, no one can deny the counterargument that more than 70 years have passed without a world war.

Military Force Is "Politics by Other Means"

The most visible instrument of foreign policy is, of course, military force. The United States has built the world's most imposing military, with army, navy, marine, and air force units stationed around the globe. The United States is responsible for one-third of the world's total military expenditures (see the "America Side by Side" feature). The Prussian military strategist Carl von Clausewitz famously called war "politics by other means." By this he meant that nations used force or the threat of force not simply to demonstrate their capacity for violence but to achieve their foreign policy goals. Military force may be needed to protect a nation's security interests and economic concerns. Ironically, force may also be needed to achieve humanitarian goals. For example, without international military protection, the people who have taken refuge in camps in the Darfur region of Sudan would be at the mercy of the violent Sudanese regime.

Military Expenditures around the World

Security is an important foreign policy goal of every country. Military force is one tool of foreign policy that countries use to secure their territory and interests. In 2013 countries around the world spent approximately $1.7 trillion on military expenditures. To put this number in perspective, the total size of the world economy was about $74 trillion in 2013, according to the International Monetary Fund,[a] so military expenditures make up about 2.3 percent of the global economy.

However, individual countries vary widely in their military spending. The United States is notable for spending far more than other countries: at $640 billion, U.S. military spending represents about 38 percent of the world's total. Among democracies, France spends the second highest, at $61 billion, or just 4 percent of the world's total.

Why does the United States choose to spend so much on its military? Why do other countries, like South Korea, which sits in a much more hostile neighborhood than the United States, spend so little?

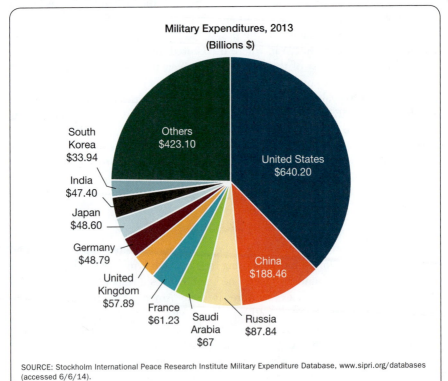

Military Expenditures, 2013 (Billions $)

- United States $640.20
- China $188.46
- Russia $87.84
- Saudi Arabia $67
- France $61.23
- United Kingdom $57.89
- Germany $48.79
- Japan $48.60
- India $47.40
- South Korea $33.94
- Others $423.10

SOURCE: Stockholm International Peace Research Institute Military Expenditure Database, www.sipri.org/databases (accessed 6/6/14).

[a]International Monetary Fund, World Economic and Financial Surveys World Economic Outlook Database, www.imf.org/external/pubs/ft/weo/2014/01/weodata/index.aspx (accessed 6/10/14).

Though force is sometimes necessary, military force is generally seen as a last resort to be avoided if possible because a number of problems are commonly associated with its use. First, the use of military force is extremely costly in both human and financial terms. In the past 50 years tens of thousands of Americans have been killed and hundreds of billions of dollars spent in America's military operations. Second, the use of military force is inherently fraught with risk. However carefully policy makers and generals plan for military operations, results can seldom be fully anticipated. For example, American policy makers expected, accurately, to defeat the Iraqi army quickly and easily in 2003. Policy makers did not anticipate, however, that American forces would still be struggling years later to defeat the insurgency that arose in the war's aftermath.

Arbitration Resolves Disputes

The final foreign policy tool is dispute arbitration. Arbitration is the resolution of a disagreement by a neutral third party. International arbitration is sometimes seen as a form of "soft power" as distinguished from military force, economic sanctions, and other coercive foreign policy instruments. The United States will occasionally turn to international tribunals to resolve disputes with other countries. For example, in 2008 the U.S. government asked the International Court of Justice to resolve a long-standing dispute with Italy over American property confiscated by the Italian government more than 40 years ago.

Foreign Policy, Democracy,
and Your Future

The harsh realities of foreign policy often clash with America's history and ideals. U.S. democratic and liberal traditions lead Americans to hope for a world in which ideals rather than naked interests govern foreign policy and in which U.S. leaders follow those ideals. Traditional American values assert that our foreign policies should have a higher purpose than narrow self-interest and that America would use force only as a last resort. But the realities of foreign policy often collide with these historic ideals, leaving U.S. policy makers to struggle to explain their actions and avoid admitting to motivations that might not sit well with the public.

International events can make it difficult to always pursue those ideals. The forces of globalization mean that it is easier than ever for small groups of extremists with violent intentions to travel to American shores and carry out their plans. On the other hand, those same forces of globalization have been the source of many positive outcomes. Greater trade reduces the price of many products for American consumers as well as for those abroad. Furthermore, many scholars believe that the increasing global economic interdependence is a force for peace: nations that trade heavily with each other are less likely to go to war with each other. What can U.S. leaders do in the future to make sure that globalization is a positive force that promotes U.S. security and prosperity?

plugin

Inform

Visit a U.S. news website, such as www.cnn.com, www.nytimes.com, or www.wsj.com, and look at the top three stories in world news. What U.S. foreign policy decisions are involved in each? Who is involved in making or influencing the decisions?

Express

Make a list of ways that international affairs and foreign policy—possibly including security concerns, the global economy, or issues like the environment—affect your life.

Connect

See how people around the world view the United States at www .pewglobal.org/database. Click "Questions by Topic" and then "U.S. Image."

Act

Consider working with an interest group on a foreign policy issue you care about, such as Amnesty International (human rights), Move America Forward (supporting American troops), or Just Foreign Policy (equality and justice from a nonpartisan perspective).

Practice Quiz

1. Which of the following terms best describes the American posture toward the world prior to the middle of the twentieth century? *(p. 439)*
   a) interventionist
   b) isolationist
   c) appeasement
   d) humanitarian
   e) internationalist

2. *Cold War* refers to *(p. 440)*
   a) competition between the United States and Canada over Alaska.
   b) the years between World War I and World War II when the United States and Germany were hostile to one another.
   c) the long-standing conflict over which nation controls Antarctica.
   d) the period of struggle between the United States and the Soviet Union between the late 1940s and the late 1980s.
   e) the economic competition between the United States and Japan today.

3. Which of the following terms describes the idea that the development and maintenance of military strength discourage attack? *(p. 440)*
   a) appeasement
   b) deterrence
   c) détente
   d) containment
   e) "Minuteman" theory of defense

4. *Bush Doctrine* refers to *(p. 447)*
   a) the idea that the United States should not allow foreign powers to meddle in the Western Hemisphere.
   b) the idea that the United States should avoid future wars by giving in to the demands of hostile foreign powers.
   c) the idea that the United States should take preemptive action against threats to its national security.

   d) the idea that the United States should never take preemptive action against threats to its national security.
   e) the idea that the United States should always secure international approval before taking any military action.

5. The Constitution assigns the power to declare war to *(p. 448)*
   a) the National Security Council.
   b) the president.
   c) the chief justice of the United States.
   d) the secretary of defense.
   e) Congress.

6. An agreement made between the president and another country that has the force of a treaty but requires only a simple majority vote in both houses of Congress for approval is called *(p. 448)*
   a) an executive order.
   b) an executive privilege.
   c) an executive agreement.
   d) a diplomatic decree.
   e) arbitration.

7. The making of American foreign policy during noncrisis moments is *(p. 451)*
   a) dominated entirely by the president.
   b) dominated entirely by Congress.
   c) dominated entirely by interest groups.
   d) dominated entirely by the Department of Defense.
   e) highly pluralistic, involving a large mix of both official and unofficial players.

8. Which of the following statements about the United Nations is *not* true? *(pp. 452–53)*
   a) It has a powerful army to implement its decisions.
   b) It gives every country one vote in the General Assembly.

c) The five permanent members of the UN Security Council are China, France, Russia, the United Kingdom, and the United States.

d) It was designed to be a channel for negotiation and a means of settling international disputes peaceably.

e) Important issues require a two-thirds majority vote.

9. Which of the following are important international economic institutions created in the 1940s? *(pp. 454–55)*

a) the Federal Reserve System and the Council of Economic Advisors

b) the North Atlantic Treaty Organization and the Southeast Asia Treaty Organization

c) the International Monetary Fund and the World Bank

d) the International Court of Justice and the Warsaw Pact

e) the Office of Management and Budget and the General Agreement on Tariffs and Trade

10. The North Atlantic Treaty Organization was formed in 1949 by the United States, *(p. 455)*

a) Canada, and most of Eastern Europe.

b) Canada, and the Soviet Union.

c) Canada, and Mexico.

d) Canada, and most of Western Europe.

e) Canada, and the United Kingdom.

11. Which statement best describes the United States' military spending compared with that of other countries? *(p. 456)*

a) The United States spends about the same as most other countries in the world.

b) The United States spends significantly more than any other country in the world.

c) The United States spends approximately as much as China.

d) The United States spends significantly less than any other country in the world.

e) The United States' growth in spending is decreasing compared with that of most other countries.

Key Terms

appeasement *(p. 440)* the effort to forestall war by giving in to the demands of a hostile power

bilateral treaties *(p. 455)* treaties made between two nations

Bush Doctrine *(p. 447)* foreign policy based on the idea that the United States should take preemptive action against threats to its national security

Cold War *(p. 440)* the period of struggle between the United States and the former Soviet Union lasting from the late 1940s to about 1990

containment *(p. 440)* a policy designed to curtail the political and military expansion of a hostile power

deterrence *(p. 440)* the development and maintenance of military strength as a means of discouraging attack

diplomacy *(p. 451)* the representation of a government to foreign governments

executive agreement *(p. 448)* an agreement, made between the president and another country, that has the force of a treaty but does not require the Senate's "advice and consent"

General Agreement on Tariffs and Trade (GATT) *(p. 443)* international trade organization, in existence from 1947 to 1995, that set many of the rules governing international trade

International Monetary Fund (IMF) *(p. 453)* an institution established in 1944 that provides loans and facilitates international monetary exchange

isolationism *(p. 439)* avoidance of involvement in the affairs of other nations

nation-states *(p. 441)* political entities consisting of people with some common cultural experience (nation) who also share a common political authority (state), recognized by other sovereignties (nation-states)

non-state actors *(p. 439)* groups other than nation-states that attempt to play a role in the international system; terrorist groups are one type of non-state actor

North American Free Trade Agreement (NAFTA) *(p. 443)* trade treaty among the United States, Canada, and Mexico to lower and eliminate tariffs among the three countries

North Atlantic Treaty Organization (NATO) *(p. 455)* an organization, comprising the United States, Canada, and most of Western Europe, formed in 1949 to counter the perceived threat from the Soviet Union

preventive war *(p. 441)* policy of striking first when a nation fears that a foreign foe is contemplating hostile action

United Nations (UN) *(p. 452)* an organization of nations founded in 1945 to be as a channel for negotiation and a means of settling international disputes peaceably; the UN has had frequent successes in providing a forum for negotiation and on some occasions a means of preventing international conflicts from spreading; on a number of occasions, the UN has supported U.S. foreign policy goals

World Trade Organization (WTO) *(p. 443)* international organization promoting free trade that grew out of the General Agreement on Tariffs and Trade

For Further Reading

Art, Robert. *The Use of Force: Military Power and International Politics.* New York: Rowman and Littlefield, 2009.

Dorman, Andrew, and Joyce Kaufman, eds. *Providing for National Security.* Palo Alto: Stanford University Press, 2014.

Gaddis, John L. *The Cold War: A New History.* New York: Penguin, 2005.

Ginsberg, Benjamin. *The Worth of War.* Amherst, NY: Prometheus Books, 2014.

Hook, Steven. *U.S. Foreign Policy: The Paradox of World Power.* Washington, DC: CQ Press, 2010.

Ikenberry, John. *American Foreign Policy.* New York: Wadsworth, 2010.

Jentleson, Bruce. *American Foreign Policy: The Dynamics of Choice in the 21st Century.* 5th ed. New York: W. W. Norton, 2013.

Mandelbaum, Michael. *The Case for Goliath: How America Acts as the World's Government in the 21st Century.* Washington, DC: Public Affairs Press, 2005.

Mearsheimer, John J., and Stephen M. Walt. *The Israel Lobby and U.S. Foreign Policy.* New York: Farrar, Straus and Giroux, 2008.

Nasr, Vali. *The Dispensable Nation: American Foreign Policy in Retreat.* New York: Anchor Books, 2014.

appendix

The Declaration of Independence

In Congress, July 4, 1776

The unanimous Declaration of the thirteen united States of America,

When in the Course of human events, it becomes necessary for one people to dissolve the political bands which have connected them with another, and to assume among the powers of the earth, the separate and equal station to which the Laws of Nature and of Nature's God entitle them, a decent respect to the opinions of mankind requires that they should declare the causes which impel them to the separation.

We hold these truths to be self-evident, that all men are created equal, that they are endowed by their Creator with certain unalienable Rights, that among these are Life, Liberty and the pursuit of Happiness.—That to secure these rights, Governments are instituted among Men, deriving their just powers from the consent of the governed.—That whenever any Form of Government becomes destructive of these ends, it is the Right of the People to alter or to abolish it, and to institute new Government, laying its foundation on such principles and organizing its powers in such form, as to them shall seem most likely to effect their Safety and Happiness. Prudence, indeed, will dictate that Governments long established should not be changed for light and transient causes; and accordingly all experience hath shewn, that mankind are more disposed to suffer, while evils are sufferable, than to right themselves by abolishing the forms to which they are accustomed. But when a long train of abuses and usurpations, pursuing invariably the same Object evinces a design to reduce them under absolute Despotism, it is their right, it is their duty, to throw off such Government, and to provide new Guards for their future security.—Such has been the patient sufferance of these Colonies; and such is now the necessity which constrains them to alter their former Systems of Government. The history of the present King of Great Britain is a history of repeated injuries and usurpations, all having in direct object the establishment of an absolute Tyranny over these States. To prove this, let Facts be submitted to a candid world.

He has refused his Assent to Laws, the most wholesome and necessary for the public good.

He has forbidden his Governors to pass Laws of immediate and pressing importance, unless suspended in their operation till his Assent should be obtained; and when so suspended, he has utterly neglected to attend to them.

He has refused to pass other Laws for the accommodation of large districts of people, unless those people would relinquish the right of Representation in the Legislature, a right inestimable to them and formidable to tyrants only.

He has called together legislative bodies at places unusual, uncomfortable, and distant from the depository of their public Records, for the sole purpose of fatiguing them into compliance with his measures.

He has dissolved Representative Houses repeatedly, for opposing with manly firmness his invasions on the rights of the people.

He has refused for a long time, after such dissolutions, to cause others to be elected; whereby the Legislative powers, incapable of Annihilation, have returned to the People at large for their exercise; the State remaining in the mean time exposed to all the dangers of invasion from without, and convulsions within.

He has endeavoured to prevent the population of these States; for that purpose obstructing the Laws for Naturalization of Foreigners; refusing to pass others to encourage their migrations hither, and raising the conditions of new Appropriations of Lands.

He has obstructed the Administration of Justice, by refusing his Assent to Laws for establishing Judiciary powers.

He has made Judges dependent on his Will alone, for the tenure of their offices, and the amount and payment of their salaries.

He has erected a multitude of New Offices, and sent hither swarms of Officers to harrass our people, and eat out their substance.

He has kept among us, in times of peace, Standing Armies without the Consent of our legislatures.

He has affected to render the Military independent of and superior to the Civil power.

He has combined with others to subject us to a jurisdiction foreign to our constitution, and unacknowledged by our laws; giving his Assent to their Acts of pretended Legislation:

For Quartering large bodies of armed troops among us:

For protecting them, by a mock Trial, from punishment for any Murders which they should commit on the Inhabitants of these States:

For cutting off our Trade with all parts of the world:

For imposing Taxes on us without our Consent:

For depriving us in many cases, of the benefits of Trial by Jury:

For transporting us beyond Seas to be tried for pretended offences:

For abolishing the free System of English Laws in a neighboring Province, establishing therein an Arbitrary government, and enlarging its Boundaries so as to render it at once an example and fit instrument for introducing the same absolute rule into these Colonies:

For taking away our Charters, abolishing our most valuable Laws, and altering fundamentally the Forms of our Governments:

For suspending our own Legislatures, and declaring themselves invested with power to legislate for us in all cases whatsoever.

He has abdicated Government here, by declaring us out of his Protection and waging War against us.

He has plundered our seas, ravaged our Coasts, burnt our towns, and destroyed the lives of our people.

He is at this time transporting large Armies of foreign Mercenaries to compleat the works of death, desolation and tyranny, already begun with circumstances of Cruelty & perfidy scarcely paralleled in the most barbarous ages, and totally unworthy the Head of a civilized nation.

He has constrained our fellow Citizens taken Captive on the high Seas to bear Arms against their Country, to become the executioners of their friends and Brethren, or to fall themselves by their Hands.

He has excited domestic insurrections amongst us, and has endeavoured to bring on the inhabitants of our frontiers, the merciless Indian Savages, whose known rule of warfare, is an undistinguished destruction of all ages, sexes and conditions.

In every stage of these Oppressions We have Petitioned for Redress in the most humble terms: Our repeated Petitions have been answered only by repeated injury. A Prince whose character is thus marked by every act which may define a Tyrant, is unfit to be the ruler of a free people.

Nor have We been wanting in attentions to our Brittish brethren. We have warned them from time to time of attempts by their legislature to extend an unwarrantable jurisdiction over us. We have reminded them of the circumstances of our emigration and settlement here. We have appealed to their native justice and magnanimity, and we have conjured them by the ties of our common kindred to disavow these usurpations, which, would inevitably interrupt our connections and correspondence. They too have been deaf to the voice of justice and of consanguinity. We must, therefore, acquiesce in the necessity, which denounces our Separation, and hold them, as we hold the rest of mankind, Enemies in War, in Peace Friends.

We, Therefore, the Representatives of the United States of America, in General Congress, Assembled, appealing to the Supreme Judge of the world for the rectitude of our intentions, do, in the Name, and by Authority of the good People of these Colonies, solemnly publish and declare, That these United Colonies are, and of Right ought to be Free and Independent States; that they are Absolved from all Allegiance to the British Crown, and that all political connection between them and the State of Great Britain, is and ought to be totally dissolved; and that as Free and Independent States, they have full Power to levy War, conclude Peace, contract Alliances, establish Commerce, and to do all other Acts and Things which Independent States may of right do. And for the support of this Declaration, with a firm reliance on the protection of divine Providence, we mutually pledge to each other our Lives, our Fortunes and our sacred Honor.

The foregoing Declaration was, by order of Congress, engrossed, and signed by the following members:

John Hancock

NEW HAMPSHIRE
Josiah Bartlett
William Whipple
Matthew Thornton

MASSACHUSETTS BAY
Samuel Adams
John Adams
Robert Treat Paine
Elbridge Gerry

RHODE ISLAND
Stephen Hopkins
William Ellery

CONNECTICUT
Roger Sherman
Samuel Huntington
William Williams
Oliver Wolcott

NEW YORK
William Floyd
Philip Livingston
Francis Lewis
Lewis Morris

NEW JERSEY
Richard Stockton
John Witherspoon
Francis Hopkinson
John Hart
Abraham Clark

PENNSYLVANIA
Robert Morris
Benjamin Rush
Benjamin Franklin
John Morton
George Clymer
James Smith
George Taylor
James Wilson
George Ross

DELAWARE
Caesar Rodney
George Read
Thomas M'Kean

MARYLAND
Samuel Chase
William Paca
Thomas Stone
Charles Carroll,
of Carrollton

VIRGINIA
George Wythe
Richard Henry Lee
Thomas Jefferson
Benjamin Harrison
Thomas Nelson, Jr.
Francis Lightfoot Lee
Carter Braxton

NORTH CAROLINA
William Hooper
Joseph Hewes
John Penn

SOUTH CAROLINA
Edward Rutledge
Thomas Heyward, Jr.
Thomas Lynch, Jr.
Arthur Middleton

GEORGIA
Button Gwinnett
Lyman Hall
George Walton

Resolved, That copies of the Declaration be sent to the several assemblies, conventions, and committees, or councils of safety, and to the several commanding officers of the continental troops; that it be proclaimed in each of the United States, at the head of the army.

The Articles of Confederation

Agreed to by Congress November 15, 1777;
ratified and in force March 1, 1781

To all whom these Presents shall come, we the undersigned Delegates of the States affixed to our Names, send greeting. Whereas the Delegates of the United States of America, in Congress assembled, did, on the fifteenth day of November, in the Year of Our Lord One thousand Seven Hundred and Seventy seven, and in the Second Year of the Independence of America, agree to certain articles of Confederation and perpetual Union between the States of Newhampshire, Massachusetts-bay, Rhodeisland and Providence Plantations, Connecticut, New-York, New-Jersey, Pennsylvania, Delaware, Maryland, Virginia, North-Carolina, South-Carolina and Georgia in the words following, viz. "Articles of Confederation and perpetual Union between the states of Newhampshire, Massachusettsbay, Rhodeisland and Providence Plantations, Connecticut, New-York, New-Jersey, Pennsylvania, Delaware, Maryland, Virginia, North-Carolina, South-Carolina and Georgia.

Art. I. The Stile of this confederacy shall be "The United States of America."

Art. II. Each state retains its sovereignty, freedom and independence, and every Power, Jurisdiction and right, which is not by this confederation expressly delegated to the United States, in Congress assembled.

Art. III. The said states hereby severally enter into a firm league of friendship with each other, for their common defence, the security of their Liberties, and their mutual and general welfare, binding themselves to assist each other, against all force offered to, or attacks made upon them, or any of them, on account of religion, sovereignty, trade, or any other pretence whatever.

Art. IV. The better to secure and perpetuate mutual friendship and intercourse among the people of the different states in this union, the free inhabitants of each of these states, paupers, vagabonds and fugitives from Justice excepted, shall be entitled to all privileges and immunities of free citizens in the several states; and the people of each state shall have free ingress and regress to and from any other state, and shall enjoy therein all the privileges of trade and commerce, subject to the same duties, impositions and restrictions as the inhabitants thereof respectively, provided that such restriction shall not extend so far as to prevent the removal of property imported into any state, to any other state, of which the Owner is an inhabitant; provided also that no imposition, duties or restriction shall be laid by any state, on the property of the united states, or either of them.

If any Person guilty of, or charged with treason, felony, or other high misdemeanor in any state, shall flee from Justice, and be found in any of the united states, he shall, upon demand of the Governor or executive power, of the state from which he fled, be delivered up and removed to the state having jurisdiction of his offence.

Full faith and credit shall be given in each of these states to the records, acts and judicial proceedings of the courts and magistrates of every other state.

Art. V. For the more convenient management of the general interests of the united states, delegates shall be annually appointed in such manner as the legislature of each state shall direct, to meet in Congress on the first Monday in November, in every year, with a power reserved to each state, to recall its delegates, or any of them, at any time within the year, and to send others in their stead, for the remainder of the Year.

No state shall be represented in Congress by less than two, nor by more than seven Members; and no person shall be capable of being a delegate for more than three years in any term of six years; nor shall any person, being a delegate, be capable of holding any office under the united states, for which he, or another for his benefit receives any salary, fees or emolument of any kind.

Each state shall maintain its own delegates in a meeting of the states, and while they act as members of the committee of the states.

In determining questions in the united states, in Congress assembled, each state shall have one vote.

Freedom of speech and debate in Congress shall not be impeached or questioned in any Court, or place out of Congress, and the members of congress shall be protected in their persons from arrests and imprisonments, during the time of their going to and from, and attendance on congress, except for treason, felony, or breach of the peace.

Art. VI. No state without the Consent of the united states in congress assembled, shall send any embassy to, or receive any embassy from, or enter into any conference, agreement, or alliance or treaty with any King, prince or state; nor shall any person holding any office or profit or trust under the united states, or any of them, accept of any present, emolument, office or title of any kind whatever from any king, prince or foreign state; nor shall the united states in congress assembled, or any of them, grant any title of nobility.

No two or more states shall enter into any treaty, confederation or alliance whatever between them, without the consent of the united states in congress assembled, specifying accurately the purposes for which the same is to be entered into, and how long it shall continue.

No state shall lay any imposts or duties, which may interfere with any stipulations in treaties, entered into by the united states in congress assembled, with any king, prince or state, in pursuance of any treaties already proposed by congress, to the courts of France and Spain.

No vessels of war shall be kept up in time of peace by any state, except such number only, as shall be deemed necessary by the united states in congress assembled, for the defence of such state, or its trade; nor shall any body of forces be kept up by any state, in time of peace, except such number only, as in the judgment of the united states, in congress assembled, shall be deemed requisite to garrison the forts necessary for the defence of such state; but every state shall always keep up a well regulated and disciplined militia, sufficiently armed and accoutred, and shall provide and constantly have ready for use, in public stores, a due number of field pieces and tents, and a proper quantity of arms, ammunition and camp equipage.

No state shall engage in any war without the consent of the united states in congress assembled, unless such state be actually invaded by enemies, or shall have received certain advice of a resolution being formed by some nation of Indians to invade such state, and the danger is so imminent as not to admit of a delay, till the united states in congress asssembled can be consulted; nor shall any state grant commissions to any ships or vessels of war, nor letters of marque or reprisal, except it be after a declaration of war by the united states in congress assembled, and then only against the kingdom or state and the subjects thereof, against which war has been so declared, and under such regulations as shall be established by the united states in congress assembled, unless such state be infested by pirates; in which case vessels of war may be fitted out for that occasion, and kept so long as the danger shall continue, or until the united states in congress assembled shall determine otherwise.

Art. VII. When land-forces are raised by any state for the common defence, all officers of or under the rank of colonel, shall be appointed by the legislature of each state respectively, by whom such forces shall be raised, or in such manner as such state shall direct, and all vacancies shall be filled up by the state which first made the appointment.

Art. VIII. All charges of war, and all other expences that shall be incurred for the common defence or general welfare, and allowed by the united states in congress assembled, shall be defrayed out of a common treasury, which shall be supplied by the several states in proportion to the value of all land within each state, granted to or surveyed for any Person, as such land and the buildings and improvements thereon shall be estimated according to such mode as the united states in congress assembled, shall from time to time direct and appoint.

The taxes for paying that proportion shall be laid and levied by the authority and direction of the legislatures of the several states within the time agreed upon by the united states in congress assembled.

Art. IX. The united states in congress assembled, shall have the sole and exclusive right and power of determining on peace and war, except in the cases mentioned in the sixth article—of sending and receiving ambassadors—entering into treaties and alliances, provided that no treaty of commerce shall be made whereby the legislative power of the respective states shall be restrained from imposing such imposts and duties on foreigners, as their own people are subjected to, or from prohibiting the exportation of any species of goods or commodities whatsoever—of establishing rules for deciding in all cases, what captures on land or water shall be legal, and in what manner prizes taken by land or naval forces in the service of the united states shall be divided or appropriated—of granting letters of marque and reprisal in times of peace—appointing courts for the trial of piracies and felonies committed on the high seas and establishing courts for receiving and determining finally appeals in all cases of captures, provided that no member of congress shall be appointed a judge of any of the said courts.

The united states in congress assembled shall also be the last resort on appeal in all disputes and differences now subsisting or that hereafter may arise between two or more states concerning boundary, jurisdiction or any other cause whatever; which authority shall always be exercised in the manner following. Whenever the legislative or executive authority or lawful agent of any state in controversy with another shall present a petition to congress stating the matter in question and praying for a hearing, notice thereof shall be given by order of congress to the legislative or executive authority of the other state in controversy, and a day assigned for the appearance of the parties by their lawful agents, who shall then be directed to appoint by joint consent, commissioners or judges to constitute a court for hearing and determining the matter in question: but if they cannot agree, congress shall name three persons out of each of the united states, and from the list of such persons each party shall alternately strike out one, the petitioners beginning, until the number shall be reduced to thirteen; and from that number not less than seven, nor more than nine names as congress shall direct, shall in the presence of congress be drawn out by lot, and the persons whose names shall be so drawn or any five of them, shall be commissioners or judges, to hear and finally determine the controversy, so always as a major part of the judges who shall hear the cause shall agree in the determination: and if either party shall neglect to attend at the day appointed, without shewing reasons, which congress shall judge sufficient, or being present shall refuse to strike, the congress shall proceed to nominate three persons out of each state, and the secretary of congress shall strike in behalf of such party absent or refusing; and the judgment and sentence of the court to be appointed, in the manner before prescribed, shall be final and conclusive; and if any of the parties shall refuse to submit to the authority of such court, or to appear to defend their claim or cause, the court shall nevertheless proceed to pronounce sentence, or judgment, which shall in like manner be final and decisive, the judgment or sentence and other proceedings being in either case transmitted to congress, and lodged among the acts of congress for the security of the parties concerned: provided that every commissioner, before he sits in judgment, shall take an oath to be administered by one of the judges of the supreme or superior court of the state, where the cause shall be tried, "well and truly to hear and determine the matter in question, according to the best of his judgment, without favour, affection or hope of reward:" provided also, that no state shall be deprived of territory for the benefit of the united states.

All controversies concerning the private right of soil claimed under different grants of two or more states, whose jurisdictions as they may respect such lands, and the states which passed such grants are adjusted, the said grants or either of them being at the same time claimed to have originated antecedent to such settlement of jurisdiction, shall on the petition of either party to the congress of the united states, be finally determined as near as may be in the same manner as is before prescribed for deciding disputes respecting territorial jurisdiction between different states.

The united states in congress assembled shall also have the sole and exclusive right and power of regulating the alloy and value of coin struck by their own authority, or by that of the respective states—fixing the standard of weights and measures throughout the united states—regulating the trade and managing all affairs with the Indians, not members of any of the states, provided that the legislative right of any state within its own limits be not infringed or violated—establishing and regulating post-offices from one state to another, throughout all the united states, and exacting such postage on the papers passing thro' the same as may be requisite to defray the expences of the said office—appointing all officers of the land forces, in the service of the united states, excepting regimental officers—appointing all the officers of the naval forces, and commissioning all officers whatever in the service of the united states—making rules for the government and regulation of the said land and naval forces, and directing their operations.

The united states in congress assembled shall have authority to appoint a committee, to sit in the recess of congress, to be denominated "A Committee of the States," and to consist of one delegate from each state; and to appoint such other committees and civil officers as may be necessary for managing the general affairs of the united states under their direction—to appoint one of their number to preside, provided that no person be allowed to serve in the office of president more than one year in any term of three years; to ascertain the necessary sums of Money to be raised for the service of the united states, and to appropriate and apply the same for defraying the public expenses—to borrow money, or emit bills on the credit of the united states, transmitting every half year to the respective states an account of the sums of money so borrowed or emitted,—to build and equip a navy—to agree upon the number of land forces, and to make requisitions from each state for its quota, in proportion to the number of white inhabitants in such state; which requisition shall be binding, and thereupon the legislature of each state shall appoint the regimental officers, raise the men and cloath, arm and equip them in a soldier like manner, at the expense of the united states; and the officers and men so cloathed, armed and equipped shall march to the place ap-pointed, and within the time agreed on by the united states in congress assembled: But if the united states in congress assembled shall, on consideration of circum-stances judge proper that any state should not raise men, or should raise a smaller number than its quota, and that any other state should raise a greater number of men than the quota thereof, such extra number shall be raised, officered, cloathed, armed and equipped in the same manner as the quota of such state, unless the legislature of such state shall judge that such extra number cannot be safely spared out of the same, in which case they shall raise officer, cloath, arm and equip as many of such extra number as they judge can be safely spared. And the officers and men so cloathed, armed and equipped, shall march to the place appointed, and within the time agreed on by the united states in congress assembled.

The united states in congress assembled shall never engage in a war, nor grant letters of marque and reprisal in time of peace, nor enter into any treaties or alli-ances, nor coin money, nor regulate the value thereof, nor ascertain the sums and expenses necessary for the defence and welfare of the united states, or any of them, nor emit bills, nor borrow money on the credit of the united states, nor appropriate money, nor agree upon the number of vessels of war, to be built or purchased, or the number of land or sea forces to be raised, nor appoint a commander in chief of the army or navy, unless nine states assent to the same: nor shall a question on any other point, except for adjourning from day to day be determined, unless by the votes of a majority of the united states in congress assembled.

The congress of the united states shall have power to adjourn to any time within the year, and to any place within the united states, so that no period of adjourn-ment be for a longer duration than the space of six Months, and shall publish the Journal of their proceedings monthly, except such parts thereof relating to treaties, alliances or military operations, as in their judgment require secrecy; and the yeas and nays of the delegates of each state on any question shall be entered on the Journal, when it is desired by any delegate; and the delegates of a state, or any of them, at his or their request shall be furnished with a transcript of the said Journal, except such parts as are above excepted, to lay before the legislatures of the several states.

Art. X. The committee of the states, or any nine of them, shall be authorised to execute, in the recess of congress, such of the powers of congress as the united states in congress assembled, by the consent of nine states, shall from time to time think expedient to vest them with; provided that no power be delegated to the said committee, for the exercise of which, by the articles of confederation, the voice of nine states in the congress of the united states assembled is requisite.

Art. XI. Canada acceding to this confederation, and joining in the measures of the united states, shall be admitted into, and entitled to all the advantages of this union: but no other colony shall be admitted into the same, unless such admission be agreed to by nine states.

Art. XII. All bills of credit emitted, monies borrowed and debts contracted by, or under the authority of congress, before the assembling of the united states, in pursuance of the present confederation, shall be deemed and considered as a charge against the united states, for payment and satisfaction whereof the said united states and the public faith are hereby solemnly pledged.

Art. XIII. Every state shall abide by the determinations of the united states in congress assembled, on all questions which by this confederation are submitted to them. And the Articles of this confederation shall be inviolably observed by every state, and the union shall be perpetual; nor shall any alteration at any time hereafter be made in any of them; unless such alteration be agreed to in a congress of the united states, and be afterwards confirmed by the legislatures of every state.

And Whereas it hath pleased the Great Governor of the World to incline the hearts of the legislatures we respectively represent in congress, to approve of, and to authorize us to ratify the said articles of confederation and perpetual union. Know Ye that we the undersigned delegates, by virtue of the power and authority to us given for that purpose, do by these presents, in the name and in behalf of our respective constituents, fully and entirely ratify and confirm each and every of the said articles of confederation and perpetual union, and all and singular the matters and things therein contained: And we do further solemnly plight and engage the faith of our respective constituents, that they shall abide by the determinations of the united states in congress assembled, on all questions, which by the said confederation are submitted to them. And that the articles thereof shall be inviolably observed by the states we respectively represent, and that the union shall be perpetual. In Witness whereof we have hereunto set our hands in Congress. Done at Philadelphia in the state of Pennsylvania the ninth day of July, in the Year of our Lord one Thousand seven Hundred and Seventy-eight, and in the third year of the independence of America.

The Constitution of the United States of America

We the People of the United States, in Order to form a more perfect Union, establish Justice, insure domestic Tranquility, provide for the common defence, promote the general Welfare, and secure the Blessings of Liberty to ourselves and our Posterity, do ordain and establish this Constitution for the United States of America.

Article I

SECTION 1
[LEGISLATIVE POWERS]
All legislative Powers herein granted shall be vested in a Congress of the United States, which shall consist of a Senate and House of Representatives.

SECTION 2
[HOUSE OF REPRESENTATIVES, HOW CONSTITUTED, POWER OF IMPEACHMENT]
The House of Representatives shall be composed of Members chosen every second Year by the People of the several States, and the Electors in each State shall have the Qualifications requisite for Electors of the most numerous Branch of the State Legislature.

No Person shall be a Representative who shall not have attained to the Age of twenty five Years, and been seven Years a Citizen of the United States, and who shall not, when elected, be an Inhabitant of that State in which he shall be chosen.

Representatives and *direct Taxes*[1] shall be apportioned among the several States which may be included within this Union, according to their respective Numbers, *which shall be determined by adding to the whole Number of free Persons, including those bound to Service for a Term of Years, and excluding Indians not taxed, three fifths of all other Persons.*[2] The actual Enumeration shall be made within three Years after the first Meeting of the Congress of the United States, and within every subsequent Term of ten Years, in such Manner as they shall by Law direct. The Number of Representatives shall not exceed one for every thirty Thousand, but each State shall have at Least one Representative; *and until such enumeration shall be made, the State of New Hampshire shall be entitled to chuse three, Massachusetts eight, Rhode-Island and Providence Plantations one, Connecticut five, New-York six, New Jersey four, Pennsylvania eight, Delaware one, Maryland six, Virginia ten, North Carolina five, South Carolina five, and Georgia three.*[3]

When vacancies happen in the Representation from any State, the Executive Authority thereof shall issue Writs of Election to fill such Vacancies.

The House of Representatives shall chuse their Speaker and other Officers; and shall have the sole Power of Impeachment.

---

[1]Modified by Sixteenth Amendment.

[2]Modified by Fourteenth Amendment.

[3]Temporary provision.

SECTION 3

[THE SENATE, HOW CONSTITUTED, IMPEACHMENT TRIALS]

The Senate of the United States shall be composed of two Senators from each State, *chosen by the Legislature thereof,*[4] for six Years; and each Senator shall have one Vote.

Immediately after they shall be assembled in Consequence of the first Election, they shall be divided as equally as may be into three Classes. The Seats of the Senators of the first Class shall be vacated at the Expiration of the second Year, of the second Class at the Expiration of the fourth Year, and of the third Class at the Expiration of the sixth Year, so that one third may be chosen every second Year; *and if Vacancies happen by Resignation, or otherwise, during the Recess of the Legislature of any State, the Executive thereof may make temporary Appointments until the next Meeting of the Legislature, which shall then fill such Vacancies.*[5]

No Person shall be a Senator who shall not have attained to the Age of thirty Years, and been nine Years a Citizen of the United States, and who shall not, when elected, be an Inhabitant of that State for which he shall be chosen.

The Vice President of the United States shall be President of the Senate, but shall have no Vote, unless they be equally divided.

The Senate shall chuse their other Officers, and also a President pro tempore, in the Absence of the Vice President, or when he shall exercise the Office of President of the United States.

The Senate shall have the sole Power to try all Impeachments. When sitting for that Purpose, they shall be on Oath or Affirmation. When the President of the United States is tried, the Chief Justice shall preside: And no Person shall be convicted without the Concurrence of two thirds of the Members present.

Judgment in Cases of Impeachment shall not extend further than to removal from Office, and disqualification to hold and enjoy any Office of honor, Trust or Profit under the United States: but the Party convicted shall nevertheless be liable and subject to Indictment, Trial, Judgment and Punishment, according to Law.

SECTION 4

[ELECTION OF SENATORS AND REPRESENTATIVES]

The Times, Places and Manner of holding Elections for Senators and Representatives, shall be prescribed in each State by the Legislature thereof; but the Congress may at any time by Law make or alter such Regulations, except as to the Places of chusing Senators.

The Congress shall assemble at least once in every Year, and such Meeting shall be on the first Monday in December, unless they shall by Law appoint a different Day.[6]

SECTION 5

[QUORUM, JOURNALS, MEETINGS, ADJOURNMENTS]

Each House shall be the Judge of the Elections, Returns and Qualifications of its own Members, and a Majority of each shall constitute a Quorum to do Business;

---

[4]Modified by Seventeenth Amendment.

[5]Modified by Seventeenth Amendment.

[6]Modified by Twentieth Amendment.

but a smaller Number may adjourn from day to day, and may be authorized to compel the Attendance of absent Members, in such Manner, and under such Penalties as each House may provide.

Each House may determine the Rules of its Proceedings, punish its Members for disorderly Behaviour, and, with the Concurrence of two thirds, expel a Member.

Each House shall keep a Journal of its Proceedings, and from time to time publish the same, excepting such Parts as may in their Judgment require Secrecy; and the Yeas and Nays of the Members of either House on any questions shall, at the Desire of one fifth of those Present, be entered on the Journal.

Neither House, during the Session of Congress, shall, without the Consent of the other, adjourn for more than three days, nor to any other Place than that in which the two Houses shall be sitting.

SECTION 6

[COMPENSATION, PRIVILEGES, DISABILITIES]

The Senators and Representatives shall receive a Compensation for their Services, to be ascertained by Law, and paid out of the Treasury of the United States. They shall in all Cases, except Treason, Felony and Breach of the Peace, be privileged from Arrest during their Attendance at the Session of their respective Houses, and in going to and returning from the same; and for any Speech or Debate in either House, they shall not be questioned in any other Place.

No Senator or Representative shall, during the Time for which he was elected, be appointed to any civil Office under the Authority of the United States, which shall have been created, or the Emoluments whereof shall have been encreased during such time; and no Person holding any Office under the United States, shall be a Member of either House during his Continuance in Office.

SECTION 7

[PROCEDURE IN PASSING BILLS AND RESOLUTIONS]

All Bills for raising Revenue shall originate in the House of Representatives; but the Senate may propose or concur with Amendments as on other Bills.

Every Bill which shall have passed the House of Representatives and the Senate, shall, before it become a Law, be presented to the President of the United States: If he approve he shall sign it, but if not he shall return it, with his Objections to that House in which it shall have originated, who shall enter the Objections at large on their Journal, and proceed to reconsider it. If after such Reconsideration two thirds of that House shall agree to pass the Bill, it shall be sent, together with the Objections, to the other House, by which it shall likewise be reconsidered, and if approved by two thirds of that House, it shall become a Law. But in all such Cases the Votes of both Houses shall be determined by yeas and Nays, and the Names of the Persons voting for and against the Bill shall be entered on the Journal of each House respectively. If any Bill shall not be returned by the President within ten Days (Sundays excepted) after it shall have been presented to him, the Same shall be a Law, in like Manner as if he had signed it, unless the Congress by their Adjournment prevent its Return, in which Case it shall not be a Law.

Every Order, Resolution, or Vote to which the Concurrence of the Senate and House of Representatives may be necessary (except on a question of Adjournment) shall be presented to the President of the United States; and before the Same shall take Effect, shall be approved by him, or being disapproved by him, shall be repassed by two thirds of the Senate and House of Representatives, according to the Rules and Limitations prescribed in the Case of a Bill.

SECTION 8
[POWERS OF CONGRESS]
The Congress shall have Power

To lay and collect Taxes, Duties, Imposts and Excises, to pay the Debts and provide for the common Defence and general Welfare of the United States; but all Duties, Imposts and Excises shall be uniform throughout the United States;

To borrow Money on the credit of the United States;

To regulate Commerce with foreign Nations, and among the several States, and with the Indian Tribes;

To establish an uniform Rule of Naturalization, and uniform Laws on the subject of Bankruptcies throughout the United States;

To coin Money, regulate the Value thereof, and of foreign Coin, and fix the Standard of Weights and Measures;

To provide for the Punishment of counterfeiting the Securities and current Coin of the United States;

To establish Post Offices and post Roads;

To promote the Progress of Science and useful Arts, by securing for limited Times to Authors and Inventors the exclusive Right to their respective Writings and Discoveries;

To constitute Tribunals inferior to the supreme Court;

To define and punish Piracies and Felonies committed on the high Seas, and Offences against the Law of Nations;

To declare War, grant Letters of Marque and Reprisal, and make Rules concerning Captures on Land and Water;

To raise and support Armies, but no Appropriation of Money to that Use shall be for a longer Term than two Years;

To provide and maintain a Navy;

To make Rules for the Government and Regulation of the land and naval Forces;

To provide for calling forth the Militia to execute the Laws of the Union, suppress Insurrections and repel Invasions;

To provide for organizing, arming, and disciplining, the Militia, and for governing such Part of them as may be employed in the Service of the United States, reserving to the States respectively, the Appointment of the Officers, and the Authority of training the Militia according to the discipline prescribed by Congress;

To exercise exclusive Legislation in all Cases whatsoever, over such District (not exceeding ten Miles square) as may, by Cession of particular States, and the Acceptance of Congress, become the Seat of the Government of the United States, and to exercise like Authority over all Places purchased by the Consent of the Legislature of the State in which the Same shall be, for the Erection of Forts, Magazines, Arsenals, dock-Yards, and other needful Buildings;—And

To make all Laws which shall be necessary and proper for carrying into Execution the foregoing Powers, and all other Powers vested by this

Constitution in the Government of the United States, or in any Department or Officer thereof.

SECTION 9

The Migration or Importation of such Persons as any of the States now existing shall think proper to admit, shall not be prohibited by the Congress prior to the Year one thousand eight hundred and eight, but a Tax or duty may be imposed on such Importation, not exceeding ten dollars for each Person.[7]

The Privilege of the Writ of Habeas Corpus shall not be suspended, unless when in Cases of Rebellion or Invasion the public Safety may require it.

No Bill of Attainder or ex post facto Law shall be passed.

No Capitation, or other direct, Tax shall be laid, unless in Proportion to the Census or Enumeration herein before directed to be taken.[8]

No Tax or Duty shall be laid on Articles exported from any State.

No Preference shall be given by any Regulation of Commerce or Revenue to the Ports of one State over those of another; nor shall Vessels bound to, or from, one State, be obliged to enter, clear, or pay Duties in another.

No Money shall be drawn from the Treasury, but in Consequence of Appropriations made by Law; and a regular Statement and Account of the Receipts and Expenditures of all public Money shall be published from time to time.

No Title of Nobility shall be granted by the United States: And no Person holding any Office of Profit or Trust under them, shall, without the Consent of the Congress, accept of any present, Emolument, Office, or Title, of any kind whatever, from any King, Prince, or foreign State.

SECTION 10

No State shall enter into any Treaty, Alliance, or Confederation; grant Letters of Marque and Reprisal; coin Money; emit Bills of Credit; make any Thing but gold and silver Coin a Tender in Payment of Debts; pass any Bill of Attainder, ex post facto Law, or Law impairing the Obligation of Contracts, or grant any Title of Nobility.

No State shall, without the Consent of the Congress, lay any Imposts or Duties on Imports or Exports, except what may be absolutely necessary for executing its inspection Laws: and the net Produce of all Duties and Imposts, laid by any State on Imports or Exports, shall be for the Use of the Treasury of the United States; and all such Laws shall be subject to the Revision and Control of the Congress.

No State shall, without the Consent of Congress, lay any Duty of Tonnage, keep Troops, or Ships of War in time of Peace, enter into any Agreement or Compact with another State, or with a foreign Power, or engage in War, unless actually invaded, or in such imminent Danger as will not admit of delay.

---

[7]Temporary provision.

[8]Modified by Sixteenth Amendment.

Article II

SECTION 1

[EXECUTIVE POWER, ELECTION, QUALIFICATIONS OF THE PRESIDENT]

The executive Power shall be vested in a President of the United States of America. *He shall hold his Office during the Term of four Years, and, together with the Vice President, chosen for the same Term, be elected, as follows*[9]

Each State shall appoint, in such Manner as the Legislature thereof may direct, a Number of Electors, equal to the whole Number of Senators and Representatives to which the State may be entitled in the Congress: but no Senator or Representative, or Person holding an Office of Trust or Profit under the United States, shall be appointed an Elector.

The electors shall meet in their respective States, and vote by ballot for two Persons, of whom one at least shall not be an Inhabitant of the same State with themselves. And they shall make a List of all the Persons voted for, and of the Number of Votes for each; which List they shall sign and certify, and transmit sealed to the Seat of the Government of the United States, directed to the President of the Senate. The President of the Senate shall, in the Presence of the Senate and House of Representatives, open all the Certificates, and the Votes shall then be counted. The Person having the greatest Number of Votes shall be the President, if such Number be a Majority of the whole Number of Electors appointed; and if there be more than one who have such Majority, and have an equal Number of Votes, then the House of Representatives shall immediately chuse by Ballot one of them for President; and if no Person have a Majority, then from the five highest on the List the said House shall in like Manner chuse the President. But in chusing the President, the Votes shall be taken by States, the Representation from each State having one Vote; A quorum for this Purpose shall consist of a Member or Members from two thirds of the States, and a Majority of all the States shall be necessary to a Choice. In every Case, after the Choice of the President, the person having the greatest Number of Votes of the Electors shall be the Vice President. But if there should remain two or more who have equal Votes, the Senate shall chuse from them by Ballot the Vice President.[10]

The Congress may determine the Time of chusing the Electors, and the Day on which they shall give their Votes; which Day shall be the same throughout the United States.

No Person except a natural born Citizen, or a Citizen of the United States, at the time of the Adoption of this Constitution, shall be eligible to the Office of President; neither shall any Person be eligible to that Office who shall not have attained to the Age of thirty five Years, and been fourteen Years a Resident within the United States.

In Case of the Removal of the President from Office, or his Death, Resignation, or Inability to discharge the Powers and Duties of the said Office, the Same shall devolve on the Vice President, and the Congress may by Law provide for the Case of Removal, Death, Resignation or Inability, both of the President and Vice President,

---

[9]Number of terms limited to two by Twenty-Second Amendment.

[10]Modified by Twelfth and Twentieth Amendments.

declaring what Officer shall then act as President, and such Officer shall act accordingly, until the Disability be removed, or a President shall be elected.

The President shall, at stated Times, receive for his Services, a Compensation, which shall neither be increased nor diminished during the Period for which he shall have been elected, and he shall not receive within that Period any other Emolument from the United States, or any of them.

Before he enter on the Execution of his Office, he shall take the following Oath or Affirmation:—"I do solemnly swear (or affirm) that I will faithfully execute the Office of President of the United States, and will to the best of my Ability, preserve, protect and defend the Constitution of the United States."

SECTION 2
[POWERS OF THE PRESIDENT]
The President shall be Commander in Chief of the Army and Navy of the United States, and of the Militia of the several States, when called into the actual Service of the United States; he may require the Opinion, in writing, of the principal Officer in each of the executive Departments, upon any Subject relating to the Duties of their respective Offices, and he shall have Power to grant Reprieves and Pardons for Offences against the United States, except in Cases of Impeachment.

He shall have Power, by and with the Advice and Consent of the Senate, to make Treaties, provided two thirds of the Senators present concur; and he shall nominate, and by and with the Advice and Consent of the Senate, shall appoint Ambassadors, other public Ministers and Consuls, Judges of the supreme Court, and all other Officers of the United States, whose Appointments are not herein otherwise provided for, and which shall be established by Law: but the Congress may by Law vest the Appointment of such inferior Officers, as they think proper, in the President alone, in the Courts of Law, or in the Heads of Departments.

The President shall have Power to fill up all Vacancies that may happen during the Recess of the Senate, by granting Commissions which shall expire at the End of their next Session.

SECTION 3
[POWERS AND DUTIES OF THE PRESIDENT]
He shall from time to time give to the Congress Information of the State of the Union, and recommend to their Consideration such Measures as he shall judge necessary and expedient; he may, on extraordinary Occasions, convene both Houses, or either of them, and in Case of Disagreement between them, with Respect to the Time of Adjournment, he may adjourn them to such Time as he shall think proper; he shall receive Ambassadors and other public Ministers; he shall take Care that the Laws be faithfully executed, and shall Commission all the Officers of the United States.

SECTION 4
[IMPEACHMENT]
The President, Vice President and all civil Officers of the United States, shall be removed from Office on Impeachment for, and Conviction of, Treason, Bribery, or other high Crimes and Misdemeanors.

Article III

SECTION 1

[JUDICIAL POWER, TENURE OF OFFICE]

The judicial Power of the United States, shall be vested in one supreme Court, and in such inferior Courts as the Congress may from time to time ordain and establish. The Judges, both of the supreme and inferior Courts, shall hold their Offices during good Behaviour, and shall, at stated Times, receive for their Services, a Compensation, which shall not be diminished during their Continuance in Office.

SECTION 2

[JURISDICTION]

The judicial Power shall extend to all Cases, in Law and Equity, arising under this Constitution, the Laws of the United States, and Treaties made, or which shall be made, under their Authority;—to all Cases affecting Ambassadors, other public Ministers and Consuls;—to all Cases of admiralty and maritime Jurisdiction;—to Controversies to which the United States shall be a Party;—to Controversies between two or more States;—*between a State and Citizens of another State;*—between Citizens of different States,—between Citizens of the same State claiming Lands under Grants of different States, *and between a State*, or the Citizens thereof, *and foreign States, Citizens or Subjects.*[11]

In all Cases affecting Ambassadors, other public Ministers and Consuls, and those in which a State shall be Party, the supreme Court shall have original Jurisdiction. In all the other Cases before mentioned, the supreme Court shall have appellate Jurisdiction, both as to Law and Fact, with such Exceptions, and under such Regulations as the Congress shall make.

The Trial of all Crimes, except in Cases of Impeachment, shall be by Jury; and such Trial shall be held in the State where the said Crimes shall have been committed; but when not committed within any State, the Trial shall be at such Place or Places as the Congress may by Law have directed.

SECTION 3

[TREASON, PROOF, AND PUNISHMENT]

Treason against the United States, shall consist only in levying War against them, or in adhering to their Enemies, giving them Aid and Comfort. No Person shall be convicted of Treason unless on the Testimony of two Witnesses to the same overt Act, or on Confession in open Court.

The Congress shall have Power to declare the Punishment of Treason, but no Attainder of Treason shall work Corruption of Blood, or Forfeiture except during the Life of the Person attainted.

Article IV

SECTION 1

[FAITH AND CREDIT AMONG STATES]

---

[11]Modified by Eleventh Amendment.

Full Faith and Credit shall be given in each State to the public Acts, Records, and judicial Proceedings of every other State. And the Congress may by general Laws prescribe the Manner in which such Acts, Records and Proceedings shall be proved, and the Effect thereof.

SECTION 2
[PRIVILEGES AND IMMUNITIES, FUGITIVES]
The Citizens of each State shall be entitled to all Privileges and Immunities of Citizens in the several States.

A Person charged in any State with Treason, Felony or other Crime, who shall flee from Justice, and be found in another State, shall on Demand of the executive Authority of the State from which he fled, be delivered up, to be removed to the State having Jurisdiction of the Crime.

No person held to Service or Labour in one State, under the Laws thereof, escaping into another, shall, in Consequence of any Law or Regulation therein, be discharged from such Service or Labour, but shall be delivered up on Claim of the Party to whom such Service or Labour may be due.[12]

SECTION 3
[ADMISSION OF NEW STATES]
New States may be admitted by the Congress into this Union; but no new State shall be formed or erected within the Jurisdiction of any other State; nor any State be formed by the Junction of two or more States, or Parts of States, without the Consent of the Legislatures of the States concerned as well as of the Congress.

The Congress shall have Power to dispose of and make all needful Rules and Regulations respecting the Territory or other Property belonging to the United States; and nothing in this Constitution shall be so construed as to Prejudice any Claims of the United States, or of any particular State.

SECTION 4
[GUARANTEE OF REPUBLICAN GOVERNMENT]
The United States shall guarantee to every State in this Union a Republican Form of Government, and shall protect each of them against Invasion; and on Application of the Legislature, or of the Executive (when the Legislature cannot be convened), against domestic Violence.

Article V
[AMENDMENT OF THE CONSTITUTION]
The Congress, whenever two thirds of both Houses shall deem it necessary, shall propose Amendments to this Constitution, or, on the Application of the Legislatures of two thirds of the several States, shall call a Convention for proposing Amendments, which, in either Case, shall be valid to all Intents and Purposes, as Part of this Constitution, when ratified by the Legislatures of three fourths of the

---

[12]Repealed by the Thirteenth Amendment.

several States, or by Conventions in three fourths thereof, as the one or the other Mode of Ratification may be proposed by the Congress; *Provided that no Amendment which may be made prior to the Year One thousand eight hundred and eight shall in any Manner affect the first and fourth Clauses in the Ninth Section of the first Article;*[13] and that no State, without its Consent, shall be deprived of its equal Suffrage in the Senate.

Article VI

[DEBTS, SUPREMACY, OATH]

All Debts contracted and Engagements entered into, before the Adoption of this Constitution, shall be as valid against the United States under this Constitution, as under the Confederation.

This Constitution, and the Laws of the United States which shall be made in Pursuance thereof; and all Treaties made, or which shall be made, under the Authority of the United States, shall be the supreme Law of the Land; and the Judges in every State shall be bound thereby, any Thing in the Constitution or Laws of any State to the Contrary notwithstanding.

The Senators and Representatives before mentioned, and the Members of the several State Legislatures, and all executive and judicial Officers, both of the United States and of the several States, shall be bound by Oath or Affirmation, to support this Constitution; but no religious Test shall be required as a Qualification to any Office or public Trust under the United States.

Article VII

[RATIFICATION AND ESTABLISHMENT]

The Ratification of the Conventions of nine States, shall be sufficient for the Establishment of this Constitution between the States so ratifying the Same.[14]

Done in Convention by the Unanimous Consent of the States present the Seventeenth Day of September in the Year of our Lord one thousand seven hundred

---

[13]Temporary provision.

[14]The Constitution was submitted on September 17, 1787, by the Constitutional Convention, was ratified by the conventions of several states at various dates up to May 29, 1790, and became effective on March 4, 1789.

and Eighty seven and of the Independence of the United States of America the Twelfth. *In Witness* whereof We have hereunto subscribed our Names,

G:⁰ *WASHINGTON*—
Presidt. and deputy from Virginia

NEW HAMPSHIRE
John Langdon
Nicholas Gilman

MASSACHUSETTS
Nathaniel Gorham
Rufus King

CONNECTICUT
Wm. Saml. Johnson
Roger Sherman

NEW YORK
Alexander Hamilton

NEW JERSEY
Wil: Livingston
David Brearley
Wm. Paterson
Jona: Dayton

PENNSYLVANIA
B Franklin
Thomas Mifflin
Robt. Morris
Geo. Clymer
Thos. FitzSimons
Jared Ingersoll
James Wilson
Gouv Morris

DELAWARE
Geo: Read
Gunning Bedford jun
John Dickinson
Richard Bassett
Jaco: Broom

MARYLAND
James McHenry
Dan of St Thos. Jenifer
Danl. Carroll

VIRGINIA
John Blair—
James Madison Jr.

NORTH CAROLINA
Wm. Blount
Richd. Dobbs Spaight
Hu Williamson

SOUTH CAROLINA
J. Rutledge
Charles Cotesworth
  Pinckney
Charles Pinckney
Pierce Butler

GEORGIA
William Few
Abr Baldwin

Amendments to the Constitution

Proposed by Congress and Ratified by the Legislatures of the Several States, Pursuant to Article V of the Original Constitution.

Amendments I–X, known as the Bill of Rights, were proposed by Congress on September 25, 1789, and ratified on December 15, 1791.

Amendment I

[FREEDOM OF RELIGION, OF SPEECH, AND OF THE PRESS]

Congress shall make no law respecting an establishment of religion, or prohibiting the free exercise thereof; or abridging the freedom of speech, or of the press; or the right of the people peaceably to assemble, and to petition the Government for a redress of grievances.

Amendment II

[RIGHT TO KEEP AND BEAR ARMS]

A well regulated Militia, being necessary to the security of a free State, the right of the people to keep and bear Arms, shall not be infringed.

Amendment III

[QUARTERING OF SOLDIERS]

No Soldier shall, in time of peace be quartered in any house, without the consent of the Owner, nor in time of war, but in a manner to be prescribed by law.

Amendment IV

[SECURITY FROM UNWARRANTABLE SEARCH AND SEIZURE]

The right of the people to be secure in their persons, houses, papers, and effects, against unreasonable searches and seizures, shall not be violated, and no Warrants shall issue, but upon probable cause, supported by Oath or affirmation, and particularly describing the place to be searched, and the persons or things to be seized.

Amendment V

[RIGHTS OF ACCUSED PERSONS IN CRIMINAL PROCEEDINGS]

No person shall be held to answer for a capital, or otherwise infamous crime, unless on a presentment or indictment of a Grand Jury, except in cases arising in the land or naval forces, or in the Militia, when in actual service in time of War or in public danger; nor shall any person be subject for the same offence to be twice put in jeopardy of life or limb; nor shall be compelled in any criminal case to be a witness against himself, nor be deprived of life, liberty, or property, without due process of law; nor shall private property be taken for public use, without just compensation.

Amendment VI

[RIGHT TO SPEEDY TRIAL, WITNESSES, ETC.]

In all criminal prosecutions, the accused shall enjoy the right to a speedy and public trial, by an impartial jury of the State and district wherein the crime shall have been committed, which district shall have been previously ascertained by law, and to be informed of the nature and cause of the accusation; to be confronted with the witnesses against him; to have compulsory process for obtaining witnesses in his favor, and to have the Assistance of Counsel for his defence.

Amendment VII

[TRIAL BY JURY IN CIVIL CASES]

In suits at common law, where the value in controversy shall exceed twenty dollars, the right of trial by jury shall be preserved, and no fact tried by a jury, shall be otherwise reexamined in any Court of the United States, than according to the rules of the common law.

Amendment VIII

[BAILS, FINES, PUNISHMENTS]

Excessive bail shall not be required, nor excessive fines imposed, nor cruel and unusual punishments inflicted.

Amendment IX

[RESERVATION OF RIGHTS OF PEOPLE]

The enumeration in the Constitution, of certain rights, shall not be construed to deny or disparage others retained by the people.

Amendment X

[POWERS RESERVED TO STATES OR PEOPLE]

The powers not delegated to the United States by the Constitution, nor prohibited by it to the States, are reserved to the States respectively, or to the people.

Amendment XI

[PROPOSED BY CONGRESS ON MARCH 4, 1794; DECLARED RATIFIED ON JANUARY 8, 1798.]

[RESTRICTION OF JUDICIAL POWER]

The Judicial power of the United States shall not be construed to extend to any suit in law or equity, commenced or prosecuted against one of the United States by Citizens of another State, or by Citizens or Subjects of any Foreign State.

Amendment XII

[PROPOSED BY CONGRESS ON DECEMBER 9, 1803; DECLARED RATIFIED ON SEPTEMBER 25, 1804.]

[ELECTION OF PRESIDENT AND VICE PRESIDENT]

The Electors shall meet in their respective states and vote by ballot for President and Vice-President, one of whom, at least, shall not be an inhabitant of the same state with themselves; they shall name in their ballots the person voted for as President, and in distinct ballots the person voted for as Vice-President, and they shall make distinct lists of all persons voted for as President, and of all persons voted for as Vice-President, and of the number of votes for each, which lists they shall sign and certify, and transmit sealed to the seat of the government of the United States, directed to the President of the Senate;—the President of the Senate shall, in presence of the Senate and House of Representatives, open all the certificates and the votes shall then be counted;—The person having the greatest number of votes for President, shall be the President, if such number be a majority of the whole number of Electors appointed; and if no person have such majority, then from the persons having the highest numbers not exceeding three on the list of those voted for as President, the House of Representatives shall choose immediately, by ballot, the President. But in choosing the President, the votes shall be taken by states, the representation from each state having one vote; a quorum for this purpose shall consist of a member or members from two-thirds of the states, and a majority of all the states shall be necessary to a choice. And if the House of Representatives shall not choose a President whenever the right of choice shall devolve upon them, before the fourth day of March next following, then the Vice-President shall act as President, as in the case of the death or other constitutional disability of the President.—The person having the greatest number of votes as Vice-President, shall be the Vice-President, if such number be a majority of the whole number of Electors appointed, and if no person have a majority, then from the two highest numbers on the list, the Senate shall choose the Vice-President; a quorum for the purpose shall consist of two-thirds of the whole number of Senators, and a majority of the whole number shall be necessary to a choice. But no person constitutionally ineligible to the office of President shall be eligible to that of Vice-President of the United States.

Amendment XIII

[PROPOSED BY CONGRESS ON JANUARY 31, 1865; DECLARED RATIFIED ON DECEMBER 18, 1865.]

SECTION 1

[ABOLITION OF SLAVERY]

Neither slavery nor involuntary servitude, except as a punishment for crime whereof the party shall have been duly convicted, shall exist within the United States, or any place subject to their jurisdiction.

SECTION 2

[POWER TO ENFORCE THIS ARTICLE]

Congress shall have power to enforce this article by appropriate legislation.

Amendment XIV

[PROPOSED BY CONGRESS ON JUNE 13, 1866; DECLARED RATIFIED ON JULY 28, 1868.]

SECTION 1

[CITIZENSHIP RIGHTS NOT TO BE ABRIDGED BY STATES]

All persons born or naturalized in the United States, and subject to the jurisdiction thereof, are citizens of the United States and of the State wherein they reside. No State shall make or enforce any law which shall abridge the privileges or immunities of citizens of the United States; nor shall any State deprive any person of life, liberty, or property, without due process of law; nor deny to any person within its jurisdiction the equal protection of the laws.

SECTION 2

[APPORTIONMENT OF REPRESENTATIVES IN CONGRESS]

Representatives shall be apportioned among the several States according to their respective numbers, counting the whole number of persons in each State, excluding Indians not taxed. But when the right to vote at any election for the choice of electors for President and Vice-President of the United States, Representatives in Congress, the Executive and Judicial officers of a State, or the members of the Legislature thereof, is denied to any of the male inhabitants of such State, being twenty-one years of age, and citizens of the United States, or in any way abridged, except for participation in rebellion, or other crime, the basis of representation therein shall be reduced in the proportion which the number of such male citizens shall bear to the whole number of male citizens twenty-one years of age in such State.

SECTION 3
[PERSONS DISQUALIFIED FROM HOLDING OFFICE]
No person shall be a Senator or Representative in Congress, or elector of President and Vice-President, or hold any office, civil or military, under the United States, or under any State, who, having previously taken an oath, as a member of Congress, or as an officer of the United States, or as a member of any State legislature, or as an executive or judicial officer of any State, to support the Constitution of the United States, shall have engaged in insurrection or rebellion against the same, or given aid or comfort to the enemies thereof. But Congress may by a vote of two-thirds of each House, remove such disability.

SECTION 4
[WHAT PUBLIC DEBTS ARE VALID]
The validity of the public debt of the United States, authorized by law, including debts incurred for payment of pensions and bounties for services in suppressing insurrection or rebellion, shall not be questioned. But neither the United States nor any State shall assume or pay any debt or obligation incurred in aid of insurrection or rebellion against the United States, or any claim for the loss or emancipation of any slave; but all such debts, obligations and claims shall be held illegal and void.

SECTION 5
[POWER TO ENFORCE THIS ARTICLE]
The Congress shall have power to enforce, by appropriate legislation, the provisions of this article.

Amendment XV
[PROPOSED BY CONGRESS ON FEBRUARY 26, 1869; DECLARED RATIFIED ON MARCH 30, 1870.]

SECTION 1
[NEGRO SUFFRAGE]
The right of citizens of the United States to vote shall not be denied or abridged by the United States or by any State on account of race, color, or previous condition of servitude.

SECTION 2
[POWER TO ENFORCE THIS ARTICLE]
The Congress shall have power to enforce this article by appropriate legislation.

Amendment XVI

[PROPOSED BY CONGRESS ON JULY 2, 1909; DECLARED RATIFIED ON FEBRUARY 25, 1913.]
[AUTHORIZING INCOME TAXES]

The Congress shall have power to lay and collect taxes on incomes, from whatever source derived, without apportionment among the several States, and without regard to any census or enumeration.

Amendment XVII

[PROPOSED BY CONGRESS ON MAY 13, 1912; DECLARED RATIFIED ON MAY 31, 1913.]
[POPULAR ELECTION OF SENATORS]

The Senate of the United States shall be composed of two Senators from each State, elected by the people thereof, for six years; and each Senator shall have one vote. The electors in each State shall have the qualifications requisite for electors of the most numerous branch of the State legislatures.

When vacancies happen in the representation of any State in the Senate, the executive authority of such State shall issue writs of election to fill such vacancies: *Provided,* That the legislature of any State may empower the executive thereof to make temporary appointments until the people fill the vacancies by election as the legislature may direct.

This amendment shall not be so construed as to affect the election or term of any Senator chosen before it becomes valid as part of the Constitution.

Amendment XVIII

[PROPOSED BY CONGRESS DECEMBER 18, 1917; DECLARED RATIFIED ON JANUARY 29, 1919.]

SECTION 1

[NATIONAL LIQUOR PROHIBITION]

After one year from the ratification of this article the manufacture, sale, or transportation of intoxicating liquors within, the importation thereof into, or the exportation thereof from the United States and all territory subject to the jurisdiction thereof for beverage purposes is hereby prohibited.

SECTION 2

[POWER TO ENFORCE THIS ARTICLE]

The Congress and the several States shall have concurrent power to enforce this article by appropriate legislation.

SECTION 3

[RATIFICATION WITHIN SEVEN YEARS]

This article shall be inoperative unless it shall have been ratified as an amendment to the Constitution by the legislatures of the several States, as provided in the Constitution, within seven years from the date of the submission hereof to the States by the Congress.[1]

---

[1]Repealed by the Twenty-First Amendment.

Amendment XIX

[PROPOSED BY CONGRESS ON JUNE 4, 1919; DECLARED RATIFIED ON AUGUST 26, 1920.]

[WOMAN SUFFRAGE]

The right of citizens of the United States to vote shall not be denied or abridged by the United States or by any State on account of sex.

Congress shall have power to enforce this article by appropriate legislation.

Amendment XX

[PROPOSED BY CONGRESS ON MARCH 2, 1932; DECLARED RATIFIED ON FEBRUARY 6, 1933.]

SECTION 1

[TERMS OF OFFICE]

The terms of the President and Vice President shall end at noon on the 20th day of January, and the terms of Senators and Representatives at noon on the 3d day of January, of the years in which such terms would have ended if this article had not been ratified; and the terms of their successors shall then begin.

SECTION 2

[TIME OF CONVENING CONGRESS]

The Congress shall assemble at least once in every year, and such meeting shall begin at noon on the 3d day of January, unless they shall by law appoint a different day.

SECTION 3

[DEATH OF PRESIDENT-ELECT]

If, at the time fixed for the beginning of the term of the President, the President elect shall have died, the Vice President elect shall become President. If a President shall not have been chosen before the time fixed for the beginning of his term, or if the President elect shall have failed to qualify, then the Vice President elect shall act as President until a President shall have qualified; and the Congress may by law provide for the case wherein neither a President elect nor a Vice President elect shall have qualified, declaring who shall then act as President, or the manner in which one who is to act shall be selected, and such person shall act accordingly until a President or Vice President shall have qualified.

SECTION 4

[ELECTION OF THE PRESIDENT]

The Congress may by law provide for the case of the death of any of the persons from whom the House of Representatives may choose a President whenever the right of choice shall have devolved upon them, and for the case of the death of any of the persons from whom the Senate may choose a Vice President whenever the right of choice shall have devolved upon them.

SECTION 5

[AMENDMENT TAKES EFFECT]

Sections 1 and 2 shall take effect on the 15th day of October following the ratification of this article.

SECTION 6
[RATIFICATION WITHIN SEVEN YEARS]
This article shall be inoperative unless it shall have been ratified as an amendment to the Constitution by the legislatures of three-fourths of the several States within seven years from the date of its submission.

Amendment XXI
[PROPOSED BY CONGRESS ON FEBRUARY 20, 1933; DECLARED RATIFIED ON DECEMBER 5, 1933.]

SECTION 1
[NATIONAL LIQUOR PROHIBITION REPEALED]
The eighteenth article of amendment to the Constitution of the United States is hereby repealed.

SECTION 2
[TRANSPORTATION OF LIQUOR INTO "DRY" STATES]
The transportation or importation into any State, Territory, or Possession of the United States for delivery or use therein of intoxicating liquors, in violation of the laws thereof, is hereby prohibited.

SECTION 3
[RATIFICATION WITHIN SEVEN YEARS]
This article shall be inoperative unless it shall have been ratified as an amendment to the Constitution by conventions in the several States, as provided in the Constitution, within seven years from the date of the submission hereof to the States by the Congress.

Amendment XXII
[PROPOSED BY CONGRESS ON MARCH 21, 1947; DECLARED RATIFIED ON FEBRUARY 27, 1951.]

SECTION 1
[TENURE OF PRESIDENT LIMITED]
No person shall be elected to the office of President more than twice, and no person who has held the office of President or acted as President, for more than two years of a term to which some other person was elected President shall be elected to the office of the President more than once. But this Article shall not apply to any person holding the office of President when this Article was proposed by the Congress, and shall not prevent any person who may be holding the office of President, or acting as President, during the term within which this Article becomes operative from holding the office of President or acting as President during the remainder of such term.

SECTION 2
[RATIFICATION WITHIN SEVEN YEARS]
This article shall be inoperative unless it shall have been ratified as an amendment to the Constitution by the legislatures of three-fourths of the several States within seven years from the date of its submission to the States by the Congress.

Amendment XXIII

[PROPOSED BY CONGRESS ON JUNE 16, 1960; DECLARED RATIFIED ON MARCH 29, 1961.]

SECTION 1

[ELECTORAL COLLEGE VOTES FOR THE DISTRICT OF COLUMBIA]

The District constituting the seat of Government of the United States shall appoint in such manner as the Congress may direct:

A number of electors of President and Vice President equal to the whole number of Senators and Representatives in Congress to which the District would be entitled if it were a State, but in no event more than the least populous State; they shall be in addition to those appointed by the States, but they shall be considered, for the purposes of the election of President and Vice President, to be electors appointed by a State; and they shall meet in the District and perform such duties as provided by the twelfth article of amendment.

SECTION 2

[POWER TO ENFORCE THIS ARTICLE]

The Congress shall have power to enforce this article by appropriate legislation.

Amendment XXIV

[PROPOSED BY CONGRESS ON AUGUST 27, 1962; DECLARED RATIFIED ON JANUARY 23, 1964.]

SECTION 1

[ANTI-POLL TAX]

The right of citizens of the United States to vote in any primary or other election for President or Vice President, for electors for President or Vice President, or for Senator or Representative of Congress, shall not be denied or abridged by the United States or any State by reason of failure to pay any poll tax or other tax.

SECTION 2

[POWER TO ENFORCE THIS ARTICLE]

The Congress shall have power to enforce this article by appropriate legislation.

Amendment XXV

[PROPOSED BY CONGRESS ON JULY 6, 1965; DECLARED RATIFIED ON FEBRUARY 10, 1967.]

SECTION 1

[VICE PRESIDENT TO BECOME PRESIDENT]

In case of the removal of the President from office or his death or resignation, the Vice President shall become President.

SECTION 2

[CHOICE OF A NEW VICE PRESIDENT]

Whenever there is a vacancy in the office of the Vice President, the President shall nominate a Vice President who shall take the office upon confirmation by a majority vote of both houses of Congress.

SECTION 3

Whenever the President transmits to the President pro tempore of the Senate and the Speaker of the House of Representatives his written declaration that he is unable to discharge the powers and duties of his office, and until he transmits to them a written declaration to the contrary, such powers and duties shall be discharged by the Vice President as Acting President.

SECTION 4
[ALTERNATE PROCEDURES TO DECLARE AND TO END PRESIDENTIAL DISABILITY]

Whenever the Vice President and a majority of either the principal officers of the executive departments, or of such other body as Congress may by law provide, transmit to the President pro tempore of the Senate and the Speaker of the House of Representatives their written declaration that the President is unable to discharge the powers and duties of his office, the Vice President shall immediately assume the powers and duties of the office as Acting President.

Thereafter, when the President transmits to the President pro tempore of the Senate and the Speaker of the House of Representatives his written declaration that no inability exists, he shall resume the powers and duties of his office unless the Vice President and a majority of either the principal officers of the executive department, or of such other body as Congress may by law provide, transmit within four days to the President pro tempore of the Senate and the Speaker of the House of Representatives their written declaration that the President is unable to discharge the powers and duties of his office. Thereupon Congress shall decide the issue, assembling within forty eight hours for that purpose if not in session. If the Congress, within twenty one days after receipt of the latter written declaration, or, if Congress is not in session, within twenty one days after Congress is required to assemble, determines by two-thirds vote of both Houses that the President is unable to discharge the powers and duties of his office, the Vice President shall continue to discharge the same as Acting President; otherwise, the President shall resume the powers and duties of his office.

Amendment XXVI
[PROPOSED BY CONGRESS ON MARCH 23, 1971; DECLARED RATIFIED ON JULY 1, 1971.]

SECTION 1
[EIGHTEEN-YEAR-OLD VOTE]

The right of citizens of the United States, who are eighteen years of age or older, to vote shall not be denied or abridged by the United States or by any State on account of age.

SECTION 2
[POWER TO ENFORCE THIS ARTICLE]

The Congress shall have power to enforce this article by appropriate legislation.

Amendment XXVII
[PROPOSED BY CONGRESS ON SEPTEMBER 25, 1789; DECLARED RATIFIED ON MAY 8, 1992.]
[CONGRESS CANNOT RAISE ITS OWN PAY]

No law varying the compensation for the services of the Senators and Representatives, shall take effect, until an election of representatives shall have intervened.

The Federalist Papers

No. 10: Madison

Among the numerous advantages promised by a well constructed Union, none deserves to be more accurately developed than its tendency to break and control the violence of faction. The friend of popular governments never finds himself so much alarmed for their character and fate, as when he contemplates their propensity to this dangerous vice. He will not fail therefore to set a due value on any plan which, without violating the principles to which he is attached, provides a proper cure for it. The instability, injustice, and confusion introduced into the public councils have, in truth, been the mortal diseases under which popular governments have everywhere perished, as they continue to be the favorite and fruitful topics from which the adversaries to liberty derive their most specious declamations. The valuable improvements made by the American constitutions on the popular models, both ancient and modern, cannot certainly be too much admired; but it would be an unwarrantable partiality to contend that they have as effectually obviated the danger on this side, as was wished and expected. Complaints are everywhere heard from our most considerate and virtuous citizens, equally the friends of public and private faith and of public and personal liberty, that our governments are too unstable, that the public good is disregarded in the conflicts of rival parties, and that measures are too often decided, not according to the rules of justice and the rights of the minor party, but by the superior force of an interested and overbearing majority. However anxiously we may wish that these complaints had no foundation, the evidence of known facts will not permit us to deny that they are in some degree true. It will be found, indeed, on a candid review of our situation, that some of the distresses under which we labor have been erroneously charged on the operation of our governments; but it will be found, at the same time, that other causes will not alone account for many of our heaviest misfortunes; and, particularly, for that prevailing and increasing distrust of public engagements and alarm for private rights which are echoed from one end of the continent to the other. These must be chiefly, if not wholly, effects of the unsteadiness and injustice with which a factious spirit has tainted our public administration.

By a faction I understand a number of citizens, whether amounting to a majority or minority of the whole, who are united and actuated by some common impulse of passion, or of interest, adverse to the rights of other citizens, or to the permanent and aggregate interests of the community.

There are two methods of curing the mischiefs of faction: the one, by removing its causes; the other, by controlling its effects.

There are again two methods of removing the causes of faction: the one, by destroying the liberty which is essential to its existence; the other, by giving to every citizen the same opinions, the same passions, and the same interests.

It could never be more truly said than of the first remedy, that it is worse than the disease. Liberty is to faction what air is to fire, an aliment without which it instantly expires. But it could not be a less folly to abolish liberty, which is essential to political life, because it nourishes faction, than it would be to wish the annihilation of air, which is essential to animal life, because it imparts to fire its destructive agency.

The second expedient is as impracticable, as the first would be unwise. As long as the reason of man continues fallible, and he is at liberty to exercise it, different opinions will be formed. As long as the connection subsists between his reason and his self-love, his opinions and his passions will have a reciprocal influence on each other; and the former will be objects to which the latter will attach themselves. The diversity in the faculties of men, from which the rights of property originate, is not less an insuperable obstacle to a uniformity of interests. The protection of these faculties is the first object of Government. From the protection of different and unequal faculties of acquiring property, the possession of different degrees and kinds of property immediately results; and from the influence of these on the sentiments and views of the respective proprietors, ensues a division of the society into different interests and parties.

The latent causes of faction are thus sown in the nature of man; and we see them everywhere brought into different degrees of activity, according to the different circumstances of civil society. A zeal for different opinions concerning religion, concerning Government, and many other points, as well of speculation as of practice; an attachment to different leaders ambitiously contending for pre-eminence and power; or to persons of other descriptions whose fortunes have been interesting to the human passions, have in turn divided mankind into parties, inflamed them with mutual animosity, and rendered them much more disposed to vex and oppress each other, than to co-operate for their common good. So strong is this propensity of mankind to fall into mutual animosities, that where no substantial occasion presents itself, the most frivolous and fanciful distinctions have been sufficient to kindle their unfriendly passions, and excite their most violent conflicts. But the most common and durable source of factions has been the various and unequal distribution of property. Those who hold and those who are without property have ever formed distinct interests in society. Those who are creditors, and those who are debtors, fall under a like discrimination. A landed interest, a manufacturing interest, a mercantile interest, a moneyed interest, with many lesser interests, grow up of necessity in civilized nations, and divide them into different classes, actuated by different sentiments and views. The regulation of these various and interfering interests forms the principal task of modern Legislation, and involves the spirit of party and faction in the necessary and ordinary operations of Government.

No man is allowed to be judge in his own cause, because his interest would certainly bias his judgment and, not improbably, corrupt his integrity. With equal, nay with greater reason, a body of men are unfit to be both judges and parties at the same time; yet what are many of the most important acts of legislation but so many judicial determinations, not indeed concerning the rights of single persons, but concerning the rights of large bodies of citizens; and what are the different classes of legislators but advocates and parties to the causes which they determine? Is a law proposed concerning private debts? It is a question to which the creditors are parties on one side and the debtors on the other. Justice ought to hold the balance between them. Yet the parties are, and must be, themselves the judges; and the most numerous party, or in other words, the most powerful faction must be expected to prevail. Shall domestic manufacturers be encouraged, and in what degree, by restrictions on foreign manufacturers? are questions which would be differently decided by the landed and the manufacturing classes, and probably by neither with a sole regard to justice and the public good. The apportionment of taxes on the various descriptions of property is an act which seems to require the most exact impartiality; yet there is, perhaps, no legislative act in which greater opportunity and temptation are given to a predominant party to trample on the rules of justice. Every shilling with which they overburden the inferior number is a shilling saved to their own pockets.

It is in vain to say that enlightened statesmen will be able to adjust these clashing interests and render them all subservient to the public good. Enlightened statesmen will not always be at the helm. Nor, in many cases, can such an adjustment be made at all without taking into view indirect and remote considerations, which will rarely prevail over the immediate interest which one party may find in disregarding the rights of another or the good of the whole.

The inference to which we are brought is that the *causes* of faction cannot be removed and that relief is only to be sought in the means of controlling its *effects*.

If a faction consists of less than a majority, relief is supplied by the republican principle, which enables the majority to defeat its sinister views by regular vote. It may clog the administration, it may convulse the society; but it will be unable to execute and mask its violence under the forms of the Constitution. When a majority is included in a faction, the form of popular government, on the other hand, enables it to sacrifice to its ruling passion or interest both the public good and the rights of other citizens. To secure the public good and private rights against the danger of such a faction, and at the same time to preserve the spirit and the form of popular government, is then the great object to which our enquiries are directed. Let me add that it is the great desideratum by which alone this form of government can be rescued from the opprobrium under which it has so long labored and be recommended to the esteem and adoption of mankind.

By what means is this object attainable? Evidently by one of two only. Either the existence of the same passion or interest in a majority at the same time must be prevented, or the majority, having such co-existent passion or interest, must be rendered, by their number and local situation, unable to concert and carry into effect schemes of oppression. If the impulse and the opportunity be suffered to coincide, we well know that neither moral nor religious motives can be relied on as an adequate control. They are not found to be such on the injustice and violence of individuals, and lose their efficacy in proportion to the number combined together, that is, in proportion as their efficacy becomes needful.

From this view of the subject it may be concluded that a pure Democracy, by which I mean a Society consisting of a small number of citizens, who assemble and administer the Government in person, can admit of no cure for the mischiefs of faction. A common passion or interest will, in almost every case, be felt by a majority of the whole; a communication and concert results from the form of Government itself; and there is nothing to check the inducements to sacrifice the weaker party or an obnoxious individual. Hence it is that such Democracies have ever been spectacles of turbulence and contention; have ever been found incompatible with personal security or the rights of property; and have in general been as short in their lives as they have been violent in their deaths. Theoretic politicians, who have patronized this species of Government, have erroneously supposed that by reducing mankind to a perfect equality in their political rights, they would at the same time be perfectly equalized and assimilated in their possessions, their opinions, and their passions.

A Republic, by which I mean a Government in which the scheme of representation takes place, opens a different prospect and promises the cure for which we are seeking. Let us examine the points in which it varies from pure Democracy, and we shall comprehend both the nature of the cure and the efficacy which it must derive from the Union.

The two great points of difference between a Democracy and a Republic are: first, the delegation of the Government, in the latter, to a small number of citizens elected by the rest; secondly, the greater number of citizens and greater sphere of country over which the latter may be extended.

The effect of the first difference is, on the one hand, to refine and enlarge the public views by passing them through the medium of a chosen body of citizens, whose wisdom may best discern the true interest of their country and whose patriotism and love of justice will be least likely to sacrifice it to temporary or partial considerations. Under such a regulation it may well happen that the public voice, pronounced by the representatives of the people, will be more consonant to the public good than if pronounced by the people themselves, convened for the purpose. On the other hand, the effect may be inverted. Men of factious tempers, of local prejudices, or of sinister designs, may, by intrigue, by corruption, or by other means, first obtain the suffrages, and then betray the interests of the people. The question resulting is, whether small or extensive Republics are most favorable to the election of proper guardians of the public weal; and it is clearly decided in favor of the latter by two obvious considerations.

In the first place it is to be remarked that however small the Republic may be, the Representatives must be raised to a certain number in order to guard against the cabals of a few; and that however large it may be they must be limited to a certain number in order to guard against the confusion of a multitude. Hence, the number of Representatives in the two cases not being in proportion to that of the Constituents, and being proportionally greatest in the small Republic, it follows that if the proportion of fit characters be not less in the large than in the small Republic, the former will present a greater option, and consequently a greater probability of a fit choice.

In the next place, as each Representative will be chosen by a greater number of citizens in the large than in the small Republic, it will be more difficult for unworthy candidates to practise with success the vicious arts by which elections are too often carried; and the suffrages of the people being more free, will be more likely to centre on men who possess the most attractive merit and the most diffusive and established characters.

It must be confessed that in this, as in most other cases, there is a mean, on both sides of which inconveniencies will be found to lie. By enlarging too much the number of electors, you render the representative too little acquainted with all their local circumstances and lesser interests; as by reducing it too much, you render him unduly attached to these, and too little fit to comprehend and pursue great and national objects. The Federal Constitution forms a happy combination in this respect; the great and aggregate interests being referred to the national, the local and particular to the State legislatures.

The other point of difference is the greater number of citizens and extent of territory which may be brought within the compass of Republican than of Democratic Government; and it is this circumstance principally which renders factious combinations less to be dreaded in the former than in the latter. The smaller the society, the fewer probably will be the distinct parties and interests composing it; the fewer the distinct parties and interests, the more frequently will a majority be found of the same party; and the smaller the number of individuals composing a majority, and the smaller the compass within which they are placed, the more easily will they concert and execute their plans of oppression. Extend the sphere and you take in a greater variety of parties and interests; you make it less probable that a majority of the whole will have a common motive to invade the rights of other citizens; or if such a common motive exists, it will be more difficult for all who feel it to discover their own strength and to act in unison with each other. Besides other impediments, it may be remarked, that where there is a consciousness of unjust or dishonorable purposes, communication is always checked by distrust in proportion to the number whose concurrence is necessary.

Hence, it clearly appears that the same advantage which a Republic has over a Democracy in controlling the effects of faction is enjoyed by a large over a small republic—is enjoyed by the Union over the States composing it. Does this advantage consist in the substitution of representatives whose enlightened views and virtuous sentiments render them superior to local prejudices and to schemes of injustice? It will not be denied that the representation of the Union will be most likely to possess these requisite endowments. Does it consist in the greater security afforded by a greater variety of parties, against the event of any one party being able to outnumber and oppress the rest? In an equal degree does the increased variety of parties comprised within the Union increase this security? Does it, in fine, consist in the greater obstacles opposed to the concert and accomplishment of the secret wishes of an unjust and interested majority? Here again the extent of the Union gives it the most palpable advantage.

The influence of factious leaders may kindle a flame within their particular States but will be unable to spread a general conflagration through the other States: a religious sect may degenerate into a political faction in a part of the Confederacy; but the variety of sects dispersed over the entire face of it must secure the national Councils against any danger from that source: a rage for paper money, for an abolition of debts, for an equal division of property, or for any other improper or wicked project, will be less apt to pervade the whole body of the Union than a particular member of it; in the same proportion as such a malady is more likely to taint a particular county or district than an entire State.

In the extent and proper structure of the Union, therefore, we behold a republican remedy for the diseases most incident to Republican Government. And according to the degree of pleasure and pride we feel in being republicans ought to be our zeal in cherishing the spirit and supporting the character of federalist.

PUBLIUS
November 22, 1787

No. 51: Madison

To what expedient, then, shall we finally resort, for maintaining in practice the necessary partition of power among the several departments as laid down in the constitution? The only answer that can be given is that as all these exterior provisions are found to be inadequate the defect must be supplied, by so contriving the interior structure of the government as that its several constituent parts may, by their mutual relations, be the means of keeping each other in their proper places. Without presuming to undertake a full development of this important idea I will hazard a few general observations which may perhaps place it in a clearer light, and enable us to form a more correct judgment of the principles and structure of the government planned by the convention.

In order to lay a due foundation for that separate and distinct exercise of the different powers of government, which to a certain extent is admitted on all hands to be essential to the preservation of liberty, it is evident that each department should have a will of its own; and consequently should be so constituted that the members of each should have as little agency as possible in the appointment of the members of the others. Were this principle rigorously adhered to, it would require that all the appointments for the supreme executive, legislative, and judiciary magistracies should be drawn from the same fountain of authority, the people, through channels having no communication whatever with one another. Perhaps such a plan of constructing the several departments would be less difficult in practice than it may in contemplation appear. Some difficulties, however, and some additional expense would attend the execution of it. Some deviations, therefore, from the principle must be admitted. In the constitution of the judiciary department in particular, it might be inexpedient to insist rigorously on the principle: first, because peculiar qualifications being essential in the members, the primary consideration ought to be to select that mode of choice which best secures these qualifications; second, because the permanent tenure by which the appointments are held in that department must soon destroy all sense of dependence on the authority conferring them.

It is equally evident that the members of each department should be as little dependent as possible on those of the others for the emoluments annexed to their offices. Were the executive magistrate, or the judges, not independent of the legislature in this particular, their independence in every other would be merely nominal.

But the great security against a gradual concentration of the several powers in the same department consists in giving to those who administer each department the necessary constitutional means and personal motives to resist encroachments of the others. The provision for defence must in this, as in all other cases, be made commensurate to the danger of attack. Ambition must be made to counteract ambition. The interest of the man must be connected with the constitutional rights of the place. It may be a reflection on human nature that such devices should be necessary to control the abuses of government. But what is government itself but the greatest of all reflections on human nature? If men were angels, no government would be necessary. If angels were to govern men, neither external nor internal controls on government would be necessary. In framing a government which is to be administered by men over men, the great difficulty lies in this: You must first enable the government to control the governed; and in the next place oblige it to control itself. A dependence on the people is, no doubt, the primary control on the government; but experience has taught mankind the necessity of auxiliary precautions.

This policy of supplying, by opposite and rival interests, the defect of better motives, might be traced through the whole system of human affairs, private as well as public. We see it particularly displayed in all the subordinate distributions of power, where the constant aim is to divide and arrange the several offices in such a manner as that each may be a check on the other; that the private interest of every individual may be a sentinel over the public rights. These inventions of prudence cannot be less requisite in the distribution of the supreme powers of the State.

But it is not possible to give to each department an equal power of self-defense. In republican government, the legislative authority necessarily predominates. The remedy for this inconveniency is to divide the legislature into different branches; and to render them, by different modes of election and different principles of action, as little connected with each other as the nature of their common functions and their common dependence on the society will admit. It may even be necessary to guard against dangerous encroachments by still further precautions. As the weight of the legislative authority requires that it should be thus divided, the weakness of the executive may require, on the other hand, that it should be fortified. An absolute negative on the legislature appears, at first view, to be the natural defense with which the executive magistrate should be armed. But perhaps it would be neither altogether safe nor alone sufficient. On ordinary occasions it might not be exerted with the requisite firmness, and on extraordinary occasions it might be perfidiously abused. May not this defect of an absolute negative be supplied by some qualified connection between this weaker branch of the stronger department, by which the latter may be led to support the constitutional rights of the former, without being too much detached from the rights of its own department?

If the principles on which these observations are founded be just, as I persuade myself they are, and they be applied as a criterion to the several State constitutions, and to the federal Constitution, it will be found that if the latter does not perfectly correspond with them, the former are infinitely less able to bear such a test.

There are, moreover, two considerations particularly applicable to the federal system of America, which place that system in a very interesting point of view.

First. In a single republic, all the power surrendered by the people is submitted to the administration of a single government; and usurpations are guarded against by a division of the government into distinct and separate departments. In the compound republic of America, the power surrendered by the people is first divided between two distinct governments, and then the portion allotted to each subdivided among distinct and separate departments. Hence a double security arises to the rights of the people. The different governments will control each other, at the same time that each will be controlled by itself.

Second. It is of great importance in a republic not only to guard the society against the oppression of its rulers, but to guard one part of the society against the injustice of the other part. Different interests necessarily exist in different classes of citizens. If a majority be united by a common interest, the rights of the minority will be insecure. There are but two methods of providing against this evil: The one by creating a will in the community independent of the majority—that is, of the society itself; the other, by comprehending in the society so many separate descriptions of citizens as will render an unjust combination of a majority of the whole very improbable, if not impracticable. The first method prevails in all governments possessing an hereditary or self-appointed authority. This, at best, is but a precarious security; because a power independent of the society may as well espouse the unjust views of the major as the rightful interests of the minor party, and may possibly be turned against both parties. The second method will be exemplified in the federal republic of the United States. Whilst all authority in it will be derived from and dependent on the society, the society itself will be broken into so many parts, interests and classes of citizens, that the rights of individuals, or of the minority, will be in little danger from interested combinations of the majority. In a free government the security for civil rights must be the same as that for religious rights. It consists in the one case in the multiplicity of interests, and in the other in the multiplicity of sects. The degree of security in both cases will depend on the number of interests and sects; and this may be presumed to depend on the extent of country and number of people comprehended under the same government. This view of the subject must particularly recommend a proper federal system to all the sincere and considerate friends of republican government: Since it shows that in exact proportion as the territory of the Union may be formed into more circumscribed Confederacies, or States, oppressive combinations of a majority will be facilitated; the best security, under the republican form, for the rights of every class of citizens, will be diminished; and consequently the stability and independence of some member of the government, the only other security, must be proportionally increased. Justice is the end of government. It is the end of civil society. It ever has been and ever will be pursued until it be obtained, or until liberty be lost in the pursuit. In a society under the forms of which the stronger faction can readily unite and oppress the weaker, anarchy may as truly be said to reign as in a state of nature, where the weaker individual is not secured against the violence of the stronger: And as, in the latter state, even the stronger individuals are prompted, by the uncertainty of their condition, to submit to a government which may protect the weak as well as themselves: So, in the former state, will the more powerful factions or parties be gradually induced, by a like motive, to wish for a government which will protect all parties, the weaker as well as the more powerful. It can be little doubted that if the State of Rhode Island was separated from the Confederacy and left to itself, the insecurity of rights under the popular form of government within such narrow limits would be displayed by such reiterated oppressions of factious majorities that some power altogether independent of the people would soon be called for by the voice of the very factions whose misrule had proved the necessity of it. In the extended republic of the United States, and among the great variety of interests, parties, and sects which it embraces, a coalition of a majority of the whole society could seldom take place on any other principles than those of justice and the general good; and there being thus less danger to a minor from the will of the major party, there must be less pretext, also, to provide for the security of the former, by introducing into the government a will not dependent on the latter, or, in other words, a will independent of the society itself. It is no less certain than it is important, notwithstanding the contrary opinions which have been entertained, that the larger the society, provided it lie within a practicable sphere, the more duly capable it will be of self-government. And happily for the *republican cause,* practicable sphere may be carried to a very great extent by a judicious modification and mixture of the *federal principle.*

PUBLIUS
February 6, 1788

The Anti-Federalist Papers

Essay by Brutus in the *New York Journal*

When the public is called to investigate and decide upon a question in which not only the present members of the community are deeply interested, but upon which the happiness and misery of generations yet unborn is in great measure suspended, the benevolent mind cannot help feeling itself peculiarly interested in the result.

In this situation, I trust the feeble efforts of an individual, to lead the minds of the people to a wise and prudent determination, cannot fail of being acceptable to the candid and dispassionate part of the community. Encouraged by this consideration, I have been induced to offer my thoughts upon the present important crisis of our public affairs.

Perhaps this country never saw so critical a period in their political concerns. We have felt the feebleness of the ties by which these United-States are held together, and the want of sufficient energy in our present confederation, to manage, in some instances, our general concerns. Various expedients have been proposed to remedy these evils, but none have succeeded. At length a Convention of the states has been assembled, they have formed a constitution which will now, probably, be submitted to the people to ratify or reject, who are the fountain of all power, to whom alone it of right belongs to make or unmake constitutions, or forms of government, at their pleasure. The most important question that was ever proposed to your decision, or to the decision of any people under heaven, is before you, and you are to decide upon it by men of your own election, chosen specially for this purpose. If the constitution, offered to your acceptance, be a wise one, calculated to preserve the invaluable blessings of liberty, to secure the inestimable rights of mankind, and promote human happiness, then, if you accept it, you will lay a lasting foundation of happiness for millions yet unborn; generations to come will rise up and call you blessed. You may rejoice in the prospects of this vast extended continent becoming filled with freemen, who will assert the dignity of human nature. You may solace yourselves with the idea, that society, in this favoured land, will fast advance to the highest point of perfection; the human mind will expand in knowledge and virtue, and the golden age be, in some measure, realised. But if, on the other hand, this form of government contains principles that will lead to the subversion of liberty—if it tends to establish a despotism, or, what is worse, a tyrannic aristocracy; then, if you adopt it, this only remaining assylum for liberty will be shut up, and posterity will execrate your memory.

Momentous then is the question you have to determine, and you are called upon by every motive which should influence a noble and virtuous mind, to examine it well, and to make up a wise judgment. It is insisted, indeed, that this constitution must be received, be it ever so imperfect. If it has its defects, it is said, they can be best amended when they are experienced. But remember, when the people once part with power, they can seldom or never resume it again but by force. Many instances can be produced in which the people have voluntarily increased the powers of their rulers; but few, if any, in which rulers have willingly abridged their authority. This is a sufficient reason to induce you to be careful, in the first instance, how you deposit the powers of government.

With these few introductory remarks, I shall proceed to a consideration of this constitution:

The first question that presents itself on the subject is, whether a confederated government be the best for the United States or not? Or in other words, whether the thirteen United States should be reduced to one great republic, governed by one legislature, and under the direction of one executive and judicial; or whether they should continue thirteen confederated republics, under the direction and controul of a supreme federal head for certain defined national purposes only?

This enquiry is important, because, although the government reported by the convention does not go to a perfect and entire consolidation, yet it approaches so near to it, that it must, if executed, certainly and infallibly terminate in it.

This government is to possess absolute and uncontroulable power, legislative, executive and judicial, with respect to every object to which it extends, for by the last clause of section 8th, article 1st, it is declared "that the Congress shall have power to make all laws which shall be necessary and proper for carrying into execution the foregoing powers, and all other powers vested by this constitution, in the government of the United States; or in any department or office thereof." And by the 6th article, it is declared "that this constitution, and the laws of the United States, which shall be made in pursuance thereof, and the treaties made, or which shall be made, under the authority of the United States, shall be the supreme law of the land; and the judges in every state shall be bound thereby, any thing in the constitution, or law of any state to the contrary notwithstanding." It appears from these articles that there is no need of any intervention of the state governments, between the Congress and the people, to execute any one power vested in the general government, and that the constitution and laws of every state are nullified and declared void, so far as they are or shall be inconsistent with this constitution, or the laws made in pursuance of it, or with treaties made under the authority of the United States.—The government then, so far as it extends, is a complete one, and not a confederation. It is as much one complete government as that of New-York or Massachusetts, has as absolute and perfect powers to make and execute all laws, to appoint officers, institute courts, declare offences, and annex penalties, with respect to every object to which it extends, as any other in the world. So far therefore as its powers reach, all ideas of confederation are given up and lost. It is true this government is limited to certain objects, or to speak more properly, some small degree of power is still left to the states, but a little attention to the powers vested in the general government, will convince every candid man, that if it is capable of being executed, all that is reserved for the individual states must very soon be annihilated, except so far as they are barely necessary to the organization of the general government. The powers of the general legislature extend to every case that is of the least importance—there is nothing valuable to human nature, nothing dear to freemen, but what is within its power. It has authority to make laws which will affect the lives, the liberty, and property of every man in the United States; nor can the constitution or laws of any state, in any way prevent or impede the full and complete execution of every power given. The legislative power is competent to lay taxes, duties, imposts, and excises;—there is no limitation to this power, unless it be said that the clause which directs the use to which those taxes, and duties shall be applied, may be said to be a limitation: but this is no restriction of the power at all, for by this clause they are to be applied to pay the debts and provide for the common defence and general welfare of the United States; but the legislature have authority to contract debts at their discretion; they are the sole judges of what is necessary to provide for the common defence, and they only are to determine what is for the general welfare; this power therefore is neither more nor less, than a power to lay and collect taxes, imposts, and excises, at their pleasure; not only [is] the power to lay taxes unlimited, as to the amount they may require, but it is perfect and absolute to raise them in any mode they please. No state legislature, or any power in the state governments, have any more to do in carrying this into effect, than the authority of one state has to do with that of another. In the business therefore of laying and collecting taxes, the idea of confederation is totally lost, and that of one entire republic is embraced. It is proper here to remark, that the authority to lay and collect taxes is the most important of any power that can be granted; it connects with it almost all other powers, or at least will in process of time draw all other after it; it is the great mean of protection, security, and defence, in a good government, and the great engine of oppression and tyranny in a bad one. This cannot fail of being the case, if we consider the contracted limits which are set by this constitution, to the late [state?] governments, on this article of raising money. No state can emit paper money—lay any duties, or imposts, on imports, or exports, but by consent of the Congress; and then the net produce shall be for the benefit of the United States: the only mean therefore left, for any state to support its government and discharge its debts, is by direct taxation; and the United States have also power to lay and collect taxes, in any way they please. Every one who has thought on the subject, must be convinced that but small sums of money can be collected in any country, by direct taxe[s], when the foederal government begins to exercise the right of taxation in all its parts, the legislatures of the several states will find it impossible to raise monies to support their governments. Without money they cannot be supported, and they must dwindle away, and, as before observed, their powers absorbed in that of the general government.

It might be here shewn, that the power in the federal legislative, to raise and support armies at pleasure, as well in peace as in war, and their controul over the militia, tend, not only to a consolidation of the government, but the destruction of liberty.—I shall not, however, dwell upon these, as a few observations upon the judicial power of this government, in addition to the preceding, will fully evince the truth of the position.

The judicial power of the United States is to be vested in a supreme court, and in such inferior courts as Congress may from time to time ordain and establish. The powers of these courts are very extensive; their jurisdiction comprehends all civil causes, except such as arise between citizens of the same state; and it extends to all cases in law and equity arising under the constitution. One inferior court must be established, I presume, in each state, at least, with the necessary executive officers appendant thereto. It is easy to see, that in the common course of things, these courts will eclipse the dignity, and take away from the respectability, of the state courts. These courts will be, in themselves, totally independent of the states, deriving their authority from the United States, and receiving from them fixed salaries; and in the course of human events it is to be expected, that they will swallow up all the powers of the courts in the respective states.

How far the clause in the 8th section of the 1st article may operate to do away all idea of confederated states, and to effect an entire consolidation of the whole into one general government, it is impossible to say. The powers given by this article are very general and comprehensive, and it may receive a construction to justify the passing almost any law. A power to make all laws, which shall be *necessary and proper*, for carrying into execution, all powers vested by the constitution in the government of the United States, or any department or officer thereof, is a power very comprehensive and definite [indefinite?], and may, for ought I know, be exercised in a such manner as entirely to abolish the state legislatures. Suppose the legislature of a state should pass a law to raise money to support their government and pay the state debt, may the Congress repeal this law, because it may prevent the collection of a tax which they may think proper and necessary to lay, to provide for the general welfare of the United States? For all laws made, in pursuance of this constitution, are the supreme lay of the land, and the judges in every state shall be bound thereby, any thing in the constitution or laws of the different states to the contrary notwithstanding.—By such a law, the government of a particular state might be overturned at one stroke, and thereby be deprived of every means of its support.

It is not meant, by stating this case, to insinuate that the constitution would warrant a law of this kind; or unnecessarily to alarm the fears of the people, by suggesting, that the federal legislature would be more likely to pass the limits assigned them by the constitution, than that of an individual state, further than they are less responsible to the people. But what is meant is, that the legislature of the United States are vested with the great and uncontroulable powers, of laying and collecting taxes, duties, imposts, and excises; of regulating trade, raising and supporting armies, organizing, arming, and disciplining the militia, instituting courts, and other general powers. And are by this clause invested with the power of making all laws, *proper and necessary*, for carrying all these into execution; and they may so exercise this power as entirely to annihilate all the state governments, and reduce this country to one single government. And if they may do it, it is pretty certain they will; for it will be found that the power retained by individual states, small as it is, will be a clog upon the wheels of the government of the United States; the latter therefore will be naturally inclined to remove it out of the way. Besides, it is a truth confirmed by the unerring experience of ages, that every man, and every body of men, invested with power, are ever disposed to increase it, and to acquire a superiority over every thing that stands in their way. This disposition, which is implanted in human nature, will operate in the federal legislature to lessen and ultimately to subvert the state authority, and having such advantages, will most certainly succeed, if the federal government succeeds at all. It must be very evident then, that what this constitution wants of being a complete consolidation of the several parts of the union into one complete government, possessed of perfect legislative, judicial, and executive powers, to all intents and purposes, it will necessarily acquire in its exercise and operation.

Let us now proceed to enquire, as I at first proposed, whether it be best the thirteen United States should be reduced to one great republic, or not? It is here taken for granted, that all agree in this, that whatever government we adopt, it ought to be a free one; that it should be so framed as to secure the liberty of the citizens of America, and such an one as to admit of a full, fair, and equal representation of the people. The question then will be, whether a government thus constituted, and founded on such principles, is practicable, and can be exercised over the whole United States, reduced into one state?

If respect is to be paid to the opinion of the greatest and wisest men who have ever thought or wrote on the science of government, we shall be constrained to conclude, that a free republic cannot succeed over a country of such immense extent, containing such a number of inhabitants, and these encreasing in such rapid progression as that of the whole United States. Among the many illustrious authorities which might be produced to this point, I shall content myself with quoting only two. The one is the baron de Montesquieu, spirit of laws, chap. xvi. vol. I [book VIII]. "It is natural to a republic to have only a small territory, otherwise it cannot long subsist. In a large republic there are men of large fortunes, and consequently of less moderation; there are trusts too great to be placed in any single subject; he has interest of his own; he soon begins to think that he may be happy, great and glorious, by oppressing his fellow citizens; and that he may raise himself to grandeur on the ruins of his country. In a large republic, the public good is sacrificed to a thousand views; it is subordinate to exceptions, and depends on accidents. In a small one, the interest of the public is easier perceived, better understood, and more within the reach of every citizen; abuses are of less extent, and of course are less protected." Of the same opinion is the marquis Beccarari.

History furnishes no example of a free republic, any thing like the extent of the United States. The Grecian republics were of small extent; so also was that of the Romans. Both of these, it is true, in process of time, extended their conquests over large territories of country; and the consequence was, that their governments were changed from that of free governments to those of the most tyrannical that ever existed in the world.

Not only the opinion of the greatest men, and the experience of mankind, are against the idea of an extensive republic, but a variety of reasons may be drawn from the reason and nature of things, against it. In every government, the will of the sovereign is the law. In despotic governments, the supreme authority being lodged in one, his will is law, and can be as easily expressed to a large extensive territory as to a small one. In a pure democracy the people are the sovereign, and their will is declared by themselves; for this purpose they must all come together to deliberate, and decide. This kind of government cannot be exercised, therefore, over a country of any considerable extent; it must be confined to a single city, or at least limited to such bounds as that the people can conveniently assemble, be able to debate, understand the subject submitted to them, and declare their opinion concerning it.

In a free republic, although all laws are derived from the consent of the people, yet the people do not declare their consent by themselves in person, but by representatives, chosen by them, who are supposed to know the minds of their constituents, and to be possessed of integrity to declare this mind.

In every free government, the people must give their assent to the laws by which they are governed. This is the true criterion between a free government and an arbitrary one. The former are ruled by the will of the whole, expressed in any manner they may agree upon; the latter by the will of one, or a few. If the people are to give their assent to the laws, by persons chosen and appointed by them, the manner of the choice and the number chosen, must be such, as to possess, be disposed, and consequently qualified to declare the sentiments of the people; for if they do not know, or are not disposed to speak the sentiments of the people, the people do not govern, but the sovereignty is in a few. Now, in a large extended country, it is impossible to have a representation, possessing the sentiments, and of integrity, to declare the minds of the people, without having it so numerous and unwieldly, as to be subject in great measure to the inconveniency of a democratic government.

The territory of the United States is of vast extent; it now contains near three millions of souls, and is capable of containing much more than ten times that number. Is it practicable for a country, so large and so numerous as they will soon become, to elect a representation, that will speak their sentiments, without their becoming so numerous as to be incapable of transacting public business? It certainly is not.

In a republic, the manners, sentiments, and interests of the people should be similar. If this be not the case, there will be a constant clashing of opinions; and the representatives of one part will be continually striving against those of the other. This will retard the operations of government, and prevent such conclusions as will promote the public good. If we apply this remark to the condition of the United States, we shall be convinced that it forbids that we should be one government. The United States includes a variety of climates. The productions of the different parts of the union are very variant, and their interests, of consequence, diverse. Their manners and habits differ as much as their climates and productions; and their sentiments are by no means coincident. The laws and customs of the several states are, in many respects, very diverse, and in some opposite; each would be in favor of its own interests and customs, and, of consequence, a legislature, formed of representatives from the respective parts, would not only be too numerous to act with any care or decision, but would be composed of such heterogenous and discordant principles, as would constantly be contending with each other.

The laws cannot be executed in a republic, of an extent equal to that of the United States, with promptitude.

The magistrates in every government must be supported in the execution of the laws, either by an armed force, maintained at the public expence for that purpose; or by the people turning out to aid the magistrate upon his command, in case of resistance.

In despotic governments, as well as in all the monarchies of Europe, standing armies are kept up to execute the commands of the prince or the magistrate, and are employed for this purpose when occasion requires: But they have always proved the destruction of liberty, and [are] abhorrent to the spirit of a free republic. In England, where they depend upon the parliament for their annual support, they have always been complained of as oppressive and unconstitutional, and are seldom employed in executing of the laws; never except on extraordinary occasions, and then under the direction of a civil magistrate.

A free republic will never keep a standing army to execute its laws. It must depend upon the support of its citizens. But when a government is to receive its support from the aid of the citizens, it must be so constructed as to have the confidence, respect, and affection of the people. Men who, upon the call of the magistrate, offer themselves to execute the laws, are influenced to do it either by affection to the government, or from fear; where a standing army is at hand to punish offenders, every man is actuated by the latter principle, and therefore, when the magistrate calls, will obey: but, where this is not the case, the government must rest for its support upon the confidence and respect which the people have for their government and laws. The body of the people being attached, the government will always be sufficient to support and execute its laws, and to operate upon the fears of any faction which may be opposed to it, not only to prevent an opposition to the execution of the laws themselves, but also to compel the most of them to aid the magistrate; but the people will not be likely to have such confidence in their rulers, in a republic so extensive as the United States, as necessary for these purposes. The confidence which the people have in their rulers, in a free republic, arises from their knowing them, from their being responsible to them for their conduct, and from the power they have of displacing them when they misbehave: but in a republic of the extent of this continent, the people in general would be acquainted with very few of their rulers: the people at large would know little of their proceedings, and it would be extremely difficult to change them. The people in Georgia and New-Hampshire would not know one another's mind, and therefore could not act in concert to enable them to effect a general change of representatives. The different parts of so extensive a country could not possibly be made acquainted with the conduct of their representatives, nor be informed of the reasons upon which measures were founded. The consequence will be, they will have no confidence in their legislature, suspect them of ambitious views, be jealous of every measure they adopt, and will not support the laws they pass. Hence the government will be nerveless and inefficient, and no way will be left to render it otherwise, but by establishing an armed force to execute the laws at the point of the bayonet—a government of all others the most to be dreaded.

In a republic of such vast extent as the United-States, the legislature cannot attend to the various concerns and wants of its different parts. It cannot be sufficiently numerous to be acquainted with the local condition and wants of the different districts, and if it could, it is impossible it should have sufficient time to attend to and provide for all the variety of cases of this nature, that would be continually arising.

In so extensive a republic, the great officers of government would soon become above the controul of the people, and abuse their power to the purpose of aggrandizing themselves, and oppressing them. The trust committed to the executive offices, in a country of the extent of the United-States, must be various and of magnitude. The command of all the troops and navy of the republic, the appointment of officers, the power of pardoning offences, the collecting of all the public revenues, and the power of expending them, with a number of other powers, must be lodged and exercised in every state, in the hands of a few. When these are attended with great honor and emolument, as they always will be in large states, so as greatly to interest men to pursue them, and to be proper objects for ambitious and designing men, such men will be ever restless in their pursuit after them. They will use the power, when they have acquired it, to the purposes of gratifying their own interest and ambition, and it is scarcely possible, in a very large republic, to call them to account for their misconduct, or to prevent their abuse of power.

These are some of the reasons by which it appears, that a free republic cannot long subsist over a country of the great extent of these states. If then this new constitution is calculated to consolidate the thirteen states into one, as it evidently is, it ought not to be adopted.

Though I am of opinion, that it is a sufficient objection to this government, to reject it, that it creates the whole union into one government, under the form of a republic, yet if this objection was obviated, there are exceptions to it, which are so material and fundamental, that they ought to determine every man, who is a friend to the liberty and happiness of mankind, not to adopt it. I beg the candid and dispassionate attention of my countrymen while I state these objections—they are such as have obtruded themselves upon my mind upon a careful attention to the matter, and such as I sincerely believe are well founded. There are many objections, of small moment, of which I shall take no notice— perfection is not to be expected in any thing that is the production of man—and if I did not in my conscience believe that this scheme was defective in the fundamental principles—in the foundation upon which a free and equal government must rest—I would hold my peace.

BRUTUS
Ocotober 18, 1787

Presidents and Vice Presidents

PRESIDENT	VICE PRESIDENT
1 George Washington *(Federalist 1789)*	John Adams *(Federalist 1789)*
2 John Adams *(Federalist 1797)*	Thomas Jefferson *(Dem.-Rep. 1797)*
3 Thomas Jefferson *(Dem.-Rep. 1801)*	Aaron Burr *(Dem.-Rep. 1801)*
	George Clinton *(Dem.-Rep. 1805)*
4 James Madison *(Dem.-Rep. 1809)*	George Clinton *(Dem.-Rep. 1809)*
	Elbridge Gerry *(Dem.-Rep. 1813)*
5 James Monroe *(Dem.-Rep. 1817)*	Daniel D. Tompkins *(Dem.-Rep. 1817)*
6 John Quincy Adams *(Dem.-Rep. 1825)*	John C. Calhoun *(Dem.-Rep. 1825)*
7 Andrew Jackson *(Democratic 1829)*	John C. Calhoun *(Democratic 1829)*
	Martin Van Buren *(Democratic 1833)*
8 Martin Van Buren *(Democratic 1837)*	Richard M. Johnson *(Democratic 1837)*
9 William H. Harrison *(Whig 1841)*	John Tyler *(Whig 1841)*
10 John Tyler *(Whig and Democratic 1841)*	
11 James K. Polk *(Democratic 1845)*	George M. Dallas *(Democratic 1845)*
12 Zachary Taylor *(Whig 1849)*	Millard Fillmore *(Whig 1849)*
13 Millard Fillmore *(Whig 1850)*	
14 Franklin Pierce *(Democratic 1853)*	William R. D. King *(Democratic 1853)*
15 James Buchanan *(Democratic 1857)*	John C. Breckinridge *(Democratic 1857)*

PRESIDENT	VICE PRESIDENT
16 Abraham Lincoln *(Republican 1861)*	Hannibal Hamlin *(Republican 1861)*
	Andrew Johnson *(Unionist 1865)*
17 Andrew Johnson (Unionist 1865)	
18 Ulysses S. Grant *(Republican 1869)*	Schuyler Colfax *(Republican 1869)*
	Henry Wilson *(Republican 1873)*
19 Rutherford B. Hayes *(Republican 1877)*	William A. Wheeler *(Republican 1877)*
20 James A. Garfield *(Republican 1881)*	Chester A. Arthur *(Republican 1881)*
21 Chester A. Arthur *(Republican 1881)*	
22 Grover Cleveland *(Democratic 1885)*	Thomas A. Hendricks *(Democratic 1885)*
23 Benjamin Harrison *(Republican 1889)*	Levi P. Morton *(Republican 1889)*
24 Grover Cleveland *(Democratic 1893)*	Adlai E. Stevenson *(Democratic 1893)*
25 William McKinley *(Republican 1897)*	Garret A. Hobart *(Republican 1897)*
	Theodore Roosevelt *(Republican 1901)*
26 Theodore Roosevelt *(Republican 1901)*	Charles W. Fairbanks *(Republican 1905)*
27 William H. Taft *(Republican 1909)*	James S. Sherman *(Republican 1909)*
28 Woodrow Wilson *(Democratic 1913)*	Thomas R. Marshall *(Democratic 1913)*
29 Warren G. Harding *(Republican 1921)*	Calvin Coolidge *(Republican 1921)*
30 Calvin Coolidge *(Republican 1923)*	Charles G. Dawes *(Republican 1925)*
31 Herbert Hoover *(Republican 1929)*	Charles Curtis *(Republican 1929)*

PRESIDENT	VICE PRESIDENT
32 Franklin D. Roosevelt *(Democratic 1933)*	John Nance Garner *(Democratic 1933)*
	Henry A. Wallace *(Democratic 1941)*
	Harry S. Truman *(Democratic 1945)*
33 Harry S. Truman *(Democratic 1945)*	Alben W. Barkley *(Democratic 1949)*
34 Dwight D. Eisenhower *(Republican 1953)*	Richard M. Nixon *(Republican 1953)*
35 John F. Kennedy *(Democratic 1961)*	Lyndon B. Johnson *(Democratic 1961)*
36 Lyndon B. Johnson *(Democratic 1963)*	Hubert H. Humphrey *(Democratic 1965)*
37 Richard M. Nixon *(Republican 1969)*	Spiro T. Agnew *(Republican 1969)*
	Gerald R. Ford *(Republican 1973)*
38 Gerald R. Ford *(Republican 1974)*	Nelson Rockefeller *(Republican 1974)*
39 James E. Carter *(Democratic 1977)*	Walter Mondale *(Democratic 1977)*
40 Ronald Reagan *(Republican 1981)*	George H. W. Bush *(Republican 1981)*
41 George H. W. Bush *(Republican 1989)*	J. Danforth Quayle *(Republican 1989)*
42 William J. Clinton *(Democratic 1993)*	Albert Gore, Jr. *(Democratic 1993)*
43 George W. Bush *(Republican 2001)*	Richard Cheney *(Republican 2001)*
44 Barack H. Obama *(Democratic 2009)*	Joseph R. Biden, Jr. *(Democratic 2009)*

glossary

affirmative action government policies or programs that seek to redress past injustices against specified groups by making special efforts to provide members of these groups with access to educational and employment opportunities

agency representation a type of representation in which a representative is held accountable to a constituency if he or she fails to represent that constituency properly; this is incentive for good representation when the personal backgrounds, views, and interests of the representative differ from those of his or her constituency

agenda setting the power of the media to bring public attention to particular issues and problems

agents of socialization social institutions, including families and schools, that help to shape individuals' basic political beliefs and values

amendment a change added to a bill, law, or constitution

amicus curiae literally, "friend of the court"; individuals or groups who are not parties to a lawsuit but who seek to assist the Supreme Court in reaching a decision by presenting additional briefs

Antifederalists those who favored strong state governments and a weak national government and were opponents of the constitution proposed at the American Constitutional Convention of 1787

appeasement the effort to forestall war by giving in to the demands of a hostile power

apportionment the process, occurring after every decennial census, that allocates congressional seats among the 50 states

appropriations the amounts of money approved by Congress in statutes (bills) that each unit or agency of government can spend

Articles of Confederation America's first written constitution; served as the basis for America's national government until 1789

attitude (or opinion) a specific preference on a particular issue

authoritarian government a system of rule in which the government recognizes no formal limit but may nevertheless be restrained by the power of other social institutions

ballot initiative a proposed law or policy change that is placed on the ballot by citizens or interest groups for a popular vote closed primary a primary election in which voters can participate in the nomination of candidates, but only of the party in which they are enrolled for a period of time prior to primary day

bandwagon effect a shift in electoral support to the candidate whom publicopinion polls report as the front-runner

bicameral having a legislative assembly composed of two chambers or houses; distinguished from *unicameral*

bilateral treaties treaties made between two nations

bill a proposed law that has been sponsored by a member of Congress and submitted to the clerk of the House or Senate cloture a rule or process in a legislative body aimed at ending debate on a given bill; in the U.S. Senate, 60 senators (three-fifths) must agree in order to impose a time limit and end debate

bill of attainder a law that declares a person guilty of a crime without a trial

Bill of Rights the first 10 amendments to the Constitution, ratified in 1791; they ensure certain rights and liberties to the people

block grants federal grants-in-aid that allow states considerable discretion in how the funds are spent

briefs written documents in which attorneys explain, using case precedents, why the court should find in favor of their client

Brown v. Board of Education the 1954 Supreme Court decision that struck down the "separate but equal" doctrine as fundamentally unequal; this case eliminated state power to use race as a criterion for discrimination in law and provided the national government with the power to intervene by exercising strict regulatory policies against discriminatory actions

bureaucracy the complex structure of offices, tasks, rules, and principles of organization that are employed by all large-scale institutions to coordinate effectively the work of their personnel

Bush Doctrine foreign policy based on the idea that the United States should take preemptive action against threats to its national security

Cabinet the secretaries, or chief administrators, of the major departments of the federal government; Cabinet secretaries are appointed by the president with the consent of the Senate

categorical grants congressional grants given to states and localities on the condition that expenditures be limited to a problem or group specified by law

checks and balances mechanisms through which each branch of government is able to participate in and influence the activities of the other branches; major examples include the presidential veto power over congressional legislation, the power of the Senate to approve presidential appointments, and judicial review of congressional enactments

chief justice justice on the Supreme Court who presides over the Court's public sessions and whose official title is chief justice of the United States

citizen journalism news reported and distributed by citizens, rather than professional journalists and for-profit news organizations

citizenship informed and active membership in a political community

civil law the branch of law that deals with disputes that do not involve criminal penalties

civil liberties areas of personal freedom constitutionally protected from government interference

civil rights obligation imposed on government to take positive action to protect citizens from any illegal action of government agencies and of other private citizens

"clear and present danger" test test to determine whether speech is protected or unprotected, based on its capacity to present a "clear and present danger" to society

collective goods benefits, sought by groups, that are broadly available and cannot be denied to nonmembers

commander in chief the role of the president as commander of the national military and the state National Guard units (when called into service)

commerce clause Article I, Section 8, of the Constitution, which delegates to Congress the power "to regulate Commerce with foreign Nations, and among the several States and with the Indian Tribes"; this clause was interpreted by the Supreme Court in favor of national power over the economy

concurrent powers authority possessed by both state and national governments, such as the power to levy taxes

confederation a system of government in which states retain sovereign authority except for the powers expressly delegated to the national government

conference a gathering of House Republicans every two years to elect their House leaders; Democrats call their gathering the caucus

conference committees joint committees created to work out a compromise on House and Senate versions of a piece of legislation

conservative today this term refers to those who generally support the social and economic status quo and are suspicious of efforts to introduce new political formulae and economic arrangements; conservatives believe that a large and powerful government poses a threat to citizens' freedom

constituency the residents in the area from which an official is elected filibuster a tactic used by members of the Senate to prevent action on legislation they oppose by continuously holding the floor and speaking until the majority backs down; once given the floor, senators have unlimited time to speak, and it requires a vote of three-fifths of the Senate to end a filibuster

constitutional government a system of rule in which formal and effective limits are placed on the powers of the government

contracting power the power of government to set conditions on companies seeking to sell goods or services to government agencies

contributory programs social programs financed in whole or in part by taxation or other mandatory contributions by their present or future recipients

cooperative federalism a type of federalism existing since the New Deal era in which grants-in-aid have been used strategically to encourage states and localities (without commanding them) to pursue nationally defined goals; also known as *intergovernmental cooperation*

cost-of-living adjustments (COLAs) changes made to the level of benefits of a government program based on the rate of inflation

court of appeals a court that hears the appeals of trial court decisions

criminal law the branch of law that regulates the conduct of individuals, defines crimes, and specifies punishment for criminal acts

de facto literally, "by fact"; practices that occur even when there is no legal enforcement, such as school segregation in much of the United States today

de jure literally, "by law"; legally enforced practices, such as school segregation in the South before the 1960s

defendant the one against whom a complaint is brought in a criminal or civil case

delegated powers constitutional powers that are assigned to one governmental agency but that are exercised by another agency with the express permission of the first

democracy a system of rule that permits citizens to play a significant part in the governmental process, usually through the election of key public officials

department the largest subunit of the executive branch; the secretaries of the 15 departments form the Cabinet

devolution a policy to remove a program from one level of government by delegating it or passing it down to a lower level of government, such as from the national government to the state and local governments

digital citizen a daily Internet user with high-speed home Internet access and the technology and literacy skills to go online for employment, news, politics, entertainment, commerce, and other activities

diplomacy the representation of a government to foreign governments

direct democracy a system of rule that permits citizens to vote directly on laws and policies

dissenting opinion a decision written by a justice in the minority in a particular case in which the justice wishes to express his or her reasoning in the case

divided government the condition in American government wherein the presidency is controlled by one party while the opposing party controls one or both houses of Congress

double jeopardy the Fifth Amendment right providing that a person cannot be tried twice for the same crime

dual federalism the system of government that prevailed in the United States from 1789 to 1937 in which most fundamental governmental powers were shared between the federal and state governments

due process of law the right of every citizen against arbitrary action by national or state governments

elastic clause Article I, Section 8, of the Constitution (also known as the necessary and proper clause), which enumerates the powers of Congress and provides Congress with the authority to make all laws "necessary and proper" to carry them out

electoral college the electors from each state who meet after the popular election to cast ballots for president and vice president

electoral realignment the point in history when a new party supplants the ruling party, becoming in turn the dominant political force; in the United States, this has tended to occur roughly every 30 years

eminent domain the right of government to take private property for public use

equal protection clause provision of the Fourteenth Amendment guaranteeing citizens "the equal protection of the laws"; this clause has served as the basis for the civil rights of African Americans, women, and other groups

equal time rule the requirement that broadcasters provide candidates for the same political office equal opportunities to communicate their messages to the public

equality of opportunity a widely shared American ideal that all people should have the freedom to use whatever talents and wealth they have to reach their fullest potential

establishment clause the First Amendment clause that says that "Congress shall make no law respecting an establishment of religion"; this law means that a "wall of separation" exists between church and state

ex post facto laws laws that declare an action to be illegal after it has been committed

exclusionary rule the ability of courts to exclude evidence obtained in violation of the Fourth Amendment

executive agreement an agreement, made between the president and another country, that has the force of a treaty but does not require the Senate's "advice and consent"

Executive Office of the President (EOP) the permanent agencies that perform defined management tasks for the president; created in 1939, the EOP includes the OMB, the CEA, the NSC, and other agencies

executive order a rule or regulation issued by the president that has the effect and formal status of legislation

expressed powers specific powers granted by the Constitution to Congress (Article I, Section 8) and to the president (Article II)

fairness doctrine a Federal Communications Commission requirement for broadcasters who air programs on controversial issues to provide time for opposing views; the FCC ceased enforcing this doctrine in 1985

Federal Reserve System a system of 12 Federal Reserve banks that facilitates exchanges of cash, checks, and credit; regulates member banks; and uses monetary policies to fight inflation and deflation

federal system a system of government in which the national government shares power with lower levels of government such as states

federalism a system of government in which power is divided, by a constitution, between the central (national) government and regional (state) governments

Federalist Papers a series of essays written by James Madison, Alexander Hamilton, and John Jay supporting the ratification of the Constitution

Federalists those who favored a strong national government and supported the constitution proposed at the American Constitutional Convention of 1787

Fifteenth Amendment one of three Civil War amendments; it guaranteed voting rights for African American men

fighting words speech that directly incites damaging conduct

fiscal policy the government's use of taxing, monetary, and spending powers to manipulate the economy

527 committees nonprofit independent groups that receive and disburse funds to influence the nomination, election, or defeat of candidates; named after Section 527 of the Internal Revenue Code, which defines and provides tax-exempt status for nonprofit advocacy groups

Fourteenth Amendment one of three Civil War amendments; it guaranteed equal protection and due process

framing the power of the media to influence how events and issues are interpreted

free exercise clause the First Amendment clause that protects a citizen's right to believe and practice whatever religion one chooses

free riders those who enjoy the benefits of collective goods but did not participate in acquiring them

full faith and credit clause provision from Article IV, Section 1 of the Constitution requiring that the states normally honor the public acts and judicial decisions that take place in another state

gender gap a distinctive pattern of voting behavior reflecting the differences in views between women and men

General Agreement on Tariffs and Trade (GATT) international trade organization, in existence from 1947 to 1995, that set many of the rules governing international trade

general election a regularly scheduled election involving most districts in the nation or state, in which voters select officeholders; in the United States, general elections for national office and most state and local offices are held on the first Tuesday following the first Monday in November in even-numbered years (every four years for presidential elections)

general revenue sharing the process by which one unit of government yields a portion of its tax income to another unit of government, according to an established formula; revenue sharing typically involves the national government providing money to state governments

gerrymandering the apportionment of voters in districts in such a way as to give unfair advantage to one racial or ethnic group or political party

government institutions and procedures through which a territory and its people are ruled

government corporation government agency that performs a service normally provided by the private sector

grand jury jury that determines whether sufficient evidence is available to justify a trial; grand juries do not rule on the accused's guilt or innocence

grants-in-aid programs through which Congress provides money to state and local governments on the condition that the funds be employed for purposes defined by the federal government

grassroots mobilization a lobbying campaign in which a group mobilizes its membership to contact government officials in support of the group's position

Great Compromise the agreement reached at the Constitutional Convention of 1787 that gave each state an equal number of senators regardless of its population, but linked representation in the House of Representatives to population

habeas corpus a court order demanding that an individual in custody be brought into court and shown the cause for detention

home rule power delegated by the state to a local unit of government to manage its own affairs

impeachment the formal charge by the House of Representatives that a government official has committed "Treason, Bribery, or other high Crimes and Misdemeanors"

implementation the efforts of departments and agencies to translate laws into specific bureaucratic rules and actions

implied powers powers that are not specifically expressed in the Constitution but are seen as necessary to allow presidents to exercise their expressed powers

in-kind benefits noncash goods and services provided to needy individuals and families by the federal government

incumbency holding the political office for which one is running **joint committees** legislative committees formed of members of both the House and Senate

incumbent a candidate running for reelection to a position that he or she already holds

independent agency agency that is not part of a cabinet department

indexing periodic process of adjusting of social benefits or wages to account for increases in the cost of living

informational benefits special newsletters, periodicals, training programs, conferences, and other information provided to members of groups to entice others to join

inherent powers powers claimed by a president that are not expressed in the Constitution but are inferred from it

institutional advertising advertising designed to create a positive image of an organization

interest group individuals who organize to influence the government's programs and policies

International Monetary Fund (IMF) an institution established in 1944 that provides loans and facilitates international monetary exchange

iron triangle the stable, cooperative relationships that often develop among a congressional committee, an administrative agency, and one or more supportive interest groups; not all of these relationships are triangular, but the iron triangle is the most typical

isolationism avoidance of involvement in the affairs of other nations

judicial activism judicial philosophy that posits that the Court should go beyond the words of the Constitution or a statute to consider the broader societal implications of its decisions

judicial restraint judicial philosophy whose adherents refuse to go beyond the clear words of the Constitution in interpreting the document's meaning

judicial review the power of the courts to review and, if necessary, declare actions of the legislative and executive branches invalid or unconstitutional; the Supreme Court asserted this power in *Marbury v. Madison* (1803)

jurisdiction the sphere of a court's power and authority

Kitchen Cabinet an informal group of advisers to whom the president turns for counsel and guidance; members of the official Cabinet may or may not also be members of the Kitchen Cabinet

laissez-faire capitalism an economic system in which the means of production and distribution are privately owned and operated for profit with minimal or no government interference

legislative initiative the president's implied power to bring a legislative agenda before Congress

libel a written statement made in "reckless disregard of the truth" that is considered damaging to a victim because it is "malicious, scandalous, and defamatory"

liberal today this term refers to those who generally support social and political reform; governmental intervention in the economy and more economic equality; the expansion of federal social services; and greater concern for consumers and the environment

liberty freedom from government control

limited government a principle of constitutional government; a government whose powers are defined and limited by a constitution

lobbying a strategy by which organized interests seek to influence the passage of legislation or other public policy by exerting direct pressure on members of the legislature

logrolling a legislative practice whereby agreements are made between legislators in voting for or against a bill; vote trading **majority leader** the elected leader of the majority party in the House of Representatives or in the Senate; in the House, the majority leader is subordinate in the party hierarchy to the Speaker of the House

majority party the party that holds the majority of legislative seats in either the House or the Senate

majority rule/minority rights the democratic principle that a government follows the preferences of the majority of voters but protects the interests of the minority

market place of ideas the public forum in which beliefs and ideas are exchanged and compete

material benefits special goods, services, or money provided to members of groups to entice others to join

means testing a procedure by which potential beneficiaries of a public assistance program establish their eligibility by demonstrating a genuine need for the assistance

Medicaid a federally and state-financed, state-operated program providing medical services to low-income people

Medicare a form of national health insurance for the elderly and the disabled

membership association an organized group in which members actually play a substantial role, sitting on committees and engaging in group projects

merit system a product of civil service reform, in which appointees to positions in public bureaucracies must objectively be deemed qualified for those positions

minority leader the elected leader of the minority party in the House or Senate **oversight** the effort by Congress, through hearings, investigations, and other techniques, to exercise control over the activities of executive agencies

minority party the party that holds a minority of legislative seats in either the House or the Senate

Miranda rule the requirement, articulated by the Supreme Court in *Miranda v. Arizona* (1966), that persons under arrest must be informed prior to police interrogation of their rights to remain silent and to have the benefit of legal counsel

mobilization the process by which large numbers of people are organized for a political activity

monetary policies efforts to regulate the economy through the manipulation of the supply of money and credit; America's most powerful institution in this area of monetary policy is the Federal Reserve Board

nation-states political entities consisting of people with some common cultural experience (nation) who also share a common political authority (state), recognized by other sovereignties (nation-states)

necessary and proper clause provision from Article I, Section 8, of the Constitution providing Congress with the authority to make all laws necessary and proper to carry out its expressed powers

netroots grassroots online activist organizations that have redefined membership and fund-raising practices and streamlined staff structure

New Federalism attempts by presidents Nixon and Reagan to return power to the states through block grants **police power** power reserved to the state government to regulate the health, safety, and morals of its citizens

New Jersey Plan a framework for the Constitution, introduced by William Paterson, that called for equal state representation in the national legislature regardless of population

New Politics movement a political movement that began in the 1960s and '70s, made up of professionals and intellectuals for whom the civil rights and antiwar movements were formative experiences; the New Politics movement strengthened public interest groups

niche journalism news reporting devoted to a targeted portion (subset) of a journalism market sector or for a portion of readers or viewers based on content or ideological presentation

nomination the process by which political parties select their candidates for election to public office

noncontributory programs social programs that provide assistance to people based on demonstrated need rather than any contribution they have made

non-state actors groups other than nation-states that attempt to play a role in the international system; terrorist groups are one type of non-state actor

North American Free Trade Agreement (NAFTA) trade treaty among the United States, Canada, and Mexico to lower and eliminate tariffs among the three countries

North Atlantic Treaty Organization (NATO) an organization, comprising the United States, Canada, and most of Western Europe, formed in 1948 to counter the perceived threat from the Soviet Union

open primary a primary election in which the voter can wait until the day of the primary to choose which party to enroll in to select candidates for the general election

opinion the written explanation of the Supreme Court's decision in a particular case

oral argument the stage in Supreme Court procedure in which attorneys for both sides appear before the Court to present their positions and answer questions posed by justices

original jurisdiction the authority to initially consider a case; distinguished from appellate jurisdiction, which is the authority to hear appeals from a lower court's decision

oversight the effort by Congress, through hearings, investigations, and other techniques, to exercise control over the activities of executive agencies

party identification an individual voter's psychological ties to one party or another

party unity vote a roll-call vote in the House or Senate in which at least 50 percent of the members of one party take a particular position and are opposed by at least 50 percent of the members of the other party patronage the resources available to higher officials, usually opportunities to make partisan appointments to offices and to confer grants, licenses, or special favors to supporters

plaintiff the individual or organization that brings a complaint in court

plea bargain a negotiated agreement in a criminal case in a which a defendant agrees to plead guilty in return for the state's agreement to reduce the severity of the criminal charge the defendant is facing

pluralism the theory that all interests are and should be free to compete for influence in the government; the outcome of this competition is compromise and moderation

pocket veto a presidential veto that is automatically triggered if the president does not act on a given piece of legislation passed during the final 10 days of a legislative session

political action committee (PAC) a private group that raises and distributes funds for use in election campaigns

political efficacy the ability to influence government and politics

political equality the right to participate in politics equally, based on the principle of "one person, one vote"

political ideology a cohesive set of beliefs that forms a general philosophy about the role of government

political parties organized groups that attempt to influence the government by electing their members to important government offices

political socialization the induction of individuals into the political culture; learning the underlying beliefs and values on which the political system is based

politics conflict over the leadership, structure, and policies of governments

popular sovereignty a principle of democracy in which political authority rests ultimately in the hands of the people

pork barrel legislation (or pork) appropriations made by legislative bodies for local projects that are often not needed but that are created so that local representatives can win re-election in their home districts

power influence over a government's leadership, organization, or policies

precedent prior case whose principles are used by judges as the basis for their decisions in present cases

preemption the principle that allows the national government to override state or local actions in certain policy areas; in foreign policy, the willingness to strike first in order to prevent an enemy attack

preventive war policy of striking first when a nation fears that a foreign foe is contemplating hostile action

primary elections elections to select a party's candidate for the general election

priming process of preparing the public to take a particular view of an event or political actor

prior restraint an effort by a governmental agency to block the publication of material it deems libelous or harmful in some other way; censorship; in the United States, the courts forbid prior restraint except under the most extraordinary circumstances

private bill a proposal in Congress to provide a specific person with some kind of relief, such as a special exemption from immigration quotas redistricting the process of redrawing election districts and redistributing legislative representatives; this happens every 10 years to reflect shifts in population or in response to legal challenges to existing districts

privatization the transfer of all or part of a program from the public sector to the private sector

privileges and immunities clause provision, from Article IV, Section 2, of the Constitution, that a state cannot discriminate against someone from another state or give its own residents special privileges

proportional representation a multiple-member district system that allows each political party representation in proportion to its percentage of the total vote

public interest groups groups that claim they serve the general good rather than only their own particular interest

public opinion citizens' attitudes about political issues, leaders, institutions, and events

public-opinion polls scientific instruments for measuring public opinion

public policy a law, a rule, a statute, or an edict that expresses the government's goals and provides for rewards and punishments to promote those goals' attainment

purposive benefits selective benefits of group membership that emphasize the purpose and accomplishments of the group

push polling a polling technique in which the questions are designed to shape the respondent's opinion

random digit dialing a polling method in which respondents are selected at random from a list of 10-digit telephone numbers, with every effort made to avoid bias in the construction of the sample

recall a procedure to allow voters to remove state officials from office before their terms expire by circulating petitions to call a vote

referendum the practice of referring a measure proposed or passed by a legislature to the vote of the electorate for approval or rejection

regulatory agency a department, bureau, or independent agency whose primary mission is to impose limits, restrictions, or other obligations on the conduct of individuals or companies in the private sector

representative democracy (republic) a system of government in which the populace selects representatives, who play a significant role in governmental decision making

reserved powers powers, derived from the Tenth Amendment to the Constitution, that are not specifically delegated to the national government or denied to the states

revenue agency an agency responsible for collecting taxes; examples include the Internal Revenue Service for income taxes, the U.S. Customs Service for tariffs and other taxes on imported goods, and the Bureau of Alcohol, Tobacco, Firearms and Explosives for collection of taxes on the sales of those particular products

right of rebuttal a Federal Communications Commission regulation giving individuals the right to have the opportunity to respond to personal attacks made on a radio or television broadcast

right to privacy the right to be left alone, which has been interpreted by the Supreme Court to entail individual access to birth control and abortion

roll-call vote a vote in which each legislator's yes or no vote is recorded as the clerk calls the names of the members alphabetically

sample a small group selected by researchers to represent the most important characteristics of an entire population

sampling error (or margin of error) polling error that arises based on the small size of the sample

select committees (usually) temporary legislative committees set up to highlight or investigate a particular issue or address an issue not within the jurisdiction of existing committees seniority the ranking given to an individual on the basis of length of continuous service on a committee in Congress

selection bias (news) the tendency to focus news coverage on only one aspect of an event or issue, avoiding coverage of other aspects

selection bias (surveys) polling error that arises when the sample is not representative of the population being studied, which creates errors in overrepresenting or underrepresenting some opinions

selective incorporation the process by which different protections in the Bill of Rights were incorporated into the Fourteenth Amendment, thus guaranteeing citizens protection from state as well as national governments

senatorial courtesy the practice whereby the president, before formally nominating a person for a federal judgeship, seeks the indication that senators from the candidate's own state support the nomination

"separate but equal" rule doctrine that public accommodations could be segregated by race but still be considered equal

separation of powers the division of governmental power among several institutions that must cooperate in decision making

signing statements announcements made by the president when signing bills into law, often presenting the president's interpretation of the law

simple random sample (or probability sample) a method used by pollsters to select a representative sample in which every individual in the population has an equal probability of being selected as a respondent

slander an oral statement made in "reckless disregard of the truth" that is considered damaging to the victim because it is "malicious, scandalous, and defamatory"

social desirability effect the effect that results when respondents in a survey report what they expect the interviewer wishes to hear rather than what they believe

social media web-based and mobile-based technologies that are used to turn communication into interactive dialogue between organizations, communities, and individuals; social media technologies take on many different forms including blogs, Wikis, podcasts, pictures, video, Facebook, and Twitter

Social Security a contributory welfare program into which working Americans contribute a percentage of their wages and from which they receive cash benefits after retirement or if they become disabled

socioeconomic status status in society based on level of education, income, and occupational prestige

sociological representation a type of representation in which representatives have the same racial, gender, ethnic, religious, or educational backgrounds as their constituents; it is based on the principle that if two individuals are similar in background, character, interests, and perspectives, then one can correctly represent the other's views

solicitor general the top government lawyer in all cases before the Supreme Court in which the government is a party

solidary benefits selective benefits of group membership that emphasize friendship, networking, and consciousness raising

Speaker of the House the chief presiding officer of the House of Representatives; the Speaker is the most important party and House leader, and can influence the legislative agenda, the fate of individual pieces of legislation, and members' positions within the House

"speech plus" speech accompanied by conduct such as sit-ins, picketing, and demonstrations; protection of this form of speech under the First Amendment is conditional, and restrictions imposed by state or local authorities are acceptable if properly balanced by considerations of public order

staff organization type of membership group in which a professional staff conducts most of the group's activities

standing committee a permanent committee with the power to propose and write legislation that covers a particular subject, such as finance or agriculture term limits legally prescribed limits on the number of terms an elected official can serve veto the president's constitutional power to prevent a bill from becoming a law; a presidential veto may be overridden by a two-thirds vote of each house of Congress

stare decisis literally, "let the decision stand"; the doctrine that a previous decision by a court applies as a precedent in similar cases until that decision is overruled

states' rights the principle that the states should oppose the increasing authority of the national government; this principle was most popular in the period before the Civil War

strict scrutiny a test used by the Supreme Court in racial discrimination cases and other cases involving civil liberties and civil rights that places the burden of proof on the government rather than on the challengers to show that the law in question is constitutional

subsidies government grants of cash or other valuable commodities, such as land, to individuals or an organization; used to promote activities desired by the government, to reward political support, or to buy off political opposition

suffrage the right to vote; also called *franchise*

Supplemental Nutrition Assistance Program (SNAP) the largest antipoverty program, which provides recipients with a debit card for food at most grocery stores; formerly known as *food stamps*

supremacy clause Article VI of the Constitution, which states that laws passed by the national government and all treaties "shall be the supreme law of the land" and superior to all laws adopted by any state or any subdivision

supreme court the highest court in a particular state or in the United States; this court primarily serves an appellate function

tax expenditures government subsidies provided to employers and employees through tax deductions for amounts spent on health insurance and other benefits

third parties parties that organize to compete against the two major American political parties

Thirteenth Amendment one of three Civil War amendments; it abolished slavery

Three-Fifths Compromise the agreement reached at the Constitutional Convention of 1787 that stipulated that for purposes of the apportionment of congressional seats, every slave would be counted as three-fifths of a person

totalitarian government a system of rule in which the government recognizes no formal limits on its power and seeks to absurb or eliminate other social institutions that might challenge it

trial court the first court to hear a criminal or civil case

turnout the percentage of eligible individuals who actually vote

two-party system a political system in which only two parties have a realistic opportunity to compete effectively for control of the government

tyranny oppressive and unjust government that employs cruel and unjust use of power and authority

unfunded mandates regulations or conditions for receiving grants that impose costs on state and local governments for which they are not reimbursed by the federal government

unitary system a centralized government system in which lower levels of government have little power independent of the national government

United Nations (UN) an organization of nations founded in 1945 to be as a channel for negotiation and a means of settling international disputes peaceably; the UN has had frequent successes in providing a forum for negotiation and on some occasions a means of preventing international conflicts from spreading; on a number of occasions, the UN has supported U.S. foreign policy goals

values (or beliefs) basic principles that shape a person's opinions about political issues and events

veto the president's constitutional power to prevent a bill from becoming a law; a presidential veto may be overridden by a two-thirds vote of each house of Congress

Virginia Plan a framework for the Constitution, introduced by Edmund Randolph, that called for representation in the national legislature based on the population of each state

War Powers Resolution a resolution of Congress that the president can send troops into action abroad only by authorization of Congress, or if American troops are already under attack or serious threat

whip a party member in the House or Senate responsible for coordinating the party's legislative strategy, building support for key issues, and counting votes

White House staff analysts and advisers to the president, each of whom is often given the title "special assistant"

World Trade Organization (WTO) international organization promoting free trade that grew out of the General Agreement on Tariffs and Trade

writ of certiorari a decision of at least four of the nine Supreme Court justices to review a decision of a lower court; *certiorari* is Latin, meaning "to make more certain"

writ of habeas corpus a court order that the individual in custody be brought into court and shown the cause for detention; habeas corpus is guaranteed by the Constitution and can be suspended only in cases of rebellion or invasion

endnotes

Chapter 1

1. The Pew Research Center for the People and the Press, "Trust in Government Nears Record Low," October 18, 2013, www.people-press.org/2013/10/18/trust-in-government -nears-record-low-but-most-federal-agencies-are-viewed-favorably/ (accessed 5/15/14).
2. The Pew Research Center for the People and the Press, "Trust in Government Nears Record Low."
3. The Pew Research Center for the People and the Press, "Trust in Government Nears Record Low."
4. Joseph S. Nye, Jr., "Introduction: The Decline of Confidence in Government," in *Why People Don't Trust Government*, ed. Joseph S. Nye, Philip D. Zelikow, and David C. King (Cambridge, MA: Harvard University Press, 1999), p. 4;
5. The Pew Research Center for the People and the Press, "The Political Typology," June 28, 2014, www.people-press.org/files/2014/06/6-26-14-Political-Typology-release1.pdf (accessed 8/26/14).
6. The Pew Research Center for the People and the Press, "Partisan Polarization Surges in Bush, Obama Years; Trends in American Values: 1987–2012, Section 4: Values about Government and the Social Safety Net," www.people-press.org/2012/06/04 /section-4-values-about-government-and-the-social-safety-net/ (accessed 6/8/12).
7. Pew Internet and American Life, "What Internet Users Do Online," February 2012 Survey, http://pewinternet.org/Trend–Data–(Adults)/online–Activities–Total.aspx (accessed 6/5/12).
8. Freedom House, "Freedom in the World Report, 2013, Essay: Democratic Breakthroughs in the Balance," www.freedomhouse.org/report/freedom-world-2013/essay-democratic -breakthroughs-balance (accessed 9/25/13).
9. See Eugen Weber, *Peasants into Frenchmen: The Modernization of Rural France, 1870–1914* (Stanford, CA: Stanford University Press, 1976), chap. 5.
10. See V. O. Key, *Politics, Parties, and Pressure Groups* (New York: Crowell, 1964), p. 201.
11. Harold Lasswell, *Politics: Who Gets What, When, How* (New York: Meridian Books, 1958).
12. Susan B. Carter, Scott Sigmund Gartner, Michael R. Haines, Alan L. Olmsted, Richard Sutch, and Gavin Wright, eds., *Historical Statistics of the United States: Millennial Edition Online*, Table Aa145–184, Population, by Sex and Race: 1790–1990 (New York: Cambridge University Press, 2006). Current data available at U.S. Census Bureau, www.census.gov (accessed 2/25/12).
13. Carter et al., "Historical Statistics of the United States, Table Aa145–184, Population, by Sex and Race: 1790–1990."
14. Carter et al., "Historical Statistics of the United States, Table Aa145–184, Population, by Sex and Race: 1790–1990"; "Table Aa2189–2215, Hispanic Population Estimates."
15. U.S. Census Bureau, "Statistical Abstract of the United States," www.census.gov (accessed 11/13/07); Claude S. Fischer and Michael Hout, *A Century of Difference:*

How America Changed in the Last One Hundred Years (New York: Russell Sage Foundation, 2006), p. 36.

16. Carter et al., "Historical Statistics of the United States," Table Aa22–35, Selected Population Characteristics.

17. Michael B. Katz and Mark J. Stern, *One Nation Divisible: What America Was and What It Is Becoming* (New York: Russell Sage Foundation, 2006), p. 16.

18. Carter et al., "Historical Statistics of the United States," Table Aa145–184, Population, by Sex and Race: 1790–1990; Karen R. Humes, Nicholas A. Jones, and Roberto R. Ramirez, "Overview of Race and Hispanic Origin: 2010," *2010 Census Briefs*, Number C210BR-02 (Washington, DC: U.S. Census Bureau, March 2011), p. 4. www.census .gov/prod/cen2010/briefs/c2010br-02.pdf (accessed 10/14/2011).

19. U.S. Census, "Annual Estimates of the Resident Population by Sex, Race, and Hispanic Origin for the United States, States, and Counties: April 1, 2010 to July 1, 2012," http://factfinder2.census.gov/faces/tableservices/jsf/pages/productview .xhtml?pid=PEP_2012_PEPASR6H&prodType=table (accessed 9/25/13).

20. U.S. Census Bureau, "2012 American Community Survey 1-Year Estimates: Selected Social Characteristics in the United States," factfinder2.census.gov/faces/tableservices /jsf/pages/productview.xhtml?pid=ACS_12_1YR_DP02&prodType=table (accessed 9/25/13).

21. Michael Hoefer, Nancy Rytina, and Bryan Barker, "Estimates of the Unauthorized Immigrant Population Residing in the United States: January 2011, *Population Estimates*, Office of Immigration Statistics, Department of Homeland Security, March 2012, www.dhs.gov/sites/default/files/publications/ois_ill_pe_2011.pdf (accessed 9/25/13).

22. The Pew Forum on Religion and Public Life, "'Nones' on the Rise: One in Five Adults Have No Religious Affiliation," Pew Research Center, October 9, 2012, www.pewforum .org/files/2012/10/NonesOnTheRise-full.pdf (accessed 5/15/14).

23. The Pew Forum on Religion and Public Life, "'Nones' on the Rise"; Michael Lipka, "How Many Jews Are There in the United States?" Pew Research Center, October 2, 2013, www.pewresearchcenter.org/fact-tank/2013/10/02/how-many-jews-are-there -in-the-united-states/ (accessed 5/15/14); Muslim population is from 2010. See Pew Research Religion and Public Life Project, "The Future of the Global Muslim Popula- tion," January 27, 2011, www.pewforum.org/2011/01/27/the-future-of-the-global -muslim-population/#the-americas (accessed 5/15/14).

24. U.S. Census Bureau, "Annual Estimates of the Resident Population for Selected Age Groups by Sex for the United States, States, Counties, and Puerto Rico Common- wealth and Municipios: April 1, 2010 to July 1, 2012," factfinder2.census.gov/faces /tableservices/jsf/pages/productview.xhtml?src=bkmk (accessed 9/25/13).

25. U.S. Census Bureau, "Growth in Urban Population Outpaces Rest of Nation, Census Bureau Reports," March 26, 2012, www.census.gov/newsroom/releases/archives /2010_census/cb12-50.html (accessed 9/25/13).

26. Thomas , Piketty and Emmanuel Saez, "Income Inequality in the United States, 1993–1998," *Quarterly Journal of Economics*, 18 no. 1 (2003), (Tables and Figures Updated to 2012, September, 2013), elsa.berkeley.edu/~saez/TabFig2012prel.xls (accessed 10/14/13).

27. U.S. Census Bureau, "Historical Income Tables, Tables F-2, F-3 and F-6."

28. "Bordering on Poverty," *New York Times*, November 18, 2011, www.nytimes.com /interactive/2011/11/19/us/bordering-on-poverty.html?ref=us (accessed 10/16/13).

29. U.S. Census Bureau, "Congressional Apportionment: 2010 Apportionment Results," www.census.gov/population/apportionment/files/Apportionment%20Population %202010.pdf (accessed 9/25/13).

30. Herbert McClosky and John Zaller, *The American Ethos: Public Attitudes toward Capitalism and Democracy* (Cambridge, MA: Harvard University Press, 1984), p. 19.

31. J. R. Pole, *The Pursuit of Equality in American History* (Berkeley: University of California Press, 1978), p. 19.

Chapter 2

1. The social makeup of colonial America and some of the social conflicts that divided colonial society are discussed in Jackson Turner Main, *The Social Structure of Revolutionary America* (Princeton, NJ: Princeton University Press, 1965).

2. George B. Tindall and David E. Shi, *America: A Narrative History*, 8th ed. (New York: W. W. Norton, 2010), p. 202.

3. For a discussion of events leading up to the Revolution, see Charles M. Andrews, *The Colonial Background of the American Revolution* (New Haven, CT: Yale University Press, 1924).

4. See Carl Becker, *The Declaration of Independence* (New York: Knopf, 1942).

5. See Merrill Jensen, *The Articles of Confederation* (Madison: University of Wisconsin Press, 1970).

6. Reported in Samuel E. Morrison, Henry Steele Commager, and William Leuchtenberg, *The Growth of the American Republic* (New York: Oxford University Press, 1969), vol. 1, p. 244.

7. Quoted in Morrison et al., *The Growth of the American Republic*, vol. 1, p. 242.

8. Charles A. Beard, *An Economic Interpretation of the Constitution of the United States* (New York: Macmillan, 1913).

9. Max Farrand, ed., *The Records of the Federal Convention of 1787*, 4 vols., rev. ed. (New Haven, CT: Yale University Press, 1966), vol. 2, p. 10.

10. Alexander Hamilton, James Madison, and John Jay, *The Federalist Papers*, ed. Clinton L. Rossiter (New York: New American Library, 1961), no. 71.

11. *The Federalist Papers*, no. 62.

12. Max Farrand, *The Framing of the Constitution of the United States* (New Haven, CT: Yale University Press, 1962), p. 49.

13. Melancton Smith, quoted in Herbert J. Storing, *What the Anti-Federalists Were For* (Chicago: University of Chicago, 1981), p. 17.

14. *The Federalist Papers*, no. 57.

15. "Essays of Brutus," no. 15, in *The Complete Anti-Federalist*, ed. Herbert Storing (Chicago: University of Chicago Press, 1981).

16. *The Federalist Papers*, no. 10.

17. *The Federalist Papers*, no. 51.

Chapter 3

1. Bradley Dennis, "Obama Administration Will Not Block State Marijuana Laws, If Distribution Is Regulated," *Washington Post*, August 29, 2013, http://articles .washingtonpost.com/2013-08-29/national/41566270_1_marijuana-legalization -attorney-general-bob-ferguson-obama-administration (accessed 11/17/13).

2. ProCon.org, "35 States with Legal Gay Marriage and 15 States with Same-Sex Marriage Bans," updated November 20, 2014, http://gaymarriage.procon.org/view .resource.php?resourceID=004857 (accessed 11/21/14)

3. *United States v. Windsor,* 570 U.S. __ (2013).

4. *Hicklin v. Orbeck*, 437 U.S. 518 (1978).

5. *Sweeny v. Woodall*, 344 U.S. 86 (1953).

6. A good discussion of the constitutional position of local governments is in York Willbern, *The Withering Away of the City* (Bloomington: Indiana University Press, 1971). For more on the structure and theory of federalism, see Thomas R. Dye,

American Federalism: Competition among Governments (Lexington, MA: Lexington Books, 1990), chap. 1, and Martha Derthick, "Up-to-Date in Kansas City: Reflections on American Federalism," 1992 John Gaus Lecture, *PS: Political Science and Politics* 25 (December 1992): 671–75.

7. For a good treatment of the contrast between national political stability and social instability, see Samuel P. Huntington, *Political Order in Changing Societies* (New Haven, CT: Yale University Press, 1968), chap. 2.

8. *McCulloch v. Maryland*, 4 Wheaton 316 (1819).

9. *Gibbons v. Ogden*, 9 Wheaton 1 (1824).

10. The Sherman Antitrust Act, adopted in 1890, for example, was enacted not to restrict commerce but rather to protect it from monopolies, or trusts, so as to prevent unfair trade practices and to enable the market again to become self-regulating. Moreover, the Supreme Court sought to uphold liberty of contract to protect businesses. For example, in *Lochner v. New York*, 198 U.S. 45 (1905), the Court invalidated a New York law regulating the sanitary conditions in bakeries and the hours of labor for bakers on the grounds that the law interfered with liberty of contract.

11. Kenneth T. Palmer, "The Evolution of Grant Policies," in *The Changing Politics of Federal Grants*, by Lawrence D. Brown, James W. Fossett, and Kenneth T. Palmer (Washington, DC: Brookings Institution Press, 1984), p. 15.

12. Palmer, "The Evolution of Grant Policies," p. 6.

13. The key case in this process of expanding the power of the national government is generally considered to be *NLRB v. Jones & Laughlin Steel Corporation*, 301 U.S. 1 (1937), in which the Supreme Court approved federal regulation of the workplace and thereby virtually eliminated interstate commerce as a limit on the national government's power.

14. *United States v. Darby Lumber Co.*, 312 U.S. 100 (1941).

15. W. John Moore, "Pleading the 10th," *National Journal*, July 29, 1995, p. 1940.

16. *United States v. Lopez*, 514 U.S. 549 (1995).

17. *Printz v. United States*, 521 U.S. 898 (1997).

18. Morton Grodzins, *The American System*, ed. Daniel J. Elazar (Chicago: Rand McNally, 1966).

19. See Terry Sanford, *Storm over the States* (New York: McGraw-Hill, 1967).

20. James L. Sundquist, with David W. Davis, *Making Federalism Work* (Washington, DC: Brookings Institution Press, 1969), p. 271. Wallace was mistrusted by the architects of the War on Poverty because he was a strong proponent of racial segregation. He believed in "states' rights," which meant that states, not the federal government, should decide what liberty and equality meant.

21. See Don Kettl, *The Regulation of American Federalism* (Baton Rouge: Louisiana State University Press, 1983).

22. Eliza Newlin Carney, "Power Grab," *National Journal*, April 11, 1998, p. 798.

23. Philip Rucker, "Obama Curtails Bush's Policy of 'Preemption,'" *Washington Post*, May 22, 2009, p. A3.

24. See Advisory Commission on Intergovernmental Relations, *Federal Regulation of State and Local Governments: The Mixed Record of the 1980s* (Washington, DC: Advisory Commission on Intergovernmental Relations, July 1993).

25. Robert Jay Dilger and Richard S. Beth, "Unfunded Mandates Reform Act: History, Impact, and Issues" (Washington, D.C.: Congressional Research Service, April 19, 2011), p.40, http://digital.library.unt.edu/ark:/67531/metadc40084/m1/1/high_res_d/R40957_2011Apr19.pdf (accessed 11/16/13).

26. Advisory Commission on Intergovernmental Relations, *Federal Regulation of State and Local Governments*, p. iii.

27. Advisory Commission on Intergovernmental Relations, *Federal Regulation of State and Local Governments*, p. 51.

28. Robert Frank, "Proposed Block Grants Seem Unlikely to Cure Management Problems," *Wall Street Journal*, May 1, 1995, p. 1.

29. Sarah Kershaw, "U.S. Rule Limits Emergency Care for Immigrants," *New York Times*, September 22, 2007, p. A1.

30. National Conference of State Legislatures, "2013 Report on State Immigration Laws," www.ncsl.org/research/immigration/immgration-report-august-2013.aspx (accessed 11/3/13).

31. Associated Press, "Justice Department Sues Utah over State's Illegal Immigration Enforcement Law," *Washington Post*, November 22, 2011, www.washingtonpost.com /national/us-department-of-justice-sues-utah-over-immigration-enforcement -law/2011/11/22/gIQAJeJEmN_story.html (accessed 11/27/11).

32. *Arizona v. United States*, 567 U.S. __ (2012).

33. Kate Phillips, "South Carolina Governor Rejects Stimulus Money," *New York Times*, March 20, 2009, http://thecaucus.blogs.nytimes.com/2009/03/20/round-2-omb -rejects-sc-governors-stimulus-plan/ (accessed 10/6/09).

34. Robert Pear and J. David Goodman, "Governors' Fight over Stimulus May Define G.O.P.," *New York Times*, February 22, 2009, www.nytimes.com/2009/02/23/us /politics/23governors.html (accessed 10/7/09).

35. The White House, Office of the Press Secretary, Memorandum for the Heads of Executive Departments and Agencies, Subject: Preemption, May 20, 2009, http://theusconstituion.org/blog.history/wp-content/uploads/2009/05/obama -preemption-memo-5202009.pdf (accessed 10/17/09).

36. Adam Liptak, "In Health Law, Asking Where U.S. Power Stops," *New York Times*, November 14, 2011, p. A1.

Chapter 4

1 ProCon.org, "35 States with Legal Gay Marriage and 15 States with Same-Sex Marriage Bans," updated November 20, 2014, http://gaymarriage.procon.org/view .resource.php?resourceID=004857 (accessed 11/21/14).

2. *United States v. Windsor*, 570 U.S. 12 (2013).

3. Alexander Hamilton, James Madison, and John Jay, *The Federalist Papers*, ed. Clinton Rossiter (New York: New American Library, 1961), no. 84, p. 513.

4. *The Federalist Papers*, no. 84, p. 513.

5. Let there be no confusion about the words *liberty* and *freedom*. They are synonymous and interchangeable. *Freedom* comes from the German *Freiheit*. *Liberty* is from the French *liberté*. Although people sometimes try to make them appear to be different, both of them have equal concern with the absence of restraints on individual choices of action.

6. *Barron v. Baltimore*, 7 Peters 243, 246 (1833).

7. The Fourteenth Amendment also seems designed to introduce civil rights. The final clause of the all-important Section 1 provides that no state can "deny to any person within its jurisdiction the equal protection of the laws." It is reasonable to conclude that the purpose of this provision was to obligate the state governments as well as the national government to take *positive* actions to protect citizens from arbitrary and discriminatory actions, at least those based on race.

8. For example, *The Slaughterhouse Cases*, 16 Wallace 36 (1873).

9. *Chicago, Burlington and Quincy Railroad Company v. Chicago*, 166 U.S. 226 (1897).

10. *Gitlow v. New York*, 268 U.S. 652 (1925).

11. *Near v. Minnesota*, 283 U.S. 697 (1931); *Hague v. C.I.O.*, 307 U.S. 496 (1939).

12. *McDonald v. Chicago*, 561 U.S. 3025 (2010).

13. *Palko v. Connecticut*, 302 U.S. 319 (1937).

14. *Abington School District v. Schempp*, 374 U.S. 203 (1963).
15. *Engel v. Vitale*, 370 U.S. 421 (1962).
16. *Doe v. Santa Fe Independent School District*, 530 U.S. 290 (2000).
17. *Wallace v. Jaffree*, 472 U.S. 38 (1985).
18. *Lynch v. Donnelly*, 465 U.S. 668 (1984).
19. *Van Orden v. Perry*, 545 U.S. 677 (2005).
20. *McCreary v. ACLU of Kentucky*, 545 U.S. 844 (2005).
21. *West Virginia State Board of Education v. Barnette*, 319 U.S. 624 (1943). The case it reversed was *Minersville School District v. Gobitus*, 310 U.S. 586 (1940).
22. *Employment Division, Department of Human Resources of Oregon v. Smith*, 494 U.S. 872 (1990).
23. *Wisconsin v. Yoder*, 406 U.S. 205 (1972).
24. *Hosanna-Tabor Church v. Equal Employment Opportunity Commission*, 565 U.S. __ (2012).
25. *Abrams v. United States*, 250 U.S. 616 (1919).
26. *United States v. Carolene Products Company*, 304 U.S. 144 (1938), note 4. This footnote is one of the Court's most important doctrines. See Alfred H. Kelly, Winfred A. Harbison, and Herman Belz, *The American Constitution: Its Origins and Development*, 7th ed. (New York: W. W. Norton, 1991), vol. 2, pp. 519–23.
27. *Schenk v. United States*, 249 U.S. 47 (1919).
28. *Citizens United v. Federal Election Commission*, 588 U.S. 50 (2010).
29. *McCutcheon v. Federal Election Commission*, 572 U.S. __ (2014).
30. Arthur Delaney, "Supreme Court Rolls Back Campaign Finance Restrictions," *Huffington Post*, updated May 25, 2011, www.huffingtonpost.com/2010/01/21 /supreme-court-rolls-back_n_431227.html (accessed 7/9/12).
31. *Hague v. Committee for Industrial Organization*, 307 U.S. 496 (1939).
32. *Stromberg v. California*, 283 U.S. 359 (1931).
33. *Texas v. Johnson*, 488 U.S. 884 (1989).
34. *Snyder v. Phelps*, 562 U.S. __ (2011).
35. For a good general discussion of "speech plus," see Louis Fisher, *American Constitutional Law* (New York: McGraw-Hill, 1990), pp. 544–46. The case upholding the buffer zone against the abortion protesters is *Madsen v. Women's Health Center*, 512 U.S. 753 (1994).
36. *Bethel School District v. Fraser*, 478 U.S. 675 (1986).
37. *Hazelwood v. Kuhlmeier*, 484 U.S. 260 (1988).
38. *Morse v. Frederick*, 551 U.S. 393 (2007).
39. *Near v. Minnesota*, 283 U.S. 697 (1931).
40. *New York Times v. United States*, 403 U.S. 731 (1971).
41. *Branzburg v. Hayes*, 408 U.S. 656 (1972).
42. *New York Times v. Sullivan*, 376 U.S. 254 (1964).
43. See *Zeran v. America Online*, 129 F.3d 327 (4th Cir. 1997).
44. *Roth v. United States*, 354 U.S. 476 (1957).
45. Concurring opinion in *Jacobellis v. Ohio*, 378 U.S. 184 (1964).
46. *Miller v. California*, 413 U.S. 15 (1973).
47. *Reno v. American Civil Liberties Union*, 521 U.S. 844 (1997).
48. *United States v. Williams*, 553 U.S. 285 (2008).
49. *United States v. Playboy Entertainment Group*, 529 U.S. 803 (2000).
50. *Brown v. Entertainment Merchants Association*, 564 U.S. __ (2011).
51. *Chaplinsky v. State of New Hampshire*, 315 U.S. 568 (1942).
52. *Dennis v. United States*, 341 U.S. 494 (1951).
53. *Broadcasting Company v. Acting Attorney General*, 405 U.S. 1000 (1972).
54. *City Council v. Taxpayers for Vincent*, 466 U.S. 789 (1984).
55. *44 Liquormart, Inc. and Peoples Super Liquor Stores Inc., Petitioners v. Rhode Island and Rhode Island Liquor Stores Association*, 517 U.S. 484 (1996).

56. *Lorillard Tobacco v. Reilly*, 533 U.S. 525 (2001).
57. *Presser v. Illinois*, 116 U.S. 252 (1886).
58. *United States v. Miller*, 307 U.S. 174 (1939).
59. *District of Columbia v. Heller*, 554 U.S. 570 (2008).
60. *McDonald v. Chicago*, 561 U.S. 3025 (2010).
61. *Horton v. California*, 496 U.S. 128 (1990).
62. *Mapp v. Ohio*, 367 U.S. 643 (1961). Although Mapp went free in this case, she was later convicted in New York on narcotics trafficking charges and served 9 years of a 20-year sentence.
63. *People v. Defore*, 242 N.Y. 13, 21, 150 N.E. 585, 587 (1926).
64. For a good discussion of the issue, see Fisher, *American Constitutional Law*, pp. 884–89.
65. *Florida v. Jardines*, 569 U.S. __ (2013).
66. *United States v. Jones*, 565 U.S. __ (2012).
67. *Maryland v. King*, 569 U.S. __ (2013).
68. *Palko v. Connecticut*, 302 U.S. 319 (1937).
69. *Miranda v. Arizona*, 384 U.S. 436 (1966).
70. *Berghuis v. Thompkins*, 560 U.S. 370 (2010).
71. *Gideon v. Wainwright*, 372 U.S. 335 (1963). For a full account of the story of the trial and release of Clarence Earl Gideon, see Anthony Lewis, *Gideon's Trumpet* (New York: Random House, 1964). See also David O'Brien, *Storm Center*, 8th ed. (New York: W. W. Norton, 2008).
72. *Furman v. Georgia*, 408 U.S. 238 (1972).
73. *Gregg v. Georgia*, 428 U.S. 153 (1976).
74. The Clark County Prosecuting Attorney, "U.S. Executions since 1976," www.clarkprosecutor.org/html/death/usexecute.htm (accessed 7/17/14); "Death Penalty," Gallup, www.gallup.com/poll/1606/death-penalty.aspx (accessed 5/22/12); Erik Eckholm, "In Death Penalty's Steady Decline, Some Experts See a Societal Shift," *New York Times*, December 19, 2013, p. A23.
75. *Kennedy v. Louisiana*, 554 U.S. 407 (2008).
76. *Snyder v. Louisiana*, 552 U.S. 472 (2008).
77. *Baze v. Rees*, 553 U.S. 35 (2008).
78. *Griswold v. Connecticut*, 381 U.S. 479 (1965).
79. *Griswold v. Connecticut*, concurring opinion. In 1972 the Court extended the privacy right to unmarried women: *Eisenstadt v. Baird*, 405 U.S. 438 (1972).
80. *Roe v. Wade*, 410 U.S. 113 (1973).
81. *Lawrence v. Texas*, 539 U.S. 558 (2003).
82. *Plessy v. Ferguson*, 163 U.S. 537 (1896).
83. *Missouri ex rel. Gaines v. Canada*, 305 U.S. 337 (1938).
84. The District of Columbia case came up too, but since the District of Columbia is not a state, this case did not directly involve the Fourteenth Amendment and its "equal protection" clause. It confronted the Court on the same grounds, however—that segregation is inherently unequal. Its victory in effect was "incorporation in reverse," with equal protection moving from the Fourteenth Amendment to become part of the Bill of Rights. See *Bolling v. Sharpe*, 347 U.S. 497 (1954).
85. *Brown v. Board of Education of Topeka, Kansas*, 347 U.S. 483 (1954).
86. The Supreme Court first declared that race was a suspect classification requiring strict scrutiny in the decision *Korematsu v. United States*, 323 U.S. 214 (1944). In this case, the Court upheld President Roosevelt's executive order of 1941 allowing the military to exclude persons of Japanese ancestry from the West Coast and to place them in internment camps. It is one of the few cases in which classification based on race survived strict scrutiny.

87. For good treatments of this long stretch of the struggle of the federal courts to integrate the schools, see Paul Brest and Sanford Levinson, *Processes of Constitutional Decision-Making: Cases and Materials*, 2nd ed. (Boston: Little, Brown, 1983), pp. 471–80; and Alfred H. Kelly, Winfred A. Harbison, and Herman Belz, *The American Constitution: Its Origins and Development*, 6th ed. (New York: W. W. Norton, 1983), pp. 610–16.

88. Pierre Thomas, "Denny's to Settle Bias Cases," *Washington Post*, May 24, 1994, p. A1.

89. *Parents Involved in Community Schools v. Seattle School District No. 1*, 551 U.S. 701 (2007).

90. John A. Powell, "Segregated Schools Ruling Not All Bad: In Rejecting Seattle's Integration Bid Top Court Majority Also Held That Avoiding Racial Isolation Is a Legitimate Public Goal," *Newsday*, July 16, 2007, p. A33.

91. See especially *Katzenbach v. McClung*, 379 U.S. 294 (1964). Almost immediately after passage of the Civil Rights Act of 1964, a case was brought challenging the validity of Title II, which covered discrimination in public accommodations. Ollie's Barbecue was a neighborhood restaurant in Birmingham, Alabama. It was located 11 blocks away from an interstate highway and even farther from railroad and bus stations. Its table service was for whites only; there was only take-out service for blacks. The Supreme Court agreed that Ollie's was strictly an intrastate restaurant, but since a substantial proportion of its food and other supplies were bought from companies outside the state of Alabama, there was a sufficient connection to interstate commerce; therefore, racial discrimination at such restaurants would "impose commercial burdens of national magnitude upon interstate commerce." Although this case involved Title II, it had direct bearing on the constitutionality of Title VII.

92. In 1970 this act was amended to outlaw for five years literacy tests as a condition for voting in all states.

93. See Douglas S. Massey and Nancy A. Denton, *American Apartheid: Segregation and the Making of the Underclass* (Cambridge, MA: Harvard University Press, 1993), chap. 7.

94. Michael Powell, "Bank Accused of Pushing Mortgage Deals on Blacks," *New York Times*, June 6, 2009, p. A16; Office of the Illinois Attorney General, "Madigan Sues Wells Fargo for Discriminatory and Deceptive Mortgage Lending Practices," Press Release July 31, 2009," www.illinoisattorneygeneral.gov/pressroom/2009_07/20090731.html (accessed 10/23/09).

95. See Jane J. Mansbridge, *Why We Lost the ERA* (Chicago: University of Chicago Press, 1986); and Gilbert Steiner, *Constitutional Inequality* (Washington, DC: Brookings Institution Press, 1985).

96. See *Frontiero v. Richardson*, 411 U.S. 677 (1973).

97. *Meritor Savings Bank v. Vinson*, 477 U.S. 57 (1986).

98. *Franklin v. Gwinnett County Public Schools*, 503 U.S. 60 (1992).

99. *United States v. Virginia*, 518 U.S. 515 (1996).

100. *Ledbetter v. Goodyear Tire and Rubber Co.*, 550 U.S. 618 (2007).

101. *Lau v. Nichols*, 414 U.S. 563 (1974).

102. Dick Kirschten, "Not Black and White," *National Journal*, March 2, 1991, p. 497.

103. *R.A.V. v. City of St. Paul*, 506 U.S. 377 (1992).

104. See the discussion in Robert A. Katzmann, *Institutional Disability: The Saga of Transportation Policy for the Disabled* (Washington, DC: Brookings Institution Press, 1986).

105. For example, after pressure from the Justice Department, one of the nation's largest rental-car companies agreed to make special hand controls available to any customer requesting them. See "Avis Agrees to Equip Cars for Disabled," *Los Angeles Times*, September 2, 1994, p. D1.

106. For more, see Dale Carpenter, *Flagrant Conduct: The Story of* Lawrence v. Texas (New York: W. W. Norton & Co., 2012).

107. *Bowers v. Hardwick*, 478 U.S. 186 (1986).

108. Quoted in Joan Biskupic, "Gay Rights Activists Seek a Supreme Court Test Case," *Washington Post*, December 19, 1993, p. A1.

109. *Romer v. Evans*, 517 U.S. 620 (1996).

110. *Lawrence v. Texas*, 539 U.S. 558 (2003).

111. *United States v. Windsor*, 570 U.S. 12 (2013); *Hollingsworth v. Perry*, 570 U.S. __ (2013).

112. From Lyndon B. Johnson, *The Vantage Point* (New York: Holt, Rinehart and Winston, 1971), p. 166.

113. The Department of Health, Education, and Welfare (HEW) was the cabinet department charged with administering most federal social programs. In 1980, when education programs were transferred to the newly created Department of Education, HEW was renamed the Department of Health and Human Services.

114. *Regents of the University of California v. Bakke*, 438 U.S. 265 (1978).

115. *Adarand Constructors, Inc. v. Peña*, 515 U.S. 200 (1995).

116. *Grutter v. Bollinger*, 539 U.S. 306 (2003).

117. *Gratz v. Bollinger*, 539 U.S. 244 (2003).

118. *Fisher v. University of Texas*, 570 U.S. __ (2013).

Chapter 5

1. Larry Bartels, *Unequal Democracy: The Political Economy of the New Gilded Age* (Princeton, NJ: Princeton University Press, 2008).

2. Emmanuel Saez, "Striking It Richer: The Evolution of the Top Incomes in the United States," September 3, 2013, http://elsa.berkeley.edy/~saez/saez-UStopincomes-2012.pdf (accessed 2/13/14).

3. Drew DeSilver, "5 Facts about Economic Inequality" Pew Research Center, January 7, 2014, www.pewresearch.org/fact-tank/2014/01/07/5-facts-about-economic-inequality (accessed 2/13/14).

4. Bruce Stokes, "The U.S.'s High Income Gap Is Met with Relatively Low Public Concern," December 6, 2013, www.pewresearch.org/fact-tank/2013/12/06/the-u-s-s-high-income-gap-is-met-with-relatively-low-public-concern (accessed 1/20/14).

5. M. Lodge and C. S. Taber, "Three Steps toward a Theory of Motivated Political Reasoning," in A. Lupia, M. McCubbins, and S. Popkin, eds., *Elements of Reason: Cognition, Choice, and the Bounds of Rationality* (London: Cambridge University Press, 2000); George E. Marcus, W. Russell Neuman, and Michael MacKuen, *Affective Intelligence and Political Judgment* (Chicago: University of Chicago Press, 2000); David Redlawsk, "Hot Cognition or Cool Consideration? Testing the Effects of Motivated Reasoning on Political Decision Making," *Journal of Politics* 64 (2002): 1021–44; David Redlawsk, Andrew Civettini, and Karen Emmerson, "The Affective Tipping Point: Do Motivated Reasoners Ever 'Get It?'" *Political Psychology* 31, no. 4 (2010).

6. Marcus, Neuman, and MacKuen, *Affective Intelligence and Political Judgment*.

7. David Redlawsk, "A Matter of Motivated 'Reasoning,'" *New York Times*, April 22, 2011, www.nytimes.com/roomfordebate/2011/04/21/barack-obama-and-the-psychology-of-the-birther-myth/a-matter-of-motivated-reasoning (accessed 3/18/14).

8. www.whitehouse.gov/sites/default/files/rss_viewer/birth-certificate-long-form.pdf (accessed 3/18/14).

9. See Karen Mossberger, Caroline Tolbert, and Ramona McNeal, *Digital Citizenship: The Internet, Society and Participation* (Cambridge, MA: MIT Press, 2008).

10. See Harry Holloway and John George, *Public Opinion* (New York: St. Martin's, 1986). See also Paul R. Abramson, *Political Attitudes in America* (San Francisco: Freeman, 1983).

11. Pippa Norris, ed., *Critical Citizens: Global Support for Democratic Government* (New York: Oxford University Press, 1999); Robert Putnam, *Bowling Alone: The Collapse and Revival of American Community* (New York: Simon and Schuster, 2000).

12. Todd Donovan and Shaun Bowler, *Reforming the Republic: Democratic Institutions for the New America* (New York: Prentice Hall, 2004).

13. Pew Research Center for the People and the Press, "Public Trust in Government: 1958–2013," October 18, 2013, www.people-press.org/2013/10/18/trust-in-government -interactive/ (accessed 7/2/14).

14. See Angus Campbell et al., *The American Voter* (New York: Wiley, 1960), p. 147.

15. CNN Poll, 2009.

16. CBS News/*New York Times* Poll, 2008.

17. Donald Green, Bradley Palmquist, and Eric Schickler, *Partisan Hearts and Minds: Political Parties and the Social Identities of Voters* (New Haven, CT: Yale University Press, 2002).

18. See Richard Lau and David Redlawsk, *How Voters Decide: Information Processing during an Election Campaign* (New York: Cambridge University Press, 2006).

19. David S. Broder, "Partisan Gap Is at a High, Poll Finds," *Washington Post*, November 9, 2003, p. A6.

20. Jennifer A. Heerwig and Brian J. McCabe, "Education and Social Desirability Bias: The Case of a Black Presidential Candidate," *Social Science Quarterly* 90, no. 3 (2009): 674–86.

21. Raymond E. Wolfinger and Steven J. Rosenstone, *Who Votes?* (New Haven, CT: Yale University Press, 1980). See also Steven J. Rosenstone and John Mark Hansen, *Mobilization, Participation, and Democracy in America* (New York: Macmillan, 1993).

22. John R. Zaller, *The Nature and Origins of Mass Opinion* (New York: Cambridge University Press, 1992).

23. Carol Glynn et al., *Public Opinion*, 2nd ed. (Boulder, CO: Westview, 2004), p. 293. See also Michael X. Delli Carpini and Scott Keeter, *What Americans Know about Politics and Why It Matters* (New Haven, CT: Yale University Press, 1996).

24. Delli Carpini and Keeter, *What Americans Know about Politics*.

25. Adam J. Berinsky, "Assuming the Costs of War: Events, Elites and American Support for Military Conflict," *Journal of Politics* 69, no. 4 (2007): 975–97; Zaller, *Nature and Origins of Mass Opinion*.

26. Richard R. Lau and David P. Redlawsk, "Advantages and Disadvantages of Cognitive Heuristics in Political Decision Making," *American Journal of Political Science* 45 (October 2001): 951–71; Lau and Redlawsk, *How Voters Decide*.

27. For a discussion of the role of information politics, see Arthur Lupia and Matthew D. McCubbins, *The Democratic Dilemma: Can Citizens Learn What They Need to Know?* (New York: Cambridge University Press, 1998). See also Shaun Bowler and Todd Donovan, *Demanding Choices: Opinion and Voting in Direct Democracy* (Ann Arbor: University of Michigan Press, 1998). See also Samuel Popkin, *The Reasoning Voter: Communication and Persuasion in Presidential Campaigns* (Chicago: University of Chicago Press, 1991); Arthur Lupia, "Shortcuts Versus Encyclopedias: Information and Voting Behavior in California Insurance Reform Elections," *American Political Science Review* 88 (1994): 63–76; and Wendy Rahn, "The Role of Partisan Stereotypes in Information Processing about Political Candidates," *American Journal of Political Science* 37 (1993): 472–96.

28. James Druckman, Erik Petersen, and Rune Slothuus, "How Elite Partisan Polarization Affects Public Opinion Formation," *American Political Science Review* 107, no. 1 (February 2013): 57–79.

29. Nicholas Carr, *The Shallows: What the Internet Is Doing to Our Brains* (New York: W. W. Norton, 2010).

30. Bartels, *Unequal Democracy*.

31. Benjamin Ginsberg, *The American Lie: Government by the People and Other Political Fables* (Boulder, CO: Paradigm, 2007).

32. Peter Marks, "Adept in Politics and Advertising, 4 Women Shape a Campaign," *New York Times*, November 11, 2001, p. B6.

33. *Roe v. Wade*, 410 U.S. 113 (1973).

34. See Gillian Peele, *Revival and Reaction* (Oxford, UK: Clarendon, 1985). See also Connie Paige, *The Right-to-Lifers* (New York: Summit, 1983).

35. Benjamin I. Page and Robert Y. Shapiro, "Effects of Public Opinion on Policy," *American Political Science Review* 77, no.1 (1983): 175–90.

36. Page and Shapiro, "Effects of Public Opinion on Policy."

37. Pew Research Center, "Mixed Views of Economic Polices and Health Care Reform Persist," October 8, 2009, www.people-press.org/2009/10/08/mixed-views-of-economic-policies -and-health-care-reform-persist (accessed 3/18/14).

38. Christopher Wlezien, "The Public as Thermostat: Dynamics of Preferences for Spending," *American Journal of Political Science* 39, no. 4 (1995): 981–1000.

39. Malcolm E. Jewell, *Representation in State Legislatures* (Lexington: University Press of Kentucky, 1982).

40. Lawrence R. Jacobs and Robert Y. Shapiro, *Politicians Don't Pander: Political Manipulation and the Loss of Democratic Responsiveness* (Chicago: University of Chicago Press, 2000).

41. Herbert Asher, *Polling and the Public* (Washington, DC: CQ Press, 2001), p. 64.

42. Michael Kagay and Janet Elder, "Numbers Are No Problem for Pollsters, Words Are," *New York Times*, August 9, 1992, p. E6.

43. See Adam Berinsky, "The Two Faces of Public Opinion," *American Journal of Political Science* 43, no. 4 (1999): 1209–230. See also Adam Berinsky, "Political Context and the Survey Response: The Dynamics of Racial Policy Opinion," *Journal of Politics* 64, no. 2 (2002): 567–84.

44. Heerwig and McCabe, "Education and Social Desirability Bias," pp. 674–86.

45. "Dial S for Smear," *Memphis Commercial Appeal*, September 22, 1996.

46. For a discussion of the growing difficulty of persuading people to respond to surveys, see John Brehm, *Phantom Respondents* (Ann Arbor: University of Michigan Press, 1993).

47. Christopher Wlezien and Stuart Soroka, "The Relationship between Public Opinion and Policy," in Russell Dalton and Hans-Dieter Klingemann, eds. *Oxford Handbook of Political Behavior* (New York: Oxford University Press, 2009), pp. 799–817.

48. Gilens, "Inequality and Democratic Responsiveness"; Bartels, *Unequal Democracy*.

49. Ryan Claassen and Benjamin Highton, "Does Policy Debate Reduce Information Effects in Public Opinion? Analyzing the Evolution of Public Opinion on Health Care," *Journal of Politic* 68, no. 2 (2006): 410–20.

Chapter 6

1. Larry M. Bartels, *Presidential Primaries and the Dynamics of Public Choice* (Princeton, NJ: Princeton University Press, 1988).

2. David Redlawsk, Caroline Tolbert, and Todd Donovan, *Why Iowa? How Caucuses and Sequential Elections Improve the Presidential Nominating Process* (Chicago: University of Chicago Press, 2011).

3. Karen Mossberger, Caroline Tolbert, and Ramona McNeal, *Digital Citizenship: The Internet, Society and Participation* (Cambridge, MA: MIT Press, 2008). See also J. E. Katz and R. E. Rice, *Social Consequences of Internet Use: Access, Involvement, and Interaction* (Cambridge, MA: MIT Press, 2002).

4. Pew Internet and American Life, "Trend Data (Adults): What Internet Users Do Online," February 2012, http://pewinternet.org/Static-Pages/Trend-Data-(Adults) /Online-Activites-Total.aspx (accessed 6/12/12).

5. Caroline Tolbert and Ramona McNeal, "Unraveling the Effects of the Internet on Political Participation," *Political Research Quarterly* 56, no. 2 (2003): 175–85. See also Bruce Bimber, "Information and Political Engagement in America: The Search for Effects of Information Technology at the Individual Level," *Political Research Quarterly* 54 (2001): 53–67; Bruce Bimber, *Information and American Democracy: Technology in the Evolution of Political Power* (Cambridge: Cambridge University Press, 2003); and Brian S. Krueger, "Assessing the Potential of Internet Political Participation in the United States," *American Politics Research* 30 (2002): 476–98.

6. Pew Research Internet Project, "Social Media Update 2013," December 30, 2013, www.pewinternet.org/2013/12/30/social-media-update-2013 (accessed 9/2/14).

7. Julian P. Boyd et al., ed., *The Papers of Thomas Jefferson*, Princeton, NJ: Princeton University Press, http://press-pubs.uchicago.edu/founders/documents/amendl _speechs8.html (accessed 5/30/14).

8. Pew Research Center, "Amid Criticism, Support for Media's 'Watchdog' Role Stands Out," August 8, 2013, www.people-press.org/2013/08/08/amid-criticism-support-for -medias-watchdog-role-stands-out/ (accessed 4/27/14).

9. Robert McChesney and John Nichols, *The Death and Life of American Journalism: The Media Revolution That Will Begin the World Again* (New York: Nation Books, 2010).

10. Darrell West, *The Next Wave: Using Digital Technology to Further Social and Political Innovation* (Washington, DC: Brookings Institution Press, 2011).

11. Pew Research Center Publications, "State of the News Media 2010," March 15, 2010, http://pewresearch.org/pubs/1523/state-of-the-news-media-2010 (accessed 9/11/12).

12. Pew Journalism Project, "State of the News Media 2013, Overview," 2013, http://stateofthemedia.org.2013/overview-5/ (accessed 4/29/14).

13. Pew Research Center Publications, "The Internet's Broader Role in Campaign 2008," January 11, 2008, http://pewresearch.org/pubs/689/the-internets-broader-role-in -campaign-2008 and Pew Research Center Publications, "*The Daily Show*: Journalism, Satire, or Just Laughs?" May 8, 2008, http://pewresearch.org/pubs/829/the-daily-show -journalism-satire-or-just-laughs (accessed 9/11/12).

14. For a criticism of the increasing consolidation of the media, see the essays in Patricia Aufderheide et al., *Conglomerates and the Media* (New York: New York University Press, 1997).

15. West, *Next Wave*; Edward Glaeser, *Triumph of the City: How Our Greatest Invention Makes Us Richer, Smarter, Greener, Healthier, and Happier* (New York: Penguin Press, 2011).

16. Pew Internet Project, "Internet Use Over Time," 2014, www.pewinternet.org/data-trend /internet-use/internet-use-over-time/ (accessed 4/29/14).

17. Pew Internet Project, "Online Political Videos and Campaign 2012," November 2, 2012, www.pewinternet.org/2012/11/02/online-political-videos-and-campaign-2012/ (accessed 4/29/14).

18. Mossberger, Tolbert, and McNeal, *Digital Citizenship*; Brian A. Krueger, "A Comparison of Conventional and Internet Political Mobilization," *American Politics Research* 34, no. 6 (2006): 759–76.

19. Antony Wilhelm, *Digital Nation: Toward an Inclusive Information Society* (Cambridge, MA: MIT Press, 2006); P. DiMaggio, E. Hargittai, et al., "Social Implications of the Internet, *Annual Review of Sociology* 27, no. 1 (2001): 307–36.

20. Karen Mossberger, Caroline Tolbert, and Mary Stansbury, *Virtual Inequality: Beyond the Digital Divide* (Washington, DC: Georgetown University Press, 2003); Pippa Norris, *Digital Divide: Civic Engagement, Information Poverty, and the Internet Worldwide* (New York: Cambridge University Press, 2001).

21. Pew Internet Project, "Broadband Technology Fact Sheet," 2014, www.pewinternet.org/fact-sheets/broadband-technology-fact-sheet/ (accessed 4/29/14).

22. Zoe M. Oxley, "More Sources, Better Informed Public? New Media and Political Knowledge," in *iPolitics: Citizens, Elections, and Governing in the New Media Era*, ed. Richard L. Fox and Jennifer M. Ramos (Cambridge: Cambridge University Press, 2012), pp. 25–47.

23. Pew Internet Project, "Social Media Update 2013," December 30, 2013, http://www.pewinternet.org/2013/12/30/social-media-update-2013/ (accessed 4/29/14).

24. Amy Schatz, "BO, UR So Gr8: How a Young Tech Entrepreneur Translated Barack Obama into the Idiom of Facebook," *Wall Street Journal*, May 26, 2007, p. 1.

25. Tolbert and McNeal, "Unraveling the Effects of the Internet."

26. Mossberger, Tolbert, and McNeal, *Digital Citizenship*. See Richard L. Fox and Jennifer M. Ramos, eds., iPolitics: Citizens, Elections, and Governing in the New Media Era (Cambridge: Cambridge University Press, 2011).

27. W. R. Neuman, M. R. Just, and A. N. Crigler, *Common Knowledge: News and the Construction of Political Meaning* (Chicago: University of Chicago Press, 1991).

28. Cass Sunstein, Republic.com (Princeton, NJ: Princeton University Press, 2011). See also Mossberger, Tolbert, and McNeal, Digital Citizenship.

29. West, *Next Wave*; McChesney and Nichols, *Death and Life of American Journalism*.

30. Oxley, "More Sources, Better Informed Public?"

31. Doris Graber, ed., *Media Power in American Politics*, 5th ed. (Washington, DC: CQ Press, 2006).

32. Bartels, *Unequal Democracy*.

33. Shanto Iyengar and Donald R. Kinder, *News That Matters: Television and American Opinion* (Chicago: University of Chicago Press, 1987), p. 63.

34. *New York Times v. United States*, 403 U. S. 713 (1971).

35. Michael Massing, "The Press: The Enemy Within," *New York Review of Books*, December 15, 2005, p. 6.

36. *Red Lion Broadcasting Company v. Federal Communications Commission*, 395 U.S. 367 (1969).

37. UN General Assembly, "Report of the Special Rapporteur on the Promotion and Protection of the Right to Freedom of Opinion and Expression, 2011."

38. Andrew Chadwick, *Internet Politics: States, Citizens, and New Communication Technologies* (Oxford: Oxford University Press, 2006).

Chapter 7

1. Michael McDonald, United States Election Project, http://elections.gmu.edu/early_vote_2012.html (accessed 5/25/14).

2. National Conference of State Legislatures, "Absentee and Early Voting," www.ncsl.org/research/elections-and-campaigns/absentee-and-early-voting.aspx (accessed 5/24/14).

3. Michael C. Herron and Daniel A. Smith, "Race, Party, and the Consequences of Restricting Early Voting in Florida in the 2012 General Election," *Political Research Quarterly* 67, no. 3 (July 2014): 646–65.

4. Alan Greenblatt, "With Major Issues Fading, Capitol Life Lures Fewer," *Congressional Quarterly Weekly Report*, October 25, 1997, p. 2625.

5. For a discussion of third parties in the United States, see Daniel Mazmanian, *Third Parties in Presidential Elections* (Washington, DC: Brookings Institution Press, 1974).

6. Alex Isenstadt, "Tea Party Candidates Falling Short," *Politico*, March 7, 2010, www.politico.com/news/stories/0310/34041.html (accessed 3/11/10).

7. The American National Election Studies (ANES), "American National Election Study, 2008: Pre- and Post-Election Survey" (Computer file) ICPSR25383-v1, Ann Arbor, MI: Inter-university Consortium for Political and Social Research (distributor), 2009-06-10, doi:10.3886/ICPSR25383 (accessed 12/4/09).

8. Karen Mossberger, Caroline Tolbert, and Ramona McNeal, *Digital Citizenship: The Internet, Society, and Participation* (Cambridge, MA: MIT Press, 2008).

9. Pew Internet and American Life Project, "Trend Data (Adults): What Internet Users Do Online," April 2012, http://pewinternet.org/Trend-Data-%28Adults%29 /Online-Activties-Total.aspx (accessed 7/26/12).

10. Sidney Verba, Kay Lehman Schlozman, and Henry E. Brady, *Voice and Equality: Civic Voluntarism in American Politics* (Cambridge, MA: Harvard University Press, 1995).

11. For a discussion of the decline in voter turnout over time, see Ruy A. Teixeria, *The Disappearing American Voter* (Washington, DC: Brookings Institution Press, 1992). See also Michael McDonald and Samuel Popkin, "The Myth of the Vanishing Voter," *American Political Science Review* 95 (2001): 963–74; and Michael McDonald, "Voter Turnout," *United States Election Project*, http://elections.gmu.edu/voter_turnout.htm (accessed 9/14/12).

12. Robert Jackman, "Political Institutions and Voter Turnout in the Democracies," *American Political Science Review* 81 (June 1987): 420.

13. Angus Campbell, Philip E. Converse, Warren E. Miller, and Donald E. Stokes, *The American Voter* (New York: Wiley, 1960); Steven Rosenstone and John Mark Hansen, *Mobilization, Participation, and Democracy in America* (New York: Macmillan, 1993).

14. Sidney Verba and Norman H. Nie, *Participation in America: Political Democracy and Social Equality* (New York: Harper and Row, 1972).

15. Jan E. Leighley and Jonathan Nagler, "Socioeconomic Class Bias in Turnout, 1964–1988: The Voters Remain the Same," *American Political Science Review* 86, no. 3 (1992): 725–36.

16. Rosenstone and Hansen, *Mobilization, Participation, and Democracy in America*, p. 59.

17. Michael P. McDonald and John Samples, eds., *The Marketplace of Democracy: Electoral Competition and American Politics* (Washington, DC: Brookings Institution Press, 2006).

18. Mark N. Franklin, "Electoral Participation," in *Comparing Democracies: Elections and Voting in Global Perspective*, ed. Lawrence LeDuc, Richard G. Niemi, and Pippa Norris (Thousand Oaks, CA: Sage, 1996), 216–35; G. Bingham Powell, "American Voter Turnout in Comparative Perspective," *American Political Science Review* 80, no. 1 (1986): 17–43.

19. National Conference of State Legislatures, "Voter Identification Requirements," www.ncsl.org/research/elections-and-campaigns/voter-id.aspx (accessed 5/24/14).

20. Matt Barreto, Stephen Nuño, and Gabriel Sanchez, "The Disproportionate Impact of Voter-ID Requirements on the Electorate—New Evidence from Indiana," *PS: Political Science & Politics* 42 (2009): 111–16.

21. See Morris Fiorina, "Parties and Partisanship: A Forty Year Retrospective," *Political Behavior* 24, no. 2 (June 2002): 93–115.

22. On the limited polarization among ordinary voters, see Morris P. Fiorina, with Samuel J. Abrams and Jeremy C. Pope, *Culture War? The Myth of a Polarized America* (New York: Pearson Longman, 2004); on growing partisan attachment among a subset of voters, see Alan Abramowitz and Kyle Saunders, "Why Can't We Just Get Along? The Reality of a Polarized America," *The Forum* 3, no. 2 (2005): 1–22.

23. *League of United Latin American Citizens v. Wilson*, CV-94-7569 (C.D. Calif. 1995); Adam Nagourney, "Court Strikes Down Ban on Gay Marriage in California," *New York Times*, February 7, 2012, www.nytimes.com/2012/02/08/us/marriage-ban-violates -constitution-court-rules.html (accessed 8/21/12).

24. Daron Shaw, *The Race to 270: The Electoral College and the Campaign Strategies of 2000 and 2004* (Chicago: University of Chicago Press, 2006).

25. State legislatures determine the system by which electors are selected. Almost all states use this "winner-take-all" system. Maine and Nebraska, however, provide that one electoral vote goes to the winner in each congressional district and two electoral votes go to the winner statewide.

26. Russ Choma, "Money Won on Tuesday, but Rules of the Game Changed," Center for Responsive Politics, www.opensecrets.org/news/2014/11/money-won-on-tuesday-but-rules-of-the-game-changed/ (accessed 11/6/14).

27. Michael Luo and Jeff Zeleny, "Straining to Reach Money Goal, Obama Presses Donors," *New York Times*, September 9, 2008, p.1; Nichols Confessore and Jo McGinty, "Obama, Romney and Their Parties on Track to Raise $2 Billion," *New York Times*, October 25, 2012, www.nytimes.com/2012/10/26/us/politics/obama-and-romney-raise-1-billion-each.html (accessed July 4, 2014).

28. *McCutcheon et al. v. Federal Election Commission*, 572 U.S. __ (2014).

29. *Citizens United v. Federal Election Commission*, 558 U.S. 50 (2010).

30. *McCutcheon et al. v. Federal Election Commission*.

31. *Buckley v. Valeo*, 424 U.S. 1 (1976).

Chapter 8

1. Alexander Hamilton, James Madison, and John Jay, *The Federalist Papers*, ed. Clinton L. Rossiter (New York: New American Library, 1961), no. 10, p. 83.

2. *The Federalist Papers*, no. 10.

3. The best statement of the pluralist view is in David Truman, *The Governmental Process* (New York: Knopf, 1951), chap. 2.

4. Baumgartner, Frank, Jeffery M. Berry, Beth L. Leech, David C. Kimball, and Marie Hojnacki, *Lobbying and Policy Change: Who Wins, Who Loses and Why* (Chicago: University of Chicago Press, 2009).

5. Baumgartner et al., *Lobbying and Policy Change*.

6. Erika Falk, Erin Grizard, and Gordon McDonald, "Legislative Issue Advertising in the 108th Congress: Pluralism or Peril?" *Harvard International Journal of Press/Politics* 11, no. 4 (Fall 2006): 148–64, http://hij.sagepub.com/cgi/reprint/11/4/148 (accessed 3/2/08).

7. Betsy Wagner and David Bowermaster, "B.S. Economics," *Washington Monthly*, November 1992, pp. 19–21.

8. David Truman, *The Governmental Process* (New York: Knopf, 1951).

9. For an exploration of lower-class interest groups and social movements, see Frances Piven and Richard Cloward, *Poor People's Movements* (New York: Vintage, 1978).

10. E. E. Schattschneider, *The Semisovereign People: A Realist's View of Democracy in America* (New York: Holt, Rinehart and Winston, 1960).

11. Kay Lehman Schlozman and John T. Tierney, *Organized Interests and American Democracy* (New York: Harper and Row, 1986), p. 60.

12. Clay Shirky, *Here Comes Everybody: The Power of Organizing without Organizations* (New York: Penguin, 2008).

13. Mancur Olson, *The Logic of Collective Action* (Cambridge, MA: Harvard University Press, 1965).

14. John Herbers, "Special Interests Gaining Power as Voter Disillusionment Grows," *New York Times*, November 14, 1978.

15. For discussions of lobbying, see Allan J. Cigler and Burdett A. Loomis, eds., *Interest Group Politics* (Washington, DC: CQ Press, 1983). See also Jeffrey M. Berry, *Lobbying for the People* (Princeton, NJ: Princeton University Press, 1977).

16. David Kirkpatrick, "Congress Finds Ways of Avoiding Lobbyist Limits," *Washington Post*, February 11, 2007, p. 1.

17. *Brown v. Board of Education of Topeka, Kansas*, 347 U.S. 483 (1954).

18. *Roe v. Wade*, 410 U.S. 113 (1973).

19. *Webster v. Reproductive Health Services*, 492 U.S. 490 (1989).

20. Julia Preston, "Grass Roots Roared and Immigration Bill Collapsed," *New York Times*, June 10, 2007, p. 1.

21. *Citizens United v. Federal Election Commission*, 558 U.S. 50 (2010).

22. Center for Responsive Politics, "2014 Outside Spending, by SuperPAC," www.opensecrets .org/outsidespending/summ.php?cycle=2014&chrt=V&disp=O&type=S (accessed 11/12/14).

23. Elisabeth R. Gerber, *The Populist Paradox* (Princeton, NJ: Princeton University Press, 1999), p. 6.

24. Olson, *The Logic of Collective Action*.

Chapter 9

1. Associated Press, "Milk Prices Could Rise if Farm Bill Looms," *Washington Post* (December 5, 2013), www.washingtonpost.com/politics/federal_government /boehner-floats-farm-bill-extension/2013/12/05/ce3510ce-5dd0-11e3-8d24 -31c016b976b2_story.html (accessed 12/10/13).

2. Mildred Amer and Jennifer E. Manning, *Membership of the 112th Congress: A Profile*, Congressional Research Service 7-5700, September 20, 2011, p. 2, http://fpc.state.gov /documents/organization/174246.pdf (accessed 1/23/12).

3. Marian D. Irish and James Prothro, *The Politics of American Democracy*, 5th ed. (Englewood Cliffs, NJ: Prentice Hall, 1971), p. 352.

4. For some interesting empirical evidence, see Angus Campbell, Philip Converse, Warren Miller, and Donald Stokes, *Elections and the Political Order* (New York: Wiley, 1966), chap. 11.

5. Congressional Management Foundation, *Communicating with Congress: How Citizen Advocacy Is Changing Mail Operations on Capitol Hill*, Partnership for a More Perfect Union at the Congressional Management Foundation, Washington, DC, 2011, http://congressfoundation.org/storage/documents/CMF_Pubs/cwc-mail-operations.pdf (accessed 1/23/12).

6. John S. Saloma, *Congress and the New Politics* (Boston: Little, Brown, 1969), pp. 184–5. A 1977 official report using less detailed categories came up with almost the same impression of Congress's workload. Commission on Administrative Review, *Administrative Reorganization and Legislative Management*, House Doc. #95-232 (September 28, 1977), vol. 2, especially pp. 17–19.

7. Ballotpedia, United States Congress Elections, 2012, http://ballotpedia.org/United _States_Congress_elections,_2012 (accessed 4/17/14). Data for 2014 are based on *Roll Call*, "Casualty List," www.rollcall.com/politics/casualtylist.html (accessed 11/6/14), and NPR, "Incumbents Who Lost Seats Tonight," www.npr.org/blogs/itsallpolitics /2014/11/04/361486490/incumbents-who-lost-seats-tonight (accessed 11/6/14).

8. See Barbara C. Burrell, *A Woman's Place Is in the House: Campaigning for Congress in the Feminist Era* (Ann Arbor: University of Michigan Press, 1994); and David Broder, "Key to Women's Political Parity: Running," *Washington Post*, September 8, 1994, p. A17.

9. Congressional Quarterly, *Guide to the Congress of the United States*, 2nd ed. (Washington, DC: CQ Press, 1976), pp. 229–310.

10. Pew Research Center, "The 2010 Congressional Reapportionment and Latinos," www .pewhispanic.org/2011/01/05/the-2010-congressional-reapportionment-and-latinos (accessed 2/24/14).

11. "Did Redistricting Sink the Democrats?" *National Journal*, December 17, 1994, p. 2984.

12. *Miller v. Johnson*, 515 U.S. 900 (1995).

13. Bernie Becker, "Reapportionment Roundup," *New York Times*, December 24, 2009, http://thecaucus.blogs.nytimes.com/2009/12/24/reapportionment-roundup/ (accessed 1/31/10).

14. L. Paige Whitaker, "Congressional Redistricting and the Voting Rights Act: A Legal Overview," Congressional Research Service, August 30, 2013, www.fas.org/sgp/crs /misc/R42482.pdf (accessed 12/2/13).

15. Chris Cillizza, "What the Supreme Court's Voting Rights Act Decision Means for Politics," *Washington Post*, June 25, 2013, www.washingtonpost.com/blogs/the-fix/wp/2013/06/25/what-the-voting-rights-act-decision-means-for-politics (accessed 12/2/13).

16. Tom Hamburger and Richard Simon, "Everybody Will Know If It's Pork," *Los Angeles Times*, January 6, 2007, p. A1.

17. Speaker of the House John Boehner, "House Repulicans Renew Earmark Ban for 113th Congress," November 16, 2012, www.speaker.gov/general/house-republicans-renew-earmark-ban-113th-congress (accessed 12/1/13).

18. David Clarke, "Earmarks: Here to Stay or Facing Extinction?" *Congressional Quarterly (CQ) Weekly*, March 16, 2009, p. 613. Jared Allen, "Lawmakers Pushing for Earmark Reform Think Obama Boosted Their Chances," *The Hill*, January 30, 2010, http://thehill.com/homenews/house/78869-lawmakers-think-obama-boosted-earmark-reform (accessed 1/31/10); David S. Fallis, Scott Higham, and Kimberly Kindy, "Congressional Earmarks Sometimes Used to Fund Projects Near Lawmakers' Properties," *Washington Post*, February 6, 2012, p. 1.

19. Congressman Pete Stark, "Constituent Services: Federal Grants," www.house.gov/stark/webarchives/Stark%20Web%20Pa ge/services/grants.html (accessed 3/5/08).

20. Associated Press, "Congress Passes Rare Private Immigration Bills," December 15, 2010, www.aolnews.com/2010/12/15/congress-passes-rare-private-immigration-bills (accessed 2/1/12).

21. Faith Karimi, "Obama Signs Bill to Grant Nigerian Student U.S. Permanent Residency," CNN, December 29, 2012, www.cnn.com/2012/12/29/world/africa/us-nigerian-obama-law/ (accessed 11/30/13).

22. Richard Fenno, Jr., *Home Style: House Members in Their Districts* (Boston: Little, Brown, 1978).

23. Edward Epstein "Dusting Off Deliberation," CQ *Weekly*, June 14, 2010, pp. 1436–442; Sarah Binder, "Where Have All the Conference Committees Gone?" *The Monkey Cage* (blog) December 21, 2011, themonkeycage.org/blog/2011/12/21/where-have-all-the-conference-committees-gone (accessed 2/7/12).

24. Rebecca Kimitch, "CQ Guide to the Committees: Democrats Opt to Spread the Power," *Congressional Quarterly Weekly*, April 16, 2007, p. 1080.

25. U.S. Senate, Senate Action on Cloture Motions, www.senate.gov/pagelayout/reference/cloture_motions/clotureCounts.htm (accessed 4/17/14).

26. Carl Hulse and David M. Herszenhorn, "Defiant House Rejects Huge Bailout; Next Step Is Uncertain," *New York Times*, September 29, 2008, www.nytimes.com/2008/09/30/business/30cong.html?pagewanted=1&_r=1 (accessed 02/04/2010); Reuters, "House Passes Bailout, Focus Shifts to Fallout," October 3, 2008, www.reuters.com/article/idUSTRE49267J20081003 (accessed 2/4/10).

27. See John W. Kingdon, *Congressmen's Voting Decisions* (New York: Harper & Row, 1973), chap. 3; and R. Douglas Arnold, *The Logic of Congressional Action* (New Haven, CT: Yale University Press, 1990).

28. Daniel Franklin, "Tommy Boggs and the Death of Health Care Reform," *Washington Monthly*, April 1995, p. 36.

29. Dan Eggen, "SuperPACs Target Congressional Races," *Washington Post*, January 29, 2012, www.washingtonpost.com/politics/super-pacs-target-congressional-races/2012/01/26/gIQAyRfnaQ_story.html (accessed 2/9/12).

30. Holly Idelson, "Signs Point to Greater Loyalty on Both Sides of the Aisle," *Congressional Quarterly Weekly Report*, December 19, 1992, p. 3849.

31. "Vote Studies 2013," in Graphics, CQ.com, media.cq.com/votestudies/ (accessed 3/17/14).

32. Alexander Bolton, "DeMint's Leadership PAC Battles Leaders in Fight for the Future of Senate GOP Caucus," *The Hill*, August 4, 2011, http://thehill.com/homenews/senate/175397 -demints-leadership-pac-battles-leaders-in-fight-for-future-of-senate (accessed 1/23/12); for a list of leadership PACs, see the Open Secrets website, www.opensecrets.org/industries /indus.php?Ind=Q03 (accessed 1/23/12).

33. Robert Draper, "How Kevin McCarthy Wrangles the Tea Party in Washington," *New York Times*, July 13, 2011, www.nytimes.com/2011/07/17/magazine/how-kevin-mccarthy -wrangles-the-tea-party.html?pagewanted=all (accessed 2/1/12).

34. Frank Newport, "Congressional Approval Sinks to Record Low," Gallup Politics www .gallup.com/poll/165809/congressional-approval-sinks-record-low.aspx (accessed 4/17/14).

35. Susan Davis, "Congress Hits New Productivity Lows," *USA Today*, November 30, 2013, www.usatoday.com/story/news/politics/2013/11/30/unproductive-congress-record -low/3691993/ (accessed 11/30/13); Dan Roberts, "Gridlocked Congress on Track for Least Productive Year in History," *The Guardian*, December 3, 2013, www.theguardian.com /world/2013/dec/03/congress-least-productive-year-partisan-tensions (accessed 12/12/13); but see also, Pew Research Center, Drew DeSilver, "Current Congress Is Not the Least Productive in Recent History, but Close," www.pewresearch.org/fact-tank/2013/09/03/current -congress-is-not-the-least-productive-in-recent-history-but-close/ (accessed 12/12/13).

36. Jonathan Weisman and Jeremy Peters, "Government Shuts Down in Budget Impasse," *New York Times*, October 1, 2013, www.nytimes.com/2013/10/01/us/politics/congress -shutdown-debate.html (accessed 12/1/13).

37. Caren Bohan and Rachelle Younglai, "Boehner Warns against Shutting U.S. Government Over 'Obamacare,'" *Reuters*, August 23, 2013, www.reuters.com/article/2013/08/23 /us-usa-healthcare-republicans-idUSBRE97L15120130823 (accessed 12/1/13).

38. Jonathan Weisman and Ashley Parker, "Republicans Back Down, Ending Crisis Over Shutdown and Debt Limit," *New York Times*, October 16, 2013, www.nytimes. com/2013/10/17/us/congress-budget-debate.html (accessed 12/1/13).

39. Rasmussen Reports, "New High: 48% Say Most Members of Congress Are Corrupt," December 31, 2011, www.rasmussenreports.com/public_content/politics/general_politics /december_2011/new_high_48_say_most_members_of_congress_are_corrupt (accessed 2/10/12).

40. *Citizens United v. Federal Election Commission*, 558 U.S. 50 (2010).

41. See Geoffrey C. Layman, Thomas M. Carsey, and Juliana Menasce Horowitz, "Party Polarization in American Politics: Characteristics, Causes, and Consequences,"*Annual Reivew of Political Science*, no. 9 (2006): 83–110.

42. John Stanton and Daniel Newhowser, "House GOP Uses Retreat to Lay 2012 Plans," *The Hill*, January 23, 2012, www.rollcall.com/issues/57_82/house_gop_uses_retreat_lay_2012 _plans-211670-1.html (accessed 2/9/12).

43. Carroll J. Doherty, "Impeachment: How It Would Work," *Congressional Quarterly Weekly Report*, January 31, 1998, p. 222.

Chapter 10

1. These statutes are contained mainly in Title 10 of the United States Code, Sections 331, 332, and 333.

2. Dan Slater, "Bush Pardon Party Goes Out with a Whimper," *Wall Street Journal*, January 20, 2009, http://blogs.wsj.com (accessed 3/20/10).

3. In *United States v. Pink*, 315 U.S. 203 (1942), the Supreme Court confirmed that an executive agreement is the legal equivalent of a treaty, despite the absence of Senate approval. This case approved the executive agreement that was used to establish diplomatic relations with the Soviet Union in 1933. An executive agreement, not a

treaty, was used in 1940 to exchange "50 overage destroyers" for 99-year leases on some important military bases.

4. For a different perspective, see William F. Grover, *The President as Prisoner: A Structural Critique of the Carter and Reagan Years* (Albany: State University of New York Press, 1988).

5. There is a third source of presidential power implied from the provision for "faithful execution of the laws." This is the president's power to impound funds—that is, to refuse to spend money Congress has appropriated for certain purposes. One author referred to this as a "retroactive veto power" (Robert E. Goosetree, "The Power of the President to Impound Appropriated Funds," *American University Law Review* [January 1962]). Many modern presidents used this impoundment power freely and to considerable effect, and Congress has occasionally delegated such power to the president by statute. But in reaction to the Watergate scandal, Congress adopted the Budget and Impoundment Control Act of 1974, which was designed to circumscribe the president's ability to impound funds by requiring that the president spend all appropriated funds unless both houses of Congress consented to an impoundment within 45 days of a presidential request. Therefore, since 1974, the use of impoundment has declined significantly. Presidents have either had to bite their tongues and accept unwanted appropriations or had to revert to the older and more dependable but politically limited method of vetoing the entire bill.

6. For more on the veto, see Robert J. Spitzer, *The Presidential Veto: Touchstone of the American Presidency* (Albany: State University of New York Press, 1988).

7. Henry C. Black, *Black's Law Dictionary*, 6th ed (St. Paul, MN: West Publishing Co., 1991), p. 539.

8. James G. Randall, *Constitutional Problems under Lincoln* (New York: Appleton, 1926), chap. 1.

9. Edward S. Corwin, *The President: Office and Powers*, 4th rev. ed. (New York: New York University Press, 1957), p. 229.

10. A substantial portion of this section is taken from Theodore J. Lowi, *The Personal President* (Ithaca, NY: Cornell University Press, 1985), pp. 141–50.

11. All the figures since 1967, and probably 1957, are understated, because additional White House staff members were on "detail" service from the military and other departments (some secretly assigned) and are not counted here because they were not on the White House payroll.

12. Article I, Section 3, provides that "The Vice-President . . . shall be President of the Senate, but shall have no Vote, unless they be equally divided." This is the only vote the vice president is allowed.

13. David Ignatius, "A Skeptical Biden's Role," RealClearPolitics.com, November 26, 2009, www.realclearpolitics.com (accessed 4/14/10).

14. Samuel Kernell, *Going Public: New Strategies of Presidential Leadership*, 3rd ed. (Washington, DC: Congressional Quarterly Press, 1997); also, Jeffrey K. Tulis, *The Rhetorical Presidency* (Princeton, NJ: Princeton University Press, 1987).

15. Tulis, *The Rhetorical Presidency*, p. 91.

16. Sidney M. Milkis, *The President and the Parties* (New York: Oxford University Press, 1993), p. 97.

17. James MacGregor Burns, *Roosevelt: The Lion and the Fox* (New York: Harcourt, Brace, 1956), p. 317.

18. Kernell, *Going Public*, p. 79.

19. Claire Cain Miller, "How Obama's Internet Campaign Changed Politics," *New York Times*, November 7, 2008; David Plouffe, *The Audacity to Win: The Inside Story and Lessons of Barack Obama's Historic Victory* (New York: Penguin Group Publishers, 2009).

20. Gallup, www.gallup.com/poll/124922/presidential-approval-center.aspx (accessed 3/14/14).
21. Lowi, *The Personal President*.
22. Lowi, *The Personal President*, p. 11.
23. Harold W. Stanley and Richard G. Niemi, *Vital Statistics on American Politics, 2001–2002* (Washington, DC: Congressional Quarterly Press, 2001), pp. 250–51.
24. Milkis, *The President and the Parties*, p. 128.
25. Milkis, *The President and the Parties*, p. 160.
26. The classic critique of this process is Theodore J. Lowi, *The End of Liberalism* (New York: W. W. Norton, 1969).
27. Kenneth Culp Davis, *Administrative Law Treatise* (St. Paul, MN: West Publishing, 1958), p. 9.
28. John M. Broder, "Powerful Shaper of U.S. Rules Quits, with Critics in Wake," *New York Times*, August 4, 2012, p. A1.
29. A complete inventory is provided in Harold C. Relyea, "Presidential Directives: Background and Review," Congressional Research Service Report 98–611 (Washington, DC: Library of Congress, November 9, 2001).
30. Terry M. Moe and William G. Howell, "The Presidential Power of Unilateral Action," *Journal of Law, Economics and Organization* 15, no. 1 (January 1999): 133–34.
31. *Youngstown Sheet & Tube Co. v. Sawyer*, 346 U.S. 579 (1952).
32. Peter Baker, "Obama Is Making Plans to Use Executive Power for Action on Several Fronts," *New York Times*, February 13, 2010, p. A12.
33. Mark Killenbeck, "A Matter of Mere Approval: The Role of the President in the Creation of Legislative History," *University of Arkansas Law Review* 239, no. 48 (1995).
34. Philip Cooper, *By Order of the President* (Lawrence: University Press of Kansas, 2002), p. 201.
35. Edward S. Corwin, *The President: Office and Powers*, 4th rev. ed. (New York: New York University Press, 1957), p. 283.
36. Cooper, *By Order of the President*, p. 201.
37. Cooper, *By Order of the President*, p. 216.
38. Robert J. Spitzer, "Comparing the Constitutional Presidencies of George W. Bush and Barack Obama: War Powers, Signing Statements, Vetoes," White House Studies 12 (October 2013): 125–46.

Chapter 11

1. Linda Greenhouse, "Justices Say E.P.A. Has Power to Act on Harmful Gases," *New York Times*, April 3, 2007, www.nytimes.com (accessed 2/15/10).
2. Environmental Protection Agency, "Endangerment and Cause or Contribute Findings for Greenhouse Gases under the Clean Air Act," http://epa.gov (accessed 2/16/10).
3. John M. Broder, "U.S. Issues Limits on Greenhouse Gas Emissions from Cars," *New York Times*, April 2, 2010, p. 81.
4. Juliet Eilperin, "EPA Needed More Data before Ruling on Greenhouse Gas Emissions, Report Says," *Washington Post*, September 28, 2011, www.washingtonpost.com/national/health-science/epa-needed-more-data-before-ruling-on-greenhouse-gas-emissions-report-says/2011/09/28/gIQABs2X5K_story.html (accessed 1/2/12).
5. Jerry Hirsch, "Hyundai, Kia Reach $400-Million Settlement over Inflated MPG Claims," *Los Angeles Times*, December 23, 2013, articles.latimes.com/2013/dec/23/autos/la-fi-hy-hyundai-kia-settle-mpg-lawsuit-20131223 (accessed 1/20/14).
6. Quoted in Leonard D. White, *The Republican Era* (New York: Free Press, 1958), p. 6.
7. "Obama's Health Care Speech to Congress," New York Times, September 9, 2009, www.nytimes.com (accessed 2/10/10).

8. Office of Personnel and Management, "Comparison of Total Civilian Employment of the Federal Government by Branch, Agency, and Area as of June 2012 and September 2012," Table 2, www.opm.gov/policy-data-oversight/data-analysis-documentation/federal -employment-reports/employment-trends-data/2012/september/table-2/; Defense Manpower Data Center, "Active Duty Military Personnel by Service by Rank/Grade," www.dmdc.osd.mil/appj/dwp/reports.do?category-reports&subCat-milActDutReg (accessed 1/20/14).

9. U.S. Census Bureau, "Government Employment and Payroll," www2.census.gov/govs /apes/11stlus.txt (accessed 1/20/14); Bureau of Labor Statistics, "Employment Status of the Civilian Noninstitutional Population, 1940s to Date," Table 1, www.bls.gov /opub/ee/2013/cps/annavg1_2012.pdf (accessed 1/20/14).

10. There are historical reasons that American cabinet-level administrators are called "secretaries." During the Second Continental Congress and the subsequent confed-eral government, standing committees were formed to deal with executive functions related to foreign affairs, military and maritime issues, and public financing. The heads of those committees were called "secretaries" because their primary task was to handle all correspondence and documentation related to their areas of responsibility.

11. Environmental Protection Agency, "Understanding the Safe Drinking Water Act," August 2009, water.epa.gov/lawsregs/guidance/sdwa/upload/2009_08_28_sdwa_ fs_30ann_sdwa_web.pdf (accessed 1/20/14).

12. For more detail, consult John E. Harr, *The Professional Diplomat* (Princeton, NJ: Princeton University Press, 1972), 11; and Nicholas Horrock, "The CIA Has Neighbors in the 'Intel-ligence Community,'" *New York Times*, June 29, 1975, sec. 4, p. 2. See also Roger Hilsman, *The Politics of Policy Making in Defense and Foreign Affairs*, 3rd ed. (Englewood Cliffs, NJ: Prentice Hall, 1993).

13. Daniel Patrick Moynihan, "The Culture of Secrecy," *Public Interest* (Summer 1997): 55–71.

14. Charlie Savage, "Obama Curbs Secrecy of Classified Documents," *New York Times*, December 30, 2009, p. A19. See the comprehensive evaluation in Citizens for Responsibil-ity and Ethics in Washington, OpenTheGovernment.org, "Measuring Transparency under the FOIA: The Real Story Behind the Numbers," December 2011, http://crew.3cdn.net /5911487fbaaa8cb0f8_9xm6bgari.pdf (accessed 1/3/12).

15. Louise Osborne, "Europeans Outraged over NSA Spying, Threaten Action," *USA Today*, October 29, 2013, www.usatoday,com/story/news/world/2013/10/28/report -nsa-spain/3284609/ (accessed 1/24/14).

16. U.S. Department of the Treasury, "The Debt to the Penny and Who Holds It," www .treasurydirect.gov/NP/BPDLogin?application=np (accessed 2/18/10).

17. For an account of the Financial Stability Oversight Council and the passage of the Dodd-Frank financial regulatory legislation, see John T. Woolley and J. Nicholas Ziegler, "The Two-Tiered Politics of Financial Reform in the United States," in Renate Mayntz, ed., *Crisis and Control: Institutional Change in Financial Market Regulation* (Frankfurt: Campus/MPIfG, 2012); the council's early activities are described in Financial Stability Oversight Council, Annual Report 2011, www.treasury.gov/initiatives/fsoc/Documents /FSOCAR2011.pdf, and in Edward V. Murphy and Michael B. Bernier, "Financial Stabil-ity Oversight Council: A Framework to Mitigate Systemic Risk" (Washington, DC: Congressional Research Service, November 15, 2011), www.llsdc.org/attachments /wysiwyg/544/CRS-R42083.pdf (accessed 1/3/12).

18. George E. Berkley, *The Craft of Public Administration* (Boston: Allyn and Bacon, 1975), p. 417.

19. Alexander Hamilton, James Madison, and John Jay, *The Federalist Papers*, ed. Clinton Rossiter (New York: New American Library, 1961), no. 51, p. 322.

20. The title of this section was inspired by Peri Arnold, *Making the Managerial Presidency* (Princeton, NJ: Princeton University Press, 1986).

21. For more details and evaluations, see David Rosenbloom, *Public Administration* (New York: Random House, 1986), pp. 186–221; Charles H. Levine and Rosslyn Kleeman, "The Quiet Crisis in the American Public Service," in *Agenda for Excellence: Public Service in America*, ed. Patricia Ingraham and Donald Kettl (Chatham, NJ: Chatham House, 1992); and Patricia Ingraham and David Rosenbloom, "The State of Merit in the Federal Government," in *Agenda for Excellence*.

22. Lester Salamon and Alan Abramson, "Governance: The Politics of Retrenchment," in *The Reagan Record*, ed. John Palmer and Isabel Sawhill (Cambridge, MA: Ballinger, 1984), p. 40.

23. Colin Campbell, "The White House and the Presidency under the 'Let's Deal' President," in *The Bush Presidency: First Appraisals*, ed. Colin Campbell and Bert A. Rockman (Chatham, NJ: Chatham House, 1991), pp. 185–222.

24. See National Partnership for Reinventing Government, http://govinfo.library.unt.edu/npr/index.htm (accessed 9/10/08).

25. Thomas E. Mann and Norman J. Ornstein, *The Broken Branch: How Congress Is Failing America and How to Get It Back on Track* (New York: Oxford University Press, 2006), p. 155.

26. The Office of Technology Assessment (OTA) was a fourth research agency serving Congress until 1995. It was one of the first agencies scheduled for elimination by the 104th Congress. Until 1983, Congress had still another tool of legislative oversight: the legislative veto. Agencies were obliged to submit to Congress every proposed decision or rule, which would then lie before both chambers for 30 to 60 days. If Congress took no action by a one-house or two-house resolution explicitly to veto the proposed measure during the prescribed period, the measure became law. In 1983 the Supreme Court declared the legislative veto unconstitutional on the grounds that it violated the separation of powers—that is the resolutions Congress passed to exercise its veto were not subject to presidential veto, as required by the Constitution. See *Immigration and Naturalization Service v. Chadha*, 462 U.S. 919 (1983).

Chapter 12

1. *Morse v. Frederick*, 551 U.S. 393 (2007).

2. Charles Lane, "Court Backs School on Speech Curbs," *Washington Post*, June 26, 2007, p. A6.

3. Judicial Business of the United States Courts, "Annual Report of the Director 2013," www.uscourts.gov/Statistics/JudicialBusiness/2013.aspx (accessed 5/20/14).

4. Michael A. Fletcher, "Obama Criticized as Too Cautious on Judicial Posts," *Washington Post*, October 15, 2009, www.washingtonpost.com/wp-dyn/content/article/2009/10/15/AR2009101504083.html (accessed 3/1/10).

5. Russell Wheeler, "Judicial Nominations and Confirmations after Three Years—Where Do Things Stand?" Governance Studies at Brookings, January 13, 2012; "Judicial Vacancies," United States Courts, www.uscourts.gov/JudgesAndJudgeships/JudicialVacancies.aspx (accessed 6/27/12).

6. *Arizona v. United States*, 567 U.S. ___ (2012).

7. *National Federation of Independent Business v. Sebelius*, 567 U.S. ___ (2012).

8. Peter Wallsten and Richard Simon, "Sotomayor Nomination Splits GOP," *Los Angeles Times*, May 27, 2009, http://articles.latimes.com (accessed 11/12/09).

9. C. Herman Pritchett, *The American Constitution* (New York: McGraw-Hill, 1959), p. 138.

10. *Marbury v. Madison*, 1 Cr. 137 (1803).

11. *National Federation of Independent Business v. Sebelius*, 567 U.S. ___ (2012).

12. U.S. Government Printing Office, "Acts of Congress Held Unconstitutional In Whole or In Part by the Supreme Court of the United States," www.gpo.gov/fdsys/pkg /GPO-CONAN-2013/pdf/GPO-CONAN-2013-11.pdf (accessed 4/20/14).

13. *Federal Election Commission v. Wisconsin Right to Life*, 551 U.S. 449 (2007); *Citizens United v. Federal Election Commission*, 558 U.S. 310 (2010); *McCutcheon v. Federal Election Commission*, 572 U.S. __ (2014).

14. *Hamdi v. Rumsfeld*, 542 U.S. 507 (2004).

15. *Hamdan v. Rumsfeld*, 548 U.S. 557 (2006).

16. *Boumediene v. Bush*, 553 U.S. 723 (2008).

17. The Supreme Court affirmed this review power in *Martin v. Hunter's Lessee*, 1 Wheat. 304 (1816).

18. *Brown v. Board of Education*, 347 U.S. 483 (1954).

19. *Lawrence v. Texas*, 539 U.S. 558 (2003).

20. *Miranda v. Arizona*, 384 U.S. 436 (1966).

21. *United States v. Jones*, 567 U.S. __ (2012).

22. *Miller v. Alabama*, 567 U.S. __ (2012).

23. Robert Scigliano, *The Supreme Court and the Presidency* (New York: Free Press, 1971), 161. For an interesting critique of the solicitor general's role during the Reagan administration, see Lincoln Caplan, "Annals of the Law," *New Yorker*, August 17, 1987, 30–62.

24. Edward Lazarus, *Closed Chambers* (New York: Times Books, 1998), p. 6.

25. *Smith v. Allwright*, 321 U.S. 649 (1994).

26. Charles Krauthammer, "Why Roberts Did It," *Washington Post*, June 29, 2012, www.washingtonpost.com/opinions/charles-krauthammer-why-roberts-did-it /2012/06/28/gJQA4X0g9V_stroy. html (accessed 4/22/14).

27. *Roe v. Wade*, 410 U.S. 113 (1973); *Griswold v. Connecticut*, 381 U.S. 479 (1965).

28. Adam Liptak, "For Justices, Free Speech Often Means 'Speech I Agree With,'" *New York Times*, May 6, 2014, p. A15.

29. Alexander Hamilton, James Madison, and John Jay, *The Federalist Papers*, ed. Clinton Rossiter (New York: New American Library, 1961), no. 10, p. 78.

Chapter 13

1. Henry J. Kaiser Family Foundation, "Health Tracking Poll: Exploring the Public's Views on the Affordable Care Act (ACA)," http://kff.org/interactive/health-tracking-poll -exploring-the-publics-views-on-the-affordable-care-act-aca/ (accessed 5/12/14).

2. *Cato Handbook for Policymakers*, 7th ed. (Washington, DC: Cato Institute, 2009), p. 281, www.cato.org (accessed 3/19/10).

3. James Dao, "The Nation; Big Bucks Trip Up the Lean New Army," *New York Times*, February 10, 2002, sec. 4, p. 5.

4. For an evaluation of the policy of withholding subsidies to carry out desegregation laws, see Gary Orfield, *Must We Bus?* (Washington, DC: Brookings Institution Press, 1978). For an evaluation of the use of subsidies to encourage work or to calm political unrest, see Frances Fox Piven and Richard Cloward, *Regulating the Poor: The Functions of Public Welfare* (New York: Random House, 1971).

5. For an evaluation of the politics of eminent domain, see Theodore J. Lowi and Benjamin Ginsberg, *Poliscide* (New York: Macmillan, 1976), p. 235 and *passim*, and especially chaps. 11 and 12, written by Julia and Thomas Vitullo-Martin.

6. Federal Reserve Board, *Selected Interest Rates*, www.federalreserve.gov/releases/h15/ (accessed 6/6/14).

7. Ronald Reagan, Inaugural Address, January 20, 1981, www.reaganfoundation.org/pdf /Inaugural_Address_012081.pdf (accessed 4/27/14).

8. Gallup, Taxes, www.gallup.com/poll/1714/taxes.aspx (accessed 4/27/14).

9. Gallup, Taxes, www.gallup.com/poll/1714/taxes.aspx (accessed 4/27/14).

10. Social Security Online, "Contribution and Benefit Base," www.ssa.gov/OACT/COLA/cbb.html (accessed 6/11/10).

11. Liz Schott and Zachary Levinson, "TANF Benefits Are Low and Have Not Kept Pace with Inflation," Washington, DC: Center on Budget and Policy Priorities, November 24, 2008, www.cbpp.org (accessed 3/11/10).

12. U.S. Department of Health and Social Services, Administration for Children and Families, LIHEAP Clearinghouse, *2010 HHS Poverty Guidelines*, www.liheap.ncat.org/profiles/povertytables/FY2012/popstate.htm (accessed 2/19/12).

13. See Martin Gilens, *Why Americans Hate Welfare* (Chicago: University of Chicago Press, 1999), chaps. 3, 4.

14. Gilens, *Why Americans Hate Welfare*.

15. U.S. Department of Health and Social Services, Administration for Children and Families, "TANF Total Number of Recipients, Fiscal Year 2009," www.acf.hhs.gov (accessed 3/12/10).

16. Center for Law and Social Policy, "Analysis of Fiscal Year 2006 TANF and MOE Spending by States," http://clasp.org (accessed 4/9/08).

17. See the discussion of the law and the data presented in House Ways and Means Committee Print, WMCP: 106-14, 2000 Green Book, Section 7, Temporary Assistance for Needy Families (TANF), http://frwebgate.access.gpo.gov (accessed 3/26/08); Rebecca M. Blank, "Evaluating Welfare Reform in the United States," *Journal of Economic Literature* 40 (December 2002): 1105–66.

18. Center for Budget and Policy Priorities, "Chartbook: SNAP Helps Struggling Families Put Food on the Table," April 18, 2012, www.cbpp.org/cms/?fa=view&id=3744#part5 (accessed 7/9/12); U.S. Department of Agriculture, Food and Nutrition Service, Supplemental Nutrition Assistance Program, ww.fns.usda.gov/pd/34SNAPmonthly.htm (accessed 5/3/14).

19. There were a couple of minor precedents. One was the Smith-Hughes Act of 1917, which made federal funds available to the states for vocational education at the elementary and secondary levels. Second, the Lanham Act of 1940 made federal funds available to schools in "federally impacted areas," that is, areas with an unusually large number of government employees and/or where the local tax base was reduced by large amounts of government-owned property.

20. See the critique in Raegen T. Miller and Cynthia G. Brown, *Bitter Pill, Better Formula: Toward a Single, Fair, and Equitable Formula for ESEA Title I, Part A* (Washington, DC: Center for American Progress, February 2010), www.americanprogress.org/wp_content/uploads/issues/2010/02/pdf/bitter_pill.pdf (accessed 5/11/14).

21. David K. Cohen and Susan L. Moffitt, *The Ordeal of Equality: Did Federal Regulation Fix the Schools* (Cambridge, MA: Harvard University Press, 2009).

22. Rich Motoko, "No Child' Law Whittled Down by White House," *New York Times*, July 6, 2012, p. A1; U.S. Department of Education, Elementary and Secondary Education, ESEA Flexibility, www2.ed.gov/policy/elsec/guid/esea-flexibility/index.html (accessed 5/11/14).

23. For a positive view of the standards, see Sonja Brookins Santelises, "Abandoning the Common Core Is Taking the Easy Way Out," The Equity Line, http://theequityline.org/wp/2014/03/31/abandoning-the-common-core-is-taking-the-easy-way-out/ (accessed 5/11/14). For a critique, see Valerie Strauss, "The Coming Common Core Melt-down," *Washington Post*, January 23, 2014, www.washingtonpost.com/blogs/answer-sheet/wp/2014/01/23/the-coming-common-core-meltdown/ (accessed 5/11/14).

24. Sam Dillon, "Obama Proposes Sweeping Change in Education Law," *New York Times*, March 14, 2010, p. A1; Veronica DeVore, " ' Race to the Top' Education Funds Awarded to 9 States and D.C.," August 24, 2010, www.pbs.org/newshour/rundown/2010/08/round-two-results-announced-for-race-to-the-top.html (accessed 11/13/12).

25. Elaine Weiss, "Mismatches in Race to the Top Limit Educational Improvement: Lack of Time, Resources, and Tools to Address Opportunity Gaps Puts Lofty State Goals Out of Reach," www.boldapproach.org/report (accessed 5/11/14).

26. Morton Keller, *Affairs of State: Public Life in Nineteenth Century America* (Cambridge, MA: Belknap Press of Harvard University Press, 1977), p. 500.

27. Henry J. Kaiser Family Foundation, "U.S. Federal Funding for HIV/AIDS: The President's FY 2014 Budget Request," January 22, 2014, http://kaiserfamilyfoundation.files .wordpress.com/2014/01/7029-09-u-s-federal-funding-for-hivaids-the-presidents-fy -2014-budget-request.pdf (accessed 5/10/14).

28. White House, "Fact Sheet: Affordable Care Act by the Numbers," www.whitehouse.gov /the-press-office/2014/04/17/fact-sheet-affordable-care-act-numbers (accessed 5/12/14).

29. Henry J. Kaiser Family Foundation, "Health Tracking Poll: Exploring the Public's Views on the Affordable Care Act (ACA)," http://kff.org/interactive/health-tracking-poll -exploring-the-publics-views-on-the-affordable-care-act-aca/ (accessed 5/12/14).

30. *National Federation of Independent Business v. Sebelius*, 567 U.S. __ (2012).

31. White House, "Fact Sheet: Affordable Care Act by the Numbers," http://whitehouse .gov/the-press-office/2014/04/17/fact-sheet-affordable-care-act-numbers (accessed 5/12/14).

32. John E. Schwarz, *America's Hidden Success*, 2nd ed. (New York: W.W. Norton, 1988), pp. 41–42.

33. Peter Dreier, Saqib Bhatti, Rob Call, Alex Schwartz, and Gregory Squires, *Underwater America: How the So-Called Housing "Recovery" Is Bypassing Many American Communities*, (Berkeley, CA: Haas Institute for a Fair and Inclusive Society, 2014), p. 8.

34. U.S. Census Bureau, "Historical Poverty Tables," Table 2: Poverty Status, by Family Relationship, Race, and Hispanic Origin and Table 3: Poverty Status, by Age, Race and Hispanic Origin, www.census.gov/hhes/www/poverty/data/historical/people.html (accessed 4/29/14).

35. See, for example, Theodore R. Marmor, Jerry L. Mashaw, and Philip L. Harvey, *America's Misunderstood Welfare State* (New York: Basic Books, 1990), p. 156; U.S. Census Bureau, Historical Poverty Tables, "Table 2. Poverty Status, by Family Relationship, Race, and Hispanic Origin" and "Table 3. Poverty Status, by Age, Race and Hispanic Origin," www.census.gov/hhes/www/poverty/data/historical/people.html (accessed 4/29/14).

36. Frederick R. Lynch, "How AARP Can Get Its Groove Back," *New York Times*, June 23, 2011, www.nytimes.com/2011/06/24/opinion/24lynch.html (accessed 2/20/12), and "Influence and Lobbying: AARP Lobbyists, 2011," www.opensecrets.org/lobby /clientlbs.php?id=D000023726&year=2011 (accessed 2/20/12). Although AARP is the largest and the strongest organization of the elderly, other groups, such as the Alliance for Retired Americans, to which many retired union members belong, also lobby Congress on behalf of the elderly.

37. Christopher Howard, *The Hidden Welfare State: Tax Expenditures and Social Policy in the United States* (Princeton, NJ: Princeton University Press, 1999); Jacob S. Hacker, *The Divided Welfare State: The Battle over Public and Private Benefits in the United States* (New York: Cambridge University Press, 2002).

38. Center on Budget and Policy Priorities, "Policy Basics: Introduction to the Supplemental Nutrition Assistance Program (SNAP)," March 19, 2014, www.centeronbudget.org /cms/index.cfm?fa=view&id=2226 (accessed 5/12/14).

39. "Panera CEO: On Food Stamps, I Can't Eat in My Own Restaurant," September 25, 2013, http://eatocracy.cnn.com/2013/09/25/panera-ceo-on-food-stamps-i-cant-eat-in-my-own-restaurant/ (accessed 5/12/14).

40. Raymond Hernandez, "Federal Welfare Overhaul Allows Albany to Shift Money Elsewhere," *New York Times*, April 23, 2000, p. 1.

41. U.S. Department of Agriculture, Food and Nutrition Service, Supplemental Nutrition Assistance Program, www.fns.usda.gov/pd/34SNAPmonthly.htmwww.fns.usda .gov/snap/ (accessed 5/12/14).

42. Carmen DeNavas-Walt, Bernadette D. Proctor, and Jessica C. Smith, "Income Poverty and Health Insurance Coverage in the United States," U.S. Census Bureau, September 2013, www.census.gov/prod/2013pubs/p60-245 (accessed 5/12/14).

43. L. Free and Hadley Cantril, *The Political Beliefs of Americans* (New York: Simon and Schuster, 1968).

44. Fay Lomax Cook and Edith Barrett, *Support for the American Welfare State* (New York: Columbia University Press, 1992); and Hugh Heclo, "The Political Foundations of Anti-poverty Policy," in *Fighting Poverty*, ed. Sheldon H. Danziger and Daniel H. Weinberg (Cambridge, MA: Harvard University Press, 1986), pp. 312–40.

45. Henry J. Kaiser Family Foundation, Health Care Costs: A Primer, http://kaiserfamily foundation.files.wordpress.com/2013/01/7670-03.pdf (accessed 5/12/14).

Chapter 14

1. Geoffrey Perret, *A Country Made by War* (New York: Random House, 1989), p. 558.

2. Stockholm International Peace Research Institute, "Trends in World Military Expenditure, 2013," http://books.sipri.org/files/FS/SIPRIFS1404.pdf (accessed 6/12/14).

3. Rupert Smith, *The Utility of Force: The Art of War in the Modern World* (New York: Vintage, 2008).

4. D. Robert Worley, *Shaping U.S. Military Forces: Revolution or Relevance in a Post–Cold War World* (Westport, CT: Praeger Security International, 2006).

5. Matthew Crenson and Benjamin Ginsberg, *Presidential Power: Unchecked and Unbalanced* (New York: W. W. Norton, 2007).

6. Benjamin Ginsberg, *The American Lie: Government by the People and Other Political Fables* (Boulder, CO: Paradigm, 2007).

7. Paul R. Pillar, *Terrorism and American Foreign Policy* (Washington, DC: Brookings Institution Press, 2003).

8. One confirmation of this is found in Theodore Lowi, *The End of Liberalism: The Second Republic of the United States*, 2nd ed. (New York: W.W. Norton, 1979), pp. 127–30; another is found in Stephen Krasner, "Are Bureaucracies Important?" *Foreign Policy* 7 (Summer 1972): 159–79. However, it should be noted that Krasner was writing his article in disagreement with Graham T. Allison, "Conceptual Models and the Cuban Missile Crisis," *American Political Science Review* 63, no. 3 (September 1969): 689–718.

9. Paul E. Peterson, "The President's Dominance in Foreign Policy Making," *Political Science Quarterly* 109, no. 2 (Summer 1994): 232.

10. Hans Morgenthau, *Politics among Nations*, 2nd ed. (New York: Knopf, 1956), p. 505.

11. See Theodore Lowi, *The Personal President: Power Invested, Promise Unfulfilled* (Ithaca, NY: Cornell University Press, 1985), pp. 167–69.

12. For information on current U.S. sanctions programs, visit U.S. Department of the Trea-sury, "Sanctions Programs and Country Information," www.treasury.gov/resource-center /sanctions/Programs/Pages/Programs.aspx (accessed 6/11/14).

13. George Quester, *The Continuing Problem of International Politics* (Hinsdale, IL: Dryden Press, 1974), p. 229.

14. The Warsaw Pact was signed in 1955 by Albania, Bulgaria, Czechoslovakia, Hungary, the German Democratic Republic (East Germany), Poland, Romania, and the Soviet Union. Albania later dropped out. The Warsaw Pact was terminated in 1991.

answer key

Chapter 1
1. b
2. d
3. a
4. d
5. c
6. d
7. b
8. a
9. a
10. d
11. e
12. e
13. a
14. b

Chapter 2
1. a
2. b
3. b
4. c
5. c
6. e
7. d
8. e
9. e
10. a
11. d
12. a

Chapter 3
1. b
2. c
3. c
4. e
5. a
6. a
7. b
8. a
9. b

10. d
11. b
12. d

Chapter 4
1. e
2. b
3. a
4. e
5. e
6. d
7. a
8. c
9. b
10. b
11. d
12. b

Chapter 5
1. c
2. e
3. b
4. d
5. b
6. e
7. c
8. a
9. b
10. a
11. b

Chapter 6
1. b
2. a
3. b
4. e
5. d
6. b
7. e
8. b

9. c
10. c
11. b
12. b

Chapter 7
1. a
2. a
3. c
4. e
5. d
6. e
7. d
8. a
9. d
10. d
11. c

Chapter 8
1. a
2. b
3. c
4. d
5. c
6. b
7. a
8. e
9. d
10. a
11. e
12. c

Chapter 9
1. d
2. a
3. b
4. b
5. a
6. b

7. a
8. a
9. e
10. c
11. a
12. a

Chapter 10
1. b
2. d
3. b
4. c
5. b
6. b
7. e
8. c
9. a
10. c
11. b
12. a

Chapter 11
1. b
2. b
3. b
4. d
5. e
6. c
7. d
8. a
9. d
10. d
11. a
12. d

Chapter 12
1. a
2. c
3. e

4. a

5. d

6. e

7. a

8. b

9. b

10. a

11. c

12. c

Chapter 13

1. e

2. c

3. d

4. d

5. d

6. b

7. c

8. a

9. e

10. d

11. c

12. c

Chapter 14

1. b

2. d

3. b

4. c

5. e

6. c

7. e

8. a

9. c

10. d

11. b

photo credits

Chapter 1:p. 2: JG Photography/Alamy; p. 8: JOHN ANGELILLO/UPI/Landov; p. 10: studentaid.edu; p. 22: AP Photo. Chapter 2: p. 28: Art Resource, NY; p. 33: Granger Collection; p. 34: Kena Betancur/Getty Images; p. 37: Granger Collection; p. 40: Library Company of Philadelphia; p. 51: AP Photo/Susan Walsh. Chapter 3: p. 62: Peter Dasilva/The New York Times/REDUX; p. 67 (top): © STEPHEN D. CANNERELLI/Syracuse Newspapers/The Image Works; p. 67 (bottom): Joshua Roberts/Bloomberg via Getty Images; p. 68: AP Photo/Charles Rex Arbogast, File; p. 74: © Richard Nowitz/National Geographic Society/Corbis; p. 76: © Bettmann/CORBIS; p. 81: AP Photo; p. 84: AP Photo/Charles Dharapak. Chapter 4: p. 92: Robert Nickelsberg/Getty Images; p. 99: AP Photo; p. 103: AP Photo/Rick Bowmer; p. 104: Clay Good/Zuma Press; p. 110: AP Photo; p. 114: AP Photo; p. 116: UPI/Kevin Dietsch/ Newscom; p. 118: Credit N/A; p. 123: © Bob Daemmrich/Alamy; p. 126: Bettmann/ Corbis; p. 128: JOSHUA LOTT/The New York Times/Redux; p. 131 (left): DON EMMERT/AFP/Getty Images; p. 131 (right): AP Photo/Richard Drew; p. 133: Signe Wilkinson Editorial Cartoon © 2003 Signe Wilkinson. Chapter 5: p. 140: Scott Olson/ Getty Images; p. 144: Bob Daemmrich/Alamy; p. 149: JAY JANNER/MCT/Landov; p. 154 (both): William B. Plowman/NBC/NBC NewsWire via Getty Images; p. 160: Bill Watterson; p. 164: Bettmann/Corbis. Chapter 6: p. 172: Sara D. Davis/Getty Images; p. 177: © Bernhard Classen/age footstock; p. 180: Nick Suydam/Alamy; p. 184: Jasna Hodzic/The California Aggie/EPA/Newscom; p. 188 (top): WANG CHENGYUN/ Xinhua/Landov; p. 188 (bottom): HANDOUT/Reuters/Landov; p. 190: Jack Plunkett/ Invision/AP; p. 192: Shannon Stapleton/Reuters/Corbis. Chapter 7:p. 198: Hill Street Studios/Getty Images; p. 202: AP Photo/Bozeman Daily Chronicle, Adrian Sanchez-Gonzalez; p. 208: Granger Collection; p. 216: Xinhua/eyevine/Redux; p. 219: Marc Piscotty/Getty Images; p. 223: Daniel Acker/Bloomberg via Getty Images; p. 227: AP Photo/Charles Dharapak; p. 235: © Jay Mallin/ZUMA Press/Corbis. Chapter 8:p. 242: Courtesy Stefanie Penn Spear/ecowatch.org; p. 246: Alamy; p. 249: Rex Features via AP Images; p. 253: © Jeff Greenberg 2 of 6/Alamy; p. 257: Ron Sachs/Pool/CNP/ Corbis; p. 263: cartoonstock.com. Chapter 9:p. 270: JIM BOURG/Reuters/Landov; p. 276: JOE SKIPPER/Reuters/Landov; p. 280: AP Photo/Ross D. Franklin; p. 285: Alex Wong/Getty Images; p. 288: Scott J. Ferrell/Congressional Quarterly/Getty Images; p. 293: STAFF/Reuters/Landov; p. 299: Drew Angerer/Getty Images. Chapter 10: p. 310: JIM YOUNG/Reuters/Landov; p. 313 (left): AP Photo/Tim Roske; p. 313 (right): Chip Somodevilla/Getty Images; p. 315: JAMES NIELSEN/AFP/Getty Images; p. 320 (top): LUCY NICHOLSON/Reuters/Landov; p. 320 (bottom): AP Photo/U.S. Consumer Product Safety Commission; p. 326: Conrad Schmidt/AFP/Getty Images; p. 328: Bettmann/Corbis; p. 331: Craig F. Walker/The Denver Post via Getty Images; p. 333: JEWEL SAMAD/AFP/Getty Images. Chapter 11: p. 340: Craig F. Walker/The Denver Post via Getty Images; p. 343: John Moore/Getty Images; p. 351: Richard T. Nowitz/ Science Source; p. 356: FOIA.gov; p. 360: CBS/courtesy Everett Collection; p. 361:

Douglas Graham/CQ Roll Call/Newscom. **Chapter 12: p. 368:** © Melvyn Longhurst /Alamy; **p. 371:** AP Photo; **p. 379:** AP Photo/Pablo Martinez Monsivais, File; **p. 383:** AP Photo; **p. 392:** AP Photo/The Decatur Daily, Clyde Stancil; **p. 393:** Chip Somodevilla/ Getty Images. **Chapter 13: p. 400:** AP Photo; **p. 408:** Scull/BloombergNews/Landov; **p. 412:** Joseph Barnell/SuperStock; **p. 416:** Jim West imageBROKER/Newscom; **p. 419:** Chip Somodevilla/Getty Images; **p. 425:** © Jim West/Alamy. **Chapter 14: p. 436:** U.S. Navy photo by Mass Communication Specialist Seaman Kyle D. Gahlau; **p. 441:** AP Photo; **p. 450:** BAY ISMOYO/AFP/Getty Images; **p. 452:** AP Photo; **p. 454:** BAY ISMOYO/AFP/GettyImages.

index

Agriculture, Department of, 348
AIDS, 420
Aid to Dependent Children (ADC), 428–29
Aid to Families with Dependent Children (AFDC), 414, 428, 429
Air America, 178
Alabama
    and comity clause, 68
    immigration law in, 129
    Montgomery bus boycott, 121
    sentences for juveniles in, 384
Alabama syndrome, 77–78
Alaska
    earmark for bridge in, 282
    employment discrimination in, 68
    TANF benefits in, 414
al-Assad, Bashar, 443
Alien and Sedition Acts, 102
Alito, Samuel, 379
ambassadors, 354, 446, 448
amendments to the Constitution, 53–56; see also Bill of Rights
    as "higher law," 54, 56
    list of, 55
    methods for creating, 53, 54
    process for amending, 45–46
    proposed, 53
American Civil Liberties Union (ACLU), 107, 387–88
American Federation of Teachers (AFT), 246
American Gas Association, 243
American population
    changes over time in, 13–18
    political knowledge of, 153–55
American Recovery and Reinvestment Act (ARRA), 85, 417, 419–20
American Revolution (1776), 11
    and balance of power among states, 35–36
    forces contributing to, 31–32
Americans for Balanced Energy Choices, 261
Americans with Disabilities Act of 1990 (ADA), 83, 130
amicus curiae, 387, 388
Amish, 101
Amnesty International, 450, 450
Amtrak, 348
Andrus, Ethel Percy, 253

Annapolis Convention, 36–37
Anonymous (grassroots organization), 261–62
Antifederalists
    and bill of rights, 95, 96
    Federalists vs., 49
    and ratification of Constitution, 48–49, 51–53
appeals, filing, 374
appeasement, 440
appellant, 374
appellate courts, 376–77
appointments, political, 345, 378–80
apportionment, 279–82
appropriations, 300
Arab Spring; see also individual countries
arbitration, 457
Arizona
    illegal aliens law in, 379
    immigration law in, 84, 84–85, 129
    and 2010 reapportionment, 280
Arizona v. United States, 84, 85
Arkansas, 316, 384
ARPA (Advanced Research Projects Agency), 341
ARRA. See American Recovery and Reinvestment Act
Article III (U.S. Constitution), 375, 384
Articles of Confederation, 35–37, 42
ASFT (American Federation of Teachers), 246
Ashcroft, John, 379
Asian Americans
    civil rights of, 128–29
    as proportion of population, 15, 16
Asians, ban on naturalization of, 15
assembly, freedom of, 103, 104
Associated Press, 178
attitudes
    about politics, 143–48
    defined, 143
    political, 143
authoritarian systems, 11
automobile emission standards, 344

B
Bakke, Allan, 132–33
Bakke case, 132–33
balance of powers, 41–47, 48
ballot initiatives, 13, 224–25, 263–64
ballots, bilingual, 123

CEA (Council of Economic Advisers), 325

cell phones, 183, 216

censorship, 105

Central Intelligence Agency (CIA), 190, 315, 348, 439, 447, 448

Chamber of Commerce v. Environmental Protection Agency, 389

charter schools, 419

checks and balances, 41, 46–47, *48*

Cheney, Dick, 326, 329

Chicago Teachers Unions, *246*

chief justice, 377

children, poverty among, 428–29

Children's Defense Fund, 429

China, 446, 453; *see also* People's Republic of China

Chinese Exclusion Act of 1882, 15

Christian Broadcasting Network (CBN), 157

Christian Coalition, 247, 450

Christian right, 450

Christian Science Monitor, 177

Christie, Chris, 189

CIA. *See* Central Intelligence Agency

Citadel, 127

cities
direct legislation in, 13
home rule for, 69

citizen interest groups, 247

citizen journalism, 183–84, 193

citizens
civil liberties as protection for, 96
critical, 148
digital. *See* digital citizens
naturalized, 15

Citizens for Asbestos Reform, 261

Citizens for Better Medicare, 261

Citizens for the American Way, 388

citizenship, 7–10
for African Americans, 15
digital. *See* digital citizenship
of President Obama, 144
and political knowledge, 153–55

Citizens United v. Federal Election Commission, 102, 233, 263

Civil Aeronautics Act, 78

civil cases, 372

civil law, 372

civil libertarians, 369–70

civil liberties, 93–117
Bill of Rights, 93, 95–96
defined, 93
and Doctrine of Incorporation, 96–97, *98*
due process of law, 110–15
freedom of religion, 99–101
freedom of speech and of the press, 101–8
global view of, 117
as protection against government, 96
right to own a gun, 108–10
right to privacy, 115–16

civil penalties, 406

civil rights, *92*, 118–33
and affirmative action, 132–34
defined, 93–94
for disabled Americans, 130
gender equality, 125–28
and immigration laws, 128–29
for language minorities, 128
for Native Americans, 129
and New Deal coalition, 209
as protection by government, 118
racial equality, 118–25
and sexual orientation, 130–31
Supreme Court cases related to, 383–84

Civil Rights Act of 1875, 119

Civil Rights Act of 1964, 122, 125, 127

civil rights movement
after *Brown v. Board of Education*, 120–21
goals of, 94
and school segregation, 120
Southern Manifesto, 76

Civil Service Act of 1883, 345

civil service reform, 358–59

Civil Service Reform Act of 1978, 359

Civil War, 207

Clausewitz, Carl von, 455

Clay, Henry, 226

Clean Air Act, 344

clear and present danger, 102

Clear Channel Communications, 179

Cleveland, Grover, 226

climate change, *331*

unfunded mandates of, 80
waning powers of, 335
Congressional Black Caucus, *274*
Congressional Budget Office (CBO), 362
Congressional Hispanic Caucus, *299*
Congressional Quarterly, 183
Congressional Research Service (CRS), 362
Connecticut, 115–16
Connecticut Compromise, 39
consent of the governed, 355
conservatism, 146, 392, 393, 430
conservatives, 83
constituency(-ies)
　of branches of government, 46–47
　of Congress, 276–77
　and congressional decision making, 293
　defined, 273
　interventions for, 283
constituents, *293*
Constitution, U.S.
　Amendments to, 53–56
　Annapolis Convention, 36–37
　Articles of Confederation vs., *42*
　balance of powers in, 41–47, *48*
　difficulties in changing, 29–30
　election rights in, 202
　expressed powers from, 314–20
　foreign policy provisions of, *449*
　future of, 56
　original jurisdiction in, 375
　as plan for the country, 29
　power of the presidency in, 313–23
　powers of president in, 446
　preamble of, 18
　ratification of, 46, 48–49, 51–53
　rights in, *95*
　and weakness of Articles of Confederation, 36
Constitutional Amendments, 53–56
Constitutional Convention of 1787, *28*, 37–41
constitutional democracies, 11
constitutional government, 11
Consumer Financial Protection Bureau, 350
Consumer Product Safety Commission, 320, 420
containment, 440

Continental Congress
　First, 34
　Second, 34, 35
contract cases, 372
contracting power, 405
contributory programs, 413–14, 424
control, public policy as means of, 403–11, *404*
convenience, of new media, 185
cooperative federalism, *77*, 77–78
Copenhagen Climate Summit, 444
Corzine, Jon, 234
cost-of-living adjustments (COLAs), 414
Council of Chief State School Officers, 419
Council of Economic Advisers (CEA), 325
Council on Environmental Quality, 325
counsel, right to, 113–14
court cases, 371–72
Courtney, Joe, 279
court packing, 378
court-related rights, 111–13
courts, *373*
　and balance of values, 21
　interest groups' use of, 259–60
　state, 372–74
courts of appeals, 373
Covered California, 422
Crawford, William H., 226
criminal cases, 371–72
criminal justice system, 68
criminal laws, 71
criminally accused, due process for, 110–15
"critical citizens," 148
CRS (Congressional Research Service), 362
cruel and unusual punishment, 114–15
Cuban missile crisis, 440
Cunningham, Randy "Duke," 283
currency, of new media, 185
cyberporn, 106–7

D
Daily Show, The, 178
Darfur region, 455
Daschle, Linda, 258
Daschle, Tom, 258, 295
Davie, William R., 41

International Bank for Reconstruction and Development (World Bank), 453
international benefits, U.S. foreign policy for, 444–46
International Convention on the Elimination of All Forms of Racial Discrimination, 444
International Court of Justice, 457
International Covenant on Civil and Political Rights, 444
international environmental policy, 444
international human rights policy, 444
International Monetary Fund (IMF), 453
international monetary structure, 453
international peacekeeping efforts, 444–46, 452
International Religious Freedom Act, 444
Internet; *see also* social media
    access to, *180*, 192
    affect of, on information consumption, 154
    and Affordable Care Act, 422
    attempts to regulate content of, 191–92
    cyberporn on, 106–7
    and elections, 174
    "going public" on, 329
    and interest group participation, 254
    and interest groups, 255
    and libel laws, 106
    as news source, 175, 179–80
    online news, 181–85
    and organization of interest groups, 250
    and political news, 182
    political participation on, 215–16
    politics changed by, 235
    politics on, 166
    public opinion surveys on, 162
interstate commerce, 72–73, 122–23
Interstate Commerce Commission, 348
intervention, of government, 409, 411
Iowa, 173, 199, 228
Iran, 441, 442, 443, 447, 454
Iraq War, 189–90, 321
    aftermath of, 457
    and Americans' mistrust of government, 5
    costs of, 347
    end of, 447

    as preventive war, 441, *441*
    service members in, 437
Ireland, 450
iron triangle, 258, *259*, 351, *353*
IRS (Internal Revenue Service), 356–58
IRS Restructuring and Reform Act of 1998, 358
ISIS (Islamic State in Iraq and Syria), 443, 447
isolationism, 439, 440
Israel, 50, 447, 450, 454
Italy, 457

J
Jackson, Andrew, 205, 226
Jackson, Robert H., 390
Japan, 79, 349, 446
Jay, John, 49
JCS (Joint Chiefs of Staff), 447
Jefferson, Thomas
    and bill of rights, 95, 96
    and Declaration of Independence, 34
    election of 1800, 226
    and Locke's work, 31
    on newspapers, 175
    and separation of church and state, 99–100
Jeffersonian Republicans, 204–5, 211
Jehovah's Witnesses, 100
Jewish Americans, 16, 450
Jewish immigrants, 14
Johnson, Andrew, 316–17, 327–28
Johnson, Lyndon
    and affirmative action, 132
    election of 1964, 209
    executive order of, 332
    public relations strategy of, 328
    as vice president, 325
Joint Chiefs of Staff (JCS), 447
joint committees, 286–87
judges
    appointed to federal courts, 378–80
    for district courts, 375
    federal, 378–80
    Supreme Court justices, 45, 370, *377*, 377–78, *379*
judicial branch, 44–45
judicial powers, of the president, 316–17
judicial restraint, 391–92

and political power relations, 186–92
and public opinion, 158, 187–89
regulation of, 191–92
rise of new media, 179–86
traditional, 175–79
Medicaid, 414
as categorical grant, 74
expansion of, 80–81, 421–23
middle class benefits from, 426
for the nonworking poor, 428
oversight of, 350
spending on, *421*
medical marijuana, 63, 83–84
Medicare, 413–14
AARP's lobbying for, 426
contributions for, 413–14
oversight of, 350
senior citizens' benefits from, 425–26
spending on, *421*
Meese, Edwin, 332
Meet the Press (tv show), *154*
Meetup.com, 216
Megaupload, 192
membership associations, 251
merit system, 345
Merit Systems Protection Board
(MSPB), 359
Mexican War, 448–49
Mexico, 79, 443
Michigan, 133
middle class, 424, 426–27
Middle East peace deal, 447
military
draft, 437
expressed powers of, 315–16
and foreign policy, 448
gays in, 131
and national security, 439–43
Military Commissions Act, 382, 383
military contracting, 405
military force, 455, 457
military spending, *436*, *442*, 456, *456*
militias, 108
Milkis, Sidney, 328
Miller, Evan, *392*
Miller, Judith, 105
Miller v. Johnson, 281–82
"ministerial exception," 101
Minnesota, 420
minorities, poverty among, 428–29
minority leader, 185

minority party, 203
minority rights, majority rule with, 21
Miranda, Ernesto, 112–13
Miranda rule, 113, 384
Miranda v. Arizona, 384
Mississippi
child care block grant in, 82
TANF benefits in, 414
Missouri, 119
mixed regime, 46–47
mobilization
and political participation, 218
by presidents, 327–29
of public opinion, 260–62
via social media, 185
of voters, 199–200
monetary agencies, 357
monetary policies, 407–8
monetary structure, international,
453
money, in politics, 236
Monroe, James, 439
Monroe Doctrine, 439
Montesquieu, Baron de la Brède et de,
31, 46
Montgomery bus boycott, 121
Montreal Protocol, 444
Morgenthau, Hans, 451
Mormonism, 227
Morse v. Frederick, 105, 369–70
mortgage crisis, 125, 424
mortgage interest tax exemption,
426–27
MSNBC, 177
MSN Latino, 178
MSPB (Merit Systems Protection
Board), 359
multiracial Americans, 15
Murdoch, Rupert, 179
Muslim, 16
mutual defense alliances, 455
Myanmar, 354, 454

N
NAACP. *See* National Association for
the Advancement of Colored
People
Nader, Ralph, 212, 250, 255
NAFTA (North American Free Trade
Agreement), 443
Narwhal (voter files), 203

personal freedom, 18–19; *see also* liberty

Personal Responsibility and Work Opportunity Reconciliation Act (PRWORA), 416

Peterson, Erik, 154

petition(s)
    freedom of, 103, 104
    right of, 257

Pew Research Center, 148, 165

philosophy, political, 31

physician-assisted suicide, 116

PIPA. *See* Protect Intellectual Property Act

plaintiff, 371, 372

Plame, Valerie, 105

plea bargains, 374

Plessy, Homer, 119

Plessy v. Ferguson, *118*, 118–19

pluralism, 245

pluralist views, 245

pocket veto, 292, 318

polarization
    of Congress, 299–300
    of politics, 153–54

police dogs, 111

police power, 66, 73

police regulation, 406

political action committees (PACs)
    and campaign finance laws, 178
    campaign funding from, 231–33
    defined, 245
    as interest group strategy, 262–63
    interest groups vs., 245
    leadership, 296
    purpose of, 201
    super PACs, 233–34, 263, 294

political appointments, 345

political campaigns. *See* election campaigns

political efficacy, 7

political environment
    as agent of political socialization, 152
    and political participation, 218

political equality, 19

political ideologies, 146–47, *147*
    conservatism, 146
    liberalism, 146
    of Supreme Court, 392–94

political knowledge
    for citizenship, 7–8
    shaping public opinion, 153–55, *156*

political mobilization, 185; *see also* mobilization

political news, 182

political participation
    and candidate characteristics, 223–24
    by citizens, 7–8
    electoral process, 224–26
    expansion of, 12–13
    forms of, 215
    issues in, 222–23
    online, 215–16, *216*
    and online news, 180, 181
    and party loyalty, 221–22
    and strength of democracy, 155
    through digital citizenship, 8, 10
    by voting, 215, 216, 218–19

political parties, 201–13, *214*
    congressional organization by, 285
    defined, 201
    development of, 201
    and electoral realignments, 211
    functions of, 201–4
    identification with, *210*, *214*
    party loyalty, 221–22
    and political orientation, 151–52
    presidents supported by, 327
    psychological ties to, 213, *214*
    purpose of, 200
    third parties, 212–13
    two-party system, 204–11

political philosophy, 31

political socialization, 148–52

political speech, 102–3

political system, urban areas representation in, 17

political values, 143–45
    and demographic changes, 22
    in future, 21–22

politicians, Americans' suspicions of, 5

Politico, 183

politics
    colonial, 31–32
    defined, 13
    electoral, 262–64
    goal of, 13
    and government, 13
    importance of media in, 175
    institutions of, 12
    on Internet, 166

Project Protect, 247
property rights, 97, 110–11; *see also*
    private property
proportional representation, 213
Protestants
    and abortion, 157
    immigrants as, 14
    as proportion of Americans, 15, 16
protests, 260–61, 261–62
PRWORA (Personal Responsibility and
    Work Opportunity Reconciliation
    Act), 416
public accommodations, 122
Public Broadcasting System (PBS), 177
public health, 420–23
public housing, 423–24
public interest groups, 247
public opinion, 141–66
    defined, 143
    in a democracy, 166
    disapproval of Congress, 298, 299,
        301
    and dominant political ideologies,
        146–47, *147*
    on economic inequality, 141–42
    on economy, 159
    on the environment, 159
    and foreign policy, 450
    and government policies, 158, 160
    government's influence on, 155,
        157–60, 189
    on health care, *140*
    interest groups' mobilization of,
        260–62
    measuring, 160–66
    media's influence on, 155, 157–60,
        187–89
    political knowledge shaping, 153–55,
        156
    political socialization shaping,
        148–52
    representing attitudes about politics,
        143–48
    shared political values, 144–45
    stability in, *156*
    on taxes, *140*
public-opinion polls, 160–66
    design and wording of, 162, *163*
    on economic inequality, 141
    inaccurate results of, 162–66
    samples for, 161, 162

public policy, 403; *see also* domestic
    policy; foreign policy
    gender and opinions about, *151*
    implementation of, 344–45
    as techniques of control, 403–11, *404*
public-relations strategies, 328
public school students, speech by, *104*,
    104–5
public-sector groups, 247
purposive benefits (interest groups),
    252, *252*
push polling, 165
Putin, Vladimir, 447

Q
Qaddafi, Mu'ammar, 321, 323, 447

R
race, and redistricting, 280–82
Race to the Top program, 419–20
racial classifications in population, 15
racial discrimination
    and death-penalty cases, 115
    in employment, 123
    in housing, 124–25
    post–World War II, 119–20
    school segregation, 120–21
racial equality, 118–25
racial immigration criteria, 14–15
racial segregation, 77
    in public accommodations, 121–22
    in schools, 120–22
    and Southern Manifesto, 76
racism, 149, *150*, 151
radio news, 175, 177–79
Randolph, Edmund, 38, 41
random digit dialing, 161
ratification of the Constitution, 46,
    48–49, 51–53
Reagan, Ronald
    bureaucracy under, 362
    fiscal policy of, 411
    on government as a problem, 345
    New Federalism, 82
    Republican coalition under, 210
    signing statements of, 332–33
    Supreme Court justices appointed
        by, 394
    and zero-base budgeting, 359
reapportionment, *281*
rebuttal, right of, 192

UN (United Nations), 192, 452–53
UN Charter, 454–55
UN Convention against Torture, 444
undersecretaries, federal, 348
undocumented immigrants, 15, 82, 332
unemployment, 428
unfunded mandates, 80
Unfunded Mandates Reform Act (UMRA), 80
UN General Assembly, *452*, 452–53
unions, 246, *246*
unitary system, 65, 79
United Kingdom, 453
  judicial review in, 381
  system of government in, 50
United National Framework Convention on Climate Change, 444
United Nations (UN), 192, 452–53
United Nations peacekeeping operations, 445
United States
  defense spending of, *436*
  government spending in, 79
  judicial review in, 381
  as member of UN Security Council, 453
  presidential powers in, 322
  system of government in, 50
  tax rates of, 410
United States v. Jones, 111, 384
United States v. Lopez, 75
United States v. Playboy Entertainment Group, 107
University of California–Davis, 133, 183, *184*
University of Michigan, 133
Univision, 178
UN Security Council, 453
upper class, 426–27
urban areas, shift of population to, 17
U.S. Court of Appeals, 376, *376*
U.S. Northern command, 354
U.S. Postal Service (USPS), 341
U.S. Public Health Service (USPHS), 420
U.S. Weather Service, 341
USA PATRIOT Act, 316
USPHS (U.S. Public Health Service), 420

USPS (U.S. Postal Service), 341
Utah, 129, 280

V
values
  Americans' support for, *145*
  conflict of, 21
  defined, 143
  democracy, 21
  equality, 19–20
  liberty, 18–19
  political, 21–22, 143–45
  shared, 144–45
  taught in public schools, 152
  underlying government, 4, 18–21
Van Ordern v. Perry, 100
veto power, 44, 46, 292–93, 318, *319*
vice presidency, 325–26
Vietnam War, 152, 189, 209, 455
violent broadcast content, 107
violent video games, *383*
Virginia
  and Annapolis Convention, 37
  election of 2012, 199, 228
  and school segregation, 119, 384
  slaves in, 40
Virginia Military Institute (VMI), 127
Virginia Plan, 39
Voices for Choices, 261
Volcker, Paul, 408
voter ID laws, *123*, 124, 219
voter registration, 203, 218–19
voter turnout, *198*, 216–17, *217*
  around the world, 220
  in 2012 election, 200
  parties' assistance with, 202–3
voting
  on bills, 291–92
  as building block of citizenship, 8
  and candidate characteristics, 223–24
  early, 199–200
  factors influencing, 218–19
  issues in, 222–23
  by mail, *219*
  party loyalty in, *221*, 221–22
  as political participation, 215, 216, 218–19
  rates of, *22*

WTO (World Trade Organization), 443
Wyoming, 108

Y
Yates, Robert, 39, 49
Yee, Leland, *383*

Yellen, Janet, *408*
YouTube, 180, 184

Z
zero-base budgeting, 359
Zimbabwe, 454

Voter Registration Information*

State	Registration Deadline before Election	Early Voting Permitted?	Identification Required to Vote?	More Information
Alabama	10 days	No	Photo ID requested	sos.state.al.us
Alaska	30 days	Yes	ID requested; photo not required	elections.alaska.gov
Arizona	29 days	Yes	ID required (nonphoto OK)	azsos.gov/election
Arkansas	30 days	Yes	ID requested; photo not required	sos.arkansas.gov
California	15 days	Yes	No	sos.ca.gov
Colorado	22 days; same-day registration permitted	Yes (all voting by mail)	ID requested; photo not required	sos.state.co.us
Connecticut	General election: in person, 7 days; by mail, 14 days Primary elections: in person, 1 day; by mail, 5 days	No	ID requested; photo not required	ct.gov/sots
Delaware	24 days	No	ID requested; photo not required	elections.delaware.gov
District of Columbia	30 days; same-day registration permitted	Yes	No	dcboee.org
Florida	29 days	Yes	Photo ID requested	election.dos.state.fl.us
Georgia	28 days	Yes	Photo ID required	sos.ga.gov
Hawaii	30 days	Yes	Photo ID requested	hawaii.gov/elections
Idaho	25 days; same-day registration permitted	Yes	Photo ID requested	idahovotes.gov
Illinois	27 days	Yes	No	elections.il.gov
Indiana	29 days	Yes	Photo ID required	in.gov/sos/elections
Iowa	10 days	Yes	No	sos.iowa.gov
Kansas	21 days	Yes	Photo ID required	kssos.org
Kentucky	28 days	No	ID requested; photo not required	elect.ky.gov
Louisiana	30 days	Yes	Photo ID requested	sos.la.gov
Maine	21 days; same-day registration permitted	Yes	No	maine.gov/sos
Maryland	21 days	Yes	No	elections.state.md.us
Massachusetts	20 days	No	No	www.sec.state.ma.us
Michigan	30 days	No	Photo ID requested	michigan.gov/sos
Minnesota	21 days	Yes	No	mnvotes.org
Mississippi	30 days	No	Photo ID required	sos.ms.gov
Missouri	Fourth Wednesday prior to election	No	ID requested; photo not required	sos.mo.gov